IN THE
SHADOW
OF AN
EAGLE

IN THE
SHADOW
OF AN
EAGLE

JAMES SAFRENO

CONTENTS

PROLOGUE

As we were eating breakfast, I looked over to Fredrick and noticed he had a copy of our great-grandfather's book, "Are you going to read that book again," I asked him?

"I've never read the book, but I remember your stories about our grandfather," he replied.

"Yes, I did tell you about him, but that was the child's version." "The original version is more graphic, but I think you will like it, it's well written." Fredrick smiled and nodded, and my thoughts went to my great-grandfather, who my parents named me after. He was very old when my great uncle wrote his book, as I am now. My great-grandfather could have written his book, he was more than smart enough, and it would have been better if he did, perhaps we would have learned even more about him that my great-uncle might have left out.

Frank White had done a great job writing about me over the years, but that was his words, his thoughts, not mine. Perhaps I should write my story myself, and if I do not finish it, Fredrick or one of my other boys will, I'm sure.

After breakfast, I got some paper and pencils, sat in the living room, and then got busy writing my story. Many hours had passed as I was writing, and I was into it so much that I hadn't notice Fredrick staring at me. Curious as to why I was writing so much, Fredrick asked me, "Who are you writing to?"

"I'm not writing to anyone; I'm writing a book about me." "I know there have been other books written about me, but those books aren't my own words or thoughts."

"That's a good idea, I was going to suggest it myself, but I'm glad you came up with it first," said Fredrick. "Why are you using paper and pencil," he asked?

"What else am I going to use."

Fredrick smiled and left the room only to come back with a computer. "No one writes with a pencil and paper anymore; use this; it will be easier for you."

"Okay, but you will have to show me how to work this thing."

"I'll tell you enough to get you started, and if you need more help, just ask." It took me a few days to get comfortable with the laptop, but it became fun after a while. My best friend is Charles Kahler, and for the longest time, he was the only real friend I had. Someone I completely trusted, and I never questioned. We never fought and never competed. We helped each other with almost everything a small boy would do from one day to another. I must admit that he helped me more than I did him. One could say we were like two peas in a pod.

I was an average boy, perhaps a little more aggressive than usual. I did not play sports mostly because no one showed me how to. My academic abilities were poor; I had a learning disability that took me more than twelve years to overcome. I was stubborn about things, and once I started something, I did not let anything stop me until I finished. Overall, I was happy until I turned nine, and my father decided to build a house in another city, and I lost my best friend. I felt alone, and everything changed; I gained a lot of weight and was depressed and sad. I spent my days keeping to my thoughts as I stayed by myself or roamed the nearby creek.

One day when I was at the creek, a dark-haired skinny kid came running near me, almost knocking me into the water, and I yelled out, "Hey, watch it."

He stopped and came back towards me, and he first looked me up and down then said with a smile on his face, "I'm your cousin Allen."

Then he took off running again, and I yelled, "Cousin or no cousin; you still need to watch it." I do not know if he heard me or not, and I did not care; I just sat down, wanting to be left alone. Being alone was not what I was going to get ten minutes later, Allen came back. He sat down beside me, so I started my life with Allen and what a miserable life it was.

Allen was just the opposite as Charles; we fought all the time. He made everything a contest with me and thought I was inferior to him. There were some things he was right, I was inferior to him, but when I admitted to it, he would rub it in. As time passed, I learned more, and his claim to superiority fell apart. I had a girlfriend in high school, at least I considered her a girlfriend, by the name of Darlene, the prettiest redhead you ever wanted to see. But she broke my heart when I found out she married someone else. I gained more weight in high school and avoided any physical education. When I went to my school counselor with the desire to go to college, she told me that I would be lucky to graduate high school, let alone college. She suggested I go into the military, which was my backup plan anyway.

1

THE BEGINNING

O n the twentieth of June, I joined the Army with a friend from high school; his name is Dennis; we went in on the Buddy system. I thought I was going to be another John Wayne but found out quickly how out of shape and homesick I was. We flew into the airport, which was my first plane ride, near Fort Lewis Washington, and there was a long wait for the military bus to the fort. In that time of waiting, my zeal for the Army vanished, and dread crept in. I was five feet eight, two hundred and sixty-five pounds, and I didn't have the confidence I would finish basic training successfully.

"Private York outside," said the head drill Instructor Donald Datwilder also known as D. D. or Death and Destruction. As I went outside, I had a feeling what he was going to say was not going to be good. "York, I've been observing you, and I feel your progress hasn't been good." I knew what he was talking about was true. "I feel if I don't do something now, you will be recycled and do this training all over again." My heart sank, I felt depressed, and I feared I was not going to make it through basic training. "I judge that what you need is extra training." "Are you willing to do this training private?"

Apprehensively I said, "I see no other way, Drill Sergeant."

"Very well, go back to the barracks and remove your shirt and meet me on the parade ground."

"Yes, Drill Sergeant," I replied, and I left to do as he told me.

He was at the traveling bars at the parade ground, and the Sergeant said, "You must go all the way down without falling to pass." These traveling bars were different from those they had in elementary school;

they rotated when you grabbed the bar, but I could not go all the way down even if they did not. "Get up there and give it a try." I climbed up and grabbed the first bar and looked down at the Sergeant with despair, and I got to the third bar and fell off. "Get up there again." I almost made it to the fourth bar and fell off again, and again he sent me up. I was getting arm weary but made it to the fourth bar.

"Alright, we will run now." I had to run around the parade ground, which was about a half-mile, and the Sergeant joined me, and I did not get to the halfway mark when I was winded. The Sergeant saw this, and he grabbed my belt and said, "You can make it," as pulled me the rest of the way. When we completed the half-mile, the Sergeant said, "You must be able to go around this twice to past." "Go rest, and I will come and get you in a few hours."

I went into the barracks and flopped on my bunk, and Dennis asked, "What happen to you?" as others stared at me.

"I think I'm going to die," I replied as I closed my eyes.

I was called out to the parade ground three hours after I laid down. Out there, this time was not only my drill instructor but also the first sergeant. The first sergeant was a small older dark skin man that, when you looked at him, anyone would know you did not want to anger him. "You are going to run first, and I will be right behind you," said the Drill Sergeant.

I was about to start to run when First Sergeant Pinto said, "Private take off your T-shirt, pants, and boots run with just your boxers." I did not argue with him that could have been dangerous. The parade ground was sandy, but occasionally, I step on a stone, causing the pain to shoot right through me. To my surprise, I got all away around without help from the drill sergeant, and I stopped; however, the drill sergeant did not, so I took off, and I ran behind him, trying to catch up to him. Every time I thought I was about to catch up to him, he would run a little faster, leaving me in the dust, and it angered me. I did not know that I attracted an audience the guys from my barracks, including Dennis, nor did I realize I ran twice around the parade grounds. We finally stopped; I thought I was going to heave a lung. The drill sergeant went over to the first sergeant to talk I could barely make out what they were saying.

"The private has short legs, he's fat and weak, but the private is stubborn when he gets mad, the young man doesn't quit, good luck with him but I don't think the private will make it," the first sergeant said bluntly.

As the two sergeants parted, the first sergeant shooed the guys of my barrack away, and my drill sergeant came over to me.

"You did well with the run, but you need a fire lit under you." "Get your clothes on and get up on the traveling bars," he demanded. I got up on the bars, got to the third bar, and fell off, and the Sergeant shook his head in disgust. "Get up, try again," he said with repugnance. I could see he was losing patience with me. I went down the bars and tried very hard and made it to the fourth bar almost to the fifth. "Get up again and keep on practicing until I get back," the Drill Sergeant said, and he left.

He returned with a backpack filled with rocks and said, "I can't be out here with you all the time you must do it yourself. Put this backpack on when you run and do the traveling bars. At the progress you are making, you must also do this extra work out after your regular training if you don't want to go through basic twice." I started pacing worriedly; I was not going to make it and regretting I ever joined the Army. I finally grabbed the backpack, put it on, and started running. It was much harder with the pack, especially when I tried the traveling bars, but I kept up with it taking two or three-minute brakes when I had to.

I was tired and hungry; it was getting dark, and I had missed dinner but kept up with what I was doing when I heard, "What the hell are you doing out here private?" said Drill Sergeant Tanner. Sergeant Tanner was another Drill Sergeant who was being trained by Sergeant Datwilder. He was an arrogant asshole; what made it worse his father was a full bird colonel.

"Maggot, what are you doing out of the barracks?" said Drill Sergeant Tanner.

"Drill Sergeant Datwilder sent me out here to train," I replied.

"I will talk with him later, get in the barracks now," he said.

As I walked over to him, I asked, "What do you wish me to do with this backpack that Sergeant Datwilder told me to use?"

He looked in the pack, started laughing, and said, "Put it under your bunk."

I went into the barracks and threw the pack under my bunk everyone was silent and staring at me when Dennis asked, "What have you been up to?"

"Training," I replied as I started taking off my clothing.

"What kind of training?"

I grabbed my towel and said, "The Army kind," and I headed for the shower as everyone's eyes followed me.

As the weeks went on, I put on the backpack, whether it was on the weekend or after a regular training day, then ran and went down the traveling bars. I had also noticed from time to time there was an extra rock placed in the backpack, but I still wore the pack. Sergeant Datwilder was not a mean man; I had a lot of respect for him. I do not know how the others of my barrack felt there was a lot of bitching but mostly towards Sergeant Tanner.

I always considered myself a good shot with a rifle thanks to the competition my Cousin Allen put me through. It came to the time when we all had to qualify at the rifle range, and I was having a hard time trying to knock down the targets.

Drill Sergeant Datwilder came over to me and said, "What's the problem, Private York?"

"I don't know Drill Sergeant; I swear I am hitting those targets; it's almost as if they are locked," I said.

"Give me that rife." He then shot at some of the targets himself. He handed the rifle back to me and said, "Shit, don't shoot anymore until I come back." He went into the spotting shack, and then there was a loud ruckus as if a fight were going on. He came back to me and said, "Try shooting now." I knocked down every target that I was aiming at, and the drill sergeant nodded his approval.

It was a Saturday late afternoon I had run around the parade ground twice, just before I had made it down to the end of the traveling bar for the first time. I was quite satisfied with myself, and I was heading back to the barracks to clean up and go to dinner when Drill Sergeant Datwilder approached me. "Sit down here on this bench; I want to talk with you." "How are you doing with your training?"

"I don't know I hope well enough to pass that P.T. test, but I feel awful weak."

"Well, you have lost a lot of weight."

"I wouldn't know I feel the same other than feeling weak."

"Tell me about yourself," the Sergeant asked.

"I've been fat since I was nine; I never did well in school, and you could say I was a couch potato." "It's funny I'm named after a great-grandfather who was a mountain man and a great Indian warrior."

"I'm part native; what was your grandfather's native name?"

"Soaring Eagle something else I don't remember," I said.

"Soaring Eagle With Many Coos?"

"Yes, I think so, you heard of him?" I asked.

"Yes, my grandfather told me stories about him; he was a great warrior for my people." "You better go in and get clean for dinner." Time went by, and the day before P.T. test Drill Sergeant Datwilder came to me and said, "You better give me your backpack you won't need it anymore." "I don't know if you will pass the test, for your sake; I hope you do, I don't have much confidence, good luck anyway." At that, he left, and I started to worry then quickly concluded that whatever is going to happen would happen, and I let the fear go.

We all marched to the P.T. test area, and there was a place where we had to do a low crawl, an obstacle course, a track, and the dreaded traveling bars. They divided everyone up into four groups. Each group had sergeants with a clipboard and other sergeants to time each of us, and they placed a number on us. The first thing I had to do was the low crawl we were lined up three across we had to go down and back. My plan was not to watch the others but to gauge how well I went down and back. We all got on the grown and headed down, and then we headed back, I felt I went fast enough, but I didn't know how well I did against the others because a sergeant ushered me to the obstacle course.

At the obstacle course, I had to go over a log barrier. Then I had to run the length of another log that went over a ditch. Finally, I had to jump over another ditch and weave in and out of a line of posts. I intended to handle the obstacle course the same way I did the low crawl. So, I started down the obstacle course, I don't know how fast I did it, but I do know that I completed it where others didn't.

As I headed for the traveling bars test, I came across Dennis, he asked, "How are you doing?"

"I don't know," I replied. As we parted, Dennis went to the low craw, and I went to the traveling bars with butterflies in my stomach. I could go down the bars a few times back on the parade ground, but I did not know what was going to happen now. It was my turn to go down the bars, and as I started moving, I found it a lot easier than when I was training on the parade ground. I got to the end and headed back the other way, and to my surprise, I made it and got off. I stared up at the traveling bars, and I was shocked and dumbfounded at what I just did. What got me out of my shock feeling was a sergeant yelling at me to go to the track.

At the track, I had to go around four times, and it was not just going around and completing it; I also had to do it fast enough to pass. There were ten of us lined up to run. When everyone got the signal to run, I headed out running with the rest of the men. At first, I stayed towards the back of the pack. By the second lap, I was in the center of those running, and many around me were breathing hard, but I was not having any trouble. When I started the third lap, I decided to go a little faster and move up in the pack near the front. I stayed there until the last half of the fourth lap, and I pour it on. I came nowhere near first others had the same idea I had, but I did finish in front of the pack. I was pleased with myself at how well I did run. The big question was how I did overall, I just did not know, and the wait to find out was going to kill me.

We got back into formation, and Dennis turned to me and whispered, "How did you do?"

I whispered back, "I don't know."

Back at the Barracks as I was getting ready to shower, Drill Sergeant Datwilder asked me, "How did you think you did?"

"I don't know, all I know is I did my best."

He nodded and said, "Well, you will find out in a few days.

Three days went by, and we were in formation Drill Sergeant Datwilder said, "I have the results of the P.T. test." "I will start from the bottom of the list to the top, and if I don't call out your name, it means you failed." "Jones congratulations, you made the bottom of the list with a score of 62 at least you passed," he said sarcastically. Anderson 64, Connors 66, Gonzales 68, Morales 70, on and on the Drill Sergeant called out names, and when he came to Dennis, he said 76, which was about the center. After he called out a couple of more names, my heart sunk, and I didn't think I made it, and Dennis saw the stress on my face.

"It will be alright you'll see," he said unconvincingly to me.

"This last sheet of paper has the top scores if you're not here you didn't make it." There was a lot of murmuring from those around me. I turned sheet white, and I thought I was going to pass out. Drill Sergeant Datwilder started laughing and said, "You people stay here for a few minutes," as he walked over to First Sergeant Pinto. "Top look at this," he said as he handed him the last sheet of paper.

When the first sergeant looked at the paper, something happened that no one ever saw before, the first sergeant smiled and started laughing and said to the Drill Sergeant, "Good job."

He came back to all of us and started rereading names. He had been reading the names and had only a few left when he stopped calling names then said, "These last names are first, second, and third I will read the highest first." "Private Less Titus, you got a score of 99; that's the highest score." "Private Michael Odom, you also did very well with a score of 98. In third place is Private Robert Bosch with a score of 96 very good." Drill Sergeant Datwilder hesitated and looked at his list then said, "Private Bosh, I hate to burst your bubble, but you tied for third." Everyone looked at each other, and I did not even hear what he said. I was very concerned that I would have to take basic training over again. "The person who tied with you worked the hardest, and I have a lot of respect for him. Of course, I did not hear nor was paying attention to him. "The private who did so well is James York," he said. The Sergeant said my name but didn't listen to what he said, but everyone else did and was padding me on my back, which confused me.

"Jim, didn't you hear what he said?" Dennis asked surprise; I wasn't ecstatic.

"What, what did he say?" I said, confused.

"You came in third, you passed," Dennis said with a smile. I thought for a minute what he said, and then everything around me started to spin and went black and I passed out.

A few minutes later, I woke up on the ground with everyone around me, and the drill sergeant said, "The excitement too much for you, York?"

When my eyes cleared, I said, "Did you say I passed?"

He nodded and said, "He will be alright." The drill sergeant, without a further word, got up and sat down with the first sergeant as Dennis helped me stand up.

As time passed, and training ended, Drill Sergeant Tanner decided to go to Hawaii. He had borrowed, or a better word would be he stole money from some of the guys knowing that he would not be back until everybody was gone. But those guys got even with him destroying everything he had, which will cost him thousands to replace.

After basic training, I thought that I would be going home, but that is not how it works. We all had to go to additional training for our military occupational specialty, M.O.S., and this was to be at Fort Lee, Virginia. Dennis wanted to get into accounting, and I didn't care, so I picked the same job he did.

We got to Virginia late Friday afternoon, and they gathered everyone in front of the headquarters building. When counted, there were forty of us, and now we had to wait to be given a barracks to house us. After a few hours, a Sergeant came out and told us to follow him, and we followed him to a two-story building. Then the Sergeant said, "You have till Monday morning to clean and pant this barracks your supplies are inside if you need anything more, I'll be at headquarters."

We went in and were shocked at the condition of the barracks. There were two inches of dirt and cobwebs on everything, the paint had peeled and was hanging down, you could not see out the windows, and the latrine was worse with toilets plugged, everything mucked up. We divided everyone up into specific areas and got to work. Dennis and I had the bottom floor bunk area to do.

It took us until late Sunday night to finish the barracks, and no one was in the mood to do anything else but shower and sleep. The next day many were grumbling at the work we had to do, and later that morning, we started school, and it was clear that it was going to be boring for me. The school was supposed to be six weeks long, and I found that it wasn't that hard, but even so, after six weeks, some failed, which surprised me, but I did pass and got promoted to Specialist Four.

They were not letting any of us go home on leave why we did not know. Dennis, some of the other guys, and I decided to visit our nation's capital in Washington. When we got back to Fort Lee, we notice that some of the bunks were empty. The ones who were still there in the barracks were packing their duffle bags. "Where are these guys with their bunks rolled up, and why are you guys packing your duffle bags?" asked Bill Morrison.

"Those who failed the class went to infantry training, and everyone else is moving for more training," Davis said.

We marched over to another barracks, and we got assigned to the 101st Air Born to everyone's surprise. "You think we are going to jump out of airplanes," I whispered to Dennis.

"I don't know, but I hope so," he said without looking at me. I looked at him as if to say, are you crazy. A Lieutenant, a Sergeant Major, and an obese Sergeant approached us. They had us line up in a formation, and the Lieutenant spoke first.

"I'm Lieutenant Bates; this is my company; you will conduct yourself always in a military matter." "You will run everywhere you go while in this company area." "You will also give me one hundred and one percent of effort; if you conduct yourself in any other way, I guarantee there will be a cost." Then Lieutenant Bates said, "This man is Sergeant Major Connors, and this is Sergeant Brown; Sergeant Brown will be over you, making sure you follow my rules."

The sergeant-major whispered something to Sergeant Brown, and he nodded. Then the Sergeant said, "You men stow your gear when I dismiss you then stay in the barracks until I get you for dinner; is there a specialist four James York here?" the Sergeant asked.

"Yes, Sergeant right here," I said.

"After you stow your gear report to the headquarters building Sergeant Major Connors wants to talk to you," he said.

"Yes, Sergeant," I replied. They dismissed us to the barracks.

"What do you think he wants?" I asked Dennis.

"I don't know, but one thing I do know you better run to the headquarters building," he replied.

I ran to the headquarters building and was told by the clerk to wait here. He went into a room, then came back and told me to sit on that bench until someone called me. After about five minutes, he ordered me to take a seat in the office while Sergeant Major Connors looked at my file. As I was sitting there, a Captain walked in, the Sergeant Major and I stood up. "Sit down and relax," said the Captain. "I'm Captain Reynolds, you know why you're here?" he said as the Sergeant Major handed him my file.

"No, Sir," I replied.

"Your ASVAB test shows you scored in the 99th percentile of the nation, yet when they tested you in basic you didn't do very well can you explain this?" the Captain asked.

"What is ASVAB, Sir?" I asked.

"It's the test the recruiter gave you," he replied.

I thought a few seconds and then said, "There was a different situation when I took both of those tests, Sir."

"What were those conditions?" he inquired.

"The first one I had eaten, I was relaxed, as well as alone, and it was quiet." "The one in basic it was two a. m., I was tired, I hadn't eaten since breakfast, they rushed everyone through the test, and it was shoulder to shoulder, noisy and others were asking for help from me."

The Captain looked at the Sergeant Major, and the Sergeant Major said, "It's possible, Sir, they are treated like cattle sometimes."

The Captain turned back to me and said, "You weighed two hundred and seventy-five pounds when you enlisted, and yet you lost over a hundred pounds," the Captain stated.

"Yes, Sir, about a hundred fifty pounds, Sir," I replied.

"Your drill instructor and first sergeant wrote some excellent statements about you." "They said you scored in the top three of your unit."

"Yes, Sir, I could have scored higher, Sir, but didn't," I said.

"Then why didn't you score higher?" he asked.

"The last two events I had to do were the traveling bars and running if I had done more bars, I'd get more points, but I didn't want to get tired before the run, it turned out the run wasn't all that hard."

"Your drill instructor said the score you got on the rifle range is misleading because the targets had gotten sabotaged." "He feels you are most likely an expert marksman," the Captain said.

"Yes Sir, the targets are the type that when you hit them, they fold down, the man or men in the observation tower locked my targets."

"How good of a shot are you?" asked the Sergeant Major.

"Well, I have never yet been able to light a matchstick, but I can break them," I said.

"James, have a seat on the bench," said the Captain.

"Yes Sir," I said and headed out the door, confused. I had noticed he just called me James instead of Specialist James, which confused me also.

"Well, what do you think, John," said the Captain.

"He is the best I have seen maybe officer material, but I don't believe he has very high self-esteem," the Sergeant Major said.

"Yes, I agree with you, I have a feeling many people picked on him since he was a small kid, but I feel he can overcome it," the Captain replied.

"I agree with you, Sir," replied the Sergeant Major.

"Then, can I assume you believe he would be an asset to our group?" said the Captain.

"Absolutely, Sir."

"James, come back in here and have a seat," said the Captain. "We are going to allow you to do something that very few get to do." "Have you ever heard of a unit called PSYOPS?" he asked.

"No, Sir," I said.

"It means Psychological Operations in a nutshell people in this unit go out in the field gathers information, bring it back, and turn it into propaganda." "The unit is unique because no one uses rank; however, eighty percent of the unit are officers, so we are on a first-name basis." "This unit has both males and females; we allow you to have your hair as long as you wish and a beard." "One other thing you should know about this unit that I feel will interest you." "There are only two units, one in this state, and the other will be in California, about twenty-five miles from where you live, I believe." "You think you would be interested in this unit?"

"May I ask a few questions, Sir?"

"Yes, what do you want to know?" he asked.

"Would I be going to O.C.S., Sir?" I asked.

He looked down at my record and then at the Sergeant Major, who shrugged and said, "We will arrange this, but I think it would be after you were in the unit for a while to see how you do."

I nodded and then said, "I came in the Army on the buddy system what's going to happen to my buddy?" I asked.

"You understand once you had finished your last training, you and your buddy could be separated," said the Sergeant Major.

"Yes, I know this could happen, but what I wanted to know is, can I finish this training with him?" I asked.

"It would be a good idea, Captain." "The unit won't organize for about three months, and the challenges of the 101st will keep him healthy, and the time will give him a little leave after this training."

"Then that will be alright, James," the Captain said. "Are there any more questions?" he asked.

"Just a couple, Sir, what are the drawbacks to this unit?"

"I would have been disappointed if you didn't ask." "It depends on what you call drawbacks." "I'll be honest with you this unit means you have a good chance to be in a combat area, and it is likely you would be working with a Special Forces unit while in the field," he said.

"The Green Berets, Sir?" I asked with great interest.

"Most likely."

"Alright, I'm willing to be part of that unit," I said.

"Great, the Sergeant Major, will get your orders written up for you, and we will meet you in California." "By the way, we don't have any specialist positions in the unit we will get your orders for your stripes, I don't think you will be corporal for very long," said the Captain. He shook my hand, and he dismissed me back to my barracks.

When I got back to the barracks, Dennis asked, "You were gone for a long time what happened?"

Others around us were also interested in knowing I said, "After this class, I will be going to a special unit called PSYOPS."

"What's PSYOPS?" he asked.

"Getting information and turning it into propaganda, I guess."

"Shit, it sounds like you are going into combat," someone said.

"They stated that I would get orders soon and orders also to make me a corporal," I added.

"Your fucked man, you are going into combat for sure," someone said again.

"I can't go to Vietnam; my brother is there," I retorted.

"So, where is this training?" Dennis asked.

"That's what's nice; the unit I will be in is near San Jose, California," I said with a smile.

"Damn, you can live at home," he said, surprised.

"Yes," I replied, still smiling.

The training was to become a parts man, but we had to run all the time and had a lot of P.T., but it was not hard. What was funny was Sergeant Brown was so out of shape he could not keep up, but he loved to make us do push-ups. One day, Dennis and I got into trouble at the morning inspection. The Sergeant said, "You both owe me eighty push-ups. He then looked at my brass buckle, and although it was perfect on the outside, he claimed it should have been shining on the inside too. I had to do another eighty push-ups all at once. He stood over me watching to make sure I did them right; I had no problem doing them and could have done much more.

Three days after the push-up punishment, Sergeant Brown said, "I have a set of orders here for Specialist James York." "It says after you finish here, you are going to a unit in California call PISSYAPS."

"Sergeant, it's pronounced PSYOPS," I said.

"Oh, yes, PSYOPS, your right," he replied.

"Vietnam, here you come," someone blurted out.

I got back into line, and Sergeant Brown had another packet of papers and, with a smile, said, "Looks like I have other orders for you York." "According to these sets of orders, you can buy me a beer at the N.C.O. club, your rank has been changed to corporal no more K.P. for you."

I also got a letter from home. My parents told me Allen wanted to be an Army helicopter pilot. They gave him a mental test since helicopter pilots are at high risk of being killed. His grandmother thinks he will be a colonel, well I don't think so, but who knows he is smart when he wants to be.

Dennis and I decided to go back to Washington, D.C.; we had been there once before with others in our unit. We did not bring anyone else with us this time; it is too hard to get a room. We got there about four-thirty on

Friday afternoon, and we went to the same hotel we stayed in last time. It was cheap by Washington's standards, and we did not have much money to spare. When we arrived, Dennis asked the hotel clerk, "We would like a room."

"Our rooms are all booked up; we have no rooms available," the clerk replied.

Dennis looked at me, and I said, "Well, let's look somewhere else."

As we walked down the street in our uniforms, there was a busload of girls from a girl's school. The girls started whistling and calling out to Dennis and me, much like a bunch of guys would to girls. I'm not comfortable with something like that, but it was flattering, and if the girls were older, who knows what would have happened. The ratio female to male in D.C. was five to one, which made it pleasant for us. Naturally, when we were hit on by a girl most of the time, it was a prostitute, and there were plenty of them. We were having a hard time finding a hotel when someone who looked important asked, "You soldiers looking for a hotel room."

"Yes, Sir," we both said at the same time.

"Follow me; I will get you a room," he said. We followed him down the street, and as we were walking, he said, "It is a lucky thing you two ran into me there is a conference here, and most of the hotels are full." He brought us to a beautiful place, and we got a room, but the cost of the room took most of our cash; luckily, we had tickets back to Fort Lee.

We made the best of our time with the money we had by sightseeing anywhere where it was free. By about five pm, we ran into some guy from George Town University; he wanted to take us to a popular nightclub full of people our age. We went down several pleasant-looking residential streets, then stopped, and he said, "Where do you think the club is?" We looked around, and the area seemed like a beautiful quiet area with some elegant houses we had no idea where this club could be.

"I have no idea where it could be," Dennis said, and I agreed.

The guy from the university smiled and said, "Follow me." We went over to a beautiful home with a small door on one side. He opened the door, and there was a flight of stairs going down, at the bottom was a large man in a dark suit and tie, he looked like something out of a gangster movie. We went down the stairs, and there was no noise or smoke that you would think there be. Next to the man with the black suit was a door with a sliding peephole that reminded me of the old speakeasies.

The man at the door said in a deep voice, "Is this your first time?"

"Yes," Dennis said, wanting to see what was behind the door.

"Then enjoy yourself no cover charge for first-timers," he said as he opened the door. We were immediately hit in the face with the noise of music, people talking, and the smoke. The place seemed packed, and many people were dancing. It was not a huge place, not what I would expect. Our guide disappeared as we moved deeper into the club, and we never saw him again. Dennis and I got some beer, and we looked for a table to sit down, not finding one we stood up towards the back of the club until a table came available. Dennis was thoroughly enjoying himself, but I am not comfortable with large crowds like this. I did not complain I did not want to ruin the fun Dennis was having, so I just put up with the situation. We finally found a couple who shared their table with us, and we sat down, but Dennis was not there long before he was up dancing with someone. I downed about three beers, and I was feeling it in my head and down below.

I was not a drinker, so it did not take much to affect me, and when Dennis came back, I said, "Stay here and save the table, I will be right back." I got up and almost fell back down while Dennis and the other couple at the table laughed at me. I found the bathroom, and it reeked, but I did not care, and when I came out, a pretty girl, who was as drunk if not more intoxicated than I, grabbed me and started dancing with me. If I weren't drunk, I wouldn't have attempted dancing, but I had no self-consciousness of myself, so I danced much to the delight of Dennis, and to tell you the truth, it felt nice holding this girl. I sat down with Dennis, nursed another beer, and as I drank, the place did not seem so bad. It was about one-thirty in the morning when we notice that the club was thinning out, so Dennis and I decided to leave.

We were very drunk, smelling like tobacco, and it took us over an hour to find the hotel. We stumbled upstairs to our room, and I passed out on one of the beds, still wearing clothes. It was light when we woke up with terrible headaches. We had about two hours before we had to leave, we couldn't afford to stay another night.

We showered and went downstairs to the main desk, and I said, "We want to check out, but we also want to have something to eat before we leave, and it's only thirty minutes before checkout time."

"You can check out now and still have something to eat before you leave, I will make sure of that soldier." "Give these two men anything they want to eat; it's on the house," the clerk said to the hotel restaurant's maître d'.

We ate then got to the bus station about noon and had to wait an additional two hours for the next bus back. Dennis and I got propositioned a couple of times, but we both said no even if we had the time, we didn't have the money, nor did we feel so good.

The days went by, and I got a letter from Darlene; it was an upsetting Dear John letter. She told me that I was a good guy and she wasn't. Darlene told me she met someone and was going to the state of Washington with him. I still intended to see if she was still in California when I got leave. The letter bothered me for some time; it wasn't long when the class ended, and it was time for us to go home.

I knew I was in better shape than I was in high school. I was less than a hundred and twenty-eight pounds with not an ounce of fat on me. We took our duffle bags, threw them on our shoulder, and ran two miles to get our transportation back home. We got to the San Francisco Airport late in the afternoon and decided to get a taxi to our homes.

2

NEW TRAINING AND DEPLOYMENT

After being dropped off home, the taxi took off with Dennis, and it would be the last time I saw Dennis. It was Saturday afternoon when I walked up the first flight of stairs to the house, and my mother spotted me. When she saw the taxi, she was already curious why a cab stopped at her house. "Jim is home," my mother said to my father, who got up and looked out the bay window to confirm what she said. My dad came out of the front door, followed behind by my mother.

"Why didn't you call?" "I would have gotten you?" my dad asked.

"Dennis and I didn't want to bother anyone, and we had the money for the taxi." I grabbed my duffle bag and went into the house.

"You have lost a lot of weight," he stated.

"Yes, over a hundred and fifty pounds." "I'll have to buy some new clothes; the ones I had before are much too big," I said.

"Maybe some of Jerry's things will fit you," my mother said.

"How long are you going to be here?" my father asked.

"Well, that's what we need to talk about." "I have about three weeks' leave; then, I have to report to my next duty station." "Normally, I would have four weeks leave, but the army assigned me to a special duty station."

"Special duty station?" my mother asked, confused.

"The unit's name is PSYOPS; it has something to do with gathering information and making propaganda out of it."

"Sounds almost like spy stuff to me," my dad said.

"That's what I thought when they explained it to me." "Anyway, I will be station there and be learning my job until they deploy me."

"Where is this unit you will be going to?" My father asked.

"I figure about twenty-five miles from here near San Jose."

"Are you going to be living there or here," my mother asked.

"Here, unless this would be an inconvenience to you," I said.

"No, you know where your room is," my dad said.

"Well, I'll bring my things up there, and then if you don't mind, I wish to take a shower," I said. As I got up to take my stuff upstairs, my mother asked if I wanted something to eat. I answered no, and I went upstairs and found my empty bed, and I started to unpack my things so that I could get some underwear, socks, and fatigues.

I stripped to my boxers when my mother said, "Boy, you are skinny." "I'll have to fatten you up."

"No, no, I'm not skinny; I'm just healthy, and I have to keep fit."

"You don't have to use those Army clothes." "Jerry doesn't use this shirt and these jeans they don't fit him and here are some socks your old shoes should still fit you," she said, and then I went into the shower.

Jerry came home, and I noticed that I was slightly skinnier than he was and somewhat taller. I was sitting outside with the dog when I asked Jerry about high school.

"Is MacDonald still the principal?"

"Yes," he said.

"What about Reynosa is he still there as a P.E. teacher."

"Yes."

"How about Reynolds?"

"Yes, he is there," he said.

"Maybe I will take a run down there Monday."

"Why?" he asked.

"I need a place to work out, and I need permission," I replied.

"Workout, you're supposed to be on vacation," he stated.

"I have to keep strong; the type of work they are going to have me do will require it," I said. "You ever heard of the Green Berets?"

"Yes, of course."

"Well, I will be working with them," I said.

"You are going to be in the Green Berets?" he asked, surprised.

"No, I wish I was, but I will just be working with them," I said then went into the house. Dinner was something my mother had to get used to,

I would eat anything, and she was surprised at how little I did eat. I could eat more, but I knew if I got started eating, I would not stop. David and Lynda came over with the baby, and he was surprised at the way I looked. I held my nephew and stood next to Jerry while someone took pictures. David joked and teased me then I went over everything that happened since I was gone. They were curious about the duty station. I told them what I knew, even though it was not much.

The next day my Aunt Dorothy and Uncle Art showed up; also, my grandmother came over to the house. "You shouldn't lose any more weight; your weight is perfect," my aunt said. As we all talked, Allen came to the front door dressed in what looked like military clothing that I've never seen before.

I started laughing and said, "Will you look at that." I went to the front door and opened it while my Uncle Art was beside me as Allen came walking up the steps. "What do you have on?" I asked with a smile.

"It's a uniform I made up for my R.O.T.C. at college," He replied.

"I have never seen anything like that before," I said. My cousin had on starched tapered jungle fatigues, polished jungle boots, braids, scarf, ammo belt, and a beret; it looked funny.

His face turned red, and he said, "Well, I better go home and change; I'll be right back," he said and left.

I shut the door, both my uncle and I started laughing, and he said, "He just made a fool out of himself." About forty minutes later, Allen came back in regular street clothes. I went to the backyard with him and didn't mention the costume he was wearing.

"How long are you home?" Allen asked.

"About three weeks, but I am being stationed near San Jose for a while and living here," I replied.

"What rank did you make?" "Corporal, but an officer told me I would get promoted soon, and they are thinking of sending me to O. C. S."

"So, what are you doing?"

"I'm in a special unit called PSYOPS." "What I do is go out in the field, gather information, and turn it into propaganda," I explained.

"Well, I'm thinking about starting a commando unit." "I would like you to be in it." "I would promote you to sergeant since you look fit now, of course, I would be your commanding officer," he said. Usually, some would think he was kidding, but he wasn't his mind was still when we were kids, but I intended not to embarrass him.

"Well, I must think about that let me know when you organize this unit of yours." We talked about the Army, and he tried to one-up me by telling me about his R.O.T.C. I could tell by the conversation that he hadn't changed much.

My aunt, uncle, and grandmother decided to leave, so I said to Allen, "Let's go over to your house, I haven't seen your parents yet nor your sister." His mother, father, and sister were always kind to me, unlike Allen. After staying with them for a few hours, I went back home satisfied that I didn't need to be around Allen.

The next day I got up early, got dressed in my fatigues and boots then started to work out. I went for a run down to the elementary school did some pull-ups, the traveling bars, and push-ups, then ran back home, by that time everyone was awake and up. "How come you are in your uniform," my father asked.

"I haven't finished working out this morning; I was just warming up." My father went to work, Jerry went to school, and I rested my breakfast an hour then started to run down Mission Boulevard towards Mission High School. It took me about twenty minutes to get to my old high school, and I went to the administration building.

"My name is James York is Mr. MacDonald available," I asked.

"What do you wish to talk to him about, Mr. York?"

"I graduated last year, and I am hoping to get permission to do something at the school," I said.

"Oh, yes I thought your name sounded familiar, don't you have a brother here?" she said.

"Yes, my brother Jerry is here."

"Let me see if he is free to see you." She went down the hall to another office then came out and said, "Mr. York, Mr. MacDonald will see you now." I walked down the hall to his office and went in, and he stood up then we shook hands then sat down.

"I don't know if you know me or not; there are many students in this school," I said.

"I remember you but don't remember much about you. Weren't you a lot heavier and a bit of a loner?" he asked.

"Yes, and my grades weren't outstanding either; however, the Army says I'm smarter than most realize, but I'm not convinced yet."

"What have you come here today to ask me?"

"The Army unit I'm in requires me to be fit to keep me alive; I wish to use the P.E. equipment if it is alright with you and coach Reynosa."

He leaned back in his seat and thought for a second and said, "I have a few questions for you."

"Why do you need to be that fit if posted so near?"

"That is where headquarters is; it's a place where I will get specialized training until I go out in the field, which means Vietnam."

"What is this job you will be doing for the Army?"

"It's called PSYOPS; I gather information and turn it into propaganda."

"Won't the Army give you that physical training you need?"

"Calisthenics, which I feel is not enough; there are many men who are dead because they were not fit enough."

Again, he leaned back in his seat and thought for a second then said, "If you can get coach Reynosa permission, it will be alright with me."

"Great, after I leave you, I will go over to the gym and ask him." At that, I got up, shook his hand, and headed over to the gym. Coach Reynosa was with Coach Reynolds down on the outdoor basketball court with a bunch of students. He was talking to them, so I sat down on the stairs that led to the outdoor basketball court about twenty feet away.

He glanced over a few times, and I smiled at him finally coach Reynolds came over to me and said, "Are you supposed to be here?"

"Yes, I've got permission from Mr. MacDonald; I've come to talk to coach Reynosa, but I don't wish to interrupt him."

He turned around and started to go back to coach Reynosa when I said, "You don't recognize me do you?"

"He turned around and said, "No, but it is evident that you are in the military, and I would assume you are a past student."

"You're right on both accounts," I replied with a smile. Coach Reynolds went over to coach Reynosa and talked to him; I assume about me because coach Reynosa took a long look at me.

"I know who he is, don't you," Reynosa said with a smile.

Reynolds looked at me again and said, "Who?"

"He has changed a lot; he is a past student his name of James York." Coach Reynosa sent the students to run two laps around the track, then came over to me and said as I got up to shake his hand, "James, you have changed quite a bit, and I see you are in the Army."

I nodded and, at the same time, said, "Yes."

"What can I do for you?" asked Coach Reynosa.

"The Army unit that I am in requires me to be very fit to remain alive." "There is a good chance I will be going to Vietnam." "I wish to use your equipment and your track to improve myself or at least not get any worse than what I am."

"Hasn't the Army given you enough training?"

"No, they only have calisthenics, which I feel isn't sufficient."

"How long will you need to be using the school equipment?"

"I'm on leave for three weeks, then the unit is near here, so it will be for several months until the army deploys me."

Coach Reynosa then said, "Is Mr. MacDonald okay with this?"

"He is leaving it up to you." His class came back from the two laps wheezing, fighting for air, and I looked over and started laughing.

"What's so funny?"

"I remember when I was out of shape like they are now, I can run all day without breathing hard now," I replied.

He smiled and chuckled himself then said, "How are you going to pay for using the equipment?"

I thought for a second, then said, "I can help with your P.E. class by making some adjustments in what you are doing."

He chuckled again and said, "Ok, we'll see what you can do, and you can use the equipment anytime you want to work out."

"Coach, are you here on Saturdays?"

"Yes, eight in the morning till about one." "I'll tell you what I will do, I will give you a key to the locker room's back door, and you can use the equipment anytime you want."

"That's great when do you want me to work with your students."

With a giggle, he said, "Tomorrow at one in the afternoon, we will see what you can do." I knew he thought I was biting off more than I could handle, but I did not care; I just wanted to use the equipment. He gave me the key to the locker room I headed home. I had gone to the store and bought some clothing, and the next day I ran down to the school in fatigues, boots, with a towel around my neck and under my clothing gym shorts. I got to the high school before anyone was there. The first thing I did, I worked on the weights, then the Nautilus machine followed by a run. I had stripped down to just my gym shorts working my chest muscles when the coaches started showing up.

"I didn't think you would show up?" Reynolds said smugly. I just stared at him and didn't say anything, and he left.

"You got a few minutes to talk," coach Reynosa asked.

"Sure." I got up off the weight bench and followed him into the coach's office, wiping the sweat off me.

"Are you prepared for this afternoon," coach Reynosa asked as the others listened to what I was going to say.

"Yes, I'm prepared."

"What do you plan to do?"

"Talk with them first." "Then I think before they do any calisthenics, I will have them run, but not like you have them run, I will put them into a formation of four across with the slower ones in front."

"Are you going to have them count cadence as they run also?" one of the coaches asked mockingly.

"Yes, their problem is they are not getting enough oxygen to their lungs." "Counting cadence while running will expand their lungs, having the weaker ones in front will cause them to move faster for longer because of the stronger ones in the back." "On the push-ups, I would rather see a weak student doing one good push-up than ten bad ones." "With sit-ups, I would eliminate them and have them do crunches; three crunches are worth ten sit-ups." "After the run and calisthenics, let me pick five or seven of your weakest students and work with them with the weights, no point having them play a sport if they are too weak to play it, it would just ruin their self-esteem."

As all the other coaches were chuckling, coach Reynosa said in a stern voice, "Alright, we will try it your way, some of it might work."

That quieted the other coaches, and I said, "Then I will go back and work out some more."

"Don't overdo it, working out too much can also do you harm," coach Reynosa said.

I nodded and said, "I have a routine, and I know when to stop." At that, I left and went to the Nautilus Machine.

After my workout, I showered and got dressed in my fatigues; it was twelve-thirty, and the P.E. class was to start in thirty minutes. The students drifted into the locker room first the athletes who were eager for P.E. and then the weaker ones who dreaded P.E; I understood this group the best. Coach Reynosa turned to me and said, "Showtime," and I went outside with him. It was Coach Maiden, Coach Reynosa, and I, as the students lined up in front of us. "Quiet down; this is James York." "He will be working with us for a few weeks, listen to him, and do what he says," said coach Reynosa.

"As you can see, I am wearing military fatigues because I'm in the Army." "Do any of you know me; I graduated last year?" I asked. A few of the upperclassmen raised their hands, and I said, "Tell the class what I looked like when you last knew me."

"You were fat and weak and couldn't do anything," said a student.

"Your right, but the Army changed me, and I went through hell changing." "I'm here to lessen the pain you must go through if you go into the military." "First, I want to rearrange you all freshmen here to my right then sophomores, juniors, and seniors."

Everyone looked at each other, murmuring but didn't move when coach Reynosa said, "You heard him move."

When everyone was where they were supposed to be, I said, "Remember where you are supposed to be, I want you there every time we meet up here." I then picked out the weaker looking kids. I formed them in four ranks, then told the rest to line up behind them. I said, "In a few minutes we are going to run, you are not to move around anyone but stay behind the person in front of you no matter how fast that person is running." "Any of you who try to go past someone I will kick your ass, I hope for your sake, you understand me." We walked down to the track, and as we walked down, I said, "When I yell jog, you jog when I say run you run." I yelled out jog, and we all jogged down the track I was watching everyone to make sure they didn't try passing anyone, and I could see that the athletes were losing it with the speed of those in front of them. We went halfway around, and I yelled for the students to repeat several sonnets as we jogged around the track. One stupid asshole decided to challenge me. He started passing others, I went after him, and I grabbed him, threw him to the ground, and yelled, "Does anyone else want to break the rules." While all this was going on, I was getting an audience of the coaches watching. No one else tried to pass again; the kids in the front were breathing heavily but did not stop.

In the last half of the track, I yelled, "Run," and we all ran, and no one stopped. When we got up to where the basketball court was, I thought the weaker frontrunners would lose a lung. "We are going to do some push-ups and crunches." "I don't care if you can only do one push-up, providing it is a good push-up the same is true about crunches." "Does anyone want to compete with me doing push-ups?" Of course, one of the senior athletes decided he wanted to try the other coaches watched to make sure everyone was doing a proper push-up. I was head to head with the high school senior who challenged me I was up to sixty-eight when the senior gave up, and I did another thirty-two pushups before I stopped.

I picked ten weak students, mostly ninth graders, and had them follow me while the other coaches took the rest. The ten I choose are students of all types; some were overweight, some very skinny, and even one small one who looked about ten. I divided them by two and had them work out doing curls. When they picked up a weight to do their curls, I told each one to drop down ten pounds lighter. To start, I had them do three sets of ten curls and made them do it right. By the time many of them complete their second set, they were glad I had them drop down ten pounds. "When you can do three sets without any problem, then you can move up in weight, but I must tell you it is not the weight that will build your muscles; it's how much you can challenge your muscle," I said.

At the end of the class, I said, "Expect your muscles to ache for a while, but the pain will go away, then I had them do a lap by themselves and into the locker room.

As the ten students went into the locker room, Coach Reynosa asked, "How did they do with the weights?"

"They will be sore tomorrow, but they are doing them right and getting a good workout."

"Well, I think you did well better than most of the other coaches, and I thought you would do."

"Thanks, you keep this routine up after I have to stop, and I'm betting that you will all see some good results and happier kids."

"We will try to keep them doing the same thing for as long as we can." "I'm interested to see what the results will also be."

I worked out and helped the coach for the next three weeks. I felt I was getting stronger but wasn't sure; I felt better, so I guess I was. About two days before I had to report to my unit, Sergeant Major Connors called.

"James, this is John Connors." "I want to know if you want a ride to the unit on Monday." "I live in the city of Hayward." "I'm near enough to pick you up."

"That would be nice Sergeant Major,"

"Good, be out in front of your house six in the morning."

"I will be there; what is the uniform of the day?"

"Do you have any civilian clothing?"

"Yes."

"Good wear them and bring all your gear and orders with you."

"Ok, I'll be waiting for you at six in front of my parent's home."

"See you Monday," the Sergeant Major said and then hung up. I packed my duffle bag and placed it by the front door the night before, and by five-thirty, I got showered and dressed.

"You know you didn't have to get up I would have been alright," I said to my mother.

"I get up at six anyway, are you coming back tonight?"

"Yes, but I don't know what time it will be I must hitch a ride with the Sergeant Major," I said as I sipped on some black tea.

As my mother fussed in the kitchen, I finished my tea; my mother said, "I wish you would have let me fix you breakfast."

"I'm not hungry, but I'm sure we will get something before the day starts at the unit," I replied.

I was out sided on the porch waiting for my ride five minutes before six and had to wait until ten after six before he came.

"Have you eaten yet?" asked the Sergeant Major.

"No."

"Well I hope you're hungry we eat at the Navy's mess hall, and they have some good cooks, we will have breakfast there." We talked about the unit, and he let me know it will be a significant change for me, but he will walk me through it and get me to the people I will be working alongside. As we rode down the road, I became quiet, thinking of how I would get to my old high school so that I could work out. The weekend would be no problem but during the week would.

"Your kind of quiet, is there something bothering you?"

"No, not really, I've been working out at my old high school, and I was thinking about how I would continue to work out." "I might have to use my old Volkswagen to go back and forth."

"How will that help?"

"Well, I could go directly to the school when I am released," I said.

"Is working out very important to you; you look fit?"

"I don't know what to expect when I do get deployed, and I don't want to take any chances," I replied.

The unit was unique as the Captain, and Sergeant Major told me. Everyone immediately accepted me as one of its members, and I made many friends. We wore fatigues during the day without any rank. However, when we left for somewhere, we wore civilian clothing, except for a military installation, such as the Navy mess or the San Francisco Presidio. I saw many have long hair, and some had beards, but the older ones groomed like a typical person in a business.

There were five of us in the gathering information and writing propaganda department; the rest of the unit consisted of command and support. But we five were the meat of the unit, and the guys varied in rank from private to lieutenant. When we weren't going to class, we practice mock scenarios for which the lieutenant who had a little training back east walked us through it. Lunch was delicious; what was great we had a choice of food. No one bothered us even though some had long hair and beards, but we did get plenty of stares and gossiping about us. We had our share of comedians in our unit, and they were funny. The unit consisted of three-quarters men and the rest women, and we were very protective of the females. We finished the day at three-thirty, and as I was riding back with Sergeant Major Connors, my thoughts were how lucky I was to get into this unit. "Make sure you let me know if you are going to take your car tomorrow," Sergeant major said.

"I'll ask my father tonight if I can have the VW and let you know when you pick me up tomorrow."

He nodded and asked, "What do you think of the unit?"

"If I knew it was like this, I would have joined the Army when I was fourteen," I replied enthusiastically.

He chuckled and said with a smile, "Remember most units aren't like this one, so be grateful you are in this unit."

He dropped me off in front of my parents' house, and I noticed that the Volkswagen was at home.

So, I went into the house and told my mother, "I'm going down to the high school to work out." When I got there, some of the coaches were still there, so I went into the locker room to work out on the Nautilus Machine. No one questioned me, so after about a half-hour, I worked out with the free weights and then went for a run; I showered and then went home.

I got home about six, and my dad had just gotten there about ten minutes before. When we sat at the dinner table, I asked my dad, "Do you think I can use the Volkswagen while I'm still here to get to the unit and back?"

"Did you lose your ride to that place you have to go to?" my mother asked.

"No, I just want to get to the high school faster to work out."

"It's your car; you can drive it when you want," my dad said.

"I plan to go see Charles also most likely Saturday afternoon."

"Charles who?" asked my father.

"Charles Kahler, my best friend, from Twenty-Eighth Avenue, I haven't seen him in years."

"So how was your first day back?" my father asked.

"It was great, they treated me good, and we ate at the Navy's mess hall, and they cook well."

"By the way, I won't need the car tomorrow the Sergeant Major is going to pick me up, and that's when I will tell him that I will have the car for the rest of the time you can take the car to work."

"No, I have the other work car I can take."

"Why have you kept the VW when you and Jerry have cars?"

"Well, you won't be in the Army forever." "You will need something when you get out beside the Volkswagen is a good running car," my mother said.

The next day the Sergeant Major picked me up at the same time, and again we ate breakfast at the Navy's mess.

All five of us that I worked with had a meeting that afternoon, but in the morning, we continued our training, and it seemed to be going quite well. I didn't find the task I had to do was that difficult, but others were having some trouble, and I couldn't understand why. At one pm, the five of us went into a room with others. Colonel Roberts, our company commander, was standing in the front, getting ready to talk.

"What you are about to see and hear is classified, and you aren't to discuss what you see." We saw a movie about some of the Soviet military equipment. As the film was running, you could hear a pin drop on the floor. Everyone was in shock at what the Soviets had, including me, and when the lights came on, the Colonel saw the expression on our faces but wasn't surprised at seeing it. "I can see that the Soviets equipment impressed you." "However, what you see is their best equipment under the best conditions most of their equipment doesn't work; this film was staged and brought to the west." "Any questions so far?"

I raised my hand and was recognized, so I asked, "Sir, if this film is a bunch of bullshit, then why is it classified?"

"Good question, and the answer is they don't know we know that their equipment is a bunch of crap." "The purpose of showing you this movie is to demonstrate how propaganda can work; you saw how well it worked on all of you."

"I will be going to each department to see how you are progressing." "I can't stress more that you must learn your craft well to convince the enemy that what you are saying is true." "I hope that you will take yourself out of the game if you think you can't do your job, but if you don't, then I will remove you."

We were dismissed and returned to our departments.

I finished the day without the Colonel coming by, but I was not worried when he would visit. When I got home, I informed my mother that I was going to school to work out. I never said anything about the movie or the Colonel. I figured there would be too many questions that would make me uncomfortable to say anything.

The Colonel came by Friday noon, "How are things going, men?"

"Very well, Sir," I said since he was nearest to me.

"What I want to do is talk to each of you men privately." "I'll start with you," the Colonel said, pointing Greg Martin. He was with Martin for about fifteen minutes when Greg finally came back, and then Sam Oaks went.

"What did he talk to you about?" asked Lieutenant Alex Sorenson.

"He went over my file and asked me some questions about what we were doing, and he wanted to know who I thought was doing the best and who the worse was," Greg said. When Sam got back, Joe Jerome went then Frank Morales after him; I was the last one who went.

He had me sit opposite him in a chair as he opened my file, flipped through the pages, then said, "Captain Reynolds and Sergeant Major Connors think highly of you, did you know that?"

"They are good people, Sir; it was very kind of them to think of me this way."

"The Captain said you have a desire to become an officer."

"Yes Sir, my brother is an officer I hope I can do as well as him."

He smiled and said, "When you finish your deployment, I will see to it that you go to OCS, you will most likely be a sergeant by then."

"You don't seem to be nervous as the others, aren't you worried that I might remove you from your department."

"No, Sir, I am learning the job quite fast and find the work easy so far, and I enjoy it; I don't see why you would remove me."

"I have no intention of removing you, who do you think is the weakest in your department."

I smiled and said, "I believe that we all have straights and weaknesses; however, we all work well as a team, and since I feel this way to ask me who is the strongest would be superfluous."

He laughed and said, "You have a point." "The others thought you are the strongest."

I thought for a few seconds letting that info sink in, then, I said, "They are good friends and being kind to me, but I feel they all have their strengths also." At that, he dismissed me, and when I got back, I did not say anything about what he told me.

The next morning, I went to the gym to work out one of the coaches was there I didn't bother him when I finished my workout and shower, I decided to go to Oakland to see my best friend, Charles. As I traveled down my old neighborhood memories flooded back into my mind, and a tear seeped from my eye of the thought of my lost childhood. When I drove to Charles's house, there was an old dark blue Volvo in his garage with engine parts all over the place. As I looked at the car out crawled a long blond hair nineteen-year-old man with a smile on his face and I said with a smile, "I heard you had some beautiful sisters and I came to see for myself."

"Your right, but they only go for beautiful guys," Charles replied.

"I guess that leaves me out," I said. We shook hands I wanted to hug Charles, but he was full of grease from the car.

"Could you use some help with your car?" "I don't know much about cars, but I am willing to help," I said.

"It wouldn't be right; besides, you would get grease on you."

"You're my best friend; there isn't anything I wouldn't do for you." "I can remove my shirt; what grease I get on me can be washed out." "What do you want me to do?" We worked on his car for hours before he quit, I did get grease on me, but I didn't care. It seemed like I never left Oakland, and our relationship was the same as when we were children. We talked as we worked, and he told me he was going to the University of San Francisco. I told him about the Army and what I was doing, and he said that he respected the men in the military.

"I have a deferment because I go to school, but my draft number is relatively high," Charles said.

"I joined, but it wouldn't have made any difference, I had a low draft number, they would have drafted me, and what's funny when I was in basic training, I did get a draft notice." "It's just as well you're not in the military; if something were to happen to you, I'd go crazy."

He put his head down, then said, "You keep careful yourself."

It was late afternoon when he stopped. Charles asked, "Do you want to clean up?" When we were little, we use to wash up in a laundry washbasin with this stuff call sand soap that I think his father got from somewhere. However, that is not what he had in mind. It turns out there was an apartment I didn't know about in the basement; it had a full bath. We went into his bedroom he stripped and went into the shower first then I jumped in. When I came out to dress, my T-shirt had some grease on it, so I left it off and put my shirt and underpants on, but I had to clean a little grease off my pants and shoes.

"Thanks for the help." "I will finish the car tomorrow."

"Do you want me to come by tomorrow?"

"If you want but I have a date you can go with me if you want,"

"No, that wouldn't be right; besides, you might get lucky," I said with a smile. We went upstairs, where I saw Charles's mother, father, and some of his siblings, including Nancy, but Caroline was not home.

The next day was Sunday, and I didn't work out. I did go to church, which I hadn't been doing while in the Army. My grandmother came over and made my favorite food a peasant dish from Spain. But I didn't overeat it because it is very fattening. My mother made a dessert I also like, but again I didn't eat much of it for the same reason; I talked a lot about Charles and his family while I ate.

Allen came over, and I hung out with him; he didn't talk any more nonsense about forming a commando unit. He talked about hunting, fishing, and the past; some of his stories seemed altered from what they were. He couldn't get over how fit I appeared to him and wondered why I didn't take better care of myself before I joined. "In high school, they didn't force me to do anything the Army is different; it is much more intense." "I got fit to stay alive," I explained.

In the next two days, we were training and got told Wednesday my department was going over to Stanford to do some mock research. The university had more than one library; our study was Indonesia. When we got there, I got lucky and found the right library. It was massive; it had three stories; everyone was wondering where to start. I went over to the card file found the location of several books while the rest of the guys were scattered around looking at titles. Since I wasn't familiar with this library,

I went over to a good-looking, blond hair female. She looked like a student and said, "Excuse me, I'm new to this University, could you direct me to where these books are."

She smiled and looked at the paper I had and said, "Third-tier, and it looks like down to the end."

"Thank you," I said.

As I started to leave, she said, "You are a freshman, then?"

I turned around and said, "You could say that, are you in your first year here."

"Yes, I'm a Chi Omega."

"Your sorority?"

"Yes, what fraternity do you belong to?"

"I haven't joined one; I live at home."

"What is your major and minor?"

I had to think quickly, then said, "Sociology and Economics."

"What your name?" I asked.

"Cathy Sweetser, and what is yours?"

"You have a sister by the name of Barbra?" I asked with a smile.

"Yes, do you know her?"

"Cathy, don't you know who I am?"

"You look familiar, but I don't know you."

"Think back about twelve years when you were a little girl."

She studied me carefully and said, "Oh my God, James, are you, James York?"

"It's been a long time, Cathy; you are as pretty as when I first knew you." We talked for a few minutes then I told her I had to go, but before I left, I got her phone number and the address.

As I passed the Lieutenant, I whispered, "Gather the others and have them follow me to the third tier." I found the books we needed, as the rest of the department joined me. As I was pulling books out, I glance down at Cathy, and she looked up at me and smiled.

"Pretty girl," said the lieutenant.

"Yes, I know her; she was a childhood friend."

"By the looks of her, she is still your friend."

"Yes, I think you're right." We got the information we needed and left the library for the unit, but not until we hit a bar first to have a few drinks and a little food.

31

When we returned to the unit, it was time to go home, so we left our notes in our office, and I left for my workout.

We had until Monday to come up with a report on Indonesia and write propaganda. I got elected to give the presentation to the Commander, the Executive-Officer, and the Sergeant Major, with the others providing their input when needed. "I will first tell you what we have learned about Indonesia with the other team members jumping in if I leave anything out." I went on to explain about the Indonesians. I was hoping someone would jump in, but they just sat back and said nothing as I talked. "I will now tell you about how we changed the information into propaganda again if I leave anything out the members of the team will jump in." I started out explaining how we took things and twisted them around. Again, no one said anything I wasn't mad; I just was a little insecure.

I sat down, and Colonel Roberts said, "I will comment first; the presentation was excellent." "It's obvious that you all have learned your jobs well, and it is also apparent that your research has been very successful." "The propaganda that you all have done is the best I've seen, to sum it up, well-done gentlemen."

The executive officer and Sergeant Major said similar things about us. When they finished, Lieutenant Sorenson said, "I must tell you something, Sir, James is the one who found the right library and where we found the information." "It was most of his notes that we use for the report and to make the propaganda."

"Is this true, James?" asked the Colonel.

"We are a team, Sir," I said, then we were dismissed.

When Thursday came, I was called into the Colonel's office and told to sit down. "I notice you don't take credit for all the positive things you do, but you choose to give credit to the whole department."

"We are a team, Sir."

"I like your loyalty; that's why I'm making you section chief you will be the same rank, but it will help when promotion time comes."

"Sir, there is a problem; there are at least two in our department who have a higher rank than me, and one is an officer."

"Yes, I know this; that's why I talked with your whole department, and they were all for it." "You have to understand that rank doesn't count here its ability."

After I talked a little longer, I went back to the office and said, "Why didn't you guys tell me about this section, chief business?"

"We thought the surprise would be better," said the Lieutenant.

Over the next month, we continued to train and perfect our trade; then we had a big meeting where the unit came together.

The Colonel said, "In three weeks we are doing training at Fort Ord, we will be staying there for two weeks." "You will only need your fatigues and maybe some civilian clothes for your off time." "We won't be wearing any rank, and I don't want you to associate with the other units' personnel." "Some problems you might face are your long hair and beards." "You females might get some harassment."

"We will protect them, Sir," said Sanchez he was in another section.

"I would prefer if there is any trouble you would come to me," the Colonel said. "I have talked to the Captain of the unit." "He told me he would inform his people to leave us alone."

I told my parents about the training at Fort Ord, and after three weeks, we left. I took my car as did some of the others and got there in the afternoon. We got stares from others, but I didn't care. Our reception at dinner was not what I would call pleasant. The girls stayed in the back of the mess hall. The rest of us were all around them in our group. As we were eating, three men from the other unit started walking towards our females, and we all stood up and blocked their progress.

"What do you three think you are doing?" I asked.

"We thought we would go over to those girls and introduce ourselves," said one of them.

"They don't want to be bothered, so just turn around and leave," said Joe from another department.

"I think they can make up their mind hippy," one of them said.

"Put that ass wipe tongue back in your mouth and leave before you get hurt," I said.

The whole mess hall was up on their feet when Cindy one of our girls came and said, "You, limp dick sons of a britches, leave we want nothing to do with you." The one who was doing all the talking looked at his two partners and then left. As we all sat down, a second lieutenant came into the mess hall angrily, expecting to see some trouble and when there wasn't any got livid and left.

At breakfast the next day, I was walked to my table with my food when four lieutenants at a table stopped me. One smart-aleck lieutenant said to me, "I don't allow dirty hippies eating in my mess hall."

As the four were laughing, I got mad and said, "Then take this shit you call food and shove it up your ass." At that, I slammed my tray upside down on their table, splattering food all over them. I was about to leave when someone was hassling our females before I could do something Jack Pendleton tried to stop them, but one of them took a swing at Jack, and the fight started. They outnumbered us, but we were putting up a good fight. Two tried to swing on me, but I knock both to the ground. The officers from the table I had trouble were getting involved. It wasn't long after our Colonel, madder than a wet hen came in, and the other unit's commander followed him.

Everything stopped when our Colonel grabbed the lieutenant that was causing me a lot of trouble, lifted him, and threw him against the wall. He then said, "Mister, I'm Colonel Roberts. You are in a whole world of hurt; you don't ever touch any of my personal again. Nor say anything to them, do you understand me, Lieutenant."

"Yes, Sir," said the Lieutenant fearfully.

"Now what's going on here?" said the Colonel. One of our guys told the Colonel the whole story, and the other unit didn't refute it.

Their company commander growled, "Except for the kitchen staff, I want my entire unit out of here and into the barracks." "You, four Lieutenants, wait for me in my office now." "Those of you who haven't eaten get your food and eat; I will be making arrangements, so you don't have to eat with them again." At that, I got another tray got some more food, sat down, and ate, but I already made up my mind that I would eat somewhere else for now on.

From that time on, my friends and I ate either in Monterey or at the Officer's Cub. Saturday, we found out there was a party in Carmel, but it was nothing and only stayed for a few hours. That night we ate at a fancy restaurant in Monterey we got drunk and made fools out of ourselves. Sunday, some of the guys and I went for a swim. The pool was huge; it had a jacuzzi and a sauna with many military families swimming. I was sitting on one side of the swimming pool with the rest of the guys when I spotted a pretty blond hair girl on the opposite side of the swimming pool, so I swam over to her.

"Hello, my name is James, do you swim here often?" I said.

"Yes, with my family."

"So, what do you like to do for fun?"

"Swim, go bicycle riding, and play at the beach."

Something strange about the girl made me uncomfortable, so I asked, "Are you in school?"

"Yes."

"What is your favorite class?"

"I like reading, writing, and oh yes, arithmetic," she said with delight.

Arithmetic, I thought, then said, "Did you say arithmetic?"

"Yes, it's like doing puzzles."

"How old are you; what grade are you in?"

"I'm in the fifth grade; I'm ten."

I turned beet red in the face. I was shocked this girl was nearly my height, and fully developed. I looked up at her and asked, "Where are your parents?"

"My mother is right over there with my brother," she said, pointing to her left.

I got up, walked over to her mother, and said, "Excuse me, but I need to apologize to you."

"For what?" she said with a smile.

"I was hitting on your daughter; I thought she was a lot older."

"Don't let it bother you; it happens all the time we are used to it." I excused myself and jumped back into the pool, joining my friends.

"Do you see that girl over there?" I asked the guys.

"You mean the one you were hitting on," said Sam with a smile.

"Yeah, guess how old she is?"

"Twenty."

"Eighteen,"

"At least twenty-one."

"I'm saying nineteen; how old is she, James?" Sam asked.

"Ten."

"No way, she can't be," they all were saying.

"She is, and I'm glad I am not the only one who got fooled." After time in the sauna and Jacuzzi, we went back to the barracks.

Monday, we went to a field training exercise, we would go to a village with the Green Berets gather information come back and turn it into propaganda. Each of us would go out with three men, who were supposed to be the Green Berets, and I went first. The whole thing went well, so when we all got back, we talked about our experience.

"It seemed kind of phony, a weak version of what we might see," said Sam.

"I have to agree with that," I said.

"I have a feeling that we may be heading to Vietnam," said Greg.

"Why do you think that?" I asked.

"The whole theme was South East Asia; I just got a bad feeling that we were going to get deployed to Vietnam."

"That's not how it works if we get deployed, it will be one at a time, not the whole team," said Alex.

"Who told you that," asked Frank.

"Captain Reynolds."

"Well, I don't think I have anything to worry about right now." "I have a brother there," I said.

"You are lucky," said Alex.

"Well, it won't do you guys any good to dwell on it, so let's get back to work," I said.

We finished our training, and it was nice being back home again away from those idiots from the other unit. Monday, I walked into the office and sat down read a manual we just got. I'm not a coffee drinker, so I had my cup of hot chocolate as I was reading the manual most of what I was reading I already knew.

About ten o'clock, Sergeant Major came in with a box full of more manuals, and he said, "The Colonel wants you to read these manuals." "He wanted me to tell all of you; you did an outstanding job during the two weeks training at Fort Ord."

"Tell the Colonel thanks for his kind words," I said. After he left, we looked at a couple of manuals, one read training in a combat situation, and the other one read surviving a prison camp.

We looked at each other, then Greg said, "Are you convinced now that we are going to Vietnam?"

No one answered him, but I said, "I am not going to worry about it until I can find out what is going on."

At lunch, I saw an open spot at Captain Reynolds's table, so I asked, "Sir, would it be alright that I sit at your table?"

"Certainly, have a seat." The captain was talked to another officer, and I waited until I could jump in and ask about the manuals.

"So, James, I hear a lot of good things about you and your section."

"We do our best, Sir."

"Sir, do you know why we got manuals to read dealing with training in a combat situation and surviving a prison camp?"

The captain's demeanor wholly changed, then he said in a somber voice, "I can't tell you much, but I would think you and your department should study those manuals." "I have to be going," he said and got up and left before I could say more.

I told the guys back in the office what happened, and they just turned around and went back to work without saying anything. That night I went home wondering if Greg was right. I didn't say anything to anyone because I just wasn't sure what was going to happen.

The months went by; no more got said about Vietnam.

I had come into the office Tuesday morning just before Sam had come in, and Greg said, "Colonel Roberts wants to see you."

"Alright, is he in his office."

"That's where he said to meet him." I went to his office, not thinking what the Colonel wanted, would happen to be a big deal.

"You wanted to see me, Sir?"

"Yes, please sit down." "You know James; I'm more than pleased with your performance here, you and your department have surpassed what I had hoped." By about this time, I was getting nervous. The Colonel continued, "You deserve a promotion, and you said you wanted to go to OCS, so this will happen when you get back from deployment."

"Deployment, Sir?" He handed me a packet of paper, and I looked at it. "It says I'm going to Vietnam; Sir, I have a brother there."

"I know the Sergeant Major told me, and I've called everybody I could, to change your orders and got the same answer every time." "You can talk to the commanding officer at the deployment office in Oakland." "If that doesn't work, you can talk to the commanding officer where they post you in Vietnam."

As I looked at the orders in shock, he said, "I'm sorry James clean out your desk and your locker, and the rest of your time, you will be on leave." In shock, I went back to the office to my desk, and I started emptying it.

The rest of the department saw something wrong, and Sam came over to me and said, "What's wrong, James." I didn't say anything I just handed him my orders, and he said, "Nam." Everyone knew then and tried to be sympathetic towards me.

"Damn, if they can send you, they can send anyone," said Greg.

The Sergeant Major told me, "When you get over there, never get complacent and listen to those who have experience there."

3

VIETNAM

When I got home, I told them that even though Bob was in Vietnam, the Army was sending me over there. "I plan to talk to the deployment commander tomorrow, but I don't think it will do me any good."

The rest of the night, everyone acted subdued, and I tried to put my deployment out of my mind. It wasn't that I was trying to get out of going, it's just the unknown of what might happen my brother was an officer in the Air Force he was somewhat safe, it wouldn't be in my case.

The next day I headed to the deployment commander office. The next day I headed to the deployment commander office. I talked to a specialist four clerk, "Corporal York, to see the commanding officer of deployment."

"What for?"

"I wish to talk to him about my deployment."

The specialist gave me an annoyed look, and just before he said something, a master sergeant came out. He said, "The Captain hears men whining about going to Vietnam all the time, and he doesn't have time for you."

"I'm not whining about going; my commander Colonel Roberts said I should talk to him about another matter about my deployment."

You could see he wasn't happy with what I said, and he said, "Wait here." He went down the hall, ten minutes later, he said, "Follow me."

We went down the hall, opened a door, and I went in, stood at attention saluted, and said, "Corporal York reporting as ordered by Colonel Roberts."

"Sit down, corporal; what do you want."

"I am not trying to get out of going to Vietnam, but I have an older brother deployed there already."

He leaned back in his chair and let out a breath of air and said, "That is different; what is his name and what unit is he in."

"He's Captain Robert York, and he is in the Air Force; in bombers or some other kind of plane, he is both a navigator and bombardier."

"When are you to deploy?" I handed him my orders, and he said, "I'll do what I can to confirm your story but if I don't get back to you make sure you are back here on time, and you must talk to someone over there to see if they can do something." I thanked him I was dismissed and left for home, knowing he wasn't sincere. Before going home, I stopped off to see coach Reynosa.

I walked up to him, handed him the key to the Gym, and said, "The Army is deploying me in seven days?"

"Where are you going?"

"Vietnam."

"Well, you are in the best shape that you ever have been in your life." "Just be careful and come see me when you come back." I thanked him for using the equipment and said I would make sure I would contact him when I came back.

"So how did it go?" my mother asked.

"He said he would investigate my story, but I think he is insincere."

"Why do you say that?"

"It's just a feeling I have."

"He said if I don't hear from him, make sure I report for deployment on time and I can talk to someone over there."

"Maybe we should write to Bob."

"A letter wouldn't reach him in time, and even if it did, he wouldn't have enough time to stop my deployment," I said. Everyone else got notified later that day the rest of the night was quite subdued.

The remainder of the week, I worked out at home. Also, down the creek, to keep my mind off my troubles. I did go down to Charles's house and let him know what was happening, and many of my relatives came by to give me their support. When Friday came, I still hadn't heard from the deployment officer; I resigned myself that I was going, and there was nothing I could do about it. My father had a barbecue, and many of my relatives showed up I could tell my mother wasn't thrilled with all of this. I left with my dad to deployment building at seven in the morning. They brought me into a room, took a copy of my orders, and went through my things, and taking almost everything. They issued me jungle clothing, and they also gave me a new set of dog tags, which were slightly different from the ones I had. After I got my things, I was taken to a place to get a physical and some shots that didn't make me feel so good. Later, I, with others, got an orientation on Vietnam. All this time, I looked for the Captain in some false hope of a last-minute reprieve, but I never saw him. We were to leave the next day they put us in a room with thirty others. It was quiet in the bunk area; everyone wondered what it would be like in Nam, and that night I had a sleepless night.

The next morning, we had our breakfast, grabbed our gear, and headed downstairs single file for a bus to the airport. They took our duffle bags and told us to pile into the transport I was about to get in when someone yelled, "York, wait a minute." I got out of the bus and saw the Captain who I talked to a week ago. "Corporal York, I tried to get your orders changed, but I didn't get the proof of your brother in time, but I did find out he is there." "Talk to your commanding officer when you get there, and I'm sure they will send you back."

"Thanks for trying," I said and turned around and entered the bus without saying another word. I was angry, I knew if the Captain had investigated when I first talked to him, he would have had the paper proof, but he blew me off.

We got to the airport, they had a chartered plane waiting for us, and there were more guys and a few females waiting to board the aircraft. We all boarded the plane; it was a stuffy, cheap-looking chartered plane, which made everyone uncomfortable because of the way they designed it. They put the females upfront and the men behind them. I was near the middle next to a window near the wings. As we moved out, the wings of the plane appeared to start flapping as the jet tried to climb, and I thought this plane would crash. The flight was a long one with a stop in Hawaii for fuel and a few hours stopover in Guam, where we ate and stretched our legs while the plane got a look over. I slept and woke up several times, we were still over the ocean, and I thought this flight would never end. We finally landed at Tan Son Nhat Airport in the late morning.

It was a warm, humid cloudless day when military staff ushered everyone from the plane into a building that had what looked like a gymnasium to it. We lined up in front of several tables, and when I got to the table, a second Lieutenant said, "Your orders." I handed him my packet, and he said, "PSYOPS, Bill, this is the one you been looking for."

The Second Lieutenant took a copy of my orders, handed the rest to me, and pointed to a person coming towards me.

"I'm Lieutenant William Henderson." "I've come to take you to your headquarters and then to your post." The Lieutenant was a six-eight black man over two hundred pounds of pure muscle he was in the Green Berets, and he had an attitude of all business. It appeared to me he didn't think much of me.

"I need to get my duffle bag," I said. The military staff brought in the duffle bags, and I found mine, and we went outside to a jeep. I threw my duffle bag in the back of the jeep, got into the front seat, and went off.

"Your headquarters is on the other side of Saigon." I nodded and didn't say much as we traveled down some rough roads. I was fascinated by my surroundings for a small country; there seemed to be people everywhere. The smells were all exotic to me, there were many colors, mostly very bright, and the vendors were everywhere hawking their wares. About forty-five minutes after we left, we rode up to a building in a compound.

I got out and was about to follow the Lieutenant when he said, "Grab your duffle bag and take it with you, you can't trust anyone here if you leave your duffle bag it won't be there when we get back."

"Even in an American compound, Sir."

"The GI's and Gooks will both steal the things you have until you can stow them away."

We walked into the building, and I noticed that the Lieutenant didn't take off his hat, but I took off mine. I went into an office and handed my orders to a Second Lieutenant who appeared to be a clerk. "The Captain wants to see you before you leave, sit down he just stepped out and will be back soon." About ten minutes later, a Captain came into the room, and the Lieutenant said, "This is your man, Captain."

I stood up and said, "Sir Corporal York reporting as ordered."

"We are informal here Corporal come into my office, and we will talk."

"I'll stay out here and watch your things," said Lieutenant Henderson. When I went into the Captain's office, he told me to sit.

"I'm Captain Paige, and I'm your commanding officer." "I received your file yesterday, and it is impressive." "We do things a little different here than what you did back in the World." "I found it is better to split the intelligence gathering from the propaganda; your job will be the gathering." "Six months from now, you will be replaced and do the rest of your time here writing propaganda, and I will promote you to sergeant."

"Your very generous Sir; there is something I need to tell you, Sir."

"What is that?"

"Sir, I'm not whining nor trying to get out of anything, but you need to know I have a brother here in Vietnam."

"Why didn't you try to change your orders when you were in the World?"

"I did, Sir, Colonel Roberts, my commander back in the Bay Area, tried but couldn't get anyone to listen." "The commanding deployment officer tried but couldn't get the paperwork in time to stop the deployment, and both said I should tell you," I said.

"What is his name and outfit?"

"Captain Robert York and he is in the Air Force as a navigator or bombardier he has done both."

"I will do what I can, but you have to know that it will take longer to get this problem corrected here in Nam than it would in the World." "At least your brother is posted near here." "Even so, I am figuring more than a month finding him and getting the paperwork." "Then, the proper paperwork will go to the commanding officer of deployment." "He will review it and send it to Washington for a recommendation to send you home that could take three to five months," said the captain.

"Thanks, Sir I won't blame you if I didn't get that promotion when I get back here." I figured I'd mention it to see what he would say.

"No, when you come back, I will promote you."

"Again, you're very generous; I will need some equipment for this post I will be going to," I said.

"I have a grip full of everything you will need when you gather your information send it back here, we will turn it into the propaganda."

"Yes, Sir."

"Then, unless you have any more questions, let's go get your grip and get you on the road; I imagine you have jet-lagged."

"Yes, Sir, but I will be alright."

"That's the attitude I want to hear." He took several copies of my orders, I got my grip, and after he talked to Lieutenant Henderson a little, we were off to who knows where.

"You hungry?" asked the lieutenant.

"Yes, a little."

"Good, we will be going to a unit near here to catch a Huey, and they have good barbecue."

"Do you mean a Huey helicopter?" I asked a little nervous.

"Yes, you will love it," he said, laughing.

As we traveled, I asked him, "You don't think much of me, do you?"

"Why would you say that?"

"It's the way you look at me and talk to me."

"I mean, you no disrespect." "You have to understand I'm in Special Forces and we work as a team each of us watching each other back someday my team might have to take you someplace, and that will be a burden to us."

"I'm not exactly weak, and I am a good shot." "I know I haven't had the training you and your friends had, but you haven't had the training I've had."

"I'll tell you what I will do; I'll consider you as one in the team who is just green, which is the truth."

"That sounds good; I must admit that it would make more sense if they would make PSYOPS part of the Green Berets that way, the person doing the job wouldn't be much of a burden."

"Yeah, your right."

"The funny thing is I always wanted to be in the Green Beret."

"Why didn't you try out for the unit then?"

"If you had seen me when I first joined the Army, you would have laughed so hard you would have had a heart attack, I was two hundred and seventy-five pounds of pure coach potato lard."

"That's hard to believe, but if it were true, you seem lean and strong now why don't you ask to try out."

"I might just do that; it's something I have to consider." We finally arrived at a military compound, and when we drove in, I could smell the smoke of a barbecue.

We stopped in front of a large tent with sandbags around it, and the lieutenant said, "Stay here and watch your things." Lieutenant came back with a smile on his face and said, "Will eat well tonight, and the Huey will be here in about three hours." "We can stow your things inside and get something to eat while we wait."

"What about the jeep?" I asked.

"I borrowed it from this unit we will just leave it here," he said as he lifted my duffle bag and I grabbed my grip.

We walked over to where everyone seemed to be having fun; the Lieutenant said, "Who's in charge of this barbecue?"

"Right here, you two help yourselves plenty of meat, food, and Buds take as much as you want," said a G. I. dressed in only pants and boots on. We both grabbed a paper plate, some plastic utensils, and we both dove into the food with Buds. To my surprise, the Lieutenant sat with me, not caring to join others that were there.

"I'm Sergeant First Class Jackson, where are you two from back in the world?"

"I'm Lieutenant Henderson; my family is from Virginia."

"I'm Corporal York; I'm from California."

"Well, I come from Missouri," said the Sergeant.

"What part of Missouri?" I asked.

"A town in the southeastern part of the state called Poplar Bluff."

"You ever hear of a town call Ellsinore?" I asked.

"Sure, it's a small-town west of Poplar Bluff, you have kin there?"

"Yes, an aunt, uncle, and a whole house full of cousins, their last name is Korenek."

"Let's see now, I know of a Paul Korenek who works for the state don't know much about him though."

"That's my uncle."

"Well, well, it's a small world."

"Lieutenant, I see you're in the Berets; where is your unit?"

"In Vietnam," he said coldly, got up, and walked away.

"I wonder what's eating him," I said.

"I tend towards being a bit nosey; I take no offense."

At that, he walked away, and I went over to the Lieutenant and said, "You ok, he didn't mean to offend you?"

"I just don't like people asking too many questions about my unit; it's not safe."

"It's not like the V.C. doesn't know where you are."

"You have a point there, but one question leads to another." We ate until we became stuffed, and about three hours, the Huey came, and I loaded my things inside as they were refueling the copter.

"Well, let's go," the crew said to us."

"It's his first time," the Lieutenant told the crew with a smile.

They all started laughing, and I said as they took off, "Aren't they going to close these doors?"

"No, just hang on." I wrapped my arm around a three-inch-wide olive drab strap as we shot up and forward. My eyes got as large as saucers at the way they were flying; everyone thought it was funny, but I didn't. It was too dark to see anything. It was just as well if I can't see down there, then maybe no one noticed us, I hoped.

About an hour and a half out, there was a bang and a ricochet sound. "What in the hell is that?" I asked, shaken. Before anyone could say anything, the gunner of the Huey, open-up with his machine gun. When he stopped shooting, the Lieutenant pointed to a bullet hole in the floor six inches from me. I curled up into a ball and never took my eyes off the hole in the Huey until we landed. As we got off the Huey with my things, others were getting on. The crew didn't stop the blades, so we had to keep bent over until we cleared the copter, and then it took off again. The Lieutenant took me to the company commander, and Lieutenant Henderson talked to him first, then I was ushered in.

"I'm Captain Gleason." "I understand you had an exciting ride out here?"

"Yes, Sir."

"I also understand you have been up for two days, are you worn out."

"I'm tired, Sir, but I still have a few hours left in me."

"I'm sure you do, but you have to be sharp out here, so I will give you a few days rest before you go out and do your thing."

"Very well, Sir."

"Sergeant Porter, get this man a bunk with some bedding, and if he is hungry, something to eat in other words, take care of him."

"Yes, Sir."

"Sir I will need a weapon I didn't come with one."

"Sergeant get him whatever weapon he wants."

"Yes, Sir."

"Are you hungry?" asked the Sergeant.

"No, not at all the Lieutenant and I had a big barbecue dinner."

"If I know the Lieutenant, he is eating again," giggled the Sergeant.

"What kind of weapon do you want?"

"I'd like a pistol, M-16, and a bowie knife if you have one, a Hawk would be nice also, but I doubt you have one."

"Pistol, M-16 won't be a problem Bowie knife we don't have, but I can give you a knife we use."

"Is it balanced well?"

"Better than any Bowie you've had."

"Good."

"What's a Hawk?"

"Sort of a hatchet light in weight and is well balanced."

"We don't have one here, but I wish I had one."

I received my pistol and M-16 with ammo and a cleaning kit when he gave me my knife. I felt it, and it felt excellent, so I tried it on a wooden box.

"Nice throw," said the sergeant. The sergeant gave me a bunk, and I put up my gear, made up my bunk, and was asleep in a few minutes.

"Hey, little man, are you going to eat," said some Sergeant.

I woke up a very sleepy and said, "Is it breakfast already?"

"No, it's lunchtime?" I went to the latrine, threw some water on my face, and found out where they had some food. After I looked at my surroundings, what I saw was a perimeter of razor wire. The jungle had been about seventy-five feet set back from the razor wire. It seemed like a top of a hill was flatten for this compound. There were sandbags everywhere for hootches and foxholes. The dress was very casual T-shirt or no shirt at all, and some had Boonie Hats, some no hats, I rather like to get a Boonie Hat.

"How's it going?" I turned around, and it was Lieutenant Henderson talking to me.

"Fine, Sir, now that I had a little sleep."

"When you get dressed and put on your boots, make sure you shake out your clothing and shake out your boots, you never can tell what will crawl up into them."

"Yes, Sir."

"Sir, is there any way I can get one of those Boonie Hats."

"Sure, go ask the supply sergeant for one he is right over there, tell him I sent you," the Lieutenant said, pointing to my left.

I walked over to a staff sergeant who was cleaning up and asked, "Are you the supply sergeant?"

"Yes, are you new to this unit?"

"Yes, I'm attached to this unit; I'm in PSYOPS."

"Yeah, I heard about you; you think that stuff works?"

"Yes, I've seen it works if done right, and I'm very good at it."

"What do you need?"

"Lieutenant Henderson said I could get a Boonie Hat."

"Follow me over to the supply hut and let me see what I have." We walked over to the hut, and the sergeant handed me a hat, and I tried it on.

"A bit small," I said. The sergeant looked at the sizes of a few hats then handed me another; it was perfect. "This one is a good one, thanks."

"If you need anything else, let me know."

"I'll do that." After lunch, I went back to my bunk and started cleaning my pistol and rifle.

As I was cleaning my rifle, one of the guys I shared the hootch with came over to me. "I'm Sergeant Greg Brooks. That guy on the bunk over there by the door is Corporal Nickerson, across from him is Corporal Peterson and across from me is Sergeant Sounders."

"I'm Corporal James York; it's nice meeting all of you."

I finished my rifle and pistol and got out my sharpening stone and started on the knife. As I was working on my knife Corporal Peterson came over and asked challengingly, "You any good with that knife?"

"Leave him alone, Peterson," said Sergeant Sounders.

"I'm alright with it," I said.

"Well, let's have a little contest to see how good you are York."

"Careful James," said Sergeant Brooks.

I smiled and said, "Well, let's see how well I can throw; what do you want to do."

"Let's go outside and find a target," said the Sergeant with a smirk. I took off my shirt and T-shirt and went outside. As we left the hootch, everyone followed, and more outside joined us, including Lieutenant Henderson and Captain Gleason.

Peterson placed a big X on a box, stepped back about fifteen feet, and said, "Closes to the center three times wins."

"Fine, you go first," I said.

"Ok, if you wish, but how about a little wager."

"What do you have in mind?"

"I won't be too hard on you how about a case of beer."

"Well, if you can get the beer here, I'll agree."

He threw his knife, it stuck, and someone pulled it out and yelled, "One-quarter inch from dead center."

"Good, but I want you to understand that I'm accustomed to throwing a Bowie knife, but I will do my best," I said with a smile. I've been throwing knives since I was ten, and I said that to him to make him feel a little cockier.

"Now, don't make any excuses now, greenhorn."

Surprisingly, the knife I had was better than any Bowie knife I had ever had, and it felt better. I studied the X, relaxed, and threw my knife.

The same guy that pulled the last knife pulled mine and said, "Dead center." The same man smeared mud into the knife marks, a less sure Peterson got ready to throw, and when he threw, he hit dead center. When it was my turn, I threw, and again it hit dead center.

It was Peterson's last turn, and before he threw, I said, "Peterson, this beer would be shared anyway, so no matter who wins, I don't want any hard feelings."

"I'm not a poor loser; I don't hold a grudge."

He threw and hit dead center and then said, "It's a tie."

"He still has his turn," said Sergeant Sounders.

"Alright, go ahead," Peterson said. I smiled, stepped back ten more feet, took the knife, threw it, and hit the dead center to Peterson's surprise.

There were loud shouts of approval and many congratulations, and I walked up to Peterson and said, "I won't hold you to the bet."

"I'd hold you; I'll get the beer." I smiled and shook his hand, and then Lieutenant Henderson and Captain Gleason came up to me.

"You surprised me, James," said the Lieutenant.

"It's not a surprise I was throwing knives ever since I was ten."

"If you want to get into the Green Berets, the Lieutenant and I will help you," said Captain Gleason.

"Well, that's very kind, and I just might hold you to that."

I went back, finished sharpening my knife, and then put it away, and I grabbed my grip and went through the things I had to do my job. I had a small thirty-five-millimeter camera with film and two lenses telephoto and wide, a small eight-millimeter movie camera with film and two lenses, small pencils, notepads, erasers, and a little Vietnamese Dictionary. I looked at the two cameras and said to Sergeant Sounders, "Does it rain much this time of year?"

"Some but not as much as it does during the monsoon season."

"Shit, I need to go to the supply sergeant."

"What's the problem?"

"If water gets on my equipment, it will be destroyed."

"Make sure you have a weapon with you." I slid my knife in my boot, and strapped my pistol on, went outside, and headed to the supply hootch.

"Nice knife throwing, Peterson needed to be beaten; he is too cocky for me," said the supply sergeant.

"He's not that bad of a guy," I replied.

"Well, what can I do for you?"

"I have a problem, the equipment I have, I can't let get wet, I need something to protect it when I'm out in the field."

"Let's see what I have here; I have some plastic, but make sure you poke some holes in it, so moisture doesn't build up."

"The plastic will do fine, thanks again."

"Anytime," he said, and I went back to my hootch.

I rapped everything I had and placed fork size holes. Jungle fatigues have more pockets than regular fatigues. So, I could put all my ammo clips in various pockets and even had room for a notepad and pencil. I then put the rest of my PSYOPS equipment in my backpack and still had some room.

We all went to eat, and I like others I ate outside. I sat in a foxhole with some other guy who had a nickname Tex for apparent reasons.

"You ever been to Texas?" he asked.

"Just the panhandle on my way to Missouri."

"Oh, those people are a wholly different type."

"The towns looked nice, but my family had a few unpleasant times with the people."

"Yes, they are uppity, go down around Amarillo, and it is a whole different situation there."

"Where are you from?" he asked me.

"California, born and raised in the San Francisco Bay Area."

"You haven't had a welcoming call from Charlie yet, have you?"

"No, what kind of welcoming do they give?"

"Oh, you will find out," he said with a grin. I finished my dinner and went for a walk around the camp, and when it was getting dark, I went back to my bunk and went to bed I was still feeling the effects of the air flight. I must have been sleeping several hours when I got knocked out of my bunk by many big explosions and gunfire.

I grabbed my rifle still sleepy and headed for the outside, but Sergeant Brooks stop me, "You stay in here, we can't lose you." He didn't get any argument from me. I waited until all the excitement ended. When the gunfire stopped, I popped out of the hootch and looked around and saw small fires and men running all over the place.

"Exciting isn't it," Peterson said with a smile as he came in.

After everyone came back into the hootch, I asked, "Does this happen often?"

"Almost every night," said Corporal Nickerson.

"Why doesn't someone go after those guys?"

"We've tried, trouble is they know this area better than we do, and they melt back in with the local villagers," said Sergeant Brooks.

I sighed and said, "I'm going back to bed and get some more sleep." I knew I would have to figure a way to get more sleep during the day.

I was woken by Sergeant Sounders, "Time for breakfast."

I ate outside again and decided after I eat to take a bath. Now bathing in the field style was a whole new thing for me. I inquired about bathing, and it was always the same story. Bathing consisted of stripping completely naked. Standing next to a fifty-gallon drum of water using your helmet pot and scooping water, you pour it over your head, and that's your bath. When shaving, you use the helmet pot also, and I planned to do both. I lost my bashfulness of being nude back in basic training. I finished bathing I felt better about it since no one took notice of it and I went ahead and shaved.

I pulled up my pants when Corporal Nickerson approached me and said, "The Captain wants to talk to you?"

"Ok, I'll go right over there as soon as I get a shirt on."

"You wanted to see me, Sir?"

"Yes, sit down." "I saw you bathe and shaved; that's good, tomorrow about eight you will be going out into the field for about four or five days." "Lieutenant Henderson will be your team leader; you will need to draw some ammo and rations."

"I have ammo, Sir."

"Draw some more it's better to have too much than not enough."

"Yes, Sir, where are we going, Sir."

"Your designation is just over the Vietnam border in Cambodia." "There is a village in Cambodia, and there are some villages along the way."

"Why Cambodia?" "I thought we weren't supposed to go there?"

"We aren't, but we believed that the Ho Chi Min trail goes through there, and this assignment comes from your headquarters."

"Well, I go where I'm told to, Sir."

"Good luck to you."

"Thank you, Sir."

"The Captain said I'm going out in the field tomorrow he wants me to draw more ammo," I said to the officer in charge of the armory.

"For what weapons?"

"The pistol and M-16." He handed me four banana clips and six pistol clips, which I didn't know where I would store them.

"What's the problem?"

"I don't know where I'm going to carry them."

"Taking a backpack right."

"Yes, but I will have it full of my equipment and food."

"Hand me your clips." He taped the M-16 clips by two upside-down from each other he gave me two hooks. "You take this one and shove it up into your rifle when you use up the clip flip it over and use the other side. You take the other two clips and hook them to your backpack straps; the forty-five clips are small, find a place for them." "Here, take these also." He handed me four grenades and said, "Hook those to your pistol belt."

"Thanks, Sir."

"No problem, good luck to you." I headed back to my hootch.

As I walked into the hootch, the others were packing their packs, they all looked at me, and Sergeant Sounders said, "You didn't think we were going to let you go alone, did you?"

"I didn't know Lieutenant Henderson was your squad leader."

"Yes, us and the next hootch over."

I smiled and went over to my bunk, deposited my clips and grenades, and headed towards the door. "Well, this will allow me to protect Corporal Peterson. I wouldn't want anything to happen to him until after he gets the beer." Before Peterson could say anything, I left for the supply hootch, but I heard a lot of laughter.

"Sergeant, the Captain, wants me to draw some rations I'm going out into the field," I said to the supply sergeant.

"How long are you going to be in the field?"

"Captain said four or five days."

He handed me twelve small cans and said, "Bon apatite."

"Thanks."

Each can contain something different in it, and I was about to leave when he said, "Wait a minute." He handed me some hard candy, and told me, "If you get a little hungry, suck on some of these."

I smiled and thanked him again, then headed back to the hootch. I took all my things out of my backpack and put the cans and the candy first;

then I put my PSYOPS gear on top. I attached the two clips and figured I had about thirty pounds in the pack I then took out the small clip I had in my rifle and replaced it with the other banana clip. I decided to put the grenades on my pistol belt just before I leave. After I finished, it was time for lunch, and I went to eat, then came back and took a nap until dinner.

After dinner, most of the guys were inside bullshitting. The only one who wasn't there was Corporal Nickerson, who was smoking. I hopped up on my bunk and shut my eyes, trying to sleep, hoping Charlie doesn't visit us tonight.

"What are you doing?" Peterson said as he came over towards me.

"Trying to get some sleep, I figure I will need all the rest I can get if we are going out at eight in the morning."

Everyone started laughing, and Peterson said, "We never leave when the sun is up, we are leaving at about eight at night so that Charlie won't have a clear shot." I got down from my bunk, and he said, "Let me check your gear."

He lifted my pack, and Sergeant Brooks said, "What is the weight."

"About thirty or thirty-five pounds with the clip," Peterson replied.

"That's a great weight," the sergeant said.

"Make sure you don't forget your grenades," Peterson cautioned.

"I won't."

A card game started, and Sergeant Sounders said, "James, you want in on this game."

"No, I'm not much of a card player."

"Suit yourself."

The Lieutenant came into the hootch as I watched the card game and said, "Everyone into the other hootch."

I grabbed my forty-five and followed the others into the hootch.

"Listen up; we are going to the villages of Pleime, Le Thanh, and Andaung Pech." "Andaung Pech is in Cambodia, and we must cross the Yang Krong River twice; it's called the Se San in Cambodia, but it is all the same river." "We will be leaving at eight pm tomorrow." "This whole exercise is for gathering information to write propaganda, which is James York's expertise." "Are there any questions?"

"Yes," I said.

"What is it, James?"

"I have some equipment that can't get wet, how deep are these river crossings."

"The water shouldn't be much deeper than your waist, but if the water is deeper, we will get your equipment across without getting it wet." "Any more questions?" "If there aren't any more questions, James, come up here and tell everyone what you need us to do."

"When we approach a village regardless of whether you think the enemy had been there or not, I do not wish to enter immediately." "I want to observe the village and its people first." "Once we enter the village, we talk to the head honcho first to sweet talk him you never know when that person will say something that I can use." "Even if you think there is nothing there, I can always find something." "Like an extremely skinny child or a hut with little foodstuffs, even a pregnant woman can be a propaganda tool." "Do we have an interpreter?" Sergeant Brooks raised his hand, and I said, "Good, stay with me when we go into the village, and when we talk to someone, let that person know that you will interpret for me and then say what I say."

"You got it," Brooks replied.

"Great, but if you think I'm saying something wrong, let me know, I not afraid of being corrected." "Peterson, I might use you to threaten the head honcho I'll talk to you about it later." He nodded, so I said, "The only other thing I can tell you is that the information I gather is more important than me, but do your best to get me back." We got dismissed to go back to do what we were doing, and I went back to the hootch and went to bed.

The next day I tried to rest but was very uptight about going out into the field. I wasn't nervous about doing my job, but I was concerned about what might happen along the way.

After dinner, I hooked my grenades on my pistol belt, waited, and at eight o'clock, we piled out of the hootches and headed to the back gate where there was less light. "Quiet, stay low," the Lieutenant said. I was placed third from the end, and we left in a single file, and we moved out. I was very nervous as we moved out but hoped that after daylight, I would feel better. We traveled for about four hours, stopping several times to check our trail ahead. I was surprised that the weight I had on me wasn't bothering me at all. When we finally stopped for a rest, the Lieutenant came back to me and asked, "How are you doing?"

"I'm fine, not tired at all."

He slapped me on my leg and said, "Good, we will be traveling till light before the next rest." After about fifteen minutes we were at it again as we went, I thought that I'm glad that I worked out the way I did it has helped. So far, we hadn't run into any trouble, which made me feel a little better. We traveled over one hill and down another, we stayed away from established trails choosing to make our own. Climbing up or downhills, we were a muddy mess, and the insects seem to eat you alive it was a good thing I had repellent.

The sun had come up, and we took another break. The Lieutenant came over to me and said, "We will be at Pleime in a few hours." We rested about an hour before we set out again; some ate, and some, like me, slept or dosed I wasn't that hungry and decided to save my food. As we traveled, there was an abundance of sounds of animals and insects. What scared me was the occasional noise of branches breaking. Every time I hear these sounds, I imagine it was Charlie, of course, it wasn't, and the noise didn't even faze the other guys.

In a few hours, we topped a hill, and down below was a small village. The Lieutenant came over to me as I took off my pack, "You let me know when you want to move down to the village."

I nodded and asked, "Does anyone have binoculars?"

"Yes, we will give them to you when we check out the village for hostiles first." I had some film in the camera already, so I added my telephoto lens to the camera and then pulled out my notebook and started taking notes. Each roll of film had a number on it, so my notes would correspond with the film. I got the binoculars, and I looked at the village, picking out possible things I could photograph. I switched to the camera and started taking pictures, a burnt hut, a water buffalo sleeping, however, it looked like it was dead and other subjects of interest. I wrote some notes and then picked up the binoculars, and after I finished with them, then I handed the binoculars back.

"I'm ready to go down if you are," I said to the Lieutenant.

"Ok, let's head out Peterson take the point." We headed down to the village, single file, I with my camera around my neck. As we traveled down the hill, I found some things to take pictures of and writing notes. As we walked into the village, we attracted a lot of attention.

We went to the head man, and Sergeant Brooks started to talk to him, "My name is John Brooks this man's name is James York he wishes to speak to you, and I will tell you what he and you say."

"It is an honor to speak to you." "I'm writing a book about the people of this land." "I would like to take some pictures and asked questions of you and your people; with your permission."

Sergeant Brooks translated what I said, and I gave a signal to Peterson to start the trouble we had discussed earlier. He came charging towards the village leader yelling with an angry face, "Where is the V.C., Where is the V.C."

Peterson grabbed the frightened man as he yelled in English, "No V.C. here, No V.C. here."

As planned, I grabbed Peterson, knocked him to the ground. As the sergeant translated, I said, "I believe this honorable person I will not allow you to disrespect him anymore."

The Lieutenant grabbed Peterson and said, "You come with me." They walked away Peterson, struggling with the Lieutenant's grip on him. I turned to the leader and said, "I wish to apologize to you, the Lieutenant will punish that man for the disrespect he showed you." Then the sergeant translated again.

The old leader was silent for a few minutes looking at me up and down then said in Vietnamese, "I speak only to you, your parents must have taught you great respect, come into my home we will talk."

"May I have John Brooks also come, so we will know what we say?"

"Yes, I like him too."

As I walked behind the older man into the hut, the Sergeant nodded to the Lieutenant, and I waited to be seated and sat down on a straw matt. The older man said something to what I assume would be his wife, and she brought us all something to drink.

As the sergeant drank, I waited, and the old man said, "Why aren't you drinking? Do you not like what my wife has prepared?"

"I have been taught that it is polite to wait until after the one who is older, wiser, and master of his house drinks first."

"You honor me, and your parents raised you correctly."

"You may ask me or any of my people any question you wish and take as many pictures as you want." I smiled and sipped my drink that wasn't too bad.

The old man got very quiet then said, "There is something I wish to tell you, but it is dangerous if I do."

"I will protect what you say."

"The V.C. and even soldiers from the North come here often they take our young and our food and ask questions about you."

"What do you tell them about us?

"The truth anything else they would kill us."

55

"When were they here last, and where did they go?

"They were here two days ago, and they went south."

"How many were there and what kind of weapons did they have?"

"There were much more than my whole village, and they had only the weapons they could carry, but some didn't come into the village who could have had larger weapons."

"Thank you for telling me this information I would like to take some pictures now."

We went out, and he followed us around the camp as I took pictures and wrote notes. Sergeant Brooks informed the Lieutenant of what we found out, and the radioman sent the message to our compound.

We walked all around the village, asking the older man many questions about life in the village. "Do you have any women who are with child?" I asked the older man. He took me to three women who were in the different months of their pregnancy. "Sergeant ask this woman what their fears and hopes for her child; you don't have to translate to me." I took pictures of the expression on her face when she spoke and then thanked her and moved on.

"Do you have any women who have had children who have died or taken?" I again asked the older man.

Then he took us to one couple when the sergeant asked about their child. I took pictures of their expressions while they talked. We came across some children playing, and I had an idea. With the help of the sergeant, I said, "I will give you something sweet to eat if you play a game with me." I pointed to one boy and said, "Show me how you would look if you were frightened." I took some pictures and said, "Now, all of you look frightened and pretend you're crying." They did, and I took some more pictures. "Now remember what you all did, now I want you to run crying and afraid do this looking back at me."

They did beautifully. After calling the children back, I rewarded them all, then went over to the Lieutenant and said, "We can leave now."

"Good, I wanted to leave a half-hour ago." I thanked the man and told him we had to go. I said to the Lieutenant we should go in another direction, so they don't know where we are going, or they will tell the V.C., and the Lieutenant agreed. We traveled for three hours and then took a break. The Lieutenant came to me and said, "I didn't have a chance to tell you that you did an excellent job." "You got us valuable information, and I will inform the Captain of this."

"Well, thanks, but I did have some help, Lieutenant."

He nodded and said, "Do you have any of that candy left?" I pointed to my backpack, and he fished some out. "This next village won't be as smooth as the one we left." "They are very unfriendly, suspicious people." "We should be there by nightfall but won't enter the village until the next day."

"Understood, I'll do the best I can with them."

"You better get something to eat and get some rest." I nodded and pulled a can out of my backpack, open it, and it was ham and eggs, and I devoured it. I then took some more notes and checked my camera; it only had a few pictures left, so I took some photos of the guys and had Nickerson take my picture. I then took another notebook and film then wrote the number down on it. I placed the notebook and pencil back into my pocket then loaded the film into the camera then I pulled my hat over my eyes and dozed off to sleep.

When several hours passed, Robertson kicked in my leg and said, "Time to go." I got up, relieved myself, then put my backpack on and left. It was dark when we came to a dirt road the lieutenant sent two guys to check it out then we went over to the other side. We continued to travel towards the village as we were moving, I was surprised that I wasn't as uptight as I was when we first left the military compound. However, I was also aware that I couldn't become complacent. It was nightfall when we got to the village, and we found a place where we could stay without being noticed until sunup.

At sunrise, I took pictures from a hidden area, and then we headed into the village. As the Lieutenant predicted, the village leader was not happy that we were there, and everything I said made him more stubborn. "So, what do you want to do, this guy isn't going to budge?" said Lieutenant Henderson.

"We played nice; now we play rough." I said, with an angry look on my face, "Translate for me." I grabbed the leader, threw him to the ground, and said, "You will answer all my questions, or you will die slowly." I pulled out my knife and said, "Who here is V.C."

"No, V.C., no V.C.," he said frighten.

I sliced him in the neck, not deep but enough to hurt and said, "Who here is V.C." He pointed to a man who ran, and our guys shot him.

I yanked him back to his feet and said, "Where are the V.C. weapons?" He wouldn't answer, so I grabbed him showed him the knife, and he pointed to his hut. We went to his hut, and the guys tossed it and found a large amount of ammo and weapons in an underground bunker. Our men threw several grenades into the bunker then burnt the hut destroying everything. As my team was doing this, I took pictures and notes of everything in the village, including the dead V.C. I made more notes of Le Thanh than I did in Pleime; I decided to wait to get a fresh notebook and new film. We left and traveled for five hours then stopped by a river the first of two. I changed out the film and loaded the movie camera with film after that I took out a fresh notebook and rapped the old notebook around the second roll of film.

Again, the Lieutenant came over to me, and with a smile, he said, "You can get nasty when you want."

"I didn't like what I did."

"Sometimes, you have to do things you don't like to achieve your goal."

"Yes, I know this; that's why I was rough with that man."

"Your actions will be noted in my report when I get back."

"I think if you want to be in the Green Berets, you should apply." "I would be more than happy for you to be on my team."

"I will consider it."

"Let me ask you one more thing." "If that man you cut had not talked, would you have killed him?"

I thought for a few seconds then said, "I would have hurt him a little more, but if he hadn't given us any information, I would figure he doesn't know much and let him go." With a smile, the Lieutenant slapped me on my shoulder, got up, and went to talk to someone else.

I had a good sleep that night even after what I did the day before; I figured that I must have been exhausted. Before sunup, the lieutenant sent someone across the river, and I saw it wasn't all that deep, so I went across with confidence that nothing would get wet but me. We walked about an hour when word came down the line that we were in Cambodia, and after that, we were at the second river crossing. As before, someone went across first, which was much more dangerous because the sun was up. I saw the water was about the same depth but running much faster. I turned around to Sergeant Sounders and said, "Keep an eye out for me if I start to slip or stumble, grab me, don't let my backpack go into the water."

"Don't worry; I won't let anything happen to you." With much effort, I got across without the help of the Sergeant. We traveled about thirty minutes when we came to a heavily traveled trail with tire and footprints.

It was the Ho Chi Minh Trail, and we moved away from it as fast as we could, but not before I photographed it. We traveled for about five hours before we stopped for the night. The Lieutenant said we should be at the village before noon tomorrow.

It was a cloudy, humid day when we headed out. The going was not as bad as when we were in Vietnam. I was filthy, and I thought even the bath I would get back at the compound would feel great about now. The plan was to get to Andaung Pech, take some pictures and interview some people and then head back to the Vietnam side where the landing zone was. As we traveled and time passed, the jungle seemed to be getting thicker, and then suddenly, we broke through to a downward sloping terrain that led to the village down below. After checking the village with binoculars, I started taking pictures then I spotted something through the camera. I put down my thirty-five-millimeter camera and pick up my movie camera with the telephoto lens and, at the same time, then pointed said, "Look over there." From the side of the village came many North Vietnamese soldiers in vehicles pulling equipment and on foot. I switch from the movie camera to the thirty-five millimeter then back to the movie camera. As I was taking the pictures, there were some shootings of resisting villagers, and suddenly, we saw a female child run straight for us. We stayed low, so we weren't detected. The soldiers were shooting at this child; I had my movie camera on her as she was getting nearer. The Lieutenant was getting uptight when the soldiers started to chase the girl up the hill.

The Lieutenant said, "It's time." Before he could say to leave, the little girl's face disappeared in a mass of blood and mangled flesh, and she went down no less than thirty feet from us. I threw my cameras in my backpack, and off we went, but sadly we were spotted, and one of our men was hit by enemy fire, but not bad. We ran as fast as we could as the enemy pursued us. We ran about five miles before we stopped, the one man who was wounded was taken care of, and after a short rest, we moved out fast again. After several hours, we slowed down a bit until the sun came down, and we stopped.

The Lieutenant sent Nickerson to check our back trail. I ate and removed my film then repacked my backpack. When Nickerson came back several hours later, he went directly to the Lieutenant. After about an hour, we headed out again. By a little, after sunup, we came to the Ho Chi Minh Trail, and there was a problem. We spotted some N.V.R. waiting for us on the other side of the road, and we couldn't wait until dark because the N.V.R. was also coming up behind us. "James, Peterson come here," ordered the Lieutenant. "You two think you can hit those two N.V.R. with your knives?"

"No problem," we both said at the same time. Peterson gave me the one on the right, we both threw at the same time, hitting both in the chest, and they went down without a sound. We all ran across the road, but we were spotted, and the fight was on. Sergeant Brooks grabbed me, and we were running, another man got shot, but he kept running. Lieutenant Henderson got hit, and it looked like it was a severe wound, but he also managed to keep going. We saw the river, but we skirted south of it while the N.V.R. pursued us.

We were moving uphill just ahead of N.V.R. I asked, "Why don't we call in an airstrike?"

"We are in Cambodia no planes or copters will come here we have to cross the border to get any help," Sergeant Brooks said.

Just then, I felt a sharp burning sting to my shoulder, I stumbled, and the wetness of blood trickled down my arm from my wound it was painful, but I kept ongoing. Sergeant Brooks took notice and asked, "Are you hit bad?"

"No, I don't think so, but it smarts." We got to the top of the hill, and it started to level out we were lucky there were many trees and bushes to give us cover.

Lieutenant Henderson wasn't doing very well, but he was still moving. Sergeant Brooks said, "We are in Vietnam and near the L.Z." The Sergeant must be right because I could see Richards, who was our radioman already calling for help. The blood was still dripping down my shoulder, but I guess I had a lot of adrenaline in me because I hardly felt it now. Two of our guys were shot in the head and went down someone got their dog tags I saw others who were wounded. We found some cover fifty feet from the L.Z., and Sergeant Brooks went with two other guys to lay some cover fire. I was with the Lieutenant, the medic, and two other men who were wounded, not bad. After a few minutes, I saw Sergeant Sounders get hit, and he didn't get up, and Corporal Suarez was injured but still fighting.

When I saw this, I knew I had to do something, so I took off my backpack and said to Sergeant Nelson, who was wounded with me, "Make sure this backpack returns to the right people."

"Where do you think you're going, Corporal?" asked the Lieutenant.

"If I don't help those guys giving cover fire, we are all going to die, and this whole trip into Cambodia will be a waste." I pulled out a letter we all carry in case something happens, and I handed it to the Lieutenant. "Tell my parents that I will always be alive in the spirit."

"I'm not going to let you go now; you stay here; that's an order."

"You have no choice, and you know it."

I was about to leave when the Lieutenant grabbed my arm and said as he took off his dog tags, "Give me your dog tags." I did, and he gave me his and said, "Wear them; they might save your life."

I put them on and moved out as bullets were whizzing all around me. I made it about halfway around to where Sergeant Brooks was when I heard the thump of Hueys coming. I went the last half of the distance to the Sergeant, and miraculously I wasn't hit.

"You got to be crazy to be here." "Why didn't you stay with the Lieutenant?" the Sergeant said.

"You know they wouldn't make it back without enough cover fire." I flipped my M-16 to semiautomatic and said, "You know how well I can throw a knife now you can see how well I can shoot." The N.V.R. started advancing, and one by one, I picked them off. They were about two hundred yards from us, and it seemed like every time I shot one-two more would show up.

"You are a good shot, too bad I won't live long enough to tell anyone," said the Sergeant.

"We aren't dead yet." The N.V.R. kept on coming, we kept on shooting them Corporal Suarez was reshot I thought he was dead. The Huey had landed the other Hueys couldn't give us cover because they didn't know where we were and the N.V.R. were. The Lieutenant had just loaded into the copter, so we tried to move out when Sergeant Brooks got shot, and we hunkered back down. I kept on shooting, keeping them off us the Sergeant patched himself up as well as he could. I finished my two banana clips and shoved in another one as the Sergeant was shooting as well as possible. As we were shooting, the Hueys were starting to fire around us, I assume the Lieutenant told them where we were, but the N.V.R. came anyway. I ran out of ammo for my M-16 except for the small clips I had in my pockets. I went through those clips fast. I grabbed what clips Corporal Suarez had but ran out again, and the N.V.R. kept on coming. I pulled out my forty-five and started shooting with that, and they rush us, so I threw a few grenades and started shooting again. The N.V.R. backed off again.

"Go save yourself," said the Sergeant.

"Go, where will I go, to the L.Z., I'm out in the open, and I will get shot." They started sneaking up again, and I started shooting and throwing grenades. The sergeant was beginning to pass out, so I took his weapons and used them. One N.V.R. got close, so I took my knife and threw it, hitting him in the chest. I grabbed the Sergeant's knife and started yelling like a crazy person, and then I got hit with what felt like a bat in the back of my head, and everything went black.

4

P.O.W.

The Hueys flew the wounded to a military medical facility near Saigon. The Lieutenant lost a lot of blood but would be alright, and he could return to duty after treatment. When Lieutenant Henderson recovered, he brought the film, notes, and equipment to the PSYOPS office. He gave the letter I wrote to the Commander. Lieutenant Henderson also wrote a report of happened and made a note as to what I contributed to the mission. He reported to his commander, and both Psyops commander and his commander sent everything to command with a recommendation on how they should recognize me for the sacrifice I made.

Planes pounded the area we were in, and then they sent troops in to clean up. When they came to where the battle was, they found more than four hundred dead North Vietnamese Regulars and our dead from the team, but what they didn't see is neither Sergeant Brooks' body nor my body. Many of the N.V.R. dead were in the area where we were providing cover fire.

The report of what they found was written and sent up to command. After a review of all statements, two officers, seven o'clock Pacific Time, rang my parent's front door. "Are you Manuel and Marie York?" asked Chaplain Werner.

"Yes," my father said concern.

"I'm Chaplain Werner."

"May we come in, Sir," asked the chaplain.

"Yes, please come in." My father showed them into the living room, and my mother joined them, confused.

"This is Captain Smith, and as I said, I'm Chaplain Werner, we are from the Defense Prisoner of War and Missing Personnel Office."

"Is this about one of my sons?" my father asked.

"Yes, Sir, Corporal James York."

"The good news, Sir, is he is missing and not counted as dead," said the Captain.

"What do you think happened to him?" asked my mother.

"We believe he is a prisoner of the North Vietnamese." "I'll tell you what we believe happen, and perhaps you will understand." "Your son was on a dangerous mission with the Special Forces; where he was, I cannot tell you, it's classified." "They completed their mission and were about to head back when they were spotted." "They tried to escape their pursuers but weren't successful." "Several men were killed or wounded, including your son, but his wound wasn't life-threatening." "They were waiting for a helicopter to come when two of the soldiers covering the injured, were wounded or killed." "James risked his life by joining the remaining person, still protecting the wounded; this act most likely saved all the others." "We moved a large force of men to retrieve the dead." "Your son and another man weren't there, and the enemy does not take dead bodies."

"When do you think they will let you know if they have him?" my father asked.

"Maybe a few months."

"Why that long?" asked my mother.

"They will be transporting him up North, and then there is the interrogation, paperwork, and notifying of the Red Cross."

"How do you think they will treat him?" asked my dad.

"I won't lie to you; they won't treat your son very well, but from what I understand, he is strong; he can handle it."

"There is something else I need to tell you that is very important," said Captain Smith. "Just before James left the wounded, the team leader exchanged his ID tags with him." "The Lieutenant's thinking was that being an officer would help save his life; his name is Lieutenant William Henderson." "Under no circumstance are you to write to him using any other name other than Lieutenant William Henderson." "Nor should you tell the press if it gets back to those holding him it could cost him his life."

"He talked to the Lieutenant and said to tell you that not to worry about him that his spirit would always be here." "It is the habit of the soldiers in combat to write letters to be sent back home just in case something happens to them. James did this also," Captain Smith said as he handed the letter to my father.

"We must be going, but I want to stress one more time use no other name other than Lieutenant William Henderson." "If we hear any more, we will contact you."

"We will be careful with the name thanks," said my father

"There is one more question I wish to know," my mother said. "What about my other son Bob he is still in Vietnam?"

"He already has orders to return home, and I would guess he is already on his way back," said Captain Smith. They shook my parents' hands and said their goodbyes and left.

My father opened the letter and read it: "Dear Ma and Dad, if you got this letter, it means something terrible has happened." "It does no good to dwell on it; it was something meant to be." "If I am gone, I am in a better place, with Bill, and that's not so bad, besides someone needs to teach him how to play Hearts." "I knew what I was getting into when I joined the Army." "I also knew what I was getting into when I agreed to the training in the field I entered, and finally, I knew I might go to Vietnam." "If it weren't me, it would have been someone else Uncle Art knew this, as did Uncle Raymond they were lucky I wasn't." "If I am gone, I will still be there in spirit as Bill is." "Take care of the dog; she is a good girl, let everyone know and then move on, Jim."

Bouncing around in the vehicle is what woke me up. Everything was blurry, and I was in a cage. My head hurt; as did my shoulder, someone was next to me in another cage, I couldn't make out who it was just before I passed out again. I was woken once more this time by the rain falling on my face. I was still hurting, and my eyes were fuzzy, but they cleared up some after a few minutes. It was dark out and raining heavily. I knew it wasn't cold, but I had the shivers anyway. I was thirsty, so I let the water from the rain drip into my mouth, and I could suck the water running down the bamboo bars of my cage. Across from me was the other cage with Sergeant Brooks in it, and he was motioning me to be quiet, he made actions to tell me fake that I was asleep. I nodded, I understood, closed my eyes and tried to relax as I lay there, I could hear people taking in Vietnamese. I opened my eyes a little enough to see the Sergeant, and he didn't look well; he only knew how I looked. I could see him all banged up with a nasty wound on his shoulder. I was able to see the dog tags that Lieutenant Henderson gave me, and I memorized what was on it. Then I closed my eyes and tried to sleep even though this cage was miserable, but I did drift off to sleep.

The rain had stopped, and it was sunup, my cage opened, and I was dragged out of the cage onto the ground, as was the Sergeant. They started kicking and beating us with a bamboo stick, screaming Vietnamese. I tried to protect myself, but with each whack or kick, the pain shot through me. The beating continued until what I thought was an officer yelled something, and they stopped.

"Stand up," the officer said with a heavy Vietnamese accent. The Sergeant and I tried to get up, but it was difficult because our arms were tied, and we were weak. As we were struggling to get up, the N.V.R. officer said something, and two soldiers each grabbed the Sergeant and me and pulled us up. They shoved a bamboo stick behind our backs and taken over to a lean-to where there was a table and another officer. They forced us to our knees as the officer across the table looked at us and then looked at the dog tags; he took from us just before they took us to him.

"What were you doing in Cambodia?" asked the officer speaking better English than the other officer. We didn't answer, and for that, we both got beat. The Sergeant keeled over as they kept beating him, so I jumped on top of him to take some of the blows. The officer said something, then they stopped hitting us, and they pulled me back up while Sergeant Brooks had passed out. The officer looked at me again and said, "What were you doing in Cambodia?"

"My name is William Henderson, first lieutenant."

"I know who you are; I have both of your identification tags; I want to know why you were in Cambodia," he snarled.

"It is my understanding that the American military is not in Cambodia." For that answer, they ripped off my shirt and beat me with a bamboo whip cutting into my back until I passed out.

I regained consciousness before the Sergeant did; we still had our hands tied behind our backs with a bamboo stick lodged behind our backs. My arm and head hurt as well as my back burned with pain from the beating I got. The Sergeant finally woke up and righted himself up.

"What did they do to you?" he whispered.

"Whipped me a good one with a bamboo whip."

"I can see your back; it's all messed up." "Why did they do it?"

"In part because they wanted to, and I didn't tell them what they wanted to know."

He nodded then whispered, "We are in deep shit; they are taking us up North." "It might be a good thing though they typically kill the Green Berets," he added.

"Too bad we had to cross the Ho Chi Minh Trail, we all might have made it," I said.

Just then, the officer who couldn't speak English very well kicked us both and said, "No talking." I sat propped up against a tree, wondering if we were going to get any water or food which we didn't, so I tried to fall asleep. I had to pee in the middle of the night, and I knew they weren't going to let me lose, so I rolled over and went.

We got awakened at dawn, or should I say beaten at dawn, pulled to our feet, and started walking. In tandem, the North Vietnamese soldiers tied a rope around our necks; I guess they figured it would slow us down if we tried to run. We walked for hours, and I was quite thirsty about an hour after we had an afternoon break, I heard some of the soldiers saying the word Laos, so I figured we were in Laos. By night, we came to the village of Ban Tasseng, and they put us in a hut under guard. A woman went into the hut with a bucket of water and a cup she gave the sergeant some water and then me, and I drank greedily and wanted more. The woman gave the Sergeant some more, and as I was getting my second cup, the guard threw her out. I closed my eyes and wondered what was going to happen next to us. I was a wreck, and the Sergeant was worse; it was miserly humid, and I was still hurting. I started to dose as the N.V.R. were eating, but I was startled awake when that girl that was giving us water came back with what looked like a slop bucket. She cup fed us, it had a bit of rice and fish many vegetable parts, it didn't taste terrific, but I didn't complain and ate as much as she would give.

The next day we were dragged out of the hut early and headed down the road. It started raining again, but I didn't mind because it seemed to cool things off, and it helped with the thirst. We walked about three hours when Sergeant Brooks stumbled, and we were whipped with those bamboo whips again. The Sergeant wasn't doing very well; I could see he had a fever. The wound he had, stop bleeding two days ago, but it looked nasty; I didn't know if he would make it to wherever we were going. We finally got a rest break, but after about forty-five minutes, we were off again. Ultimately, we stopped for the night I looked over to the Sergeant and whispered, "How are you doing?"

"I'm in bad shape; my wound got infected, and I'm weak."

Every night that we stopped, that officer who tried to question us would walk by and sneer, tonight was no exception. When he walked by me, I said, "If you don't get him some medical attention, he will die, and I'm sure your superiors wouldn't be happy."

For that, a soldier with him started beating me with a leather whip instead of the bamboo one. The officer smiled with that sneer he had and walked away. I had dozed off when there was a bunch of noise next to me. A soldier was stripping the shirt off the Sergeant then looked at his arm. The soldier touched the wound, which caused the Sergeant to scream. He poured some water on the wound and washed it, then he put a salve on the wound and then bound it. He forced open the Sergeant's mouth, poured some powder into his mouth then forced him to drink some water. Then the soldier looked at me in disgust, and I stared back. All three of them got up without saying a word and left.

I sat back and smiled, and the Sergeant whispered, "You pulled a nice one, but I wouldn't press your luck."

"It was worth it," I replied.

The next day we were on the road for about an hour when we came to a deep river. The Sergeant and I struggled to get across the river; the only good thing was that we could stick our faces into the water to drink some water a few times before we got out. When we stopped, I looked over to the Sergeant, and I whispered again, "How are you?" The sergeant just nodded his head that he was alright.

The next day after traveling several hours, we came to a fork in the trail, and we stopped and rested there. When we started again, three-quarters of the N.V.R. went to the right fork as did all the vehicles, the Sergeant and I were forced down the left fork. We traveled until dark then stopped for the night. The lack of food, water, and the beatings was starting to take a toll on me. The Sergeant and I laid back, looking forward to another night of no food and water. So, as the N.V.R. ate, you could imagine how surprised I was when a very young-looking soldier came over to us with two buckets of water and food.

"I have gotten permission to feed you," said the young soldier.

"You speak English very well," I said.

"I was in a special class to learn your language." He started first with the Sergeant and said, "I am sorry this is not very good what they have given me, but it is better than nothing.

"It was kind of you to bring it," I said.

"I do not like the way they treat you; we are not all like them."

"I understand my people are the same way," I said. He finished with the Sergeant and started with me.

"Why are you here?" he asked me.

"Are you asking me here in Vietnam or here with you?"

"Why are you and your people in my country?"

"In my army, we follow orders and don't question them; this goes for all armies, including yours."

"Why do they order you to come to my country?"

"They did not teach you how this war started?" The young soldier shook his head no. "Your people are two people; there are people who wish to be socialist like you, and those who want to be capitalist like in the south." "Before the Americans came, there was the French was here we came in part because the government in the south asked us." "When the French didn't do very well and got kicked out, the people of South Vietnam asked the United States for help." "Most people in the United States do not like the policies of socialism." "So, the United States Government was more than happy to come."

"So, how do you feel about being in my country?"

He gave me a drink of water, and I said, "I believe that the people of the North and South should talk in good faith without fighting to decide what they want." "The United States should only help when asked but not to help with violent things."

"I believe this, too," he said.

"Then live long for you are very wise," I replied.

He got up and left, and the Sergeant turned to me and said, "That was smart of you." "I think you might have made a friend who may help us." I smiled and knew he thought I was playing a head game with the young soldier, but the truth was I meant everything I said.

The next day we crossed another river not as deep as the first river we cross. We didn't get any food or water the next day, but the day after we did with our young friend and I asked him, "I am curious, how old are you?"

"Fourteen."

"Is it common for one so young to be in the army?"

"No, I lied about my age; my brother and father are serving, and I wanted to also."

"Do yourself a favor when this war is over, go back to school." "You're too smart to be risking your life," he nodded and left.

The Sergeant chuckled and smiled as we sat there. The next day before we rested for the night, we came to another fork in the trail, and when we stopped for the evening, I asked the young soldier where those paths went, and his whole demeanor changed. "If I offended you, I am sorry," I said.

"I think you ask to escape?" said the young soldier.

"I am in no shape to escape, and the Sergeant is worse than me." "I would not leave him."

He thought for a few seconds then said, "Those trails lead back to the south." Two days later, we crossed a major road, and the next day we left Laos and entered Vietnam, North Vietnam.

Even though we were in the North, we still were moving North East for most of the day until we came to a camp near the Lang Mo village. There were several buildings for the guards, cooking, supply, medical, a large building for that were the commandant office, and his quarters. There were also two rows of twenty kennel size cells, each made of what looked like corrugated tin and wood surrounded by dirt. Two N.V.R grabbed me, removed the rope from my neck and arms, then dragged me to the first cell, opened the door, and threw me in, and immediately close the door. It was pitch black in there as I lay on what felt like a stone floor. From across my cell, I heard the same thing going on with the Sergeant. My eyes started to adjust to the darkness, and I found small holes in the front of the cell that light came through. I tried to look out one of the little holes, and I couldn't see much, but I could see soldiers standing around smoking and laughing. I could see a twenty by twenty raised platform for which I didn't know what they used it for, but I saw nothing else. I figured I would have to find a way to make the hole larger.

After about an hour in the cell, my eyes adjust well enough to see my surroundings I had a raised six-foot-long, two-foot-wide rock platform for which I figured it was for sleeping. There were two buckets at the far end of the cell one was apparently for a toilet, and the other had water in it, I would guess for drinking. The height of the cell was about five feet, and the width was about four feet. I tried standing and could if I bent my head down. I looked around the entrance of the cell, and it had a wood door. It had several nails; some of them bent over for which I started to see if I could loosen any, and I was lucky I manage to pry one up with great difficulty. I got worn out from trying, so I drank a little water and laid down on my stone bunk. As I laid there, I could hear brushing sound from the next cell over. I thought it was a rodent, but then it hit me there was someone next door. I thought about yelling to get my neighbor's attention but figured I shouldn't the N.V.R. would just beat me, so I just closed my eyes and tried to get some sleep.

I awoke, and it was dark outside. I felt around for the small hole in the wall, found it, and looked out there was some dim light far off, and I could hear the N.V.R. in the distance. I knew there was a guard nearby but not very close. I couldn't see that nail I worked on earlier, so I felt around for it and finally found it. I worked on it hoping I could pull it out, and after several hours I did. It gave me some sore fingers in removing it, but now I had a tool to make a bigger hole to see out of, and perhaps I could think of other things to do with it. I dug up some soil with the nail from around the rocks and pushed it into the hole left by the nail. After sharpening the nail on a stone, I started to enlarge the hole in the front of the cell. It took several hours to widen the hole enough for me to see very good but not so big for them to notice. I stuffed that hole with dirt; then, I was about to hide the nail when I heard that brushing sound again, so I went to the wall and tapped "a shave and a haircut." I waited then I heard two taps I knew Morse code, so I tapped out, "I am Lieutenant William Henderson," then I paused, then tapped it out again and crossed my fingers.

I got rewarded with, "I am Lieutenant Michael Susmann U. S. Navy pilot what branch are you?"

"Army Green Beret, Sergeant Greg Brooks and I were both captured."

"Thank God, you are both trained in survival." I thought if he ever knew the truth, he would be incensed, but I couldn't tell him otherwise. "I am the ranking officer here." "If you don't mind when the commandant interrogates me again, I will tell him that you are the in command of us, prisoners, maybe you can get him to treat us better."

"I think you are making a mistake, but if you do, you better come up with a story on how you know my rank," I tapped.

"Smart, I will do that," he tapped.

"Good, I am tired I need to sleep now," I replied. I hid my nail, then laid down and drifted off to sleep.

It was sunup, but that wasn't what woke me the door to my cell busted open. The Vietnamese dragged me out, and I was roughly stripped and then kicked and beaten with clubs when they finished, I was bloody, and I was thrown back into my cell with some dark blue pajamas. I laid on the floor, trying to recover from the beating. I tried to protect my head but only had limited success. I think my nose might be broke, and I might have a concussion because everything is blurry and spinning in my head. Also, I felt like I had a severe migraine, and I couldn't hear very well. I was bleeding around my body, and I knew I had or will have many nasty bruises. I moved around a little it was painful, but I didn't think I had any broken bones. What nearly knocked me out was when someone kicked me in the groin. After about five minutes, my head started to clear, they split my lip, the guards chipped one a tooth, and I was almost sure that my nose broke at least it felt that way. I could hear someone else being beat, so I got my nail and poked out the hole to see them beating Sergeant Brooks. He was a mass of blood, so I looked away; I didn't want to see anymore. I was sitting on my bunk when I heard tapping on my wall.

"What condition are you in?"

"Badly bruised, maybe a broken nose, possible concussion, I think the Sergeant is in worse shape."

"They beat everyone when they first come, sick N.V.R welcome."

"You can say that again."

"They won't bother you for a couple of days now."

"When do we eat?"

"Afternoon sometime only one meal."

Sometime in the afternoon, the door to my cell open and it was the young soldier we met moving up North. He handed me a small container with and a wooden spoon, and then he looked around and gave me two pieces of bread.

"How is my companion? I asked.

"He lives, but I cannot talk." He shut the door, I took off my shirt, rapped one slice of bread in my shirt and started on the vegetable soup. Of course, it tasted terrible; it had about a tablespoon of rice, vegetables, and it tasted like pumpkin, which dominated it, and the soup they watered down. I ate it anyway with one of the slices of bread I knew it was all I was going to get for the day.

A different soldier picked up the container and spoon, and I settled back on my bunk as best I could. It was a hot, humid day; I was sweating a lot, which is something I seldom do. After about an hour of doing nothing, I was getting bored, but I found that if I went into a fantasy, I could pretend I was somewhere else.

I was deep in thought when I snapped out of it by the noise of some guards nearby. Then the door of Susmann's cell was opened, and I heard him drugged out, so I looked through the hole in my cell, and two guards had him by the arm and were hurrying him towards the commandant's office. I laid back down and wondered what he was going to go through. A little more than two hours had passed when the Lieutenant was dragged back to his cell in worse shape than when he left.

I went over to the wall and tapped, "How are you?"

"A bit beat up, but I will live." "I don't know if I did you a favor or not, but you are the new prisoner commander. Expect to be taken to the commandant tomorrow," the Navy Lieutenant tapped.

"I'll want to know what he is like and what to expect, but I will ask you tonight, get some rest for now." At that, I laid back down and went back into one of my fantasies.

It was dark out, so I went over and tapped, "Are you up to talking?"

"Yes."

"Tell me about this commandant and what to expect."

"His name is Major Dac Kien, and he is a very educated and cunning man who speaks English very well." "I believe that his education was in America." "He will most likely try to study you to find out your weaknesses; he is very narcissistic." "He will find some way to justify him, giving you a beating to establish who is in control, but he doesn't do the beating." "The one I wish to break his neck is Sergeant Major Anh Dung. He is the one who hands out the beatings with such glee." "I would suggest that you hold out as long as you can then give him something that doesn't mean anything," the Navy Lieutenant tapped.

"Has Major Kien have any weaknesses?" I tapped.

"He likes a strong-willed person." "When the Major knows he isn't going to get what he wants, the Major will negotiate, but it is tough to get him to that point, and he likes to hear things that will make him think."

"Thanks, that will be useful." "I am going to sleep now." I laid back on my bunk and started thinking of what I could do to get better treatment. As I rested there, I took out the second piece of bread and started eating it. The next day after I relieved myself, I drank some water and then used my shirt and a little water to give myself a sponge bath. Then using a splinter of wood and my shirt as an abrasive, I cleaned my teeth. I sat back and rested to wait for the ordeal I knew I would be going through today. We got something to eat, the same as before, but I only got one piece of bread this time the young soldier wasn't the one handing out the food today. I ate quickly, so I would be able to finish before they came and got me. The young soldier was the one who picked up the containers, and when he did, he pulled from his shirt a piece of bread, and I said, "Thank you, but you be careful you don't get caught." He didn't answer; he just shut the door and left. I had to find a new place to hide the bread. I dug around a rock the size of my fist, at the foot of my bed. I found I could remove the stone. Underneath the stone was sandy clay, I dug down about four inches, placed my bread inside, and replaced the rock; you couldn't tell I removed the stone. All this took me a little longer than an hour. I laid down using my shirt as a pillow and started to doze as I got lost in my thoughts.

I was standing up, relieving myself when I heard the guards coming, I finished just as they opened the door and the guards dragged me outside. They tied my arms behind my back, shoved a bamboo pole behind me, and raised the pole so that my joints in my shoulders felt like they were going to pop out. They hurried me up to Major Kien's building as we went; I was in extreme pain. We went into the building, and they sat me on a stool lower than the commandant, a blatant power move. That Sergeant was there with that officer who tried to question the Sergeant and me as we got transported North.

Major Kien was eating something when he said, "Excuse me for my eating are you hungry." I didn't say anything, and he looked at the Sergeant who knocked me to the ground and then started beating me with a split bamboo cane. He then pulled me back up on the stool. He looked at one of the soldiers, and they took his food away.

The Major then picked up a dog tag. He said, "So Lieutenant Henderson tell me your identification number and blood type."

"Lieutenant Henderson, O 793561949 blood type A positive."

He smiled and said, "I heard that some of you low life thugs like to switch, what did you call it dog tags." I didn't answer him, and then he said, "Do you know Navy Lieutenant Susmann" I looked at him but didn't say anything, and for that, I got beat again. "Lieutenant Susmann has given up his command of the prisoners and gave the command to you." I kept silent, and he went on, "The thing I want to know is how he knew who you are." I was not saying anything, and I could see he was losing his patients. He looked at the sergeant said something in Vietnamese, then the sergeant smiled. The Sergeant jerked me up a rope was thrown over a beam of the building, and then it was tied to the bamboo stick, and I got hoisted up into the air. I thought my arms were going to get ripped off, and the pain was terrific. I found if I tried to pull the stick into my back, the pain seemed less. "If you talk, you wouldn't have to go through this unpleasantness," the Major said with a smirk.

The Major looked at me, waiting for an answer, but he didn't get one. The Sergeant dropped me to the floor, started beating me with that bamboo cane, kicked me with his boot, and I blacked out.

I woke up on the floor of my cell. I could see it was dark out even though one of my eyes had nearly closed. I manage to get on my bunk, and I reached for the bucket of water. I threw some water on my face and flushed my mouth out. Then I drank some water and tried to clear my head. I tried to rub my shoulders to work out the pain. My lip had split again, but I decided to eat the bread I had hid. When I finished my small meal, I drank some more water, then leaned my back on the wall and tried to shut my eyes. I then thought I should talk to the Navy Lieutenant. I got my nail out and tried to stand, but I was a little shaky. I then sat on the floor and tapped out, "Are you awake."

"Yes, how are you."

"A bit beat up, but he never broke me."

"Good for you, but expect more tomorrow."

"I have a plan that I hope will get us better treatment."

"That would be great."

"The Major tried his power play on me, but I got him upset when he could not break me."

"You think you can withstand another day of beatings?"

"I must."

"Tell me what you said to him when he asked how you knew my name, rank, and branch," I tapped.

"I told him I heard your name spoken when you first arrived."

"Good." "I am going to rest now and try to recuperate." As I laid back on my bunk, my thoughts drifted to Aunt Adeline and her family and how fond I was of them all; as I was fantasizing about them, I drifted off to sleep.

The next morning was sunny and hot in the cell after I used the toilet I clean up and check the outside through the hole. Everything was clear, so I went over to the wall and asked Lieutenant Susmann, "When do we get toilet cleaned out and new water?"

"Once a week for sure that is in two days, the N.V.R do not like the smell any more than we do."

"Good."

"They will grab one of us to do the dirty work." "Feeling any better?"

"Still sore, but doing better today, I will talk more tonight.

"Right, good luck today."

At lunch, I got an extra piece of bread again, and I hid it away in my concealed place. Not a half-hour had passed after they picked up the containers that they came and got me.

"We will try this again." "How did the Lieutenant know you?"

"My name is Lieutenant William Henderson." That's all I got out when the Sergeant knocked me to the ground again and beaten with a wet split bamboo cane, then he jerked me up tied a rope on my arms, and I got hoisted up.

"It will only get worse for you if you don't answer," the Major said.

"I would think someone educated in the United States would know how to play the game," I said with difficulty.

"How can you tell my education was in the United States?"

"Just guessed, and you have an American accent." The Major motioned the Sergeant to put me down.

"It was a good guess I went to U.C.L.A."

"I've been there."

"So, what is this game you are talking about?"

"You give me what I wish, and if I can, I will answer your question." He stared at me for what seemed forever, and I showed no emotion, but I just stared back.

"Oh, yes, wheel and dealing." "I know this, I will give you what you wish if I can, but you will answer my questions."

I shook my head no, then said, "I think you misunderstand I will answer one question for granting me one thing I wish."

You could see the major's anger, but he composed himself very quickly and said, "Alright, each thing you request will cost you so many questions."

"As long as it's no more than three questions and you are fair."

He nodded and said, "How do you know I will honor your request."

"You appear to be a man of principle and honor at lease more honor than this sadistic Sergeant." The Major smiled chuckled, then said something in Vietnamese, and I was knocked to the ground then beat with the cane. When beating stopped, I said, "If you do not honor our agreement, you get no more cooperation from me again."

He gave me a nasty look and finally said, "What is it, you wish?"

"Let my men and me out of our cells an hour a day so we can get some exercise, chat, and check on the welfare of my men."

"You gangsters might escape or try to harm my brave soldiers."

"In our shape, we are lucky we can still walk, there will be no escape or harm to your soldiers while we are out." "Besides, your brave soldiers are many, and we are few." What I said he did not like my sarcasm.

"I will give you forty-five minutes."

I nodded and said, "What will it cost me?"

"How did the Navy Lieutenant know who you are?"

"I'm not sure, but I would assume he heard the Sergeant and me talking when we first came, we addressed each other by rank." The Major just stared at me, so I added, "Ask your Captain he was there."

He looked over at the Captain, then the Captain whispered something in his ear, and then the Major said, "I will accept that." "What is your job in the American Army?"

"My request is not worth two questions, but I will answer you. I am a team leader in the Special Forces, that's why the Navy Lieutenant wanted me to command I'm guessing."

"The Green Berets?"

"That's three questions, but yes."

"You're very small for the Green Berets."

I smiled and said, "Another American expression Major, a big thing sometimes comes in small packages."

He smiled, then said something to the Sergeant, and the beating started. When he finished beating me, he raised me with a rope. He started hitting me again with a wet leather whip, and the last thing I heard the Major say was, "Don't ever try my patients again, Lieutenant."

Again, I woke up on the floor of my cell, and as I lay there, I thought at least this time that sadistic Sergeant didn't hit my head. I got up with difficulty; it was dark outside. I must have been out for some time. I wet my shirt and washed myself everything hurt, including my shoulders. I had welts all over me; some were bleeding. I drank a little water, got my extra bread out, and ate that slowly.

After I finished eating, I looked out the hole and seen a couple of guards smoking some distance from me. There was also a lot of buoyant clamor coming from the soldier's quarters. I laid back down using my shirt as a pillow and rested, wondering if the Major would keep his word. If he didn't, it would be the last bit of information he would get from me. I was starting to doze when I heard some tapping on my wall. I got up, got my nail, and waited, but he didn't tap, so I tapped as I did at first, "A shave and a haircut." He came back with two taps.

"I was not sure if you were up to talking."

"It was brutal, but I am in better shape than yesterday."

"How did it go?"

"Very good if he is an honest man." "He is supposed to give us forty-five minutes outdoors so that we can exercise, talk, and check on the condition of the men."

"That was a significant concession you got from him what did you have to do to get it?" tapped the lieutenant.

"I told him how you knew who I was also I'm in the Special Forces."

"I am surprised he did not ask for more."

"I think he knew his error when he agreed to give me this because he became surly."

"Well, I will look forward to talking to you."

"We haven't gone out yet let us see if he honors his agreement if he doesn't, he will never get anything out of me again." "Just in case we do go out, give me a list of the men we have and their condition."

"I will do that and let you know."

"Great, you will be my XO."

"Thank you for the position, but I think you're making a big mistake." "I am not a very good officer."

"No, you are the ranking officer, and I will need you to unite your people with the Sergeant and me."

"Understood, I'll contact you later." I put the nail away, laid back down, and went into my fantasizing. After several hours, I got the names and the condition of the men. There were a few who were in bad shape. The next day I waited to go out, but that didn't happen nor the next day, but we did trade out our water and toilet. I was beginning to think the Major wasn't going to honor our agreement, but then my door flew open, and the guards motioned me out.

I came out, and the Major was there he came over to me and said, "Get your men out of their cells and have them line up."

"Lieutenant Susmann, gather the men and put them into a formation let them know who is in command." I went over to the Sergeant's cell, the guard opened the door, and he came out.

"I'm in command, don't forget, I am Lieutenant Henderson."

"You're in command?"

"I'll explain later and give you a briefing on what's going on."

"How's your arm?"

"It's ok now, but I had a fever for days, but I cleaned it out good and drank a lot of water lucky the bullet went right through."

"By the way, you're the first sergeant."

"Let's go help the Navy Lieutenant," I said.

"You do know that a Navy Lieutenant is a higher rank than an Army Lieutenant."

"I know, but he gave up command to me because he thinks I'm in the Special Forces."

"Special Forces, how did he get that idea?"

"I told him."

"You did; did you."

"Yes." We got all the men lined up some needed help I was out front with the Lieutenant Susmann and Sergeant Brooks.

"I have graciously given you criminals forty-five minutes a day out of your cell because of your Commander's cooperation." "Do not abuse this privilege; if you try to harm or show disrespect towards my brave men, you will get punished severely." "You will lose this gracious privilege." "If you try to escape, everyone will get punished in the same manner." "Now, other small privileges might be granted if all you cooperate also." At that, he turned around and left, not happy with himself.

I turned around and said, "This is First Sergeant Greg Brooks we will need someone familiar with medical, someone, who is a good scrounger and a Chaplain, someone who knows scripture."

"If you don't mind having a Mormon Chaplain, I can help you with the scripture," said Ensign Pickett.

"I don't care what church you're from; you're the chaplain," I said.

"Leave the medical to me to do, Lieutenant," said Sergeant Brooks.

"I think I know a good scrounger Lieutenant J. G. Grey," said Lieutenant Susmann.

"Good, let's enjoy our outside time." Lieutenant Susmann, the Sergeant, and I first checked on the sick. "How are they, Sergeant?"

"These two are bad; they need a doctor soon these others, I will clean their wounds and tell them how to take care of themselves."

"What are their names, Michael?"

"He's Jeff Rollins; he is Donald Twist; they're both Lieutenant J. G."

"Sergeant, when you have finished here, I'll need you to translate."

"Yes, Sir," he said with a smile.

"Do you think the commandant will send these men a doctor out of the kindness of his heart?" I asked the Lieutenant Susmann with a smile.

He laughed and said, "No, you must offer him something."

"That's what I was afraid of."

"Sir, as far a religion, what do you wish me to do?" asked Pickett.

"Sunday, give a fifteen-minute sermon and comfort the men with words of the Lord."

"When is Sunday, Sir?"

I looked at the Lieutenant, and he shrugged his shoulders, and I said, "I will find out, by the way, don't use too much of your church's doctrine unless the men want to hear it."

"Yes, Sir."

Sergeant Brooks joined us, and I asked, "Sergeant, I am going to try to get a doctor for the men who are the worse."

"Doing this, I might have to give him some information do you think to tell him about our trek through Cambodia will cause any harm?"

"They will use it for propaganda depending on what you tell them, but I don't believe it will harm our troops."

"Do you know when Sunday is?"

"Yesterday, isn't it?"

"If I can't find out what day for sure Sunday is, we will say it is six days from now," I said to Ensign Pickett.

"Let's go talk to one of the guards, Sergeant." I got the attention of one of the guards, and I told the Sergeant, "Tell him I wish to talk to Major Kien."

The Sergeant did, and the guard said, "He is too busy, you can tell me what you want." Then the Sergeant said what he said.

"Tell him what I have to say is for the Major's ears only and that if he doesn't tell the Major when I do talk to him, I will tell the Major that he didn't tell him, and the Major will punish him." The Sergeant told him, and the guard wasn't happy, but he agreed to let the Major know.

"Ask him what day it is."

"Monday, he said, Sir."

"There you go, Ensign Pickett."

"Yes, Sir." The guard went with a frown to inform the Major.

"Which cells are those men who need medical attention in?" I asked Lieutenant Susmann.

"The last two on our side."

"Sergeant, do you know Morse code?"

"Yes, I do."

"Good use it to communicate with the men on your side."

"Lieutenant find out who knows Morse code and those who don't know it then teach them."

"Sergeant, let's go find Lieutenant J. G. Grey."

"Lieutenant, see if you can scrounge up some nails and small splinters of wood we can use for cleaning of teeth."

"I'll get on it." My back was itching, so I took off my shirt and tried scratching it.

"Let me see that back of yours," said Sergeant Brooks concerned.

"How does it look?" I asked.

"It looks like raw hamburger, but at least it isn't infected, whatever you are doing keep doing it."

As I was briefing the sergeant on what was going on, Sergeant Dung charged me like a raging bull. He knocked me to the ground tied my arms behind my back, then he pulled me up and hurried me up to the Major's hut.

An angry Major Kien alleged, "You insulted one of my men for that you will pay."

"That's not true."

"Are you saying he is a liar," an enraged Major said.

I raise my voice, which was a bad mistake when I said, "I don't know if he is a liar or not; I only know what I said." For raising my voice, I was caned on my back again. I was regretting leaving my shirt on the ground back by the cells.

"Then tell me what you think happened."

"I asked the soldier that I wish to talk with you; he refused; he wanted me to tell him what I wanted to say to you." "So, I told him that if he didn't tell you that you would punish him when you found out."

The Major said something to the Sergeant, and the Sergeant left. A few minutes later he returned with the soldier, and I assume he asked him just what I said. The soldier looked very nervous and started sweating. Then he said something, and the Major got very mad and told the Sergeant something, and the guard took him out.

I looked at the Major, and he said, "What is it you wanted?"

"I have two men Rollins and Twist; they are both officers; they have life-threatening wounds, and a doctor needs to take care of them." "You will find them in the last two cells from my cell."

The Major just stared at me and then said, "This will cost you." His Captain whispered something to him, and he said, "What was your mission, and why were you in Cambodia?" It was time to put on a good show I put on a look of concern at answering his question.

"You ask something difficult for me to answer." I waited a few more seconds and displayed a little anxiety then said, "Getting medical is essential for the survival of those men." "If I answer your questions, can my Sergeant, who speaks Vietnamese, and I observe your doctor working on the men."

He smiled with a smirk and said, "You may observe, but you will not need your Sergeant; the doctor speaks English almost as well as I do."

"Good; you wanted to know what my mission was." I hesitated again and said, "We are aware of the trail you go down to the south; we call it the Ho Chi Minh Trail. We knew it went through Cambodia, but we didn't know where it was exactly and how far south it went." "We also didn't know if large equipment traveled down it." "We were ordered to go to Cambodia and find the trail, talk to the locals and find out as much as we could about troop movement," I said.

"And what were your superiors going to do with this information?"

"I can only guess I'm too low in rank to know, but I would guess bomb the trail and set up ambushes." The Sergeant had come back in, Major Kien told him something, and he left. While he was gone, I asked Major Kien, "Would it be alright the days it rain, and my men and I are out of our cells if we strip and bath in the rain."

"I do not care what you wear when you are outside."

A few minutes later, the Sergeant returned with a woman carrying a bamboo box with a sling. The Major said something to the woman while the Sergeant grabbed my arm, and we went down to where the cells were.

"You are a doctor," I asked the female.

"Yes, you are surprised?"

"No, not really."

Surprised, she asked, "You have female doctors in your country?"

"Yes, many." As we walked, I grabbed my shirt, and the Sergeant wasn't pleased that I got it. He was about to hit me when the doctor said something angrily to him, and he stopped unhappy.

"I wouldn't do too many things like that; the Sergeant would love to beat you to death."

"I think he has tried that a few times, but thanks for the advice." The sergeant ordered the guard to unlock the door, and the doctor told me to go into the cell and bring out Lieutenant Rollins.

"She's a doctor, Jeff; she is going to work on that wound of yours."

"I have no painkillers and what I have to do will hurt I'll need everyone to hold him down," she said. I gave Jeff his shirt rolled up to bite down, and then she washed the wound and dried it. Then, she took out a scalpel and cut it into the wound. Jeff screamed, and the Sergeant started laughing. The wound was open enough to drain pus, the smell nearly caused me and everyone else to gag, but the doctor seemed to take it in stride.

"You must be used to the smell; it doesn't bother you," I said to the doctor.

"This smell is nothing I have smelled worse." She put a yellow power on the wound, took out a syringe and a bottle, and gave Jeff a shot into the wound. She sewed up the wound, put a salve on the injury, and bandage it. She got out a white power, put it into a cup with water, and told Jeff to drink it. It amazed me that Jeff didn't pass out from what the doctor did.

"Keep the wound clean you may develop a fever drink a lot of water and rest." It took the guard and me to get him back into his cell; then, we went to Twist's cell. Again, a guard and I had to help Donald out of his cell. Donald had a leg wound; the doctor told a guard to get two bamboo sticks.

The doctor said, "He has a broken leg; it is his fibula; it could be worse." "He is worse than the last I do not know if I can save his leg," she said.

"Do your best, that's all I can ask of you," I replied. As before, I rolled up Donald's shirt and stuck it in his mouth, then she made an eight-inch-long incision along the leg Donald screamed as she was doing this, but he passed out. The doctor cleaned and flush out his leg repeatedly. I could see the broken bone on his leg as she worked. She kept on mumbling in Vietnamese as she worked, and she removed some of the infected muscle from around his wound. She then squirted some liquid that seemed to burn his leg and then flushed it. There was blood all over the place much more than Jeff's wound. After her last flushing, she set the bone, applied some of that yellow power on the lesion, and gave him a shot then sewed him up. She took the two sticks, splinted his leg, and told me how to care for him.

"I have a Sergeant who has some medical experience; he will take care of him." She nodded then one of the guards, and I placed him back into his cell.

I got escorted back to my cell, but before I went inside, the doctor said to me, "Let me look at your back." The Sergeant argued with the doctor, but the doctor put him in his place. "Keep your back clean your back is healing just fine."

"Thank you for all you have done."

"It's my job," she replied, turned, and left, and the Sergeant threw me to the floor of my cell.

The guards didn't take me into the commandant's office for the next few days, and that suited me just fine. The guards took others in including the Sergeant I wasn't worried he was thoroughly brief. Rollins and Twist were in better shape, considering everything. We were due to go out in the next few hours, and I wanted to get with Lieutenant Susmann to discuss the food. I also wanted to address the mental condition of the men and what we could do about it. I laid on my bunk and went to my little world, thinking of home and relatives. I could remove myself from this place and have a short happy time after about two hours, it came to me, and I snapped out of my dream world. I knew how to improve the mental condition of men.

"We need to have a meeting I am going to need the Chaplain, the Sergeant, and Greg," I said to Lieutenant Susmann.

"I'll go get them," he said.

First, the Sergeant came, then the rest arrived, and I said, "How many pieces of bread have you all been getting each meal." Lieutenant Grey and Lieutenant Susmann both said one, the sergeant said two, and then I said I was getting two. "Find out who is hurting the most for the lack of food," I said to Ensign Pickett. "I'm going to talk to the Major to see if we can get more food, but I need to find something to bargain with him." "I'm worried about the mental condition of the men, find out who is suffering, and the ones who aren't, find out what they do to keep themselves mentally fit," I said that to everybody. "How are you coming along, finding nails and wood splinters?" I asked Lieutenant Grey.

"Wood splinters, I have more than enough but nails I'm having a hard time with I only have three so far," he said.

"That's better than I thought you would say. Give the wood to the sergeant to be handed out for teeth cleaning and hand out the nails to those who know Morse code, keep on looking for nails until we have enough for everyone, how many know Morse code?" I asked.

"About half know it, and we are training the others," said Lieutenant Susmann.

"Great, let's get to our tasks," I said and then went off talking to some of the other men. When we went back into the cell, I laid down tried to figure out how to get these men more food. Two days had passed, and it was Chaplain Ensign Pickett day to give a sermon, and to my surprise, he gave a great one. The Sergeant and I gave up our extra bread to those in more need than we were. Back in the cell, I laid down and tried to get my mind off where I was, I finally doze off to sleep but was waken when my door flew open, and a guard grabbed me and hauled me out of the cell. Up to the Major's Kien building, we went. My wrists were bound behind my back as I sat, waiting to find out what the Major wanted. I looked around and saw some video recording machines, and I had a feeling what he wanted.

"Lieutenant, we discussed your mission do you recall."

"Yes."

"My superiors want you to discuss this again so that we can record it for our records." I just stared at him, and he became impatient and said, "Are you willing to cooperate, or do we have to use some persuasion," he said with a smile.

"What you and your superiors want is record me to use it for propaganda. As for your persuasion, you already know that it doesn't work on me." At that, I got a severe beating with a bamboo cane on my back, but I didn't cave in, and the Major was furious.

"You are a very difficult person, what do you want for doing this?" the Major snarled.

"Only what are any fundamental human rights, an increase in our food rations. At least two pieces of bread per meal and some more things in our soup or stew, like extra rice, vegetables, and an occasional bit of meat, wouldn't hurt." I waited for the Major to say something, but he just stared at me for the longest time, but then with the surliest voice I've heard in a long time, he said something to the Sergeant in Vietnamese, and the Sergeant left. About fifteen minutes of silence later back came the Sergeant with another man.

The Major said something to the other man and then turn to me and said, "I told him to give each man two pieces of bread."

"What about that soup or stew you provide us with?" He said something to the man again, turned to me and said, "Your containers will contain more rice, vegetable, and on occasion meat of some sort."

"You have always honored what you say, so I won't question you now when you want to start recording?"

"Tomorrow, we will give you and your men time out of their cells early, then you will be taken to be clean up, and we will record," I nodded consent. I was then led back to my cell with a smile on my face.

The next day I informed Susmann and Brooks what happened. "We will see if we get more food today or not if we don't, I won't be doing any recording." I waited for lunch, and then I check to see if everybody got the same by looking out my hole. Sure enough, we all got two pieces of bread and a much more and fuller container of food. I wasn't sure about everybody's container. I assume if everyone got two hunks of bread and if I got a full vessel, then everybody did. I hid the extra piece of bread and finished the meal just in time because they came and got me to clean up. They took me to a stream where I bathed and saved under close supervision. After cleaning up, they took me to the Major's office; a woman, to my surprise, did the interview, while a man was holding a camera. I got told to change into a new uniform, which I did. Afterward, I was put back in my old clothing and into my cell.

5

HANOI HILTON

A week after the recorded interview, everyone seemed to be in better shape. However, even with the extra food, no one was gaining any weight. We had modified the Morse code to make it much simpler so that everyone could use it. It was a Tuesday morning, and as I was looking out the hole, I saw several N.V.R. gather around the platform. Sergeant Major Anh Dung got up on the platform and started doing some martial arts of some sort. After about fifteen minutes, he had a Vietnamese soldier come up on the platform, and he was showing him some moves. Then he had another soldier come on the platform, and he jumped off.

The two soldiers had what looked like a contest. This training went on for three days. On the fourth day, it was the same, but then two guards came and grabbed one of my men. The guards forced my man up on the platform, and they used him as if he was a combat dummy. They knocked him around, finally knocking him off the platform only to put him back up again. By the time they finished, they had to drag him back to his cell. As I laid on my bunk, I started thinking I had better try to learn offensive and defensive moves before I had to go up on the platform. That night I did a lot of stretching and exercises as I did them, I found out through weaker I wasn't that far out of shape. The next day when we got to go outside, I checked on the man who they beat. He had very severe bruises, but he had no broken bones. I asked the Sergeant when we were alone, "Do you know any offensive and defensive moves in martial arts that could help?"

"Yes, but if I show you them, the guards might cause us some harm."

"Just describe how to do them, and I will figure it out the best way I can." He taught me what he could for the next two days. On the third day, they took another man with the same results. As the first man but again other than some bruises, he was alright. As they worked that man over, I once again observed those men, especially when Sergeant Dung made his moves. I saw I would have to become more limber, and that required a lot more stretching. More than a month had passed, and six men suffered the fate as the first one. Those men sustained a concussion and were off their feet for more than a week. At that time, I could predict what those soldiers that were inflicting the punishment were going to do before they did it. I don't know if what I was doing in my cell would help, but it felt right, but there was one thing I did want to learn that was to use my legs as a weapon. At our out time, I talked to the Sergeant about using the legs, and he told me some things I could do, but it would be hard to practice in the cell because of space. I knew I had one advantage over them; I believed I was faster moving than they were. As the days went by and the one thing I noticed was that the moves the Sergeant and his men made were all the same. I did my best to learn how to use my legs, but as Sergeant Brooks said it was difficult.

Another ten days had passed, and they beat two more men. We already had been let out for our forty-five minutes, and I was resting thinking about home and my aunt in Missouri when my cell door flew open. The guards took me to the platform where a soldier was waiting. I acted like I was weak to give him more confidence, and once on the platform, I turn my body, so he had a smaller target. Major Kien stepped out of his building with his hands on his hips. The soldier charged me, and I moved out of the way. He then tried to swing at me, and I was able to block every move, which upset him, and it worsened when his comrades started laughing. He tried to deliver another blow, but again I prevented it, and in his frustration, he tried a reverse back kick. I blocked that too and slammed my fist into his genitals, and he folded. The soldiers who surrounded me stopped laughing, and the Sergeant was enraged. He was about to come on the platform to beat me when another soldier begged him to try, and the Sergeant relented. I knew that this soldier would be much more talented than the last, and I found out he was a lot faster and sure of himself. He tried to give me a few kicks they were either missed or blocked, I gave a not so pretty roundhouse kick and caught him on the side of his head, and he flew off the platform. The Sergeant went ballistic, and his men went for their rifles. As the Sergeant started to come up onto the platform, a voice rang out over the din, the Sergeant stopped, and the soldiers quieted. It was Major Kien as he came up onto the platform, he told the soldiers to disperse then the Major said something angrily to Sergeant Dung, and he left with his head down.

"You violated our agreement you harmed some of my men."

"I violated nothing; it was your men who brutally beat my men for no reason, and they were going to do the same to me." "Besides, I agreed that my men and I would not try to escape or harm your troops while we were outside."

"This exercise will get suspended; my men won't use your men anymore." He motioned two guards to take me back to my cell. When I got back to my cell, and the guards were gone, I tapped to Lieutenant Susmann what had happened.

Several months went by, and I didn't even see the Major then one day two cars drove up to the Majors building those who got out of the cars looked like officers and they went into the building. They were there for about an hour then left two days later everyone was ordered to stand formation. We waited for about thirty minutes, then finally Major Kien came to the formation; we came to attention, and he addressed us. "This camp is shutting down, I and some of my men will transfer up north to Hanoi." "You criminals will go to the Hòa Lò Prison I will be commanding there; we will all leave in three days."

"Major, may I talk to you privately I have some information you may want to hear."

As the guards placed the prisoners back into their cells, we stepped away from everyone, and the Major said, "And what will this information cost me?"

"Nothing, it's free." "I would assume that the soldiers that don't go with you will go into combat?" I said, and he nodded yes. "Do you see that young soldier to my left carrying a bucket?" Again, he nodded yes. "He told me he is fourteen, but I think he is a lot younger." "He is very bright; it wouldn't be good for one so young and bright to be killed."

"Why are you concerned about him he is your enemy?" he asked.

"He is a child, and I have no hate or anger towards him; he is not my enemy." At that, he nodded, and I was sent back to my cell.

The next day Lieutenant Susmann asked if anyone ever heard of or know anything about Hòa Lò Prison, and no one did. Sergeant Brooks said he had a feeling it wasn't going to be a happy place. We were all loaded up into two trucks I went in one, and Lieutenant Susmann went in the other.

On the way up North, we had to pull over several times, in the distance, we heard explosions, which Lieutenant Twist said was B-52s bombing. They stopped the trucks at a large plaza, we were all taken off the truck and lined up two by two, and they forced us to walk through the street to face a jeering crowd and the occasional flinging of mud or trash at us. We came in sight of the depressing prison, and someone from behind me said it looks like we are here at the Hanoi Hilton, the Hanoi Hilton stuck as our name for this prison. We were taken down a narrow hall single file and placed into cells. The cell was roomier than the last. It had a platform to sleep on, a hole on the floor for a toilet, also faucet for water. I got two meals a day of rice, bread, and a nasty tasting soup.

It was the next day, two guards took me to a courtyard and then to an office. There was Major Kien, another officer, and a prisoner, I didn't know. "This is Lieutenant Colonel Danh he commands here I am his executive officer all previous agreements are now void." "This criminal next to you is Commander Harry McBride." "He is the highest-ranking prisoner, but he doesn't want to command, do you still want to."

"It has worked out just fine before; I will continue being the commander." "May I talk to Commander McBride?"

The Major looked over to the Lieutenant Colonel for approval, and he nodded yes then said, "But here."

"We have about forty men; how many do you have, Sir."

"Maybe forty-seven men."

"And their condition, Sir?"

He first looked at the Lieutenant Colonel Danh then nervously said, "They are as well as you could expect." I noted that he was troubled at answering and that he gave me a safe answer.

"Can I see all the men?"

"No, not now," said the Lieutenant Colonel abruptly.

They took me back to my cell, and after dinner, my door opened Major Kien walked into my cell. He said, "I was supposed to be in command of this jail, but my superiors felt that they could get more information and cooperation from Lieutenant Colonel Danh." "I would advise you to cooperate with the interrogation he has no honor and will cause you more pain or death than you can imagine." He was about to leave when he turned around and said, "That young soldier you told me about works here now." I had dozed off to sleep for how long I do not know, and I awoke when my door flew open, and I was drugged out of my cell and down the hall. We pass through a courtyard to a building, and they forced me to sit on a bench; there was a small platform with a large container of water at one end. There were various types of whips, and on the ceiling, there was a ring with a rope hanging from it. There was a table with all sorts of things on it, and I knew I was going to have some pain. The guards yanked me up off the bench; they stripped my clothing and made to stand in front of a desk. Then into the room came the Major and the Lieutenant Colonel who sat down.

"I want the location of your unit, and how many criminals are there?" asked the Colonel sternly.

I looked at him then said, "My name is Lieutenant William Henderson; my serial number is 079356." I got no more out than that when they first hit me in the mouth. Another guard slammed something into my genitals, and I went down and curled up into a ball, trying to catch my breath and recover from the blow. I hadn't recovered yet when I got yanked up off the ground.

"Answer the question," he said.

"My name is Lieutenant William." I got hit again, then fell to the ground and dragged over to the platform. They rolled me on my stomach, grabbed my hair, then shoved my head into the water and held it there. I fought to get my head out of the water, but it did no good. When I couldn't hold my breath anymore, the water rushed in, but just before I passed out, they pulled my head out, and I coughed out the water, and then they beat me until I passed out.

I woke up when they threw cold water on me. Two men came into my cell and bound my wrists behind my back. Then they tied me tight my lower arms then my upper arms causing a tremendous amount of pain. After this, they tied my ankles then tied a rope between my ankles and my arms and pulled them together tight, they threw more cold water on me and then left me. The pain was terrific; I laid there for hours, and my arms and legs went numb. They put a container of food in my cell, laughing at me, and I could move where I could get some of it, but it was all over me. Every movement was an ordeal to get around after they removed the food. I tried to move over to the water, and I could open the spout enough to get some water. Once I drank enough, I attempted to rest; it took a lot out of me to try to get the food and water. As I was still lying on the floor, I couldn't get up on the bunk, and as I lay there, I watched as a rat crawled under my door and started to eat what food was still there on the ground. Then a second rat came, I must have watched them for about ten minutes when the door flew open, and the two rats scurried over me and into the toilet. There were three guards; two of them grabbed me and threw me on the bunk, and shackled my feet and attached it to the cot, and then they left, and my two rat friends came back shortly after that to finish their meal. Food was brought in and placed just out of reach of me. I had to pee very bad, so I relieved myself where I lay. By the second day or so, I was getting weak for the lack of food and water. In my weakened state, I could hear others screaming from what I assume was the treatment they were getting. The interrogators and guards were frustrated with me because I kept silent. They didn't know I had a high pain tolerance, but I knew that I wouldn't be able to keep it up for long as I got weaker. I could hear dinner coming, and I knew the guard would put it far enough away to torment me.

When the door flew open in walked the young soldier that the Sergeant and I befriended shaking his head, he said, "You should talk it would be easier for you if you did."

"Yes, but it wouldn't be the honorable thing to do." He gave me some water, I drank greedily, and some bread and rice with a little more water, but he had to stop because someone was yelling for him down the hall, so he left. That night I was unshackled and brought down to the interrogation room. As I went, I stumbled quite often because of how they bound my legs.

"Are you ready to answer my questions?" asked Colonel Danh.

"Not unless you grant me and my men some basic human rights."

"Human rights, you are all criminals no better than an animal."

"My name is Lieutenant William Henderson; my serial number is O." They started whipping me with a wet bamboo cane, and when I didn't cry out, they grabbed my hair, dragged me to the container of water, and plunged my head in, and that is the last I remembered. I woke up shackled to my bunk again and in a lot of pain, but I got it under control. I laid there for hours, and at that time, I thought of those I left-back in the world, and soon I was there in my mind.

"Why are you smiling?" I don't know how long I was in my fantasy, but Major Kien brought me out of it.

"I was in a different place."

"I don't understand?"

"During World War Two, when the Nazis put the Jews in the concentration camps, there was one Jew who always seemed in good

92

spirits." "A young German soldier noticed this and finally asked him how he could be in high spirits when there was so much misery here." "The old Jew smiled and said, young man, you can imprison my body, but never my mind for my mind will always be free." I could see that the Major was disturbed by what I said.

"What will it take for you to answer the Colonel Danh's questions?"

"Let me see my men at lease every other day and treat us all humanely."

"Do you trust my word?"

"Yes, you are an honorable person."

"The Lieutenant Colonel thinks he does treat you fairly considering who you are." "If you trust me, I will do what I can little by little, but you must wait until I replace Colonel Danh," the Major said.

"You are replacing him?"

"Yes, I also have friends high up who will replace this fool with me; they are not happy with his results."

"I believe what you say, Major, and I know you will keep your word, but the Lieutenant Colonel must agree let me see my men every other day or more."

"If he agrees, you will answer his questions."

"Yes, if I know the answers, you need to know I had only been in Vietnam a short time when your people captured me." He nodded and started to leave, and I said, "May I ask you a question?" he stopped and looked at me "Is there any more men I came here with still locked up in a cell."

He looked outside the cell and said, "Some have talked only a little, but since they talked, we removed them to a dorm, a few have not talked, so they are still here, and some have died."

"Died, how many are still here, and of those who have died was Sergeant Brooks one of them or Lieutenant Susmann?"

"They are both alive; there are three still in a cell, like yours." I was relieved and said, "Tell them I said for them to say something even if it isn't that important, so they can go to the dorm and please don't remove me to a dorm until all my men are there." He nodded and left, and I laid back, wondering when they would interrogate me again.

I laid there several hours when I heard other doors open and close down the hall. I assumed they were the other three prisoners they were interrogating, and I hope they would tell them something to get them out of their cells and into a dorm. It wasn't until the second day when they took me to see Colonel Danh.

"Where is your base?"

"Do we understand that I would be able to see and talk to all my men every other day." Lieutenant Colonel Danh looked over at Major Kien and then nodded his head yes.

"My base is on hill three forty-nine about sixty-five kilometers from Cambodia and about seventy-five kilometers from Laos."

"How many men on that base?"

"It varies but about five to six hundred."

"How many are the Green Berets?"

"About four hundred to four hundred and fifty."

"What kind of weapons do they have?"

"M-16s, fifty calibers, mortars, anti-tank weapons, M-60s, M-79s, forty-five pistols, and a few AK 49s and shotguns."

"Where are the weak areas of your base?"

"I am not sure I was only at that base a short time; I can only guess."

"Then guess," he snarled.

"I wouldn't believe there aren't any weak spots; there are land mines all around the base and barb wire." If there were an attempt to take the base, it would fail, they would call in planes if your people tried." I was sent back to my cell. They untied my arms; they remained numb and swollen, and one shoulder, I believe, was dislocated. The first thing I did is drank a lot of water and then bathed. I devoured my food and my two rat friends with no food to feast on left unhappy.

The next two days, I had restless nights feeling came back to my arms, and the pain from the dislocated shoulder was terrific. They gave me clean clothing by order of Major Kien, I'm sure. A few hours later, I was taken out of my cell by two guards and escorted into a courtyard where Major Kien was.

"Are all the men in dorms now?"

"Yes, the last left yesterday." I assumed the last one was Sergeant Brooks as we walk over to another building.

"When will I get to see all the men?"

"Whenever you wish."

"Then tomorrow if that is alright with you."

"Yes."

"Thanks for the clean uniform." He just nodded, and I was led into a large dorm with about twenty-eight men in it. After the guards left and they shut the door, I looked to see how many I knew; several men came over to me, including Sergeant Brooks and Ensign Pickett.

"Do I look as bad as I feel?"

"You're very thin, bruised up, and your back has fresh strips," said the Sergeant. He grabbed my shoulder, and I moaned.

"What's wrong with your shoulder?"

"I think they dislocated it."

"Sit down here on the bunk, and I will set it."

"For you men, I have not met, I'm Lieutenant William Henderson, the commanding officer."

"What happened to Commander Harry McBride?" someone asked.

"He gave up command to me; he is not in good shape." I was held down by two men, then the Sergeant set my shoulder with a snap, and I groan with pain at the ordeal.

"Take it easy for the next few days so that your shoulder has a chance to heal," said the Sergeant.

"So, what did you get for information?" asked Ensign Pickett.

"From Colonel Danh, every other day, I will visit all the men."

"Is this place, bugged?"

"No," someone said.

"From Major Kien better treatment in time."

"Did Danh agree to the better treatment?" someone asked.

"No, but Major Kien has always kept his word."

"I'll believe it when I see it," said the same cynical soldier.

I walked over to him and said, "Do you have a problem?"

"No, Sir," he answered, stunned at my anger for what he said.

"Then end the negativity, mister, and that goes for everyone."

"We need a morale officer," I said.

"That would fall on me, Sir," said Ensign Pickett.

"No, I have other plans for you; you're still the chaplain."

"Then Sir, let me suggest Lieutenant Brinkerhoff he is Air Force and quite a caricature, he is amusing."

"Sounds like just what we need."

"Lieutenant Brinkerhoff, come here." "Lieutenant, you're the new morale officer." "Go around the room and find ideas you can use to give us a little entertainment, then report back to me."

"Yes, Sir," he said with an upbeat tone.

"You look tired; you should lie down and rest," said the Sergeant.

"That's not a bad idea." "I'll think I'll try to get some sleep."

I woke up when Ensign Pickett grabbed my foot, for which I jumped ten feet; it was time to eat. As we ate, I said, "Brinkerhoff, what did you come up with for morale.

He said, "Some suggested we play word games, others think maybe exercise might be good to do, and there were a few who wanted to do a sing-along."

"Good suggestions, we will do them all, also storytelling and on Sunday bible stories." "I think maybe funny stories of ones' pass would be amusing and perhaps autobiographies." Also, anyone who has some talent can give classes; get it organized."

The Sergeant was sitting next to me, and I said, "If I can, I will evaluate the health of the others and see if I can take you with me to treat some of the men." He nodded his approval, and I said, "I will also see if Pickett can give sermons to the other dorms once a week."

"Good luck with that," the Sergeant replied.

That night the guys had a sing-along. It was so unusual that the guards came in a few times. They seemed to be amused by what was going on. The most important thing was the men were getting into it and having a great time. Since Lieutenant J. G. Grey wasn't in this dorm, I would have to find another scrounger for this dorm.

The next day after I ate the young Vietnamese soldier who spoke English that I knew, and another guard came and got me to visit my other men. "You have been very kind to me, but I don't know your name."

"Huu Phuoc," he said as we went down the hall a short distance. We went into another dorm with about twenty-five men also, and immediately I spotted Lieutenant Michael Susmann. He came over to me with a smile. "We will wait outside," Huu said.

"William, I'm sure glad you're alive." I shook his hand and said to everyone, "I am Lieutenant William Henderson, your commanding officer, Commander McBride gave up command to me." "I will be able to visit you every other day, your commanding officer for this dorm will be Lieutenant Susmann."

"There is Lieutenant Whitman, who has more time in grade than I."

"Lieutenant Whitman, do you prefer to be in command here?"

"I leave it up to your judgment, Sir."

"I know Lieutenant Susmann, so he is your dorm commander." "Listen up, pick yourself a morale officer someone who will come up with activities to lift-up your spirit." "He can organize a sing-along, games, storytelling, and classes from those who have talent." "Also, pick a Chaplin." "I'm going to see if Chaplin Pickett can give a sermon once a week, but I don't know if that will be possible." "Also, it is important to pick yourself a scrounger." "We have someone with medical experience in my dorm." "I will try to bring him for your medical needs, but if I can't, pick the best person." "Above all, I don't want to hear that there is negativity here." "Are there any questions?"

"How many have died, Sir?"

"I know some have died, but I don't know yet how many, but I will find out." "When you get interrogated, hold out if you can." "However, don't lose your life over some information; your life is more important, and no one will blame you for talking, or they will answer to me."

"What's the news from home, Sir?"

"Well, New York Mets and the Baltimore Orioles were the two best teams in baseball the last I heard looks like they are both heading to the World Series."

"The Mets impossible," someone said.

"There were some great movies Butch Cassidy and the Sundance Kid, Easy Rider, Midnight Cowboy."

"Sounds like all cowboy movies."

"No, Easy Rider is about a motorcycle rider, Midnight Cowboy is about a male prostitute."

"Who is staring in that Midnight Cowboy movie?"

"You interest in becoming a prostitute Randy," someone asked.

"Jon Vought is the prostitute; Dustin Hoffman plays his sick friend."

"What's in the world of politics?"

"The hippies are still protesting the war, and the Republican Richard Milhous Nixon is the new your President."

"I'll answer more of your questions the next time; I want to talk to Lieutenant Susmann before I have to leave." "Are there any here that need Sergeant Brook's attention?"

"No."

"Good, Major Kien promised better treatment when he could get around the Colonel; there's a power play between those two, I think."

"I'll try to get us more and more privileges as time goes on, but it won't be easy."

He nodded as the door open, and Huu said, "We must go."

We went down the hall, around the corner, and into the next dorm. This dorm was entirely different; there were about twenty men, who were quiet and depressed; there was an atmosphere of dreariness and gloom. I spotted Commander Harry McBride, but he didn't even come over to me. "I am Lieutenant William Henderson, your commanding officer." No one responded, and then I barked, "Get off your pathetic asses and act like American officers are supposed to act when their commanding officer comes in."

One angry man came towards me saying, "What are you going to do if we don't?"

I smack him right between the eyes, and he went down, and then I said, "I don't want to hear any more negativity here get on your feet." The door opened, and the two guards saw the man on the floor, and I said, "He slipped on a bar of soap."

"Soap, no soap here," said Huu.

Everyone laughed, and I said, "I know Huu, everything is alright." They both went back out the door, and I continued, "Who is the highest-ranking officer here?" I knew what the answer would be, but I asked anyway.

"Commander Harry McBride," someone said.

"Commander, are you capable of commanding this dorm?"

"I don't know; perhaps it would be better if it were someone else."

I stared at him a few seconds then said, "No, I think you're the man, but I will give you some help."

"Who is the second-highest rank here?"

"I believe I am Sir, Lieutenant Kyle Zelinksy."

"Good, you're the executive officer under Commander Harry McBride." "Both of you are to pick a morale officer." "He can organize a sing-along, games, storytelling, and classes from those who have special talent do anything that you can think to do." "Also, pick a chaplain I have one and will try to bring him if I can." "Pick also someone with the best medical experience." "I also have someone with experience with medicine, and I will bring him if I can." "I do not want to hear anything negative from this dorm, get organized, and take care of yourself; I will be coming by every other day." "The guards came and escorted me back to my dorm."

I informed everyone in my dorm of the other dorms' conditions and what I did to correct it. I had no plans of contacting Major Kien to see if he would let Sergeant Brooks and Ensign Pickett could go with me at least not for a while to give time for the other dorms to get organized. That night was storytelling night, and I told the story about my great, great grandfather Soaring Eagle With Many Coups.

That night as I laid down, I was trying to think of the date, and I didn't know, so I yelled out, "Does anyone know what the date is?"

"August twenty-second nineteen seventy," came from someone.

As the weeks went on, Lieutenant Susmann's dorm was getting organized much like mine. However, Commander McBride's dorm was struggling; they were better than what they were initially, but I wasn't satisfied with their progress. I had decided to see if I could take Ensign Pickett with me the next time and when the guard came to the door, Sergeant Brooks told the guard I wanted to talk to Major Kien. About an hour and a half later, Major Kien went to the dorm. "I wish Ensign Pickett to go with me tomorrow and once a week after that."

"Why?"

"He is our spiritual leader, and I feel it would do the men some good to hear some religious message."

"It will cost you."

"I figured that I would also like to take Sergeant Brooks he has medical experience."

"Someone is ill?"

"No, I will only take him when he is needed."

He said something to the guard and told me, "It will cost you some other time soon, hopefully." He left, and I wondered what he was insinuating. It hit me he was talking about when Lieutenant Colonel Danh was relieved.

The next day Ensign Pickett and I left for the dorms. At Susmann's dorm, Ensign Pickett gave an excellent sermon and then talked to some men. Ensign Pickett had a knack for being a good listener and one who could give good advice. The talent Pickett had come in handy at the next dorm where there were many troubled men, including Commander McBride, who he spent some time with him.

As we walked back to our dorm Ensign Pickett asked, "Sir, can I bring some of my own beliefs into my sermons and especially when I talk to the men privately."

"Why."

"I believe I can be more effective."

"I have nothing against your church, but others might, but I will let you if you're not too pushy."

"Yes, Sir."

"You might bring up some of the Book of Mormon stories on Sunday bible story night."

"That would be excellent, Sir," Ensign Pickett said with enthusiasm.

About a month went by when Huu showed up and took me out into the hall. "The Major wish me to tell and warn you that Lieutenant Colonel Danh is in trouble." "He needs to get valuable information from you and your men and will do anything to get it."

"Thanks," I told the men in my dorm and informed the other two dorms. Five days later, men got taken to be interrogated and came back in bad shape. When it was my turn, I could see, the Colonel was desperate; he wasn't getting anything from my men. He thought if he squeezed me enough the other men or perhaps, I would give him something to impress his superiors. I got beaten brutally every time I went, and Sergeant Brooks would patch me up. It was on the fourth visit when I was near passing out from the vicious beating when the door flew open. Two official-looking men and a female in what appeared like an officers' uniform came in, followed by Major Kien. They looked at me first; I was a pathetic bloody mess, and then the female said something to a worried Colonel Danh. Two guards lifted me and took me out of the room. As I left, I heard some shouting coming from the room, and I had a smile on my face.

Sergeant Brooks did the best he could with me in the dorm. I told him about what happened. The next day a Vietnamese medical person came into the dorm. He spoke no English, but Sergeant Brooks talked to him I was examined carefully. The Vietnamese medical people put a salve on my wounds and gave me some medication to drink. He gave the Sergeant extra medicine with instructions to give me some every day. Soon I was feeling better, and I was visiting the other dorms. There were no more beatings from Colonel Danh, and things started to get back to normal or as normal as you could get for a P.O.W. camp. About a week later, they took me into the commandant office. Major Kien had replaced Colonel Danh, but now he was a Lieutenant Colonel. On his desk, he had some food, and he offered me to eat with him.

"Please help yourself take as much as you want."

"No, thank you; I will eat what my men eat."

"I'm in such a good mood, tell me what you want, and I will grant it."

I smiled and said, "Send my men and me home."

He smiled and said, "You know I cannot do that."

Well, there are only two other things I wish right now."

"What are they?"

"Give us our Red Cross packages and let my men and I go outside and get some sun at least a few times a week."

He thought then said with a smile, "I'll grant you both."

"What's it going to cost me?"

"You have already paid me; you help me get rid of Danh."

"Yes, and I may have helped you get a promotion also."

He laughed and said, "Maybe."

He motioned for the guard to take me back to my dorm then stated in a solemn voice, "I am in a good mood today, but tomorrow I may not be, there will be demands, and you better do as I say." I walked back to the dorm a bit happier that day; perhaps things were looking up.

That night we got our Red Cross packages much to the delight of all. The next day I visited the other dorms; they got theirs also. I told all dorms not to throw anything away; everything is useful to make something. By the end of the week, we went outside, and I walked over to talked to Lieutenant Susmann, who was talking to Ensign Pickett.

"How long do you think this honeymoon period will last with the commandant?" asked Lieutenant Susmann.

"Not long, I have a hunch that someone most likely me will come under his thumb."

The Lieutenant and I went walking off alone, and he said, "It's amazing how you can help all these men."

"I've done nothing; it's been everyone I have delegated that deserves the credit."

"You have done plenty, you have gone way beyond the call of duty and delegating is a sign of a good officer."

"My father is an admiral if we ever get out of here, I'm going to tell him the whole story about you."

I laughed and said, "If you only knew who I am."

"Oh, I think I know who you are James, you know Napoleon was a corporal also."

"How long have you known?"

"I knew there was something wrong the first time I taped Morse code; then, I pressured Sergeant Brooks into telling me the truth."

"Who else knows?"

"Just the Sergeant, I and no one else needs to know it would cause a lot of trouble if anyone else found out." "You're a natural leader and are doing an excellent job much better than anyone I've ever known; you should be a commander."

"Well, thanks for what you said I did want to tell you about me, but I think my past shouldn't be talked about anymore."

"I agree."

Ensign Pickett joined us, and he said to Lieutenant Susmann, "Could I talk to Lieutenant Henderson privately."

The Lieutenant smiled, patted the Ensign on the shoulder, and said, "Sure," then left.

"You know I've talked to every one of the men, and it occurred to me that I haven't spoken to you yet." "You must be under tremendous pressure with all you have gone through and trying to help everybody as well as keep them alive."

"I'm alright, considering where I am."

"How are you coping?"

"You want the truth?"

"Of course."

"I have high pain tolerance, and I don't think about what will happen to me."

"A lot of time, I go into a kind of fantasy and remove myself mentally from here," I added.

"Still, you must be under a lot of stress with all the responsibility."

"You know I have a lot of help from others, such as yourself." "I also have a tendency to focus on the future after I leave here, and I keep a positive attitude," I said.

"Well, if you need to talk, I am always here to listen and give you what advice I can."

I nodded, and he was about to leave when I said, "Ensign, how are you coping?"

"I pray a lot, Sir, and trust in our heavenly father."

"Good, but if you need to talk to someone, I'm here, as are all your friends."

Three days after I talked to Ensign Picket outside, I was sleeping, as was everyone else when I got dragged off my bunk. A guard motioned me to go with him, I dressed and left.

"Sit down, I couldn't sleep, and I knew you knew how to play chess."

"You start," he said. I move a pond forward, and as I did, one of the guards placed two glasses out and filled them with brandy.

"You know I don't drink," I stated.

"Yes, but you owe me, so by drinking with me, you can pay off some of your debt."

"Alright." I sniffed the brandy first, then took a sip it and thought it taste good.

"I thought you didn't drink."

"I didn't say I didn't drink what I said I wasn't a drinker."

"So, tell me, Lieutenant, why do you hate my people?"

"I don't hate your people."

"Then why does your country hate my people?"

"You lived there; you know the people of my country don't hate the Vietnamese they dislike your government."

"What do you think is wrong with communism?"

"Colonel, your country isn't communist, nor is any other country you are a socialist, and the United States isn't a democracy; it is a republic."

"Alright then, what is wrong with socialism everybody shares everything no one goes without unlike the United States?"

"You only want to see what you want, Colonel." "Not everyone has a car or fancy clothing, and more importantly, your people don't have a right to say what they wish, worship the way they want, and travel where they want." "Growth in your society is slow." "Look at any country that is a republic at what they have compared to a socialist country like yours."

"France, Greece, and Italy all have socialist governments, and they are doing just fine."

"Yes, you're right; if their government doesn't make the people happy, they will have a different government, come next election, unlike a system like yours." "All three of those countries have something your country doesn't have, and that's guaranteed human rights," I added. Colonel Kline was getting irritated at what I said, and he knew I was right, so I did a changeup, on him. "Even though I said all of this, Colonel, I can understand why a country like China and Vietnam went socialist."

He perked up at this and said, "What do you understand?"

"Many countries such as yours were under the thumb of European colonists." "They were raping the country of all their wealth, caring little for the people who lived there."

"You believe this?"

"Of course, every school child in American knows this."

"Then what is the United States doing in Vietnam?"

"There are many people in America who don't think we should be here, as you know." "The only thing for sure I know is that we were asked for help by the government in the south."

"Perhaps because your government wants military bases here, maybe they want the oil in the China Sea, or perhaps they want to colonize us like the French."

"I don't know, but if I were a betting man, I would bet you they don't want to colonize Vietnam." I finished my brandy and said with a smile, "Checkmate Colonel."

He looked down, surprise, and said, "Very good one more game."

As we were resetting the chessboard, I asked, "Colonel, how long did you spend in the United States?"

"About two years."

"Then you don't know that much about the American people."

"No, my English wasn't good when I first went to your country."

"There is a book called "A Light In The Forest" if you could get it, it would be an excellent book to read." He nodded; he understood what I said, and we continued playing the game. Since the Colonel paid more attention to the game, he beat me, which made him extremely happy. I was about to leave when I asked him, "Colonel, do you think you could get us a bible and a Book of Mormon?"

"What is this Book of Mormon?"

"It is a religious book some churches read."

"I will think about it if I can find them," at that, I went to bed.

Two weeks passed; the guards took me back to see Lieutenant Colonel Kien. I sat down and noticed that Colonel Kien had a clever look on his face. He grabbed two books and said, "I believe you requested these."

They were the Book of Mormon and a bible. "Yes."

"I wish something from you and your men first."

"And what would that be?" I asked suspiciously.

"I want you and some of your men to do a film answering questions." He wanted propaganda, but one could twist the propaganda and use it against them.

"I am uncomfortable with your people filming my men." "However, I will agree if you give not only the books but all the Red Cross packages that are sent to us and let me choose the men you will film."

He thought for a few seconds then said, "I will agree to this." "I will want you and three others."

"I must first talk to the men first to see if they will agree."

"Why don't you just command them to do it?"

"It will be easier for you to have their willingness."

"I need to know by Friday."

"If I have access to the other dorms, I can tell you today."

"I will let you all go outside today, and you can ask there."

"That would work out well."

I picked Sergeant Brooks, Lieutenant Susmann, and Ensign Pickett, and they all agreed. I explain to them what I wanted to do to turn their propaganda against them. I also told them risk if caught.

"Say anything you can to send a message back home of what we go through here."

"I am uncomfortable with being filmed," said the Lieutenant.

"I understand but understand this if we refuse, they will torture, not just us, but the rest of the men until we give in."

"I guess you're right, but I am still uncomfortable with it."

"What are they going to ask us?" asked Ensign Pickett.

"Your guess is as good as mine; just do your best with it."

"Are we going to get anything for doing this?" asked Sergeant Brooks.

"Yes, all of our Red Cross packages for now on and something else that I want to be a surprise."

As we were going into our dorms, Colonel Kien was waiting for me, and I said, "When do you want to do it?"

"Monday."

I nodded yes, and he handed me the two books and said, "You will get your packages tonight." Again, I nodded approval, he left, and I went into the dorm.

"I have an announcement the Red Cross packages will be here tonight Ensign Pickett come here."

I handed Ensign Pickett a thick black book, and he said with a smile, "A Bible, and it is a King James version."

"Oh, but I am not finished yet." I pulled out a Book of Mormon.

"I am shocked that the Colonel could find one, but I am grateful."

"You give good sermons, but now I expect great sermons; it cost us to get those two books."

"Monday, we will be going through our ordeal."

Monday came, and Sergeant Brooks, Ensign Pickett, and Lieutenant Susmann went one at a time. I wasn't allowed to be in the room, but they looked confident when they came out. It was my turn, I went in and sat on a regular chair, and there was a small table in front of me a camera, microphones and a North Vietnamese flag draped behind me. Colonel Kien was there; it was evident that he was there to observe. They had a thin man in his forties running the camera, a younger man assisting running the audio, a young woman, and an official-looking man doing the interview. They had a set of questions ready to ask me.

"You will read this statement, and then we will ask you questions." They didn't bother telling what their names were, and they acted very arrogantly. If I were going to film a prisoner, I would have had a run through to see what I was going to say, but they didn't, their mistake.

"The United States is illegally in Vietnam; they kill innocent women and children." I made sure it was evident that I was reading this, and I acted as if I was having a hard time understanding. It went on and on how terrible the United States was and how the innocent Vietnamese were suffering. They didn't stop me or correct me; they were either incompetent or inexperienced, but it appeared I got away with it.

"Do you think the United States should be here killing innocent people in Vietnam?" asked the male interviewer.

"No, we should not be killing innocent people, and I don't think we should be in Vietnam unless Vietnamese ask us." The way I answered the question went right over the interviewers' head.

"What do you think of the people of my country," asked the female interviewer.

"I have not seen much of the people here up North, including in Hanoi, but they seem to be honest, hard-working people trying to get by, stressed by the conflict from the North and South."

"You say you do not know much about the people of Hanoi, but haven't you been treated well since our heroic troops capture you?"

I looked over to Colonel Kien, then smiled and said, "Lieutenant Colonel Kien is an honorable man." "He keeps his word; however, if, after the war, I come back to visit, I don't think I would want to stay in the same hotel that I am in now nor eat in the same restaurant."

"I can understand that being a prisoner of war is not comfortable, and you must greatly miss your loved ones," she said.

"Yes."

"I was talking to Lieutenant Colonel Kien about your thoughts about our socialist form of government."

"You told him that a country like China and Vietnam socialism was needed to get rid of the oppressive colonialist." "Please commit to your discussion," said the male interviewer.

"Many countries have been taken over by other nations like the European countries for their profit with little regard for the people." "These countries took natural resources from these countries, leaving the population in a terrible state." "The only way for the oppressed nation to get out from under the thumb of their oppressors was to unite and throw them out sometimes violently, such as what the United States did with England in 1776." "China and Vietnam chose to be socialism, and it worked they kicked out the Europeans now they have other oppressors."

"Do you think the United States does the same as the Europeans?"

"No, I don't know of any country they colonized."

"What about the Philippines and here in Vietnam?"

"The United States kicked out Spain, who was exploiting the Filipinos." "While it is true the United States occupied the Philippines for forty years; they never exploited them." "After World War Two, they gave them their independence."

"With Puerto Rico which the United States acquired at the same time the people were given the choice of independence, statehood, or to remain a commonwealth and they chose more than once to remain a commonwealth." "In Vietnam, the United States is not colonizing; the south asked us to come and help." The questioning went on, and on they tried to trap me into saying things. Every time they did, I turned the question around to make it sound like there was more than one meaning or forced me to answer the way they wanted. I finally went back to my dorm satisfied they didn't get anything from me, and more importantly, they didn't know what I was doing.

A week passed, and we were still joking about the interview. Several guards came into the dorm and dragged Sergeant Brooks, Ensign Pickett, and me out of the room where we joined Lieutenant Susmann. They took us to the same individual cells we were in when we first came to this place. After about an hour, I heard a door open and close and figured that Colonel Kien would save me for last. It was late at night when they took me into Colonel Kien's office.

"You must think I'm stupid."

"No, Colonel." I was knocked to the ground, stripped and beaten for saying anything, and then placed back on the stool.

"You may have deceived those two fools who interviewed you, but you didn't trick me. I checked the film after they broadcast it." I didn't say anything and, of course, got beat for it. "I hold you entirely responsible for what all of you did."

"What are you saying we did that has upset you, Colonel." I was beaten with a wet cane and laid on the floor bleeding all over.

"You will confess everything."

"I don't know what to admit to," I said weakly. We went on this way for what seemed like hours, and when I passed out, a bucket of water was splashed on me to revive me until I wasn't coming out of it anymore. I woke up in the dorm with Sergeant Brooks tending me. "You look like shit," I said to the Sergeant.

"If you think I look like crap, you should see yourself."

"How's Ensign Pickett?"

"Better than you."

I got up and was dizzy then I said, "How long have I been out."

"Three days."

"Wow, have you seen any sign of Colonel Kien?"

"No, I assume you didn't say anything to him when he interrogated you," the Sergeant said.

"No, did you or anyone say anything?"

"I know Ensign Pickett, and I didn't, and I assume Lieutenant Susmann didn't."

"Has Kien taken anything away?

"No, which surprises me."

"Well, maybe he had a change of heart," I said with a smile.

"Yeah, right."

"I need to get into the other dorms to check on the men."

"Dinner will be in about an hour; we can ask then."

After we ate, Sergeant Brooks and I went to the other dorms. Lieutenant Susmann was up and doing well, but Sergeant Brooks look at him anyway. We informed Lieutenant Susmann of what happened, and our suspicion about the Lieutenant was correct; he didn't say anything. We checked the last dorm and then back to our dorm.

Ten days after I woke up from my ordeal with Kien, the guards took me to see Colonel Kien.

"You seem to be resilient after what you received the last beating; I didn't think you would recover so quickly."

"It's all this good food you give us." I was about to be hit for saying that when the Colonel waved the guard off.

"You take a lot of chances."

"Life is a chance." A guard poured us both tea and brought sweet cakes. I thought it best that I eat and drink some. I knew he wanted something he was treating me too kind not to want something, but I went back to my dorm, not finding out what he wanted.

A month passed, and I had made many visits to Colonel Kien's office, but this last time he said, "We have a special guess coming here, and I want ten of your men and yourself to meet this guess." "I do not want any of those who did the film except for you." "I won't tolerate any nonsense like before; I will carefully watch."

"Who is the person that is coming?"

"I think you must wait and see, but I will tell you this person is a well-known person in the entertainment industry."

I went to the dorm and told the Sergeant what was said. "It would be best just to go along with Kien and not to cause any problems."

"You know that they are allowing this person to come just because they want to create good propaganda."

"Yes, but what more disturbs me is that this person coming here sounds like a traitor to me," I informed Lieutenant Susmann about it. He was happy he wasn't going.

I picked ten men and told them, "I don't want you to cause any problems, but it doesn't mean you have to put on an act for the sake of the commandant." "You can be respectful but unemotional if you wish." "I don't care how you act if it doesn't bring down the wrath of the Colonel." "To tell you the truth, I frankly think this person is a traitor."

They told us to bathe and shave, and then they gave us new clothing to wear. Then the guards paraded us into a room, and six men stood up behind a table, and five of us sat down, I was in the center of the five who were sitting down. There were two guards inside the room and a lot more outside. There was also a new camera crew; I wondered what happened to the other people. Kien wasn't there yet, but I was sure this time he would be running the show. We waited over twenty minutes then a door across of us open in walk an officer I knew. Then Lieutenant Colonel Kien followed by an official after he came a good-looking young woman another official and out the door, I could see more guards. I didn't know who the girl was, but I assume she was a celebrity.

"Hello, I'm Jane Fonda, the kind people of North Vietnam have allowed me to come to visit you to see how well the Vietnamese people treated you." No one said anything I couldn't believe she was that stupid to trust anything they said. She looked a little confused at the silence, then she said, "I'm an actress I have made a lot of movies as have my family."

"We know who you and your family are, Miss," I said.

"He is Lieutenant William Henderson, the commander of the prisoners," said Colonel Kien. "Have your men introduce themselves to our most honored guest," Kien said.

I nodded to Ensign Richard Peterson, and he said, "Ensign Richard Peterson U. S. Navy." Each man introduced himself the same way when it came back to me. I told her who I was and in what branch I was in also. She shook our hands as we introduced ourselves. She then went on and on how courageous the North Vietnamese people are and how terrible it was that America was killing women and babies. She finally left, and we went back to our dorm after returning the new uniforms and putting back on the old dirty ones. Unfortunately, three of my men tried to slip her a note when they shook her hand, and the next day they got a beating. We assumed that Jane Fonda must have handed over the messages to our captives. I would have punished the men for taking the chance, but since they got beaten up, I didn't; I was afraid they would die from their beating; fortunately, none did.

Twelve days later, at night, I was taken into Colonel Kien's office for another round of chess.

"Why didn't you try to slip a note to Miss Fonda?"

"I'm not stupid," I replied without taking my eyes off the chessboard. "I didn't trust Fonda the first time she stepped into the room, I believe, she is a traitor."

"She is a great actress."

"Colonel, what would you think if you were in my place."

He thought, then smiled and said, "You are right; she is a traitor."

"She not that good of an actress either."

He won the first game while we were playing the next game, he said, "Your country and mine are in Pairs negotiating an end to the war." I looked up, shocked at what he said, "You might be going home soon." Of course, I lost the game since I couldn't focus because of the news.

When I got back to the dorm, I let everyone know what happened, and in the next days, I told the other dorms.

"You think he is telling you the truth?" Lieutenant Susmann said.

"Yes, you have any idea how long these negotiations might go on for."

"Not really, but I would assume because of all the protesting going on about this war, it won't be that long maybe five or six months."

"Well, the good thing is that there is hope," I said.

6

RETURNING HOME

Christmas came and went Ensign Pickett gave a beautiful sermon, and we played games and sang songs. Suddenly, the food changed for the better about the middle of January, and we got medical treatment. We were spending more time outside now, and I figured we were to be released soon. January ended, and February started. I was sitting on my bunk early in the morning, getting lost in my thoughts. I had a feeling as I did often, that something was about to happen. Twenty minutes later, the door to our dorm opened and in walked Huu. "Everyone clean-up, bath and shave then put these on."

He brought in brand new uniforms, all size fitted all type, and was about to leave when I asked, "Are we going home, Huu?" He didn't say anything as he shut the door, but he had a big smile when I asked him. "I think this is it we are going home," I said with enthusiasm. We all took turns cleaning up and getting dressed in our clean clothing, which took more than an hour. We had to wait another hour when a guard came and got us. We were marched single file down the hall and across the courtyard, and Huu was standing there.

"Huu, come here?" He walked over to me, and I stepped out of line. "You make sure you go back to school; you're brilliant, and your country needs smart people and be proud that you served honorably."

"I will go to school as you say you are not what I thought Americans were." I shook his hand, then got back in line.

They loaded us into buses Klein was there, and I stepped out of line again and asked, "What is going to happen to you?"

"I will be assigned to another unit again this time, a combat unit, I believe." "I hope you do not have any hate towards me."

"I hate no one, Colonel good luck with your future in the military."

I offered him my hand, and he took it and said, "Good luck to you in whatever you intend to do." I got on the bus with the others. The bus took us to an airport where we went into a hanger to receive a package of souvenirs. I thought it was funny and then boarded an American Jet. Everyone held their breath until they were up in the air and out into international space, then a cheer went up.

I sighed and turned to Sergeant Brooks and said, "I need to tell the men who I am."

"Why," said Lieutenant Susmann.

"Because they have a right to know." I got the staff's attention on the plane and said, "I have something to tell my men."

"Now, Lieutenant?"

"Yes, it's important."

"Well, come with me, and I will let you use the mike."

"Quiet down; I have something to tell you." Everyone quieted down, and I went on, "It has been an honor to have served with you, to me, you are all heroes."

"It's you who's the hero, Sir, you saved all of us," someone yelled, and everyone confirmed.

I put up my hand to quiet the men again. I then said, "There is something I need to tell you, I am not Lieutenant William Henderson; he was my squad leader." "I am Corporal James York." "I am not in the Special Forces although I would like to be, I was in a unit called PSYOPS." "Lieutenant William Henderson gave me his dog tags hoping the N.V.R. wouldn't kill an officer." "I'm sorry I had to deceive you if the N.V.R. found out they would have killed me."

Commander Harry McBride stood up and said, "I don't give a rat's ass who you are." "You saved all of our lives and made conditions a lot better for us, and you suffered in doing this." "To me, as far as I'm concern, you are still my commanding officer, and I salute you, Sir."

I turned beet red and said as everyone who agreed with him, "Thank you for your kind words." I sat down, and Lieutenant Susmann smiled and shook my hand.

"Looks like you're a lieutenant a little longer, and you deserve to be an officer permanently," said Sergeant Brooks.

"Yeah," I said as I laid my head back and closed my eyes. The plane's crew started to tell us about all the things we miss since being a prisoner of war. We got a snack to eat, and they said they couldn't give us much more until the doctors ok it. We were going first to the naval base Subic Bay in the Philippines for about two weeks; then, we will be taken to Hawaii if we are healthy enough. In about three hours, we landed in the Philippines. We got taken to a hospital after the handshakes and news people. We were all taken to three large hospital dorms, cleaned up, and immediately changed to hospital clothing. The nurses took blood and vital statistics, then they started to debrief us. While I was waiting for my debriefing, I got a full checkup. The doctors said they would work on my damaged back first, but most of the work on my back will be in the states.

"I'm Commander Talbot; this is Lieutenant Arnold and Baxter." "We have several questions for you if you're up to it."

"Alright." It was time for my debriefing, and from what someone told me it would take some time, these three men were all Navy officers.

"From what I understand, you commanded the prisoners," said Commander Talbot.

"Yes, Sir."

"Why?"

"My squad leader Lieutenant Henderson gave me his dog tags hoping they wouldn't kill an officer, so I took his identity." "When Sergeant Brooks and I came to the first prison camp, my cell was next door to Lieutenant Susmann." "We were able to communicate via Morse code." "He told me who he was, and I said I was Lieutenant Henderson and in Special Forces." "I figured the fewer people that knew who I was the least likely the N.V.R. would know." "He was elated and gave over command to me, and I accepted." "I figured that I could handle the pain that the N.V.R. would inflict on me during interrogation because I have a high pain tolerance." "I also knew hope was a powerful thing, and it gave hope to the men that an officer from Special Forces commanded them." "I thought that the training I had in PSYOPS would help in dealing with the N.V.R also." "I didn't know that Sergeant Brooks had told Lieutenant Susmann everything at the first chance he could."

"When you went to the prison camp in Hanoi, why didn't you let Commander Harry McBride command?" asked Lieutenant Baxter.

"I would have been happy to give up command." "However, soon after I was there, the commandant took me into his office." "Commander

114

McBride was there, and in terrible shape, so he gave up command at his request."

"I understand you had two different commandants, a Major Kien and a Colonel Danh," said Lieutenant Arnold.

"Yes, Sir, Colonel Kien, and Colonel Danh," I said, correcting their title. The questioning went on some time about how they treated the men and me, what information the Vietnamese wanted, and what the men and I told them.

After about three hours, Commander Talbot said, "Your answers will be helpful, James, you must be debriefed a few more times in more detail as you move through the process."

"Yes, Sir, I would assume that the Army will want to talk to me."

"You assume right and Air Force also," the Commander said.

The next morning after breakfast at about seven o'clock, I was on my bunk when a female petty officer third class came to me and said, "Sir, you have a phone call."

"A phone call," I said, surprised.

"Yes, Sir, come with me." I went into an office, and an Ensign handed me the phone.

"Hello."

"Hello, Jim."

"Dad," I said, shocked to hear him.

"Are you alright?"

"Yes, I'm a bit thinner and beaten up a bit, but I'm alright."

"Did they hurt you?"

"You don't want to know, and I don't want to talk about it."

"What are they doing to you there in the Philippines?"

"They are giving me medical treatment and debriefing me." "I should be going to Hawaii in about two weeks."

"Yes, we know, we saw you in the news."

"Oh yeah."

"It wasn't a good picture, but we could tell it was you."

"You know I was using a different name."

"Yes, we knew the military told us."

"How is Bob?"

"He is fine; he is at Travis Air Force Base near Sacramento."

"Good."

"Have you heard from Charlie?"

"Who?"

"Charlie Kahler, my best friend."

"Yes, he called once, I think."

"How is Ma and everyone else?"

"Everyone is fine."

"Good."

"Sir, you need to go to have your back worked on," said the Ensign.

"I have to go, Dad; they want to work on me." "I'll call you when I get to Hawaii your number is the same, isn't it?"

"Yes."

"That's good; goodbye."

"Goodbye."

The next two weeks were full of physical therapy working on my back and debriefing. Sergeant Brooks and I decided to work out in the gym. I was feeling better; they worked on my teeth, filling a few cavities and clean them. By the end of the two weeks, I had gained about twelve pounds. Seven o'clock that night we boarded a jet for Hawaii with a stopover in Guam, the whole trip took eighteen hours. When the plane landed in Honolulu, the men decided that I would be the first to leave the aircraft. After me, Sergeant Brooks, the Navy according to rank and then the Air Force according to rank, would depart the plane. I protested this saying it should be Commander Harry McBride or Lieutenant Susmann going first. However, Commander McBride said I was the commander of the P.O.W.s until the military reassigned us, and everyone agreed. We had a two-hour wait over in Guam we got to get off the plane but had to stay in a hanger where they fed us, and we used the facilities. The military gave us dress uniforms to wear. The dress uniform Sergeant Brooks and I chose were khakis to wear, so we blended with the Navy since they wore khakis also.

After several hours in the air, the pilot came over the loudspeaker and said, "Gentlemen, we should be landing in Honolulu in about an hour and a half. It is a clear day there with light trade winds; the temperature should be about eighty-five degrees when we land."

"Are you all staying in the military when we get back?" I asked those around me.

"I will see when I get back, but I don't think so," said Ensign Pickett.

"Most likely, I had planned to make the Navy my career anyway," Lieutenant Susmann said.

"I'm an old Army warhorse I eat the military up." "I wouldn't know what to do without it," said Sergeant Brooks.

"What about you, James?" asked Lieutenant Susmann.

"I don't know I guess I will see what they will offer me first; I don't have any plans." They gave us battery-electric shavers and a comb and mirror with several towel wipes. I shaved and handed the shaver to Sergeant Brooks. While he was shaving, I combed my hair and gave him the mirror to finish up. I cleaned up with the rest of my towel wipes, then laid back and tried to sleep.

I woke up when someone said excitedly, "I can see an island." Sergeant Brooks looked out the window, and sure enough, there was an island far off. I was starting to get nervous, would there be people outside yelling obscenities or spit at us, I think I would go crazy if they did. I could feel the descent of the plane as we got nearer to the airport, and there was an excited chatter of the men.

I finally felt the wheels hit the runway. The Captain of the plane saying, "We have just landed in Hawaii welcome back home," as jet rolled down the tarmac towards some terminals.

We were informed to remain seated. A naval officer came on board and said, "Welcome home, in a few minutes, you will disembark." "I've come to warn you there are many people out there to welcome you, including the press, celebrities, military personnel from all branches, and even President Nixon." "When you leave the plane, proceed down the stairs at the bottom of the stairs you will find a red carpet." "There will be Generals and Admirals lining the carpet to welcome you, salute them, shake their hand and proceed to the chairs." "I will go first when I get to the bottom of the stairs you come down James all others follow him." He looked out, smiled, then said, "It's time to go."

"That's a cue for me to go, I guess." I got up and went to the door.

"Lieutenant James York."

"No Corporal James York," I said

"You were the commander of the P.O.Ws., as far as I am concern, you are their commander until everyone gets reassigned."

"Yes, Sir."

"When I get to the bottom, come down," he said with a smile. He walked out the door, down the stairs, and then I followed him.

When I step out, I looked around and said with astonishment, "Oh my God, look at all the people." I walked down the latter while Sergeant

Brooks and the others followed me. As instructed, I saluted and shook each of the Generals and Admiral's hands then sat down where a naval officer said to sit. Music was playing; there were flashes of cameras and cheers from the crowd.

Within twenty-five minutes, everyone had sat down, and the crowd quieted down. General Westmoreland got up and said, "I wish to welcome home all these brave men you see before you." "I also like to recognize the dignitaries that are here today." "Our Commander and Chief President Richard Milhous Nixon, the governors of Hawaii, California, Utah, Texas, New York, and Florida," he went on and on. "There are also several senators and congressmen too many to cite." "We also have Johnny Cash and his wife June Carter, Dolly Parton, Bob Hope, and John Wayne and others." "Representing the media are all the networks and several newspapers too many to mention." "I would like to introduce now our first speaker General Arnold of the joint chiefs." He got up and said, "What you see here to my right are over eighty of the most courageous men the arm forces of the United States have to offer." "They have endured many years of things too graphic to speak about in front of you." "There is no reward I could give these heroes that would satisfy the service they performed." "However, today, we will do our best to give them the recognition they deserve." "These men represent the men from the Navy, Air Force, and Army." "I will tell you, men, with all sincerity well done, you have the gratitude of a grateful nation." "I won't take up any more of your time; I will turn it back over to General Westmoreland."

"We will next hear from our Commander and Chief President Richard Nixon."

"I am quite proud to call you soldiers and citizens of the United States." "Many don't fully realize the sacrifice the American soldiers make, especially these men." "They give up their careers, family, schooling, and risk their lives just to keep America free." "These men didn't ask to fight this war nor to be captured and endure terrible conditions, but they did it anyway." "Like the Generals both said and now I, we want to give you a warm welcome back home."

"We are going to hand out awards to these men then they will have a little private time with their families in hanger nine after this if anyone wants to talk to the press, we will allow it." "We will hand out awards by branch starting first with the Air Force, then the Navy, and finally the Army." "You will come up here, receive your awards, and then go back to your seat." We will only mention the significant awards all the men will receive others. "Giving out the Air Force awards will be General John Daniel Lavelle," said General Westmoreland.

"Captain George Irvine." "Captain Irvine has earned, amongst others, the Air Force Cross, Airman's Medal, Bronze Star, and the Purple Heart."

And so, it went with the Air Force, and then Admiral William F. Bringle for the Navy got up to hand out awards. The First one called was Commander Harry McBride he won the Purple Heart, the Distinguished Flying Cross, and the Bronze Star, amongst others. They called Lieutenant Susmann; he won Purple Heart, the Distinguished Flying Cross, the Navy Cross, and the Silver Star, among others. "We are also promoting you to Commander." "Is there anything you wish to say, Commander Susmann?" asked Admiral Bringle.

"Yes, Sir." "I did little compare to the rest of these men, especially my friend and commanding officer James York; he is the most heroic man I have ever met." "Without him, many of us would have been dead." He turned to me, then said, "I salute you, Sir." He sat down, and they went through many of the Navy men.

Then Admiral Bringle said, "Ensign Samuel Pickett." Ensign Pickett, who was behind me, got up then started walking towards the podium, and I looked at him and smiled as he walked to the Admiral. Suddenly, he turned sheet white wobbled and began to fall. Before he hit the ground, I was up and down to him, as was Commander Susmann, Sergeant Brooks, and Commander McBride. The medical personnel tried to rush in, but we prevented them.

"Get him some water, now," I said to the medical people.

"Just a little dehydrated," Sergeant Brooks said.

"Are you able to go to the podium, Sam?" I asked.

"Yes, Sir."

I helped him up and was about to escort him to the podium when Commander Susmann said, "Sir let Commander McBride, and I escort him." "He is Navy, after all."

"Alright." As I looked at the men, most of them were on their feet clapping; they sat down once he got to the podium. I remained standing worried Sam might be in worse shape than what Sergeant Brooks felt. A Navy medical person came, gave him some water, and then let him hold onto the container if he needed some more.

"Can you continue Ensign?" asked the Admiral.

"Yes, Sir."

"Good, we have awarded you the Purple Heart, the Distinguished Flying Cross, the Navy Cross, and the Silver Star." "We have also promoted you to lieutenant." "Do you wish to say anything, Lieutenant?"

"Yes, Sir." "I want to thank our Heavenly Father for bringing us home safely, and for our commander James York for without him, we would have all perished." "I think I better sit down now."

"James wet this handkerchief and put it on his head," said Sergeant Brooks. As Lieutenant Pickett pasted, I stopped him, took his water, poured some water on the handkerchief, and then put it on his head.

"Thank you, Sir."

"It's alright, Lieutenant; if you are feeling sick, have someone call the medical people over."

"Yes, Sir." He finally got back to his seat, sat down, the ceremony went on, and General Arnold handed the medals to the Army. He called up Sergeant Brooks.

"Staff Sergeant Greg Brooks, it is my pleasure to award you with the Purple Heart, Silver Star, the Soldier Medal, Distinguished Service Cross, and Meritorious Service Medal."

The President then got up and said, "It is my pleasure to award you with the Army Medal of Honor the highest recognition your country can give you." Then General Arnold stepped back in.

"Sergeant, we also are promoting you to Master Sergeant you make all of us proud, do you wish to say anything."

"Yes, Sir." He looked down at his Medal of Honor that the president draped around his neck then said, "I'm quite surprised at getting the Medal of Honor." "I was just doing the job that my country expected of me." "The one who deserves it is James York he acted way beyond the call of duty more than once." As he talked, I held my head down as I did with everyone who spoke about me. I was uncomfortable with people giving me accolades I didn't think I was any different from anyone else. "This is a man who dreamed of being in the Special Forces, and he performed as good as any Green Beret I've seen." "James is a man who had a desire to go to officer's candidate school when he returned to the United States." "However, he didn't need to because he is the best officer I ever knew." "I could tell you much of how he suffered for all of us, and I know this because since I had a medical background, I was assigned to be the medic, and I treated him often." "Well, I don't want to take too much time, because I know these men want to be with their loved ones, so I will just say thanks for the support and all the awards." At that, he saluted the general and went back to his seat next to me.

I smiled at him and whispered to him, "You know that stuff you said about me was a bunch of bullshit."

"No, I met every word of it," he replied.

General Westmoreland joined General Arnold. General Westmoreland got up and said, "Before General, Arnold makes his presentation I wish to speak about this next man." "This young man was an overweight, high school student when he joined the Army; his drill instructor didn't think he was going to get through basic training." He went on and on how I built myself up, went into PSYOPS, and was rated the best. "While in Vietnam he was assigned to a Special Forces unit and on their first trip out the enemy attacked them." "Some men got killed; those who lived, lived because James stayed behind to protect the wounded while they were being picked up by Hueys. After we retook the battle zone, we found the body count of over four hundred and fifty of the enemy dead; most contributed to this man." "He assumed the identity of his squad leader to fool the enemy." "Then, at the first prison camp, he took command of about forty men, taking all sorts of abuse to acquire some basic human rights." "Afterwards, James and his men moved to Hanoi, where he took command of over eighty men and again took the abuse to help his men." "He also created a health care system, a spiritual system, and an entertainment system; this is only a small part of what he did." "This person is Corporal James York, James, come up here."

I looked around, and all the men were on their feet, saluting me, and I said, "Thank you, but please sit down." For some reason, my heart was beating fast as I approached the podium.

The Generals shook my hand. General Arnold said, "We are awarding James the Distinguished Service Cross, Silver Star, Bronze Star, Joint Service Commendation Medal. Also, there are many other medals, too many to mention." General Arnold pinned some of the medals on me then handed me a box with the rest I was shocked at the number of awards they gave me.

General John Daniel Lavelle of the Air Force stepped up he said, "It doesn't happen very often, but the Air Force felt they should award James the Air Force Cross."

Admiral Bringle stepped forward; he said, "Like the Air Force, the Navy felt they should award James the Navy Cross."

Then the president stepped forward and said, "From a grateful nation, Congress has awarded James the Army Medal of Honor." "Frankly, I feel you should have had two Medals of Honor for what you did with your squad and what you did for your fellow prisoners." He shook my hand and placed the medal around my neck. Then the President said, "When you finish here, and after you go on leave, I want you to come and stay in the White House."

"Yes, Sir, just send me the orders, and I will be there," I replied.

General Arnold said, "For four years, you acted as a first lieutenant and commander of these brave men." "From what I understand, your performance as an officer had been exceptional." "So, I don't see why you shouldn't be an officer." "Since you have been an officer for four years, I believe you should be a captain as of the first day you took command." "Congratulations, Captain, you are the most decorated man in the Vietnam war; if not ever in the history of the nation, would you like to say a few words, James."

"Yes Sir, I guess I should," I said, shocked and overwhelmed at what happened. "I am surprised at what happened to me here, and I feel that these men are just as good or better than me." "Frankly, Lieutenant Henderson saved my life." "To me, he is my hero; I wish he were here." "I also wish to say how grateful I am for Sergeant Brooks, who supported me from the beginning right along with Commander Susmann." "Without these two, I couldn't have done what I did." "And then there is Lieutenant Pickett who kept all of us level-headed with his spiritual words; I hope the leaders of his church sees how great of a man he is." "It would have been nice if my family were here to see what has happened, but I know it would have taken a miracle for my mother to get on a plane."

"James, your family, are here," General Arnold said.

"Where," I said, surprised. The General pointed to my left, I looked, and there was my aunt Dorothy and my Brother Dave waving at me then my dad stood up. "Dad, your here." After I composed myself after the shock of seeing my family, I said in closing. "I wish all of you to know that every man you see here served with honor and bravery." "There have never been finer bunch men in the military." I turned and saluted the General and went back to my seat.

"My family is at the far end to the left of us; I didn't think they would come."

"Why would you think that?" asked Sergeant Brooks.

"They don't have the money to travel, and my mother doesn't like planes or boats."

"Gentlemen, attention." We all stood up. General Westmoreland said, "An escort will escort Captain James York to hanger nine everyone else is to follow him roll by roll." I headed out but looked back one more time to see if I could see my family, but they were far off.

"Do you have family here, Sergeant?" I asked. "Just maybe my ex-wife and boy, he should be nine by now."

"Great age, you should have a lot of fun with him."

"Yeah, if he is here."

"Here or not, why don't you join me with my family?"

"I'll do that." We entered the hanger, and there were tables and chairs all over the place each table had names on them, I got pointed to the directed of my area. Fortunately, the Sergeant's table was right next to my tables, so we just combined them. I placed my box of medals on top of the table and looked for Lieutenant Pickett.

"I'm going to check on Lieutenant Pickett," I said to the Sergeant.

"I'll go with you."

We found him in the center of the hanger, and I asked, "How are you feeling?"

"I'm fine, Sir," Pickett said as the Sergeant felt his head.

Sergeant nodded his head, then said, "Keep on pushing the liquids."

"I'll do that, Sergeant."

We walked back over to our tables, which were next to a platform.

"I wonder what that is for," I said.

"I would imagine it is a makeshift stage," replied the Sergeant. The families started drifting in and filling the hanger; when I looked over to the Sergeant, there was no look of expectation. I had a smile ear to ear; when my family, and to my surprise, Charles Kahler, all came in.

After all, the welcoming and I introducing Sergeant Brooks, we sat down, and I asked, "How were you all able to afford coming here?"

"We didn't have to pay anything the government paid for it all," said my dad.

The Sergeant gave up hope of anyone coming when a sandy long hair little boy came up to him and said, "Daddy, are you, my daddy."

That was the first time I ever saw tears seep from his eyes, and he said, "Josh, is that you, Josh?" He picked him up into his arms and said, "Who brought you here, Josh?"

"Mommy."

A nice-looking woman came over to him and said, "I thought I would come to see if you want to give it another try."

He lost it, grabbed her, brought her close to him, and said, "Of course I want to," he said.

I smiled and said, "I always liked a happy ending."

We talked for about fifteen minutes from behind the Sergeant, and I came, "Captain York come to attention when a superior is present."

I stood up at attention as did Bob the Sergeant turned his head around and smiled, but I didn't notice. "I don't think he is talking about you, Bob."

"A Major still outranks me, but you don't have to stand, salute, or take off your hat if you're a Medal of Honor winner."

At that, I turned, then smiled and said, "Sit down, Bob; he is here for us." Sergeant Brooks was hysterical with laughter, in front of us stood a smiling six-foot-eight black man, all muscles, with a green beret on his head, and a package in his hand. "I like to introduce you to the man who saved my life; this is the real Major William Henderson." I went over to shake his hand, but I didn't get away with that he gave me a big bear hug and then gave Sergeant Brooks one also.

"I can't stay very long; I have to head back to my base, but I have this for you, James." He handed me a wrapped package and told me to open it. I open it and, in the box, was a green beret, I looked back up at Major Henderson confused, and he said, "You told me you wanted to be in Special Forces, do you still want to?"

"Yes."

"Put on the hat you're in the Green Berets." "You must do some of the training, and some of it I will wave, but as of now, you are in the Army Special Forces." "Sergeant Brooks, you think you can get this man into shape and train him while you are here in Hawaii."

"Yes, Sir." He handed the Sergeant and me a packet of orders. Mine said to report to Fort Brag, I was to report the end of June for additional training and that I was already in the Green Berets.

I looked up at him startled and in disbelief, and he said, "It's true, and I will be your commanding officer, but you need to know I will not give you any special treatment." "I will see you at the end of June."

"Yes, Sir." The Sergeant and I shook his hand; he said his goodbyes to our families, and then he was gone.

"What's the Green Berets?" asked my Aunt Dorothy.

"It's an elite unit in the Army; only a few are qualified to be in it." My brother David wanted to look at my beret, and I handed it to him. I asked my brother, Bob, "Are you sure about not saluting or wearing my hat when I want."

"Yes."

"That's correct James when you are a medal of honor winner or in the Green Berets," said Sergeant Brooks. I got the hat back from David after he put it on as my Uncle Art and my brother Bob went through my box of medals looking and making commits on them.

"What did they do to you in that prison camp?" my mother asked.

"You don't want to know Ma; the doctors are taking care of me."

"Can I see you without your shirt on?"

"Not now, maybe when I come home, let them work on me for a couple of months." All the celebrities came into the hanger and up to the stage. Bob Hope and John Wayne put on a small show, and they were funny.

Bob Hope called me up on the stage and cracked some jokes about me then asked, "Did you see any of my U.S.O shows while in Vietnam?"

"No, the commandant of the prison camp wouldn't allow it."

That got a laugh, and then John Wayne said, "I like your Beret."

"Well, you are in part responsible for me getting it, Mr. Wayne."

"It's Duke; how am I responsible?"

"I saw your movie."

"Well, you have good taste in movies." Bob Hope crack a few more jokes, and then I sat down, and he started in on other things.

Johnny Cash and June Carter had finished singing. Dolly Parton had begun when a female Ensign came to me and whispered, "Captain, the press would like to talk to you for a few minutes."

"The media wants to talk to me; I'll come back, don't go anywhere."

I went to a raised platform with a podium. Along the way going there, the Ensign said, "If there is any personal information asked about the other men, it is classified confidential. You're not to answer them." "Also, if you are asked any question you think might be damaging to the military or America, just look over at me. I will shake my head if you should answer or not."

"Alright." I got behind the podium and said, "I am Captain James York; I wish to set a few rules." "I will start to my right you may ask one question, and a follow-up one, which I will answer if I can, then I will move on to the next person." "I do this because I don't like the chaos of a news conference and wish to get back to my family." "Besides you, all took me away from Dolly Parton, and yes, they are real, at least from where I was sitting." After the laughter, I said, "When you ask a question, please tell me who you are and who you represent."

I then pointed to the first person. "John Dailey of the New York Times, of the men in the prison camps, how many didn't come back alive?"

"Are you talking about under my command?"

"Yes."

"They all came back." "However, when we left the smaller prison camp and moved to the Hanoi Hilton Commander McBride was in command after several days of interrogation, some men died." "The Vietnamese had taken me into a room, and Commander McBride turned over command to me from that point everyone else returned home."

"Clarify Hanoi Hilton?"

"Name we gave for the Hỏa Lò Prison turned into a prison camp."

I pointed to the next person, and he said, "Jack Richards of the Oakland Tribune, what was wrong with Commander McBride to give up command?"

"Are you of the Oakland California Tribune?"

"Yes."

"Do you have an extra newspaper with you?"

"Sorry, no."

"Too bad that is the paper I grew up reading." "Your question is confidential, and I can't answer, ask another."

"What were you tortured for?"

"Several things like information, to assert control, their pleasure, perceived disrespect."

"Are you related to Sargent York of the First World War?"

"I'm not sure." "I've asked my father, who said he might have been a distant cousin."

The questions proceeded when we came to, "Walter Cronkite CBS news." "It is said you killed four hundred and fifty men first is this number correct and how many rounds of ammunition did you carry."

"No, I believe that number was an estimate." "I had that day about two hundred rounds of ammunition when I ran out of ammo; I took more ammo off those who were either dead or too wounded to fight." "I had a lot of hand grenades, two of the N.V.R. I killed with my knife."

"Harry Reasoner ABC new, were you in Cambodia, and what was your mission when they attacked you."

I looked over at the Ensign, and she shook her head, yes. I said, "Yes, we were in Cambodia in a non-combat role." "I was in a unit called PSYOPS, which is gathering information and turn it into propaganda." "David Brinkley NBC, "I notice you wearing a beret, are you in the Green Berets, or is PSYOPS part of the Green Berets?"

"PSYOPS at present is not part of the Army Special Forces or what you would call the Green Berets." "I at the time wasn't in the Green Berets but wanted to be." "Someone of a higher rank than I decided I earned the beret, and when I got here, I just received orders for the unit." "I must do some training that they go through, but regardless I am in the Green Berets as you call it." The questions went on until everyone had two questions answered, then I excused myself. When I got back, Dolly Parton was talking to my family, and then she came over to me, giving me a big hug and a kiss much to everyone's delight.

"So, does this mean we are married now?"

"Now Captain you just got back home there are plenty of women out there that would love to have you, but if none are suitable for you, look me up," she said with a smile then left.

I asked everyone, "What are your plans while you are here?" They were going to Kauai except for Bob; he had to get back to his base and my Aunt Adeline and Uncle Paul, who had to get back home. "Aunt Adeline, Uncle Paul, I would like to talk to you privately before you leave."

"Alright, we leave tomorrow," said Uncle Paul.

"What is the name of your Hotel?" "I will leave you a message as to where we can meet later today?"

"The Hotel is called Hyatt room 342."

"Alright, I will give you a call."

We were all taken to different facilities according to our branch of service. Sergeant Brooks and I went to Schofield Army Base for further medical, psychological treatment, and more debriefing. It was at my request that I stayed in the same room as Sergeant Brooks.

A Lieutenant Fergusson wanted to run a bunch of tests on me, but I said, "Not now I have some personal business to take care of."

"You don't have any choice, Sir, your business must be taken care of another day."

"I looked at him and said who is going to stop me."

"The M. Ps. will stop you, Sir."

"I looked at him and said, well, you call those M. Ps. but let me tell you what will happen." "I will get into a fight with the M. Ps. most likely hurting some, and then they will take me to the stockade." "The press will find out that a Medal of Honor recipient and a hero of the Vietnam war got arrested because he wanted to do some important business." "Now, who do you think the brass will come down on?"

He thought then said, "You think you will be available tomorrow?"

"Yes," I said with a smile.

At that, he left, and the Sergeant started laughing and said, "What is so important that you need to do now?"

"My aunt and uncle from Missouri are going back home tomorrow morning, and I need to see them before they go."

I got a jeep and got to the hotel by five. The whole family was there; my father came down and said they were going to dinner and wanted to know if I wanted to go. "Sure, but I need to talk to Aunt Adeline first."

"They were across the hall from us." I went up to their room, knocked on their door, and they told me to come in.

My aunt and uncle had a big smile on her face then my Uncle Paul said, "What is it you want to talk about?"

"Is there any land that butts up to your place for sale?"

"About five hundred acres across the road, good land, they have a spring running through it."

"Has it been for sale for a while?"

"Yes, about two years, I would like to buy it but don't have the money it has a house, barn, and sheds on the property," said my uncle.

"How much do they want for it?"

"Adeline, you know how much they want for that place?"

"Last I heard they wanted about fifteen thousand because it had water on the property."

"Will you do me a favor?" "As soon as you get back, offer them ten thousand if they take it great if not get it at whatever price you can." "Let me know, and I will send the money."

"You want to live in Missouri, James?" my aunt asked.

"Yes, and if I get the property, I will tell you why."

My father knocked and asked, "Are you ready?"

"We're coming," my aunt said.

"I need your telephone number." My aunt wrote it down and gave it to me. "I'll call in a week." We went downstairs where everyone was waiting; at dinner, I sat next to Charles and talked about home.

The next day they worked on my back, removing several bamboo splinters. They didn't knock me out; they gave me a local, so when medical people finished, they sent me to see a therapist for a mental evaluation. Afterward, the Sergeant and I had enough time to work out and go for a run. After we ate, I was bored, so I went back to the gym to work out some more, and then I went for a swim.

"Where did you go?" asked Sergeant Brooks.

"To work out again and swim."

"You should have told me I would have gone with you."

"Well, I figured you would be tired to work out, for a man of your age," I said, smiling.

"Wait until tomorrow; I will show you tired."

I went to sleep that night and then awoke when the Sergeant and a nurse shook me. "You were yelling in your sleep," said the Sergeant

"Did you have a bad dream, Captain?" asked the nurse.

I looked at Sergeant Brooks and said, "I had a nightmare about that little girl killed by the N.V.R." I went back to sleep, and I woke again, but this time it was for breakfast, I was dragging with fatigue. "Do you think I'm tired because I did that extra work out I did?" I asked the Sergeant.

"No, most likely the fitful night you had worn you out." We went to breakfast then I had a meeting with a psychiatrist.

"I heard you didn't sleep well last night."

"Yes, it was a nightmare."

"You have these dreams often."

"No, this was the first one I've had."

"Do you know what caused you to have this dream?"

"Not really, I did work out extra hard yesterday."

"Your dreams may increase, and you may have them during the day just remember they are just a dream and that you need to be concentrating on what is real at the time." I nodded, and we went on talking about other things. The Sergeant and I worked out for three hours, and then I had to go for some more work on my back. Later the Sergeant and I worked out again, and that night I slept better. The next day about seven in the morning, they gave me a complete set of uniforms with everything sewed on. I was just about to go to the gym with Sergeant Brooks when I got a phone call.

"Jim, can you get away today we are going home tomorrow we would like to spend the day with you?" asked my father.

"Let me go ask, are you at the hotel."

"Yes."

"Give me your number, and I will call you back in about twenty minutes." I talked to the officer in charge of me to see if I could go with my family. I got the ok, and so I went to speak to Sergeant Brooks.

"My family is going home today; do you mind if I spend the day with them instead of working out during the day."

"No, you go with your family, and we will exercise even more tomorrow." "I have things to do today, and I would like to spend more time with my ex and son," he added. I called my dad and told him that I would be wearing fatigues, and I didn't have any money yet, I wouldn't be getting that for about a week, so we planned for him to pick me up at the front gate of the Fort.

My father picked me up about an hour after I had called him, and I spent the day shopping, seeing the sights, and eating. They tried to talk to me about what I went through, but I didn't say much. "I may be buying some property in Missouri," I said to my father.

"Yes, Adeline said something about it; how much land is it."

"About five hundred acres, it has a spring on the property, a house, barn, and sheds; it also butts up to Aunt Adeline's place."

"How much do they want for the property fifteen thousand, but Aunt Adeline is going to offer ten if they take it."

"It sounds good; how much back pay they plan to give you?"

"I think about seventy or eighty thousand."

"You should invest some of it."

"I plan to." I got dropped off in front of Schofield Army Base about seven o'clock, and I walked backed to my building. I had been sitting on my bunk for about a half-hour when the Sergeant arrived. "You ready to go to the Gym?" I asked.

"Sure, let me get into my shorts."

"How did your day go?" he asked me.

"Good, and what about you?" I asked.

"Oh, it went well, my ex and I are still building a relationship." "How do you feel about jumping out of an airplane?"

"Well, I'll try anything once if I have a parachute."

"Good in two weeks you will go airborne."

I looked at him like he was crazy, saying, "Don't worry, I will teach you everything you need to know before you make your jump."

"You need to get your wings if you are going to be in the Berets,"

I found out that my offer for the property in Missouri got accepted over the next two weeks. I arranged for them to send me the paperwork on the property, which I had to have notarized, then I would mail everything back to my aunt with a check for the place.

Sergeant Brooks and I were working out at a fever pitch, and he had been instructing me on doing a jump with the Eleventh Airborne Division. Medical had been working on my back and filling both the Sergeant and me with mega doses of vitamins, minerals, and I believe steroids. The doctors didn't know we were going to do a jump this soon; they wouldn't have approved it. Sergeant Brooks told the commanding officer of the Eleventh Airborne Division we just had to requalify our jump. Every two years, this must get done; this was true for the Sergeant but a slight lie about me. As we walked to the Airborne unit, I said, "You know I was in the Hundred and First before."

"Did you do a jump there?"

"No, did a lot of running and pushups." Most of the men jumping went to the airport by truck, but they took us by jeep because of who we were. About sixty-two paratroopers, including ourselves, loaded up into a C-130 Hercules and started to taxi down the runway. I sat next to Sergeant Brooks, and we both got stares from everyone. I guessed we became somewhat of celebrities; we were both on television and in the newspapers. One of the things that the Sergeant didn't warn me about is that a C-130 Hercules is not pressurized, and I could feel it. I turned to the Sergeant and said, "Thanks for letting me know that the plane is not pressurized; what else didn't you tell me." He chuckled but didn't say anything. When we got to the right location, we got told to stand and hook up. I watched the guy in front hook up, and I did the same, then a light changed from red to green, and we started jumping. When it was my turn to go out the door, I did what the Sergeant said, look straight forward and jump out the plane without looking down. My heart and lungs jumped up into my throat; another thing the Sergeant didn't tell me. He did say once I feel a sudden jerk on my harness to look up to make sure my chute opened all the way, which fortunately it did. There were many parachutes all over the place. I didn't know which one the Sergeant was, but I assume he was near-by. To the far left of me was one trooper that had what's called a Mae West a malfunction of the chute, I saw him struggling to fix the chute, and when that didn't work, he then pulled his emergency chute. I looked for the marker on the ground we were supposed to hit, and I was to the far right. Sergeant Brooks told me if I pulled on the ropes on the left side of me, I would go right. I tried that, and I did go right when I thought I moved right far enough I let go and I stop moving right and then I hit the ground with a jarring thump. I stumbled a little but was able to keep standing, and I pulled in my chute and crammed it back into the pack so that someone could retrig it correctly. I looked around, spotted the Sergeant coming towards me. I was within twenty feet from the target, which was a good jump. Sergeant Brooks did much better; he was within ten feet.

With a big smile on his face, Sergeant Brooks asked, "Well, what did you think?"

"You say we only have to do this once every two years."

"Yes."

"Good."

He laughed, "Well, you did a good jump better than most of these guys." I nodded and smiled, and we walked to where the others were and waited for transportation back. We received everything we need to show proof of the jump.

When we got back, Major Bartley, one of our doctors, was standing there, and he didn't look pleased. "I heard you boys have been doing an exercise with the Eleventh Airborne Division."

Sergeant Brooks smiled and said, in a strongest southern accent, he could muster, "Why Major, whatever are you talking about?"

"York, did you get your wings?"

"I sure did Major," I said as I walked into my room. The Major shook his head and walked down the hall the opposite way.

By the end of the first month in Hawaii, I had sent the notarized papers and a check back to my aunt in Missouri with a note saying you can place their cattle on the property and use the spring. I also told her I would be coming for a month after I spent time with my parents. I had also sent a substantial check to my father to invest and bank. I found the amount of money they paid me was more than enough to live on and had a lot of money left over.

The Sergeant and I were starting to bulk up from the workout we have been doing and medical treatments. I felt excellent except for my back. I did feel a lot stronger than when I left for Vietnam, and I was happy that I felt stronger because I didn't know what to expect when I went to Bragg for training.

Monday Sergeant Brooks spent time with his ex-wife and child, so after I worked out in the morning, I decided to go sightseeing. I was in the town of Waimalu, and I came across a martial art school. There were many of children learning; I watched for a while until an instructor came over to me and said, "Can I help you?"

"Well maybe, I'm in the Army Special Forces I will be leaving in about a month." "I learned some martial arts in Vietnam." "I would like to learn some more can you work with me."

He looked at me for a few seconds then said, "You're that war hero James York, aren't you?"

"Well, I don't know about being a war hero, but I am James York."

"I read about you; your story is incredible." I smiled, and he continued and said, "I will give you a free lesson on day by day basis until you go back to the mainland." "You want to start now?" he asked.

"Sure, but I don't have a gi."

"That's alright." "I have an extra; you can use mine."

"I changed into the gi and came out the children who were there were waiting around the mat."

"What are we going to do?" I asked the instructor.

"I thought that it would be good to see what you can do to me." "It would also be good for you and the children."

"Alright." I wasn't happy with the children being there but didn't say anything. I got in one corner, and the instructor at the other we both bowed. I kept my eyes on him, and as I was bowing, he attacked me before he made contact, I gave him a blow to the chest, and he went flying. I didn't know an older Asian man was watching from the corner of the room. The instructor got up mad and tried to do a kick, but I went down and swept his leg, and again he fell to the ground. I stood up and said, "What is it with you?" But he didn't say anything he got up furious and came at me I gave him a wicked kick knocking him out. I looked at him in disbelief, as did the children.

The old man came on the mat and said to me, "He does not work here any longer; he is without honor."

"You are that soldier who won the Medal of Honor?"

"Yes, Sir."

"Fighting style comes from Vietnam?"

"Yes, Sir, I was hoping to learn some more but not from that one."

"I will train you if you will honor me."

I smiled and said, "Yes, Sir."

By this time, the instructor that I knocked out came to, and the Asian man told him, "You may leave."

Without a word, he got up and left, and I said, "This is his gi."

"No, it is mine; you may use it." He trained the children until another instructor came, and then he worked with me. The old man's name was Wang; he agreed he would make time for me each time I arrived, and I learned much even this first day. I went down to the dojo three times a week; the Sergeant believe it was a good idea.

Friday after breakfast, a Frank White from Penguin publishing company called me. "Yes, Sir, I am Captain James York."

"I wish to talk to you about a book deal."

"Alright, when."

"How about now?"

"Here or where you are?"

"I will come and get you." "I'll be there in about forty-five minutes."

"Alright." I phoned the Army JAG office, and they agreed to go with me to make sure I signed a reasonable contract. Twenty minutes later, a female JAG officer came, and we walked to the front gate talking.

"This is Lieutenant Mary Reap; she is a JAG officer to make sure everything is honest and straightforward," I said.

"I'm Frank White, and this is Henry Penn, who handles the contracts." We drove to a nice quiet restaurant in Honolulu, and Frank White said, "You look strong, but you're not as I pictured you to be in my mind." "Well, let's get down to business Penguin wants to write a book about you and they want me to be the writer," stated Frank White.

"Alright, I will go with you; however, I have some conditions before I consent to a book as you likely figured there would be."

"Okay, what are your conditions?"

"I wish this book to be successful, so I don't want it written in an autobiography style but in an exciting novel style." "I want it to be real and truthful, don't sugar-coat it, make it as accurate as possible."

"Well, I will try my best to make it sound like a novel I like the idea, and I promise you I will keep it honest."

"I know you will I want it put into the contact."

"Okay, what else."

"Well, I have some questions, first from what point to what point in my life are you going to write?"

"What do you think it should be?"

"Birth to when I got awarded the Medal of Honor."

"Sounds good to me."

"If something happens, after that point, we can negotiate a new contract."

"Do you think something new is going to happen in your life?"

"I have these feelings that come true, and yes, I think there will be other things happening."

He looked at me for a few seconds then said astonished, "You're serious, aren't you?"

"Yes."

"Then, if you go with us, I will agree to this."

"Any movie deal I want a percentage in the deal and say on how the movie people make it."

Frank White looked at Henry Penn with a smile and said, "Have you ever negotiated a contract before?"

"No, but I am not stupid."

"I will agree to this also and put it in the contract."

"How many books does Penguin think will sell?" asked Lieutenant Reap.

"Minimum of five million."

"At what cost per book."

"Twelve to fifteen dollars a book for a hard copy and eight to nine dollars a book for a paperback."

"What is the cost to make one hard copy and paperback?" asked the Lieutenant.

"Hard copy about three dollars and paperback about a dollar."

"I figure that Penguin will make near sixty million dollars, how much does Penguin plan to pay Captain York?"

"Two dollars a book and a hundred thousand in advance."

"Four dollars a book and two hundred thousand advances are better."

Frank wasn't smiling anymore. Henry Penn whispered something to him and then said, "The best we can do for an unknown person is three dollars a book and one hundred and fifty thousand in advance."

"Unknown you just told me that the Penguin would sell at least five million copies." She looked over at me, and I smiled at how well she negotiates then nodded yes.

"Alright, Mr. White, I think he should get more, but he has agreed to the amount."

That brought a smile to both Mr. White and Penn, and I said, "This does not include any movie deal."

"That's correct," said Mr. White.

There are a couple of smaller things I wish, a couple of cases of hardback books so I can give them out." "I want you to understand when you gather the information you need from me; you can't interfere with my military job." "There will be things that I can't disclose."

"I understand, Captain York, but why are you going to stay in the military? Penguin will make you a very wealthy man?"

"Do you think I joined the Army for the money, I joined the Army to defend my country; it is the right thing to do?"

"I understand," he said.

"Well, make sure you put everything in writing, so we both understand." "I can't force others to talk to you about me; you must persuade them to talk to you, Mr. White."

"That's alright you let me handle them."

"When will the contract be ready, I'll want to see it before the Captain signs it?" asked Lieutenant Reap.

"By the end of the week, it should be available with the money."

"Good." We all shook hands and went back to Schofield Army Base.

I told my father and Sergeant Brooks what happened, and by the end of the week, I received my money and sent most of it home. Frank White agreed he would start interviewing me in California after the first week I was there. For the rest of my time in Hawaii, I did physical training, also medical treatment. I got my orders to go on leave for two months, then report to the Pentagon and Fort Bragg.

7
LEAVE

I said my goodbyes to Sergeant Brook and his family and caught a flight back home. It was about seven-thirty p.m. overcast and cold when the plane landed in San Francisco. When I left the plane and entered the terminal, a crowd of people greeted me with a cheer, and there were flashes from cameras from news reporters. "Do you have anything to say to us, Captain?" asked a reporter.

"It surprised me to see so many people here and the press too."

"Don't you know you have been the topic of much discussion?"

"No, I don't watch television nor had time to read much."

"Will you answer a few questions for us, Sir?"

"Alright."

"What will you be doing here in California?"

"Enjoying my leave with my family."

"I have heard you have signed a book deal with Penguin."

"That's true."

"Will you tell us what the deal was?"

"I'm afraid you must ask the people at Penguin about that."

"Do you plan to stay in the military, Captain?"

"Yes, until after my Special Forces training is finished, I will see what the Army will do with me and reevaluate what I will do?"

"Do you plan to live in California, Sir?"

"I haven't left the Army yet." "California is my home, but I did buy some property in Missouri; I like the countryside of the Ozarks." "I really must be going; I wish to go home." I left to get my baggage and catch a cab, but as I went, they continued asking me questions. By about nine p.m.,

I was unloading my luggage from the taxi and paid him. My father and mother came to the front porch as I carried my things up into the house and placed them in the kitchen.

"I would have come to get you if you would have called," my dad said.

"I had the money, and I didn't want to bother you besides the press was there, and it was chaotic."

"Are you hungry?" my mother asked.

"No, I'm alright." We talked for about an hour, and then my dad started yawning, so I said with a smile, "It may be time for bed."

"Well, you know where your bedroom is," my mother said. I went to grab my bags when through the sliding glass doors, in the kitchen, my dog wagged her tail. I opened the door, sat down on the stairs next to her as she went nuts with excitement. She calmed down, and I went upstairs with my bags with my mother following me. I got some hangers and started to hang up my clothing when Jerry came home.

"Well, you look better than you did," said Jerry.

"You think so?"

"Yeah, how long are you going to be here?"

"Three or four weeks, I will be spending a month in Missouri."

"Oh yes, I remember you bought some property there." I finished hanging my things up and decided to take a shower before I went to bed. I had stripped down to my short when Jerry said, "Jesus, you look like you went through hell."

My mother came into the room and said, "Your wounds look terrible; Manuel come here." My parents looked at my back real close, and they were in shock at what I went through.

I said, "My back isn't as bad as it seems to you; the treatment the military has been giving me makes it look worse."

"Well, at least you seem strong," my father said.

"Yeah, better than that fat I use to have."

The next day I went for a run and did some calisthenics. It was Saturday, and my father was just waking up when I finished. I went into the house and said to my dad, "I'm thinking of buying a vehicle today if you can take me down to a lot."

"I'll take you, but why buy a car when you have the VW?"

"I don't want a car I need a pickup, and I don't want to bother you with your work car beside I want to drive back to Missouri, the pickup will be good for the place I bought."

"Alright, but I would buy a good used one; the engine bugs will be out by now."

"Whatever you say."

"After we eat, I will take you to a car lot."

"I prefer Ford."

"Alright."

After breakfast, my father took me down to a car lot, and I found a red and white nineteen seventy F-100 long bed. It was only two years old the body looked perfect, as did the interior. It had air-conditioning and V-8 302 engine I didn't know much about engines, but my father told me it was a small engine but would do.

The salesman came out; my father said, "How much for the truck."

"Nice one, isn't it thirty-five hundred dollars."

"It's too much," my father said.

He started to walk off the lot, I followed him, and the salesman said, "Wait a minute, maybe I can work out a deal lets negotiate."

"I have cash what do you want to offer," I said.

"How much cash do you have?"

"Enough."

"I'll have to know to make you a deal."

My father looked at me, said, "Let's go to another lot."

We started walking again, and the salesman said, "What are you willing to pay?"

My father went back to the truck, looked at the odometer, and said, "You have high mileage on this truck twenty-five hundred."

"That's not giving me a much profit." We started walking again, and he said, "Let me ask my boss."

"Alright," I said.

"What is your name?"

"James, Captain James York."

The salesman stared at me then went into an office, and I turned to my dad and said, "You think he recognized me from the newspapers."

"I wouldn't be surprised."

"Maybe if I would have worn my uniform, it would have been easier." After a few minutes, an older man came over to us.

"Hi, I'm Robert Bird." "I own this and other car lots, have you, young man, served in Vietnam."

"Yes, Sir."

"You're not that Medal of Honor winner that I saw in the newspaper."

"Yes, I am, Sir." "I'm on leave with my parents, who live here."

He shook my hand and said, "It is an honor, Sir."

"Well, thank you."

"I'll take care of this, Doug," the owner told his salesman.

"Now, what vehicle were you looking at?"

"The red and white pickup."

"I should give it to you for free, but it has been a rough month I had to lay off two men."

"Doug said you are willing to pay twenty-five hundred for it."

"Yes, if a mechanic looks at it first."

"I assure you the engine is in excellent shape, but you can bring it down to a mechanic if you wish." My father knew a mechanic not far from the car lot, and we took it over to him.

After about an hour, he had finished going through the truck and said to my father, "It looks good." I paid the mechanic twenty-five dollars, and we went back to do the paperwork. A half-hour later, I was driving the Ford back to the house.

I walk over to my Cousin Allen's house to say hello. I never got along very well with him, but I liked the rest of his family. I rang the doorbell and Evana, his mother, opened the door, "Do you recognize me?"

"Yes, Jimmy, come in." I went into the house, which hadn't changed much. "Alex and Allen are in the backyard. I'll go get them." In walked Allen with a smile on his face, and right behind him was Alex.

I shook both their hands, and Alex said, "Sit down."

"Where's Sandy?" I asked.

"She married now to a man named James Pradels, and they live up north," said Alex.

"You didn't know?" asked Evana.

"No, I just got here last night I haven't had time to catch up."

"Didn't your parents go over to Hawaii to see you?"

"Yes, but there was a lot of chaos, you know, with the press, medical, and all that I didn't spend much time with them." "Someone might have said something, but if it was said, it didn't register," I added.

"I hear you are an officer and won a bunch of medals," said Allen.

"Yes, I am a captain in the Green Berets, and yes, I did get a lot of medals I am so far, the most decorated, I even have the Medal of Honor." I could see he was green with envy, but I didn't care.

"Do you have your Beret yet?" Allen asked.

"Yes, it's with my dress greens."

"Can I see it?"

"Sure, we can go over to my house after I finish visiting here."

"How long are you going to be here?" asked Alex.

About three weeks to a month then I will go to Missouri for about a month, I bought some property there." I didn't say anything about the White House or the training I was getting at Fort Bragg I didn't want to rub it into Allen.

"Were you wounded?" Allen asked.

"Yes, and when my family saw me last night just before I went into the shower, they were shocked at how much damage my body got."

"What are your plans while you are here?" asked Alex.

"I plan to work out a lot, see relatives and friends, and check-in with medical for some follow-up."

We finished talking, and I walked back to my house with Allen when he said, "So it was rough over there in Vietnam."

"Yes."

"I was going to go over there as a helicopter pilot."

"So, I heard, whatever happen to that?"

"Oh, they don't pay enough for the danger of the job, and I was the only son, so I didn't want to worry my parents about me."

I shook my head and said, "Stop the bullshit, Allen." "I know why you didn't go in, tell me the truth if you could, would you go in?"

"Yes."

"Is the only thing wrong with you is your feet."

"Yes."

"I will be seeing some generals, including the Joint Chiefs of Staff and the President, when I go to Washington, D.C." "If I can, I will try to get you in if you want, there is no guarantee, but I will see what I can do."

"Why are you doing this for me?"

"Two reasons, you have a fantastic photographic memory, and you didn't know it, but in a way, you helped keep me alive."

"How did I do that?"

"Before we moved to Niles, I never touched a rifle, real or toy."

"Do you remember those times we broke matchsticks with a BB gun and all those times we went shooting at the rifle range."

"Yes."

141

"Well, I'm an excellent shot because of it."

We got to the house, went to my room with Allen, and pulled out my uniform. He looked at all the medals and then the beret and handed it back to me.

"Can I see your wounds?" I took off my shirt, and he became fixated on my wounds then said, "Gee, they mess you up bad."

I put the shirt back on and said, "There will be some scares, but most of what you see will disappear in time."

We went outside, and he asked, "Whose truck is that?"

"Mine."

"You must have gotten a lot of back pay."

"Yes, but I got more on the book deal."

"You're getting a book written about you?"

"Yes, the writer may talk to you."

"That property you bought in Missouri, how large is it?"

"Over four hundred fifty acres."

"Any deer on it?"

"I don't know I haven't seen the property yet, but it butts up to my Aunt's and Uncle's place, which is six hundred plus acres."

The next day I went to church with my father, and Monday after I did my run and exercise, I drove down to Mission San Jose High School in my dress greens. "May I see the principal, please?"

The secretary smiled and stared at me at first then said, "I will see if he can see you, Captain York."

"Principal Nelson will see you now."

"Mr. Nelson, thank you for seeing me."

"He looked up and said it's Dr. Nelson or Principal Nelson." I clenched my jaw; I couldn't stand a person who was arrogant about their title, but I had to deal with him.

"I graduated from this school and joined the Army and went into a special unit." "When I came home on leave, I asked the last principal if I could use the physical education facilities." "He gave me his approval if it was alright with the head coach Reynosa." "I am in the Special Forces, and I'm going to get extra training." "I would like to use the facilities again for three to four weeks."

He stared at me, grabbed his phone, and said, "Have Randle come to my office." "The only reason I am considering this is because of who you are; otherwise, I would have said no."

"I was wondering if you knew who I was, I understand I've been in the media."

"I think everyone knows who you are." Just then, there was a knock at the door, and in came Coach Randle.

I stood up and shook his hand and asked, "Do you remember who I am, coach?"

"Yes, of course, James, you come to train again."

"Yes, if I can get permission."

"You have mine."

"Then, you don't mind?" asked Principal Nelson.

"No, not at all the last time he was here he was helpful with the PE program." "Some of the things he did we still use today."

"Alright, Captain, you have my permission," said the principal.

I got up and shook his hand, and coach Randle said, "Why don't you come down to the gym with me, and I will introduce you to everyone." He introduced me and gave me the same key as I had before as I left students were coming into the locker room, and I got plenty of stares and murmuring. Coach Randle told me Coach Reynosa was working as a head coach at Ohlone College, so I went to see him. I found him in his office, talking to a student. When the student left, I knock on the door jam, and he looked up and smiled, then stood up and offered his hand, which I took.

"I saw you on TV congratulation on your Medal of Honor."

"Seems like a lot of people have seen me?" "So why did you stop working at the high school?"

"More money and most of those kids I coached at the high school didn't want to be there." "I did everything I could there, so I needed a new challenge."

"I see you with that hat, are you in a special unit or something?"

"Yeah, the Green Berets."

"Wow."

"Back when I was in high school, did you ever think that things for me would ever end up as they did?"

"No, not at all." We talked for about forty-five minutes, and I left.

The next three days, I filled with me getting up before light, working out, eating breakfast, and going down to the high school to work out again. Wednesday afternoon, I check into Oak Noll Naval Hospital. I got an examination, and they especially checked out my back. They probed my back, removing bamboo splinters. "You're most likely for some time are going to have splinters coming up on your back; otherwise, you're in great shape considering what you have gone through," said Doctor Parker.

"When you get to Washington, I want you to get another checkup at Walter Reed," he added.

"Yes, Sir." They released me; it took me all afternoon to finish my exam, and I didn't get home until six-thirty that night.

The next day after I worked out at the school, I went to my old PSYOPS unit in the south bay. Everyone had moved on except for Sergeant Major John Connors. The Sergeant Major introduced me to the new company commander Colonel William Pike. The Sergeant Major, Colonel, and I went to the Navel mess hall to have a bite to eat and talk. "The information you gathered proved to be very valuable, and most of it we used did you know this?" asked the Sergeant Major.

"No, I wondered what became of it." I didn't know how they got this information.

"What are your plans?" "Are you coming back to PSYOPS?" Sergeant Major Connors inquired.

"The powers above are not sending me here; after leave, I'm to report to the Pentagon, then to Bragg, after Bragg, who knows."

"How would you improve PSYOPS James?" asked Colonel Pike.

"You may not like what I say, Sir."

"That's alright; say what's on your mind."

"Alright, I think PSYOPS should be made up of nothing but Special Forces personnel at lease those who go out into the field." "I, for what I had to face, the training did not prepare me, and I could have put those men in the Special Forces in danger."

"To tell you the truth, Sir, I've felt the same way about it; our people don't have the training for what they must do," said the Sergeant Major.

"I can't argue with your opinion; I agree with both of you." "I think when I get back, I'll write a letter to General Harper about what you said," the Colonel said. We talked a little longer, and then I went back home.

The next three weeks went by fast, I had gained more weight, mostly muscle mass, Frank White was interviewing me for a few hours a day, and I gave him the instructions on how to get to my aunt's house in Missouri. When he wasn't interviewing me, he talked to everyone else, including Allen, who agreed was a pompous ass. I also saw many of my relatives either they came over to the house or I went to see them. I did see Charles a couple of times, and while in Oakland, I visited with my old neighbors the Parcells. Bob came down, and David came over several times. However, the relative I drop in on the most was my Aunt Dorothy, who is my godmother. As time drew nearer for me to go to Missouri, I went to the bank. I withdrew fifty thousand dollars in a cashier's check to open an account in Missouri.

I bought a big toolbox for the back of the pickup and filled it with every tool I thought I would need for the Missouri property. I also picked a ton of oranges and lemons for my relatives in Missouri. I tried to get some walnuts from my uncle in Pleasanton, but he wanted money for them, and what he was asking was just too much. It made me somewhat mad after all; it was his sister. I turned in my key to the high school locker room on Monday and shook the hands of the coaches who were there. I tried to thank the principal, but he was at the district office. That Thursday, I put my duffle bag and suitcase in the back of the truck. I tied a tarp over the top of everything, leaving a corner easy to untie so I could add things if I bought anything during the trip. The next morning, I ate breakfast with my parents, well, my father anyway my mother hardly ever ate with the family. I got into the truck and headed out I intended to travel down highway forty, the Southern route because it was a shorter route.

I went down interstate five for several hours and then cut across to Bakersfield, where I stopped at a fruit stand. I bought several fruits that I felt my aunt would have a hard time getting, then went to the nearest gas station and filled up. I traveled for several days, staying in motels with weight rooms. I pushed it to Springfield, Missouri, and stayed at the Holiday Inn. I slept in late because I was going to drive to Ellsinore without stopping. I figured it would take four hours. I took off about ten-thirty in the morning and headed down the highway, and in about four hours, I was in Ellsinore.

I got gas at the two-pumper gas station on the highway, and I knew that my aunt lived down the dirt road directly across from the gas station. I went down that dirt road and came to a white house with a barn next to it, and Val was in the front when I drove up. "I hear you are the smartest and hardest worker in all of Missouri."

"No, Sir, who told you that?"

"A little bird."

"Birds can't talk."

"Are you sure?"

He nodded yes just then Tom and Mike came to the front of the house they had heard the conversation between Val and me. "Haven't you ever heard of a parrot talking?" Tom said to Val.

"Yes, but he said little bird, parrots aren't small."

"He has a point, Tom," I said.

"Do we know you?" asked Mike.

"Yes, I'm your brother James or at least wish I was your brother."

Mike and Tom smiled, but Val looked confused, "You're my cousin James," said Tom.

"I would rather be your brother James." Val went into the house to get his mother; when she came out, she had a big smile on her face.

"James, I was wondering when you would be here."

"Well, you got me a little more than a month."

"Mama, is he my brother?" "He said he was?" asked Val.

"No, he is your first cousin."

"I said I wish I were your brother Val."

"I have surprises in the front seat and the back of the pickup."

"What kind of surprises?" asked Val.

"Go look." All three went first to the front seat and pulled out a ton of fireworks. They were so excited that they forgot about the back and went off to blow them up.

"Where do you want me to put the truck, so I can untie the back and bring in the things I brought everybody?"

"Just put the truck on the other side of the road." I drove the pickup to the opposite side of the road and untied the back of the truck.

My aunt looked in the back of the truck, smiled, and said, "This will be a treat?"

"I tried to bring things that I thought would be hard to get." We carried the things I brought into the house, and then I sat down.

"You'll be staying in Val's room," said my aunt.

"I could get a room in Poplar Bluff." "I don't need to be putting a burden on you and Uncle Paul."

"No, you are going to stay here."

"Are you sure Uncle Paul wouldn't mind either I don't want to cause any trouble?"

"He would be mad if you didn't stay."

"Well, okay, then I'll bring my things in." When I brought in my suitcase and duffle bag, my aunt took me down the hall and went into a room next to her room.

"Wasn't this Mike's and Tom's room?"

"Yes, but they are across the hall now; Val will sleep with them."

"Val can sleep with me if he wants."

"I'll ask him, but I think he will want to sleep with his brothers." My aunt went back to work in the kitchen. I offered to help, but she refused, so I sat, and we talked.

About an hour after I sat down to speak to my aunt, Mike, Tom, and Val came into the house, I turned around and said, "Did you go through all those fireworks already."

"No, we are going to save the rest of them until tomorrow," said Val.

My aunt had finished what she was doing in the kitchen and said, "Let's sit in the front room." "So, tell me how everyone back in California is?"

"They're okay, some of them put on the dog at times."

My cousin's head popped up at what I said, and my aunt smiled and said, "Do you normally talk like that?"

I thought for a second, trying to figure out what she was talking about, then it hit me, and I said, "Well, you have to blame Mike and Tom for the way I talk."

"What do you mean?" Tom asked.

"Remember when you came to California, and both of you slept in my bedroom. I think I was about eleven or twelve then."

"I remember," said my aunt and Mike.

"Well, you all made an impression on me." "I was awestruck at some of the ways you two talked and acted, and it stuck on me, I don't know why you didn't have the same effect on anyone else."

"Your father should be home in another hour you boys got your chores done," said Aunt Adeline to the boys.

All three went outside, and I asked my aunt, "Tell me about the property?"

"You should hear it from your Uncle Paul; he knows about it better than I do, but I can tell you it is a good piece of property."

"Maybe you and Uncle Paul can go over there after dinner with me."

She said yes and changed the subject and said with all seriousness, "You know, James, I've always wanted you to come and stay with me."

I looked at her, she had a longing look on her face, and timidly I said, "You must mean my brother David, your godson."

"No, you."

I was silent for a few seconds then said nervously, "I didn't know, but had I, you might have made a big mistake because I would have never left." I got shaken up and headed to the door, then stopped and said meekly,

"Would you answer me a question, truthfully?" She nodded, yes. "Are you my mother?"

She looked at me with a tear in her eye and said, "No."

"Well, you ought to be." I moved closer to the door and said, "I am here now and have a home right next door we need to talk more about this later," at that, I went outside. I went over to my truck and checked the oil and water. Then I searched for Mike and Tom, who were working on a tracker near the barn.

"Need some help," I asked.

"No, not really, we're just about finished."

I look over to the vegetable garden and seen Val by himself pulling weeds, so I went over to him and said, "Looks like you could use some help." He nodded yes so, I got next to him and helped him. About forty-five minutes later, Uncle Paul came home in his old pickup, and everyone went to greet him. I got up, washed off my hands, went over to him, and shook his hand. I sat in the living room, and after my uncle had finished cleaning up, I asked, "What can you tell me about the property?"

"That's a good piece of property that you bought?"

"Did you put your cattle on it yet?"

"No, I was waiting for you."

"You didn't have to wait?"

"I'll move them over there Saturday."

"How bad are the buildings?"

"Not as bad as I first thought, but all the buildings are boarded up and overgrown with vines and plants, so I can't see inside."

"I'll take you over to the place after dinner."

"Great."

"I'll need to go to a bank tomorrow I have cashier's check for fifty thousand dollars. I wish to open an account and put one of you on the account, so if you have an emergency or if some more land comes up, you can buy it." I got my deed and started reading it carefully. It said that I own not only the property and buildings but everything in those buildings.

At dinner, I told everybody about Frank White that I expected him soon. However, he would be staying in Poplar Bluff; after we ate, we all drove over to the property in my truck. There were a chain and lock on the old rickety wooden gate, and Uncle Paul said, "We'll have to climb over the fence."

The lock was old and rusted, so I said, "Wait, I have a new hacksaw, I'll cut the lock." It just took a few minutes, and with the help of my uncle and cousins, we pushed open the gate and drove in. The place was thick with trees, brush, and vines just as my uncle said, the house was overgrown, and everything appeared boarded up.

"I have some work to do." "Do you have a chainsaw, Uncle Paul?"

"No, I don't."

"I'll pick one up tomorrow." I tried pulling some of the plywood off the windows but didn't have much success. I walked around the building, as I did, I notice some of the plants were roses, and I said, "I have plenty of roses Aunt Adeline."

"Yes, you do, but they need cutting back."

I stepped back to see the roof, and at least it wasn't sagging. I was near one of the two sheds I had, and I tried to look in through a crack, but it was just too dark inside, and it was the same as the other one.

I then went over to the barn it looked sturdy, but I ask my uncle, "You think this here barn is a good one and sturdy?"

He just stared at me with a smile, then Tom said, "We taught him how to talk that way?"

He chuckled and said, "Yes, I do, and I think it is bigger than mine."

It was too dark inside to see anything. I walked to the back of the barn and asked, "Where is the spring?" My uncle pointed to the left of us, "Does it run all year long?" I asked.

"Yes, but not as much as it does in the winter and spring."

"Where is your property?"

"Over that way."

He pointed straight back, and I asked, "Does it come out next to where your old house use to be?"

"Yes."

"Do you know where I can rent a bulldozer?"

"There is a place in Poplar Bluff, what do you want it for?" asked my uncle.

"I want to build a pond out here that the spring feeds; also, I want to cut a road from my front gate to your property if that's alright."

"Yeah, you can do that I figure you will need the bulldozer two or three days."

"I'll most likely need a backhoe or loader also." My uncle nodded yes, and we headed home, I was getting tired anyway.

The next day I got up before light, I thought I would be up before anyone, but my aunt and uncle fooled me they were already up. "I'm going over to the house to take off the plywood and air it out."

"Wait a minute why don't you sit down and eat," said my aunt.

"I'm still full, from last night's meal. I'll be alright until noon."

"Here are the keys to the house," said my aunt.

"Are you going to be able to go with me to Poplar Bluff later?"

"Yes, I will walk over to your house when I am ready."

I drove over there, went to the back of my truck, pulled out a crowbar, and started on the plywood that someone hammered over the door. It took some time, but I was able to get the plywood removed. The door was ornate with fancy glass and what looked like mahogany wood. The door was locked, so I tried the key, and it unlocked the door. The door was sticking a little, so I put my weight on it, and the door swung open. I could see many things inside I decided to get as much sun into the house, so I started on the windows. It took me several hours to get all the plywood off, and as I finished, my aunt showed up. We went into the house and looked around, and she said, "It seems the same as it did when she was last here many years ago." "What are you going to do with all these things?" asked my aunt.

"Well, I'm going to separate everything into three piles stuff I want to keep, stuff that I want to think about, and things I don't want."

"I can use the things you don't want, or I will give them away."

"Alright." We opened all the windows to air the place out. It had a smell of mildew, older people, or something I couldn't make out. Then I locked the door and left with my aunt to Poplar Bluff.

We first went to the bank; I open a savings account arranged so my aunt could withdraw money from it. We then went to a roofer and hired him to do all the buildings on the place. I gave him the instructions on how to get to the house, and he agreed to be out tomorrow morning. We went to a hardware store where I bought a lopper, a medium-size chainsaw, a sharpener, and a gas can. After the hardware store, we went to a small construction company; I arranged for a D nine bulldozer and a backhoe to be brought to my place for three days with an operator. It would cost me eight hundred dollars, and everything would be at my home in two days.

It was about noon, and I said, "Let me treat you to lunch."

"That would be nice, but you don't have to," my aunt said.

"No, I want to," I replied. We went to a restaurant that my aunt knew of was reasonable and good tasting. Along the way, I saw Colonel Sanders and said, "So you don't have to cook tonight; I will buy more than enough fried chicken for dinner tonight."

"That would help out." We ate, and I said I would take her to a grocery store; some of my cousins will be coming home for the weekend. I knew she could use some things, so I would pay for them besides, I needed cleaning things, and she would know what to buy. Along the way to the store, I saw an electrician's office, so we stopped.

"I need someone to come out and check out my house to see if the wiring is alright so that I can turn on the power."

"I can be out to your home by nine in the morning."

"That's fine; my aunt will tell you how to get there." After the electrician's and store, we picked up the chicken with all the trimmings.

8

MY HOME

After dropping off my aunt with her things, I went back over to my house. I started in the master bedroom and moved everything and placed it in the living room. I opened the closet door and saw it packed with clothing and things. I grabbed the garments and checked everything and found money and jewelry; the garments I put in the back of my truck to give to my aunt. I took down a big wooden inlaid box on a shelf and opened it; it was full of jewelry. On the left side of the shelf was an attaché case I opened it, and it looked like some valuable papers, so I put those things in the truck's front seat. I found some old photo albums, and in the back of the closet was an old twelve-gauge shotgun these I put in the back of the truck with a box of pills and other medicines I found. Then I took down several pictures on the walls, placed them in the living room, rolled up a dirty carpet, and removed it. When I removed the rug, I noticed that the floors were beautiful hardwood, maybe oak. It was getting late, so I took the curtains and locked the front door, and left.

I drove back to the house and told my aunt that I had some things in the truck I didn't want, and some things that I felt might be valuable; I also informed her about the money. She asked me to put them in the large family room, and we would go through them after dinner. I brought in everything, but the last thing I brought in was the shotgun. Mike and Tom took an interest in the shotgun picking it up and checking it out.

"Do you all have jobs yet?"

"No," Val said seriously.

I smiled as did Mike and Tom, "We have a part-time job cutting wood for a charcoal company; they shut down for a while."

"You three want to work for me."

"Doing what?" asked Mike.

"Clearing the brush, vines, and trees around the buildings other things as I come across them."

"How much you going to pay us," asked Val.

"Two dollars an hour."

"Two dollars is better than nothing; we will do it," said Tom.

"You'll have to ask your mother first."

Val went running into the kitchen and asked his mother, "Ma, James will pay us two dollars an hour to work around his house is that alright?"

We all came into the kitchen as Val was asking, and she said, "You shouldn't get paid for doing something for a family member."

"No, I wish to pay them what I want them to do isn't easy besides they can use the money."

"You all write down your time each day on a piece of paper you start tomorrow." I had to get gas for the chainsaw, so I took Val with me, and we went into the town of Ellsinore to get a couple of gallons I already had the oil to mix with it. I had gotten the two gallons and mixed the oil right there. I then went to the general store to pay the bill, but not until I bought about five gallons of vanilla ice cream and some chocolate syrup. A happy Val and I got home almost at the same time as Uncle Paul did.

As we were all eating, I had told my uncle about the things I brought back from the house when Tom asked, "So James, when you have to leave, what are you going to do with the truck?"

"I will leave it here for all of you to use when I get leave to come home; I'll have something to drive." After dinner, we went into the family room, and Aunt Adeline checked all the clothing and decided what is suitable for clothing; the rest can be rags. The shoes and boots were in good shape, so my aunt kept some and others she intended to give away.

Uncle Paul looked at the shotgun and said, "It's an old one, but in excellent shape, it's worth maybe two hundred dollars."

"I think I will keep it, is it alright to leave it here?"

"Sure, maybe I will use it for bird hunting." The pills my uncle and aunt agreed they should dump them. I then showed both my aunt and uncle the inlaid box and the jewelry. I asked if they thought it was real or costume.

"Some look real, I don't know for sure, but there is a jewelry store in Poplar Bluff," my aunt said.

I then showed them the valuable papers, and they looked at them and said, "They look like stocks," said Uncle Paul. "Maybe someone at the bank can tell what they are worth."

"I'll take them to Popular Bluff when I've gone through everything who knows what else I will fine."

"Is there a lot there?" asked my Uncle.

"I haven't even put a dent in it yet."

The next day I was over to the house before light. I started to use the loppers to cut some of the vines and bushes back, and as soon as there was enough light, I went into the house. I looked around, and I decided I wanted to save the master bedroom bed and dresser. I put the bed back in the master bedroom and placed the mattress on the veranda. I then went through the dresser setting the clothing in the truck. I did find more jewelry and a little more than two hundred dollars as I was removing the garments. I didn't want the two lamps, so I took those two outside to bring back to my aunt's house. I went through a secretary desk in the room, and there were plenty of things in it including money it seemed these people who lived in this house stuck money everywhere. However, I am not surprised my mother does the same. There were two locked drawers that I did not have a key for, so I tried to pick the lock with a small screwdriver and a piece of wire. After about twenty minutes, I finally open one of the locks in there was two old books titled The Fables Of Aesop volume one and two. They were quite old, leather-bound, and gold-leaf books in excellent condition. Aesop, I have heard about these might be valuable books. I found other papers that looked important, like those I had brought over to my aunts' house. I left the books inside the desk but took everything else out. I then started on the next drawer; it was down below the one I open; it was narrower and deep.

As I was working on it in came Mike, Tom, and Val, "Ma will be over here in a couple of hours," declared Mike.

I looked at Mike and Tom and said, "You two ever use a chainsaw."

"Sure, lots of times," replied Tom.

"Where are your gloves?"

"Don't have any," said Val.

"You have a driver's license, Mike?"

"Yes."

"Take my truck and go into Ellsinore pick up some gloves, sodas, snacks, and anything else you think you might need and take Val with you;

he will need to get fitted for gloves." "It's ten after nine I'll agree you three have started working at nine, stop off at your place and give your mother the clothing in the back ask her if she wants the mattresses." I pulled out forty dollars, my keys then gave it to him, and he and Val went.

"Come with me, Tom?" We started to walk around the house, and I said, "Any tree that around this house, and those buildings I want you to cut them down and anything not worth keeping remove. He nodded we walked to the front of the house, and I pointed to the chainsaw, gas, and loppers and then went into the house.

I went back to picking the lock, and in about twenty-five minutes, I had the drawer unlocked. I looked inside, and the first thing I grabbed an engraved silver pistol with ivory grips that happen to be loaded, so I unloaded it. The bullets said forty-five, and the gun said Model P Peacemaker M1873. It was a fine-looking pistol I put it to the side and grabbed a grey metal box with a lock on it, and it was heavy. Of course, it also was locked, I look inside the drawer again, and all that was left was loose bullets and a thick, yellowed envelope which I open. There were two packs of one-hundred-dollar bills and a key that fit the lock in the grey box. In the box were several gold coins, and there were some Standard Oil stocks. I put all the valuables back in the desk and then looked at the paintings. They were all oils in beautiful frames, so I kept them all to find their worth later. I was about to go upstairs when the electrician showed up.

"Hello, I'm Bill Myers. I'm looking for Captain York."

"I'm Captain York."

"I have come to check out your wiring."

"Good, where do you want to start?"

"Outside first, then the rest of the house and buildings."

"Alright." I was going to go upstairs but went into the kitchen. There was nothing in the kitchen I wanted, so I put everything outside. The electrician then went into the master bedroom, and I followed him. He opened all the outlets and then closed them again and went into the kitchen. About this time, Mike and Val came back, and I told them to pile the brush to be burn later.

"Mama said she would look at the things you have that you want to get rid of later when she gets here."

The electrician finally finished the kitchen and the living room. He said, "Everything looks good, but I would change out the fuse box and put in a circuit breaker, and I would put in some safety plugs I could do that now if you want."

"Go ahead and put them in." As the electrician was working, my aunt came, and I pointed to the things on the porch.

I went up to my aunt, whispered into her ear, "When the electrician leaves, I want to show you something." She nodded, and I said, "What you want I will load it in the truck about forty minutes after loading the pickup the electrician handed me a bill and left. We went into the master bedroom, and I said, "Look." I pulled out the two drawers, and she looked at everything in amazement.

"You better bring this back to the house." I agreed and put everything in the front of the truck.

We went back into the living room, and I said, "I don't want any of these chairs." "I must bring it over to the house tomorrow." That stove and refrigerator I don't want but the pictures, cabinets, rugs, and vases I moved everything into the master bedroom. I open one cabinet that had glass doors; it was full of old books.

My aunt went to a closet at the foot of the stairs, opened it, and said, "This is a linen closet." "Do you want any of these things?"

"Take them, but go through everything you never know what you will find." I pulled a book out of the cabinet, and the author had signed it; it was also the first addition. As I went through each book, some were signed; some weren't, but they were all first additions. I then turned my attention to another cabinet with solid doors, but it was locked, so I started picking the lock.

Meanwhile, my aunt said, "The truck is full."

"Give me a minute, and I'll drive the truck back to your house."

"What are you doing there?"

"Most of these locks don't have keys, so I had to pick them." Just then, the locked opened, and I said, "I'm getting so good at unlocking these locks, I should be a locksmith." I looked in the cabinet; it turned out to be a gun cabinet.

"Some of those rifles are old," said my aunt.

"Yes, I must come back for them." I called the boys in and said, "Tom, see if you can squeeze in the back of the truck if you can't get in the middle of the cab." "Mike, Val sit here on the porch and take a break from your work watch for the roofer, and when he shows, tell him to go ahead and start." "I'll be back in a few minutes." Tom couldn't fit in the truck's back, but he managed to squeeze in the cab, and we went back.

We unloaded the truck. Then my aunt called the power company who said they would be out early the next day. I called the roofer, and he said he would be there within the hour. My aunt decided to stay back; she was going to make some calls and then some bread, so Tom and I headed back. "Let's try going cross country, which way Tom?" He pointed to where the old house was, and we started our bumpy ride slow. "Let me know when I'm on my property."

He nodded, and when we traveled about a hundred yards, he said, "That tree line is your property."

"I want a ten-foot-wide path through that, so cut down those trees."

We went up and down dips, and I told Tom what to cut, we finally came up onto a grassy area and Tom pointed to the left and said, "That is where the spring is."

We drove over to it, and it was like a small stream, but it was enough to do what I wanted. I looked for where it was coming out and found a rock outcropping. I walked down about ten feet and said, "From here to about fifty feet down the stream, I want you and your brothers to cut everything out." "How far across the water is mine?"

"About fifty yards, but it varies."

"Cut everything back fifteen feet on that side; that's after the path is cleared between your place and mine."

We got back to the house Mike, and Val was sitting on the front porch, and the roofer wasn't there yet. "Go ahead and take the chainsaw, Gas, and loppers put them in the truck." "Tom knows where I want you to cut next." Tom sat in the driver's seat as Mike and Val put the things in the rear of the truck, then Val climbed in the back as Mike sat in the cab of the pickup and off, they went. I went back into the house and looked in the chest that fortunately wasn't locked when I opened it a strong smell of cedar hit my nose. It was a hope chest; the first thing I saw was a large homemade quilt I intended to keep this. The people who lived here made the quilt quite well, and it appealed to me. There were photo albums, an old journal, samplers, little mementos, and two smaller but much older quilts. But what caught my eye was a beautiful engagement and wedding set in two boxes, which were gold and had diamonds. These I would keep who knows I might get married someday. I carried the chest into the master bedroom and placed everything in it on the desk, intending to take it back to my aunt's place.

I looked at my watch, and it had already been an hour since I called the roofer, I was going to give him another hour, and if he didn't show up, I would get another roofer. I thought there was another cabinet against the wall with a tarp over it. I went over to it and removed the tarp, and to my surprise, it was a piano with a seat. It was old but looked in good shape, so I sat the bench down and played each key. It was out of tune, but each key worked, so I tried playing something. I was about halfway through a piece when there was a knock at the door.

"I'm the roofer, are you, Captain York."

"Yes, I almost gave up on you."

"Sorry, I had a hard time finding the place."

"Well, I will show you what I want." We stepped back from the house; I pointed to the roof and said, "I can tell from here it needs a new roof." "I want a green color asphalt shingle."

"I can do that."

We walked to the back of the house, and I pointed to the two sheds and said, "Do the same with them." Then I turned left and said, "On the barn, I think a metal roof would be appropriate."

"Alright, I must go up on the roofs to check them out.

"Alright, good luck with the barn." I went back in the house, into the bathroom and took everything out then threw it away. There was another closet in the living room, but before I got to that, I rolled up the carpet and put it outside. I then opened the closet, took out an old vacuum cleaner that I didn't want but intended to use it on the rugs before I gave it to my aunt. I found an old grey civil war uniform and a saber for which I placed in the master bedroom. There were several boxes; one had a hat that went with the civil war uniform. There was a box full of sports memorabilia and one full of letters I put them in the bedroom. The rest of the containers had miscellaneous items that I would take a second look at later, and there were four boxes full of leaded glass and silver things. In the back corner of the closet was a two-foot by two-foot by eighteen-inch black safe. It was locked, but there was a series of numbers in the grey box inside the desk, so I went to find them. It didn't take me long get the numbers, but before I could use them, the roofer came down off the roof and put his latter against the first shed he climbed up and climbed back down look first from the inside of both sheds and the barn. There were padlocks on all three buildings, so I asked, "Do you have a bolt cutter or a hacksaw?"

"No bolt cutter, but I do have a hacksaw." I cut the lock off and went in; there were many oil cans and other lubricants; I also saw a lot of old tools. The roofer looked up, then went back out and climbed onto the roof. At the same time, I went to the next shed. I opened it up and found some burlap bags that rodents had gotten into also more tools more for the garden than a workshop. I was halfway to the barn when he went into the next shed and then on the roof. I cut the barn's lock, but the barn also had boards nailed across the barn door. I went and got my crowbar to remove the boards when I got the boards off, I slid the doors open, and we both walked in. There were two big things tarp in the center of the barn and a bench with something else tarp next to the workbench. Several items were hanging up, which looked like some horse tack. They were next to a couple of saddles. There was an old buckboard and many other things that I would have to check on later after the house.

"The roof looks in good condition; there are no holes in it." "I don't think you need a new barn roof that should save you a few dollars."

"The house and sheds will cost you eight hundred dollars if I don't need to do any sheathing if you want me to do them."

"Alright, when can you start and how long will it take."

"I can start on Monday." "It shouldn't take no more than two or three days."

"That will be all right."

"Great, I will get the contract for you to sign, and I will need a two-hundred-dollar deposit."

We went over to his truck, and he wrote out a contract which I read and signed. I then gave him two hundred dollars in cash, and he gave me a receipt. "You realize if you don't do this by Thursday of next week, I will go with another company."

"It will be done before Thursday." I shook his hand, and he left.

I went back into the house to open the safe, and the numbers worked. I looked in and shook my head; these people must not have believed in banks; the safe appeared loaded with cash, stocks, bonds, and many old or rare coins. I got the valuables from the bedroom, then put them in the safe and closed it. I went out of the back door after this and started in the laundry room. There was an old wringer washing machine I didn't want. Also, two drop leaf tables, a washbasin, an ironing board, an old treadle sewing machine, and shelves full of other cleaners; I will give them to my aunt. I opened the cabinets that were on the walls and had bolts of cloth, which I thought my aunt would like. I examined the room; it was all screened in and thought it would make an excellent sunroom like my childhood friend Charlie had in his backyard. About this time, my truck went flying past the house, so I went to see what was going on.

"Giving up on me?"

"It's quitting time," Mike said.

I looked at my watch and said, "You're right; let's load up the truck and go back to your house." We loaded the things from the bedroom and all the rifles from the cabinet. I was going to get into the cab, but all three boys filled the inside, so I hopped in the back, and off we went, and it was a wild ride. We unloaded the truck, and I headed back with Val to get more. We loaded the back of the pickup with the bolts of cloth, the treadle sewing machine, the soap and cleaners, ironing board, and few things I could fit from the bedroom. Of course, Val grabbed the soda and snacks, and off we went. My uncle had come home by the time we got back, and all help bring in things into the house.

"We are going to have to do something with these things. If not, we are going to run out of room in here," my uncle said.

"Yes, I have more things to bring," I said.

"Well, we'll go through this stuff after Val gets a shower, and we eat," my aunt said.

"Oh, ma, I'm not that dirty."

"Yes, you are, and you are to James."

"Alright, I'll shower after Val." I looked at the rifles, as did my uncle. Mike and Tom joined us, admiring the weapons.

I heard the shower stopped, and I looked up and was about to get a towel, so I could shower when I heard my aunt say, "Don't worry about them; they can't see you."

"I can't believe he is bashful you sure he is your son Uncle Paul, Mike and Tom were never bashful."

"I always wondered if he is my brother," Tom said. My uncle gave Tom an angry look, and Tom shut up quickly.

"Do you have a towel I can use?" I asked my aunt.

"Go ahead and get into the shower, and I will get you a towel." I got a change of clothing and got into the shower I washed up and then got out looking for a towel. My aunt came in and seen me when I had nothing on, and she focused on the scares on my body and said, "My God those men in Vietnam hurt you worse than I thought."

"My scars looked worse before the Army worked on them; they will heal and fade as time goes on." She gave me the towel, and I dried myself and got dressed.

"I called some people who could use some of those things that you want to get rid of James," my aunt said.

"I'll help you load your pickup after we eat if you wish."

"That 'd be great."

"I found a safe in that house today and was able to open it." "Those people who lived there must not have believed in banks." "There was a lot of money and valuables in that safe."

"How much?" asked my uncle.

"I don't know I didn't count it, but it's a lot."

"I want to disconnect that stove and bring it over tomorrow, but it is a gas stove; I don't know if I can disconnect it."

"If the gas shut off, it should be safe to disconnect it," my uncle said. We went through the things I had brought, and then Mike drove the pickup to the back door, and we loaded it up.

The next day I was at the house again before light. I rolled out the rugs and got the vacuum ready; I then went over to the stove, unhooked the gas stove, and moved it to the porch. I also moved the refrigerator and washing machine out by that time the sun was up. I then went upstairs, there was a closet at the top, I opened it, and it was full of bedding. I was carrying them downstairs when in walked Val.

"You're early."

"Yeah, I know," he said as if he had something on his mind.

"Well, you can help me in the house until your brothers get here."

"You're like a brother."

I hugged and kissed him on the forehead and said, "Thank You, I wish I grew up here with you all." We went upstairs and took the rest of the blankets and linen downstairs, which emptied the closet. We then went into one of the two bedrooms; it had an old metal twin bed, a small dresser, and an end table with a lamp. There were shelves with some old metal toys, and that is where Val's eyes went. I got the toys down and said, "You can play with these until your brothers come." I started to take the bed apart while Val sat on the floor with the toys.

I took the end table and the lamp downstairs. I looked inside the drawer of the end table; it had some old comic books and a yo-yo and top and some small cars, which I set aside. I went back and got the dresser, Val had gotten lost in his play, I took the drawers down one at a time they had clothing mostly in them. I went into the bedroom closet, there were more toys and games and clothing, and I brought them all down and started in the next room. There were similar things in the other bedroom as there was in the first bedroom.

I was downstairs taking a break, and I thought you would think that there be some fancy dinnerware. I was looking at where the stairs went up, which was in the kitchen I walked into the kitchen, and I went to the wall and pounded on the wall it sounded hollow. Then I went back into the living room and beat on the wall surrounding the fireplace again; it also seemed hollow. I looked in the closet, and at first, I didn't see anything, but near the door, jamb was a latch. I unhooked it and pushed on the shelves, and the closet moved back, and there was a room. It was too dark for me to see, there was a light switch, but my power was not on. I went upstairs to work first, checking in on Val, who fell asleep on the floor.

I had just finished emptying the second bedroom when the power company and the man with the bulldozer and backhoe showed up at the same time. I looked at my watch, and I figured Tom and Mike should be here any minute.

"I'm here to turn on your power, where is your meter." I Pointed to the right side of the house, and he left to do his work.

"You hired me to do some bulldozing and digging with the backhoe."

"Yes, I will show you what I want; go ahead and unload the equipment."

He turned and left to get his equipment off his truck, and the power man came to me and said, "Sign here."

"Did you turn on the gas also?"

"No, you are on propane; I don't touch that." He left, and I went upstairs, pick up Val, who was still sleeping, and I carried him downstairs.

Val woke up, and I said, "Are you sleepy." He shook his head yes and laid his head on my shoulder and closed his eyes. With one hand, I laid one of the twin mattresses down, put Val on it, and threw a blanket on him. I then tried the lights, and they came on, then I went outside. The heavy equipment man drove up with the backhoe, and I went up to him and said, "Follow my truck, and I will show you where to park that backhoe." I drove to the spring and got out of the pickup. He parked the backhoe and came over to me. I said, "I want you to dig a pond here ten-foot-deep tapered up on the banks, it can be about fifty by fifty or whatever you think is best, but I want you to cut a road first." "Get inside the truck; I'll show you where."

We drove towards my aunts' place along the way I came across Mike and Tom, and I told them, "Val is asleep at my place take the gas chainsaw and loppers and work on the spring." They did as I said, and we proceeded to my aunts' road. When we got there, I said, "This is my aunt's place." "I want a road to go from this road to my front gate along the path I will travel now." We drove back to my home, and I stopped at the fence. "Try to make it as smooth as you can."

"I'll do the best I can."

"After you finish with the road, cut a road to the spring and get busy with the pond." He nodded and hopped out of the truck, and I drove back to the house. Before I got out of my pickup, the bulldozer started down my driveway and towards my aunt's house. I went into the house Val was oblivious as to what was going on, I went upstairs. I got the toys, and then I tried the light in the hidden room, and it lit up, and there were the beautiful dishes, silverware in a box, crystal, and other fancy things. I don't know why they didn't show off their beautiful silverware and put the safe and other items back here. I turned around, there was Val, and I said, "Did you have enough sleep?"

"Yes; did you see Mike and Tom?"

"Yes, they are down by the spring, but I have something for you to do here, vacuuming the rugs, and then we will hang them outside." I plugged in the vacuum, and Val started cleaning. I tied a rope between two trees, when Val finished with the rugs, I hung the carpets up, and then we loaded up the truck. I was cautious with the beautiful dinnerware wrapping them in blankets and sheets.

I told Val, "Get in the front seat of the cab." Off we went to his house to unload the truck, and then I went to Ellsinore to pick up soda and snacks.

Val went over to the toys and looked at them, and I said, "Go ahead and get one, Val." He studied toys and then picked one out, and I paid for it and then went back to the house. The bulldozer had made one pass and started another when I stopped him and asked, "How is it going?"

"I made the first past, and I will make two more, there have been no problems." "Good, I'll let you get back to your work." Val and I loaded more things in the truck, and then I sent Val to get his brothers. I decided to go to the barn and see what was under those tarps. I took off the tarp next to the bench, and I couldn't believe my eyes there in front of me was a 1915 Harley Davidson model 11 J. It looked like it was in great shape, or so it appeared that way to me. I put the tarp back on the Harley and went over to one of the other tarps and removed it and again I was shocked it was a 1928 Ford Model A sedan again it appeared to be in good shape. I pulled the other tarp, and it was a 1947 GMC pickup. I would have to get all three painted and restored, but they appeared to be in good shape. I saw a bunch of old tools and two bicycles they had wooden wheels, which I've never seen before, and a nameplate by the name of Orient. Of course, there was the tack the saddle had engravings in the leather. I heard a noise outside and figuring it was my cousins. I went out to talk to them.

"Val and I got refreshments; go help yourself." We all sat on the front porch, and I said, "I'll pay you guys tomorrow night." "Does your mother have a telephone book?"

"Yes," said Tom.

"Good, I'll need to hire someone to paint and remodel this place."

"We can paint this house," said Mike.

"No, I have other plans for you three." "How much more work do you have over by the spring?"

"Enough for a few hours, it's thick there," Mike said.

"You see that area in front of us." They all nodded, and I said, "Does it look like to you it could have been an orchard at one time?"

They all looked carefully, and Tom said, "Yes, but it is all grown over with brush and other trees."

"I want to restore the orchard so after your finish with the spring, clean up this place, remove the brush and non-fruit tree, then prune up those fruit trees that are left."

"That's going to take some time," said Tom.

"Yes, but look how much money you will earn."

As we talked, a man on a horse came onto my property, and I said, "Looks like we have company."

"That's Mr. Schumacher he's a Mennonite he doesn't believe in using modern things, and their kids don't go to public school, he's your neighbor," said Tom. I've read about these people, so I knew some of their ways. When he came up to the house, and I stood up as he got off his horse.

"Hello neighbor," I said as I stuck out my hand to shake his.

He shook my hand and said with a thick German accent, "My name is Günter Schumacher."

"My name is James York; would it be easier for you to speak in German?" I said in German.

He smiled and was surprised; I spoke German and said, "I prefer it."

"Good, these three young men are my cousins."

"Yes, I know who they are; their mother is an exceptional person."

"Yes, she is; I hope the activity and the noises aren't disturbing you."

"No, it isn't."

"That is good, and then what can I do for you?"

"I have been watering my sheep at your spring; I would like to get permission to continue to water them." "I will pay you for the use."

"I know nothing about farm animals." "My uncle has about sixty head of cattle, do sheep and cattle get along."

"I have never known them to fight."

"That is good; then feel free to bring your sheep to the spring as much as you wish, and the only payment I want is your friendship."

"That you have?"

"I do have a few requests that you do not have to agree to?"

"What are they?"

"It appears there was an orchard there once."

"Yes, there were many years ago."

"I plan to bring it back; you see how high that grass is."

"Yes."

"It is my understanding sheep will eat to the bare ground." "I would like you to bring your sheep here and let the sheep eat the grass."

"I will bring them here after I water them."

"Good, it is my understanding that your people are great barn builders." "I would like you to see my barn and tell me what kind of condition mine is in."

"I can look right now if you wish." He tied his horse to my porch, and we walked to the barn.

"I would love to talk to you someday about your religion and customs."

"Are you thinking about converting?"

"No, my aunt is a Catholic as I am, and she would kill me if I did." "I am just always interested in learning new things."

He thought for a second and said, "Why don't you come to dinner Sunday, and we will talk."

"That would be great, but shouldn't you ask your wife first."

"No, it would be alright; she would be pleased."

"Alright, I'll be there what time do you want me?"

"Five o'clock at night." He first looked on the outside of the barn, then on the inside, and he said, "This barn was built by my brethren many years ago, we made things to last it is in excellent shape."

"That is good to hear." "I have plans for it."

"What do you plan to do with your land James?"

"Well, as I said, I am not a farmer or rancher, so I plan to turn it into a park." "I should tell you something else the boys are removing trees around the spring; I will be building a large pond I hope this doesn't upset the watering of your sheep plans."

"No, it is a good idea."

"I would suggest you water your sheep after five at night when all the work by me should end. The bulldozer man will finish the pond sometime tomorrow afternoon." We walked back, and he went back home. Tom and Mike went back to work, I took Val in the truck, and we went down the new road to his house to unload the pickup. The road is excellent, and the operator was working on the access road to the spring when we passed. About the second load to the house, my aunt came home and couldn't believe everything I brought over.

"About half of the things I will be keeping, I'm going to have the house and buildings around it remodeled and didn't want them destroyed."

"How much do you have left at your house?"

"In the house one more load, but I would like you to come to the house between now and Saturday so that I could show you something."

"I could go now." We all got into the truck and went over to the house.

"Let me show you what I found." I showed her the secret room next to the stairs then how it locked, I also showed her the safe and what I had left in the house, and I told her what plans I had for the bathroom and kitchen.

We went out to the barn, and I showed her the vehicles and asked, "Do you think if it would be ok, I stored everything out here?"

"I would think so if you get them back in the house before winter, and you cover them up with plastic."

"Then, I will start to put things in the barn, and I will bring things back from your house." We headed back to her house, but first I stopped at the spring. The bulldozer had started ripping up the ground to make the pond. Mike and Tom had finished up what they were doing, so I loaded everything and everyone up in the back, including Val, and headed to their house.

"Do you think I can take Val with me to Poplar Bluff tomorrow?"

"I don't see why not; he will be excited to go." When we got back, I loaded up the truck and headed back to the barn. I had checked out the phonebook and found an antique store and a jewelry store. I found a contractor, which I plan to talk to also. I told my aunt and uncle about Mr. Schumacher. Val was in the shower again, and I was going to shower after him, and while I was waiting, we looked at the things I had.

The next day before daylight, I was at the house I opened the safe and bagged in several pillowcases all the valuables I had and then locked them in the truck cab. I moved all the things I had in the house into the barn. By that time the sun was up, so I went back to my aunt's house and gathered up the valuables, all in all, I had nine pillowcases and three sheets that I rapped money and things into them.

My cousins were up and eating, and I told them, "Mike and Tom get busy on the orchard." "Occasionally, check on that guy using the bulldozer, make sure he is doing what he is supposed to be doing." "Val, you are with me today we are going to Poplar Bluff I should be back about two or two-thirty."

"Where are the chainsaw and things?" asked Mike.

"On the table, out front."

"Aunt Adeline, do you want anything from Poplar Bluff?"

"I can't think of anything."

"Alright, then as soon as Val finishes, we will be off."

We left about eight-thirty the bank didn't open until nine, so I would get there just in time before too many people showed up. Val and I got to the bank about five minutes before they opened their doors.

"We will wait here until they open their doors." "What are you going to do with all that money you earned?"

"Oh, I don't know; maybe save it and buy a boy's bicycle or some toys I just don't know yet."

"You don't like the bicycle you have now?"

"It's a girl's bike, besides it is pretty old and worn out."

"Oh, I can see how that could be a problem."

"Why don't you go and see if those doors are open yet."

He left and then came back and said, "They just opened up." I locked the cab of the truck, and Val and I went into the bank.

I said to the teller, "I would like to talk to the head person here."

"That would be Mr. Beaker; he is our branch manager; may I ask what you wish to see him about?"

"About a substantial sum of money, I want to deposit I need to talk to him about it first."

The teller left her window, knocked on a door, and went in. A few seconds later, a man came out, looked at me, and said, "Your Captain York."

"Yes, Sir."

"What can I do for you?"

"I have a substantial number of valuables I need to bring into this bank for deposit." "It's too much for these tellers to handle." "I'll need about two or three people to help me bring it in, and perhaps we can bring it into your office."

"You have that much?"

"Yes."

"Alright, Sally, come with me and bring a cart just in case."

"Val, you can open the doors for us," I said. We went out to the truck, and I unlocked the passenger door, and I started to load up the cart the sheets went first then I was about to put five bags on top of the sheets. The teller and manager took two bags each, I pushed the heavy cart into the bank, and we all went into his office.

"Sally, go get Robert and tell him to come into my office and then go back to your window."

"Yes, Sir."

Mr. Beaker then cleared his desk of everything on it. We started to stack everything into organized piles according to what they were. As we were doing this, a man came in and began to help us, and Mr. Beaker said, "Take that adding machine and start counting." When he stopped, he had nine hundred and fifty thousand in paper money, which they immediately added to my account. Then he began to count the gold coins while Mr. Beaker was looking at the stocks and bonds. "I will have to call someone in St. Louis for the value of these stocks and bond." He looked up a number in his Rolodex, and then he dialed a number. "Hello, this is John Beaker at First National Bank in Poplar Bluff." "I have some stocks and bonds that I wish you to tell me the value." He started to inform the person he was talking to the names of the stocks and bonds and how many I had as Mr. Beaker did, he wrote down some numbers. When he hung up, I could see he got worked up, and he left his office with the figures. About ten minutes later, he said, "I check the numbers twice these stocks and

bonds are worth one million two hundred and sixty-five thousand dollars."
"You're a wealthy man Captain."

"Sir, how do you want to value these coins?"

Mr. Beaker looked at some of the coins then said, "Do it by the weight." He weighed the gold, and it was two hundred eleven thousand four hundred and fifty-six dollars. Altogether I had a total of two million four hundred seventy-six thousand four hundred and fifty-six dollars was on deposit in the bank.

"What about all this jewelry?" I asked. "Go down to Rubenstein's Jewelry, they will give you a better value than I," said Mr. Beaker.

Val and I went down to Rubenstein's, which was about a mile from the bank. "May I speak to Mr. Rubenstein, please?" I asked.

The clerk smiled and said, "There isn't any Rubenstein Mr. Walker felt the name sounded more like a fancy jewelry store, I'll get Mr. Walker."

"I'm Mr. Walker, can I help you."

"Mr. Beaker at the bank said you might buy my jewelry."

"Yes, I will buy it if it is real." I lifted the pillowcase with the jewelry then empty it on his counter. "May I ask you where you got this?"

"I bought a house with everything in it, and this was in the house." He got a pad, pencil, and a loupe and checked each piece of jewelry and had and wrote a number down. When he had finished, he took the pad he wrote the numbers on, put them in a calculator, and said, "I'll give you seventy-five thousand."

I looked at him with a smile and said, "That means they are worth one hundred and fifty thousand."

"I have to make a profit?"

"I'll tell you what you can have them for seventy-five thousand if you throw that pearl necklace in, all wrapped up nicely with a bow."

He pulled out the pearls, looked at them, and said more to himself than me, "Two thousand dollars." He looked at me and said, "Wait a minute." He left the pearls on the counter, went into his office, then came out with a magazine and said to his clerk, "Wrap this and put a gold ribbon on it."

"We have a deal Captain York," sticking out his hand to shake it. He showed me a life magazine with a picture of me on the front cover.

"It was taken when I first stepped out of the plane in Hawaii."

"Will you sign it?"

"Sure." I signed the magazine; then, he wrote me a check for seventy-five thousand, and his clerk handed me the pearls box.

"Ok, Val, let's go back to the bank."

"Do we have to go to the bank?"

"You want to get paid, don't you; it will only take me a few minutes."

I was just about to go out the door when Mr. Walker said, "Captain, that jewelry was worth one hundred and twenty-five thousand." I shook my head and went out the door and down to the bank.

I deposited the check, which gave me over two and a half million dollars. Then I told the clerk, "I need three envelopes put in sixty dollars all in fives in two of them and sixty dollars all in ones in the third." She did as I said, and I wrote Val's name on his. I had the address of a company that remodels houses. I told Val that after I talked to the person from the remodeling company, we would go to get something to eat and maybe a surprise for him.

"Hello, I wish to hire your company to remodel my home, barn, sheds, and perhaps build an addition to the house."

"Ok, we can come out to your home Monday morning to look and make a decision on what you want to do." I agreed, I signed some papers and gave the lady who was helping me instructions on how to get to the house. We left and headed to a restaurant. It was early still only about a quarter to twelve, so I stopped at a bicycle store that was just down from the restaurant.

"Alright, Val, pick yourself out any bicycle you want."

"Really."

"Yes." It didn't take him long when he chose a green Schwinn Pea Picker. When I paid for it, he got very excited, we put it in the back of the truck and put a tarp over it and then went to eat. We had just gotten what we ordered when a familiar face came into the restaurant, it was Frank White. I stood up to shake his hand and said, "Do you want to order something?"

"Maybe coffee and a Danish."

He ordered his food, and I said, "This is my cousin Val he, and his siblings are more like brothers and sisters to me."

"Hello, Val, I'm Frank White." "I'm writing a book about James."

"Why?"

"Well, he is a very famous person, and people who don't know him would like to know him."

"When do you want to start the interview?" I asked.

"Tomorrow, I just got in from New York, and I'm tired."

"You have the instructions on how to get to my place?"

"Yes, I do; they're right in my wallet."

"Let me see them." I made some changes to them and said, "There should be someone at my aunts' house, but if no one is there right across from their front gate, you will see a newly cut road go down that road, and you will come to my house."

"Are you going to interview my aunt, uncle, and cousins?"

"Oh yes, even Val." "I have some good news for you," said Frank.

"Oh, what's that?"

"I'm just about finish with gathering information for this book, and I should have your book finish in less than a week."

"Good."

"Ah, but the excellent news is Penguin wants me to write a second book about you sort of a follow-up to this present book."

"Will this mean a new contract?"

"Yes, but I will discuss this after the first book is finish and out in the bookstores."

"Why is Penguin willing to do the second book when the first book isn't published yet?"

"You just don't know how popular you are, Captain." We talked for about twenty minutes; he finished his coffee and Danish. Then he excused himself, stating he would see me tomorrow.

Val and I finished our meal, and I said, "We have three more places to go, then we will go back home."

"What are the three places?"

"I need to go to a place where they fix cars, a place that sells old things, and a place where I can buy some plants." We went to a car restoration place called Todd's Restorations. The business was a more sizeable place than I figured it would be Val, and I went into the office.

"Can I help you?"

"Yes, I have three old vehicles that I want to get fixed."

"You're that captain that has been in the newspapers and magazines, aren't you?"

"Yes, I guess I am," I said with a smile.

"Well, it is an honor to serve you, so what kind of vehicles do you have."

"I have a 1915 Harley Davidson model 11 J, 1928 Ford Model A sedan, and 1947 GMC pickup all seem to be in good shape."

"Will you need us to pick them up?"

"Yes."

"We can be there tomorrow before noon; in fact, Todd himself will be there."

"That would be great."

"Can I ask you a question about your business?"

"Ask away."

"This is not a large area for a business like yours, how do you survive?"

"We get customers from all over the nation." "We moved here because we like the small-town feel." I nodded, and after I gave her the address and instruction on how to get to my place, Val and I left for an antique store.

We walked into an antique store, and an older man and woman greeted us. I told them about all the things I had that I wanted to sell them. "We don't buy antiques; we are retiring in a year or two and get rid of all these things." "Even if we were to buy things from you, we couldn't give you a fair amount for your items." "I will tell you what, I will give you the address in St. Louis that will buy your things and give you a fair price, and I will also give you an address to an art and book dealer."

"That would be great."

Val and I left for a nearby nursery, as I walked in Val wandered off by himself. I talked to one of the clerks and told her that I wanted to buy many trees and other plants. The clerk spoke to an older man, and he came over to me and said, "I'm Rick Paner I own this nursery what can I do to help you."

"I live near Elsinore and want to buy trees of all types, but what I am interested in, is pine and redwood trees if they will grow there."

"How many do you want?"

"Two or three hundred to start, maybe twenty fruit trees."

"I have the three hundred trees you want, but I would have to order the redwood trees, but I can get them in about a week."

"Alright, get me a hundred redwoods."

"Ok, then I will figure up how much four hundred trees will cost you."

"Why don't you throw in about a hundred bushes that have color and fifty that have edible fruit."

"Alright, that will be two thousand four hundred and fifty dollars we require half now and then the total when you receive everything."

"Will you deliver?"

"Sure will." I handed him my credit card he took it, and about five minutes later I completed the sale, and I was looking for Val who was running in and out the trees and bushes. We headed home and got back by twenty after two. I dropped Val off at his house and unloaded his bicycle, which he ran into the house to show his mother. I headed back to my place, stopping at the springs to see what the operator had done. The pond got dug out precisely the way I wanted and was filling up real fast with water. I continued down to the house where Mike and Tom were still working in the orchard, and I waved at them as I went to see the operator who was loading his equipment.

"You did an excellent job, what do I owe you?"

"We will send you a bill." I shook his hand and went to join Mike and Tom.

"Do you know what kind of trees these are?"

"No, but a lot of them are not very healthy," said Mike.

"I'll have to get your mother down here to check them out." "I have some more fruit trees coming to replace the dead ones, and I hope to add a few more rows of trees." They both nodded their heads, and I said, "Looks like the sheep did an excellent job cleaning the grass up."

"Yeah, and they did a bit of fertilizing," said Tom.

"Give it another twenty-five minutes and then call it quits, then put the chainsaw and loppers in the barn but leave the gas out away from the barn." They both nodded yes, and I headed to the sheds and started to pull things out of there and put them in the barn. Mike and Tom showed up to the barn as I was carrying an item in the barn.

"Are you two working this weekend?"

"Do you want us to?"

"I want you to do what you want to do."

Mike looked at Tom, who shrugged his shoulders, and Mike said, "I think we will rest this weekend besides mama would never approve of us working on Sunday?"

"Alright, hop into the truck, and I'll drive you back as soon as I lock the barn and house." We drove back to their house, and it was three-thirty when we arrived. My uncle wouldn't be home for another forty-five minutes, and I wanted to catch him before he went into the house, so I stayed outside until he came. I had to wait nearly an hour before he came, I stopped him and said, "Before you go into the house, come to the barn with me."

"What's going on?

"You'll see," I said with a smile.

We went into the barn, and I said, "I sold all that jewelry for seventy-five thousand."

"Good God, that is a lot of money."

"Yes, but I found out afterward it was worth a hundred and twenty-five thousand dollars." "Even though I only got seventy-five thousand, the jewelry owner gave me this for Aunt Adeline."

"What is it?"

"You have to wait and be surprised when she sees it."

"Ok, why don't you give it to her?"

"It's not right; it's your job, besides I think she would be much happier if it came from you if you know what I mean."

"Yeah, I think I do," he said, and he stuck the box in his lunch box.

He went into the house through the front door and me through the side door. He laid down the lunch box and went to clean up, and I went into where I took a shower is to wash my hands and face.

"How did it go today?" asked my aunt.

"Good, Val was bored until he got his new bicycle."

"Yes, but you shouldn't have spent so much money on him."

"I love him, and besides, I have plenty of money now."

She looked at me and said, "You are sure not like your brothers or your cousins back in California and here."

"Oh, I don't know I feel very comfortable with Mike, Tom, and the rest." At that, Denise, Ray, Toni, and Patricia walk in; they had just come home from school in Springfield. Chris was in the Navy somewhere, so she wasn't here.

"Do you know your cousins, James?" my aunt asked me.

"Of course, they are like my sisters." They all smiled, and I went over to hug them. Mike and Tom came into the kitchen and started to tease them.

"Where did Val get that fancy bicycle?" asked Toni.

"James bought it." "I hope he comes back for dinner," said my aunt.

"If he doesn't show, he doesn't eat," said Uncle Paul as he hugged his daughters.

Val did come back in time for dinner, just in time; he was washing up when we sat down for dinner. Val was all excited about the bicycle, and I asked, "How does it work, is it fast?"

"It works well, and it is really fast."

I smiled, then Uncle Paul said, "Adeline, did you clean out my lunch box."

"No, not yet."

"You better, I left some food in it that might stink."

She got up, got the lunch box, opened it, pulled out a box, and said, "What is this?"

"For you."

She sat down with the small package with the gold bow and stared at it, and Tom said, "It's not going to open by itself, Ma."

She looked up and said, "I know Tom, it's not every day that I get a present for no reason I want to admire it before I open it." I was worried that Val might say something, but he wasn't near me he was looking at the watches, so I didn't think he saw what I got.

"Open it, Mama I want to see what it is," said Val.

"Ok, I'll open it." She opened the package very slowly then finally she opened the box, and my aunt was speechless.

"Put them on, Mama," said Ray.

Uncle Paul helped her put them on, and Toni said, "They look real."

My uncle looked at me, I nodded, and he said, "They are."

"How could you afford this, Paul?" asked my aunt.

"Don't worry about it; you deserve it."

"Let me go look in the mirror," my aunt said with a smile.

She came back in a few minutes and said, "You best eat or your food; it will get cold."

When dinner ended, and we were still sitting at the table, I pulled out three envelopes, "It's time that I paid you three." I handed the two envelopes to Mike and Tom, and then I gave Val the one with the sixty ones.

Val looked inside his envelope; his eyes seem to pop out of his head. He then looked at what his brothers got who had already removed the money, and he said, "I think I got more than they did."

Mike and Tom looked at the pile of ones that Val had pulled out of the envelope and smiled, and I said, "Well, you worked hard."

"Yes, I did." At that, everyone laughed, and Val happy ran off to put his money away.

"James, you did pay us more than the hours we put in," Mike said.

"You two deserve more for the work you did; you keep the extra money."

The next day I was at the house emptying the sheds. Most of the things I had in the outbuildings will be going to an antique store in St. Louis. I had gotten out everything in the sheds when a truck pulling an extended flatbed trailer came; it was Todd from Todd's Restoration. He got out of the cab of his truck, and I shook his hand and said, "The vehicles are in the barn."

He looked at a piece of paper and said, "I understand you have 1915 Harley Davidson model 11 J, 1928 Ford Model A sedan, and 1947 GMC pickup?"

"Yes."

"If you are correct about those vehicles, they are valuable and will be a pleasure to work on." I showed him the Harley, and he asked, "How did you know what kind of Harley it was?"

"There is a plate on it as there is on the other two vehicles."

He squatted down, looked at it, and said, "It's all original and in good shape, when was it last run?"

"I don't know this property sat vacant for a long time."

He looked in the gas tank and asked, "What do you want to do with it."

"Restore it, so it looks like it just came off the showroom floor and make it be able to drive."

"Great, that's what I thought, it would cost you about three hundred dollars to get it the way you want it unless I have a broken part then it will cost you more."

"Alright." He rolled the motorcycle out of the barn without starting it and then placed it at the front of the trailer and secured it. The next one I showed him was GMC pickup; he looked at the engine, then the interior, and finally looked at the body.

"I suppose you want to restore this to showroom also?"

"Yes, and No, I want to have it restored to showroom condition, but I want to change the color to a two-tone black and khaki or tan." "I would also like a sign on the doors that say York Estates."

He looked at the truck for a minute and said, "The color is an excellent choice, and I will redo the wood bed in the back." "I'll make the chrome pop, but I think it would be better if I don't put the sign on the door, but what I will do to all three vehicles and make a plate that is attached to the license York Estates it will look better that way."

"Alright."

"This one will cost you about six hundred dollars, again if I don't have to replace any parts."

"The price is okay." "Now, to get this truck on the trailer is going to be a challenge." "You drive; I'll push."

"Ok, but I have a wench on the trailer, so once we get it to the trailer, it will go up easy." He got in, released the brake, and I pushed the truck as he steered it. When we got to the trailer, he put a cable on the axle, wrenched it up, latched it down, and then went to get the Model A sedan.

After checking the car out, he asked, "What do you want to do with this car."

"Like the truck, I want to change the color to a two-tone black and kelly-green."

"Good choice, and I will make everything pop with this one also. It will cost about five hundred dollars, not counting extra parts."

"That's fine; let me push this one while you drive again." We loaded the sedan on his trailer, then he filled out some papers and had me sign them, and I asked, "How long do you think it will take you to finish?"

"I want to do a good job; it will take about three months."

"Alright, I should be back by then for about two weeks leave." At that, we shook hands, and he left.

About ten minutes after he left, my aunt and uncle showed up in his pickup. At the same time, I was drawing rough sketches of what I wanted to get remolded to the house, barns, and sheds. "Let's go see what you did with that spring," said my uncle.

"Alright, but I want you to check out the orchard first." "I wish to know what kind of fruit trees they are."

We walked out to the trees, and my aunt said, "There are several different kinds of trees here, I see cherry, peach, apricot, and apple."

"Good, I have about twenty-five more fruit trees coming and another four hundred and seventy-five trees coming some which are redwoods." "And there are also a hundred and fifty bushes coming."

"That is a lot of trees and bushes how are you going to water all of them until they get big enough to survive on their own."

"I saw a trailer with a big water tank on it just outside Poplar Bluff, and it was for sale."

"I'll see if I can get the boys to water the trees while I am gone, I'll pay them of course."

"I can do that, and I could use the money besides the boys will be working at the charcoal company soon," said my aunt.

"Ok, if you want to, however, you do understand if either one of you needs money, you're welcome to use what I have."

"No, that is your money we will get along just fine," my aunt said.

We walked over to the spring the water looked like it just reached its crest and the pond was emptying into the stream. "Someday, I will stock it with fish, but it is ready to go skinny dipping now," I said with a smile.

"How deep is it?" asked my uncle.

"Ten feet in the center, but it slopes to that ten feet." "I'll be putting trees all over here, creating a small forest type park."

"Why don't you bring your cattle over here?" I asked.

"If you give me a hand, I will do that," said my uncle.

"I've never done that before, but I will give it a try." We moved the cattle over to my property, which had much more feed and water; it was easier than what I thought it would be. The next day we went to church, it was the same building as before when I was a child, but they had a different priest. The number of Catholics attending was perhaps slightly more than what I remembered.

I was introduced and welcomed by everyone. My aunt, uncle, and cousins were talking to other people. An older woman and man came up to me and said, "We own the property next to you." "Paul and Adeline told me you are going to make a park out of the property."

"That's correct."

"Are you going to open it up to the public? I've never thought about it, but most likely not until I am very old if I do." "However, I might let church groups, boy or girl scouts use it."

They both looked at each other and said, "I own over six hundred and fifty acres; it's overgrown with trees and brush, and it's not level ground, but I am willing to sell it to you." "The only thing I wish is to keep my house and orchard."

"How much do you want for it?"

"You paid ten thousand for yours, how about fifteen thousand."

"I paid ten thousand, but I had buildings on it, but you all seem like nice people, so fifteen thousand will be just fine."

"We will get the papers filled out at the title company, and they will be ready by Monday for you to sign," they said.

"Great, and I will have a cashier's check for you," I informed my aunt and uncle, who thought I might have paid a little too much.

I thought it better if I went over to Mr. Schumacher's place dress in civilian clothing. The Schumacher's had seven children. They were quiet and polite as was Mrs. Schumacher; when I spoke in German, they warmed up a little. Everything Mrs. Schumacher made was from their farm, including the milk straight from the cow. I drank some then stared at the mug that had the milk in it.

"What is the problem, Mr. York, don't you like milk?" "I could get you some water or perhaps cider?"

"No, I love the taste of the milk I haven't had milk fresh from the cow since I was a child when my aunt Adeline introduce me to it." We talked about his church, the customs that they practice, and his farm. I informed him that I bought more land and my tree planting plans. "Your family and church are welcome to picnic or camp on the property when you wish." We finished eating, then went and sat in the living room. "Perhaps I should help your wife with the dishes."

"No, it's not our way, and my wife would feel uneasy if you did, but she will feel grateful that you offered." There was a knock at the door, and Mr. Schumacher opened the door and in walked two older men from his church. I stood up to show respect; Mr. Schumacher introduced me, then I offered them my hand, which they shook.

"Perhaps I should leave Mr. Schumacher."

"No, they are here to speak to you, Mr. York."

"Oh, alright, then."

I sat back down, and one of the older men said, "I understand you are interested in our faith."

"Yes."

"And of what faith are you?"

"Catholic."

They all looked at each other, and the other man said, "Our faith has had a bad history with the Catholic Church."

"Many religions have had a bad history with the Catholic Church; I know this."

"How large is your property, and what do you plan to do with it, farm it, or raise livestock?"

I thought it curious that they were asking me all these questions. I didn't want to seem impolite in Mr. Schumacher's home. I said, "I have at present over a thousand acres, and I have no intentions of farming or raising cattle. I am going to turn the property into a park."

"That won't do, what will you do for a living?"

"I am in the military, and I have a lot of money." "A publisher is writing a book about me." "Also, a second book on the way." "With maybe a movie someday, all of which I will get paid a lot of money." All three shook their heads, and the one person who was asking most of the questions posed, "Are you willing to leave the military?"

"Why would I do that?"

"We do not believe in violence, especially war, and you would not be able to join the church if you are in the military."

"I would like to debate you on your beliefs on violence, but all this matter not, you misunderstand me." "I believe that all churches have a truth, some more than others, in believing, this I believe no church is perfect at least none since the apostles died off." "What I am trying to say is I seek the best from all religions, and I will let the Holy Spirit tell me what is good and what isn't." "Until the Spirit tells me I will not join any church or leave the Catholic Church." They weren't happy because of what I said, and I had a feeling Mr. Schumacher wouldn't be telling me much more about his church nor inviting me to his house for some time. About five minutes after what I said, the two older men left without shaking my hand. I turned to Mr. Schumacher and said, "I should be going; I wish to thank you and your family for your hospitality." "I apologize if I sounded like I was rude." He opened the door and shook my hand without saying anything, and I left. I informed my uncle and aunt as to what happen and then went to bed. The next day I was at my barn trying to figure out how I was going to get everything I didn't want to St. Louis, I finally settled on renting a trailer. I went back doing rough drawings of how I wanted the place, and about seven o'clock, the roofer came. I worked in the orchard until Tom and Mike showed up, which was eight-thirty.

"Where is Val?"

"I think you might have lost him," Tom said.

"Oh well, Tom, why don't you go into town and get some snacks." I handed him the keys and some money, and he left.

"Mike, let's see if we can get the water running in this old house."

"I would guess the water is pumped in from a well someplace with an electric pump like my house," said Mike.

"Where is yours located?"

"In the shed in the back of the house."

"Then that's where we will look for mine." We went in the back of the house, and the first shed we went into, we found not only an electric pump but also a gas one too, which was its backup. Burlap sacks covered the pumps, that is why I didn't notice them when I came in the sheds the first time. "Let's clean these pumps up." We got some rags and brushes and did the best we could, and then I said, "I'll check the electric motor to see if it is in working condition you check the gas motor." I checked all the wires and hand moved the pump; nothing seemed seized up, but I did see a place to put a little oil. "How's your pump?"

"Looks like it has never got used." "The good thing is there is no oil or gas in it."

"When Tom comes back, go back into town and get another gas can, and oil for the gas motor and the electric motor." "I don't want to turn it on until I know the motor is well lubricated."

"Alright." We went to work in the orchard, and about twenty minutes later, Tom came back, and after getting some money from me Mike left, and Tom took his place.

When Mike got back, we all went over to the shed and first lubricated the electric pump got some water down in the spring, Mike and Tom primed the electric pump then we started it. "Let's go see if it is working." We went into the house and turned on the bathroom water at first just air came through, then there was a sputter then water. I then checked the toilet, which was filling up. I went into the kitchen, and I had water. Tom and Mike joined me in the washroom where the water heater was, and it was filling up.

"I'd let the electric motor run for an hour and then shut it off and run the gas motor for an hour," Mike said.

"Will you do that?" "I'm going to Poplar Bluff."

"I sure will," I asked Tom and Mike if they wanted anything, both said chewing tobacco and I left first for my Aunt Adeline's house and then to the neighbors to see if the deal was still on. After talking to my aunt and neighbor, my aunt wanted nothing, and the sale was on with the property. I was to meet with them in about an hour at the title office in Poplar Bluff.

I got a cashier check for fifteen thousand and met the neighbors at the title company. Papers were signed, and we shook hands, and I had the property. I checked the remodelers, and they said they would be out by one. I stopped off where my vehicles were getting worked on, and it seemed to be going well. I picked up the tobacco, then got a trailer and headed back to my house. As I drove through the front gate of my property, I saw a truck and two men unloading some of the trees I ordered. I drove the truck to the barn, and Mike and Tom joined me.

"If you're just about finish with the orchard string a water hose to these trees, the fruit trees need to be separated from the others."

"You want us to finish the orchard first?" asked Mike.

"How long will it take to finish?"

"A couple of hours."

"Yeah, go ahead." The men were still unloading the trees, so I started to load the things I was going take to St. Louis fifteen minutes later, they finished. The paperwork said I had two hundred and fifty trees, so I counted them, and it was correct, as was the number of bushes. "Which ones are the fruit trees?" They showed me the fruit trees, and I marked the cans. I then asked, "When are the other two hundred and fifty trees coming?"

"They will be here on Friday." I signed the paperwork, then gave me a receipt and left, and I again started loading the trailer and truck. The remodelers finally showed up, and I did a walkthrough, then I showed them the drawings of what I had in mind.

"We will draw up some blueprints drawings, and by Friday, we will be back to see if you have any changes to the designs," they said. They then took some measurements and left. By three o'clock, Mike and Tom came over to me as I put a tarp on the truck.

"Tom, I haven't watered the trees yet, so why don't you do that while Mike helps me."

"Alright." About twenty minutes later, we had everything covered and tied up and just about when Tom finished watering, and the roofers stopped for the day.

When they left, I said, "You two ever been on those six hundred and fifty acres I just bought?"

"No."

"Not even when you were younger?"

"No, we were told not to go there."

"Well, let's go exploring?" The new property was dense with brush and trees; it wasn't flat; it had many swales an excellent place to build trails and campsites. I drove to the new pond and told Mike and Tom how and where to plant the trees and bushes.

"You want to do the orchard first?" asked Tom.

"Sure, that way, by the time I get back from St. Louis, you can use the truck."

The next morning, I headed to St. Louis I planned to go to an antique store first then to a rare bookstore finally to an art gallery. Three hours after leaving my aunt's house, I got to St. Louis and a place called Tin Roof Antiques. "Hello, I'm James York; may I speak to the owner, please."

"I am Jack Summerfield, what can I do for you?"

"I bought an old ranch near Poplar Bluff, and I brought a lot of old things that I think you would like to buy?"

"Maybe let's go see what you have." I took off the tarp on the trailer, and Jack looked in.

"Yes, all these things I will buy off you."

"I haven't shown you everything?" I took the tarp off the truck bed and said, "The books and paintings are going somewhere else, but all these toys I wish to sell also."

His eyes bulged out, and he said, "These are very desirable. Let's get your things into the store." We took everything in the store, and I covered the truck again. He went through everything then said, "Well, I'll give you twelve thousand for all your things."

"Sounds a little light, but I will tell you what let me store my trailer here until I leave, which will be no later than tomorrow, and I will accept twelve thousand."

"You can leave your trailer, and I will go down the street with you to my bank to get you a cashier's check.

After the antique store, I went to Barucci Gallery and brought in all the paintings that I had. "I'm Mary Swartz; can I help you."

"Yes, I would like to sell these paintings to you."

"Well, let's see what you have." She went through my paintings, and she put two aside. With a smile, she said, "These paintings are worth about two to three hundred dollars I will give you two hundred and fifty for each." "These two are different; this one is a Monet, and this one is worth five hundred thousand, and this one is a Whitely; it may be worth two hundred and fifty thousand." "Let me call someone in New York so I can give you a fair price." She got on the phone and was on it for about twenty minutes. Then she came back and said, "I guess I made a mistake; the people I talked to in New York will guarantee my gallery slightly over two million dollars." "I will give you two million for the two pictures."

"Will you give me the two thousand for the others also?"

"Yes."

"We have a deal." I got paid then went to Bauman Rare Books store.

I went into the store and told the owner about the books I had, and he told me to bring them into the store. The owner's name is Richard Tanner, and he looked at each book carefully and wrote some numbers down. I had told him about some of the autographs and that they were first editions. Mr. Tanner finally finish checking out the books, and he came over to me and said, "You have several books." "For all of them, I will give you a million five hundred thousand." I received a check, which made me nervous because it wasn't a cashier's check, but he gave me enough paperwork if he tried something. I picked up my trailer and headed back home.

It was seven at night when I drove up to my aunt's home. I parked the truck and went into the house.

"How did you do?" my aunt asked.

"About three and a half million."

"Wow, that's a lot of money," my aunt and uncle both said.

"You think I can call California?"

"Yes, you should have called a long time ago," my aunt said. I phoned my parents' home, and my mother answered the phone.

"Are you ok?" asked my mother.

"Yes, I have just been busy with this property." "When I bought the property, everything on the property was mine, including everything in the house." "There were a lot of valuables that I sold and placed the money into the bank."

"How much money did you get?" she asked.

"Over five million, that's one of the reasons I've called I want to know from dad if I should invest it or not."

"That's a lot of money, Jim; I'll get your father."

"Jim, your mother said you did well with this property."

"Yes, I have a lot of money." "I wanted to know if I should let it sit in the bank or invest it."

"If you invest it, how much do you plan to invest?"

"I thought about two million."

"Alright, what are you going to do with the rest?"

"I want to have a significant amount on hand because I am remodeling and turning the land into a park. Also, if more land comes up for sale, I will buy it and add it to the thousand acres I now have."

"That's a lot of property."

"Yes, and it's wonderful, I have at least one spring that flows all year long and a large pond which someday I will stock."

"What do you want to invest in?"

"I don't know that's what you are good at."

"Alright, send me the money, and I will invest it."

"How do I send that large amount of money?"

"You can do a bank transfer."

"With all that money, are you going to stay in the Army?"

"Yes, for now, I want to see what the Army is going to do with me."

"Won't I need some numbers and maybe an address to send this money to you?" I asked.

"Yes, I will get them for you, hold on." He gave me the numbers, address, and telephone number, so I asked, " Do you want to talk to Aunt Adeline or someone?"

"Yes." I handed the phone to my aunt and sat down. When she finished talking and hung up the phone, she came over and sat down beside me. I planned to drop off the trailer tomorrow and then go to the bank. I told my aunt and uncle what happened in St. Louis and then showered and went to bed.

The next day I got up after sunrise much to the surprise of the boys. I ate some breakfast and left for Poplar Bluff. After dropping off the trailer, I went to the bank. I spoke to the branch manager. He was happy to help me transfer the two million to the place where my father said to send the money. The rest of the money I had I deposited in my account except for some cash I wanted on hand to carry. I checked to see if the trailer with the water tank was still for sale, and it was. I looked at it a little closer; it was a seventy-five-gallon tank with an opening on top and a hose at the bottom just what I wanted. I found the owner and offered him a hundred dollars, which he took.

I headed back to my place, and when I got there, I was happy to see that the roofers were hard at work, and Tom and Mike were digging holes in the orchard. I dropped off the trailer and joined my cousins, digging holes.

"Is that the last fruit tree?"

"Yes, except for the one apple tree you said to save," Mike said.

"You two take the truck pick up the pine trees and plant them where I told you to plant them." I looked at my watch it was nearly eleven in the morning, and I said, "When you drop off the trees, go into town and get some things to snack on then you can get busy afterward." "I'm going to stay here and prune these older fruit trees."

"Do you want us to bring you back something?" asked Tom.

"No." I hadn't exercised since I left California, and I needed to start working out soon. I got the chainsaw and punning loppers and got busy on the trees. Noontime, the roofer, had finished their work, and I look at their job. Everything seemed to look good; in fact, it was much better. Now I needed to get these buildings remodeled and painted.

After the roofers left, I went back to work until about two when I put everything away and ran to where Mike and Tom were working. They had planted about six or seven trees, and I said, "Let go back to my house load up the trailer and fill the tank full of water and then you can water the trees by the time you finish it will be quitting time."

I changed my routine every morning I go running for a few hours, and at the end, I carry a load of wood to my aunts' home before I go to my house, and at night I do the same thing. My cousins thought I was crazy, but I knew I had to stay in shape, and I knew if I didn't, I would be in big trouble when I went to Bragg, so I pushed myself. Friday, the rest of the trees came in, including the redwoods, the remodelers came about one in the afternoon. I showed them what I wanted, and I liked all their ideas; the only thing I added was for them to build a brick wall or fence and entrance. "Can you start the remodeling Monday?" I asked the designer, and he agreed.

That night I paid both Mike and Tom a hundred dollars, which is more than what they would have usually gotten.

Saturday, I thought I start working on a trail in the wooded new property area. Sunday, I watered then did a lot of exercises. On Monday, Tom and Mike went back to digging holes; I waited for the remodelers who came at ten in the morning and then went back to working on the trail. By Friday, I paid Mike and Tom and found out that I was losing them because of their Job. There were several trees to plant, and I only had a week to do it. So, I started the trees Saturday and planted twelve trees. Monday, my aunt came over to me, and I showed where to water the trees. Wednesday, I planted all the trees and half of the bushes the last apple tree and the rest of the bushes I plan to plant at the end of the trail at a clearing. By the end of the day, I had made it to the clearing and had cleared out all the brush, then headed back to the main road and seen my aunt finishing watering the trees, so I went over to her.

"What are you going to do with that apple tree?" she asked.

"Do you see that worn-out path that I just came down?"

"Yes."

"It leads to the tree line; at the end of the trail, there is a clearing I will put the tree in the middle of the clearing. If you're finish watering, we can bring the trailer back, and I will show you the place."

"Ok." I put the tree and the bushes in the back of the truck, and we drove back to my place to unload the trailer. My aunt wanted to fill the water tank that day, so it would have water in it the next time she watered. So, I put the hose in the tank and let it fill while we went to see what the remodelers had done and when the tank filled up, and we headed down the trail.

"It will look like a long distance to the clearing than what it is because of the trail switchbacks through the thicket of trees and brush." It took us about twenty minutes to get there I unloaded the tree and bushes then headed back to my aunts' house.

I had ordered several loads of road base. It was to be delivered, spread, and compacted by tomorrow.

I was sitting in the living room when a car drove up to my aunt's home. It was Mr. White; he had two large boxes in his hands that he struggled to bring into the house. I went out, grabbed one box out of his hand, and went into the house.

"Where have you been all this time?"

"In New York, writing your book and doing other things."

"How's it going?" I asked.

"We can't make them fast enough, and we need to talk about that and other things."

"What's in the box?" asked my uncle.

"The books that James requested," said Mr. White

"Let's look at them," I said.

There were sixty hardcover books with a picture of me receiving the Medal of Honor on the dust cover.

"I better call my parents to see how many they want."

"I know I want one," said my aunt.

I handed one to my aunt, and my uncle said, "Sign it."

"Frank, do you have a pen?"

"Yes, and I want you to sign my book also."

"Alright." I signed both books, then we all sat down.

"What else is on your mind, Mr. White?" I asked.

"Let me give you this." He reached into his pocket, pulled out a check, and handed it to me. It was two hundred and fifty thousand dollars.

"So, what is this for?"

"We have sold a lot of books, and that check will not be the last one; it's just the beginning."

"The reviews on your book have been off the chart, and your idea of making it a story and not a biography has paid off, and Penguin loves it." "They love it so much they want to do the second book."

He pulled out a contract and handed it to me, and I compared it with the contract from the first book. It was pretty much the same, except they gave me more for each book sold, and they are to provide me with another five hundred thousand dollars for writing it.

"Do you have the check for five hundred-thousand-dollars?"

"Yes."

"How are you going to write this second book?"

"The same way."

"There won't be as many interviews, I would guess?"

"No, I will follow you around and see what comes up."

"Well, then let me sign that contract." I signed the contract, and Frank gave me a check for five hundred thousand dollars.

"Do you think they will make a movie?" I asked.

"We are already negotiating a contract."

"It looks like you're going to be famous, James," said my Aunt.

"Mrs. Korenek James is already famous."

"I will contact you once you get to D. C. I need to be going now."

"When Frank White left, I said, "Maybe I should call my parents."

"Go ahead," said my Uncle.

"Jim, let me get your father I'm cooking right now," said my mother.

"Jim," said my dad.

"Hi, Dad, did you get the money transfer?"

"Yes, and I invested it."

"Great, the book that the publisher wrote about me is out, and I have some copies do you want any?"

"Yes."

"Do you want me to sign them?"

"Yes."

"Alright, I will send you thirty of them."

"They started to write the second book about me, and they are going to start making a movie very soon."

"That sounds great."

"Yeah, they also gave me two checks, one for two hundred and fifty thousand and another for five hundred thousand."

"What are you going to do with the money?"

"I think I will open another account to be used to pay off my credit card and to have some operating money for the place I have bought."

"Well, alright." I talked some more and gave the phone to my aunt.

9

WASHINGTON

After working out the next morning, I planted the Apple tree in the center of the clearing. There was plenty of room for the truck to turn around, and just as I finish planting the tree and the bushes, the first truck came then spread his load. By noontime, they finished the trail and started on the road, which was easier to do. For the remainder of my time in Missouri, I decided to clean up the area where the lone apple tree was. By the end of the day they finished spreading the rock, and they were packing up to leave, I went over to them and paid them. Then I went to the house to see what had got done. As I walked out of the house front door, I saw a lone rider on a horse coming in it was Mr. Schumacher.

He rode up to the house, got off his horse, and said, "I've come to apologize for my actions towards you, Mr. York."

"There is nothing for you to apologize." "I take no offense for anything."

"Nevertheless, when you came for dinner, and the elders came, you were treated poorly by them and me."

"You and your elder friends saw me as a threat to your faith and an intrusion in your life; I who should apologize to you." "Let us shake each other's hand and start over," I said. We shook hands, and I said, "Would you like to see what I have done with the property?"

"I had seen the many trees you had planted when my boys and I watered the sheep."

"But you haven't seen the trail, and I would like to show it to you and get your opinion on it."

"Alright, let's go see your trail." We decided to walk, and it took forty-five minutes to get to the clearing.

"Do you see that tree?"

"Yes."

"Do you know what kind it is?"

He walked over to the tree and said, "An Apple."

"Yes, it represents the tree in the garden of Eden."

Mr. Schumacher looked around and said, "I do not know if this is a good thing, James."

"This park, that I am trying to create, I want it so beautiful I wish it to come near to the Garden of Eden."

"I understand what you are trying to do, but I just don't know what to make of it."

We walked out back towards the house, and I said, "Some religions think the Garden of Eden was right here in Missouri."

"Yes, I've heard that." We shook hands, and he left.

After church Sunday, I talked to my aunt and uncle about taking the money I owed out of the bank. I also said use the money to buy land that borders either my uncle's property or mine. My aunt and Val were going to drive me to the airport in St. Louis in my truck after breakfast. It meant that Val would have to get up early, which he wasn't pleased.

The next day I dressed in my dress greens, and just as the sun started to rise, we headed to St. Louis Val sleeping most of the way. I went into the terminal with my bags and said to a woman at the information desk, "Excuse me, I am looking for the correct plane I should be on."

"I know who you are, your Captain York."

"Yes."

"Would you sign my book?"

"Sure." She handed me the book she was reading, and I sign it.

"You want Continental; they do all the military flights here."

"Thanks."

"Thanks for signing my book."

I check-in, and they recognized me also. My flight was to leave forty-five minutes from terminal nine, so my aunt and cousin followed me down to the terminal. There was a gift shop, and I went in and bought Val, a toy and a candy bar. I asked my aunt if she wanted anything, but she didn't. We got plenty of stares and finger-pointing as we went to the terminal. I hadn't sat down fifteen minutes when the press came wanted me to make a statement.

"What do you want me to tell you?"

"Where have you been these past few months?" A reporter asked.

"After I spent some leave with my parents in California, I came to Missouri to be with my aunt, uncle, and I bought some land south of here."

"Where are you going?"

"Washington D. C."

"What are you going to do there?"

"I don't know I will report to the Pentagon when I get there."

"How are you feeling?"

"I feel healthy and happy."

"It's time to board the plane parents with children and handicap first," the Continental people said.

No one moved; everyone looked at me, and I was confused at why they weren't boarding. I looked at my aunt, and she didn't have a clue when one of the passengers said, "Captain, we want you to board first."

There was a roar of approval, and I shook my head no and said, "I serve my country; the country doesn't serve me, please do me the honor to board first." There was applause, cameras were flashing, and I finally left for Washington.

As we were in the air, I didn't know the reporters would call ahead and let their sister news agencies know I was coming. When we landed, A stewardess told me to stay on the plane until everyone was off.

Two M. Ps. came on the plane and said, "We're here, Sir, to get you through the crowd of reporters."

"I have two bags I need to get in baggage pickup."

"A duffle bag and suitcase, we have them both."

"Good." As we walked off the plane and into the terminal, I couldn't believe how many reporters there were flashing their cameras and screaming at me.

As I was walking, I spotted a well-known journalist, and I said to the two men escorting me, "Wait, let me say a few words."

"What is it you wish to know?"

"Why are you here in Washington?"

"I'm going to the Pentagon; they will tell me what I will be doing."

"Your book that just came out how accurate is it?"

"I haven't read it yet, but I know the writer, and I trust it is one hundred percent correct."

"Will you be visiting Walter Reed?"

"It is my understanding that I will."

"How's your health?"

"I feel healthy."

"I have to go now; either the Pentagon or the White House will soon have a news conference." At that, I left with the M. Ps. while the reporters were still yelling at me.

We left in a sedan to the Pentagon, which I had never seen before. It took us some time to get to where we were supposed to park.

The M.Ps. and I got out of the car, and they said, "This way, Sir."

"What about my bags?"

"We were told to leave them in the car, Sir."

We went into the building, a female Air Force staff sergeant picked up a phone and called someone, and a lieutenant came out and said, "Follow me, Sir."

At that, the two M.P.s left, and the lieutenant and I went the opposite way. We went down the hall and then down corridor six, and we turn down another hallway to General Arnold's office.

"Please have a seat Captain, the General will be back in a few minutes," said the General's secretary.

"I must be going, Captain," said the Lieutenant. I shook the Lieutenant's hand, and he left as I sat down.

Ten minutes pass then General Arnold walked in I stood up and removed my beret. He shook my hand and said, "James, it is good to see you come into my office." The General pointed to a chair, but I waited for him to sit first.

"I tried to get that book of yours, but every time I tried, they were all sold out."

"I have extra books, Sir; you can have one."

"That would be great."

"So, what have you been doing on your leave?"

"I spent a little time with my parents in California and then with my relatives in Missouri, where I bought some land with a house on it." "I have been improving the property."

"How is your health?"

"I feel just fine, Sir; I've been working out, and I am feeling strong."

"What about your back?"

"Occasionally, I feel a sliver coming up, but I ignore it."

"Well, you will have a full physical at Walter Reed tomorrow."

"Yes, Sir."

"You'll need to get some dress blues."

"Yes, Sir, but what for?"

"You will be staying at the White House, and there will be a party."

"Yes Sir, Sir, are you aware of Frank White, the writer of my book?"

"Yes, he contacted me and asked permission to do some book signings and interviews here and in New York."

"Great."

"Is it possible to get at least a two-week leave after my training at Bragg?"

"I'll see what I can do."

"Thank you, Sir, do I have a set of orders?"

"Yes, and I will get you your paycheck; we owe you for two months." "You will be staying at the White House; there will be a tailor for your dress blues."

"Yes, Sir."

"James, my name is Henry you need to loosen up."

"I only wish to show you the respect you deserve, Sir."

"I understand, but do you answer your friends with such respect."

"No, but how would you like me to address you."

"In private, Henry in public perhaps just general."

I smiled and said, "Alright, Henry."

He smiled back, shook my hand, and said, "Let's get you paid and settled in at the White House."

I got paid two months back pay, and my orders then the General and I went over to the White House.

"Have you ever been to Washington before James?"

"Yes, with a friend many years ago, I think President Johnson was president then."

We drove to a driveway with guards standing there, but we didn't have to stop we went right in.

"Do me a favor, Henry?"

"What favor is that?"

"This party they are going to have here make sure you're there."

"I'm going to be there for that event."

"Great, at least there will be someone I will know."

We entered the White House and then escorted to another room where the President and Mrs. Nixon greeted us. "It's a pleasure to meet you again, Captain York," said the President.

"The pleasure is mine, Sir."

"I'll take you to your room; it's the Lincoln room," said the President. We went up to the room, and he was explaining the room wasn't where Lincoln slept, but the bed and other furniture was his.

I saw my duffle bag in the room, and I went over to it and said, "Mr. President, did you get my book yet?"

"No, I haven't." I pulled two books out and handed one to the President and the other to General Arnold.

"I don't know if it is good or not, I haven't read it yet," I said.

"The way they are selling, I think you have a winner here," said the President.

The President gave me a tour of the White House when we got to the fitness room I asked, "Mr. President, may I use this room?"

"Yes, of course." The room not only had every kind of exercise equipment and weights, but it also had a full indoor pool I would be using this tonight. As we continued our tour, the President showed me the scar of where the White House got burnt in the war of eighteen twelve. I was surprised you could still see the scars of that war.

The President and his wife had to excuse themselves and said we would see me at dinner. The General also had to leave, and he said, "You need to go to Walter Reed tomorrow by 0 ten hundred hours."

"Alright, Henry."

I went back to my room, pulled out my book, and started to read it. I had read an hour, and I got amused that it made what happen to me sound more like a superhero story than what it was. There was a knock at the door, and I said, "Come on in."

It was a butler, I believe, and he said, "Sir, there is a Mr. Frank White who wishes to see you."

"Can he come into the White House?"

"Yes, Sir, he is here now."

"Ok, take me to him."

I walked into a room, Mr. White was standing there, and I went over to him then shook his hand.

"Well, Captain, when can you be ready to sign some books?"

"Anytime I guess, but tomorrow at ten in the morning, I have to go to Walter Reed."

"Well, get into your uniform, and let's go I arranged for a book signing." So, we went to a bookstore and put me behind a table with a bunch of books; then, the people lined up to get a signed book.

I was to sign for two hours, and then they would cut it off, but after two hours, there were so many people that I agreed to sign for a while more. As I left the bookstore, a young boy asked me to sign his book.

I was tired, but I took his book and said, "I'm surprised you would be interested in this kind of book, young man."

"My father was killed in Vietnam?"

I stared at the boy and asked, "What was your father's name?"

"Ronald Gleason." The name shot right through my heart.

"Was he a captain in the Army?"

"Yes, did you know him?"

"Yes, he was a good, brave man and my commanding officer."

His eyes started watering up, and I said, "Where do you live?"

"In Maryland."

"How did you get here?"

"By bus."

"Come with me." "I will get you a ride home." I hailed a cab, and along the way, I found out his name was Robert.

"I'll walk with you to the door." Robert opened the door and called for his mother, who was in a panic that her son was gone. When Mrs. Gleason saw me, she became taken aback, I assume, because I was in uniform and a Captain in the Green Berets.

"Hello, I'm Captain James York, I don't know if you know me, but I was at a book signing, and your son asked me to sign his book." "You will find your late husband's name in the book; he was my C.O." At that, she lost it and begged me to come into her house, which I did.

"Tell me about my husband."

"It was a long time ago, and I was an enlisted man I didn't know he had gotten killed, but the little time I spent with him, he seemed to be a good person, well organized and a take control person." I could see she was disappointed, so I asked, "Do you mind if I make a long-distance call, I think I know someone who knew him better than I."

"Yes, go ahead."

I went to her phone and called Fort Bragg. "Is Major Henderson there?" "I am Captain York."

"He is getting ready to leave, Captain."

"Tell him who I am and that this is important."

"What's going on York change your mind about training?"

"No Sir, this is something else, I'm in the home of Captain Ronald Gleason talking to his wife and son."

"Oh, please put her on the phone."

While they talked, which was for some time, I sat with Robert; we spoke of the military and his plans as far as the military. When he told me he wanted nothing to do with the Army, I said it wasn't the Army that killed his father; it was the enemy. I told him serving is the greatest gift one could give to his country. I said, "I respect your decision about the military but do it for the right reasons."

He put his head down and said, "My dad would have said the same as you."

"Major Henderson wants to talk to you, Captain," said Mrs. Gleason.

"Major."

"You will be here in about ten days?"

"Yes, unless General Arnold changes my orders."

"How are you feeling?"

"Sad but healthy."

"Understood."

"Major, do you have my book yet."

"No, I tried to get one, but the store sold out."

"I have a signed copy for you and Sergeant Brooks."

"Great, can't wait to read it."

"I better let you go Major it is a long-distance call."

"Alright, I will talk to you when you get here."

"Well I need to be going, can I use your phone to call a cab?"

"Yes, but I will drive you back."

"Thank you, but I think a cab will be better," I called a cab who said they would be there in ten minutes. I expressed my goodbyes, and in twenty minutes, I was back at the White House.

"Dinner will get served in ten minutes," said a servant. In ten minutes, he came back and showed me where to go. At the dinner table, the President and his wife were there as well as Vice President Ford and his wife, and they seated me by Mrs. Ford.

"It's a pleasure to meet you, James," the Fords said.

"It's an honor to meet both of you."

The first course came, and I said, "I wish to apologize to all of you before I start eating." "I have never learned etiquette when it comes to things like this; please correct me if I do something wrong it's the only way I will learn."

"Don't worry about your manners; we all had to learn at one point or another," said the President.

"Captain, I tried to get your book, but they sold out," said Mrs. Ford.

"I have extra copies; after dinner, I will get you one."

"We are having a ball in your honor Saturday," said Mrs. Nixon.

"I hope my dress blues are ready by then."

"They will be James," said the President.

"Who is going to be there, Sir," I asked the President.

"Senator Stuart Symington from Missouri, Congressman Richard Bolling also from Missouri, Congressman Craig Hosmer from California, Senator John Tunney also from California, joint chief of staff, General Abrams commander of European forces, General Mark Clark commander of NATO, and some dignitaries from around the world also a few celebrities."

"Sounds like a big party."

"Yes," said the President with a smile.

"You think you can add Frank White to that list."

"Who is he?" asked the President.

"He is the one who wrote my book and now is writing the second."

"It's as good as done," he replied.

"So, tell me, James, what's your party?" asked the President.

"Conservative Democrat, Sir, as is my father who voted for you."

"Oh, that's great what does your father do for a living?" asked President Nixon.

"He has his fingers in a lot of things he owns a lot of property; I believe my father is part owner of a bank, he does something for public works." "I can remember many people in his community coming to him for support for one cause or another."

"Your father sounds more like a Republican than a Democrat," said the Vice President.

"Well, that's my feeling; also, he votes for the man he is most comfortable, and most of the time, it is a Republican."

"Who do you vote for most of the time Captain?" asked Mrs. Nixon

"I've never been able to vote yet."

Mrs. Nixon was confused. The President said, "He was only eighteen when he started the military, and he was a prisoner of war."

"Oh, I'm sorry, Captain," Mrs. Nixon said apologetically.

"That's alright." We talked for the rest of the night about Vietnam and my childhood. Then I went to my room and gave the Fords a copy of my book.

The next day I headed to Walter Reed, and when I got there, Frank White was waiting for me.

"Mind if I follow you?"

"No, by the way, you are invited to the ball Saturday, don't say I never did anything for you."

"Great," I reported in and was told to wait, and when my turn came up, Frank and I went into the examination room, much to the hospital staff's objection. They gave me a full workup and then looked at my back and had me lay on my stomach while they worked on it. The hospital released me and said if I had any problem to report to medical at Fort Bragg.

"We have time for an interview," Frank said.

We talked with David Frost, and he asked, "What is off-limits for us to talk about, Captain?"

"I'll let you know if I can answer a question or not, but I can't think of anything right now."

"I would ask you not to take any cheap shots at me if we can agree to that." They prepared me for the interview then I went on a stage of sorts, and he started interviewing me.

He was fair with the interview, and there weren't any questions that I wouldn't answer; he seemed satisfied. After the interview, he said, "You know I have read your book, and I am surprised at how articulate you are."

"Well, if you speak honestly, one doesn't get nervous and say something they shouldn't." As Frank White and I got into a cab and left, I turned to him and asked, "How did I do?"

"Much better than I thought you would." "I have to arrange some things in New York tomorrow, so you won't have to deal with me tomorrow until night, then I will want to talk to you."

"Alright."

I got dropped off at the White House, and I went up to my room. I decided to talk to my parents and aunt, so I called my aunt first.

"Hello."

"Hello, Aunt Adeline, this is James."

"Jim, are you alright?"

"I'm alright, I thought I'd give you a call, can you guess where I'm staying and calling you from?"

"The White House."

"Yes, but in the Lincoln Room."

"Why that's wonderful?"

"Lincoln was a Republican."

"He was a different kind of Republican than they have now."

"How's my place," I said chuckling at what she said, she was a die-hard Democrat.

"It's fine; they are working hard on it."

"Well, let me know if there is any trouble."

"I will; I won't be watering for a while; it has been raining."

"I understand that."

"Well, say hello to everyone, and I will let you go."

"Alright, bye, Jim." Next, I called my parents; I figured my dad would just be coming home from work by now.

"Hello," answered my mother.

"Hello, this is Jim." "I'm in Washington D. C., at the White House and sleeping in the Lincoln Room."

"You are, how are you?"

"Yes, and I'm fine; I don't know when I will be able to call again with training and all."

"You want to talk to your father?"

"Yes."

"I'll go get him."

"Hi, dad."

"So, you're staying at the White House."

"Yes, in the Lincoln Room."

"Like I told Ma, I don't know when I will be able to call again because of training."

"Have you seen the President yet?"

"Yes, in fact, I had dinner with him and his wife also the Vice President and his wife."

"They are supposed to give me a big party on Saturday."

"So, when do you go for your training?"

"Next week Thursday."

"I'm guessing it's going to be rough."

"Oh, yes, I've been working out, and I feel strong." We talked a little more, then said our goodbyes.

I called for a servant, and when he came, I asked, "Tomorrow, I would like to tour Washington." "I was wondering if there is anyone here at the White House that would take me."

"Yes, Sir, it is my day off, but I am willing to take you."

"If it is your day off, I will pay you."

"That's not necessary, Sir."

"I insist, and I'll see you at about eight in the morning then?"

"Yes, Sir."

I put on my swimming trunks under my sweats and headed to work out. I didn't know that the last tour of the day was still visiting the White House. When I entered a corridor, they spotted me, and there was a clamor of noise, so I walked up to them and said, "Hello, I'm Captain James York."

"We all know who you are, Captain," said the tour guide.

"Is anyone here from California or Missouri?"

"I'm from California," said a female tourist.

"What part of California?"

"Downey."

"I've been to Downey; I am from the San Francisco Bay Area, born and raised there."

"Would you sign my book?" asked a tourist with a Texas accent.

"Sure, from what I understand, you're lucky to be able to find my book to buy."

I signed his book, and he asked, "I've read about half the book it sounds like you went through a lot of hell is it accurate?"

"I haven't read the whole book myself, but what I have read the book is true, and since I know the writer, I believe he has been truthful." "There will be a second book and movie about the first book soon from what I understand," I added.

I could see the tour guide want to get going, so I said, "Well, I have to be off now." "It's nice to meet you all." Everyone thanked me for talking to them, and I walked off to work out.

The next day William Baxter, the servant who told me he would give me a tour of Washington, was right on time. We had toured for three hours, mostly seeing the Smithsonian. We went through the Capital Building, where I spoke to some representatives. I then said to William, "Do you know any good place to eat William?"

201

"There are a lot of good places here to get something to eat."

"Any place is good for me; however, I do not prefer spicy food or anything with pumpkin in it, but any food is good to me."

"Have you ever been to James Town, Sir?"

"No, but it sounds like a good name for a town," I said with a smile.

"Mostly colored folk like me there, but there is a good place there if you don't mind going there," He said more seriously.

"Let's go?"

We ended up at a soul food restaurant in James Town.

As we got out of the cab, a young black man standing near the restaurant came up to us with an aggressive stance and said, "Old man, why you bringing that honkie here?"

"Don't you sass me negro this man here is a hero and a good person."

He looked at me up and down and said, "You take this honkie out of here before you, and he gets hurt." By this time, a crowd had gathered, and I was starting to get irritated.

"We are going in." "Neither you nor any other lowlife is going to stop us," said William Baxter as he grabbed the doorknob of the restaurant. This troublemaker wasn't going to let William get away with that and tried grabbing him but didn't quite make it.

I grabbed his wrist in a tight vice type grip, and I said, "You will be making a big mistake if you try anything, my friend."

He roared, "Fool, I'm going to kick your fuc." He didn't finish his sentence, and I had him on the ground. He got up like an enraged bull and charged me, bad mistake. I swung my fist, it sounded like an ax hitting a log, and he went down for good.

I grabbed him by the arm and lifted him and said, "Come on, I'll buy you lunch." He was a little woozy from the blow I gave him and didn't resist as we entered the restaurant.

We sat down, and a large black lady came up to us carrying water and said, chuckling, "You sure did show this mush head fool a lesson."

"Well, I didn't mean to hurt anyone."

"Don't worry yourself over a fool like him."

"Hello Mable, I brought you a very famous person."

"Well, introduce him, William."

"This here is James York hero of Vietnam?"

"You that white man I saw on TV get all those medals in Hawaii."

"Yes, I got a lot of medals."

By this time, the young man's head clear enough for him to say, "Yeah, the black man goes to war and gets kill the white man gets medals." Many in the restaurant were agreeing with him.

"Shut up, fool you want your ears boxed in again," said Mable.

"It's alright for him to express his opinion, you're right a lot of black people died and a lot of whites; also, it was a nasty war." "You're also right to the degree that more black people should have received more recognition; it was a black man who saved me; he is a real hero."

"Who is this black hero you are talking about?" asked Mable.

"Major William Henderson."

"How come we never heard of him?" someone asked.

"There is a book out about me, and in that book, it praises him for the way we interacted and what he did, and from what I understand, there will be a movie."

"Tell us more about him," the same person said.

"Let me get his order first?" said Mable.

"I'll have fried chicken." After ordering, I said, "Major Henderson is in the special forces, the Green Berets as I am now."

"At the time, he was a Lieutenant and my squad leader." "He led us with honor, thinking not of himself, but everyone else, and he was wounded doing so."

"Where is he now?" asked Mable.

"Fort Bragg, North Carolina."

"He commands the Green Berets training center, that's where I will be under him in a few days."

We got our food, and Mable said, "To think Major Henderson, a black hero and he is a major such a high rank."

"I only mention him because I know him there are others like General Colin Powell, who I am sure you will hear a lot about in the future." William and I finished eating and went back to sightseeing, and then I paid him and went back to the White House.

About seven o'clock that night, Frank White showed up, and I went downstairs and talked to him. "Tomorrow, we will leave early for New York. We will do a book signing first; then, you will have two interviews with Walter Cronkite of CBS and the Tonight Show with Johnny Carson."

"Alright."

"Then the next day we will go to Virginia for a book signing."

"Alright, what's with the movie?"

"Oh yes, I'm glad you reminded me, we will be signing contracts and the producer will talk with you tomorrow."

"It seems like everything has been going well."

"Better than good wait till you see the next check for your book you will get when you get back from your training."

The next day I joined the President and First Lady for breakfast, "How has your time been here, James?" asked the President.

"Great." "I'm going to miss it when I go to North Carolina."

"What are your plans for today?" asked the First Lady.

"Frank White is taking me to New York for interviews and a book signing."

"I finished reading your book very well written and almost unreal," said the President.

"I've read it also; it's true, Sir." It irritated me that the President had doubts, but Frank White was true to his word he wrote it as it was.

I had just finished breakfast when Frank White showed up, and we caught a cab to the airport. We went to the book signing, and after nearly two hours, Frank had to get more books because the store ran out. I signed books for about another two hours and then we went to lunch. We then went to an interview with Walter Cronkite. I met him first while I was in makeup, and he asked, "Is there anything that you don't want me to ask."

"I don't think so if there is, I will tell you and let you know why."

At the interview, he said, "I have read your book, and it was very gripping."

"Yes, Frank White did an excellent job writing it."

"How much input did you have in writing?"

"He interviewed me and those around me; all I told him was I wanted the truth and not to make it sound like a biography."

"You have read the book?"

"Yes, this is your interview, but I think it would be a good idea to bring Frank into this conversation he is here."

"I would agree with you, and after the break, we will see if Frank White will join us." Frank went to makeup, and they brought in an extra chair for the interview.

"You have made a lot of money because of you and your comrades' trials."

"What do you consider a lot of money?" I asked.

"Well, I understand you are worth millions of dollars."

I laughed and said, "I don't know who researches for you, but he or she needs to get talked to."

"You say you're not a millionaire?"

"No, I'm not saying that what I am saying is the person doing the research needs to find out where I got that money."

"So, where did you get your money?"

"My father has wisely invested a lot of money from my back pay." "I bought some property in Missouri, which contained a lot of valuables on it, and yes, I did make some money from royalties of the book."

"So, you're saying you didn't do well from the royalties of the book."

"James made at this point considerably less than a million on the book," said Frank.

"Mr. Cronkite, what is your concern about how much money I made?"

"None, but there were a lot of other men involved in what happened."

"Yes, and everyone I consider a hero," I said.

"Mr. Cronkite, I have interviewed everyone who is still alive none felt like they were getting a raw deal." "Everyone was thrilled that the story was going to be published," said Frank.

"Alright, let's go on to another subject," said Walter Cronkite.

"Captain, as I said, I read the book, and to me, you seemed invincible, almost like a superhero." "Especially how you admitted you were before you went to Vietnam."

"You should interview Major Henderson or better Sergeant Brooks, who was with me from the beginning; all that is in the book is true if it weren't someone who was with me would have said something."

"Where are these two people?"

"Fort Bragg." The conversation went on for about another thirty minutes before it was over, then Frank and I left irritated.

We headed to the Tonight Show and made it in time, and they took both of us to makeup and then to the Green Room. I remember watching Johnny Carson bring a guest on his show who wrote books, and he acted as if he had read each book, but I thought it was all an act, but it turns out he reads every book, and in my case, it was the same. The interview went well; he had embarrassing pictures of me when I was young, but I didn't care. What interested me was Jimmy Stewart was the next guest after me. I was a huge fan of his.

"Our next guest is Jimmy Stewart," Johnny Carson said. Frank and I both stood up to shake Jimmy Stewart's hand.

"James, did you know that Mr. Stewart was in the Air Force?" asked Johnny.

"Yes, he is a retired General, and it's an honor to sit beside him; he is my favorite adult male actor ever since I was a child."

"Who is your most favorite female actor?" Mr. Stewart asked.

"Katherine Hepburn." The rest of the show went on with Johnny Carson talking and joking with Jimmy Stewart, and then we said our goodbyes, we left to meet with the movie people about my film.

"Just what do you wish, Captain, regarding this movie we hope to film?" asked the representative of the film company.

"I wish it to be exciting, gripping, and true, don't sugar coat it." "Get some good, well-known actors, in other words, don't make it a B movie." "I would suggest you film either in the Philippines, Thailand, or even Fort Bragg, North Carolina." "Where you can use the Army and especially the Green Berets, but it's up to you."

"So how much do you want?" the film people asked.

I looked over to Frank, and the people representing the Penguin Group. Todd Zimmerman from Penguin said, "Three hundred thousand guarantees and twenty percent of profit and the Captain also has the final say on the script."

The film people looked at each other astonished at what he demanded, then they said, "Let us talk about this privately."

"Alright."

"They will come back with an offer, but I think we got them," said Frank.

"Alright, gentlemen, this is what we feel is fair." "We will give Captain York three hundred thousand and ten percent of the profit, and we have a problem with the Captain having the final say on the script, so no on that."

"Ten percent is too small eighteen percent, and Penguin will take three percent of the eighteen, and the Captain has last say on the script," said the Penguin people.

"So, what you are saying is that we don't have to pay Penguin anything?"

"Yes, and no, we will take three percent of the eighteen, and James will get fifteen."

"We will agree to that, but I still have a problem with the Captain having control over the script."

"You won't have any problem with me unless you decide to make a cheap B movie."

"Do you think we would make a cheap movie, Captain?"

"It has happened before, and I am not willing to take the chance what I want is this movie to be an award-winning academy movie."

"I will know right away what kind of movie it will be by the actors that you get and your script."

They all looked at each other and then said, "If we give you a list of the main actors and the script, will you listen to us the reason we want to do something a certain way."

"Of course, as I said, you will have little trouble from me unless you try to cheapen the movie." "Besides, I am going to be busy with the military, so I will only have so much time to deal with it."

"Then I believe we have a deal," said the movie people. After this, I went back to Washington D. C. without Frank, who said he would see me tomorrow to take me to Richman, Virginia.

The next day about ten in the morning, Frank and I went to Virginia to sign some books.

Saturday came, and one of the White House servants brought me my dress blues that afternoon. The party wouldn't be starting until about seven that night. "Is there anything I can help you with, Sir?" asked William Baxter.

"No, well, maybe is there anything I should know, so I don't look like a fool at the party, you know, etiquette."

"I could coach you on a few things, Sir, if you wish."

"That would be great." It turned out that the President sent William for this purpose, so I got instructed for the next couple of hours.

"William, will you be at this party?"

"Yes, Sir."

"Good stay close to me and let me know if I do something wrong."

"Yes, Sir," he said with a smile.

I went downstairs and stood in the receiving line, and I had white gloves on as instructed by William, and as the people filed passed, I greeted everyone. The place seemed festive with decorations; there was plenty of food and drinks, and what looked like a Marine Band.

After the receiving line, the President, First Lady, and I mingled with the guest. After talking to many of the guests, including the representatives of California and Missouri, I ended up with General Arnold, General Clark, and General Abrams. "After your training at Fort Bragg, where do you wish to be posted, James?" asked General Arnold.

"I'm not sure, perhaps Germany." "I understand there is a lot of problems there, or maybe I will just retire."

"What do you mean, my people in Germany are in great shape?" said General Abrams surprised at what I said.

"I'm willing to bet they aren't, but it's not your fault those company commanders have a way of covering up things."

"I think you are wrong, Captain," General Arnold replied disbelievingly.

"General, I'll bet you I could pick any unit at random." "If you don't tell them we're coming, I will show you overwhelmingly evidence of sloppiness, drugs, security breaches, and faulty equipment."

"And what do you want if you're right, and what do I get if you are wrong?"

"If I'm right, I wish your friendship and a promotion to major," I said with a smile.

"I consider you my friend no matter what, but what do I get if I'm right?"

"I'll serve you anywhere you want for another three years."

General Abrams looked at General Arnold and Clark with a devious smile on him. Then he said, "Alright, after you finish your training at Fort Bragg, I'll send orders for you to report to me in Frankfurt where we will hammer out the details."

"Can I still get a two-week leave after my training finishes first, General Arnold?"

"Yes, I would like to see what you will find in Germany."

"General Abrams, then the bets on, but just don't tell your troops to clean up their act."

"I won't, and you, young man, watch me win this bet."

After talking to General Arnold about my cousin Allen, I went to speak to Frank. Frank said, "You got an excellent deal with that movie contract."

"Oh yeah, how much do you think I will make out of it?"

"Several million, I would think."

"Several million?"

"Maybe as much as fifty million."

"Really?"

"Yeah."

"When do I get to see any of the money?"

"Oh, you will see plenty by the time you finish training."

"By the way Monday, I want to take you to Chicago for another book signing and interview."

"Alright."

"So, what was the conversation with the generals all about?"

"I have a bet with General Abrams if I win, I will get promoted."

"And what happens if you lose?"

"He can do what he wishes with me for the next three years."

"You think you will win?"

"Don't know, but I believe so."

The rest of the night, I talked to the remainder of the people there. The Austrian ambassador I spoke about my love for music. I told the California representative about my father, who he was interested in meeting, and the Missouri representative I told him about my home in the south of the state. After the party, I was thinking how much my life could have been different if I didn't go into the military those many years ago. However, then there is good and bad no matter what path one goes down.

Sunday, I decided to go to church. I decided to try a Mormon Church to see how it compared to what Lieutenant Pickett preached. It was much like what he preached and described. Many there recognized me, and I talked to some about Lieutenant Pickett. They wanted me to come to their other meetings, but I declined and went back to the White House to do another workout.

Frank and I went to Chicago and Detroit for book signings and interviews they went pretty much the way they did before, but it was hectic with all the traveling. In the end, Frank and I went back on separate planes. He told me before we departed that he wouldn't be bothering me for a while and said good luck at Fort Bragg.

The day I was to leave, I had breakfast with the President and First Lady, I thanked them for their hospitality, then I packed up my things and left for Fort Bragg North Carolina.

10

FORT BRAGG

I arrived at Fort Bragg just before eleven in the morning. I got instructed at the main gate on how to find the Special Forces unit. I swung my duffle bag over my shoulder, grabbed my suitcase with the other hand, and started walking. I didn't get far when a Sergeant in a jeep asked, "You going to the Green Berets headquarters?"

"Yes."

"Thought so, hop in, I'm Sergeant Carl Edwards."

"I'm Captain James York, and I would assume you are in the Berets."

"You would assume correct, and I do know who you are, Sir, we have been expecting you." He dropped me off in front of the headquarters building, and I went in with my duffle bag and suitcase.

"Captain York reporting to Major Henderson," I said to a Sergeant.

"Yes, Sir, we've been expecting you." He pressed a button and said, "Captain York is here, Sir." "You can go right in, Sir."

"Thanks." I grabbed my things, entered Major William Henderson's office, and said while handing him my orders, "Captain York reporting as ordered."

"Sit down, relax James, your training won't start until tomorrow." Just then, there was a knock at the door and in walked Sergeant Major Brooks.

"James, I see you didn't decide to pass up the training," the Sergeant said with a smile. I notice that the Major didn't like what the Sergeant said, and I think I know why.

"I guess there are some in this room who thought I wouldn't."

The Sergeant started laughing, and the Major said, looking at the Sergeant and then me, "I thought because of the way I last saw you, you might not come, but I can see physically you have shaped up." He looked at my orders, and personal file then said, confused, "When did you go airborne?"

"Hawaii." The Major looked at the Sergeant, who stopped laughing. "I did pretty well, I think."

"How good?" asked the Major.

"He was twenty feet from the target and was standing when he hit the ground," said the Sergeant."

"That is pretty good."

"Yes, Sir, it sure is," said the Sergeant.

"We are going to wave some of your training, so it isn't as long, but don't think it will be any easier."

"I don't want to be treated differently from the rest."

"You won't be, I can care less about your rank, what you went through, or our friendship while you are going through the training." I nodded, and he continued, "You won't have to go through airborne training, Sergeant Brooks said you could speak German, how well?"

"I speak, read, and write German like a native?"

"Think you can pass a language test?"

"Yes."

"Good, you pass it, and you won't have to take a language course."

"You must specialize in two areas I would suggest Intelligence and Operations some of the training I can wave."

"That would be just fine."

"What will be your other specialty?"

"Weapons," I said.

"Yes, good choice I may be able to wave part of the training on this one, but I want to see how good you are."

"Yes, Sir."

"There is some other training I can wave, all in all; your training will be for about three months."

"Yes, Sir."

"Now to put you somewhere, how about building three is there any room Sergeant."

"Yes Sir, three quit their training yesterday."

"Understand James; we are not your friend until you finish your training."

"Yes, I understand."

"Alright, Sergeant, take him to his quarters." I got up and started to leave when the Major said in German, "You forgot something, didn't you?"

"What did I forget, Sir?" I replied in German.

"The book."

"Oh, yes."

I pulled out two books, then handed one to the Major and the other to Sergeant Brooks and asked, "What's with the German?"

"Just testing you."

I started to leave and said, "Did I pass?" I didn't wait for an answer as I went; I heard him say yah while he was laughing.

I entered the barracks, and I chose a lower bunk.

"Your rank won't matter here, and if they want to know where you come from, tell them that you came from another unit."

"Don't you think that some of these guys might recognize me?"

"I don't know some might; then you are on your own." "There is one guy here that thinks he is God's gift to the Green Berets, and he will try to push you around."

"He won't be able to."

"I don't know he is a pretty big guy."

"I'll try not to hurt him too badly."

The Sergeant had left, and I had already hung up my things and had been resting on my bunk reading when I heard some of the Green Berets candidates coming, so I put my book away.

Little by little, they all trickled in eyeballing me as they came in finally one big guy came to me and said, "Who in the hell are you?"

I looked up and said, "A voice crying in the wilderness."

"Oh, a comedian well I'm Luther Parks, I'm the toughest mother fucker you ever saw, and I run this team."

"Parks, don't let your parakeet ass overpower your alligator mouth." "I don't intend to take any shit from you unless someone orders me to," I said. He turned beet red and grabbed for me, but before he could get me, I kicked him in the nuts, and he went down moaning. "If you're wise, you will just lay there and thank heaven you can still make babies." He got up breathing fire and came at me; I let him have it with a right hook that could be heard back at the headquarters building, and he stumbled back but didn't fall he came at me again, and he swung his big meat claws, but he was too slow. I came back with another right to the face and a left hook to the side of his head, and he went down he got back up but was shaky, and I gave him a crescent kick, and he went down for good much to the shock of the others. "I believe the Green Berets operate as a team not run by one individual, I'm James York, and I am here to finish training." "I'm not here to cause trouble but will handle it if it comes."

Someone drugged Parks to the shower, and he woke up and didn't bother me anymore that day. The next day we were divided into several groups, and I went to the weapons range we shot everything that they had. I had to figure out how some of the weapons worked but still could shoot expert with all of them, however, at the pistol range something happen that hadn't happened for a long time. I started to fire, then every target turned into the N.V.R., and I was back in Vietnam again.

"Nice shooting York," said an instructor. That is what woke me from my trance, I looked at the targets, and everyone I shot square in the head. I didn't say anything to anyone after I finished lunch. I then went back for more training. We went to an obstacle course, which I did with ease, and then some P.T. before the day was ended. Those men who I was with were impressed with how well I did that day.

As we went back to the barracks, one soldier named Allen Green asked me, "Are you that same York from Nam."

"Yes."

"I thought so, but didn't they make you a Green Beret already?"

"They did, but they felt I could use some more training."

The next day I was told I didn't need weapons training and was sent to a building to take a language test.

"What language do you speak," asked a female proctor.

"German."

"And how well do you speak it?"

"I am fluent in reading, writing, and speaking."

"What dialect are you most comfortable in?"

"East Upper German Central Bavarian."

"Alright, then we will start with the reading." She handed me a test booklet. The questions were easy; I would read a paragraph and answer questions from it. The test took about an hour when I finally finished; then, she handed me a piece of paper with a topic written in German. I had to write at lease a three-hundred-word essay on my thoughts on people wearing lederhosen or short leather pants. I thought a moment then started writing in German, correcting the notion that all lederhosen were short pants. It took me only about forty-five minutes to complete the essay, and that surprised the proctor.

"Wait a few minutes, and we will get someone to give you the last test, I didn't expect you to finish so soon," she said. She was correcting my first paper when she finally finished. She couldn't do the second test because she couldn't read German, the person who was coming would have to read it and grade it. I had to wait about twenty minutes when an older man came in and said something to the female proctor, and then she handed him my essay and pointed at me. The older man motioned to me to follow him.

"You're in luck I am Austrian," He said in German.

"Where are you from in Austria?"

"A small village called Mondsee, the town is near Salzburg."

"And where are you from?"

"Now or when I was a child?"

"Where did you grow up?"

"California San Francisco Bay Area."

"You speak German well is that your nationality?"

"Yes and no, I am German, Spanish, and Portuguese."

"Oh, then you learn German while in school."

"No, not really, I took German in high school, but it was a different kind of German I think High German."

"I learned German when I was a little boy at a very young age."

"Why, German?"

I turned red in the face and then said, "I always wanted to be a Vienna Choir Boy."

"Could you sing?"

"Yes, very good."

"Why didn't you try out for them?"

"My parents didn't have the money to send me for an audition."

"Well, there were plenty of excellent choirs in the United States."

"None like the Vienna Boys Choir; they are the world's best."

"Your right?"

"Let me look at your paper." He started laughing and said, "Most of what you said is correct, but I notice you write like a schoolchild, I assume because of your lack of practice."

"Yes," I said with a smile.

"Have you ever been to Europe?"

"No, but in a few months, I will be going to Frankfurt, Germany."

"That's wonderful."

"I feel you passed that essay with a mark of very good?"

"Good, what's next?"

"What's next, what do you mean next?" He said, confused.

"I was told there are three parts to this test."

"Yes, you already took the third part?"

"I do not understand."

"The third part is carrying a conversation which you did very well."

"So, you are saying I passed your entire test."

"Yes, and it was nice talking to someone who speaks German as well as you do." "I'll send the results to your commanding officer."

I went into the headquarters building and said, "I finished the language test." "What am I scheduled next to do?"

"P.T. then a survival class," said a sergeant who was a clerk.

"I thought I didn't have to take any survival classes?"

"Well, they have you down for it, Sergeant Major Brooks and Major Henderson are over at the mess hall go talk to them about it."

I went over to the mess hall, got a tray, and went to where the Major and Sergeant Major was then said, "Mind if I take a seat."

"Yes, go ahead," said the Major.

"I heard about your ruckus at the barracks," said the Major.

"Wasn't much of a ruckus Parks wanted to push me around as he does with the others, and I wasn't going to allow him to do it to me."

"He'll try to get even with you," said the Sergeant Major.

"Wouldn't be advisable on his part, but maybe he is one of those people who likes pain."

"One of these days you will come up against someone who will be too much for you to handle," said the Major.

"Yes, but those people I make my best friends like you two," I stated with a smile. "Major, why am I being sent to a survival class?"

"Because you have some extra time, and that class will help you with your wilderness survivor test." "How was the language test?"

"Oh, I passed it easily; they will send you the results."

The class was about edible plants and animals. After taking the course, I felt better about it, but many of the plants I knew of already. It appeared the edible plants were in the west somewhere. The training during the following week was bodybuilding and survival training, which suited me just fine. Wednesday, we did take a break from our routine; instead, we did some rock climbing, which I wasn't very fond of but completed. Of course, Parks took great joy in seeing my misery; he was good at it. Saturday, I decided to go for a run when I got back to the barracks; everyone was staring at me. I sat down on my bunk to remove my boots when Parks came over and threw my book on my bunk.

"So, you're a Captain and a big-time war hero."

"I thought my things in my locker were personal and private."

"We have a right to know."

"Why, what difference does it make?"

"He is right; it makes no difference," said Tom Willingham.

"Shut up, Tom," replied Parks.

"He has the C.M.H.," Tom added.

"It makes no difference I'm the top dog here he just got lucky the last time," he retorted.

At that, I got up and said irritated, "Any time you want to challenge me, go right ahead, you're not top anything to me."

"Not now, but the time will come soon."

I grabbed my book, and Tom Willingham said, "When you finish that book, you think I could read it."

I looked at him and said as I handed the book to him, "It's yours."

The next week was the same as the last, including rock climbing, and we had to find our way from one point to another, which was twenty miles away. The one good thing about that exercise was that the men in the barracks got divided in half, and Parks wasn't in my group. After this last training three days later, we all went to an area where there was a raised platform about two feet off the ground. When I saw the platform, I immediately started to sweat and had a flashback of the first prison camp but quickly got over it. We got told to move around the platform and sit down, then an instructor got up on top of the platform and said, "I will be showing you some advance hand to hand techniques."

"Now, can I have two volunteers?"

Parks jumped up on the platform and said to me, "York, why don't you come up here if you're not afraid or are you a coward." I got up and hopped on the platform. The instructor explained something, then put Parks and me together. Parks had a smirk on his face, and I knew he was up to something. We got instructed to make a move where Parks would attack me in a certain way, and I would block and prevent it. We got into position, and the instructor told us to move. I must have gotten sloppy because Parks didn't follow what he was supposed to do. He started out doing it right, but when he got near to me, he swung his big meat hooks connecting to my cheek, drawing blood, and I went flying onto the mat in a daze. My head cleared up quickly, and I looked up and saw Parks laughing and acting smug. The instructor came back on the platform to protested Park's actions, and that was my cue to get up as he pushed the instructor away and said, "I won't kill him. I just want to hurt him."

"Cheap shot Parks," I said.

Parks turned to me and said, "No cheaper than what you did."

Like a charging bull, he charged me, and I slammed my size nine into his stomach, and when he bent over, I let him have it with a left to the side of his head. He was stung, but he didn't go down; that was his mistake. He came at me clumsily I either block his swings or avoided them. He even tried to throw a kick, but he was too slow and missed. I hit him several times in the face and then did a roundhouse kick to the head and Parks few off the platform. He tried to get up but was unable to and fell back to the ground. The instructor got on the platform and said, "Now that was interesting."

Nothing happened to Parks or me, and I was all right with that. I figured that the Major and Sergeant Major knew about it but let it ride. Parks again left me alone and didn't bother me, but by no means were we friends. I had not known that Frank White had been at Fort Bragg all this time watching me from a distance, and he saw almost everything. Everything we did for the rest of the time was to build ourselves up physically, to be able for the team and me to survive and to complete the mission. I was doing good most of the guys liked me; however, there were a few followers of Parks that wanted nothing to do with me. Finally, we were all gathered, I had not seen Major Henderson or Sergeant Major Brooks for some time, but they were both there and, in the back, was Frank White with a smile on his face. Major Henderson and Sergeant Major Brooks stood up in front of us, and the Sergeant quieted us down. The Major came forward and said, "Next week, all of you will be flown to an undisclosed place at night and dropped off for your final survival exercise." "You fail this exercise will mean you do not meet the requirements of the Army Special Forces." "The first three days, no one will be hunting you after that an attachment of Marines will go after you." "You will have twenty days to reach your goal should you get captured; it doesn't mean you have failed; you will be in a prison camp, and it won't be pleasant." I had no intention of going to any prison camp. "This will be the first time you will go on this exercise with the rank you came into this unit." "That makes Captain James York your team leader."

"That doesn't give us a fair chance, Sir," Parks protested angrily.

"What doesn't give you a fair chance Sergeant Parks?

"That Captain will get us all captured."

"Why do you say that?"

"He was so incompetent he got himself captured in Vietnam."

You could see the anger on Major's and Sergeant Major's face, and the Major said, "What do you know about Captain York?"

"Just what people told me, he was on a mission and was captured."

"I was his team leader on that mission, and Sergeant Major Brooks was with him at the prison camps." "It was I who got many men killed, and Captain York and Sergeant Major Brooks captured." "We were able to medivac out because the Sergeant Major and James stayed behind holding the enemy back." "So, Parks, do you have any more objections?" Parks shook his head no and remained quiet. Just what I had thought we loaded up into a plane and headed west, I knew this because I had a compass on my knife handle. I calculated the number of hours we were in the air as to how far west we went. I figured we were near the Sierra Nevada Mountains, perhaps more on the Nevada side. We were going to jump out of the plane, and I wasn't pleased about that, but I jumped. When we hit the ground, I surveyed the area, and I saw some high ground with some rocks to protect us from the elements, so we all headed for that area.

I sent two out to get wood for a fire, and Parks said, "Any fool would know a fire might be detected."

"You forget Parks for the first three days they won't hunt us."

"Why don't you take two guys and go look for food, animal tracks, and any dangers out there."

"What are you going to do?"

"Tell you what to do now, move out." We got our campfire started and then about an hour and thirty minutes later, Parks, and the two men he took with him came back and sat around the campfire with the rest of us. "What did you find?" I asked Parks. "I found some deer tracks a lot of birds but nothing else except a tree that had some fruit on it." I notice he took all the credit for himself.

"Was the fruit edible?"

"Of course, they were apples," he said irritably.

"Alright, we will go to the tree at first light and pick as much fruit as we can carry."

"What for we have food we need to get to our pick-up point quickly or do you want to get captured," Parks growled.

"What happens after the food runs out in a few days besides what I said isn't up for debate; we go get the apples at first light." Parks was angered enough to do something but didn't and sat down across from me. "I figure we are in the Sierra Nevada's on the east side."

"You don't know that for sure there is no way anyone could know," Parks said arrogantly.

"I kept an eye on my compass as we flew on the plane and then calculated the time, and I didn't feel circling." "Besides, I use to roam the Sierra Nevada Mountains as a kid, and I know there is a Recon Marine base on the Nevada side," I said.

"That doesn't mean anything," Parks said.

"You know Parks; you're starting to get on my nerves." Parks laid down on his back, pulled his gunny hat down over his eyes, and acted as if he didn't want to hear anymore.

I had a habit of waking up before dawn, and this morning was no different. I woke everyone up, saying, "Five minutes, we move out." Parks and the two other men showed us where the apples were, and we picked and packed away as many as we could. Some were eating the apples already, and I said, "Bury the apple core when you are finished." I looked over to Parks, and before he could say anything, I said, "If the Marines finds a core, they can track us." We hiked for about seven hours, checking where we were every hour or so. I assigned myself because I had the map and two others to check our location to make sure we headed in the right direction. By early afternoon, we started to get into some rough country, so I found a safe spot with some cover, and we took a break. After about ten minutes, I could see Parks was getting antsy. It wasn't long before he said not too friendly, "We should be hiking towards our pick-up point instead of wasting our time sitting here."

I was going to say something, but one of the other men said, "Shut up, Parks, the Captain is doing just fine."

This enraged Parks, but I said, "Parks is right." "I figure those Marines will calculate how far we will travel and try to pinpoint us." "I think we should push it and get in as many miles as possible it will confuse them; they won't expect it until the end."

"See I was right, let's go?" We all got up and headed out after about six hours I spotted a place we could sleep for the night, but it was an hour away. When we got there, it was dark, and everyone was exhausted, even Parks, we must have traveled nearly fifty miles today.

Someone was about to light a fire, and I said, "No more fires, eat something and then get some sleep we move out before dawn."

The next morning, I picked two men to take point with the instructions to check with me every hour and two men to follow drag. We traveled for eight hours when we came to a gorge that I couldn't see how we could get across. "Well isn't this just fine you led us all this way to what, fine commander you are," said Parks.

"Shut up, Parks."

"Don't tell me to shut up, what are you going to do."

I about had it with Parks, so I pulled out my knife and got into his face and said with fury, "If you say one more word to me, I will cut your damn tongue out and shove it in your ass." He backed off, and I sent two men to scout out a way across the gorge to the left and right. We waited for about an hour, and the man who went left returned and didn't have any good news. However, about ten minutes later, the man who went right had better news; there was a way across, but it wasn't going to be easy. We all headed to the crossing, and the man was correct; it wasn't going to be easy, but it was possible. We slowly crossed the gorge, which took about two hours to travel about six hundred yards. Once over the other side, we hiked for another two hours before we stopped for the night.

The next day as we were going, I had two new people walking point and drag. I notice that Parks stayed to himself or with his followers; it was just as well I didn't want to talk to him anyway. Before noon, we came upon some water, which was a good thing because we were just about out. At our noon break, I said, "Today is the official day for the Marines will be looking for us so for now on keep quiet and keep your eyes open." I figured that would shut up Parks without telling him directly. In the next few days, we continued traveling towards our goal, knowing that we were in more danger as we got nearer. We came to a stream, and I had an idea I asked everyone if they had any apples left or any rations. When I got what I wanted, I told two men, "Go upstream about one or two miles. Throw an apple core on one this side of the bank, and on the other, throw an empty wrapper and break a few small twigs on the far side of the bank and leave some footprints then walk back down here through the water to us."

Of course, Parks complained about waiting at the stream and wanted to know why I sent the two men upstream. When I told him, he still wasn't satisfied, and I just ignored him. About an hour later, the two men came back, and we went in the water downstream about three miles. I looked for an area to leave the stream and found it with an outcropping of flat granite that we all walked out on.

We had traveled for two days, and there were still no signs of the Marines. Food was getting low, and some were grumbling, mostly Parks and his followers. We found some food sources but not enough; this area had been used so much from past teams; it brought the quantity of food low. As the days went by, we took it slower and slower because of the lack of food and sometimes water. The good news was we were within thirty to thirty-five miles by my estimate from our pick-up point over some very rough terrain. I figure it should take, at the rate we were moving, about three or four days to reach the place if we did not get caught first. We had been lucky so far; we hadn't run into the enemy yet, but I thought I did see some smoke far off. There were plenty of copters flying around that we hid from with lots of camouflage and cover. We had been out fourteen days when we came to a canyon that we had to pass through. It had a stream running through it, so we filled up our canteens. As I look up the canyon, I thought it would be a reasonable place for an ambush. I looked around and saw a faint trail to the left of me going along the canyon wall. "We are going to go up the canyon wall instead of going down through the canyon floor."

"What for, it's easier and quicker going through the canyon floor?" Parks said.

"Yes, you're right, Parks, but it is an easy ambush place, and we are near our pick-up area where better to do an ambush."

"I'm tired of you; I'm going down the canyon who's going with me."

"I'm not going to fight you Parks, but if you go you will be disobeying a direct order, and I will report it."

"We'll see who gets in trouble when I tell them what you put us through, now who will go with me." Two of his friends joined him, and we headed up the canyon wall as they went down the canyon. We traveled for about three hours, and it was starting to get dark, but I knew we had to keep moving until we could find a large enough place to rest for the night. On the canyon floor, I could see a small fire just where I would figure Parks was, and I did not doubt that he was going to get himself captured. After climbing another hard hour, we did find a wide enough spot to camp for the night. I posted guards both above us and down below us. I was woken very early in the morning by some pops I looked down the canyon and seen a lot of sparks coming from Parks' campfire, and then the campfire got larger. I knew he got himself captured, so I woke up the men and sent someone down to get the guard down the trail, and we headed out slowly, picking up the guard in front of us.

The sun was up an hour when we came to a fork in the trail, one going up to the rim, the other heading back down towards the Canyon floor. I had five guys go up towards the rim for about five hundred yards and then come back here. I then had everyone rest until I got back, and I went down the trail to see if we were getting followed. I traveled for about an hour, and I could see the path for quite a way back, so I waited. My wait got rewarded with the sighting Marines coming up the trail, and Parks was in the front leading them. I moved out quickly back to my men, "Parks is leading the enemy towards us, and I am guessing there are Marines some place at the end of this canyon, but I have an idea." The trail dropped quickly. I had the last man wipe out our tracks from the path as we went. We kept as quiet as possible as we got nearer and nearer to the bottom. I had my eyes open for concealment and near the bottom of the hill, and I found it. There were several boulders with some brush around it was enough to conceal us, and we moved behind them and waited. Twenty minutes later, about twenty-five Marines passed us going fast up the trail. We waited for about fifteen minutes, and then we headed out of the canyon and towards our pick-up place. We had to move out quickly before they figured out what we did. The pick-up point was only three miles beyond the canyon.

We were a mile from the pick-up point when the man I had back in drag came running up and said, "They're coming fast." We moved out at a run and made it to the pick-up site before the Marines. We sent out a signal to be picked up and then took cover.

The Marines came running into the clearing, and I went out behind them and said, "The exercise is over; we made it to the pick-up point."

"You made nothing; we never let any of you Army heroes get by us."

"Well, we just got by you."

The Marine I was talking to lost his patience and said, "I had enough of this grab him we will take him and the rest of them when we find them to the prison camp." Two Marines tried to grab me. I knocked one to the ground with a single blow to the face, and the other I grabbed his rifle, and by doing this, I flipped him over my head.

That got the attention of the rest of the Marines, but while they were pointing their rifles at me, my men pounced on them, and I said, "I told you the exercise is over, we won."

"You won't get away with this; more will be pouring in here soon."

"Then I will tell them the same thing." Just then, I heard the thump of helicopters coming. Two Chinook helicopters landed in the clearing not far from us. Then out hopped Major Henderson and Sergeant Major Brooks with some other men.

"What's going on here, James?" asked the Major.

"These Marines don't like to lose."

"Explain."

"Well, Sir, all except three, we manage not to get captured and made it to the pick-up point, and we contacted you."

"These Marines somehow knew where the pickup point was and followed us up here at a fast pace." "When I informed them, we made it to the pick-up point and contacted you. They wanted to take us to the prison camp anyway, even when they knew the exercise was over." "I disagreed with them as did the rest of the men, so we disarm them until you came."

"Who are you, Lieutenant?"

"I'm Lieutenant Morris, Sir."

"Is what the Captain said, correct?"

"Some of it, Sir."

"What part isn't incorrect?"

"We found them here because we track them, Sir."

"You tracked us running; you must be the world's greatest tracker," I said. Just then, many more Marines showed up with a Lieutenant Colonel.

"What's the problem here, Major?" asked the Lieutenant Colonel.

"Seems like your Marines tried to capture and bring back my men to your prison camp when they had already reached the pick-up point and called us." "I said, tried because my men captured and disarmed them when they wouldn't listen to Captain York tell them the exercise was over."

"Lieutenant, how did you know where the pick-up point was?" The Lieutenant Colonel asked the Lieutenant in charge of the Marine team.

"We track them, Sir."

"They couldn't have they were running for several miles trying to get us, and then they stopped at the pick-up point, Sir," I said.

"Who are you?" "Captain James York."

"Oh yes, you're the reason I join in this operation."

"Lieutenant, I will give you one chance to come clean on how you knew about this pick-up point." "If I must do an investigation, you will be in danger of losing your commission."

"We might have run across a map of where they were going to get picked up, Sir."

"I'll talk to you more about this later, Lieutenant."

"My apologies, Major, your men did an excellent job, but we do have three of your men."

"Yes, Sir, Parks, Jenkins, and Sollie." "I'll talk to you about it in private."

"Alright, James, but I think I know what went on."

"Colonel, they are prisoners of war put them through your prison camp." We gave the Marines back their rifles and started to load up in the Chinooks.

"Major, do you mind if I hitch a ride back with you and the Captain."

"No hop on board." The Lieutenant Colonel told the Marines to bring the three prisoners back to the prison camp and return to duty.

Back at the Marine base, we showered, were given full physicals, and were fed. I sat at the same table as the Lieutenant Colonel, the Major, and the Sergeant Major. As we talked, in walked Frank White, and we made room for him at the table. "How well did the Captain do Major?" Frank asked.

"Better than I thought he would."

"Then I take it he passed."

"Well, Mr. White James didn't have to pass anything; he is already a Green Beret; this was just training for him." The Colonel talked a lot about the book and wanted me to sign his, which I was happy to do. We stayed at the Marine base overnight. Then we flew back to North Carolina but not until I talked to the Major and Sergeant Major about what happened with Parks and his two companions.

"Parks refused and disobeyed me as did two of his followers Jenkins and Sollie, and in doing this, they got captured, but what was worse was Parks led the Marines to where we were."

"Are you sure of this?"

"Yes, I watched as the Marines coming up the trail behind us, and Parks was in the lead."

"Alright, I will deal those three when they get back to Bragg and will most likely have a few more words with you about this matter later."

"Yes, Sir."

"Sergeant, when those three jokers finish with the prison camp, place them under arrest and bring them back to Bragg for a hearing."

Back at Bragg, I had another full physical, and they looked over my back close. Major Henderson invited me to his home, where his mother and wife prepared an excellent southern meal. I got to meet his children, two girls and a boy who seemed very polite for being children their age. "Who is the one responsible for the excellent meal?" I asked.

"I have to admit mama Henderson is an exceptional cook. She taught me everything I know, which is not nearly as much as she knows," said the Major's wife.

"Is your mother a good cook, captain?" asked the Majors' mother.

"Yes, she is, she cooks in the Spanish style, and my aunt, who I live next to, is also good, she cooks in the German style." We talked into the night, and then the Major drove me back to the barracks.

When I went into the barrack, Parks, Jenkins, and Sollie's bunks rolled up, and I asked those in the barracks, "What's with the bunks?"

"They won't be coming back; they are in the stockade." The next day I was called into the Major's office Sergeant Major Brooks was there.

"I am assuming you know already about Parks, Jenkins, and Sollie."

"Yes, Sir."

"So, what do you think should happen to them?"

"Their problem is that they don't know how to work as a team, and they have a bad attitude." "I would like to talk to those men before I give you my answer as to what should happen to them," I said.

"Alright, I'll give the stockade a call and make the arrangements." He called the stockade, and that afternoon I went over there.

I was led to a twelve by twelve room with bars in front, and I started to have flashbacks of my P.O.W. time. Three ashen looking men hunch over and shackled came to the front. I was shocked at how they looked. They were all in their twenties, yet they all looked like little old men. They sat across from me, and I said, "The fact that all three of you disobeyed orders, I can deal with that." "I can also deal with the fact that none of you are team players." "What I have a hard time dealing with, why you Parks led those Marines to us?"

Parks remained silent for a few seconds then said, "They convince us that it would be better for all you to get the prison camp over with it." "They said you were going to get captured anyway, and we might as well relieve you of your discomfort." "They also promise us better treatment, so we told them; it was only an exercise anyway."

I stared at him for a few seconds then said, "This wasn't their idea; this was your idea; take responsibility for your actions." He nodded, and I said, "What you did was treasonous; you had no faith in me." "You Parks wanted to do it all by yourself, and you two are followers look where it got you." Everyone was silent for a short time; none of them could look at me when I said, "Do you three want to give up trying to get in the Green Beret?"

All three shook their heads no, then Parks said, "Doesn't look like there is much chance for us to get in now."

"The major wants my opinion on what should be done with you three if I decide in your favor and they go along with it, it won't be easy for any of you, what do you wish me to do?"

"If you can help us, please do," said Jenkins.

"He won't do it because of me," said Parks.

"I may or may not; I have to think about it." They all nodded, and I told the guards to take them away, and then I left. I walked back to the Major's office because I wanted time to think. Sergeant Major Brooks wasn't there, but the Major was, and I went into his office.

"I saw the three men; they look terrible."

"Don't let that bother you; they got what was coming to them."

"I know this, but it still surprised me."

"You wanted me to give you my opinion on what to do with those three men."

"Yes."

"I would forfeit some of their pay, give them one lower grade in rank, and give them retraining in teamwork after they got a good chewing out."

"You wouldn't kick them out of the Special Forces training."

"No, I feel with proper training they would make good team members, of course, I would put them on probation for a while to make sure they don't slip back to their old ways."

"I'm surprised at your attitude; I would have been quite angry, but I will consider your recommendations and make my decision."

"Will you let me know what it is?"

"Sure." I then saluted and headed back to the barracks.

It was graduation day we were in an auditorium with sixty other members of the Green Berets. In front of us were Sergeant Major Brooks, Major Henderson, Colonel Daugherty, and Brigadier General Collins, the last two men I didn't know. After all the speeches by these men, we got called to receive a certificate and beret. When it was my turn to go up, I shook the Sergeant Major's hand he gave me my beret and then the Major gave me the certificate. I then shook the Colonel and General's hand, and the General said, "Captain the Colonel and I would like to talk to you after the ceremony."

"Certainly," I said and then went back and sat down.

After the ceremony, the men got dismissed to join the other men. I went up to the General and Colonel and then said, "General, you and the Colonel wish to talk to me?"

"All four of us would like to talk to you."

"Alright, where shall we go," I said.

"Let's go across the street to my building; there is a conference room there," said the Colonel.

"I am impressed with your performance here at Fort Bragg," said the General.

"Thank you, Sir."

"James, you wanted to know what was going to happen to those three men?" said the Major.

"Yes, Sir."

"After consulting with Colonel Daugherty and General Collins, we decided to go along with what you wanted except we will let them sit in the stockade until tomorrow."

I nodded and then said, "That will be just fine."

"You know a lot of important people," said the General.

"I've met a lot of people, some of them very important."

"Is one of those people, General Arnold."

"Yes, he is a good man, Sir."

"He has different plans for you other than a Green Beret team."

"I'm to go to Europe and do some business with General Abrams," I said.

"Yes, after a three-week leave." He handed me my packet of orders, and I looked at them, smiling and said, "It says here I leave a day after tomorrow."

"Yes."

"You care to say what you will be doing in Europe with General Abrams," asked the General.

"Well, it's no secret." "I have a bet with the General." "I can pick any unit at random." "He will find it is in terrible shape; you know drugs, security problems, maintenance problems, etc."

"And what do you get if you win?" asked the Major.

"Promotion."

"You just got promoted not too long ago," stated the Major.

"Yeah, I know, but he agreed to it, I think he likes me."

"Captain, they have I.G. inspection there," said the Colonel.

"Yes, they are a joke; the units know they are coming months ahead of time and, so they clean up their act."

"How do you know the shape of the military in Europe?" asked the General.

"While I was in the Philippines, I talked to a few officers who had been there, they told me about the conditions." "I wouldn't have believed it if my information came from just one person, but many men told me, and so I think I might just win this bet."

"What happens if you lose?" asked the Major.

"He can do what he wants with me for the next three years." We talked about Vietnam, the Colonel, and General let me know they couldn't get my book, so I gave them both one after I went back to the barracks.

One by one, the men of the barracks rolled up the bunks, said their goodbyes and moved out to the new assignments. I packed my things, went over to the headquarters building, and said goodbye to the Sergeant Major Brooks and Major Henderson. "I'll give you a ride to the airport," said Sergeant Major Brooks.

As we walked down the hall, Parks, Jenkins, and Sollie came walking towards the Major's office, they stop, and Parks said, "Thanks."

"Good luck to you," I replied, and we moved on.

11

LEAVE AND EUROPE

I had called my parents at the airport in North Carolina and said I would be coming for a short visit before I went overseas. My parents said there was a package from some movie company at the house they got two days ago. I assume it was the script for me to look at; it would have to wait until I got there. It took over five hours to reach the Oakland Airport, and I caught a cab to my parent's house. "Why didn't you call?" "I would have picked you up?" asked my dad.

"There is no need to bother; it was just as easy to catch a cab."

"Are you hungry?" my mother asked as she always does.

"Have you eaten yet?" I asked.

"No, I was about to fix something."

"Why don't we go to a restaurant I'll pay."

"No, I don't feel like getting all dress up when I can fix something here," she answered. My mother didn't like to stray far from home unless she had to.

'Alright, then instead of you cooking, why don't dad and I go get takeout maybe Chinese food or something."

I put my things in the bedroom, came downstairs, and asked, "Where is Jerry?"

"He's at the college, but he doesn't always come home we think he stays at some girl house sometimes," my dad replied.

"Haven't you met her yet?"

"No, not yet we asked, but he doesn't talk about it much," my mother said. My father and I went over to the next town of Union City and picked up some Chinese food and American Food my father didn't like Chinese food.

After we ate, I sat in the living room and asked, "How are my investments coming along."

"Very good, I'll show you downstairs later," said my dad.

"I better look at that packet from the movie people." In the packet was a letter, a list of actors and the script.

I picked up the letter and said, "I'll read the letter out loud." "Dear Captain York as per our agreement we have sent you a list of the actors and the script we will use, please give us a call when you have read the script and reviewed the list of actors." "It gives the phone number, address, and name of the person I am to contact."

"Who are the actors?" my dad asked.

"I don't know any of them; they have these guys by the name of Kurt Russell and Brandon Cruz, who is going to play me." I handed the paper to my father, who didn't recognize any of the actors either. I started reading the script, which was nearly correct; I didn't have any complaints about it. I'll finish reading it tonight and then give the movie people a call tomorrow.

The next day I got up late much to the surprise of my mother. "This is a bit late for you, isn't it?" my mother asked.

"Yes, I was up all night reading the movie script." "Besides, I don't need to exercise much my training is over, I'm going to take it easier now."

"You hungry?"

"A little, but I can make something myself."

"Your father left his work car for you to use." "He's still working; he doesn't need to with the amount of money I sent him to invest; he should take a percentage for himself."

"No, that's your money?"

"Well, I'll have a talk with dad about that." "I have to make a phone call to the movie people in a few minutes, is it alright?"

"Go ahead."

It was nine in the morning; I figured that there would be someone in the office, so I called the movie people. "Hello, Paramount Pictures, how can I help you?"

"This is Captain James York I wish to talk to William Morris; he is doing a movie about me."

"I will transfer you over to his office, Sir."

"Hello William Morris office, how can I help you."

"Hello, I'm Captain York." "The movie people told me to call Mr. Morris."

"Oh, yes, Captain, he has been waiting for your call give me a second and I will connect you."

"Hello Captain, this is Bill Morris."

"Hello, Sir."

"Have you had a chance to review the packet I sent you?"

"Yes, Sir."

"What do you think?"

"The script is alright, but I don't know any of the actors."

"I'll admit some of the actors fairly unknown, but you don't know Kurt Russell he has been in many movies even Disney has used him."

"Alright, but who is Brandon Cruz?"

"Oh, he is an upcoming child actor who will play you as a child."

"Alright well I guess you know what you are doing do you need anything from me."

"Well, yes, I would like to send Kurt Russell and Brandon Cruz out to meet you and one of the directors."

"Alright, but I have to tell you I am only going to be here in the Bay Area a day or two. Then I will be at my ranch in Missouri for about two weeks after that I will be on duty in Europe."

"Well, is it alright for them to come to your ranch."

"Yes, you need to know it is in the middle of nowhere and I don't know the condition of my home I am having it remolded; they may have to stay in a motel in the next town over."

"That would be alright."

"I'll give you instructions on how to get to my home." "I'll also tell you how to get to my aunts, which is next to mine." After giving him the instructions and a telephone number, I asked one more question, "Where are you going to film the bulk of the movie if you don't mind me asking."

"We picked out a small town in California, but your Vietnam experience will get filmed in Thailand." "The Army has agreed to help us."

"Good choice." The conversation ended, and I hung up the phone.

I spent the rest of the day visiting my Aunt Dorothy and my grandmother. When my father came home, we ate and then went downstairs to discuss my investments. "As you can see, I've invested your money in several different areas."

He showed me the books, and I said, "It's all Greek to me."

"You have made so far is a little more than a hundred thousand."

"Alright, why don't you take a percentage for your time taking care of this?"

"No, that's not necessary."

"No, it's alright, I have more money than what I gave you in other accounts, and I will be getting a lot more."

"Well, I will see I have to think about it a little."

Later, Allen came over to the house; he wanted to talk to me. "Well, did you talk to anybody about me?" asked Allen.

"Yes, I talked to General Abrams, who is the commanding general of the European forces and General Arnold, who is head of the joint chief of staff."

"What did they say?"

"General Arnold said he would consider it but hasn't got back to me yet." "I will see General Abrams in about three weeks, and I will press him on it."

"I thought you might have done this already."

"I've been in training all this time, but I assure you, you will be the main topic of discussion when I see him."

"Do you think he can do anything?"

"More than I can, he has a direct line to General Arnold." "I guess General Arnold has been busy and has forgotten."

"You have a good rapport with this General Abrams?"

"Yes, and it will be even better when I get to Europe."

"What kind of training did you go through?"

"Special Forces."

"Did you pass it?"

"Yes, of course, it wasn't easy, but I overcame the training."

"What was hard for you?"

"Jumping out of a perfectly good plane."

"Oh, you mean airborne, I would like to do that."

"Well, it's not for me, and I hope I never have to do it again."

"I'd think your training would have been a lot longer than it was."

"Normally, it would have, but a lot of the training got waved." "I did do my survival training near the Primitive Area here in California."

"Oh yeah."

"They use the Marines as the enemy to hunt us down, if we got caught, we go to a prison camp, and it's my understanding they don't treat their prisoners very good."

"Did you get captured and had to go to the prison camp again?"

"No, three of my men were, but most of us got away without going through that prison camp."

"They must have gone easy on you because of what you went through."

"No, I just outsmarted them."

We talked for about another half hour on what he was doing. In the end, I said, "Make sure you are ready, in about two months something should happen between you and the Army, in any case, I will try to call you to let you know what is happening."

The next morning, I had informed my parents that I was leaving the next day in the morning. "I'll drive you to the airport," said my dad.

"What about work?"

"It will be alright; besides, you said I didn't need to work anymore."

"Alright, I have to be at the airport by seven in the morning."

"That will be fine?" My mother, I feel, was glad I was leaving. She didn't like the company, and now I was considered the company. I would have called my Aunt Adeline and told her that I was coming, and I needed a ride, but I didn't want to trouble her. I would take a bus or taxi to Ellsinore. Jerry and David showed up that day we talked about what I was up to and the movie, of course, David teased me.

The next day my father drove me to the Oakland airport, and I got on a plane bound for St. Louis, Missouri. I landed just about eleven in the morning and retrieved my entire luggage by eleven-thirty. I took a cab to the Trailways bus station and, within forty-five minutes, boarded a bus to Poplar Bluff. I arrived in about three and a half hours, and the bus driver said to me, "I go to Springfield next; I can stop and drop you off at Ellsinore if you like."

"Yes, how much more will it cost?"

"No cost at all?"

"I have two bags; will they be a problem."

"No problem at all; we leave in about fifteen minutes." I got left off at the two-pumper gas station on the highway, got my bags, and started walking down the dirt road to my aunts and uncle's place. I had been walking for about fifteen minutes when I heard something coming behind me. I stopped and turned around, and there was Val on his bike with a big smile on his face.

I figured he just came from school, "James, your back."

"Yes, for a little more than two weeks."

"You should see your house."

"I plan to, why don't you ride home and tell your mother I will be there shortly and tell her don't bother picking me up, I want to walk."

"Alright," then he took off. I had noticed that his bike was a little scratched up and dented from when I first bought it for him, he must have done a lot of hard riding. About thirty minutes after Val left, I came out of the forest and next to the open field next to my aunt's house. As I got closer to my aunt's home, Val grabbed my suitcase and, with great difficulty, brought it to the house.

"Do you have room for a vagabond like me?" I asked my aunt, who was waiting for me outside the house.

"I think I could find some room for you come on in I'll have Val move his thing over to the other bedroom."

"So, how is that place of mine?"

"You'll just have to go over there and see it yourself."

"I'll do that tomorrow."

"How long can you stay this time?"

"Oh, about sixteen or seventeen days, then I think I should be going."

"Overseas?"

"Yes, to Germany."

"And how long will you be there?"

"Don't know." Later, Tom and Mike came home, and then Uncle Paul, I talked about what I've been up to and my parents. About ten o'clock, I went to bed, as did everyone else.

I woke up about six but stayed in bed until seven in the morning when I got dressed and went into the kitchen. "Are you using the pickup today?" I asked my aunt.

"I have no plans to, but I will use the other truck if I have to."

"Alright, I'm going to be using it today."

"Do you wish to eat?"

"No, I'm going to Poplar Bluff this morning, and I will get something there, do you want anything?"

"No." I drove over to the house; it appeared to me to be almost finished except for the two-bedroom bungalow on the other side of the deck. I went into the house, and all the rooms seemed completed and ready for more furniture, the things I kept in the barn are now stored in the house my relatives must have put them in here. I walked to the barn, the apartment up in the loft was near finish except for some detail work. The shop below got fixed the way I wanted it to be, and the floor of the barn now had a cement floor.

The men working on my place started to show up, and I walked over to one of them and asked, "Who is running this crew?" He pointed to a Hispanic fellow, and I walked over to him. "Are you running this crew?"

"Yes, Sir, I am," he said with a slight accent.

"I'm the owner how soon can you have that barn finished?"

"The inside today, Sir."

"Good, I'm bringing three vehicles, and I want to park them in the barn."

"They will not be in the way," the foreman said.

"Today or tomorrow, I want to give you some more things I want to add to this place."

"That would be good."

"Alright, then I will let you get back to work." I check all my trees and then went back to my aunt's house. I plan to get something for the family even though my aunt said she didn't want anything. I needed to find out about the vehicles I was having restored, and I needed furniture. I went to the car restorers' shop and talked to his wife, who guided me to the shop where everything was.

"Well, is everything finished?"

"Just about, I'm finishing up the motorcycle; I will finish everything by tomorrow."

"Good." I looked at them and said, "Well, they look great. I assume you will deliver them?"

"Yes, I sure will."

"That's good let me know what I owe you and I will have a cashier check waiting for you when you drop off the three vehicles."

I went to the bank, got a cashier check then went to the only furniture store Poplar Bluff had. "I need to furnish my whole house." "I like to see what you have."

"Yes, Sir, what we don't have we can order."

"How long would it take me to get them?"

"No more than five days."

"That would be good." For the next two and a half hours, I chose what I wanted, including appliances, rugs, and curtains that they said they would hang. I next went to a department store and got things like sheets, dishes and everything that goes with them. I knew there would be other things I would need, but I would get them later. As I was going to the bakery right, next door was an art gallery since I knew I was going to need pictures on the wall I went in. They had several paintings of local artists, some good some bad.

As I was looking, a woman said, "Can I help you, Sir?"

"Yes, I'm looking for some pictures to place on my walls."

"Anything, in particular, you are interested in."

"Yes, something that shows something that might not be there in fifty years from now." "Like a mill, house, and storefront, anything that would preserve a memorable moment in local or national history."

"Come with me." "I think I have just what you want." She led me into another room, and the room had what I wanted. I started to point to what I wanted, and then I went into another room with pictures of still life's I picked four of them. I took a few more paintings for the guest rooms, and the lady said, "That will be twenty-eight hundred dollars." I handed her a credit card, and after she ran it, she said, "It will be thirty or thirty-five minutes before they will be all wrapped."

"That will be fine." "I have to do some errands anyway." I went to the Bakery, bought some rolls and pastries then went to the grocery store. It took me nearly an hour to get back to the art gallery, and it was a good thing that it took me that long because she was still rapping the last picture when I walked in. She helped me load the pickup with the paintings, and then I headed for home.

I stopped at my aunt's place to drop off the things I bought for the family, and my aunt said, "James, you didn't have to do this."

"I'm an extra mouth to feed besides I know you could use these things and I'm not training so much anymore I just want to maintain myself I've already gone through the hard stuff."

"But still, you are a guest."

"I was hoping I was a little more than guest."

"Well, you are, you know what I mean."

I smiled and said, "Yeah, I need to drop off some things at my place and see where these guys are in the construction."

"Alright, I will see you at dinner."

A few men were going in then out of the barn, but most were working on the bungalow. I dropped off the things I had bought at the house and then went over to the foreman. "Do you have some time to spare and come with me, so I can show you the other things I want you to build?"

"Yes, Sir." He grabbed a clipboard off we went to the front of the property next to the road.

"I want some kind of wall here and a wooden fence with an electric gate, if it isn't on the list to do already." We walked to the back of the house and said, "I want a large greenhouse next to the shed, and I don't know if I have you scheduled to redo these sheds, but go ahead and do it." "That shed to the right has two pumps in it, so you must be careful." We walked down the dirt road towards my aunt's house, and we stopped at the side road to the pond. "I want you to put a four-room toilet here; you must dig a septic tank." We walked down to the pond, and I said, "I want four picnic tables built here."

"What about barbeque pit?"

"Yes, put four in." We walked down to the forbidden apple tree, and at the far side of the tree, I had him build another toilet but with eight rooms. "I also want you to drill a well with a hand pump at both places." I finally told him to put eight picnic tables with eight barbeque pits. We headed back to the house where his work crew was cleaning up for the day, and I locked up the house.

"We have a storm coming," my aunt said as I walk into the house.

"Think it will rain much?

"It's coming from the south; it will be a lot of rain."

"Well, it will be good for the trees, and it will give me a chance to see if there are any leaks in any of the buildings."

"James, what do you think of the improvements on your property?" asked my uncle while sitting at the dinner table.

"Everything looks perfect."

"The vehicles that I sent out to get restored should be here tomorrow." "I will park them in the finished barn, and the furniture and appliances should be here in about five days."

"What else are you going to do with the place?" asked Mike."

"Fencing, picnic tables, toilets out by the pond and lone apple tree, and a large greenhouse."

"What's a greenhouse?" asked Val.

"It's a place you can grow things that won't grow in Missouri like orange and lemon trees.

"Is that what you plan to plant, James?" asked my aunt.

"Yes, amongst other things as I think of them." Before we finished dinner, the rains came, and they came hard with lighting and thunder. "It should stop sometime tomorrow morning, I think," said Tom.

It thundered and rained all night long, which caused me to have a nearly sleepless night. The next day I didn't get up until about eight after taking care of my bathroom duties I went into the living room and looked out the rain had stopped the sky was still dark with clouds but at least, it had stopped raining. "Do you want something to eat?" asked my Aunt.

"I'll eat just dry cereal." When I finished eating, I went to my house and started to hang the pictures.

Around nine-thirty quarter to ten in walks, Val, "James, do you have a job for me?"

"Are you bored, or do you need the money."

"A little of both?"

"Ok, how long do you want to work?"

"Just today."

"Ok, that is just about twenty dollars' worth." I got a rag and some furniture polish and handed it to him, "Do you see the scratches on this old furniture?" He nodded yes, and I said, "Dab a little polish on this rag and rub it over the whole piece of furniture the scratches should come out." "When you finish this room, there is more in the other room, and don't forget to do the piano."

He took the rag and got busy, and I went back hanging pictures until Val came running and said, "There's a man with your cars here."

"Well, let's go see what they look like." We went outside, Todd, who restored all the vehicles, started with the pickup and drove it off his flatbed trailer and into the barn.

Val and I looked at the three vehicles, and Todd said, "It was a pleasure to work on them if you want to sell any of them give me the first crack at buying them."

"I'm not selling them, but if I do you will be the first, I offer them to."

"These vehicles take regular gas; don't put in any higher octane."

"How often do they need to be run?"

"Once a week would be best." "Once a week would be best." He handed me the keys, and I gave him the check, he thanked me and headed back to his shop.

It wasn't long before I finished up in the house as did Val, and I got the chainsaw and loppers and headed for the lone apple tree with Val. For the rest of the day, we cleared brush from under the trees, and by the time I decided to quit, Val got mighty tuckered out. "Why don't we go down into Ellsinore and get something cold to drink," I said to Val.

"Sounds good to me."

We drove to the general store and went in, and I said to Val, "Go get us a soda."

"What flavor do you want?"

"Grape or orange." He came back with a Coke and a grape Nehi. As we went into the store, I noticed a large, used riding mower for sale, so as I paid the clerk, I asked, "Who can I talk to about that mower?

"That would be Buck over at the feed store."

"Do you know Buck, Val?"

"You mean Mr. Perkins sure do; Mr. Perkins is a friend of my daddy."

"Go get him for me and tell him I am interested in the mower." Off he went, and while he was gone, I got thirty, one-dollar bills from the general store to give to Val tonight when we got back home.

"Val said you are interested in that mower?" asked Buck.

"Yes, I am, how well does it work?"

"Like it was new."

"I'm turning my property into a park do you think it will cut the wild grass growing on my property."

"You're that hero of Vietnam, Adeline's nephew, aren't you?"

"I don't know about being a hero, but Adeline is my aunt."

We shook hands, and he said, "It will work just fine at your place, and I'll tell you what I'll give you a good deal, three hundred dollars."

"Sounds good to me can I leave it here overnight?"

"Sure." We went back to the store, and I used my card, then he said, "Use regular gas and check the oil at times, it does use oil."

"I'll do that." At that, Val and I went home, and fortunately, before my cousins and uncle came back from work, I got into the shower first.

We were at the dinner table, and the conversation was going as it usually went. I asked my Uncle Paul, "Why haven't you moved the cattle over to my property?"

"Because the cattle would eat your trees you planted down to a nub besides, we have enough feed and water for them here." After dinner, I told Val to stick out his hand, and I count thirty, one-dollar bills much to Val's delight. I went to bed early that night, expecting to get up early the next day.

The next day early, I ran down to Ellsinore to pick up my mower. I check to see if it had oil and gas in the engine. I hopped on the mower and took off back to my aunt's house. The mower moved faster than I thought it would, and when I got to my aunt's house, I went down my back road. When I got on my property, I adjusted the mower to the proper height and then started mowing. By noon, I had twenty acres cut, having to stop several times to remove large rocks. As I was lifting a big rock, Val came and got me for lunch. "What are you going to do with all the rocks, James?"

"I don't know yet."

"Why don't you place them along the road?"

"Sounds like a good idea." Since I was getting low on gas, I decided to go ahead and place the rocks along the side of the road, which I have a lot of after lunch. After placing the stones, I thought I would be tired from bending and lifting all those hours. However, I wasn't, and as I walked up to the house, the rock carrying reminded me of the story of my great-grandfather, the mountain man doing the same when he was a child. They were doing the finishing work on the bungalow when I talked to the foreman. "How much longer on this building?"

"We will be finished with everything by tomorrow."

"That's good, when will you start the new projects?"

"Monday, and I will have a new contract for you to sign."

"Alright, that's great." Before I went back to my aunt's house, I went into Ellsinore and picked up five gallons of gas for the mower.

The next day I mowed for about two hours, then stopped and went to the house when the furniture truck came. As they were unloading the furniture and appliances, I had them place the furniture, in the places they were supposed to be in and the furniture for the bungalow I stored in the sunroom. As I signed the receipt for furniture appliances, the person who hangs the curtains came and started on the house. It took several hours to do the house and the barn, so I went over to the bungalow and asked the painters that I wanted to hang some curtains how long they would be painting. They told me another forty-five minutes and to give the paint a half hour or more to dry. By the time the curtain people finished, the house and barn, the bungalow was ready to receive their curtains. I spent the rest of the day setting up the room in the barn and could get a little done with the house. When everyone left, it was time for me to go back to my aunt's place. As I was driving back, I thought the next time I come here; I would be staying in my home. I needed to tell my uncle and aunt this, and I needed to get a hold of the phone company before I went back to work in my place.

The next day I had finished setting up the house and bungalow; the phone will get turned on sometime today. I was about to go into the barn when a black limousine came down my driveway. I figured it was the movie people. Sure enough, as soon as the limo stopped a man about my age and a small boy got out, followed by a woman I thought was the boy's mother, then an older man and the driver. "Hi, I'm Kurt Russell; I'm looking for Captain James York."

"I'm James York."

"Oh good, this is Mrs. Cindy Williams."

"I'm Brandon's mother."

"This is John Hopkinson, one of our directors and Leon Madkins, our driver."

"Well, come into the house, and we will talk, so I know just what you all want to do." "I'm sorry to say I don't know any of you, but you do have a hint of familiarity with Mr. Russell."

"Maybe you saw me in one of my movies."

"Unless you were a child actor like Brandon, I don't think I would have had the opportunity to see one of your movies."

"I was a child actor; in fact, I worked for Disney for a while."

"Maybe that was it, well now what do you wish to do. I only have about four or five days when I have to be leaving."

"We just wish to observe you, so we can take some of your traits and portray them in the movie," said John Hopkinson.

"How many days do you wish to do this?"

"I think two would be fine," said John.

"Alright, but if you truly want to know me, you should stay here at the house."

"We couldn't impose on you; we will get rooms in that town near here," said Mrs. Williams.

"I'm afraid you wouldn't like those rooms, oh don't get me wrong they are clean, but they are old and run down. All they have to offer is television if you're lucky a color one." "The house, bungalow, and barn got finished recently; I just have to get some food to eat."

"Well, I will pay for the food," said John.

"If that is what you want, I think you and Mr. Russell will be happy with the bungalow; it has two bedrooms." "Mr. Madkins can have the barn loft they both have a full bath, Mrs. Williams can have the Master bedroom and Brandon I think you will like the bedroom to the left on the second story, I'll take the one on the right."

"You should have the Master bedroom?" said Mrs. Williams.

"No, it's alright." "I've been staying at my aunt's place, so it's no big deal to me." While everyone was settling in, I went to my aunt's house. I told her about the actors and that I would be staying at my home.

We ate in Poplar Bluff and then got some pizza, chicken, soda and other things for the house. "You're not a coffee drinker, Captain?" asked Mr. Russell.

"No."

"Have you ever tasted it?"

"Oh yes, but I don't care for it, its hot chocolate or tea for me." "Are your rooms adequate?"

Everyone said yes, and then Mr. Hopkinson said, "You have a nice place here."

"You should have seen it four months ago; you wouldn't have thought so." "I go to church any of you are welcome to come if you wish."

"What kind of church do you go to, Captain?" asked Mrs. Williams.

"Catholic, it's a small country church, maybe thirty people."

"Brandon and I are Presbyterian, but we will be pleased to go."

"Services are at ten in the morning; we must leave at nine-thirty."

"I also run in the morning, so I will be up early, which means I will go to bed shortly."

The next day I was up at five after doing sit-ups and push-ups for an hour I put on my boots and started to leave my room when Brandon Cruz met me at the top of the stairs. "You're up kind of early."

He nodded and asked, "You always up this early?"

"Yes, but not when I was as young as you."

He stared at me, and I asked, "You want to go for a run with me?"

"I don't run fast, and I get tired easily."

"That's ok if you can't keep up or get tired, I'll carry you."

"Alright." We went into his room while he dressed, I made his bed up and then went outside. It was a slow jog running with Brandon, but it was alright I didn't want to push the boy too much, but it wasn't long when Brandon started wheezing, so I picked him up and picked up the pace. I ran to the apple tree, then stopped and put him down, and we went over to the apple tree. "Do you know what kind of tree that is?"

"No."

"It's an apple tree."

"There are no apples on it," Brandon said.

"Yes, it is too young in a few years it will have some red apples." We stared at the apple tree for a few seconds. I think that Brandon was a bit confused, and I said, "It's just is a symbol of the tree in the Garden of Eden." He nodded his head, he understood, and I said, "Are you ready to go again?"

"Yes." I picked him up again, and off we went towards the pond. When we got there, and I put Brandon down, he picked up some rocks and tried to skip them on top of the water.

We walked to my aunt's house, and she was making breakfast. "Who's this?"

"Brandon Cruz, he is going to portray me as a young boy."

"Well, he looks a little like you when you were a child, but he is thinner." "You two hungry?" I looked at Brandon, and he nodded his head yes. We sat down to an excellent breakfast, and Brandon couldn't get enough of it. I informed my aunt that the movie people would be going to church with me, and then Brandon and I headed back. Everyone went to church except for Leon Madkins, the driver. After church, everyone came to my place, asking many questions about my youth and how I was in the Army.

"Mr. Russell, how are you going to look like me when I first came into the Army, I mean I was heavy?" I asked.

"We use a special type of clothing and a lot of makeup," said Mr. Hopkinson.

"And Brandon should be at least twenty-five or thirty-pound heaver."

"Yes, he will have a lot of makeup, also." We talked some more, and finally, my relatives went home. I changed clothes and went to work, mowing the grass as they all watched. Later I saw Brandon take everyone to the pond, and then they headed to the apple tree.

That night we talked again, and towards the end of the night, I said, "I don't know if by you coming has done any good for you all, I don't think I have any unique traits you could copy."

"Oh, I've seen several things I could use in the movie," said Kurt.

"And you told us much about your life," said Mr. Hopkinson.

"Well, I didn't think I did anything special."

The next day after breakfast, the movie people left. I took all the food I had to my aunt's house, and I asked my relatives to either use the vehicles or start them up every one or two weeks. I also asked them to keep an eye on the workers and let me know if there is any more land to buy. My aunt took me to Poplar Bluff bus station, she wanted to take me to St. Louis, but I said no the bus would be good enough and by nine in the morning, I headed to the St. Louis airport.

My orders were to call General Abrams when I arrived in Frankfurt. I landed early at about six-thirty in the morning the next day, and by the time I got my baggage, it was seven-thirty. I found an official-looking person in a uniform and asked in German, "Would you please show me a phone I could use?" He directed me to a payphone, and I called General Abrams.

"General Abrams office Lieutenant Mark Rogers speaking."

"This is Captain James York; General Abrams ordered me to call when I arrived."

"Oh, yes, we were expecting you." "I'll send someone to pick you up."

"That would be great." I waited for a little over an hour before I saw a Sergeant enter the terminal.

"Captain York."

"Yes."

"I'm Sergeant Monday; I'm here to drive you to command." It took us a little more than thirty minutes to get to where we were going. We both grabbed my things we went into the building and down several hallways and then into an office where a receptionist was.

"The general will be with you shortly, Captain, please have a seat," said a Lieutenant. We put my things down, then the Sergeant left. I had to wait for a long time when a Major General, who I didn't know, came out of an office to the right of me, followed by General Abrams.

"James, let me introduce you to General Norman Schwarzkopf."

I shook the General's hand, and he said, "I heard a lot of good things about you; there is no denying you did a phenomenal job in Vietnam."

"Thank you, Sir."

"Come into my office, and we will talk," said General Abrams as General Schwarzkopf left.

"So, how was your training and leave?"

"The training was as tough as you can imagine, and the leave was just what I needed after the training."

He started laughing and then said, "I know what you mean." "You will be staying with my wife and me at my home not far from here until we can decide what we are going to do with you."

"I can't impose on your wife and you, Sir."

"Nonsense, my wife knows you're coming and wouldn't want it any other way besides you won't be there but a day or two." "We will go over the bet at my house to set some ground rules."

"Just one question, Sir, does anyone know what we are up to?"

"No, and no one will know, not even my driver or aid until we go." We got to the Generals' house, and he said, "This is my wife, Betty."

"Very nice to meet you, Captain."

"The feeling is mutual, and thank you for letting me stay here." We sat in the living room, and we talked about how we were going to proceed. "We pick a unit at random, and you let me find the deficiencies, you are to decide who wins," I said.

"You trust me to make that decision."

"Yes, I believe that the evidence will be overwhelming."

"And if you win, what do you want?"

"You promote me on the spot to major."

"And if I win?"

"You have me for the next three years working any place you wish."

"Alright, you have a deal." "I figure, either way, I win."

"How's that, Sir?"

"If I lose, I find out how bad the men are." "If I win, I get you and still know about the troops are." "I should tell you though we had I.G. inspections, and the data say the troops are in fine shape."

"I don't think much of those I.G. inspections."

"Well, we will see."

"Yes, I guess we will."

"Let's pick the unit." He gave me a binder and said, "These are all the Army units pick one."

I flipped the binder open to a page and placed my finger on the right side of the binder. "This says the third battalion seventh artillery," I said.

"Let me see." General Abrams took the binder, looked at what I pointed to, flipped towards the back of the binder, and said, "This is a Hawk missile unit commanded by Colonel Brain Greenhill."

"Do you know him, Sir?"

"Yes, I've met him, he's near retirement, seemed like a good officer."

"I'm sure he is he just unaware as to what's going on."

"Maybe you're right; they have five units you pick one of them." I got up and looked, headquarter, unit A, and unit B were in a city called

Schweinfurt. Unit C was in a city called Bamberg and unit D in a city called Reiterswiesen.

"This one, Sir."

I pointed to company C, and the General said, "Alright, we will leave at six in the morning." He got on the phone, called two people then said to them, "Be at my home no later than by five to six."

"Well, I assume you have jet lag, I will show you to your room."

"Before I go, Sir, there is one more thing I wish to discuss with you."

"What's that?"

"I wish to ask you for a favor." "When I was in Washington, I talked to you, and General Arnold about my cousin, do you recall this?"

"Vaguely remind me again."

"I have a cousin that I grew up with; he has a desire to be in the Army as an officer." "I know he did several years of R.O.T.C."

"Why doesn't he just join up then?"

"He has a foot problem and can't stand formation because of it, so I think he might be four F." "Even if he isn't four F, I don't think he would be terrific in the field." "However, he would be outstanding in an office situation; he has a photographic memory."

"What kind of grades did he get in school?"

"He had an A/B average; I had to fight for every grade; he could look on someone else's paper memorize it and get an A or B."

"His incapability of going out in the field concerns me."

"Don't let it concern you that much he used to go hunting every season, and he is as good a shot with a rifle as me if not better."

"What other problems does he have?" "

"He, at times, lets his alligator mouth overloads his parakeet ass."

The general stared at me for a few seconds then started chuckling and said, "I just got it." "What do you want me to do?"

"Get his problem overwritten and let him come into the Army."

"What did General Arnold say about this?"

"He said he would consider it and see what he could do, but I think it slipped his mind."

"Do you have his name, address, and telephone number?" I handed him a piece of paper with the information he wanted. General Abrams went over to the phone and called a number. "This is General Abrams wishing to speak to General Arnold."

"Bill, what can I do for you?"

"I have Captain York here with me."

"Well, tell him good luck with his bet."

"I will Henry, do you remember James telling you about his cousin."

"No, I don't recall."

"He has a cousin that has an excellent mind who wishes to go into the Army as an officer, but it turns out he is four F." "He was in R.O.T.C., but he has a foot or leg problem that prevents him from standing formation. I don't think it's that much of a big deal; he is quite a hunter." "I have his contact information."

"What do you think, Bill?"

"I think we should give him a chance." After he gave him the pertinent information, he said, "I'll send you a letter just in case you can't get to it for a while."

"Alright, Bill, let me talk to James."

"Hello."

"Captain, what do you think the outcome will be from your bet."

"Before the end of the week, I will not be Captain York anymore."

"You're awful sure of yourself."

"Yes, Sir."

"What are your plans if you win?"

"I don't know I must see what the Army offers me."

"Alright, let me talk to Bill." I handed General Abrams the phone.

"Bill, win or lose, offer him a command position, I hate to lose him."

"Alright, Henry, I'll do that."

I woke up just before five and took a shower and shaved I went downstairs. Mrs. Abrams was up, and I asked her, "I have a headache likely because of jet lag, do you have an aspirin that I could have?"

"Sure, I'll get it for you."

The General showed up and asked, "What's the matter with you?"

"A headache probably because of jet lag, but I'll be alright." We ate and left for Bamberg with Sergeant Ricks and Captain Branch.

12

VICTORY AND COMMAND

I t was going to be a two-and-a-half-hour trip by car. We informed the
Captain and Sergeant at what was about to happen as we drove. "You
know General this reminded me of that story, "A Connecticut Yankee in
King Arthur's Court," where King Arthur goes to see what his kingdom
is like," I said.

The General smiled and said, "You haven't won yet, Captain." We just
passed Schüsselfeld, a small town about thirty miles from Bamberg, and
the General said, "Pull over, Sergeant." We all got out of the car, and the
General pulled out a map and said, "The Barracks is in Bamberg on the
American compound, but their missile site is away from there, and it's right
there." "Sergeant, do you think you can find that site?"

Ricks looked at the map and said, "No problem, Sir, it's right next to
the autobahn." We got into the car and headed for the site.

We turned off the autobahn and then turned again onto a dirt road,
and I said, "Get out your clipboards ready, gentlemen." The dirt road had
trees and bushes on both sides, and at the end of the road was an open
field with a gated compound. We drove up to the gate, stopped a PFC
came out of a small guard shack, open the gate, and waved us on. "Stop,"
I said. The Sergeant stopped, and everyone got out. "Why did you let us
in?" I asked the guard.

"Your car had stars on it." I looked at the General, and he wrote down
the lack of security.

"Where is your rifle?" The guard pointed at his shack; I walked over,
grabbed the rifle that wasn't loaded, and asked, "Where is your clip?" He

grabbed his clip from a pouch he had and handed it to me. "Do you know who I am?" I asked.

"No, Sir."

"I'm a Russian spy, and I just disarmed you." I looked down the barrow of his rifle, it was dirty, and I handed it to the General who looked also. I then looked at his clip, and it was green with corrosion then I gave the clip to the General.

The General put the clip in the rifle. Then the General said to the guard, "Don't let anyone in unless you know who they are, understand."

"Yes, Sir," the Private stammered. We walked over to what we figured was the guard shack and walked in. The room was thick with smoke and scraps of pizza lying around. What was most disturbing was the half-empty beer bottles lying around.

"Attention said, and Specialist Five." Everyone stood up, confused and sloppy with disarrayed uniforms.

"Everyone outside," the General said.

"Sergeant watch these men make sure they don't try to warn their associates," I said. We took the Specialist Five with us, and he pointed out the motor pool, but we went all the way to the main buildings. We stopped at what looked like a parade ground and got out.

"Run back and tell the Sergeant that he can come up here now," Captain Branch told the Specialist. No one seemed to pay us much attention until a sharply dressed man came towards us with two first sergeant pins on his collar and one on his cap.

"General Abrams I'm First Sergeant Jack Bennett, I'm surprised to see you here."

"We are here to look around, Sergeant?" the General replied.

"I'll get the C.O., Sir."

"No, don't do that, Top," I said.

"This is Captain York, Sergeant," said the General.

"Yes, I know, it's an honor I've read your book, Sir."

"Thanks, I think we will let the commander find us." "What's this building to my right," I asked as Sergeant Ricks joined us?

"Parts and communication."

"Perfect, let's go look." We walked into the building; it was a small office with three men in it with their feet up on the desk, one sound asleep. There were trash and parts all over the place. "Don't you stand when an officer comes in here," I said angered.

"No, not when we are working," the Private said. I lost it; I lifted the Private off the chair and threw him against the wall.

That got the others on their feet, and then Captain Branch said, "Why are these parts lying around?"

"Some of them don't work, and some we haven't put away yet."

"What's all the commotion going on here?" a Warrant Officer said.

"Who are you?" asked the General, not happy at all.

"Warrant Officer Wayne Houser, Sir, I run the parts department and communication."

"It doesn't look like anyone runs this shit hole," I said.

"What's in that trailer out there?" the General asked.

"Working parts, Sir," said one of the clerks.

"Sergeant Ricks why don't you go check it out," I said.

"Alright, Sir." The Sergeant went to the trailer, and the rest of us went into the communication room.

It was in better shape but barely, "Does that radio work Specialist?" I asked.

"Off and on, but when it does work, it doesn't work very well."

An annoyed General said, "Let's go see some of the missile equipment."

As we left the building, Sergeant Ricks joined us and said, "The shelves are bare, and some broken parts mixed with good parts."

"Top what do you think of this unit?" I asked.

"It has its problems, Sir."

"Why haven't you corrected this unit's shortcomings First Sergeant?" asked the General.

"I just follow orders, Sir." As we walked over to the missile control center, a disheveled unsaved man came over in a dirty T-shirt.

"I'm Captain Leon Morgan, the commanding officer here who in the hell are you?" It was apparent that the Captain had either been drinking or taking drugs, most likely both.

"I'm General Abrams, are you intoxicated Captain?"

"No, Sir."

"Top, where are your I.G. reports stored at?" I asked

"Back at the barracks, Sir." The General, Captain Morgan, and I went into the missile control center.

It was small and crowded in there. I watched as the General asked, "Soldier is everything in working order?"

"Yes, Sir," the soldier stammered without conviction.

"General have him track a friendly as if it was the enemy, I said."

"Do what he said."

"Yes, Sir." I stepped out and looked the missiles were moving, but I notice something.

"How's it looking, General?"

"Everything appears to be good, but I don't know much about this."

"Specialist stop tracking and put your hand on that silver knob next to your left hand." I went back outside and yelled back into the control center, "Move that knob." He did, and the missiles started moving again. I looked around at the radars and noticed several men working around them. I also saw a Warrant Officer standing on the platform with the First Sergeant. I said to the Warrant, "Are you the officer in charge of this control center."

"Yes, Sir."

"I have a question for you." "In wartime, when an enemy plane is coming, doesn't this system lock onto the plane and follow it automatically?"

"We have to lock onto the plane, but this system does follow the plane automatically."

"I see."

"General Abrams, have those two operators join me outside."

"You heard him; let's go."

We all met on the parade ground, and I turned to the General and said, "I think we all had the wool pulled over our eyes?"

"What do you mean?" asked the General.

"I don't think this system is working."

"What makes you think that?"

"Too many men working on the equipment and the operator's hand moved the missiles when it should have been automatic."

The general face looked beat red, and he exploded, "I'll give you one chance; is this system working, or isn't it."

The Warrant Officer responded, "No, Sir."

"Who are you?"

"Warrant Officer Bill Shafer, Sir."

"Are you the one responsible for this system not working?"

"Yes, Sir."

The General stared at him for a second and said, "Well, at least you take responsibility."

"First Sergeant is there a phone I can get an outside line?"

"Yes, Sir."

I and the rest waited on the parade ground while Top and the General went into another building. "Right here, Sir, just dial one first."

Top told the clerk to leave, and the General said, "Stay here, First Sergeant."

"Let me talk to Colonel Greenhill; this is General Abrams."

"Yes, General, to what do I deserve the honor."

"I'm in Bamberg at your missile base; how quickly can you come down here," the General asked irritated.

"I'll be there in less than an hour."

"Meet me at their barracks."

"Yes, Sir."

"Am I going to be unhappy with what I see over there, First Sergeant?" asked the General.

"There is a good chance, Sir."

The General and First Sergeant came out of the office, and the General said to me, "I've seen enough here, let's go to the barracks."

Along the way, the First Sergeant said, "You might want to check Captain Morgan's office." No one said anything, and twenty minutes later, we stopped in front of a run-down building. We all walked into a large hall and then an office where there was a clerk, and the First Sergeant said, "Give me all the I. G. inspection reports." There was a thick packet of reports and recommendations. Top handed to the General as the company commander came in.

"Where is your office Captain Morgan?" asked General Abrams.

"Over there, General." General Abrams tried to go in, but the room was locked.

"Unlock it."

"Wouldn't you rather go to the mess hall where you would be more comfortable?"

"Open the damn door."

The Captain stuck his hands in his pockets and said, "I must have left my keys back at my house."

"Excuse me," I said. I then slammed my size nine into the door, and it flew open."

"Thanks, James."

"Your welcome, Sir." Captain Morgan was in shock at what transpired.

"Sit on the couch Captain Morgan." The General sat at the desk and started to review the first page. He then checked his pockets for something to write with, not finding anything. He opened the long desk drawer, and there was a child pornography magazine.

I left and whispered to the clerk, "Call the military police and tell them General Abrams wants them here on the double."

"Yes, Sir." As I turned around, Captain Morgan bounded towards the door, and I knocked him out with one punch.

To my surprise, the First Sergeant said, "Outstanding, Sir."

I dragged him back into his office and told the clerk, "If Colonel Greenhill comes or the police show them in."

"Yes, Sir." At that, I went inside and shut the door.

"Perhaps, Sir, we should go through the whole desk."

"No, I think we will wait for the military police." It wasn't ten minutes later when the military police showed up.

"I'm Captain Mills company commander, Sir."

"Arrest him," the General said to Captain Mills, pointing to Captain Morgan.

"What is the charge, Sir?"

"Derelict of duty and child pornography to start with." They handcuff Captain Morgan as he started waking up. Then they began to go through the desk and found several magazines of the same type, and they found one large drawer that was locked.

"We need something to pry open this drawer," Captain Mills said.

"I'll find something," I said. As I went out, Colonel Greenhill and his aid went into the office. I said to the clerk, "Go find something to pry open a desk drawer."

"I'll go down to supply, Sir."

"Good."

I went back into the office and said, "The clerk is going to supply to see what he can get." The General didn't say one word to the Colonel, and you could see he was fuming. I was starting to regret ever making this bet with the General. The clerk finally came back with a small crowbar. Captain Mills took the crowbar and got to work on the drawer. In a short time, the drawer was open, and the General and Captain Mills looked in the drawer in disbelief.

Captain Mills pulled out kilo after kilo of hash, which was a drug-related to marijuana. There were even a few kilos of something white, which I thought was opium or cocaine. Finally, the Captain pulled out several different colors of pills and said, "We should go through this room with a fine-tooth comb," said Captain Mills

"Alright, I want to talk to the Colonel anyway." "I'll use the Ex. Os' office," said General Abrams. All the non-essential people left the office, and when we were out, the General said, "I wish to talk to the Colonel alone."

"Sir, may I speak to you privately first?" I asked.

"Alright, come into the office."

The Ex. Os' office was unlocked, and the General sat down first, then I did and started talking. "I can see the anger in you; I understand, and I wish to apologize for making this bet and putting you through this."

"No, this was good; it opened my eyes to the work I have to do."

"I wish to say, don't let your anger ruin the Colonel's career." "As I said, the way these I. G. inspections get done, they are almost useless." "I'm suspecting the Colonel got fooled by Captain Morgan."

"He should have done some surprise inspections."

"Yes, but how many have you done."

"Good point, alright, I won't be too rough with the Colonel."

I left the room, and the Colonel went in, then I told the First Sergeant, "Top, get the Ex. O in here."

"Yes, Sir." Top got on the phone and called the missile site and then turned to me and said, "He should be here in about twenty or thirty minutes, Sir."

"How is the mess hall, Top."

"The building could use some fixing up, but the food is the only good thing that Charlie has going for it, Sir."

I smiled and said, "I'm a little uncomfortable being called Sir, my name is James, and I haven't been an officer that long."

"Yes, Sir."

The General was in the office for some time when the Ex. O showed up and was briefed by Top before the General came to the door. "James, come into the office."

"Yes, Sir, the Ex. O is here, and Top briefed him."

"What is your name?"

"Lieutenant Marc Dizon, Sir."

"You and the First Sergeant come in also." We brought in a few more chairs into the office and sat down. "I'll come right to the point after talking with Colonel Greenhill; we've concluded that this unit is a disaster, and the blame falls on Captain Morgan." "His career has ended; in fact,

I can assure you, so has his freedom ended for many years." "That leaves this unit without a commander." "The Colonel and I wish to give the command to you, James."

I was a little taken back, then said, "Wait a minute; you have an Ex. O. here that is next in line, and there are other problems."

"Captain, I just came into this unit a month ago, replacing the last Ex. O. besides, I don't have time in rank to be promoted to Captain."

"Well, James, what do you say?" asked the General.

"This is a Captain position, and we had a bet that I believe I won."

"You were a Major before I left Frankfurt." "I have your orders in my briefcase, James, and since this is my command, I make the rules, the Colonel, and I will allow you to command this unit."

"And how do you feel about this Top?" I asked.

"It would be a breath of fresh air, Sir." I thought for a second, and then there was a knock at the door.

"What do you want we are having a meeting?" the General said."

"Captain Mills wishes to speak to you, Sir," said the clerk.

"Have him come in."

The door opened, and Captain Mills said, "We finished with the office, it's quite a mess we plan to go to his quarters next."

"Alright, when you file your report, send a copy to the new company commander of this unit."

"Yes, Sir."

After he left the attention was focused back on me, and I said, "This unit is a mess how much support can I expect from both of you?"

"Anything you need, ask Colonel Greenhill if he can't get it; you call me, and I will get it."

"It most likely will get expensive to get things the way they are supposed to be."

"I don't care how much it cost you need it; I'll get it."

"I would like the authority to promote and demote anyone below Major without having to go through all the red tape."

"You got it?" said the General.

"I want you both to understand I do things a little unorthodox, what I'm trying to say I wish a free hand with these troops."

"You got it," said the Colonel.

"General, would you before you leave call the post commander and tell him not to give me any troubles."

"Yes, but why?"

"Since Colonel Greenhill is in Schweinfurt, Charlie is considered outsiders here." "I don't want more problems."

"Understood."

"Then, I guess I will accept at least until I get this place functioning correctly, then I'll reevaluate my future." We left the office; I asked for a piece of paper and wrote down Major James York. "This is my name." "I'm your new company commander, write some orders saying I'm you C.O. and send them to the mess hall for Colonel Greenhill to sign."

"Yes, Sir."

"Does the mess hall have a phone?" asked the General.

"Yes, Sir," replied the Lieutenant.

I walked into my new office, and it was a mess, so I turned to Top and said, "Who would be best to fix this door, jamb?"

"I'll get the Supply Sergeant on it and have someone clean up your office."

"Don't bother cleaning the office, tell him to bring up a bunk and bedding."

"I'll get right on it."

"Then join us."

"Yes, Sir."

We all sat down in the back of the mess hall everyone had coffee, but I had some chocolate milk, and I had the Mess Sergeant sit with us. He brought a pan full of chocolate chip cookies, which were excellent. "What's your name, Sergeant?" asked the General.

"Henry Hill, Sir."

"Top said you and your cooking were the only bright thing in this unit," I said. Just then, Top came in and sat down with us.

"The First Sergeant tends to be a bull shitter at times, Sir."

"Since when."

"Since when it comes to food."

"Alright, you might have me there." "Everything is being taken care of, Sir."

"Good," I said.

"When the General and Colonel go back home, I want to have a meeting with you, Lieutenant, and you Top." "That reminds me, General, all my things are at your home."

The General smiled and said, "No, they aren't, they're in the trunk I had them put there while we were having breakfast, just in case."

"I better go make that call to the post commander."

"We have a staff meeting every second Tuesday of the month," said Colonel Greenhill.

I nodded and said, "Would it be alright if I bring the Ex. O with me."

"Yes, that would be fine."

"Colonel, until I have a staff meeting with my unit, I won't know how bad this place is." "I need to tell you it may be some time before this unit is operational."

"Understood Major, just give me a report on this unit's status, and when you think you will be up and running by next Tuesday."

"It will get done, Sir."

People started to pour into the mess hall, and the Mess Sergeant yelled, "The officers eat first."

"No feed the men first Sergeant," said General Abrams. "You know James, at the rate you are going you will outrank me."

"That's kind of hard to believe, Sir. I've never gone to college let alone West Point it is amazing that I have got as far as I have."

"Well, since the Colonel and I are here, is there anything you can think of that you need Lieutenant?" the General asked.

"General, we can't come online until we get a rotator gear replacement on the low power radar."

"Did you order one Lieutenant?" I asked.

"Yes, Sir, but it is stuck in supply somewhere in the states, I think."

I looked at the General, and he said, "It will be here in seventy-two hours just right down what the part is before I leave Lieutenant."

"I like to know what the priority was put on that part when you ordered it," I said.

"We can look when we go out to the missile site, Sir," Top said.

"I'll do just that, Top."

We got up, grabbed a tray, and got our food the Mess Sergeant was going to serve us, but the General said no. What surprised me is when the men came in, they didn't pay much attention to us as I thought they would. We did get stares when we got up to get our food, but mostly everyone was quiet; of course, there wasn't that many who came in. While we were eating, the company clerk entered the mess hall and over to us. "General, the Majors' orders are on my desk back at the office."

"Alright, Specialist, I'll get them after we eat." After we finished, we walked back to the barracks, and just before we went in, the General said, "Sergeant Ricks get my briefcase and bring in the Major's things."

"Yes, Sir." We all went in, the General and Colonel signed my orders and handed them to me. Sergeant Ricks brought in the Generals' briefcase and then went back outside to get the rest of my things. The General then opened his briefcase and pulled out my papers for promotion and three brass leaves, signifying that I was a Major.

"Well, James, we should head back to Frankfurt; good luck, and don't forget to call me if you need anything."

"That goes for me, too, Major, and I'll see you next week." I nodded and brought my things to my office. The door hadn't gotten fixed, nor my bed and linen brought up to the office. Another thing that upset me was that there was no one in the clerk's office.

"Top, for now, have someone from the mess hall bring the clerk something to eat. I want someone to staff this office at all times."

"Yes, Sir."

"Major, I'm going back out to the site," said Lieutenant Dizon.

"Wait, I want to talk to both of you let's go into your office." We went in, and I said, "I don't know who to trust, by tomorrow morning; I want a list of the officers and career NCOs that I can trust."

"Yes, Sir."

"Before you go out to the site tomorrow, both of you see me."

"Yes, Sir."

They both left, I went into the office, picked up books, and stacked them in the corner of the room. The couch looked alright as did the two chairs I put the couch on the wall to the right and the two chairs to the left. There was a stench in the room I am assuming from the drugs, so I opened a window. There were two flags, an American and a unit flag that I move to one corner. I heard some noise in the clerk's office; I found it was the clerk. "Has the Top talk to you yet."

"No, Sir."

"Where is the supply room?"

"Downstairs, Sir," he said, pointing.

I found the stairwell and went down to a dark hallway with bunks and mattresses stacked next to the wall. There was a light coming from a room to my left, so I went in that direction. "Private, is this the supply room?"

"Does it look like it?"

"Is this how you show respect to an officer," I said with anger.

"I have too much work to be wasting my time with you."

I was in no mood for this disrespect I blew up just as the Supply Sergeant came in. I grabbed the Private and threw him across the room into some shelving. I then yelled, "As long as I am in command here, you will respect every officer and me in this unit, do you understand."

"Ye-yes, Sir," the frightened Private said.

I looked at the Sergeant and yelled, "Who in the hell are you?"

"Sergeant Mike Hurst, the Supply Sergeant Sir."

"Why hasn't my door been fixed?" "And also, a bunk and linen brought to my office?"

The Supply Sergeant looked at the Private angrily and then said, "It's my fault, Sir, I'll fix it right away and bring everything up."

I looked at the Sergeant and in a calmer voice and said, "No, it wasn't your fault, but I think I know whose it was," I then left.

"Where are the brooms, buckets, and mops?" I asked the clerk.

"In the latrine, Sir, I'll get it." I went back to my office and picked up all the other stuff on the floor. The bookshelf was in good shape, so I put that to the side. The Supply Sergeant came into the room with a bunk followed by the Private who had his head down and carrying a mattress. I glared at him but didn't say anything.

"After you put the mattress down, go get some bedding," the Sergeant said to the Private. "Where do you want it, Sir?"

"I need to clean this place first just put it anywhere." They put everything on the floor, and the Private left in silence as Sergeant Hurst looked at the door jam. "When you finish inspecting the doorjamb, check this desk."

The clerk came back with a broom, mop, a bucket of water, and some disinfectant, which smelled like Pine-Sol. "I thought you might want some disinfectant, Sir; do you wish me to clean?"

"No, I'll do it, but what I do want you to do is to pull everyone's personnel file, and when I'm finish cleaning in here, bring them in."

The Supply Sergeant went over to the desk, looked at it, and said, "I can fix it, Sir, but I don't think it will look pretty."

"Do your best."

"Can I take the drawer?"

"Yes, go ahead." I swept and mopped one side of the office, then the other after this, I put everything in place.

"Try to find me some rags," I told the clerk.

"Would paper towels work, Sir?"

"Yes, that would be fine." He took off just about the same time the Supply Sergeant came back and started working on the door. "I'd like a key for the lock."

"I have a couple of spares, Sir."

"Good, when you get a chance get me one." I started to work on the windows, then wiped all the furniture and took the cleaning supplies out for the clerk to put away. I placed the books in the bookcase and put all writing things inside the desk. The Supply Sergeant finished the door; then, he went back downstairs. The clerk came into the room with the personal files, and I said, "Specialist, what is your name?"

"Specialist Chris Farmer, Sir."

"Chris, give me also the I. G. reports."

"Yes, Sir." I pulled out a pencil and pad, flipped open the first file and ran into trouble I didn't know what each MOS meant.

I asked the clerk, "Do you have something that can tell me what the different MOS means?"

"Yes, Sir, and so should you." He got up and handed me his, and I checked to see if I had one and didn't.

"Chris, order me a copy of this I don't have one."

"If I type one out, it might be quicker, Sir."

"Go ahead and do that, but you must do it while I'm not using yours."

I work on the records for hours. I didn't realize that my clerk had left, and a Second Lieutenant had replaced him. "Who are you?"

"Lieutenant Keith Kallstrom, Sir."

"Are you going to be here all night?"

"Yes, Sir."

"Is there anything special that supposed to happen tonight?"

"No, Sir."

"Then stay till midnight then go home, I'll be here."

"Yes, Sir."

It was about eleven at night when I finished. It appeared that most weren't working in their MOS; many had been in trouble several times for petty to significant things. What disturbed me the most was the trouble with some of my career NCOs and officers, apathy and indifference to the whole unit was noted in many personal folders. There were some bright spots; Top overall was a good soldier, as was Lieutenant Marc Dizon. I next studied the I. G. inspection reports I did that until Midnight writing notes down on what department was continually lacking. Overall, the reports stated what I figured it would; the unit had months to prepare. I finish writing my notes. I got a knock at my door. "Sir, I'm leaving now?"

"Alright, Lieutenant." I got up, went to the clerks' office, and wrote a note on a piece of paper that read; If you need help wake me, I'm in the commander's office sleeping, then I signed it Major James York commanding.

I got about four hours of sleep and was up about five in the morning. I immediately went into the latrine, relieved myself, showered then shaved. I got dressed in my fatigues, and by the time I got dressed, Chris, the clerk came in.

"Chris, go eat but tell the Mess Sergeant to have someone bring me something to eat, tell him no coffee, but tea and or milk will be fine."

"Yes, Sir."

Top came in after Chris left and said, "Do you want me to get someone to cover this office."

"No, I had Chris inform Sergeant Hill that I would be eating here." "Why don't you get some food and join me."

"I've already eaten, but I'll get some coffee."

"Hurry them up with the breakfast I'm hungry." Top was back in fifteen minutes, followed by a KP with a tray, we both sat down in my office, me eating and him drinking coffee.

"Are you going to go to morning formation, Sir?"

"No, I don't want to meet the troops until I have a staff meeting." "Do you have a list of people I can trust?"

"Yes, Sir." He grabbed from his pocket a list of names consisting of only career solders. I checked them against the list I had and placed the paper in my pocket.

"When does Lieutenant Dizon come in?"

"He should be here in about twenty minutes."

"Good."

"Do you have anything pressing today?"

"No, Sir."

"Good, you're my chauffeur today." "You should know I'm going to be depending on you a lot." "I need pictures for the wall, don't you think, Top?"

"It would help, Sir." Chris came back with another cup of coffee for Top, followed by Lieutenant Dizon with milk for me.

"Do you have that list of names Marc that I asked you to compile?"

"Yes, Sir," he said, handing me a sheet of paper."

I checked it against my notepad and Top's list and said, "We will talk about this when I get out on the site today."

"It's time for morning formation," Top said.

"Alright, I'll watch from the doorway." There weren't many that attended the formation, which disturbed me. Before the men got dismissed, I went back into my office and told Chris to take the dishes back to the mess hall.

Top and the Lieutenant came into my office. I asked, "Are there that many people at formation all the time."

"In the morning, yes," Top said.

"Why?"

"Well, some are on-site, some in the mess hall, some off-duty, and some just don't want to get up to eat and stand formation."

"Is the later the biggest reason."

"Unfortunately, yes."

"Alright, Top is going to take me around today so that I can get settled in we will be out to the site this afternoon," I said to the Lieutenant.

"I'll take the jeep, Sir."

"No, take the sedan."

"Yes, Sir," said Lieutenant Dizon as he left.

"Specialist come in here." "Turn around." Chris did as I said, and I said, "He's dress sharp, Top." "I don't like brown-nosier, so don't try it, but otherwise, considering how the unit is, I'm impressed with you."

"Thank you, Sir, and there won't be any brown-nosing."

"What's the talk in the barracks about me, and about what has happened?"

"They think you might be a hard nose, Sir." "They are worried you will give them a hassle; they are confused about why Captain Morgan got arrested." "Many are thinking about asking for a transfer."

I smiled and told him, "You can tell them I am going to give them a hassle if I have to, and if they want a transfer, they aren't going to get one unless they have a damn good reason."

"Yes, Sir."

"Here is the list of MOS." "I'll be on site this afternoon."

"Yes, Sir."

"Where to?" asked Top.

"I need to talk to the MP commander, and you can tell me what each building is as we go if I need to stop at any particular building, I will let you know." We first stopped at the quartermaster store. I got some majors pins and patches that I could sew into my uniform, and I got some information on where I could get my dress blues altered. We came to a large parade ground on the left-hand side of the road was a long four-story building that was medical, and I instructed Top to stop. I grabbed my medical records and went in with Top.

There was a large nurse station that we went up to, and I was greeted with, "Take off your hat in my hospital."

"Besides outranking you, I'm in the Green Berets and a Medal of Honor winner."

"I don't care who you are; this is my hospital, and you will take off your hat," the nurse said louder."

I smiled at the balls this nurse had while I took off my beret, and Top said, "Sir, this is Captain Maggie McCall, and if I weren't married, I would pursue her."

"I'll have none of that, Jack, or I'll tell your wife," said a much friendlier Captain.

"What can I do for you, Major?"

"I'm the new commander of the Third of the Seventh; this is my medical records."

"She took it, opened it up and raised an eyebrow, and said, "You went through some hell over there, didn't you?"

"A bit."

"Are you that prisoner of war person I read about in Stars and Stripes?"

"Most likely."

"Why don't you and Jack come back in about an hour or two, and I'll go over your medical jacket with you."

"We'll do that, and I'll have my beret off."

"You better."

We hopped back into the jeep, and Top said, "She likes you, and she is a good friend to have."

"Tell me about her."

"She is as tough as nails and doesn't take shit from anyone, but she is the best nurse I've ever seen." "I also understand she did two tours in Vietnam."

"Interesting." We next went to the MP barracks and Captain Mills' office. "Major York to see Captain Mills," I said to a Staff Sergeant.

The Captain came out and said, "Major, how can I help you?"

"I've come to ask you about my quarters."

"Come into my office." Top stayed outside, and I went in.

"I hate to tell you this, but Major John Preston, the housing officer, took over the house he is going to give it to someone else."

"What! where can I find him?" I growled.

"Over at the headquarters building, but I have to tell you he is the brother-in-law of Colonel Nicolas Cromwell; the post commander and he is a real asshole."

"I don't give a dam." "Do yourself and me a favor if you hear that there is trouble at the headquarter building in the next ten minutes wait a while before coming." He nodded, he understood, and I left.

As we drove up, the street Top said, "What's the matter, Sir?"

"A Major Preston stole my quarters."

"Oh, he is a real asshole, Sir, who hates our unit."

"If he doesn't give me my house back, he will be in the hospital, watch my back Top." I stormed into the headquarters build and asked some clerk, "Where is Major Preston office."

"Down the hall, you can't miss it," he said while pointing. As we went down the hall, I tried to compose myself, but it wasn't working. We went past a bunch of typists. We came to another receptionist, a Second Lieutenant at the back of the room.

"Where's Preston's office?"

"Do you have an appointment, Major?"

"You got about three seconds to show me his office."

"Wait, and I'll see if he can see you." He got up, knocked on a door to the left of him, and stuck his head in; I was right behind him he said, "This Major here is demanding to see you, Sir."

"Demands, tell him I'm busy to make an appointment."

At that, I pushed the Lieutenant to the side, went in, and said, "Your busy playing solitaire; you'll see me now."

"What do you want and take off that hat," he said irately.

I didn't take off my hat but said, "I'm the new commander of the Third of the Seventh, and I want the key to Captain Morgan's house; it belongs to me now."

"Your unit lost that house; you can go on a waiting list and take off that ridiculous beret." I lost it, came over the desk, grabbed him, picked him up, and slammed him against the wall that the Colonel shared. It had knocked the wind out of him. He slid down the wall like molasses pouring out of a bowel.

"What's going on here?"

I turned around; there was standing a full bird Colonel, Cromwell. "This desk jockey fool is trying to give my quarters away to someone else."

"And who are you, Major?"

"Major James York."

The Colonel's jaw dropped, and he asked, "Are you the same Major York that General Abrams called me about yesterday."

"I am."

"John, get the paperwork and the key to that house."

"But Nick, I'm giving it to my friend Lieutenant Shafer."

"He doesn't outrank a Major do as I say." "Major, come into my office."

As we left Major Preston's office, the Lieutenant receptionist said, "I called the MPs, Sir." Sure enough, in came Captain Mills with about a half dozen MPs.

"It's alright, Captain," the Colonel said.

"Why don't you join us, Captain Mills," I said.

When he came up to me, I said, "You only brought six."

"I figured it would be enough."

"It would be if I didn't have Top."

"Join us also, Sergeant," said the Colonel.

"You might instruct your Major about my beret," I said to the Colonel.

"You'll have to excuse him; he is a pain in the neck, but he is my wife's brother, or else I would have gotten rid of him long ago." "I'm going to catch hell from my wife when she finds out about this."

"I don't have to excuse anyone who acts the way he does I hope for your sake I don't have any more trouble from him."

"You won't." The Major came in and abruptly put the documents and keys on the Colonel's desk, not looking at me.

"John, for your information, the Major here is a Green Beret and a Medal of Honor winner." "He doesn't have to remove his hat or show anyone any respect."

"I don't care about his metal or his beret," he said smugly.

"You're to give him anything he wants, do you understand?" the Colonel said, getting upset.

"I understand, but I don't have to like it."

He left the room, and I said, "Wife or no wife, if I were in my command, I would get rid of him."

"I'll talk to him again when you all leave, and he cools off."

I took off my beret and said, "Captain Mills, how did you find the house, and what is the status of Captain Morgan?"

"The house was a mess even before we got there; it's worse now that my boys went through it."

"Did you find anything?" I asked.

"Oh yes, drugs and some evidence that he might have had some children there that he was having sex with them." "I'm going over there today with the local German police to check it out." "I have an extra key to the place that I will leave in the house."

"Can I go into the house?" I asked.

"Yes, but wait until tonight after the German police, and I have had time to take a look."

"And Captain Morgan?" I asked.

"He won't talk, and he has a lawyer." "We have plans to throw the book at him; I don't see how he can get out of this one."

"I might be coming by in a few weeks to ask you a favor captain, would that be alright?" I asked him.

"Sure, what's the favor?"

"Troubles with my unit I'll talk to you when I see you next."

"Alright, and I'll send you a report when I have more information."

"I'd like one also," the Colonel said.

"You'll have one, Colonel." At that, we left and went to the PX. At the PX, I got a large map of Europe and appropriate pictures for my office some colored paper and some Elmer's glue. I also got a hot plate, glass coffee pot, hot chocolate, tea, instant coffee that Top picked out, and a small card table and a few other things.

"Top, do you know where Captain Morgan's house is, and do you think we have time to drive by it?"

"We have just about thirty minutes before we need to meet with Maggie." "I think we can make it, Sir."

"Great, let's go." In a few minutes, we were there; it was a single level older white home with unkempt bushes weeds and trash around it with a small garage to the left of the house. The place had a rusty swing, slide, and a messy sandbox, and there was yellow police tape roping off the area.

We headed back and walked into the clinic with my beret off, and the first thing Maggie said is, "You're late."

"Only about three minutes," said Top.

"You two come with me she said as she grabbed my file." We went into a conference room, and she went through the file page by page shaking her head as she read it.

"Your weight was two hundred and seventy-five pounds when you joined the Army?"

"Yes."

"It looks like to me; the Army saved your life." She read some more and said, "How's your stomach?"

"It's fine."

"Your back still giving you problems?"

"Only occasionally."

"Well, does it bother you now?"

"No, but I'm used to the way my back feels."

"Well, take off your shirt and let me see it." I stood up and took off my shirt, Top could only stare, and Maggie said, "Well, it looks like it has healed good what's your biggest problem with your back."

"A splinter will come up now and then; it's a pain in the ass."

"If you have a problem, just come and see me, I'll take care of you."

"Thanks, Maggie."

"I thought we were supposed to get some coffee here?" Top complained.

"It's right over there, go serve yourself, you old goat."

Top got up to get some coffee, and I asked Maggie, "Do you think you can do me a favor?"

"What is it you want?"

"Dam, this coffee tastes like mud."

"That's the kind you drink isn't it," Maggie replied."

"Maggie, I notice a lot of men in my unit have profiles I was wondering if you could recheck them."

She nodded and said, "We have a doctor here that will grant you anything you wish, whether sick or not."

"I'll look at them if you wish."

"It won't be for a few weeks there is a lot more I need to do before I get to that."

We left and went back to the barracks so that I could put away my things. "You want to eat here or at the site, Sir."

"Let's eat at the site." When we drove up to the gate, the private looked first, opened the gate, and Top drove through without stopping. We got out at my office and Top, and I walked into the building. Three-quarters of the building was a mess hall. In the back was a small office for a clerk and another for the ranking duty officer.

"Where is Lieutenant Dizon?" I asked.

"At the low power radar."

"What's your name?"

"Specialist Four Todd Ricker."

Top and I started to go out the door when I stopped and said, "Specialist Four Todd Ricker if you want to remain, my clerk, you better start saying Sir at the end of your answers do you understand."

"Yes, Sir."

"Better." At that, we left to find the Lieutenant.

We went up a hill where the big radar was, and sure enough, there was Lieutenant Dizon. "Marc, I thought you couldn't get this radar running until you got that gear?"

"You're right, Sir, but there are other things that need to get done, so when that gear comes, and we installed it on the radar, it will be working."

"Good thinking, after lunch we will go over some things."

"Yes, Sir."

"Grab a clipboard, and let's walk the premier until lunch comes Top."

"Yes, Sir."

We started walking along the fence, and I said, "Top put down a road around the premier." We came up to the motor pool a private seen us coming and went into a large tent. We made it to the side of what I figured was a grease pit next to the fence. I noticed a large hole under the fence, I turned to Top and said, "Put down fix whole under the fence by motor pool. Put a side note that we need to have a roving guard every hour during the night until it's fixed." As I was talking to Top, a Sergeant First Class walked up to us.

"Can I help you, gentlemen?"

"Sir, this is the motor pool sergeant, Sergeant Pete Walker, Pete, this is our new C.O. Major James York."

I shook his hand and said, "I notice the hole in the fence have you had any trouble, Sergeant."

"Yes Sir, we have had gas and diesel stolen."

"I'll have to see what I can do about that." As we were talking, I saw the mess truck coming down the road.

"Gentlemen, I think it's time to eat," I said.

As we went back, Top said, "There is a formation before we eat, Sir."

"I'll be in my office."

"Yes, Sir," Top said a little disturb.

"I don't want to meet the men formally until I have a full staff meeting; it will be a couple of days."

"It's just that the men are wondering about you, Sir."

"That's just what I want." "What do you think of Walker Top?"

"He's a good man, Sir."

"That was my first impression."

"Let me know when the formation is over."

"Yes, Sir."

I was in my office underlining the names that matched on Lieutenant Dizon's list and Top's. There was a knock at the door, and I said, "Come in."

It was Lieutenant Dizon, "Formation is over, Sir."

"Alright." I left my paperwork on my desk and joined Marc.

"We can jump in front of the line, Sir."

"No, let the men eat first." We got in the back of the line, and I was pleased to see more than enough food for the men. I saw some of the men smoke in the mess hall after they ate, I didn't say anything, but this would stop. After everyone left, I got my paperwork and sat down with the Lieutenant, and Top then said, "First Top I want signs in here saying no smoking."

"I'll get on it after the meeting, Sir."

"There are about eight names on both of your lists that are the same we will get back to them later I want to know why you disagree with the others."

"Can I see the names, Sir?" asked the Lieutenant. I gave the two lists to the Lieutenant. "Well, Sir, I can tell you the names that Top put down I just don't know those men to have an opinion."

"What about you, Top?"

"May I speak freely?"

I nodded yes and said, "That's how I wish you to speak to me all the time."

He put his head down, grabbed the list, and said, "All these Second Lieutenants seem to me to be a bit immature." "I've heard them whining and bickering in front of the men." "And this Staff Sergeant, I believe he is more comfortable with enlisted men than he is with a career person." "He might be doing drugs with the enlisted men."

I looked at the Lieutenant, and he said, "As I said, I'm new here and don't know the men that well the First Sergeant could be correct."

"I think I won't take any chances and go with Top's list."

"Tomorrow at eight hundred, I want to have a staff meeting with all officers and head sergeants of each department." "After the meeting, I want a second meeting with these men on Top's list."

"Spread the word, gentlemen." "I'm going to survey the rest of the site. I believe you have things to do Top."

"Yes, Sir."

"Alright, give me a clipboard and that list we started, and I'll do it myself." I walked back down to the motor pool. I went into a large tent that was being used as a garage to work on vehicles.

"Can I help you, Sir?" asked Sergeant Walker.

"No, I'm just looking." I left and followed the fence to the gate. The guard was sitting in a chair, leaning against the guard shack, and he didn't move as I walked up to him. I looked at him and then the guard shack, which was dirty and needed a paint job which I noted. All this time the guard didn't move, and it irritated me, so I swept the bottom of the chair with my foot, he flew on his back, hitting his head against the shack. "I just wanted to see if you were awake since you didn't show me any respect." He didn't say anything, and I headed for the guards' barracks. The outside needed paint cleaning up around it. I went in I didn't see much food and not any liquor, but they were smoking in there while playing cards and the place was dirty.

Everyone stood up slowly a Specialist Five came up to me and said, "Sir, I'm the sergeant of the guard is there anything I can do for you."

"You can clean up this place outside and inside and put out those cigarettes."

"Yes, Sir."

"Who are you?"

"Specialist Five Brain O'Farrell." I nodded and started going out, and Specialist Five Brain O'Farrell said, "Sir, are you a Green Beret?"

I turned around and said, "A day after tomorrow, you and everyone else will know who I am." I moved on; to the left of me, I could see a thicket of trees, and as I came near an embankment, I saw a bunch of kids who spotted me run back into the trees when I got up to where they were. I noticed a hole under the fence and tracks going up the embankment. I climbed up the embankment and looked around, and you could see everything. I noted the gap under the fence, and I continued down the fence, knowing that the kids were watching me as I went. I ultimately went all the way around the site, and I headed out to one of the mobile missile launchers I didn't like them out in the open, and I noted that. I walked over to where one of the high-power radars was, which was also out in the open. They looked old, and a few men were working installing a part. "Will that part fix the radar?"

"I hope so, Sir."

"Point to a part that you know is working." "Pull that part out." They looked at me as if I was crazy, but they pulled it. "What's this part called?"

"A directional altitude monitor."

I wrote some numbers down that was on it and said, "Reinstall it."

"When was this part last replaced?"

"Two months ago."

"Has this part in any of the other radars been replaced?"

"No, Sir, it doesn't break down very often."

"Alright." I then left for where the generators were. There were three large generators, all running and looking old. I felt the generators could use a shed and mound around them. A fourth generator would be helpful so that each generator could have maintenance run on them. I walked to the parts and communication building but stopped at the armory trailer first. The armory had a lock on it; I felt it should be easier to access noted it and went to the parts department. "Who is the section chief here?"

"I am," said a smiling Specialist Four.

I wrote down the name of the part and the part number those men told me at the radar and said, "Show me where this part is."

He looked at what I had written nervously and said, "You don't have the part with you?"

"I shouldn't have to." He went outside to the trailer, and I followed him the place was a mess. He went up and down the trailer looking for it; however, I found it very fast stuck in the wrong place.

Out of frustration, he said, "Major someone must have already gotten it, or it is in for repair."

"No, I just think you don't know what you are doing." I pulled the part and put it on the ground, then said, "Follow me." I went to the communication side and found Warrant Officer Wayne Houser.

"Is this man a section chief of the parts department?"

"Yes, Sir."

"Why is the parts department a mess, and no one seems to know what they are doing, especially this man?"

"I have no answer to that, Sir, but will get right on it."

"Yes, you will, is this man working in his MOS because he sure doesn't know what he is doing."

The Specialist shook his head no, and the warrant said, "No, Sir."

I turned to the Specialist and asked, "What is your training?"

"Missile repair."

"Fix this department, Warrant," I said, aggravated and left. I walked around the building, thinking, did I make a mistake taking on this job. I shook that thought off and started thinking I could use a Quonset hut and a helicopter pad, and I wrote that down and went to find Top.

"Top, who has the key to the armory?"

"You should, I do, and Lieutenant Eric Lee, the armory officer."

"Let's look at what's inside." It was full of M fourteens, forty-fives, a couple of M sixties, M79s, and ammunition. I wrote down that the rifles were outdated and needed to get replaced.

"I'm going to need a vehicle Top."

"Take the sedan."

"How are you going to get back in?"

"I'll get in the jeep with the Lieutenant and get back."

"Well, I'll be here for a little bit I need to make a few phone calls first." I then called Captain Mills to see if they took any keys off Morgan. He said they didn't but thought there were some at the house.

13

TRANSFORMING A UNIT

I ate in the mess hall and then drove out to my quarters. There was a flight of about five stairs and a small porch, which led to the front door. The door was unlocked, so I went in, found the light switch, and I looked around at the mess. The place stank of rotten garbage and another smell, which I guess, was drugs. I walked through each room, finding the same. On the kitchen counter was some keys I grabbed them cracked two windows then locked the place up. I would need some help cleaning this house up, but it had to wait until Saturday. When I returned to my office, I again told the duty officer he could leave at midnight and then got busy putting up the maps and pictures I had bought. I used colored paper to make frames around everything. Then set up the card table, hot plate, placed the tea, coffee, and cocoa in a metal container, then put four mugs next to the coffee pot. I then took out the German driving test handbook that Top got for me and started studying.

At eleven o'clock, I got restless and decided to go out in front. I was admiring the stars when I heard a clang. My head immediately swung towards the right at the garbage cans that were half full of giant rats larger than any rats I've seen, I stared in disbelief then went in. I decided to walk the halls of this building, and I started with the third story. I found without exception, loud music and the smell of drugs waffling down the halls. Someone came out of a room and immediately went back in, and the noise from that room quieted down. I didn't confront the men that would come later.

The next morning, I got up at the same time I did the day before showered and shaved then called down to the mess hall to bring me breakfast.

273

I put water in the glass coffee pot and turned on the hot plate, thirty minutes later, in walks a K.P., and I told him to leave it on my desk. Soon Top came in, and I said, "Grab yourself a mug and help yourself to some coffee."

He did as I said and then said, "You going to use that milk, Sir."

"No, take it, but I thought you drank your coffee black."

"It depends on the mood I'm in, Sir."

"I hope you are in a good mood Top."

"Excellent mood, Sir." When Lieutenant Dizon came in, I offered him a cup, and he used the rest of the milk.

"I will be at formation tomorrow at noon; that's when the party these people have been having will end."

"Yes Sir," said both the Lieutenant and Top.

"Has everyone been notified of the two meetings today?"

"Yes, Sir," they both said.

Top went out to the site with the Lieutenant; I had a few things to do. I got all my uniforms out and put them in the backseat of the sedan. I had to go to have my uniforms cleaned and rank put on them after the two meetings. I went downstairs to the supply room and said, "Where is the supply sergeant."

"It's not my...; he's out at the site, Sir," the same arrogant supply clerk said as he looked up. I left and went to the site for the meeting.

The guard opened the gate, and I drove through, not stopping and not knowing if the guard recognized me. I walked into the office and Top, and Lieutenant Dizon was there; it was ten minutes to eight, and I sent both into the mess hall and then told the clerk, "Get lost until someone comes and gets you."

"Alright, I mean, yes, Sir." I watched the clock, and thirty seconds before eight, I walked into the mess hall and sat down. Top and the Lieutenant had the room set up where everyone was facing me. Top and the Lieutenant were on both sides of me with a table in front of us. Almost everyone except Top and the Lieutenant was sitting when I walked into the room, and they sat down after I sat down.

"It disturbs me that so many of you showed me disrespect when I walked into this room except for the two men sitting beside me." "However, I'm not surprised after seeing the rest of this unit's condition, which is pitiful." "I'm warning you now you had better change your ways or face the consequences." "I have the authority to promote, demote, and throw your asses in the stockade." "I hope for your sake; I make myself clear." "I am your new C.O., my name is Major James York, and I am the opposite of Morgan." "I will call out a department, and those who have anything to do with it will talk about how to improve it, I may question you." "Let's start with the motor pool."

Sergeant Walker stood up and said, "Sir, my main problems are first not having enough personnel to do the work."

"How many do you have, and are they working in their MOS?"

"I have two Sirs, one private and one specialist, the specialist is working in his MOS, but private isn't, however, he is a great help."

"How many are you supposed to have?"

"Four, Sir."

"Top how short are we on personnel?"

"We are down by forty men, Sir."

I wrote this down and asked, "Anything else, Sergeant?"

"Replacement parts Sir, I'm having a hard time getting them."

I wrote that down also and said, "When you order anything from now on and can't get it, let me know, and I will make sure you get it." "How many vehicles are down, Sergeant?"

"I've managed to keep everything running, Sir, but I don't know for how long."

"Who is the officer in charge of the motor pool?"

"I am Sir, Warrant Ron Duden."

"Have you investigated these problems, Mr. Duden?"

"Well, Sir, perhaps not as well as I should have," he said nervously.

"I better see you paying better attention to your duties than you have been, Mister."

"Yes, Sir."

"Anything things else from you two."

"No, Sir," they both said at the same time.

"I have one more question for you two." "Could you use another generator and building and berm to protect the generators?"

"Yes, Sir, I've asked for a fourth generator often but was rejected," said Sergeant Walker.

"By whom?"

"By command, Sir."

"You'll have your fourth generator, Sergeant." We went on to other departments. Their needs vary, but the one thing that stood out was people weren't working in their MOS.

The phone rang in the office, and Top got up to answer it a few seconds later, Top whispered, "The gear for the low power is at headquarters."

"Top, go find someone to drive down there and pick it up."

'Yes, Sir."

As Top left the conversation continued, then a Second Lieutenant asked, "I see you are in the Green Beret, Sir." "Do you intend to run this unit as if it is a special forces unit."

"Who I am and what I plan to do will be announced tomorrow at the noon formation I will not talk about it now." Top had come back and as I went to the last two departments. "Let's talk about communication Warrant Officer Wayne Houser." "What if any are your problems?"

"I'm having problems getting a strong enough signal from headquarter on the shortwave and men with the proper MOS."

"Alright, why are we having problems with the shortwave if it isn't working, we will be in trouble when we get attacked."

When I said when we get attacked, there was a bit of murmuring going on, and Lieutenant Dizon said, "Quiet down."

A surprised Warrant, Officer Houser, said, "What do you mean by when we get attacked, Sir?"

"You all will find out tomorrow, answer the question I asked you."

"Well, Sir, if we get attacked, there is a good chance the shortwave won't work."

"Why?"

"I don't know for sure; unfortunately, communication isn't my field, and I'm still learning." I couldn't believe my ears; the officer in charge of communication doesn't know what he is doing.

"Keep on working on it, and I will see what I can do." "Now let's talk about the parts department, as you have heard, almost everyone is having a hard time getting replacement parts."

"Yes Sir, the personnel I have are not performing very well, but I've started cleaning up the mess."

I nodded and said, "That section chief you have I want him out of there; he does not know what he is doing." "I checked, and we don't have a man who has a MOS in parts, so when I get one, I will transfer him someplace where he is better trained." "For now, leave him there; don't trust him to do anything correctly."

"Yes, Sir."

"Is there anything else that needs to get discussed?" No one said anything, and I said, "Then you are all dismissed except for the ones that Top will read off now." Top read off their names most was already there a few he would have to get. While Top was gone, I told Lieutenant Dizon, "Top sent someone for that gear for the low power it's at headquarters." "How long will it take to install?"

"Three or four hours."

"Alright, have it done by noon tomorrow."

"Yes, Sir."

"Once that is fix will the whole system be up and running."

"I'm not sure, Sir, Mr. Shafer, he's right there he would know."

We walked over to him, and I said, "The gear for the low power will be here today once you repair that low power will this site be operational."

"No, Sir, one of the high powers is giving us trouble and one missile launcher."

"The mobile missile launcher?"

"No, Sir, one on the trailer."

"Do we have the parts to repair them?"

"I'm not sure you know how the parts department is."

"Have the parts brought to the parts room after this meeting."

"Yes, Sir."

I sat down with the Lieutenant when Top came in with the rest of the men. Then I said, "You men have been chosen by the three of us because we believe you are so to say untouchable." "You haven't fallen so far in the mire of this unit as most have." "Now, I'm not saying there aren't others who are just as trustworthy as you." "I'm sure there is, but we three could not come up with a consensus." "The reason for me gathering you men is in part that this unit is full of illegal drugs, and I am suspicious that there has been some sabotage of some of the equipment." At that, there was a shock expression on everyone's face. I continued, "When we go into combat, and I assure you we will be going into combat, I will bury three-quarters of these men." "With you men, I am determined to change everyone so that they can be trusted." "In the next two to three weeks, we will strike." "I will have another meeting with you just before."

"Are there any questions?"

"Sir, do you have any direct evidence of sabotage?"

"No, but I will have some by the time we meet again." I could see that many of the men were having their droughts, so I said, "I know many of you think I am talking out of my ass, but…" I had an impression as I had last night, and I said, "After this meeting, every one of you except Warrant Shafter, meet me in the parts room." Everyone looked at me, confused, but I didn't care. "Is there anyone who thinks that there isn't a problem with drugs in this unit?"

"It isn't that we don't think there is some in this unit using drugs, but we just don't think it is that bad," said Warrant Shafter.

"I would have to disagree with you?" Top said.

Everyone looked at him surprised, and I said, "Either way, we will find out, and I hope you all are right, but I don't think so." Gentlemen, what I discussed here is secret; nothing leaves this room."

"Warrant Officer Shafter go get your two parts; we will meet you at the parts department." Top had sent the unit clerk back into the office as we went over to the parts building. We all walked in, and I said to the clerks in the parts office, "Go take a break until I come and get you." Warrant Officer Houser peeped into the parts room also, and I said, "Houser come over here." "I want you to see what is about to happen." He did as I said, then Warrant Officer Shafter came in with two parts, a circuit box and board just as the feeling I had it would be. "Bring those parts over here." He did as I said, and I looked at the circuit board, and then I popped off the top of the circuit box and said, "Warrant Houser and Shafter look at this and tell me what you see."

They looked at the box for a few seconds, then the circuit board, and they both shook their heads. Warrant Officer Shafter said, "They have gotten cannibalized, components have gotten cut out." "Everyone look at it," I told them vindicated. No one questioned me now; they all looked at the parts in disbelief.

Everybody went back to their department. Warrant Officer Shafter and Houser stayed with me as I called the parts clerks back in their office. "I need these two parts." The section chief took the two parts and went out to the trailer and started looking and, of course, couldn't find the replacement, so Warrant Officer Houser went and helped him. He found one of them but was having trouble finding the other. I went into the trailer, and with the help of Warrant Officer Houser, I found the last circuit board. I gave the two parts to Warrant Officer Shafter and then told Warrant Officer Houser and the section chief to follow me into the parts office.

"I want you all to stop what you are doing and clear both sides of this office of everything." "Pull every part in the trailer and put it over here to my right and put everything that needs to be repaired over there to my left, then write down what the part is and where it goes. Send the damaged parts out to get them repaired."

"Yes, Sir."

"I will be back to see your progress."

"Yes, Sir." At that, I left in the sedan to get my uniforms fixed.

I dropped off my uniforms then headed to the place where they test you for your European driver's license. It took me a while to finish the test; most of it was the many different types of signs, but I got lucky most of them were easy for me, and I passed the test. After the test, I went to supply, "Sergeant, do you have any gloss OD paint and some gloss white or grey paint." "I'm going to need a brush and pan also."

"Yes, Sir."

"Bring them up to my office."

"Yes, Sir." After I left the supply room, I went to the PX and picked up some cleaning supplies, Plastic bags, and polishes then dropped them off at the house I then headed to the mess hall to eat.

"Sergeant Hill came over and sat with me, and I said, "This building could use a paint job, don't you think, Sergeant."

"Yes, Sir."

"Maybe a logo over your serving line also."

"Sounds good, Sir."

"You got any of those chocolate chip cookies?"

"Yes, Sir, I'll go get some."

He came back, and I said, "You know these are better than my mother can make."

"Thank you, Sir."

After I finish eating, I went back to the missile site. I parked my sedan next to my office, and Top joined me as I went towards the parts room. "The gear for the radar is here, and Lieutenant Dizon is working on it," Top said.

"Good, if I get a chance, I'll see if I can learn something." I looked into the trailer; it still looked like a mess with parts lying on the floor and other parts shoved anywhere. We walked into the building, and again people's feet were propped up on their desks with only a few parts pulled out. I went into a rage as did Top I knocked one of the men to the ground and one out the door screaming, "You think I'm playing a game." Top slammed another against the wall as Mr. Houser came in. "I thought I gave you a direct order Houser yet little or nothing has gotten done. You remain being an officer is greatly in question," I yelled.

"I was busy with communication," he answered nervously.

"Not anymore, you're relieved of communication duty until this section is made right."

"Who else is going to take care of communication?" he yelled.

"I'll find a private he would do a better job than you."

"Now, get out to that trailer and start pulling those dam parts as I said."

"I don't have to take this." "I'm not doing anything you say." That was the last thing he said I knocked him out.

"Too bad, he tripped over this garbage Top."

"Yes, Sir."

"Call the MPs; have them throw this man in the stockade for insubordination and derelict of duty." "Then take those idiots and place them on KP and bring the KPs here on special duty."

"Yes, Sir."

"Lieutenant Dizon, can I speak with you for a second." He came down the hill, and I told him what happen.

"I don't know if I would have handled it quite that way, Sir, but I felt he was a bit incompetent."

"Any time you get these feelings, you let me know?"

"Yes, Sir." "Do you think he will bring charges against you?"

"No witnesses to support him, but I have Top to back me."

"Even if he does, I don't care; I'm getting rid of him, the only thing that concerns me is I don't know if he has a family."

"He doesn't."

"I need to replace him." "I know Warrant Officer Shafter has got too much on his plate, but what about that quiet Warrant Officer Ron Duden?" "What is he over again?"

"Motor pool and supply, I believe he just became a warrant about a month ago, but he seems like a good man."

"You know where I can find him?"

"I saw him walk into the mess hall about five minutes ago." I left the Lieutenant and headed to the mess hall. I found him looking at a manual, "Warrant Duden."

He stood up and said, "Yes, Sir."

"In my office." We both went into the office and sat down. "I understand you are in command of the motor pool and supply."

"Yes, Sir."

"They appear to be in good shape, is it because of your talent."

"No, Sir, both Sergeants are excellent at what they do, Sir." I liked his answer; he was honest. Just then was a knock at the door.

"Yes."

"Sir, the sergeant of the guard, said the MPs are here at the front gate."

"Have the MPs come to my office."

"I like your honesty as you said the motor pool and supply don't need you right now." "I'm putting you over communications and parts impress me, and I will promote you."

"I just made warrant, Sir."

"I know, and I can promote anyone I wish at any time; it's an opportunity for you, are you willing to do it."

"Yes, Sir."

"Come with me." We went outside just as two MPs drove up.

"You have some troubles here, Sir?" asked one of the MPs.

"Yes, follow me."

All four of us went into the parts room there stretched out on the floor was Warrant Officer Houser still knocked out. Both MPs smiled, and one said, "What's the charge, Sir."

"Insubordination and derelict of duty."

"How long do you want us to keep him?"

"Till Monday, then send him to my office. I'm going to transfer him."

"How did he get knocked out?"

"Slipped and fell on this trash hit his head on the floor."

"Ok, Sir, sounds good to me." They handcuffed him, dragged him to the sedan, threw him into the back seat, and then drove off.

"I want you to spend eighty percent of your time here in parts until its running properly." "Then, you can spread your time evenly between both departments," I said to Mr. Duden.

"Yes, Sir."

"Come over to the communication side."

"Warrant Duden runs these two departments now, understand?"

"Yes, Sir," the shocked enlisted men said.

"Let's clean this place up a little and start bringing in parts."

"Yes, Sir." As we worked, I told him what I wanted to do, and we just about gotten the place cleaned up when Top came with the replacement personnel.

"You men will be working here with Warrant Officer Duden until Monday." "Then you can go back to normal duty unless you want to stay permanently; in that case, I will consider a transfer of duty." By the end of the day, we had pulled every part out of the trailer. Then we cleaned the trailer out. "Before you leave, I want to show you how to record these parts and place them back in the right place." I picked up one part and said, "Each part has two numbers and a name you will write the name down on this pad and the two numbers then you will find a place for it in the trailer then mark the place where it is next to the item on the pad." "Understand?"

"Yes, Sir."

"Good job today." I was suspicious that some of them were high. I drove back with Top, and he asked, "Are you a drinker, Sir."

I smiled and said, "I have known to drink at times."

"Would you like to have a beer on me?"

"German beer?"

"If that's what you want, but I prefer a good cold, Bud."

"Sure." He drove me to the Sportsman's Club and walked in there wasn't anyone there, so we grabbed a table next to the bar, and he ordered two beers for which I agreed to drink a Bud with him.

"So how do you think things are going, Top?"

"Well, Sir, it's only been a few days, but we're sure heading in the right direction."

"You haven't seen anything yet."

"What do you plan to do with Warrant Houser?"

"I don't know yet and won't know until Monday; you have any ideas?"

"I wouldn't transfer him or demote him."

"Lieutenant Dizon thought he was incompetent."

"Yes, he was incompetent working where he was working, but I wouldn't write him off in another department."

"I'm surprised you are an advocate for him, I'll tell you what if he doesn't get mouthy with me Monday, I'll give him Warrant Duden's department with some conditions. We stayed there for another thirty minutes and then headed back to the barracks.

I went down to the mess hall to see if I could get something to eat. I was eating alone when Sergeant Hill came over with a coffee cup in his hand and said, "Could you use some company?"

"Sure, sit down."

"I hear there has been some excitement out on the site today."

"Yeah, I had to shake up some things."

"So how long do you intend to keep those men on KP?"

"I'll let Top decide that."

I was just about finish with my meal when the Sergeant said, "I'll get you some chocolate chip cookies for you to eat tonight."

"I love your cookies, but I don't think it would be a good idea with all the rats that run around here."

"The rats don't like to be around people, but I will give you a canister that should keep those critters away."

I spread the Stars and Stripes on the floor of my office and cleared off my desk and pulled the drawers then started to paint the desk with the glossy OD green after it dried, I put a second coat on it. I was much more particular with this layer. While the second coat dried, I cleared out the drawer, mixed the white paint and the OD, and started on the drawer faces with the lighter color. After the second coat of paint on the drawers, I cleaned everything up and left my office with the windows completely open to air the place of paint fumes. I informed the duty officer I would be back around midnight then he could go home.

I headed out to the site when it was ten at night when I got to the gate; I waited for the guard to open the gate. However, no one came, so I honked my horn several times, and a man finally rolled out of the guard shack half awake and opened the gate. I went in, stopped, and said, "You were sleeping, weren't you, and before you answer, you need to know I hate liars."

"Yes, Sir, I dozed off?"

"What disturbs me is that you didn't know who I was, did you?"

"No, Sir."

"Normally, I would have given you KP or put you in the stockade, and if this were wartime, you would have gotten shot." "However, I'll forget about this, however, when I leave, I catch you sleeping again you will wish you weren't born, understand."

"Yes, Sir."

"Don't go back in the shed."

"Yes, Sir."

I went to work in the parts room, recording names and numbers of working parts and putting them in their proper place. I didn't move at a fast pace opting to do a decent job the first time. About eleven-thirty, I stopped got in my sedan and left. When I got to the gate, the guard was different and awake; there was no problem this time. At the barracks, I sent the Lieutenant home, and I posted my sign that I would be in my office if needed. The desk and drawers had dried, and the fumes, although still present, seem to have lessened. I put everything back the way it was supposed to be, then I felt the windows open; I went to bed. About four in the morning, I woke up with a headache. I assume it was from the paint fumes still lingering. I got up, grabbed a manual, and went to the clerk's office to read until my head cleared. In about an hour, I showered, shaved, and laid back down then dozed off. I felt someone grab my foot, and I shot out of bed with my knife, which I always kept with me in my hand since I came to this unit.

"Whoa, it's just me," said Top.

"Sorry about that, Top, but what are you doing here?"

"It's time to get up." I looked at the clock; it was six-thirty, and Top said as he fixed a cup of coffee, "You must have been tired."

"Yeah, this paint smell kept me up most of the night." As I got my clothing, I said, "There are some cookies in the other canister." I fixed myself a cup of tea and grabbed a cookie. "At noon formation, I want the officers to the left of me, career NCOs to the right, and the rest in the center."

"Yes, Sir." I felt better after I finished my tea. After morning formation, I headed out to the missile site and into my office there. I looked at my roster of names and MOSs and found a Specialist Four Michael Brooks, who was a communication specialist.

I called my clerk back at the barracks and said, "Pull Specialist Four Michael Brooks personal file."

"Yes, Sir." "I got it, Sir."

"Tell me his ASVAB score."

"He scored high ninety-seven percent in the nation."

"How did he do in basic train P.T. test?"

"Above average."

"How about his AIT test?"

"Ninety-nine percent, Sir."

"Alright, thanks." Why he was working on radars, I don't know.

Top came into my office, and I asked, "Top why isn't Specialist Brooks working in the communication?"

Top sighed and said, "He's a bit of a problem."

"What's his problem?"

"He has a chip on his shoulder; he thinks that every white man is out to get him, and he has been in a few fights."

"Has anyone tried to talk to him?"

"Yes, when he gets into trouble."

"I think I'll give it a try."

Top smiled and said, "Good luck." As we went outside Top and I notice some trouble at the parts office, so we walked over there.

"What's the problem here?" Top demanded.

"These three men said they are supposed to be working here," Mr. Duden said to me.

"Do you want them?" I asked.

"No, Sir, we are doing fine without them."

"You three go over to my office."

"Top, join me in my office."

I showed Top the MOSs of the three men, and Top said, "I'm afraid you are going to find a lot of men with the same problem."

"Well, take this man and put him to work in his MOS and let me talk to the other two until you can come back and get them."

"Yes, Sir, I'll be right back."

"You two still want to work in the parts section, or do you want to work elsewhere."

"In the parts department, Sir," they both said.

"Why should I trust you two?"

"We were just following what our section chief said to do, Sir," said PFC Collins.

"Yet, you ignored me."

"Sir, we were put in the middle, and since we had to work with the section chief, we went with the section chief," said PFC Tanner. Top walked into the room, and I said to the two men I will review your file and make a decision Monday morning for now you will work where Top will put you."

"Top I will be in the parts section until noon formation."

"Yes, Sir." I worked with the men for the rest of the morning, and we were able to replace three-quarters of the working parts. "Time for the noon formation," Top said. Everyone gathered at the parade ground in front of the missile command center. When I walked out, I had Lieutenant Dizon to the left of me with Top in front of the Lieutenant, and the rest of the men are as I requested.

"Company, come to attention and report." Every rank without exception said, "All present or accounted for." Then Top turned around and said to me, "All present Sir or accounted for."

"Let's do that again." "I want to know where everyone is Top," I said loud enough for everyone to hear. Top made a more accurate count of the missing men, and everyone was legitimate except for a few.

"Have the cooks come out stand formation and have the clerk stand outside by the door." Top did as I said, and then I told Top to have everyone stand at ease, and I addressed the whole company. "My Name is Major James York, I'm your commanding officer, and I belong to a group of men called the Green Berets." "I was a prisoner of war in North Vietnam for several years, any other information about me, you can read it in my book or wait for the movie." "I want you to understand that I am not anything like Captain Morgan; his career because of his choices is over." "He left this unit in a mess; however, I don't blame him completely; you are all responsible for what happened to this unit, but that is going to change, it must change." "I have something to tell you, this unit will get involved in an armed conflict, a war, and at your present shape, I will bury three-quarters of you, but that is going to change." "Everything you have done in the past is in the past from this point on you screw up on something that you could prevent I'll have your ass." "So, you had better have a good reason why something went wrong." "Some things I will not tolerate are illegal drugs; I know many of you have been using and have them." "I am warning you to stop using and get rid of them, or all hell is going to come to you." "On a related topic is I don't care if you drink on your own time; however, if you drink or are drunk while on duty, I will make you regret it." "Pornography, I'm not talking about Playboy or Penthouse; I'm talking about child pornography." "I find out you have it you will pay for it." "If you molest any Germans civilians, not only will you face my wrath but also the German police wrath?" "I had better not find any more sabotage of the equipment. If you get caught sabotaging or have unauthorized possession of military parts, I'll make your life miserable." "I want to talk to you about racial bigotry." "My great-grandfather was adopted into the Shoshone Indian Tribe when he was a small child." "He grew into a mighty warrior; some of my present family are Native." "I have several black relatives in my family. If you go far enough back in my family tree, you will find some African ancestors on my mother's side." "My grandmother's maiden name is Martinez, so you can see bigotry is not in my blood, and I won't tolerate it here."

"So, what are you saying I'm going to have to sleep with a honkie?" asked a black soldier.

"No one said you could speak," Top replied angrily.

"I'll answer that question." I walked over to the man and asked, "What is a honkie?"

He looked at me surprised that I didn't know which I did, and he said, "A white man."

"Can a white woman or a child be a honkie?"

"Yes," he said cautiously.

"Then it is alright to call you a nigger." I could see the anger on his face and many of the other black men in the formation. "I can see you and others around you getting angry, why?"

"You don't have any right to call a black man a nigger."

"What gives you the right to call a white man a honkie?"

"Because our people were slaves of the white man," came a voice from the formation.

"Is he right?"

"Yes," said the man I was talking too.

"Has anyone here grown up as a slave?"

No one raised their hand, but the soldier I talked to said, "My people's ancestors were slaves."

"I said I have African blood in me, who knows how it got there?"

"The Moroccans from Africa invaded Europe and enslaved many whites, especially from what is now Spain," said Lieutenant Dizon.

"Yes, and in about a hundred years later, the Europeans returned the favor." "My point is all races have been slaves at one time or another." "And to answer your question, no, you don't have to sleep with anyone." "What I would like you to do is break away from your groups and learn about other people, and maybe you will learn something." "I've told you about my dislikes about this unit; now I'm going to tell you some of the things I'm going to do about it." "I'm going to clean up this unit by each department." "I'm going to enforce military prodigal, and I'm going to whip you all into shape."

"Who's going whip you into shape?" said a man in the front rank.

I walked over to him, grabbed him by the noise and pulled him away from the rest of the men and said, "Open your mouth again I'm going to knock you on your ass do you understand."

"Yes, Sir," he said, frightened as I held onto his noise. I then gave him a shove back to where he was standing.

"Let me tell you something that I don't think anyone knows because I am a Medal of Honor winner, I can quit the Army anytime I wish." "I don't need the money I already have more money than I can spend in a lifetime." "I can promote or demote anyone below me, and I have been given a free hand in handling those around me, and that means if I must knock someone out, I will do it, drought me at your own risk." "As time goes on, I will let you know more precisely what I intend to do." "Now, are there any questions?"

"You said war is coming should I send my family home," asked Warrant Duden.

"No, I don't see an immediate problem, nor do I see that great of a danger to civilians now."

"Where are you getting this information, Sir?" asked Sergeant Hill.

"I can't tell you that, but believe me, war is coming."

"You said what a man has done in the past is forgotten." "What about Warrant Houser?" asked one of his men.

"That will be determined Monday, but I must tell you he won't be returning to his old department; it doesn't suit him." "Any more questions?" No one said anything, and I said, "I have an open-door policy if you don't want to talk to me drop me a note, I will treat you fairly." "Gentlemen, you can be either my best friend or my enemy; it's your choice." "The following men, I point to step forward." I looked around and picked three men; one was a big black man, and I said, "I want you three men to report to my office after lunch." I looked at the formation again and said, "Specialist Michael Booker step forward." The same black man who questioned whether he had to sleep with a white man stepped forward, and I said, "You also meet me after you eat."

"Am I in trouble?"

"No, I took no offense at your opinion, it's another topic I want to talk to you about." He stepped back into line, and I told Top, "Dismiss them, First Sergeant."

"Company, attention, dismissed."

After we ate, I went into my office. I was with Top and said, "How do you think I did."

"Just fine, you shook them up good."

"Good."

There was a knock at the door, and my site clerk said, "Sir, the men are here as ordered."

"Have Specialist Booker wait, send the rest of the men inside." "I need you, men, to do some work tomorrow, meet me in front of the barracks by seven in the morning." I could see they weren't happy, and I said, "It won't be all that bad, and I will make it worthwhile for you."

"What will we be doing, Sir," asked specialist Glen Gerbert.

"Captain Morgan left a messy house; we are going to clean it."

"I have KP Major," said Private Washington.

"I'll replace you," said Top.

"Then I'll be happy to; it's better than KP."

"Do any of you have any music you can bring?"

"Yes, Sir," said Glen Gerbert.

"Oh, he only has that Country Western music I'll bring some Blues, you got a recorder Major?" asked Washington.

I smiled and said, "There is a system there; perhaps one of you can work it, and I like both Country Western and Blues."

"Alright, you're dismissed to go back to your departments and make sure you're in front of the barracks by seven."

"Top send in Specialist Booker."

"Please sit-down, Specialist Booker."

"I'm a little confused you seem to have an issue with every place you are placed why?"

"I don't like the people there."

"Why, what is it about the people you don't like."

"They show me disrespect, and they act like I don't know what I am talking about."

"Why do you think they do that?"

"Because I am Black."

"Have you ever worked in communication?"

"Yes."

"Where and what was the result?"

"Here, and every time I told those honkies, I mean white fools, anything, they wouldn't listen."

"Why didn't you assert yourself you're not a dummy?"

"They were white and outranked me."

"The three men who are there aren't any higher rank than you."

"Not them that jerk Warrant who backs them."

"Warrant Officer Houser?"

"Yes."

"Where did you grow up and go to school?"

"Oakland, California, I went to public school at Hawthorne and Saint Elizabeth High School."

"My house was on twenty-eighth avenue, my house butted up to Hawthorne, and I attended Saint Elizabeth." "I went to religious instruction there." "What street did you live on?"

"East Seventeenth."

"Well, we were almost neighbors I use to play in that creek and Sandborn Park that was behind the grammar school."

"Me too." That was the first time I saw him smile.

"Do you like communications working with radios?"

"If I don't have to work with jerks, I know it the best."

"You are going to have jerks no matter where you work, but if you are in charge, it doesn't make any difference, do you agree?"

"Yes."

"Come with me." We got up, and all three of us went over to the communications office.

"Radio headquarters private."

"I can't do it, Sir, there is just static, I can't get a signal."

"Michael, can you call them up." He looked at the wiring in the back and asked for stripping pliers and a screwdriver. He pulled a few wires and removed the coating off them. He then went outside, I followed him, and he adjusted the antenna then went back in.

"Move, he told the private, he adjusted some knobs and switches." "He radioed headquarters, through the speaker came a highly static, "Headquarters Sergeant Wellman what do you want Charlie."

"This is a test just working the bugs out of our radio Sergeant."

Booker looked up at me, and I said, "Great but still a lot of static; it's hard to hear him."

"I can improve it a little, but I think the problem might be from the other end like I told these fools."

"Warrant Duden come here."

"Yes, Sir."

"Specialist Michael Booker MOS is in communications; he is your section chief." "You need to know anything about radios you ask him."

"Yes, Sir, but we are only supposed to have three in this section."

"Michael, in the next few working days, find out which one you want to give up and tell Top who it is, and he will reassign him."

"Meanwhile, tear this radio apart and make it perform the best you can." "We will do something about headquarter end after you've done everything you can here."

"Welcome to communications Specialist Booker," said Mr. Duden.

"Let's go check out the parts section, Mr. Duden." They had finished the working parts and had started on the ones in need of repairs, and I said, "Well done, can you have this done by the end of the day?"

"Yes, sir, but there are many missing parts I have no idea where they are."

"I can help you with that; just get the rest of these damage parts logged in."

"Yes, Sir."

"Top I need a driver to take these parts in for repair."

"I'll get on it right away, Sir." I worked with the damaged parts until Top came back with someone to drive the truck. "Pick up anything ready to come back and then place them on this desk in the back."

"Yes, Sir." He loaded the three-quarter-ton pickup, and off he went.

I worked in the parts room for the rest of the day, and we had everything recorded in a couple of hours. I went over to the flip file. I said, "This is supposed to hold all the parts that are supposed to be here." "Monday, start on this and compare it to the list you have."

I was just about to get up and go over to the communications side when the driver who took the broken parts came in with some working parts and said, "I've got a packed truck with parts."

Warrant Duden sent everyone out to help bring in the parts, and I said, "Well, here are some of your missing parts."

"Why weren't these parts brought back sooner, driver?"

"If you mean days ago, Sir, it's because no one sent me down to get them in two weeks, and some are brand new."

"Alright, we have another load to take down; you can do that Monday."

"Yes, Sir." While they were working on the new parts, I thought I peek in on what was going on in the radio room.

Radio parts were all over the place Booker was arguing with one of the other specialist fours. I walked over to him and asked, "How're things going, Michael?"

"It would go a lot better if they would do as I say."

I turned and looked at the three men and asked, "Why aren't you doing as he says?"

"He doesn't know what he is doing he has made a mess in here now we will never fix it we'll have to get all new radios, and that will take months," snarled the specialist that was arguing with Booker.

"This is his MOS; he is the section chief; he knows this better than any of us."

"It doesn't matter what his MOS is or if he is the section chief, let's face it Major; his kind just doesn't have it mentally; they always mess up everything."

Booker was just about to jump on him for saying what he did when I grabbed him and pushed him back and said to the specialist, "You said his kind, what kind is he?"

"You know a dumb nigger." I grabbed him by his shirt, picked him up, and threw him across the room, and he landed on the ground. I picked him up again as Warrant Duden came into the room and threw him through the door. Warrant Officer Duden tried to stop me, but I shoved him aside and went after him. Afraid he tried to get his footing to get away from me. Someone must have informed Top and Lieutenant Dizon because they came running.

Top grabbed me and said, "He isn't worth it, Sir." The Lieutenant grabbed the specialist and picked him up.

Seeing that Top had my arm trying to calm me down, the specialist got very brave. He said, "My father is a congressman when he hears what a nigger lover has done to me; you won't be a Major anymore."

Enraged, I broke free of Top, but it didn't matter, Lieutenant Dizon became infuriated. He backhanded the specialist so hard that you could hear the punch clear back to the barracks. He crumbled to the ground, and a trickle of blood seeped from his nose.

"Top take that boy and put him in the stockade, then throw his things together he is out of this unit I'll call Colonel Greenhill." Top grabbed the specialist by his collar and threw him in a jeep and left.

I had gathered quite a crowd, and the Lieutenant came over to me and said, "Maybe you should calm down some before you call the Colonel, Sir."

"Good idea."

"What did he do other than calling you a name?"

"It's not just the name-calling, he is a bigot, and he is why the radios weren't working." "He started using racial slurs towards Specialist Booker then totally disrespected me after telling everyone about racism." I went back into the communication's building to a smiling Booker.

I looked at the two other men and said, "I better not hear about any more trouble."

"No, Sir," they both said at the same time. I then looked at Booker and said, "The situation wasn't funny, but I understand why you are smiling." I then left to make the phone call.

"Colonel Greenhill, Major York here."

"Yes, James, what can I do for you?"

"I'm throwing a man out of this unit as soon as I demote him and sending him to you for whatever you want to do with him."

"What has he done?"

"He was insubordinate." "Because of his bigotry, arrogance, and the fact he didn't try to learn anything about radios, he sabotaged communications." "He won't work with a man who does know about radios because he is black."

"Alright, I will inform the commander of headquarter that he is coming."

"I should also tell you his father is a congressman, and he threatened to call him because I rough him up."

"Would it be Specialist Joshua Depew?"

"Yes, Sir."

"I had him transferred to you because he caused trouble here."

"If his father calls have him contact me, I could hurt his reelection."

"Good idea, where is he now?"

"In the stockade."

"Leave him there; in fact, I'll call the stockade and tell them to hold him; I'm going to talk to General Abrams; maybe I can get him out of Europe."

"Yes, Sir; Colonel, I don't think he will be the last I kick out of here."

"Understood Major, how're things otherwise going?"

"I have a list of things I need not counting personnel, but I will talk about this list with you Tuesday. Otherwise, slowly things are turning around by next week parts, and communications should be working as well as possible, and so are the radars and missiles are up and running."

"That's good." "I will talk to you, Tuesday, James."

"Alright, I'll let you go so you can call the stockade, Sir."

I went back to the barracks with Lieutenant Dizon. I informed him what the Colonel said.

Then I said, "Monday, I want to have a meeting with you and Top in the morning before we go out to the site."

"Yes, Sir." I walked into my office, pulled out my notes, a pad of paper then started to make a clean list of things I wish.

While I was working, Top came in and said, "You cool off, Sir?"

I looked up and said, "Why Top I don't know what you are talking about."

He smiled and asked, "You talk to the Colonel yet?"

"Yep, when he found out who it was, he said to leave him in the stockade until he can move him out of Europe."

"Thank God, maybe we will get a better replacement."

"Yeah, say do you want to go to the club and have a beer on me."

"Sure." I went to the mess hall first to tell Sergeant Hill to leave me something to eat. I bought Top and I a couple of beers, and the bartender brought us some peanuts and sat down with us. "Major this is Sergeant Major David Weatherly retired." "I shook his hand and said, "Nice to meet you."

"The pleasure mine Major, I've read your book."

"I'm surprised you can read at all," said Top.

"Better than you can, you old mule."

"Well, it's getting better Top you move from an old goat to a mule."

"Yeah, pretty soon I'll be an ass." The place was filling up real fast with NCOs and enlisted men; there were even a few officers. After a short while, the sportsman's club started to get rowdy, and I wasn't in the mood for that, so we left back to the barracks. I had eaten, and it was near midnight when I finally finished rewriting my list of wants and then went to sleep.

The next morning, I went to breakfast and then at seven o'clock went out front and to my surprise the three men were waiting. "You two take the jeep and go get a truck and meet me next to the theater." "Your Washington, am I right?"

"Yes, Sir."

"You're with me." We drove to the PX in the sedan, and I bought some tools for the outside of the house. I also purchased some donuts I figured that they could drink water. Washington was eyeing the donuts but didn't try to take any as we drove to the theater. We waited for about twenty minutes, and while waiting, I made small talk with Washington. "Where is home for you, Washington?"

"Detroit Major."

"Did you join or get drafted?"

"I joined, Sir."

I looked at him and said, "Seems like there is a lot of jobs there in the auto field, why did you join."

"I'm not interested in the factories, and my neighborhood isn't the best." "I figured that the military was a better thing to do, so here I am."

"You plan to reenlist?"

"I don't know Major I've been in the Army for a year and a half, and I'm only a private."

"Have you ever been in trouble?"

"No, Sir, I do as someone tells me."

"Well, show me something, and I will promote you."

"I sure will try Major." The truck came and followed me to my house. We went into the house; the men let out a sigh of disbelief, and Washington said, "It's not so bad it reminds me of home."

"See, if you can find clean glasses to drink out of if not clean one out, here are some donuts to give you some energy." They all cleaned themselves a glass to drink from then dove into the donuts.

Washington was on his second when he asked, "Major, aren't you going to eat any."

"No, they are all for you guys." "I need one to work outside around the house who will that be?"

The smallest man, a private Joseph Fernando, said with a smile, "I'll do it, my people are used to it anyway."

"Some tools are in the sedan; take some bags with you, make sure you bag those garbage cans and throw it in the back of the truck." When Fernando left, and I said, "You two pick the cleanest room, disassemble the furniture if it can be, and store it in that room," pointed to the left side of the house. I got busy in the kitchen; it took about an hour to wash all the dirty things. I took a break and went over to the phone and check to see if it was on.

Washington and Stockwell finished moving the furniture, so I said, "One clean the windows and dust, the other sweep up." "When you get finished, one mop the room while the other starts in the next room."

"We'll start in this room, but first I got to piss," Washington said while pointing to the master bedroom. When Washington came out of the bathroom, he said, "I thought my bathroom was dirty back at home, but this one is unbelievable; I open up a window." I got busy cleaning the stove and refrigerator. The refrigerator wasn't in bad shape, but it stunk. I disconnected it and went to work, throwing all the food in it away and scrubbing it with ammonia diluted in water. That took me about thirty minutes; then, I tackled the hard part, the stove. I sprayed the whole outside with an oven cleaner then let it soak for a few minutes later wiped it off I had to repeat this three times.

By the time I finished with the outside of the stove, Stockwell had come out of the room with two bags of trash and asked, "Sir, what do you want to do with Captain Morgan's things?"

"Bag them and put them in the trunk of the car." It was eleven in the morning; I grabbed the phone and called for pizza. I had gotten a number from Chris, my clerk, and I dial it. "I would like to order five pepperoni pizzas with a case of beer," I said in German.

"That will be two hundred marks where do you live?"

"1742 West Forest Street, you want my telephone number?"

"Yes."

"Eight, four, five, two, two, one."

"I should be there in about an hour."

"Very good." I went back to work cleaning out the cupboards and mopping the floor while Washington and Stockwell work in the second room. While going through the cupboards in walks, Fernando and I asked, "All finish?"

"Yes, I did all I could," he said as he grabbed a donut.

"Alright, what you can do next is move the furniture from that room and put it in this room," I said as I pointed to the two rooms. Fernando got on it, and I was just about to mop the floors when the pizza and beer came.

"Two hundred mark." I handed him two hundred and twenty marks. "Thank you?" he said and then left. "Lunch Time, I yelled to everyone." Everyone came out to the kitchen, and I said, "I didn't know what kind of pizza you ate, so I got pepperoni."

"Right on," Washington said with a smile as he flipped open one of the boxes.

Glen Gerbert picked up one of the bottles of beer and said, "I thought you said we couldn't drink while we were on duty, Sir."

"You're not on post nor duty; all of you are volunteers." They all grabbed a beer and started in on the pizza, within a matter of minutes, the first two boxes were finished mostly because of Washington. I finished the kitchen and moved to the bathroom; the other men had started working in their rooms. The bathroom was a discussing mess. I scrubbed everything and disinfectant it. I then went to work on the basin and did the same to it. You would think the toilet would be the hardest thing to work on, but you would be mistaken; it was the bathtub. Three times, I scrubbed it, the shower the curtain wasn't worth saving, so I threw it out.

"Hey, anybody home?" came a voice that sounded like Top. I went into the living room, and he said, "It looks like you got this place looking good, Sir."

"Thank Top; it also doesn't smell so bad now."

"I've come to help if there is anything left."

"There is always something."

"My wife will be here in a few minutes, always nice to have a woman's touch."

"Well, grab a beer if you don't mind German beer, and there are pizza and donuts."

"Today is Saturday; I'll drink any beer."

I laughed and said, "I might as well let these guys go." "Throw this garbage behind the truck and find a dumpster and dump the garbage, then take the truck back to the site."

"Are any of you sober enough to drive?"

"Oh, I am, Sir, it takes a lot more than those few beers I drank to get me drunk," said Washington.

"You guys did a fine job." "I won't forget it."

Washington had his head down and said as he pulled a paper bag from his shirt, "Um, I think I need to give this to you, Sir, I found in that room when I was moving the furniture."

I looked inside it was full of drugs, and then I looked at him and said, "Good work Washington," as I handed the bag to Top. "It's a good thing you gave it to me," I said as I patted him on the back. I knew his first thought was to keep the drugs but then had a change of heart. The men left, and I got back to work, and Top worked on the third bedroom. It wasn't long when I got disturbed again.

"Hello, Jack, Major."

I walked out and said, "Hello."

"Don't be an ass, Jack; introduce me."

I started laughing and said, "Well, there you go, Top, you finally made it to ass status."

"The abuse I get, Major this is wife Maryann, Maryann this is Major James York."

"It's nice to meet you," I said while shaking her hand.

"Hello," came from someone walking up the porch and into the house. A woman walked in, followed by Lieutenant Dizon.

"We've come to help," said the Lieutenant.

"This is my wife, Helen, and this is Major James York."

I shook her hand and said, "Nice to meet you; there are donuts pizza and beer help yourself."

"Well, Helen, what do you want to take the bathroom or the kitchen?" asked Maryann.

"Kitchen."

"I've already done the kitchen, and I'm just about finish with the bathroom."

"Get out of the way, Major, you're a man and couldn't clean if you tried," said Maryann.

I was going to protest, but Top said, "No use arguing with them you'll just lose."

"What do you wish me to do, Sir?" asked the Lieutenant.

"It's James, Marc, and I guess we can clean up and polish up some of the furniture then put it in its proper place."

When Top finished the one room, he worked in the living room, and after a couple of hours, everything got done. "You need a shower curtain, and this place could use a coat of paint," said Maryann.

"Our place could use a paint job also," Top said.

"So, could we," said Helen.

"I haven't looked in the garage, yet I hope there are a washer and dryer there," I said.

"Let's go see," Top said. We walked into the garage wasn't much in there, but it did have a washer and driver.

Maryann and Helen looked at it, and Maryann said, "It's better than mine but not much better."

"Well, we better be going," Maryann said.

"Us, too," said Helen.

"Wait a minute all that food and beer; I can't bring it back to the barracks; you all divide it amongst you."

"I don't want it, Maryann, you take it," said Helen.

"You're sure?" asked Maryann.

"Yes, go ahead and take it."

I locked the house and headed to MP's barracks to drop off Morgan's things and the drugs that we found. I then drove to a car lot that was just across the street from the post. "I'm looking for a car in good condition." The car salesman showed me every expensive car he had. I could have bought any of them, but my eyes focused on a light green Volkswagen, and I headed for it. The inside looked clean; I looked at the engine; it looked good, so I asked to start it up. The engine sounded good. I tried the clutch and bakes, and it was alright. I turn to him, and I said in German, "How much."

"Four thousand two hundred marks."

"No, this car is three years old; a new Volkswagen is less than five thousand two hundred marks."

"It is in good shape, but I will come down a little three thousand eight hundred marks is the lowest I can go."

I looked at the car then at him and said, "Three thousand six hundred marks or I will go somewhere else."

He had a frown on his face, as he looked at the beetle then he asked, "Are you going to finance?"

"No, I will pay cash."

He looked at the car again, then stuck out his hand and said, "It is a deal, but you Americans drive a hard bargain."

I smiled and filled out the paperwork and paid the dealer. I then dropped off my military sedan and afterward got my car. I slept well that night; the first time since I took over this unit after I ate, I drove my VW downtown to buy some things for the house. I drove to the center of the city where there was a large plaza with plenty of parking. I saw many cars park halfway on the sidewalk and roadway, but I didn't want to do that unless I had to. Every road I saw, including the plaza, was cobblestone, which gave it a quaint look. There was a large cathedral in the square with people going in, so I decided to go in. The church looked like something from the medieval period. It had rich dark wood with grey stone and beautiful stain glass windows. It was a Catholic Church, and I figured it would be fun to hear mass in German. I sat down in a pew towards the center so that I could soak up everything. When I sat down, I sat next to a beautiful woman about my age and a male child about seven. The child looked upset, so I said in German, "Hello, what is your name?"

"Frederick Muller, are you an American?"

"Yes, my name is James York; how did you know I was an American?" "Was it because of my accent?" He nodded yes and looked straight forward with a nervous look.

I looked at the woman I assumed was his mother and said, "I hope I didn't frighten him."

"I don't know why he is acting this way; he is usually friendly."

"What is the matter, Frederick," asked his mother.

"Nothing," he answered but still looked anxious. I notice that the woman didn't have a wedding ring on, and there was no husband, so I assume she was single.

I enjoyed church very much, and after church, I said to the woman, "I couldn't help but notice that you don't have a wedding ring on, nor your husband isn't here; are you single."

"Yes, my husband died two years ago."

"Would you do me the honor to let me take you and Frederick to lunch?"

"I would love to, but today is my only day off, and it's a day I spend with Frederick unless it is alright with you, Frederick." Frederick shook his head no, which surprised his mother, and she said, "I do not know what has gotten into him perhaps some other time."

"Alright, but what is your name?"

"Maria Muller."

"Let me give you my address and telephone number if you find the time, I would love to take both of you out, and if you need anything call me, I will help you."

I gave her a card, and she said with a smile, "Thank You."

I found a store that looked like a department store, and I could find most of the things I needed then I saw a bakery and got some bread and pastries. I asked the lady at the counter, "I have a home near the military there are large rats I'm concern about the rats getting into the house and eating this bread what should I do?"

She laughed and said, "Yes, our rats are large." "I wouldn't be to concern; they mainly rummage through the garbage cans and you Americans' waist a lot."

"Unfortunately, we do." "I will get a bread box if a rat tries to get at it, I will know, thanks for everything."

"Your welcome, come back again."

"I surely will if the things I bought taste as good as they smell."

I went to the PX for groceries and everything else I didn't get from downtown. I placed some food in the refrigerator, putting the rest of the things away in their proper place. I made up my bed and, for some reason, the beds in the other bedroom next to the bathroom. I bought three Down Blankets, stored those in the third bedroom, and closed all the windows, and I sprayed some air freshener throughout the house. I had a couch and an Easy Chair that could use something to drape over them, I also had a kitchen table with four chairs. They weren't that bad in shape; I could use a tablecloth. I had nothing else in the kitchen or living room. I needed pictures in all the rooms, rugs, a bookcase with books in the living room and maybe a small TV. I locked up the house, parked the car in the garage, then walked back to the barracks, which was about two miles away. As I walked, I couldn't get that girl and her son out of my head. I hoped I would see her again, but I could kick myself for not getting her address or phone number. I loaded up all my clothing much to the men's delight in barracks who thought they would have free reign again. I also took something for me to study. I then went down to the mess hall to eat, and afterward, I headed to my quarters.

14

FINDING MY SOUL MATE

I was up at four, but I wasn't tired. By the time I cleaned up, I had got to the barracks just after five. I placed the manuals and my notes in my office and then went to get breakfast. I just started eating when Top came to my table and sat down with a cup of coffee. "I'll be at morning formation." "I want everyone to be there who aren't too sick."

"Yes, Sir."

"I'll have to stay here till Warrant Houser arrives, so I want to meet with you and Lieutenant Dizon before you go out to the site."

"Yes, Sir."

"Thank you and your wife for giving me a hand with the house."

"Oh, think nothing of it, Sir, I take it you slept there last night."

"Yes." I finished eating, and we went to my office where Lieutenant Dizon was waiting, and then I told him the same thing I said to Top. Formation started just as it had every morning. When Top turned and said all present and accounted for, I said, "Where are the accounted for at?" The squad leaders said they didn't know, so I said, "Career NCOs and Officers go into the barracks and bring down those who aren't here no matter what state of dress unless they are sick." They all ran in the barracks, then almost immediately, the men came pouring out of the barracks in various states of dress. When it appeared that the last man came out, I asked, "Is this everyone?"

"We believe so, Sir," said one of my Lieutenants.

"You believe so; Lieutenant Dizon, stay here with these men while the First Sergeant and I make sure." We went to each room on the first floor and the latrine they were empty as was the rooms on the second floor there was one in the shower and I said, "Out now mister."

"I have soap in my hair," he protested.

"If you don't come out, I'll go in and drag your ass out," I said again.

He came out with a towel, and a soapy head and Top said, "Get in formation."

"But I don't have any clothes on."

"To bad move," I said with force. About halfway checking the rooms, there was one man in bed, and I kicked his bed and said, "Why aren't you at formation?"

"Kiss my ass I'm off today." I went down to the foot of his bed, grabbed his mattress, and yanked it off his bunk. He went flying onto the ground Top, and I then dragged him outside.

I then grabbed him and said, "Get your ass into formation before I break your jaw." We went back in to finish checking the rooms we did find some sick, and I left them alone, but what both Top and I saw was a messy barracks reeking of marijuana.

"Lieutenant, they are now all present and accounted for." I turned to the men and said, "For your information, you are in the Army like it or not." "I don't care if you are off duty or on leave, you will attend morning formation if you are in this building unless you are too ill, and you better be sick." "I hope I make myself clear there won't be a second chance." "I want to warn you again, get rid of any illegal drugs you may have, and I had better not find any parts you have taken from the military equipment." "After formation, I want to see Mr. Duden, Mr. Shafer, Specialist Murphy, Specialist Pichler, and Private Roby in my office." "Do you have anything, Lieutenant?"

"Yes, Sir." "Everything is working, so we will most likely be up next Sunday, that means a full staff." "All missile crews and radar crews make sure you keep your eye on any problems."

The Lieutenant nodded at me, and I said, "You got anything Top."

"Yes, Sir."

"You better get yourself together." "The Major is not playing games; he will put you in a whole world of hurt."

"Alright, Top dismiss them." I went into my office with the Lieutenant and Top following me. When I got in, I pulled out the list of wants I had and said, "Look at this and see if there is anything you want to add."

The Lieutenant looked at the list and said, "It looks good to me."

Top finish looking at it and said, "It looks fine to me, but you might have to call General Abrams on three-fourths of this stuff."

"I will if I have to." "I'll meet both of you out on the site."

"You don't want me to stay, Sir?" asked Top.

"No, it's not necessary." He stared at me, and I said, "I'm not angry Top, and I assure you I will keep calm."

"Alright, Sir."

I called out, and I said, "Mr. Duden and Shafer, please come in." They both reported in, and then I said, "Every part that comes in to get repaired, I want it checked to see if it gets sabotaged. I want you, Mr. Shafer, to check it and tag who pulled it before it gets to the parts room and you Mr. Duden to recheck it once you have it."

"Yes, Sir," they both said.

Mr. Shafer, you may leave, but you, Mr. Duden, stay here."

"Yes, Sir."

"Specialist Murphy, Pichler, and Private Roby come in." They came in and just stood there, and I said, "You three know how to report?" They reported sloppy. "You still want to work in the parts room?"

"Yes, Sir," they both said.

"Are you two going to do your job properly?"

"Yes, Sir," again, they both said.

"Well, you two better, that place has been completely redone with the help of such men as Mr. Duden and Murphy and others." "You both on probation if you screw up you will pay for it." "Specialist Murphy will you work one more week in the parts room show these two how it is supposed to be?"

"Yes, Sir," he said with a smile.

"Mr. Duden, do you have any objections to these two working in the parts room?"

"No, Sir."

"If they give you any trouble, let me know, and they will pay for it."

"Yes Sir," Warrant Duden and Specialist Murphy said.

"Alright, get out to the site and finish putting that place in order."

They left, and I grabbed my list and handed it to the clerk and said, "Type this up and give me two copies, this is confidential and isn't to be talked about, understand."

"Yes, Sir," said Specialist Chris.

"Oh yes, get me the phone number of the stockade," I added.

I called the stockade and said, "This is Major York C. O. of the Third of the Seventh when are you going to release Mr. Houser?"

"About an hour and a half, Sir?"

"Would you have him report to my office at the barracks?"

"Yes, Sir, we will."

"I'll be back in thirty minutes," I said to Chris. I had to get my uniforms, so I figured I would get that out of the way. It took me ten minutes to get them, so I dropped them off at my house then headed back to the barracks. I was reading a technical book on the missiles systems when Warrant officer Houser came into the office.

"Sir Warrant Officer Houser here to see you," said Chris.

"Have him sit; I will let you know when to let him in."

"Yes, Sir." I made him wait for about twenty minutes I wanted him to sweat a little before he came in front of me.

"Chris, let him in."

"Sir, Warrant Houser, reporting as ordered."

"Sit down, Mr. Houser." I walked to the door and said, "Hand me his personnel file, Chris." He already had it ready, and he handed it to me.

I sat down and looked at his file, as I was looking, he said, "Sir, I wish to apologize to you for my actions last week and my lack of ability."

I looked up and asked with a somber voice, "You want to stay in the Army and keep your rank?"

"Yes, Sir."

"What did you do before you became a warrant officer?"

"Supply, Sir."

"As a kid, did you ever work on cars?"

"Yes, Sir."

"Whose idea was it to put you in command of communication and parts?"

"Captain Morgan."

"Ever do any drugs?"

"I've tried marijuana, Sir."

"When was the last time you use?"

"It has been years, Sir."

"Your record shows this has been the first time you have been in trouble, at least in the military."

"Yes, Sir."

I rechecked his record and said, "I don't play games, this unit is a mess; I can't afford you screwing up, war is coming."

"Are you going to screw up again?" "I need to know now."

"Not on purpose, Sir."

"A good player on the team will tell his coach that he is having troubles are you going to be that good player Mr. Houser?"

"Yes, Sir."

"Well, you can stay in the Army with your rank." "However, I will not put you back in charge of the communication and parts department." "You will be over the motor pool and supply you have two good sergeants running those two departments listen to them."

"Yes, Sir."

"Go to your quarters, clean up, get some rest, tomorrow, make sure you are at morning formation, and understand you are on probation."

"Yes, Sir."

I went out to the site after passing the gate I was halfway down to the parade ground when I saw a couple of children on the embankment looking around. I ignored them and continued to the parade ground I spotted Top and called him over. "Let's go into the mess hall." "Don't get close to the window, but look upon the embankment."

"Those dam kids again, I'll take care of it, Sir."

"No, wait fifteen minutes then head towards those kids, I'll be on the other side of the fence." "If you yell at them or run over to them, they will crawl under the fence and be in the woods before you get there, and they will be back." Top nodded, then I went out of the mess hall, hopped into the jeep, and said just before I left, "Fifteen minutes Top."

"Yes, Sir."

I drove back out, moving at a reasonable speed, the guard opened the gate before I got there, and I stopped the jeep and headed at a breakneck pace towards where those kids were. After a few minutes, I spotted the children, but they hadn't detected me yet. One was a small blond-haired boy and the other an older looking boy with light brown hair. As I was, creeping upon them, both boys got up and ran for the fence the older boy got under before I could get to him, but the younger one got his pants caught on the fence. I walked to the boy as Top, and Private Washington came over the embankment and down to the fence. As I unhooked the child's pants and pulled him through to my side, he had his head down and wasn't saying anything when I lifted his head; I was shocked to see someone I knew. "Frederick," I said, surprised.

"You know this boy, Sir?" Top asked.

"Yes, I met him and his mother in church Sunday his name is Frederick Muller." By this time, Frederick starting to cry, and I said in German, "What do you have to say for yourself?"

"I'm sorry," he replied meekly.

"Are you a spy?"

"No," he said frighten.

"I don't know if I can believe you, but we have ways of getting at the truth come with me." I took Frederick by hand, and we walked back to the jeep him crying all the way. As we got to the jeep, Sergeant Hill came through the gate with lunch, and I had a great idea. I placed Frederick in the jeep and said, "You stay there," and I drove into the site. I parked at the mess hall Top and Washington met us.

"What are you going to do with him, Sir?" asked Washington.

"Scare him, then take him to his mother." Washington went back to work; Top joined me, then all three of us went into the mess hall.

"Sergeant Hill, do you have some of those chocolate chip cookies?"

"Yes, Sir."

"Sergeant Hill, Top, can either one of you speak German?"

"Not me, Sir," said Sergeant Hill.

"I can, Sir," said Top.

"Play along with me, Top."

"Yes, Sir."

"Frederick, you sit right here now tell me what government you are working for?"

"No government, I don't work yet."

"Do you believe him, Sergeant?"

"No, not at all?"

"How much are they paying you to spy on us?"

"I have no money I've never got paid."

I looked at Top; he shook his head, then I said, "I think we must torture him Sergeant to get any answers from him."

"Yes." I motion Sergeant Hill to bring the milk and cookies, and I told Frederick, "Eat this and then drink some of that." Reluctantly he ate the cookie slowly, and then when he tasted it, he ate it a little faster. "It doesn't seem to be working do you think he might have to eat another."

"Yes." He devoured the second cookie drinking milk in between.

"Maybe I should eat another?" he asked with pleading eyes.

"Yes, eat another and more milk to drink."

"I like this kind of torture."

"If you eat another cookie, your mother is going to torture me."

"You want to eat lunch here with the Army men."

"Yes."

"Sergeant Hill, do we have enough food for this young man."

"Yes, Sir."

"James, I am not in trouble?"

"No, not by me but your mother might say something, is she working today."

"Yes."

"What time is she off work?"

"About five."

"You will stay with me until then, and I will take you home."

"It's almost formation time, Sir," said Top.

"Ok, the company clerk can watch him," I said to Top.

"Come with me, Frederick." I took him by his hand to my clerk and said, "You watch him while I'm at formation."

"Yes, Sir."

After formation, Frederick and I waited in line and got lunch. Frederick wolfed his food down I don't know where he was putting it. After we finished eating, we walked over to the communication and parts. "How are things going on here?"

"Very well, Sir," said Warrant Duden. "All parts are in their proper place, or we shipped them for repaired, and all missing parts have gotten found."

"Great, let me see how communications are doing." There were parts still all over the place, and I asked, "How are things going, Specialist Booker?"

"Ok, it would go a lot better if I had these parts, they need to get replaced."

"Get him the parts, Warrant Duden?"

"Yes, Sir."

"And if you have a problem getting them, just let me know also take that list of parts and have the clerk type two copies."

"Yes, Sir."

I took Frederick by the hand and said, "Let's go see the missiles." Frederick was all excited when we went to the missile's launchers.

"Can those missiles go to the moon?" he asked.

"No, they are a little too small; they are like bullets they knock down airplanes." We walked over to the mobile missiles, and I opened the door and helped Frederick in. "Now, don't touch anything?"

"I won't." After the missiles, we went to see the radars. He was fascinated with everything, but a missile site was no place for a boy, so we went back to where my sedan was.

Sergeant Hill was there with a bag, and he said, "This is for the boy."

"Frederick, the Sergeant, has something for you." He looked at me, then the bag, and I said, "Go and take it."

He smiled and said, "Its cookies."

"Are you going to thank him?"

"Thank you, Sergeant Cookie."

I smiled and said, "Frederick gave you a new name you're now Sergeant Cookie."

Sergeant Hill smiled and ruffled Frederick's hair and said, "Your welcome."

"Well, let go, Frederick." I put him in the sedan, and off we went. I stopped at the barracks and picked up the two lists of wants I had then headed to my house so that I could clean him up. When we got out of the car, Frederick immediately went to the sandbox with the swing and slide. I went over to him, grabbed his hand, and said, "Let's go inside and get cleaned up."

"Is this your house?" "It's nice, much nicer than mama's and mine."

"You think so."

We went in, and Frederick peeked into every room when he came to the other bedroom that I made the beds he asked, "Is this my room?"

"That would be nice, wouldn't Frederick."

"You have a big house; mama would like it, and so do I."

"Come into the bathroom so I can clean you up." By the time I finish cleaning up Frederick, it was three o'clock, he had to use the toilet, so I walked out of the bathroom. I parked the sedan and got the VW, and we headed downtown.

"Why are you not in school today?"

"My teacher is mean, and I don't like school."

"How is your teacher mean?"

"He yells at me and sometimes spanks or shakes me."

"For what?"

"For talking to others in the class or for not paying attention."

"Does your mother know you get spanked at school?"

"I told her."

"And what did she say?"

"I had to go to school, to stop talking when I am not supposed to and pay attention."

"Sounds like your mother is right."

"I try, but I can't help it, or I get blamed for what someone else does."

"Well, I have to tell you if I were your daddy, I would pull down your pants give you a spanking for not going to school today." He frowned, and I added, "But of course, if I were your father, you wouldn't have the problems with that teacher after I finished with him."

He looked up at me and said, "I wish you were my daddy." I put my arm around him, and he snuggled against me.

"Where does your mother work?"

He pointed to a small restaurant we had an hour to wait before she got off, so I took Frederick shopping." I took his hand, and we walked into a toy store. As we walked in, Frederick's eyes were as large as saucers looking at all the toys. "Get what you would like, Frederick?"

"For me to keep?"

"Yes, even though you were bad today." He looked at the toys and then at me and said, "No, I was bad; I should not get anything." I looked at him and said, "It is alright you can have a toy I am not your father it is your mother who will punish you."

He looked at the toys real close, then picked one and said, "Is this alright?"

"Of course, you can have anything you want."

"I wish this."

I paid for the toy; we still had almost thirty minutes, I thought maybe some flowers would smooth over his mother and Frederick wouldn't get in too much trouble. I got a small bouquet of various flowers for Frederick to give to his mother and a bigger one from me. I handed the flowers to Frederick and said, "You give those flowers to your mother; maybe she won't be too angry with you."

"Why do you have flowers she is not mad at you?"

"Yes, I know."

He looked at me for a few seconds and then said, "Oh, you want mama to like you even more."

"Now, you understand." We had a few minutes, so we stood across the street until his mother came out. She came out of the restaurant looking tired but still could smile when she spotted us holding flowers.

She walked over and said, "What are you two doing here?"

"Well, I have come to give you flowers and Frederick well he has something to tell you."

"Oh, what is it, Frederick?"

Frederick looked at me, and I said, "Go ahead, tell your mother."

"I was bad today."

"Oh, Frederick, what did you do?"

"I didn't go to school?"

"Frederick, not again." "He does not get along with his teacher, and I think the teacher does not get along with him," She said to me.

"Yes, he has told me, have you tried talking to the teacher?"

"Yes, he is a no-nonsense person, and he treats the children like they were adults working for him; he won't listen to me."

"He told me that the teacher spanks him and shakes him."

"I do not know what to do?"

"Keep him home tomorrow, and let me see what I can do."

"Would you, that would be a great help."

"Sure, but I think there is something else Frederick needs to tell you, is that not right Frederick?"

"I did something else bad."

"What else did you do, Frederick?"

"I was at the American rocket base."

"Frederick, you could go to jail for that."

"He and another boy climbed under the fence. They were looking at the missiles they had been doing this for some time." "The danger is one of my men might shoot at them, especially at night."

"I assure you, James, he will be punished."

"Well, that is up to you, but he might have gotten punished enough already."

"What did you do?"

"I scared him treated him like a real spy, didn't I Frederick?"

"Yes, he tortured me too."

"Tortured?" questioned a concern, Maria.

"Tell your mother how we tortured you."

"They asked who I was working for, and then when I told them no one, they force me to eat chocolate chip cookies and drink milk."

"It doesn't sound like you got forced very hard." Frederick smiled and shook his head no.

"Sergeant Cookie gave me some to take home; they taste good."

"They are," I said.

"I then got to eat lunch with the soldiers." "After lunch, James took me to see the rockets up close; they aren't the rockets that go to the moon."

"Well, thank you for taking good care of him; he is all I have."

"Have you eaten yet?"

"No."

"Well, I will take you both to dinner."

"I can't I have to go to the store and get some groceries."

"I can do something about that also." I put Frederick in the back seat of my car and Maria in the front. "I am assuming you don't want to go to the place where you work."

"No, the food is not very good."

"You point the way." We went across town to a small restaurant. I ordered chicken, fries, and beer, as did Frederick except he had milk. Maria ordered fish with a beer. I grabbed a french-fry and threw it into my mouth then I grabbed the leg of the chicken and tore it off, and I was about to take a bite when I notice everyone was staring at me. "What is the matter?"

"Do you always eat with your hands?" asked Maria.

I put my chicken down and said, "In America, some foods such as french-fries and fried chicken, we eat it with hands." "However, I am not in American; please correct me if I do something wrong."

"Good, and I will say something."

"I think it is a good idea to eat with my hands," said Frederick.

"You eat with a knife and fork Frederick," said Maria. Eating French fries with a fork wasn't so hard, but the chicken was something else. At least, I could drink the beer out of the bottle without committing a German taboo.

"Mama, James took me to his house and washed me."

"He did, did he."

"Yes, he has a big house with a bedroom for me."

"He does."

"Yes, he bought me a toy, also."

"Even though you were bad today."

"Yes, he said that he isn't my daddy yet that you would punish me."

"Oh, not your daddy yet," she said with a smile.

Frederick then got up and whispered in his mother's ear, but I could hear him; he said, "I think he loves me."

"I am sure he does."

"I think he loves you too."

"Well, we will see about that."

"No, he is correct, and I know it is sudden, but there is something wonderful about you and Frederick that I feel deep inside."

"He would make a good daddy, mama."

"We will see Frederick."

"Go kiss her young man, don't they kiss girls in America," said an old woman at another table.

"Well, I don't have chicken grease on my hands; I guess it would be alright." I got up and kissed her much to the delight of everyone. We finished eating, and after Frederick had some ice cream, we went to the PX, and I told Maria, "Get whatever you wish, I will pay for it."

"You have already shown Frederick and me too much kindness."

"Maria, I have a lot of money; this is not any trouble for me."

"Well, I will not get too much."

"No, get what you want." We went through the PX and started picking out things; I explain what some of the products were. She wasn't taking much, but I fixed that by putting the amount she should have, and I added a few more things that she didn't choose. We headed to her apartment, which was down from the train station. Her building was a worn-out drab yellowish looking building five stories high. She handed Frederick her key as we went up two flights of stairs carrying groceries. Inside the apartment, I found out why Frederick thought my quarters were great. It had a bedroom kitchen combined with one large bed and a bathroom on the left side of the bed. It was a tiny worn-out place with one window over the sink. I had to give Maria credit; she did have it very clean. As I helped Maria with the groceries, Frederick played on the floor with his toy.

We finished putting the groceries away, and she said, "I've never had this much before." "James, would you like some coffee or tea?"

"I don't drink coffee, but tea sounds good."

As she boiled some water, she said to Frederick, "Frederick, you can play with that toy tomorrow; you need a bath now." Without argument, he shoved his toy under the bed and removed his clothes.

"Maria, would you like me to run his water?"

"That would be helpful." I grabbed the dishwashing soap and went to the bathroom. "What are you going to do with that soap?"

"It's an American custom, a bubble bath." Frederick followed me to see what I would do; I plugged the drain and added the soap and adjusted the water. Immediately bubbles started to form much to the delight and squeals of Frederick.

Maria became curious, looked in, smiled, and said, "We don't use any dish soap like that, but it does look fun."

"It also helps clean Frederick, and it will keep the tub cleaner." When the water rose high enough, I lifted Frederick and placed him in. I gave him things to play with while he was in the tub.

I turned around, and Maria said, "Thank you." Then she kissed me passionately, and I returned the favor then held her in all the right places. We had tea and talked, then she said, "I need to wash Frederick's hair, or he will just play in there."

"Why don't you relax and let me do it?"

"Alright."

"Alright, Frederick, it's wash time." His face, to wash, was a challenge I had to shampoo his hair twice, and it came out five shades lighter. When I dried him, he was yawning, so I took him to bed.

I was surprised to see Maria completely nude, and she said, "It's my turn to bath would you like to wash my hair."

"Absolutely." She pulled back the blanket, and I gently laid him down and pulled up the blanket as he stuck his thumb in his mouth, then I kissed him. "Well, do you want me in the tub with you?"

"Of course, how else are you going to wash my hair."

"I should warn you I have a lot of scares from the war." I got in first; then, she got in front of me. I started to move my soapy hands over her much to her pleasure and mine. After we bath, we both got in her bed then made love while Frederick slept. About midnight, I had to go back. I gave her a goodnight kiss as well as Frederick. At home, I got some sleep with a smile on my face, and by five forty-five, I was heading for my office.

I met Top in the mess hall drinking coffee. "You look like you're in a good mood," said Top.

"I had an interesting night."

"That German boy's mother?"

"Yeah, and it's been a long time." Top laughed, and then Top, and I walked over to my office, Lieutenant Dizon was waiting for me.

15

IMPROVING THE UNIT AND RELATIONSHIP

After formation, Mr. Duden approached me and said, "Sir, I ordered the parts that Specialist Booker needs, but it would be nice if we could get them quicker."

"Do you have a list of the parts?"

"Yes, Sir."

He handed me the list, and I said, "I'll see what I can do." Lieutenant Keith Kallstrom was put in command while Lieutenant Dizon and I were gone with instructions to listen to what Top says. We left early in the morning, so I could get what Booker needed. It was the first time I was in Schweinfurt. It was made famous for its ball-bearing factory bombed continuously in World War Two, and they still make ball bearings there. We drove into the post; there was a guard at the gate; it was a smaller, more compact place. There was a row of large buildings, to my left and mixed sized buildings to my right and far down the end of the street; it looked like an aircraft hangar. We stopped and headed for the first building, which Lieutenant Dizon said was the Head Quarters building. Across the street from the building was a small building with several large antennas. The door was open, and I saw men sitting around, I figured it was the radio building. We went into Head Quarters and approached a clerk. "Major James York to see Colonel Greenhill."

"One moment Major." He got on the phone and called the Colonel, "Go upstairs, Sir to the next floor turn right the Colonel's office is halfway down on the right there will be a receptionist there." Without saying a word, the Lieutenant and I did as the clerk said and found the Colonel's office and went in.

"Major York to see Colonel Greenhill."

"Go right in, Sir." The receptionist pointed to a door on the right.

"Colonel Greenhill, it's good to see you."

"You too, James."

"This is my X.O. Lieutenant Marc Dizon."

"Yes, I remember you, Lieutenant."

"Well, sit-down, gentlemen."

"I have a lot of things I need to get to make Charlie working properly." "Do you wish to discuss them now or later, Sir?"

"Is it a long list?"

"Yes Sir, that unit is in bad shape, but getting better."

"Why don't we wait until after the meeting?"

"Alright, Sir, I won't say anything unless it comes up in the meeting."

"I do have another list of parts that I was given this morning for radio parts." "I was wondering if I could get them from your radio shack, and when we get the replacement parts, we will give them back."

"I'll call communications building." He dialed a number and said, "Lieutenant, this is Colonel Greenhill come to my office."

He hung up the phone and said, "So how are things going."

"It's a struggle, Sir, but things are getting better slowly; it will get much better when I get the things I need."

"And what is your opinion of the condition of the unit Lieutenant Dizon?"

"Major York is doing a fine job, Sir, things are heading in the right direction."

"At this time, I have seven men I trust and are an asset to my unit." "Lieutenant Dizon is one of my best and will make a fine company commander someday."

"Sounds good, James."

"Did you ever get into your quarters yet?"

"Yes, it took a lot of cleaning with a lot of help."

There was a knock at the door, and the receptionist poked in his head in and said, "Lieutenant Brown is here to see you, Colonel."

"Send him in."

"Lieutenant Brown, reporting as ordered, Sir." He was a young, thin Second Lieutenant with short hair and with black horn-rim glasses.

"Lieutenant, this is Major James York." "He is Charlie's company commander; they need some radio parts that he will replace when his parts that he ordered comes in."

"Yes, Sir." I handed the list of parts to the Lieutenant, and he looked at it then said, "Yes, Sir, I have these parts in stock."

"Good, gather them up, and the Major will pick them up later."

"Yes, Sir."

"Lieutenant Brown, would it be alright if I sent a man down here for a couple of days." "I would like to put him in your communications department to see how a proper communications department works?"

"Yes, that would be just fine, Sir."

"Thanks." Lieutenant Brown left, and Lieutenant Dizon gave me a look like I was crazy but didn't say anything. We did some more small talk, and then the Colonel told me where the meeting would be and told me that he had some things to do to prepare for it, so we left. When I was alone with the Lieutenant, I said, "I'm sending Specialist Booker here to find out why we have a weak signal at the site."

"You trust Booker."

"Yes." "Let's go see what that communications Lieutenant has for us." The first thing I noticed when I went into the communication building was the men's laid-back attitude and the lack of activity. "Sergeant, Lieutenant Brown has some parts for me, I'm Major York."

"Lieutenant, do you have any parts for a Major York," the Sergeant yelled without getting up. The Lieutenant came into the room, carrying a large box full of parts. I took the box, thanked him, and left with Lieutenant Dizon to the sedan to put the box in the trunk.

I turned to Lieutenant Dizon and said, "What did you observe when you went into that communication's building?"

"I don't know they seem laid back, not too busy."

"Yes, laid back, lack of activity, and a Lieutenant who appeared not knowing what he is supposed to do."

"Yes, your right, Sir."

"Should be interesting when Specialist Booker comes to see what he can come up with." We had time, so we walked around to see what the post looked like, there weren't that many buildings, but there was plenty of room to build some. As I said before, they did have a hanger for planes, but they used it for the motor pool. They had two mess halls right next to each other, which was interesting. They also had a small P.X., and movie theater tinier than the one in Bamberg.

We went back to the meeting in the conference room all the company commanders of the other units were already there. I sat down, and the Captain next to me said, "Major, the Colonel will throw a fit if he sees you haven't taken off your beret."

Everyone stared at me to see what I would do or say, and then I said, "Captain, what's your name?"

"Captain David Dring, Sir."

"Captain Dring, I am a Major in the Green Berets." "I am also a Medal of Honor winner." "Having a Medal of Honor, and being in the Green Berets gives me certain privileges." "These privileges include removing my hat or beret if I choose not to; however, I do respect Colonel Greenhill; so, I will remove it." At that, I removed the beret as everyone's mouth hung open; Lieutenant Dizon chuckled as Colonel Greenhill walked in.

We all stood up as he sat down, then we sat down, and the Colonel said, "Major York is correct in what he has said." "He also has the privilege to quit the Army when he wants the Major stays because he wishes to." "The Major doesn't need the money." "I suggest you read his book, and that's all I'll say about that except he is the new C.O. of Charlie."

"Well, hopefully, you'll straighten that place out, we are tired pulling your duty," said a Captain.

"I didn't think Captain there was someone as arrogant if not more arrogant than me; I stand corrected." "For your information, Charlie has been up and running for the last two days, and this coming Sunday, we are willing to take our turn and go on full duty."

"Alright enough of that, James, your unit will go on full duty, and the rest of you will continue to do the normal rotation." "I believe it would be best if we start by everyone introducing himself, "Lieutenant, you start."

"I'm Lieutenant Marc Dizon, the X.O. of Charlie."

"What are you doing here, Lieutenant, babysitting the Major?" said the arrogant Captain.

I turned beet red with anger and said, "Shoot your mouth one more time, Captain, and I will break your jaw."

"You won't have to James, that's insubordination." "Captain, James is a superior officer I'll have your bars, and you will find yourself out of the Army if I hear any more of that," said the Colonel.

"Yes, Sir," said the Captain.

"James, continue."

"Major James York, company commander of Charlie."

"Captain David Dring, Headquarters Company."

"Captain, I wish to talk to you after this meeting," I said.

"Yes, Sir."

"Captain Paul McMullen, Alfa Company," said the arrogant Captain.

"Captain Tom Riggs, of Bravo Company."

"Captain Joe Martin, Delta Company."

"Ok, we have another I.G. inspection in two months." "I expect everything in perfect order," the Colonel said.

"Sir Charlie may not be one hundred percent." Captain McMullen started to chuckle, and it irritated me.

"I need to know why James."

"Sir, when I speak to you after this meeting, you will understand."

"Alright, James." "Besides the inspection, we are sending a missile team to Crete for some training."

"What is this training, Sir?" I asked

"Crete is where we do live fire, James." I wouldn't mind sending a team there, I thought.

"When are you sending the team, Sir?" asked Captain Riggs.

"A week after the I.G. inspection, I will let you know a few days after the inspection."

"Do any of you have any problems you want to talk about?"

I waited, but no one said anything, so I said, "Yes, Sir, I wish to bring a few things up."

"Go ahead, James."

"As Captain McMullen pointed out Charlie has been down more times than it has been up, I'm trying to change that, but one trouble is parts breaking down, and we don't have any replacement parts." "The parts are either getting ordered or repaired, yet other units have the parts on hand why can't I call another unit and get the parts?"

"Because we need the extra part on hand in case our working part breaks down," said Captain McMullen with a smirk.

"So, what you are saying in a combat situation, it's better for one unit to be inoperable while another unit has a part that could bring it operational."

"Well, when we are at war, then maybe we can accommodate you."

"By that time, it will be too late, and I assure you we will be in a war in a year or less."

That got everyone's' attention, and the Colonel said, "Where did you get this information, James?"

"I know what I am about to say will sound a little odd, but I am confident that war is coming." "While I was a prisoner of war, I developed the ability to sense something was about to happen." "I am so good with this sense that I have, I've never been wrong."

"Oh, swell, we have a psychic commanding a missile unit," said Captain McMullen.

"When it comes, you will bury half your men."

"Alright, alright, let's get back to the issue gentlemen whether James is right or wrong about this war we should all get prepared as if he is right." "Frankly, James, you are right, for now on if you need a part right away, you can call the other units, and if they have an extra part, you will send it to the unit that needs it."

"What else, James?"

"I've read the T.M. on the Hawk missile, and I've talked to my best men on the Hawk." "Correct me if I'm wrong, but is it true that the new Migs the Russians have the Hawks are just too slow for them and is barely fast enough for the other Migs."

"I'm surprised you have figured this out so soon, and I am also surprised that the rest of you men haven't figured it out." "I can't go into detail mostly because I don't know much, but they are developing a far more advanced missile." "Of course, this is classified, and is not to talk about it outside the room."

"So, Sir, what are we to do in case of an attack," asked Captain Riggs.

"Just do your best, Captain."

"Anything else, James?"

"Yes, we have M fourteens; why not M sixteen, and what about getting some LAWs?"

"Good question, it's something that I should have been taken care of long ago, and I've let the ball drop, but I'll get on the phone today and take care of it you should have the new rifles in two weeks." "Why do you want the LAW?" asked the Colonel.

"You never know what you are going to run into, especially out in the field the units should have had them a long time ago."

"It makes sense, I'll get them also, the only problem I have is how to qualify the men with the weapons, but I'll figure something out."

"Anymore, James?"

"Anything else, Sir, I'll talk to you after this meeting."

"Alright, if there is nothing else, I will see you here next month."

The men got up and started to exit the door. I turned to Captain Dring and said, "Would you be able to house one of my men for a couple of days?" "I want him to study your communications."

"Yes, anytime I'll let my First Sergeant know he is coming."

"Great, and thanks."

The Colonel directed us to his office, and we sat down. I opened my briefcase and handed the list of things I needed to the Colonel. "Let's talk about why you won't be ready for the inspection first."

"Because with all the things that need to get done, it might not get done in time." "Look at the list."

He looked at the list, shook his head, and said, "Most of this, I can't do anything about."

"Then I must call General Abrams, but everything on that list is needed."

"What is this about more men?"

"I'm down on men I can't keep on maintaining that unit with the men I have."

"Well, I can get you some men."

"Sir, the Vietnam war is over; I don't need infantry people or artillery people; I need people with MOSs that fit the jobs I have."

"That would be nice, but the reality of it we seldom get those people we get what we can get."

"Where are all those men going, I know the MOS classes are full?"

"I don't know."

"Well, if you can't get me these things, I will get them from the General."

"You'll have to; I'm limited to what I can do."

"I hope there are no hard feelings for me going over your head."

"No, do everything you can to improve Charlie." At that, the Lieutenant and I excused ourselves and headed back to Bamberg. We got something to eat on the way back to the site my mind was thinking of that meeting with the Colonel and how he couldn't get me most of the things I needed. I liked the Colonel but thought he was near retirement and didn't want to be bothered. It was disappointing when I told them that war was coming, but if I were in their place, I wouldn't believe it either. We drove into the missile site and parked outside my office.

"Sir, do you care if I go home and change into fatigues."

"No, go ahead, take the sedan but let me get some things out first."

I put my briefcase in my office and asked the clerk, "Have you seen the First Sergeant?"

"He's down at the motor pool, Sir."

I went over to the communications building with the parts and said to Booker, "Once you get these parts installed, will the radio work at least at this end?"

"Yes, Major, but it is like I told you the main problem is at Headquarters." Progress! He called me Major for the first time.

"Michael, before you start, come with me I have something to discuss with you." We went back to my office, and I had him sit down. "There is something I want you to do?"

"What's that, Major?"

"After you finish putting that radio together, I want to send you down to Headquarters communication building to do a little spying to see why they are so screwed up there." He nodded, and I continued, "You must go down there and act like you know little or nothing." "You're not to tell anyone even if you have friends."

"Are you going to kick some ass, Major?"

"That's just what I intend to do."

"Do you want pictures?"

"That would be good." "I'll see if I can get a camera."

"No need I have one just get me the film."

"Your cover is your just down for a couple of days for training."

"You will report to the head quarter's First Sergeant who will give you housing."

"Alright."

"Michael, don't argue with anyone, and for sure, don't fight with anyone."

"I won't, Major."

"How long will it take for you to put our radio back together?"

"It will be done before the end of the day."

"Good, you will go tomorrow morning."

After Booker left, I pulled out the wish list from my briefcase and was about to call the General when I got a knock at the door, "Door is unlocked." In walked Top and I had him sit, and I said, "What's up?"

"We had another break-in, someone came under the fence over by the motor pool, and they took some gas and diesel."

I leaned back and thought about it for a second then said, "Have the motor pool Sergeant come here we got to get these guys." Top got on the phone and called Sergeant Pete Walker.

"How did it go at Headquarters, Sir?"

I smiled and said, "I think you know already." "I like Colonel Greenhill, but I feel he's just hanging around waiting for retirement." "About the only things I got were some M-16s and Laws we will talk about that later, and we can now get parts from the other units when we need them right away." "I'll have to call General Abrams on the rest of this list." "I'm sending Booker tomorrow down there to spy on their commutations."

"Alright."

Sergeant Walker came into my office and sat down, and I grabbed a calendar and said, "Ok, last night, our fuel got raided when was the time before last night Sergeant Walker."

"About a day before you got here, Sir."

"Alright, and the time before that?"

"About a week, Sir, for the same amount."

"There is a pattern, Sir," said Top.

"Yes, and we are going to spring a trap, but first, I'm going to contact the German police before someone gets killed."

The motor pool Sergeant left, and then I called General Abrams. Top was going to leave, but I told him to stay. "Major James York, wishing to talk to General Abrams."

"One moment Major."

"General Abrams."

"General, it's James York."

"Oh, James, what can I do for you?"

"Well, I hope you're ready to spend some money."

He chuckled and said, "Alright, what do you want, and did you try to go through Colonel Greenhill first."

"I did try, but he said he couldn't do anything."

"Alright hold on, I'll put you on a conference call, and I'll get my secretary in here she will write down the list." I started telling him what I wanted when I got to the improvements to the site he said, "Justify why you want these things."

"Two weeks ago, I had two small boys climb under the fence and watch what we are doing. Last night we had from another area someone came under the fence and stole some of gas and diesel, which wasn't the first time this has happened." I went on and explained all the reasons for my wants.

"Alright, James, I'll get you all of this, but I might have to us the C.B.s instead of the Army Core of Engineers they are tied up."

"It's alright with me, Sir."

"Why don't you hire a local German company to work on your barracks and mess hall?"

"Sounds like a good idea, Sir."

"Anything else, James?"

"Yes, Sir, I need about forty men with the correct MOS."

"Correct MOS?"

"Yes, what has been happening when men get sent down here, we get men with MOSs like infantry and artillery etcetera."

"Do you have a list of MOSs you need?"

"Yes." I gave him the list I needed, and I told him that this had been a problem affecting the whole battalion. He said he would do something about it, and I said make sure the men's orders say they are to come to me or go to other units.

"Anything else, James?"

"Yes, you might get a phone call from Colonel Greenhill about something I said."

"What about?"

"I said we would be at war in Europe within the year."

"Where did you get that information?"

"Intuition that I develop while I was a prisoner of war; I've never been wrong, Sir."

"I'm not knocking your intuition, but I need hard evidence if you ever get any let me know."

"Yes, Sir."

"I'll get right on this list you gave me." "You should see some results in seven to ten days."

"Thanks, Sir."

"How's the unit shaping up?"

"I've straightened out some departments, and we are operational, but once I get those things on the list, I will be at one hundred percent."

"Sounds like you're doing good."

"Thank you, Sir."

"If there isn't anything else, I'll get right on this and let me know if you want anything else."

"Yes, Sir, I will." I looked at Top and said, "We got everything."

"Yes, Sir, nice to have a general for a friend," Top said.

"We go on full duty Sunday; we'll need to let everyone know. "I better go check that parts section to see how it is coming along." I got up and went across to the parade ground with Top joining me. "How are things going here?" I asked.

Mister Duden turned and around and said, "Well Sir, everything is straightened out, and we have ordered the parts we need, but I have to tell you I sure could use a sections chief someone who knows what he is doing." "This place takes a lot of my time, and I wish I could spend more time in communications."

"Help is coming; I will explain more in tomorrow's morning formation." By the end of the workday, Booker fixed the radio. Well, as good as it was going to get fixed, just as he said. Everything was up and running, so; I headed back to the barracks with Lieutenant Dizon while Top took the jeep. I told the Lieutenant and Top that after morning formation, I would be doing some military and personal business. After checking with my clerk, I left for home, and when I got there, I had a premonition something wasn't right. I got out of the sedan and quietly went up the stairs to the front door. I found the door open, so I went in, on the kitchen table was some bread, condiments, lunch meat, milk and a used glass that had milk in it. I grabbed a butcher's knife, checked the master bedroom, found no one there, and all the windows I had closed. I then went to the bathroom and found it had gotten used, but no one was there. I went into the bedroom next to the bathroom and discovered my burglar. There sound asleep on the bed was Frederick. He was dirty from what I assume was playing in the sandbox. I kissed him on the cheek and then went back into the kitchen to put the knife and food away. Then, I went back into the bedroom with a wet washcloth, removed his shoes, socks, lederhosen, and shirt, then washed him the best way I could. In the process of this, he woke, I kissed him and told him to go back to sleep which he did. I put the blanket on him, drew the shade down, and then picked up his clothes and shut the door. I placed the dirty clothes on the chair and went into my bedroom to change. I was down to just my shorts when in walked Frederick rubbing his eyes and yawning. "Frederick." He came over to me, so I pick him up, and he laid his head on my shoulder then closed his eyes. I sat down in the easy chair that rock and rocked him for a few minutes.

"Do you love me?" he asked.

"More than you could understand."

"I love you too."

"Are you going to be my daddy?"

"Do you want me to be?"

"Yes."

"Have you talked to your mother about this?"

"Yes, she said you would make a good daddy."

"Well, your mother and I would have to get married, and I don't know how she feels about me."

"She loves you."

"She told you this?"

"Yes."

"She used the word love?"

"Yes."

"Well, I love her too, but we just met we need to take our time just in case there is something she doesn't like about me."

"Mama said that too."

"I need to get dress and clean your clothes your mother is going to get off work soon." I got up, placed Frederick back in the chair then went into my bedroom as he rocked himself contentedly.

After cleaning his clothing, I made the bed he was in, then we went outside to get the V.W., and we were off. We met his mother just as she came out of the restaurant. "Frederick, you didn't go to James missile base again?" Maria asked.

"No, mama, I went to his house," he said enthusiastically.

"Frederick, you shouldn't go there; it isn't your house."

"I'd rather he be there than around that missile base beside it is safe, and I have plenty of food."

"It's alright, mama, we are going to live there someday when you know that there is nothing you don't like about him."

"What do you mean, Frederick?" his mother asked.

"He is going to marry you and be my daddy."

"Sounds like a good idea to me," I said.

She looked at me, taken aback by what I said then replied, "Really?"

"Yes, I know we haven't known each other for very long, but I have a deep feeling an instinct that has never failed me besides, I love you and Frederick very much."

"See, mama."

"Yes, Frederick and I have that feeling also but let's wait for a little to make sure."

"Of course," I replied. I talked Maria into going to my place, so I could cook a home cook meal and besides, I didn't feel like eating out.

I got Frederick a few more toys to keep him occupied, which excited him, and then we headed home. When we arrived at my house, Frederick excitedly wanted to show his mother everything. After Frederick calmed down and started to play with his toys on the floor, I said to Maria, "Why don't you go ahead and bath while I start dinner."

"Alright, what are you going to fix?"

"Tonight, my darling, we are going to eat Italian style or at least American Italian, spaghetti with meatballs, garlic bread, and red wine, milk for Frederick." She went into the master bedroom, removed her clothing, then walked into the bathroom. She was a beautiful woman, not a blemish on her. She had shoulder-length blond hair and blue eyes. She was about five feet seven and weighed maybe about a hundred and fifteen pounds; however, I was never a good judge. She was one of the most beautiful women I ever saw, like my high school sweetheart, who I felt was very beautiful. As I was preparing the food, I could hear her singing in the shower, and she had an excellent voice. "Frederick, can you sing as good as your mother?"

He stared at me then where his mother was singing from and said, "I don't know."

"Well, we must see someday." Frederick went back to playing and me fixing dinner. The shower finally stopped. Maria came out of the bathroom with a towel on her head and another one wrapped around her.

"Do you have anything I could wear?" Maria asked.

"I have sweats."

"Sweats?"

I smiled and said, "Let me show you." I grabbed the sweats and gave it to her she got dressed, and we both went into the kitchen to finish fixing dinner, and then we all sat down to eat. I tied a dishcloth around Frederick's neck, knowing what was going to happen once Frederick dove into the spaghetti.

Quickly, Frederick finished eating so he could get back playing. I washed his hands and face removed his dirty bib, and somehow, he still got spaghetti sauce on his shirt and pant, so I removed them and let him play in his underwear. "I'll wash these after we eat," I told Maria.

"Do you have a washer, perhaps I can wash my things also."

"Yes." I gave her some slippers, and we both went to the garage to do the washing. We went into the house. Maria sat on the couch as I cleaned the dishes, she wanted to do them, but I said no, just relax.

"It's warm tonight," said Maria.

"Yes, it is, is this normal?" I said as I had my back to her.

"No, I think I will take off my shirt."

"That would be nice." I turned around, and Frederick was on the couch with his mother nursing him.

I stared for a while with a grin on my face; finally, Maria said, "Does this bother you?"

"No, it is probably healthier I just never seen any child nurse at his age; in fact, I've never seen a baby nurse." "Well, it's alright with me just leave me a little Frederick," I said with a smile.

"The last person I dated objected, and I never saw him again."

"That won't happen to me."

"I'm glad." I finished the kitchen and joined Frederick and Maria on the couch. Frederick left his mother's arms, climbed onto my lap, and started snuggling.

"Can you stay the night I'll drive you home about eight when I return for Frederick."

"Yes, of course." I took Frederick to bed covered him up. I then picked up his toys and sat on the couch with Maria, and we embraced. We moved our passion to the bedroom where we made love then fell asleep in each other's arms. Sometime that night, I woke with movement on my bed, and I found out Frederick was crawling between us. I kissed him, and I fell back to sleep.

By about four in the morning, I went to the bathroom to shower and shave, leaving Maria and Frederick sleeping. When I got out of the shower and shaved, I headed to the bedroom to get in my dress greens, but Maria was up making breakfast. "You should be sleeping." "I could get something to eat at the base."

"I do this because I wish to besides, I'm hungry too."

"Alright," I said with a smile and went into the bedroom to change.

After I ate, I headed to my office at the barracks, and there was Top and Lieutenant Dizon.

"A bit late, aren't you, Sir," said Top with a smile.

"I had a late one with a friend, and she made breakfast for me." Both Top and the Lieutenant had shit grins on their faces, and I said, "It would have been impolite not to eat her breakfast."

"Yes," they both said with a smile.

"Well, it would have." "I want to have a meeting with all department heads tomorrow and with our special group again after the meeting."

"Yes, Sir," they both said.

We all went out to the formation. After everyone got accounted for, I started in by saying, "In the next few weeks, there is going to a lot of changes coming." "This building and the mess hall I plan to renovate, I will be getting contractors today to do the work." "The C.B.s will be improving and adding buildings to the site." "We will be getting rid of the M-14s and getting M-16s." "We will also be getting some LAWs you will all have to qualify with these weapons how that's going to happen you will find out later." "I want to remind you again if you have any contraband or illegal drugs get rid of them or pay the price." "You will be on full duty starting Sunday." "I want you to take inventory of all your field equipment anything you have missing give a list to the supply sergeant." "Do you have anything, Lieutenant?"

"No, Sir."

"What about you, Top?"

"Should I announce the meeting tomorrow?"

"The first meeting, yes."

"There will be a staff meeting tomorrow at O nine hundred for all department heads NCOs' and officers."

"Specialist Booker do you have what you need for your stay at headquarter?" I asked.

"Yes."

"You will leave when you get to the site." The formation got dismissed, and I went back into my office as Top followed me. "Top, are you driving Booker."

"Yes, Sir."

"Make sure he has some film for his camera."

"He has it, Sir."

"Good, I'll be gone most of the day."

"Yes, Sir."

"Things are about to pop around here if you know what I mean."

"Yes, Sir," he said with a smile.

I headed back to the house and found Frederick was bathing. "Maria, why don't you go ahead and get yourself ready, and I will finish Frederick."

"Alright." I finished washing him, then I lifted him out of the tub and dried him off. By the time I had him dressed and his hair comb, Maria was dressed and had made lunch for him. I placed a couple of chocolate chip cookies in his lunch, and then off we went back to Maria's Apartment.

"Does Frederick have any schoolbooks or things he needs?" I asked Maria.

"No."

"I don't like that you have to walk to work; I should come back and get you."

"No, I have two hours to be there, and I still need to put on some makeup."

"You don't need any makeup."

"That's nice of you to say, but my boss insisted on it."

"Alright, I will see you later."

"Yes, I would like that." It took me about thirty minutes to get to Frederick's school with Frederick telling me which way to go.

"Now, Frederick, you let me do the talking; you just sit quietly in the seat unless someone asks you a question." He nodded yes, and in we went, Frederick showed me where the headmaster or principal office is. "I wish to see the headmaster," I asked the secretary.

She first looked at me, then Frederick, and said, "Do you have an appointment?"

"No."

"Well, I will see if he has time to see you."

"May I ask why you are with Frederick?"

"He is my son."

"Son, what is your name?"

"James York." Frederick smiled but didn't say anything. The secretary looked at me, confused, knocked on a door then went in.

A few minutes later, she came out with an older man, and he looked at Frederick and me and said, "Please come in, I am Headmaster Burger." "I didn't know Frederick had a father."

"Do you speak English?"

"Yes."

"Good, then let us speak English Frederick doesn't speak the language yet."

"I am Fredericks's stepfather, but I do not care for that term for a father is one who loves his children."

"Very well, what brings you here?"

"Frederick has not been to school for several days."

"Yes, I was going to contact his mother."

"Have you ever asked Frederick why he doesn't come?"

"Well, no."

"Don't you think it is unusual for a child to miss so much?"

"Yes."

"If you get his record, I would guess he didn't miss those many days last year."

"I'll get it." He went to the secretary's office, came back with a folder, and studied it then; he said, "You are right, do you know why?"

"Yes, it's his teacher; he has been abusing him for minor offenses."

"In what way?"

"Shaking and spanking in front of the other children."

"I find it hard to believe he is a fine teacher a bit strict, but a good teacher, perhaps you just don't know our customs here in Germany."

"I know what abuse is, and it doesn't matter what country you are in abuse is abuse." "I'm guessing that if you check the files of the other children in that class, you will find that absents are higher than normal."

"I'll check on that."

"So, what are we going to do with this teacher?" "You don't approve of spanking or shaking, do you."

"Of course not, but the teacher must maintain disciplined."

"If something does not get done about him, he may not be teaching much anymore, especially if he touches Frederick." "I assure you since I'm very wealthy, the news media and courts will hear of this."

"What would you like me to do?"

"Replace the teacher, but somehow I don't think you are going to do that because you believe he wouldn't do such a thing."

"No, I don't."

"Why don't you call him in here and ask him to see what he says, and talking to some of the other students also."

"I'll call one of his students first." He got up again and told his secretary to bring one of Frederick's classmates into his office. While we waited, he asked Frederick, "Frederick, what else does Mr. Shuler do besides spanking and shaking you?"

Frederick looked at me, and I said, "You can answer him."

"He yells at me and sometimes throws things at me."

"Has he ever hit you other places besides your bottom?" I asked.

"Sometimes, my head and he hit my hands with a ruler."

"Do you see him doing this to others?"

"Yes, but mostly boys." There was a knock at the door, the secretary showed a little girl in, and she sat next to Frederick.

"Do you know her, Frederick?" I asked.

"Yes, this is Greta; she is in my class."

"Greta, I want you to tell me the truth has Mr. Shuler been mean to anyone in your classroom, especially the boys?" the principal asked.

She got terrified, put her head down, and said, "Yes, he is mean to everyone, but don't tell him because he will spank me."

"Does he spank a lot of boys and girls, including Frederick?"

"Yes, especially Frederick."

"Alright, you can go back to your classroom," the principal said.

She got up and started to leave when I said, "Greta, don't say anything about what got asked in here." "If you get asked, just say that the headmaster told where to go after school."

"Yes."

I looked at the principal, and I was livid, then he said, "I can see you are angry, but I think I should talk to the teacher first."

"We will talk to this teacher," I said.

"Yes." He told his secretary to get him and stay with the class until she was relieved. A short time later, an older tall, stern-looking man walked into the principal's office, he stared at me, and if looks could kill, I would be dead.

"What is this American swine doing here?" I tensed up, and if Frederick weren't here, I would have put this fool through the wall.

"Carl, he is an American soldier, and he speaks German."

"I do not like Americans, especially military Americans."

"Let me guess you were a Hitler Youth," I said discussed.

"I was if it is any business of yours, and I was an officer in Wehrmacht, which I am proud of."

The principal was shocked to learn of his background. He recovered fast enough to ask him, "Is it true that you have been handing out corporal punishment to your students."

"I have my methods of discipline."

"Does that include hitting on the hands and head and throwing things?" I snarled.

"Sometimes, I must use all means like for that one in the back who won't learn; by the way, I don't answer to you."

I tightened my jaw at what he said I wanted to knock him out but didn't, and the principal said, "No, you don't, but you have to answer to me, and I'm telling you your fired you may leave this school."

"You would fire me because of this American degenerate who isn't even Arian and that mental defective you should destroy."

"Get out; get out now before I turn the Major lose on you."

He stood, and I said, "Shuler, for your information, I am German, as are my uncles who fought to remove that fool who destroyed Germany." "My son Frederick is far smarter than you will ever know; consider yourself lucky I don't put you through the wall." At that, he stormed out of the office much to my and Frederick's delight.

"Major, would you please go to the classroom with Frederick while I call for another teacher to replace Mr. Shuler."

"Do you want me to tell your secretary what happen?"

"Yes, her name is Miss Rosenberger; don't go into any detail the class should know too that will make them happy."

"Alright."

"Oh yes, I wish to thank you for revealing how bad a teacher Mr. Shuler, was."

"It's alright; I would do anything for Frederick." "Alright, Frederick, show me your classroom." As we walked down the hall, I said, "Frederick, do you know what has just happened."

"Yes, Mr. Shuler is not my teacher anymore."

"Yes, you're right, do you think you can stand up in front of your class and tell them what you know?"

"Sure, I'll tell them everything."

"Very good."

We walked into the classroom, and I said to Miss Rosenberger, "Frederick has something to say to his friends."

"Go ahead, Frederick," said Miss Rosenberger.

With a smile, Frederick started in and told the class everything. The children opened with a roar of approval. Frederick continued, "Mr. Shuler said some mean thing to my daddy, and he got mad when Mr. Shuler said bad things about me." "The headmaster threw him out of the school." The class shouted their approval again.

"Go sit down, Frederick," I said. "I want to tell you all as Miss Rosenberger will tell you this doesn't mean that the rules have changed, that means no clowning in class, no talking when you are not supposed to, this is a place to learn you know when you are bad."

One young boy said, "Are you not an American soldier when did you become Frederick's father?"

"Frederick can explain everything to you later." "All that is important is I love Frederick very much."

"Daddy, tell us a story," Frederick stood up and said.

The rest of the class approved of Fredericks's request, and I said, "Frederick, this is not my class Miss Rosenberger is in charge until your new teacher gets here."

"It is alright with me, Major, if you have the time."

I looked at my watch, it was still early, and I said, "Alright." The only story I could think of was the story of my great-grandfather, who I was named after. "This is a true story of my Great Grandfather James York or Soaring Eagle with Many Coups."

"What is a Coup?" asked a little girl who stood up.

"It's an American Indian word for a brave act; my grandfather was a Shoshone Indian." I went on with the story, a short G rated version of it without interruption. Sometime during the story, the headmaster and the new teacher entered the classroom but didn't interrupt.

When I finished, Miss Rosenberger said, "That is quite a story."

"It is true I told the short version there is a book out that tells the more graphic story."

A boy stood up and said, "What happened to Soaring Eagle?"

"No one knows perhaps he went back to live with the Shoshones maybe a bear got him no one saw him again after he left his home in Salt Lake City." "It looks like you have a new teacher who is a lot smarter and more interesting than me."

A dark-haired woman stepped forward and said, "I don't know about that Major, my name is Mrs. Baecker I will be your new teacher for the rest of the year I think we will have an interesting time."

"Frederick, you go straight home after school, understand?" He nodded, then we all left and let the teacher do her job. I shook the secretaries and headmaster's hand. I excused myself, and after getting directions, I headed downtown to find the police station.

"Can I help you?" a German officer said.

"Yes, I would like to talk to someone about a German and American problem in private, if possible."

"Lieutenant Faust will help you."

We went into his office, and I said, "I am Major James York." "I am the company commander of a unit at the American post." "I believe German civilians have been stealing fuel, and they have been doing it several times." "There has been a pattern to their stealing, and I plan to spring a trap to catch them." "I wish to know if you want to be involved in apprehending these criminals."

"Yes, they are most likely teenagers."

"That's what I felt we set our trap a week after next Wednesday; they usually sneak on the base at about one in the morning." "We will set up about midnight can you have your men meet me about eleven-thirty."

"Yes."

"I have another bigger problem." "I believe there is a large drug problem in my unit, and those responsible are getting drugs from civilians." "I'm going to conduct a raid on my unit, and I'd like to know if you want to take part, you might find some of the information useful."

"You are letting me take part in your base?"

"My base is part of Germany; of course, these drugs affect the Germans and Americans."

"We do have a problem." "I would like to find out who is behind it."

"Then you will join us?"

"Yes, when will you strike?"

"About midnight a week from Sunday." "I will call you if you can give me a phone number." He gave me the number, and I said, "Lieutenant, keep this quiet." "I don't want to let anyone know what's coming."

"I'll will Major."

"Let me warn you this may get nasty." "I do not like illegal drugs and plan to put pressure on those I find who have it."

"Understood Major." I shook his hand again and asked him where I could go to hire a company to do some painting and repairs. He directed me to go across the street and a few doors down.

"Hello, I wish to hire some company to do some painting and repairs, an honest and reasonable person."

"I know someone who would be just perfect, but why don't you get someone from your military to do the work?"

"It would be a long time for the military to do the work, and I am afraid they wouldn't do as good a job as a German contractor."

"This is a first for us Major, let me call the person for you." "Mr. Zimmermann, I have an American soldier here who wants to hire you, do you wish to talk to him?"

"Yes."

"Hello Mr. Zimmermann, I'm Major James York, and I have a lot of work for you."

"I'll be happy to do it for you no matter what it is; perhaps we should meet at the site of the work."

"That would be great how about tomorrow at ten in the morning I'll give you the instruction on how to get there." After hanging up, I said to the clerk, "I also need someone to get rid of some rats."

"We do have some big ones, don't we?"

"I could call someone for you, but I'm afraid you would just be wasting your money."

"What do you mean?"

"For every one rat that gets killed, two more takes its place." "What we have here are the Norwegian roof rats; they don't go into homes they are found jumping in and out of overfilled garbage cans and factories." "It would be cheaper to get some rat poison and let them take it back to their nest." "Where can I get some?" She wrote down an address and how to get there, then I thanked her and left.

There were several types of bates, so I asked the man who worked in the shop, "What is the best rat poison to get?"

"That depends on what you want to put it around."

"A military barracks, dining hall, and residential houses."

"This doesn't smell to humans, but for rats, they love it and will take it back to their nest."

"How much do you think I need?

"How many buildings?"

"About twenty."

"About twelve kilograms should last you about three months."

"Alright."

"Just apply it heavier and more often where there is a bad problem." I got three large bags, which I placed in my trunk.

It was near lunch, so I decided to go where Maria worked, to eat and tell her about Frederick. I walked in, and the staff just stared at me. Maria came out of the kitchen area with some food and quickly served it. She started to come over to me when a stern-looking older man stopped her and said something that upset her, and she came over to me. "You must go, the owner doesn't like Americans, especially American soldiers." "If you stay, I will be in trouble and may get fired."

"Does he know we see each other?"

"Yes, and he doesn't like it."

"I don't care what he likes, I love you, but I will go for your sake." I turned to leave when I saw the owner and Shuler having an amicable conversation. I left and went to M.P.s barracks to talk to the C. O. After telling him about the drug raid and the Germans taking part, I asked for his help. The commander agreed, and I said have the M.P.s meet me at the mess hall at midnight a week from this Sunday I let him know it might get nasty.

I went to supply to drop off the rat bait, "Sergeant Hurst, I have some rat bait I need someone to put some around the garbage cans."

"Yes, Sir."

"I'll write down the instructions on how to apply it."

"Yes, Sir."

"If anyone in our unit wants any for their homes, let them have it with a set of instructions." "Give me about a half-pound of bait."

"Yes, Sir."

"I'm going down to the mess hall to get something to eat."

"Can you have that bait ready by the time I get back?"

"Yes, Sir."

After I ate and got my bait, I headed out to the site to see if everything was going alright.

"How did things go?" asked Lieutenant Dizon.

"Good for the most part, I have a man to come look at the barracks and mess hall to see what he can do to clean it up."

"Sounds good."

"I also not only got some rat poison for the barracks and mess hall but also for those who live off post."

"Very good."

"How did it go with Frederick?"

"It ended up good, but I thought there would be a fight." "They fired the teacher on the spot he turns out to be a Nazi, fought in World War Two, and hates Americans." "I thought I wouldn't see him again." "When I left Frederick's school, I went to go have lunch where Maria works." "The restaurant owner doesn't like Americans either, and after Maria got chew out for me being there, she asked me to leave before there was trouble." "Before I left, I saw the owner and that teacher together talking."

"Too bad, Maria must be miserable."

"I would think so; I'm hoping to remedy that soon." "Has everyone been notified of the meetings tomorrow afternoon?"

"Yes, Sir."

"Do you know if Booker got off, alright?"

"I wasn't involved Top took him, and Top didn't say anything, so I assume everything is fine."

"Where is Top now?"

"I saw him go into the mess hall just before I talked to you."

"Alright, I'm going to go talk to him."

"You Ok, Top?"

"Yes, Sir, just thinking," he said as he stood up.

"What are you thinking about?" I asked as we both sat down.

"This will most likely be my last duty."

"How many years you got in?"

"Twenty-six."

"Well, you have four more years to get your thirty, and you're a fairly young man to be retiring."

"Oh, I won't completely retire, I'll open a store or gas station I've saved some money."

"Are you getting tired of the military?"

"It's just not as exciting as it used to be." "The men are different, and now that the Vietnam war ended, things are going to get boring."

"I know that a lot of people think I am crazy, but I assure you that there will be all the excitement you will want within a year." "I also guarantee that in about a week, you will have a lot of fun."

"Yes Sir, well it will be a while before I leave, I'll see how things go."

It was four I drove home Frederick wasn't there, so I assumed he was at his apartment, so I went there after I put out some rat bait. When I knocked on the door, Frederick opened it and then, seeing me, jumped into my arms. I kissed him, put him back down, and said, "Let's sit at the table, and you can tell me all about today."

"I have a lot of homework; I have to catch up."

"Have you done any of it yet?"

"Yes."

"Very good."

"I have all this to read and answer these questions."

"Is there anything else besides this reading you have left?"

"No, just this, but it is a lot."

"Alright, I will help you with it, but first, tell me about your teacher."

"Oh, she is a good teacher I like her."

"That's good, and how did the boys and girls treat you."

"They were happy that Mr. Shuler was gone."

"They talk about me?"

"Yes, they wanted to know if you were my real daddy."

"And what did you tell them?"

"Yes, you will marry mama soon."

"Bring your books and a pencil, and we will go get your mother." He did his homework while I waited for Maria, Frederick read aloud, and I corrected him as he read. She finally came out, and she looked shaken up. I told Frederick to stay in the car, and then I went to her. "Are you alright?"

"I'm just upset because of how my boss treated me bad he doesn't want me to see you anymore."

"What do you want?"

"I want you; I love you, but I'm afraid I will lose my job."

"I told you I am very wealthy if you lose your job; I will support you and Frederick."

She smiled and said, "I know you would."

"I'd marry you now if you said it was alright."

She kissed me and said, "I know this too, but I think we should take more time."

I filled her in on Frederick's school, and she was happy with that. "Your boss and Frederick's ex-teacher are friends you think your boss is a Nazi?"

"I don't know he could be."

"I think I might know how to deal with him."

"I'll get you and Frederick something to eat, then take you home."

"That would be nice."

Frederick finished his homework just before the meal came, and after we ended eating, we went back to Maria's apartment. I carried Frederick up to the apartment and put him on the bed. As I was undressing Frederick, Maria said, "I will bath him tomorrow morning. He had a big day and is too tired." I tucked him into the bed, kissed him, then turned my attention to Maria, who didn't resist me. Maria finally felled asleep, so I covered her and left.

16

PROPOSAL

Mr. Zimmermann showed at ten, and I took him to see what was needed we went into the men's sleeping quarters I said, "These radiators don't work very well, and these windows need work."

"This building is old; the radiators most likely need to be drained, and we will do that and fix the windows and doors also."

"I also want doors placed in the toilet stalls and do what else you think is needed," then a little after eleven, he left.

At the staff meeting, I asked, "Are there any problems that need discussing?"

"Yes, Sir, it's the men, more, and more of them are getting profiles," said Sergeant Griffin.

"I know I assure you that is going to change in due time, be patient."

"Sir, we need more men," said Lieutenant Bryant.

"I'll second that Sir, I'm having a hard time filling the quota for K.P. and guard duty," said Top.

"More men should start coming by next week I don't know how long it will take to get to full complement, but if it isn't fast enough, I'll give General Abrams a call again." "For those who live off post, supply has rat bait if you want it, a quarter pound is more than enough." "I talked to a company that is going to do repairs and painting on the barracks and mess hall, and if he does well enough, I'm going to have him do the off-post housing also." "He will start a week from next Wednesday, which will be about the same time the C.B.s will be here." "The barracks and mess hall will be painted a pastel yellow with white trim with light green inside; there was a lot of stirring of approval for that." "We talked about a few other things, and then everyone was dismissed except for those for the next meeting."

"It took everyone about twenty minutes to come to the mess hall and settle down before the second meeting started." "The clerk got told to go somewhere, and I said, "What is going to get said is secret a week from Sunday we, along with the M.P.s and the German police, will meet in the mess hall at midnight." "You will get an assignment where you will be when we shake down the men." "If any of the doors are locked, they will be kicked in." "You are to move fast and remove all men to the dayroom no, matter their state of dressed." "Now, I'm going to tell you something you are not going to like." "Since Morgan was an officer and we know what he did, it wouldn't be fair for us only doing the enlisted man." "Everyone, including me, will get searched." "I realize some children and wives will be involved, so after dealing with the enlisted men, we will call in the off-post personal." "Then the off-post personal will go with M.P.s to each home and do a casual inspection of the homes taking care not to upset the families."

"Sir, this is going to disrupt a lot of families," said Lieutenant Dizon.

"I realize this, but it is necessary, it will only happen this one time."

"Why use the Germans?" asked Sergeant Hill.

"I believe the drugs come from German dealers, and perhaps some of these men are selling drugs to the Germans." "Besides, I feel it will build a better German and American relationship."

"Just what are you going to do to the men who have drugs?" asked Warrant Duden.

"It won't be pretty, and it all depends on how much they are involved in the drugs, how they cooperate, and their attitude."

"I'm concern someone might get hurt," said Warrant Duden.

"Because of my anger?"

"Yes."

"Someone might, but Top will be there when I confront them as will Lieutenant Dizon and others." "I assure you, Mr. Duden, no one will get killed." There were no more questions, and they got dismissed.

I went into my office, grabbed the phone and called the Israeli Consulate in Frankfurt." I spoke German and told them who I was, then I told them about Frederick's ex-teacher and Maria's boss, and they said they would investigate. I was doing some paperwork when I got a knock at the door. "Yeah."

"Specialist Booker here to see you, Sir."

"Send him in." He came in, and to my surprise, reported to me correctly, then sat down.

"Did you have any luck, Michael?"

"I found out why nothing works down there, and what needs fixing, I took a lot of pictures also to prove it Major."

"Very good, how bad is it?"

"What are you referring to the personnel or the equipment?"

"Both."

"They are worse than what I thought, and what is sad they don't know it."

"Can you fix it?"

"The equipment, yes, the men someone else would have to do that."

"What do you think of that Lieutenant they have?"

"He seems nice enough too nice his main problem the lieutenant doesn't have a clue what he is doing, and he doesn't have the balls to get those other guys to work."

I pulled out a pad of paper and said, "Would you write a detailed report of what you found and what your recommendations are."

"Sure, Major."

I handed him the pad of paper and said, "I need it today."

"It will be done in about an hour." "By the way, Major, some of those guys in Schweinfurt, I talked to say their commanding officer would not go online when it is their turn, so we must stay online."

"I'll take care of that, Michael."

I received the report and film from Booker, and I took it home with me over the next few days I studied the report, which was very good and got the film developed. I also spent as much time as I could with Maria and Frederick. Maria was coping with her job by keeping away from her boss as much as possible. Frederick was excelling in his class now that he had a new teacher. Sunday, we went on full duty, but I got away to spend some time with Maria and Frederick. Monday, I stayed at the office at the barracks and called Colonel Greenhill. "Sir, could you take some time for me today?"

"Yes, James, what is the problem?"

"I'd rather talk to you in person." "I'll be there in about forty-five minutes."

"Alright, I will be expecting you." I drove up to Schweinfurt and made it in forty minutes I went into Colonel Greenhill's office. "Now, what's the problem, James?"

"There are two problems we are running full duty." "I got word that the next unit that goes up won't go up." "I have to go down." "I have something going on with the unit."

"What do you have coming up?"

"I rather not say now, Sir, but I will say it will make or break Charlie."

"Alright, if the unit scheduled to go up next doesn't, then the other unit will come up."

"I think they are all going to pull the stunt."

"Don't worry; I will take care of it." "What else do you have?"

"My communication department is fully functioning from my end, but the reception is terrible." "My section chief said the problem is here at headquarters."

"I know that the radios aren't the best in any of the units, but I don't think the problem is here."

"I have proof of what I believe, Sir."

"What proof?"

"I made arrangements for my section chief, who is an expert with radios to do a little spying." I pulled out the report with pictures and handed them to the Colonel. He studied them, picked up the phone and called Captain Dring, and Lieutenant Brown then told them to come to his office. Minutes later, both came into Colonel's office.

"Major York has said that your communications department is in bad shape so bad that it's the cause of poor communication in all the units." Both the Lieutenant and Captain were about to defend themselves when the Colonel said, "Don't try to deny it; here is the evidence." The Colonel handed them the report and pictures, which they started studying.

"I would take it that young soldier you sent us was more knowledgeable than what we believed?" stated Captain Dring.

"He is an expert in communications."

"Why didn't you come to me and just talk about this?" "I would have done something about this."

"It's a problem with the arm forces here in Europe to cover up something instead of fixing it." "Frankly, Charlie and the rest of the units have said something to you in the past." "You didn't follow through." "I have said that war is coming regardless of how you feel I can't afford to have a thing as vital as communications not working." "I realize that you Lieutenant may not have personnel working in their MOS, but you must adapt." "There are recommendations in the report that, if followed, will improve your section."

"Yes, and you will follow those recommendations to the letter Captain Dring and Lieutenant Brown," said Colonel Greenhill.

"Yes, Sir," they both said at the same time.

"You two; are dismissed," said the Colonel.

They were just about to leave when I said, "Captain, are you and the Lieutenant angry with me?"

"I, for one, am not happy, Major," said the Captain.

"Your angry will leave you in less than a year, and both of you will understand." At that, they both left.

"You think war is coming, don't you?" said the Colonel

"I know it is coming Colonel, and what's sad, I know you think I'm delusional and these units will lose a lot of men."

"I don't think your delusional Major; I just don't think your right." "I don't want you to bring up war talk again to the rest of my battalion; it upsets them," the Colonel said irritated.

"Understood Colonel may I leave now," I said while putting my beret back on which the Colonel noticed and couldn't say anything.

"You're dismissed." I got up to leave and just started when the Colonel, who had regretted his harsh words, said, "James, we are going to have disagreements it's just human nature don't let it ruin our friendship." I stared at him and left without saying more.

That afternoon I was sitting behind my desk when Top came in and said, "Rough day, Sir?"

"Yeah, kind of."

"Want to talk about it?"

"I went down to see the Colonel; it started fine." "When I brought up my feeling about the war, I believe that is coming." "He got irritated, and the other unit commanders are not happy with me."

"Screw them."

I smiled and said, "You think I'm nuts about the pending war."

"No, Sir, you know who General Patton was, Sir?"

"Yes."

"He was one of the reasons I joined the Army he died just before I got in, but I read a lot about him." "The reasons he commanded, the way he did was because General Patton had premonitions, and he acted on them successfully." "You, Sir, are a lot like Patton, maybe not as arrogant, but your style is similar, so I believe you when you say that war is coming."

"Your confidence is a ray of sunshine to me, Top."

"Yes, Sir."

Wednesday, I got a call from General Abrams, "James, how're things going for you."

"Fine, Sir, but I would assume you would know that because I didn't call you with a problem."

"Yes, your right." "I got a call from Colonel Greenhill; he is concern that you are angry with him."

"Yes."

"What is your story as to what happened?"

"Everything went fine at first; I talked to him about my unit being on full duty and how the other units are refusing to come up." "Then I told him of a problem with communication at headquarters, and I presented him with the evidence he called in the appropriate people." "He wasn't happy that he had a deficiency in his command." "When I talked to the people, my belief of a pending war came up, and he became angry and told me not to speak of it again."

"And how do you feel about this?"

"I feel he is very foolish, for I know I am right."

"James, I feel he is a good officer, and he is in command."

"I have cooled off I have no intention to bring up the war again."

"Good."

"You wouldn't want to bet that war is coming?"

"After the last bet, no."

"What's to worry about, you don't think war is coming, but that's alright." "I have to tell you if war doesn't come, I will be resigning."

"Well, let me think about this bet."

"Alright, General, have you gotten me any men yet?"

"I'm glad you asked, you should get about twelve tomorrow, and you will get some more the following week."

"Right, MOS?"

"Yes."

"Great."

That night I went to get Frederick then I went into town to pick up Maria. She came out all excited and wanted to tell me all that went on. "James, today the police came and took away my boss and then later his wife came into the restaurant and announced that she would be running the restaurant for a while."

"Is she any better than her husband?"

"She is a worse cook, and I don't think she can run a restaurant very well, but she doesn't bother me as her husband does."

"Well, that's good."

"I wonder why the police took him."

"Maybe because he was just a bad man like Mr. Shuler." She looked at me for a few seconds and said, "You didn't have anything to do with this, did you?"

I smiled and said, "I'm just a soldier what could I possibly do."

"I think you can do many things."

"Well, I think you should just be happy that work is much better."

The next day while I was on-site, I got a call from my clerk back at the barracks. "Sir, there is a lot of new men here."

"Have them wait in the hall; Top and I will be in shortly."

"Yes, Sir."

Top and I walked into the hallway, I glanced at the men waiting, and some of the men were smoking. "Chris, collect their files and bring them to me."

"I have them already, Sir."

"Top you think we should do them all at once or one at a time?"

"Let's get it over with and do them all at one time."

"Alright, let's move to the dayroom where there is more room to deal with all of you."

Top said, "Leave your things against the wall and follow us."

I grabbed a table and two chairs, and Top told everyone to line up against the wall. "I normally would have given you a couple of days off to get used to this unit and Germany." Unfortunately, I can't; we are down too many men, and I need you now, but I will give you the rest of this day when we finish with you." "I'm going to tell you like I told the rest of the men war is coming if you are not prepared you are going to die." "You are to do your job to the best of your ability anything less Top, or I will jump in your shit." "If I catch you with drugs, I will make you miserable." "If you take military parts for your personal use, I will make your life miserable." "You will treat all personal with respect; if not, I will make you miserable." "I will not stand for any of you to disrespectfully treat a German civilian; you know what will happen if you do." "I have the power regardless of rank or time in rank to promote or bust you down to private." "I also have the power to knock you on your ass or throw you in the stockade, don't test me." "I would assume you are all fresh from the state's, answer if I am not correct?" No one said anything, so I said, "I am fairly new to this unit; I replaced the old commander who now sits in the stockade." "This unit was one of the worse units in the Army, but I am changing that, you best not give me any trouble while I do this." "Top you got anything."

"You best listen to the Major; he is not playing with you." "If you are in this building during morning formation regardless if you are off or on leave, you will attend that formation." "If you are on-site, you will attend the afternoon formation."

"Before we talk to you individually, I want to know if you are good with calculus," I said

"I took calculus and trigonometry in high school, Sir."

"What's your name?"

"Specialist four, Nickolas Lee."

I wrote that down and said, "Top get the supply sergeant to bring up some bedding for them."

"Yes, Sir."

"While we are waiting, are there any questions?"

"Major, is this a Green Beret unit."

"No, I'm in the Green Berets, but this unit isn't."

"Are you the same Major York that was a prisoner of war?"

"Yes."

"What's this about a war?"

"Less than a year, we will be at war, it won't last long, I think."

"With whom?"

"It will come from the eastern countries but backed by the Soviets."

Just then, Top, Sergeant Hurst, and his clerk came into the room with the bedding.

"That was quick," I said to Top.

"Chris called supply; they had it ready by the time I got down there."

"You think he is bucking for a promotion?"

"Yeah."

"He might get it." "Alright, first-person Nickolas Lee."

I opened his file; his MOS indicates that he was a missile operator and did very well in his class. His ABVAB test was also high, and I asked him, "You planning to make the Army a career?"

"I haven't decided yet."

"You could have gone to any school you wanted or gotten any Job why the Army?"

"It costs money to go to school, and I couldn't get a scholarship, and where I live, there aren't any jobs that I could get."

"Do you want to go to college?" "I will see what I can do."

"I have to think about it, Sir."

Top gave him a bunk assignment and directions to get to his room, and I did about five more men, then I called up Specialist Steve Freeman. "You are a parts specialist."

"Yes, Sir."

"You will most likely be a section chief." "That section has just been straightened out." "Make sure you don't screw it up, understand."

"Yes, Sir."

Top and I went back to the site. "Top I want you to get Mr. Shafer and Lieutenant Dizon and meet me in my office." Shortly after all three men entered my office and sat down, I said, "The reason I call everybody together is to discuss the problem with the Hawk." "As you know, it's too slow to knock down the faster Soviets jets." "Do any of you have any suggestions on how to remedy this problem?"

"I think the only thing we can do is let the air force take care of the faster planes," said Lieutenant Dizon.

"Do you all agree with that?" Everyone nodded yes, then I said, "Any of you been skeet shooting or deer hunting?" They all nodded yes again, and I said, "When someone shoots a skeet up into the air, do you aim directly at the skeet with the shotgun, and when a big buck is moving fast, do you shoot directly at the deer?"

"No," all three of them said.

"Why?"

"Because the birdshot and bullet are moving too slow to hit the target," said Mr. Shafer.

Just then, they all got it, and Lieutenant Dizon said, "There is a big difference between a missile and a jet and a shotgun and a bird."

"No, not really, it's the same principle." "I want you to find people who are good at calculus preferable someone who works with radars." "Tomorrow, you will be getting some new men; one of them will be a Specialist Lee; he is good at calculus, check the other men."

"Yes, Sir."

"Do mock simulations in the command center?"

"Yes, Sir."

"Good." "Once you find someone who can calculate how far ahead you have to lead a plane." "Do some scenarios every day of different planes, including their fastest MiG until you do them perfectly," I said.

"Yes, Sir," they both said.

We all exited hadn't walked more than ten feet when a MiG flew over us, moving fast. I looked at the radars none of them were tracking the jet. "Mr. Shafer, why weren't we tracking that jet?"

"It's no big thing, Sir; the MiG fly over us all the time; they are just testing our defenses we do the same with them."

Sure enough, less than ten minutes later, the MiG came back just as fast followed by two NATO jets. "Do you remember Hiroshima the Japanese thought that we were just testing their defense I want all hostel planes at lease tracked I don't want to take any chances."

"Yes, Sir."

"Also, keep a record of how often they fly over."

"Yes, Sir."

I turned to Top and said, "They think I'm nuts, but they will soon find out." I got a call and got informed that the M-16s and LAWs would be coming tomorrow morning.

The next day Top and I went and talked to Lieutenant MacDonald.

"Lieutenant, we need to open up the armory and take out all of the M-14s and ammunition that goes with the rifles." "Also, we need to replace the M-14s that the guards have with forty-fives until we get the M-16s this morning, Top, and I will help you."

"Yes, Sir."

We managed to get all the M-14s, and at just a little after ten came a duce and half with the new arms. The paperwork took time, we had to check every rifle and then have every round, and clip counted. When finished Top and I carried the M-16s with one loaded clip for each rifle to the guards, "I want you guards to clean these rifles, and when you finish bring one to the gate guard, then one of you bring down the forty-fives to my office."

"Yes, Sir," said the Sergeant of the guard.

On the way back, I said to Top, "We are going to need loaded forty-fives for each man who are going to be in the shakedown."

"Yes, Sir, I'll bring back enough pistols and clips."

"Very well."

That night a few hours before dark, I took Maria and Frederick to my house for a home cook meal, which gave Frederick time to play in the sandbox. I cooked a ham while Maria cooked rice and vegetables. I plan to have Maria and Frederick stay overnight, and the next day about nine p.m., I would drive them back home. Frederick played outside playing in his sandbox, coming in only to go to the toilet or get a drink of water. Each time Frederick went into the house, he was dirtier than before. While the ham cooked, I sat down on the couch with Maria and kissed her then asked, as Frederick walked in, "Will you marry me?" I pulled out a box with the wedding rings I found at my house in Missouri, Frederick just stood there with his mouth open.

She kissed me and said, "Of course I will." I handed her the box with the rings as Frederick was going nuts with joy.

"I told you, mama, that daddy loved you and wanted to marry you and that we would live in this big house."

"Yes, Frederick, I know you told me."

"Daddy, are you going to marry me too?"

"Yes, if your mama will let me." Maria nodded, yes, and I smiled.

"Daddy, when are we going to move into this big house?"

"Not for a while, Frederick, it will take time to arrange everything so that we can get married," said Maria.

"This place is small compared to the house in America, Frederick?"

"How big is your house in America?" asked Maria.

"We have six bedrooms, four bathrooms." "We have about eight square kilometers of land that I'm turning into a park." "We have at least one spring with a pond and an orchard."

Maria had her mouth open in shock at the size of the place, and then she said, "James, you must be wealthy."

"We are very rich, and I told you that I had a lot of money." Frederick came in for the night, and before we ate, I bathed him. We ate, and then Frederick sat on the floor playing with his toys. Maria and I sat on the couch, snuggling and talking about the pending wedding. When Frederick started yawning, I picked him up and said, "It's time for bed." Maria followed me, pulled down his bedding. I tucked him in and kissed him. We then shut the lights out and went into our bedroom to make love.

The next morning, we woke up with Frederick in our bed. Maria and I let Frederick sleep while we went and took a shower together. Maria went to the stove to put on some hot water for tea and coffee while I went to the bedroom to put something on when the phone rang.

"Hello, Major York."

"Sir, this is Lieutenant Kallstrom none of the other units will go up."

"Shit, give me five minutes, then go offline no matter what," I said irritated.

"Yes, Sir."

"What's the matter?"

"Some of the other Army units are screwing with me."

I phoned battalion, and I got switched to headquarters. "Captain Dring, the other units won't come up, and we finished our week."

"I guess you are just going to have to stay up," he said bluntly.

"Captain, I hope you can hear me we are down, and we won't go back up." "If you and the other three clowns don't like this, I suggest you call Colonel Greenhill goodbye." I didn't give him a chance to respond, and I knew he would call the Colonel.

After dressing, I called the site, and they told me that they were down, and another unit went up. When I finished talking Maria had dressed and sat down at the table with me, and we ate breakfast. As we were eating, a sleepy Frederick came out of the bedroom and into the bathroom. I planned to take Maria and Frederick shopping and buy T.V., rugs and maybe a few toys. I got the tee-shirt Frederick was using last night, and when he came out of the bathroom, I put it over his head and took him to the kitchen table. After we finished eating, I cleaned the kitchen as Maria cleaned and dressed Frederick then we went to church. After church, we went shopping much to the chagrin of Frederick, who wanted to go home and play. I picked up a small T.V. and a few rugs and then we went clothes shopping. I took Frederick to the boys' department, and Maria went off to get her clothing. After I paid for everything, Frederic said, "Daddy, I think it is time we go back home?"

"We need to go to one more store."

"But I don't want to go."

"I'll tell you what if you don't want to go to the next store; I will take you back home."

"Alright."

We walked down to the toy store, and before I could ask Frederick if he wanted to go in, he went in. I gave Maria some cash, and she went into the bakery. "Daddy, can I have this one?"

"Is that an indoor toy or outdoor toy?"

He looked at it for a few seconds then said, "Indoor."

"Then, you will need an outdoor one also." He went and looked for another toy when he was satisfied; I paid for them. When we got home, Frederick couldn't get out of the car fast enough. I carried the rugs and T.V. while Maria carried in the clothing. Frederick was a blur changing clothes and going outside with his new toy.

I worked on the T.V., got it up and running when there was a knock at the door, and I yelled, "Come on in."

In walked Top and Maryann, "We saw you were home, so we stopped," said Maryann.

Maria came out of the bedroom and said, "Hello."

Maria, this is Jack and Maryann Bennett." "Jack, Maryann, this is Maria Muller Frederick is outside."

"It's nice to meet you, Maria," Maryann said.

We saw Frederick; he is playing with my daughter Catherin." "He told Catherin that his name was Frederick York," said Top.

"Yes, Frederick loves James, and we are to be married," Maria said while showing her ring.

"I proposed last night," I said.

"So, when is the wedding?" asked Maryann.

"We haven't set a date yet," said Maria.

"I have to get permission first not only for the wedding but also for adopting Frederick; of course, you are both invited," I said.

"Well, Helen and I could help with the wedding," said Maryann.

I looked at Maria, and she said, "That would be wonderful."

Just then, Frederick and Catherin came into the house, and I said, "Do you have a new friend Frederick?"

"Yes, we're hungry."

Maria got them something to eat while Top and I talked. "We still on tonight?" asked Top.

"Absolutely, you have the pistols?"

"They are in my trunk."

"I'm leaving at eleven fifteen if you want to go with me," I said.

"Alright, I'll call Lieutenant Dizon also the fewer vehicles, the better."

17

CLEANING HOUSE

I had taken Maria and Frederick home a little later than I had intended. However, it still left me plenty of time to be back to meet with Lieutenant Dizon and Top. I got dressed in my fatigues and took a nap on the easy chair until I heard a knock at the door.

"You ready, Sir?" asked the Lieutenant.

"Yes, let me throw some water on my face, and we will be off."

Top drove us, and when we passed the barracks, several rooms had what looked like a ghostly light. Sergeant Hill was already there with one other. We took out the forty-fives and waited inside. Within ten minutes, all the men showed up, including the Germans. It was past Midnight, and the MPs hadn't shown, so I called their barracks. "This is Major York is Captain Mills there."

"Sir, he and two squads of MPs should be at your location in about five minutes."

"Alright, I'll wait for them."

A few minutes later, they showed up, and Captain said, "Sorry we are late, Sir, I had some transportation troubles."

"That's ok, listen up this is how things are going to work I want two men in front of the barracks and two in back just in case something gets thrown out the window once we have everyone in the dayroom you can come in." "We will first post, men on every floor, and we will strike all at once." "Our first objective is to remove each soldier from their room and place them in the dayroom under guard." "If there is any resistance, use appropriate force." "After this, I want four MPs and Mr. Duden to go out to the site." "Two of the MPs will stand guard at the gate; the other two will escort the men on the site to the dayroom, Mr. Duden, you will handle the phones at the site." "You will be relieved as soon as possible." "When all the men are secured, we will start going through the rooms we are looking for drugs, military contraband, any illegal pornography." "Also, anything you may want to show me." "I want these rooms torn apart, pull out drawers, go through clothing, any place they might hide something." "Are there any questions?"

"Do we bring up the men as we go to their room?" Top asked.

"Yes."

"What about the off-post people, Sir?" asked Mr. Shafer.

"We will deal with them after the men in the barracks."

"How you want to handle those men that we find something on?" asked Captain Mills.

"We will detain them, and once we have all the innocent men back to where they are supposed to be, we will question them and decide what we want to do with them." There were no more questions, so we proceeded to the barracks. When we were all in place, I entered the first room turning on the lights as I did, I said, "Everyone down to the dayroom, move it." There were only a few that caused trouble, and they were dealt with quickly. The men were caught off guard and didn't know what was happening. After we brought all the men into the dayroom and the men from the site came, I addressed them. "I want everyone sitting on the floor, move now." "Now I will explain what's going on since I've been in command, I've told you day after day to get rid of the drugs." "I've told you how I felt about military contraband and illegal pornography. Yet I, as well as others, have walked these halls and smelled dope. So now it is time to pay the price." "For those who are innocent, I'm sorry that you must go through this, but it's necessary." "I also want to let you know that you people are not the only the ones who will get hit everyone off-post will go through this also, including me." "Top, let's get started?"

"The men in three twenty stand up you men walk in front of me and go to your room." We tore their bedding apart first, and then I started on the first locker and got rewarded with a homemade pipe. "Let's see who this is," I said more to myself than anyone else on one of the shirts it said, Jennings. The MP put makeshift handcuffs on Jennings, and Sergeant Hurst wrote down what Jennings did. I did two more lockers without finding anything import and; then, I hit the jackpot on the fourth locker. I found twelve kilos of what looked like hash and another kilo that was white. I looked at Lieutenant Faust and asked, "You know what this is?"

He sniffed it then, to my surprise, tasted it and said, "Cocaine."

I looked at Brenner, whose locker it was, and I motioned for the MP to cuff him. I also found other things that had to do with drugs and then checked the last locker, which was clean.

I told the three men who were clean to straighten up the room and stay there until someone told them otherwise. We then took the two handcuffed men downstairs and put them in a section away from the rest, and I said to the MPs, "If they try to escape, stop them with any means including shooting them."

"Yes, Sir."

As we did the other rooms, I found small amounts of drugs and pipes; I didn't find any pornography that I was concerned with, and a few rooms were clean. I had two more rooms to do when Top came into the dayroom, and I said, "You find anything?"

He lifted a bag with several kilos and said, "Oh yes, I finished the rooms down here you want me to come with you?"

"Yes." "Mr. Shafter, go get me enough men to man the site and relieve the men who are there?"

"Yes, Sir."

The next room had Washington and Booker in it, and I looked at both as they got up and said, "I hope I'm not going to be disappointed with both of you."

"I don't do that shit, Major; it ruins your mind," said Booker.

"I feel the same, Sir," said Washington.

We went through the room, and fortunately, Booker and Washington were clean, but I did find a pipe and a small amount of hash with someone else in that room. As I started to leave the room with the one soldier in handcuffs, I turned around and said, "Washington, Booker well done, I would have hated to lose you two." "I would have hated to lose any of you other men too." At that, we left and went downstairs to get the last bunch. As I was going back upstairs with the last of the men, Lieutenant Dizon was coming down.

"The cooks said they need to start breakfast," the Lieutenant said.

"Are you finished yet?"

"No, I have two more rooms."

"Top find a couple of KPs that we cleared?"

"Yes, Sir."

356

"Sergeant Hill, gather your cooks if we cleared them. Have them cook something simple soup and sandwiches something the men, including the KPs, could finish quickly today and get some rest."

"Yes, Sir." The Lieutenant went to his floor. I went to mine and finished up with the last room and found nothing that mattered. With all the evidence of what we got, I went into my office and waited for Lieutenant Dizon.

We had thirteen men so far, and I turned to Lieutenant Faust and said, "What do you think of all of this?"

"I am not interested in the small stuff, but the larger things we got, I am very interested where they got them and who they sold it to."

"Me too." "Top call the off-post people in and put them in the mess hall."

"Yes, Sir."

"Captain Mills, get me two of your men."

"Yes, Sir."

"Sergeant Hurst, would you please get Mr. Duden."

"Yes, Sir."

Ten minutes later, Lieutenant Dizon finished and came into my office, as did the two MPs and Mr. Duden. "I'm sending you men to all the homes of the off-post personal." "Again, I don't want you to upset or disturb the families of these men just do a walkthrough."

"If we find anything, what do you wish to do?" asked one of the MPs.

"Bring the offender to me."

"Yes, Sir."

They left, and I said to everyone else, "The way this is going to work is we will call in the non-drug-related people first, then we will deal with the drug people from least-worst to worst." "After we talk to the individual, we will send him out of the room to decide what will happen to him." "Expect much theatrics from me, and I hope that you will join in." "What do we have first?"

Lieutenant Dizon handed me the first item: a few photographs of the parts of radars and missiles. He then said, "These pictures show equipment that is classified confidential or secret."

I looked at the tag as to whom they belonged to specialist Michael Underwood, "Bring in Underwood." Underwood got brought in handcuffed, and top shoved him on the chair. In my sternest face, I said, "You know why we have handcuffed you?"

"No, Sir."

"These yours," I said as I placed the photos in front of him.

"Yes, Sir, I met to send them home."

"Are you aware that these pictures show classified equipment."

"No, Sir."

"I could have you put in the stockade for some time, isn't that right Captain Mills."

"Yes, Sir, I'll take him now if you wish to, Sir."

When he came into my office, he was afraid, but now since the young man heard what Captain Mills said, he was in a panic. "Take him into the Ex O's office while we decided what is going to happen."

Two MPs took him, the door to my office was closed, and I said, "Does anyone think he knew the equipment was classified."

"He might have, but he doesn't know it was any big deal," said Lieutenant Dizon.

"Lieutenant Faust, what would you have done in a similar situation?" I asked.

"It depends on how severe it was, most likely a least a good lecture at the most sent home for a day or two without pay."

I nodded and said, "Did he have any other pictures that were alright to have?"

"Yes, Sir," said Lieutenant Dizon."

"I'm thinking a day of KP and guard duty, and I won't put it on his record." "How does everyone think of that?"

"Sounds good to me, Sir," said Top.

Specialist Underwood came back into my office, and I said, "I can't prove you knew what you were doing; however, you should have known." "We decided that you will get one day of KP and guard duty." "You will not go to the stockade or lose your rank, and I will not put this on your record, but if I ever catch you with these types of pictures again, your ass will be mine understand?"

"Yes, Sir."

"Take the handcuffs off him and get him out of here."

"The next thing was an altered forty-five pistol holster." Painted on the holster were flowers, and I said to no one in particular, "You think this paint is removable, and this holster can get restored."

"With some effort, Sir," said Top.

I was not a happy camper about this, and it showed I said, "Bring in Price."

The MPs brought in Price and said, "The men from off-post are coming in, Sir."

"Let me know when they are all in."

"You know why you are here, Price?"

"Yes, Sir, I think so."

"You have destroyed this military piece of equipment." "This act will get you thrown into the stockade; it's not fun there, Price." "Where did you get this?" He didn't say anything, and that made me mad, "You got about two seconds to answer before I kick the shit out of you and hand you over to Captain Mills."

A very nervous Price said, "I bought it from James Holen, Sir."

"Specialist James Holen rotated back to the states just before you came, Sir," said Top.

"Take him to the Ex O's office."

"What I am thinking about doing is making him clean the holster and restore it to the way it was supposed to be if he can't, he will pay for it." "I think a week of KP is in order, and this will get written up in his file."

"Yes, Sir."

"Bring him back in."

"I won't send you to the stockade, but you will restore that holster, and if you can't restore it, you will pay for it." "You also have a week of KP, and this will be on your record, and if you do it again, you will do time in the stockade, and I will bust you to E one, understand."

"Yes, Sir."

"Get him out of here."

"What's next?" Lieutenant Dizon pulled out a flashing toy made from parts at the site. I turned beet red and said, "Bring John Wooton in here."

"Did I not tell you to get rid of this type of thing?"

"Yes, Sir."

"And yet you kept it; you think I'm someone you can ignore?"

"No, Sir."

"Yet you have."

"Mr. Duden, have you had any equipment sabotaged since you have been checking?"

"No, Sir?"

"How long have you had this thing, Wooton?"

"For a long time."

"Take him to the Ex O's office."

"I'm thinking a reduction in rank, three hundred dollars fine, and a week of KP and a note in his file."

"Sir, I would make it a temporary reduction in rank, the fine and a week of KP with a note in his file," said Lieutenant Dizon.

"Very well, send him back in here."

"The price you will pay for ignoring what I told you, you will have a temporary reduction in rank for three months, a fine of three hundred dollars, a week on KP, and a note on your file." "This happens again you will be dishonorably discharged and placed in a prison for some time, do you understand?" He nodded, and I said, "Get him out of here before I lose control."

"What's next?"

"We have some homemade pipes, some with drugs one with no drugs found," said Lieutenant Dizon.

"If they have pipes, they are using start with the one without any drugs on him."

"Yes, Sir, Private Kerr," said Top.

I placed the pipe in front of him and said, "Now, you will tell me all I want to know or else." I pulled out my forty-five. "The one lucky thing for you is there was no dope in your locker, but we both know you are using am I correct."

"I've smoked a bowl before."

"Quite a few bowls, I would guess."

"Have you ever had drugs of your own?"

"Once."

I got up, walked around to the front of the desk then demanded, "Who did you buy them from?"

At first, he didn't answer; I knocked him out of the chair, grabbed my forty-five, and then screamed, "Who did you buy them from?"

The scared private said, "Jeff Willock."

I yanked him back in the seat and said in a stern voice, "Where did Willock get the drugs from?"

"I think a taxi driver from Bamberg and someone in Würzburg."

"Do you have any questions, Lieutenant Faust?"

"Yes, did either of those men mention names or anything else that can make it easier to identify them?"

At first, he didn't say anything, then I grabbed his shirt, and he said, "I don't know any names, but I believe the taxi driver in Bamberg and the one in Würzburg are friends at least one of them is not German."

"Anything else, Lieutenant Faust?"

"Not now."

"Does anyone else want to ask anything?"

No one answered, so I said, "One more thing private do you think you have a drug problem?"

"No, Sir."

"Take him to the Ex O's office."

"We find anything on Willock?"

"Yes, Sir, a lot of drugs and drug-related items," said Top.

"Let's see if that name holds up." I looked at the pipe and said, "I wonder where he got the parts for this pipe."

"Looks like motor pool parts to me, Sir," said Sergeant Walker.

"I think I will give him three hundred dollars fine also, a week of KP; he is already a private."

"We could bust him down to an E two," Top said.

"Alright, bust him down to an E two." I looked at Lieutenant Dizon and said, "Temporary reduction to E two." The Lieutenant nodded his approval, and I said, "Give him three days of guard duty, and I intend to restrict him to post for two months bring him back in." I explained to him what was to happen, and he got sent to his room.

"The rest of these men had drugs of various amounts," Top said.

"Well, let's start in on them." Getting any information was tough. In the end, all pointed to the same one and another one by the name of Brenner. They both had similar stories where they got their drugs. They got a reduction of rank, three hundred dollars fine, a week of KP, and a mark on their record.

"Sir, the off-post men are here."

"Let's take a break while I talk to the off-post personal."

"Good, I have to take a piss," said Top.

I told the off-post men the same thing I said to the enlisted men but added, "Care will be taken not to frighten your families." Just then, Mr. Duden and the MPs came in, and I said, "Take three or more men at a time."

"Yes, Sir."

I looked over at the nine men that were left to interrogate and spotted the next one I wanted. "Top, take Sims for the next one, and put him in the Ex O's office first."

"Yes, Sir." "Sims follow me."

"I think to speed things up and get better cooperation from these idiots; I'm going to use Sims to frighten the others just play along with me, bring in Sims."

After asking Sims the same questions, I asked everyone else. I said, "You have disrespected me, and this unit, perhaps time in the stockade, will do you some good." "I'll let those guards work you over, and maybe you will become a girlfriend to someone." I could see a tear was seeping from his eye, and I said, "Take him to the Ex O's office and let him think about all the fun he is going to have." "He'll keep his rank, but he gets a week of KP, a fine, a note on his record, and two months of post restriction any objections?" No one answered, so I said, "I spoke to him roughly because I want him to do some acting for us; just go along with me." "Captain Mills, you have shackles for his legs."

"Yes, Sir, I'll have one of my men get them."

I could hear sobs coming from Sims, and I said, "Wait a minute." I looked at Sims and said, "You going to do any more drugs, Sims?"

"No, Sir," he said sobbing.

"I'll tell you what; I'll cut you a deal do you want a break Sims."

"Yes, Sir," he said a little more hopeful.

"A week of KP, three hundred dollars fine, a note on your file, two months post restriction, and we want you to do a little acting."

"What do you want me to do?"

"I'm going to act like I'm beating you, you're going to scream in pain and say some obscenities." "There are going to be things thrown around, and then I'm going to fire off my forty-five for which you will scream as if you are in pain." "All this time, everyone will say things and act as if they are trying to stop me." "Someone will go downstairs to get a stretcher you will be carried out of here moaning and screaming in pain." "You screw this act up Sims; you will pay the price for screwing it up." "So, you had better act well." "Top go out to the hallway and start smoking act like you are taking a break." "Make sure the eight men see you when you start hearing the commotion." "Don't come but act like you are listening, and then when you hear the shot come running."

"Yes, Sir."

"I'll start yelling then we'll trash the room then the gun, don't screw this up Sims." As I started yelling, Sims told me where to get off with a few cuss words. Then we started making all sorts of noise tossing my office. They yelled at me not to hurt Sims, then I took my forty-five and fired. Sims screamed, and Top ran in as Lieutenant Dizon, and an MP ran downstairs for a stretcher.

"It's working great, Sir," said Top.

"Great."

We got some Ketchup and smeared it on him and put Sims on the stretcher, and he started moaning as they took him out in sight of the eight. Sims was taken down to the mess hall to wait.

"We'll wait for a couple of minutes then bring in another one Top.

"Yes, Sir,"

Lieutenant Faust and his men were having a hard time composing themselves from laughing, as were the rest of us. When we got ourselves back under control, the next man came in, and I had no trouble out of him. He answered everything as did the next five men, and one even had the name of a civilian. "These next two all bets are off, no more acting, don't try to stop me at what I might do, you all understand." Everyone said yes, Sir, cautiously. "Lieutenant Faust, that name that we got do you know him."

"Yes, Major, he has been under suspicion for some time."

I looked at Top and said, "Bring in Willock."

Willock came into the room, and right away, I could see an attitude he sat down and gave me that hard look. "Knock off the attitude." He looked at me as if he was bored with the same attitude, and I smiled, then place my size nine in his face, and he went flying. I grabbed him and pulled him back up and said, "You think I'm playing Willock."

"You can't do that to me; it's illegal." I smashed him in the face again, and this time he lost the attitude.

"You will answer all the questions asked because I don't care if you live or die." "These next few minutes will determine if I put a bullet in your head for escaping; I hope you understand." "We already know you and your buddy Brenner are the main drug dealer your customers ratted you out what I and the rest of us want to know is where you got the drugs from?"

"I don't know?"

I grabbed my forty-five, cocked it, then shoved the pistol in his mouth and said, "You might ask yourself if it is worth dying for."

"Alright, alright," he mumbled, and I withdrew the pistol.

"Our supply use to come from a taxi driver in Bamberg by the name of Ahmed." "I think he is a Turk."

"Where else?"

"What do you mean?"

I grabbed the pistol again, smacked him in the face with it, and said, "Where else?"

"We used to get it from another guy in Schweinfurt; I think Brenner......."

He hesitated what he was about to say, so I grabbed the pistol and said, "Brenner what?"

"I think Brenner killed him and took his drugs."

"Weren't you there?" asked Captain Mills

"No, he told me this, and he did have the drugs."

"How did he kill him?" asked Captain Mills again.

"With a knife?"

"What was the drug dealer's name?" asked Lieutenant Faust.

"Imad, I think he was from Lebanon."

"Where did this white shit come from?" I asked.

"That was from a new dealer who lives in Würzburg."

"Name?"

"Akbar, I think he is from Iran or somewhere near there."

"Is he a taxi driver also?" asked Lieutenant Faust.

"I don't know what he does, Brenner, and I only bought from him twice both times we met in a Hofbräu." "He is a big mean-looking, man, someone you wouldn't want to cross, and he has bodyguards."

"How do you contact him to meet?" asked Captain Mills.

"Telephone Brenner has a number in his wallet."

"You two men see if he has his wallet on him or look in his room."

"Yes, Sir."

The two MPs came back shortly with his wallet. Top went through it and found several cards, but one had Akbar's name on it. Top went to hand it to me, but I motioned for him to give it to Lieutenant Faust, who took it, wrote down the number, and handed it to Captain Mills. "Any more questions for this man?"

"Yes," said Lieutenant Faust. "Who did you and this Brenner sell the drugs to?"

Again, Willock wouldn't say anything, and I slapped him across his face, and I said, "Answer him."

"I just sold it to guys in this barrack and guys on the post."

"So, what you are saying, you just sold it to American soldiers?" asked Lieutenant Faust.

"Yes."

"Was one of the people you sold it to Captain Morgan?" ask Top.

"Yes, but most of the time, it was given to him to get out of some duty I didn't want to do."

"What about Brenner, who did he sell to?" asked Faust.

"Anyone who would buy from him."

"Germans, German children."

"Yes."

"How young?" he asked angrily.

"Any age."

"Any more questions?"

No one said anything, so I said, "Take him away."

"Major, what is going to happen to me?" asked Willock.

"Dishonorable discharge, a fine, and prison time." Willock put his head down, and I added, "I wouldn't worry about going to prison; the Germans may want to put you in one of their prisons."

Willock looked at Lieutenant Faust, shocked that might happen. Lieutenant Faust said, "It would depend on how you will cooperate."

At that, two MPs took Willock away, and Lieutenant Faust said to Captain Mills, "I want access to him." Captain Mills nodded, yes.

I got up, walked around to stretch my legs, then spotted Mr. Duden. "How's it going?"

"Very well, Sir, we haven't found anything yet, Sir?"

"How many are left to do?"

"Three more and then you, Lieutenant Dizon, and the First Sergeant should take about thirty to forty-five minutes."

"Very well?"

I went back into the office and said, "Gentlemen, it's three in the morning, and I'm tired; let's get this over with bring in Brenner."

Willock's attitude didn't compare to the defiance that Brenner had. "Don't even bother to ask me any questions I'm not answering, and I am not afraid of you," Brenner said to me.

"You think you're a real gangster, don't you?" "Let Captain Mills and Lieutenant Faust tell you what you are facing."

"Numerous drug possessions for sales each is a five-year sentence." "Five counts of child abuse and endangerment, which carries a five-year sentence for each, murder which carries the death penalty." "There are other charges too numerous to say now," said Captain Mills. I notice all the time that Captain Mills was talking, Brenner was smiling, and I was getting uptight.

"We don't have the death penalty, but you will have a long prison sentence, and you will hate it." "You are facing pretty much the same as what Captain Mills was saying." By the end of what Lieutenant Faust said, Brenner was laughing and mocking him.

"I don't fear you Germans, your just bunch of punks that need to get smacked around." I had enough, and I backhanded him across his face. I got him to stop mocking, but he still had that arrogant smile on his face.

"Does anyone have any questions for him?"

"Yes, where did you sell drugs to the children?" asked Lieutenant Faust.

I said I wasn't going to answer any questions."

"Answer him," I snarled.

"Fuck you." I picked up the forty-five shot him between the legs grazing him in the leg near his groin.

He screamed and said, "You can't do that; it is against the law."

"I'm an excellent shot; I can kill a flea off a gnat's ass the next shot you will lose your balls answer the questions." Most of the others in the room were disturbed at what I did but knew better to say anything. "Where did you sell the German children drugs?" I demanded.

He hesitated, so I lifted the pistol, and he said, "At schoolyards?"

"What schools?" Lieutenant Faust asked.

"All of them, you should have seen what those little fuckers would do to get a taste," he said with a smile, so I smacked him with the pistol.

"We know you got your drugs here in Bamberg, Schweinfurt, and Würzburg, where else did you get your drugs?" asked Captain Mills.

"No other place."

"Did you or Willock sell your drugs in any other city other than Bamberg?" asked Captain Mills.

"Yes."

"Where?"

"Every town between here and Schweinfurt and Würzburg."

"To children?" asked Lieutenant Faust.

"Sure."

Lieutenant Faust was livid and said, "This one we will prosecute."

"Any other questions?" I asked. Again, no one answered, so I said, "Get this piece of shit out of here."

"You aren't going to be able to prosecute me after what you did, you'll be lucky if they don't kick you out of the Army," said Brenner.

"You mean when you tried to grab my pistol, and it went off in the struggle, and you were wounded."

"That's not what happened."

"Is that what you saw Top?"

"Yes, Sir, he tried to grab the gun to kill you."

"What about the rest of you guys?"

"Yes, Sir, that's just what happened," everyone said.

"This piece of shit said I shot him I said he tried to grab my pistol, and in the struggle, the gun went off who's right," I said in German.

"We believe your version is correct, Major," said all three Germans.

"Have a nice time in prison, Brenner," I said with a smile.

The MPs took a shocked and not so smartass Brenner away, and Captain Mills said with a smile, "Major, I would get rid of that chair and do something with the floor."

"I'll do that, Captain."

"We must be going Major I wish to thank you; you have done the German people a great favor," said Lieutenant Faust.

"Lieutenant, are you still on for Wednesday's stakeout?"

"Yes, we will be there."

After the Germans left, I dismissed the rest of the men except for Lieutenant Dizon and Top. "We are the last of post personal for the MPs to go through Mr. Duden should be here soon."

"Yes, Sir," they both said.

"I believe you might have gone too far; you pushed it to the edge, Sir," said Lieutenant Dizon.

"I found ever since I was a prisoner, sometimes it is necessary."

"Would you have shot his pecker off, Sir?" asked Top.

"His wound would have been worse; fortunately, it didn't come to it." Mr. Duden had arrived, and I handed my keys to Top and said, "I'm staying here you two walk them through my home."

"Yes, Sir," they both said.

I shut the door of my office, cleaned the place up, took the chair that Brenner was sitting on, put it into my sedan then drove off the post. I went into the next town of Gereuth. I found a dumpster there, then broke up the chair and threw it away. By the time I got back, Top and Lieutenant Dizon were already there.

"What have you been up to, Sir?" asked Top.

"I had a broken chair had to get rid of it."

"You don't say," said Top

"How are you going to fix the floor?" asked Lieutenant Dizon.

"Wednesday, Mr. Zimmermann will be here to remodel this place if there is an investigation before it gets repaired; well, there is the story."

"Nice."

"Let's go to the mess hall and get some coffee," said Top.

18

THE START OF NEW BEGINNINGS

At morning formation, I said, "I know we are all tired; you will just have to make the best of it and get a good night rest tonight." "What happened this morning was regretful, but it was necessary." "For you, off the post, I hope your families weren't traumatized too bad, and I hope this won't have to happen again." "From this raid, about fifteen got caught various degrees of illegal items." "You will notice two are no longer here." "I wish to warn you again, stay away from those items you know you shouldn't have or pay the cost." "I know there have been many changes since I've taken over this unit." "Some things you don't like, but what will happen in the next couple of days, I believe you are going to like a lot." "The C.B.s will be here to redo the site, so I can cut out the roving guard when they are finished." "Two new buildings will be placed out there one will be a weight room you will be placed into groups and assigned times to use the weights also there will be a track that goes around the fence line." "At the same time, a German company will clean up, paint, and remodel the barracks and mess hall." "Once the barracks get done, the dayroom will get a T.V. and weights to work out with, again the time to use the weights will be given out." "Do not disturb the German or C.B. workers unless it is on business." "Any questions?"

"Is it true you shot someone this morning?" asked a Specialist.

"Top you want to answer that one."

"Yes Sir, the first shot you might have heard was a little acting no one was shot or injured; you can ask Sims about that he was the main actor."

"The second shot was another man, unfortunately, was shot while trying to pull Major York's pistol from him; the man didn't die, but he could have.

"Any more questions?" No one answered, so I said, "You people just don't get it a war is coming; I'm trying to keep you alive."

"Where is the proof no one else believes it?" Someone said.

"You're right; no one else believes it, and there is little proof, but do you notice that MiG's have been flying over more often." "I'm so confident that war is coming in less than a year that if it doesn't come, I will resign my commission and leave the Army." Formation ended, and I went out to the site with Lieutenant Dizon. "I'm thinking that most of the men are hoping that war won't come, and I will leave the Army," I said to the Lieutenant.

"You're probably right, but don't let that bother you when war comes everything will come together."

"So, you believe war is coming?"

"Weirdly, you have a way of saying something, and it comes true."

"Yes, I wish others would understand this, especially the higher-ups."

"I hear you are engaged."

"Yes, we haven't set a date yet, Maryann is supposed to get with your wife and get everything organized.

"She has already talked to Helen."

"I guess I'll have to talk to Colonel Greenhill and General Abrams."

I stayed at the site until one-thirty and then went back to the barracks, and I was there a half-hour when I heard a commotion outside my door. I got up and opened the door, and it was Major John Preston making a lot of noise. "What do you want, Major?"

"I am acting in command while Colonel Nicolas Cromwell is out of town, so why wasn't I told about this raid at your barracks?"

"Because it was none of your damn business, I thought that was made clear to you."

"Everything that happens in my post is my business."

"File a complaint I don't care now get out of my barracks before I throw you out."

"I will see about this?"

"I guess we will." I went home tired, but my love for Maria and Frederick motivated me to go down to get them and bring them back to my house. Maria cooked this time while I helped Frederick with his homework and then checked it. After homework and supper, Frederick bathed and played with his toys until bedtime, and Maria turned her attention to me.

"You're tired, aren't you?" said Maria.

"Maybe I'm just getting old." "I want you to take the Volkswagen tomorrow; you can drive Frederick to school, and you won't have to walk to work or walk back."

"Alright."

"How many days' notice must you have to give your landlord to move from your apartment?

"Thirty days."

"Good, give notice I want you and Frederick to move in here."

"Alright, I paid my rent Wednesday, and I will give notice then."

"About two weeks, we will start moving your things over here."

"I'm going to get permission to marry you tomorrow."

"Suppose your commander says no?"

"They won't, but if they do, I will quit the Army, and they know that, and they don't want me to quit." Frederick came up on the couch and started falling asleep, so I picked him up and put him to bed. Then Maria and I retired to the bedroom for a little lovemaking and much-needed sleep.

I was in my office by five the next day, and by the time Top came in, I had hot water boiling for hot chocolate and coffee for Top. "You feel rested, Top?"

"Yes, Sir."

"I want you to divide the men into groups of five, make sure there is someone who has some muscle on him in each group."

"Yes, Sir, what's your plan for them, Sir?"

"P.T., Top make sure everyone is on a list regardless of rank, and don't worry about mixing ranks." "The only three excluded from these groups are you, Lieutenant Dizon, and me." "We will rotate group to group."

"Yes, Sir."

"We won't start until the site, and barrack's area gets completed." "I haven't eaten; let's go down to the mess hall."

"Sounds good to me, Sir."

I saw some of the punished men were doing K.P., which served them right. Breakfast was filling even Top ate a little while I had been eating, I asked Sergeant Hill the next time he made some of his famous cookies to send some down to my office. After formation, I decided to stay for a little while so I would have the opportunity to call Colonel Greenhill and General Abrams about my pending wedding. It was nine-thirty when I got a call from Colonel Greenhill. "Major, what in the hell is going on down there?" "Why were you insubordinate to the Bamberg post commander?" he asked angrily.

"Good morning, Colonel," I said calmly.

"What?"

"I said, Good morning."

"Oh, good morning."

"The person who claimed to be the post commander isn't." "He is Major John Preston, who is the brother-in-law of Colonel Nicolas Cromwell, who is the post commander." "The Colonel knows that this Preston and I don't get along." "The good Major barged his way into my office, trying to stick his nose into my business, and after I told him that it wasn't his business, I threw him out of my barracks."

"Oh, he passed himself off as Colonel Cromwell when I get a chance, I will call the Colonel and let him know what he pulled."

"I had stayed in at the barracks for the very purpose of calling you." "Yesterday morning a little after midnight with my handpicked men, the commander of the M.P.s also his men, and the German police we had a drug and illegal contraband raid on my men." "This raid netted fifteen men, two of which were major drug dealers and one committed murder." "One of the two men was shot, not bad when there was a struggle with a forty-five." "A full report will be sent to you and General Abrams when it is ready."

"Oh, alright."

"The raid was only one of the reasons I was going to call you; it used to be that one had to get permission to get married is this still true."

"Yes, there are some forms to fill out."

"If I have your permission, would you send me those forms?"

"Yes, you have my permission, and I will send you the forms; who's the lucky lady?"

"Her name is Maria Muller, and she is the prettiest girl I've ever seen, and she has a seven-year-old son named Frederick, who I love." "Of course, you and your wife are invited to the wedding."

"That's very kind of you, and she sounds like a lovely woman."

"Will I need to sign some papers to adopt the boy?"

"I'm not sure I must check."

"I will ask you later who else you think I should invite."

"That will be fine."

"The C.B.s should be here tomorrow to work on the missile site." "Mr. Zimmermann should be here tomorrow." "He is the owner of the German company to work on the barracks and mess hall."

"That sounds good."

"Is there anything else, Sir."

"No."

"Well, then I know you are busy when things get a little further along in our wedding plans; I will send you an invitation."

"That sounds good, James."

"Chris, I need a full report on what happened in the raid do you know how to do it?"

"Yes, Sir, but I'm going to need information from you, Lieutenant Dizon, and the First Sergeant."

"I'll get it for you today." I went to the site and talked to Top and Lieutenant Dizon about writing up what happened yesterday morning and that I needed it by the end of the day. I went into my office and called General Abrams, but he wasn't available. By the end of the day, I gave Chris the statements and told him I wanted it tomorrow.

The next day I stayed in my office at the barracks and waited for Mr. Zimmermann. I told Top to let me know when the C.B.s came, and I started looking at the report that I was going to send to Colonel Greenhill. Everything looked good, so I handed it back to Chris and said, "Make me four more copies."

"Yes, Sir."

I decided to call General Abrams again, and this time I got him.

"Yes, James, what's up?"

"I'm getting married, Sir, and I want to invite you and your wife."

"Great, when is the date."

"Don't know yet, but I will send you an invitation when I know."

"That will be just fine."

"I will probably ask you who else to invite later if that is alright."

"Yes, that will be fine, by the way, how are things going down there."

"Good, I had a drug and illegal contraband raid on my men and nabbed fifteen mostly for drugs." "Two will be doing jail time; one got shot trying to grab my forty-five."

"How bad was he shot?"

"He was just grazed."

"I don't think he will ever get out of jail; the Germans want him also." "It turns out he killed someone to get his drugs, and they were also supplying Captain Morgan." "I'll send you a report." "The German contractor to redo the barracks and mess hall should be here anytime and the C.B.s to do the site."

"That's good, James; I'll have to come down to see what you have done soon."

"That would be great, Sir." "Well, I know you are busy; I'll let you go."

"Alright, James, call me if you need something."

Twenty minutes later, Mr. Zimmermann showed up with five men. "Mr. Zimmermann, it is good to see you."

"Yes Major, I'm anxious to get started, where do we start?"

"I think these three offices, the three bathrooms, the dayroom, and hallways first. Do you want the furniture moved out?"

"No, we will work around it, but we may have to move it around when we work on the floors."

"That would be fine." "When you start on the bedrooms, perhaps you could do two rooms at a time, I will move the men into the hallway."

"That would help, and I will do one bathroom at a time, so your men will have someplace to go." "The mess hall we will do last."

"That will be good."

"I will leave you to your work."

"Very well, Major."

I went back to the site and checked the areas to make sure everything was working well. "Marc, have you found a couple of men who can calculate the plane's speed and how much we must lead it to hit it?"

"I found one, Sir."

"See if you can find a backup and run any simulations using this one man you have so far."

"Yes Sir, I have run a simulation already, Sir."

"What are the results?"

"We hit the target eighty percent of the time."

"Keep on practicing until you're one hundred percent consistent with both men."

"Yes, Sir."

As I talked to the lieutenant, I had a funny feeling; then I stared out into space, it was the Lieutenant who snapped me out of it. "James, are you alright."

"No, you remember me telling you I get these premonitions."

"Yes."

"Well, I just had one big one; we are going to get attacked in May."

"Are you certain?"

"Yes."

"Something else is about to happen within the next two to three weeks." "Just keep on practicing Marc until it is a hundred percent."

"Yes, Sir."

I left the Lieutenant, went over to communications, and talked with Specialist Booker. "Michael did headquarters ever get their radio working."

"Yes, Major, it is crystal clear now it took them long enough to do it."

"Keep communications maintained and check to ensure that the site radios are working to full capacity."

"I'm already on it, Sir." "I ordered more Como wire, and I have the other two men running maintenance on the other departments."

"Very good."

As the C.B.s rolled into the site and I met with their company commander. "I'm Major James York, the company commander."

He shook my hand and said, "Lieutenant Bill Forrester."

"I will get your people some quarters, Lieutenant."

"No need, Sir; we brought our quarters where can we set up?"

"Well, let's walk, and I can show you where to set up and what I want to get done."

"Sure."

We walked down by the guard shack, and I pointed to an area for the C.B.s to set their camp, then Lieutenant Forrester had one of his men set up the campsite. We then walked around the site, and I pointed to the things I wanted to get done. "I assume you wish to eat in our mess hall?"

"If that would be alright, Sir."

"No problem, how many men do you have?"

"Fifteen."

"Let's go to my office, and I will show you how I want the Quonset hut, and I will call our mess Sergeant and let him know of the extra people."

As we walked, I asked, "Did you bring your toilets and showers?"

"Yes, Sir."

"Good, my men were ordered not to bother you if they do let me know." "Have your men stay in your quarters tonight night." "We have been having trouble with someone coming on our site and stealing fuel tonight we and the German police are going to set a trap for them."

"Alright, Major, do you want us to assist you?"

"No, but if you want to join the party, your welcome, I'll check in on you just before we set up."

At eleven o'clock at night, the German police met me at the barracks, and I rode with them to the missile site. We parked the German squad cars by the mess hall and walked to the guard sack. "Double the guard at the fence," I told Specialist Five Renner.

"Yes, Sir."

"Washington is that you."

"Yes, Major."

"You're with me." I showed the German police where the trouble is. We went over to the C.B.'s quarters, got Lieutenant Forrester, and another officer then headed back to the motor pool. Lieutenant Faust suggested a few things, and I said, "Since the people stealing fuel, I believe are Germans, why don't you run this operation."

"That's very generous of you, Major." He posted some of his and my men on the other side of the fence in a hidden area. The rest were on the site side of the fence and hidden behind a berm, and then we all waited.

"It's nearly one-thirty; do you still think they are coming?" Lieutenant Dizon asked me.

"Yes, and soon."

About fifteen minutes later, we all heard the clanking of cans and someone whispering.

"Let me go first." "Then you, Franz, you stay on this side of the fence Andreas, we will hand you the cans."

"Dieter, don't forget to get the extra diesel."

"I won't forget now, be quiet, or these stupid Americans will wake."

Lieutenant Faust put a whistle in his mouth, raised his hand, then lowered it and blew the whistle, and all hell broke loose. Some of the men went on top of the berm while everyone else swept around both sides. The men on the other side of the fence surrounded the one who was on that side. All three of them were caught entirely off guard. One of the two thieves on my side of the fence made a break for it, and Lieutenant Faust yelled halt. He kept running unfortunately for him he ran right where Washington was, and Washington clotheslined him.

"Well done, Washington," I said as I walked over to him.

The German police handcuffed all three of them and took the fuel cans for evidence. All three of them got taken down to the mess hall. I dismissed my people, letting them know there is no need for a roving guard, and they went back to their guard shack. I then thanked Lieutenant Forester and the other officer, later Top, Lieutenant Dizon, and I joined Lieutenant Faust.

"Major, do you wish to interrogate these prisoners?"

"If I'm going to interrogate them, I best put my forty-five away."

"That would be a good idea, I think," he said with a smile.

Lieutenant Dizon and I gave our forty-fives to Top, and he put them back in the armory. I let Lieutenant Faust take the lead; he took everything out of their pockets. "Have you stolen fuel from any other place?" Lieutenant Faust asked.

"No," they all said.

"Has there been any other besides you three who stole fuel." They didn't answer, and Lieutenant Faust went nuts yelling at them.

"Lieutenant, they just answered by not answering," I said.

"Yes, and I'll get the names out of them." "Do you have questions?"

"Yes." "How long have you and your friends been stealing fuel here?"

"Nearly two years, maybe."

"You still think that my soldiers and I are stupid." They didn't answer, and I told Lieutenant Faust I had nothing else to ask. They took them away, and we all went home to get a few hours' sleep.

In the next couple of days, the site and barracks were coming along. I had called General Abrams and asked where the replacement personnel I had requested. He informed me that they would come starting five men a week until we had enough men. The weekend Maryann and Helen came over and talked to Maria about the wedding. I let them know I didn't care how much it cost. I wanted a beautiful wedding. Then Marc, Top, and I went to the sportsman club to drink a couple of beers while Frederick played with Catherin around the house. It was Tuesday morning, and I was out at the site and decided to walk around the fence line to see what had got done. I just about came up to the forested area when I spotted a couple of men dress in black with cameras sneaking around. When they spotted me, they ran back into the thicket, and out of sight, I walked over to where they were standing, and the only thing I could see from that point was the high-power radar. I walked up to Top and said, "I saw two men dress in black, taking pictures where Frederick crawled under the fence; what do you make of it?"

"I don't know, but it doesn't matter the C.B.s are laying the rock and track today no one can get in then."

"Yeah, but I'm getting that feeling again."

"Well, I could post a roving guard again."

"No, what's going to happen is going to happen."

I went to my office to do some paperwork, and about ten-thirty, I got a call from Chris, "We have some new men, Sir."

"Alright, I'll be there in about thirty minutes." I went outside and found Top, and we both headed for the barracks. There were five men as we walked into the office, and I told Chris, "Give me a few minutes, then send in all five into my office."

"Yes, Sir."

"We will give them a day to settle in then put them to work."

"Sounds good to me, Sir."

There was a knock at the door, all five walked in, and Chris handed me their files. "Chris, call supply and get these men some bedding."

"I already did it, Sir."

"Are you bucking for a promotion, Chris?"

"Yes, Sir."

"At least he is honest, Sir," said Top.

"I'm going to tell you all what I expect from you, so there is no misunderstanding." "War is coming to Europe; some don't believe this you had better believe it, or there is a good chance you will die." "We just had a crackdown on drugs and contraband in this unit; fifteen were caught two will be spending a lot of time in prison one was shot." "I'm sure you will hear about this from the others in this unit." "Morning formation is mandatory regardless if you are off or not, as is afternoon formation if you are on site." "I expect one hundred and ten percent effort in your duty." "I have the power to promote or demote, regardless of where you work." "I can also throw your ass in prison or make your life miserable if I wish." "Top, do you have anything to say?"

"Yes, Sir." "The Major is not just flapping his lips; he means what he says I would suggest you do as he said." "Check your gear, see what you are missing, and give the list to Chris, our company clerk." "Do not disrespect the other soldiers in the unit and especially the German civilians." Top indicated he didn't have anymore. Top and I went through each of the men's files at the same time supply came up with the bedding and instructions to come down to the supply room, and they would issue the rest of their combat equipment. By the end of the week, the fence got fixed with a running track. The Quonset hut was up and getting modified. They had started on knolls around each missile system. At the barracks, Mr. Zimmermann had finished the three latrines, the office area, hallways, and even started in the day room. My plan for the weekend was to have some fun with Maria and Frederick, but that got changed when Maryann and Helen decided to take Maria shopping for a wedding dress. Frederick and I went and did things together, and the first place we went to was the P.X. As I was shopping, Frederick wandered off, and when I had finished shopping, I went and found Frederick, not in the toy area but the children's clothing. Frederick was looking at a child's Army fatigues that looked very much like mine, except it had the old color patches. I took Frederick to the dressing room, the uniform fitted perfectly, so I bought it. "All you need now is a hat and a belt."

"Yes, daddy, then I will be a real soldier."

"We will give you an Army name; how about Private Winkie."

"Private Winkie?"

"It comes from a famous person who played a soldier, and it is also a poem."

"Private Winkie is a good name." We went to the quartermaster store, and I pick up the smallest hat and belt. I had an old ruin fatigue shirt with some paint on it, but what I wanted is the name tag, which I cut off. "Daddy, are we going to eat in the Army restaurant?" "I'm Private Winkie now."

"No, not today, Sergeant Cookie is not here today."

We drove to Munich, where there was a festival for children going on. Frederick had fun and ate all the food that was no good for him, which he enjoyed, then after several hours, we headed back home. As we drove, I asked Frederick, "Don't they teach you English in your school?"

"Yes."

"Then let me hear you say something in English, you know you are going to have to speak it."

"We all stand up, we all sit down," he said in broken English.

"Do you know what that means?"

He thought a minute then said, "We stand up, and we sit down."

"Very good."

"What else do you know?"

"I would like to drink Coke Cola, please."

"Very good."

"Yes, very good English."

"What does it mean in German?"

"I would like to drink Coke Cola."

"Please," I said.

"I would like to drink Coke Cola, please."

"That is very good for now on try to speak English as much as possible, and I will try to teach you also."

"What about mama?"

"We can both teach her, but I think you will learn faster."

"I think so too."

When we got home, Frederic and I bathed. Frederic stayed in the tub longer to play, which gave Maria, and me time together. Unfortunately, it wasn't long when we heard, "I'm ready to get out."

"Say it in English."

There was silence, then he said, "I finish I want out."

"Very good, but say I am ready to get out."

Silence again, then he said, "You are out, Daddy."

"Your right."

"He is speaking English well," said Maria.

"Yes, and you need to learn also."

"To learn a new language is very difficult."

"Yes, but it is possible."

"Don't be afraid to try even if you make a mistake you will learn."

"I will try," Maria said as she got up to dry off Frederick.

Maria insisted we eat something better than what we had been eating. As we sat at the table, Frederick said, "Daddy is going to teach us good English."

"Yes, I know."

"I think I am going to hire a tutor for you and Frederick when you quit your job and come here to live that way; you will both learn faster." "Meanwhile, I will do the best I can, and you should tell Maryann and Helen your desire to learn English, and you Frederick can learn from school and your friend Catherin." Frederick went to bed, and I got his shirt and started to sew on the name tag, but Maria took over and did a much better job than I did.

Monday came, and I got a report that one of my men saw someone wearing back by the fence taking pictures. By Wednesday, the Quonset hut got finished; the C.B.s were working on the weight room, and the generator shed. Mr. Zimmermann's crew started on the rooms three at a time, which took about two and a half days to three days. He had hired some more men to begin painting the outside of the building. I was in my barracks office Thursday waiting for some new men who were coming when two things happen. An investigator for Willock and Brenner came to my office and asked me about the shootings. He didn't get much out of me, but he wanted to look over the room. "Go ahead, but I am staying here."

He went over the whole room covering every inch of the place and then said, "This place got remolded."

"Yes, I thought it was obvious." "It was scheduled for some time."

"That's not what Major Preston said."

"Talk to General Abrams or Colonel Greenhill; they both know."

I walked him out of the building, and driving up with a big soldier was Major Preston. "These Germans must go I gave no permission to have this done remove them from my post, or I will remove them."

"You'll remove no one." "This work was approved by General Abrams."

"I don't care what that General said you didn't have my consent."

"Let's talk to Colonel Cromwell; I'll call him."

"It doesn't matter what the Colonel says, it's my department, and I say what happens."

"I'm losing patience, Major."

"I don't care." At that, he grabbed Mr. Zimmermann's worker, and I went ballistic. I seized him, threw him to the ground, his sidekick came at me and gave me a glancing blow that I shook off. He came at me again, and I slammed him with a left to the face, which staggered him. What I didn't see was Major Preston gave me a sucker shot to the head that stung, then I saw a big black blur of Private Washington fly by me and pounced on the Major. By this time, his bodyguard had recovered and came after me, but I quickly took care of him, giving him a couple of shots to the head and a crescent kick knocking him out. I looked over at Major Preston, he was a bloody mess, and there was a crowd looking on.

Mr. Zimmermann asked, "Do you wish us to continue to work?"

"Absolutely."

"Washington, give me a hand throwing these two fools in my jeep and follow me to the post command building in their car."

"Yes, Sir."

We got to the headquarter building with the two men still knocked out. Washington grabbed one of them, and I grabbed the other and dragged them into the building. "The Colonel in?" I asked the clerk.

"Yes, but." He didn't get another word before I kick the Colonel's door in, and we deposited the two men in his office."

"Put a leash on this fool, or I will make your life feel like hell."

Washington threw the car keys on the desk. As we left, the Colonel called us, "Please come back to my office to discuss this." Against better judgment, we turned around and went into his office, as some men dragged the Major and his partner out. "I told him to leave you alone, but he has a vendetta against you." "Let me tell him again not to bother you, and if he does, wife or no wife, I will transfer him out of Germany."

"You should transfer him now; your career might be in danger."

"I can understand how you feel, but the reason I don't transfer him is that his behavior is partly my fault." "For too long, I have been letting him get away with this behavior without consequence." "So, I wish to lay the law down on him and give him one more chance."

"If I have any more trouble like I just had, General Abrams will hear of it." At that, Washington and I left for the barracks.

By Friday, everything got finished, including the helicopter landing pad. I had Sergeant Hurst order two complete sets of exercise equipment and a large T.V. set. By the middle of next week, Mr. Zimmermann's crew had finished the third floor, and he got halfway done on the second floor. They had also started on the mess hall, and the men's attitude was changing for the better. Mr. Shafer informed me that they were ninety percent accurate, knocking down a target for which I told him that is good. However, I still want a hundred percent consecutively. We had gotten five more men in, and we were due another fifteen. Maria, Maryann, and Helen had gotten the cathedral plus a priest, so they set a date for the wedding. I had signed papers and obtained approval to marry Maria and to adopt Frederick. What I hadn't done was tell my family back in the states yet, and Maria got after me, so I plan to do it tonight. "Hello, Aunt Adeline, this is James."

"James, I was wondering when you were going to call, we hadn't heard from you in some time."

"I've been busy, and there is a lot I need to tell you."

"There are some things I need to tell you also, but you go first."

"Alright, the Army promoted me to major, and I command a missile base."

"That is wonderful, is it nice where you are?"

"It's wonderful and beautiful but a lot of hard work, though." "I met a beautiful young lady and fell in love with her; we are going to get married." "She has a small son who I am adopting." "Her name is Maria, and the boy is Frederick."

"That is just wonderful, when is the date?"

"September twenty third, we will have the wedding here."

"Is she there with you now?"

"No, they are back at their apartment, but even if she was here, she and the boy don't speak English yet, but they are learning fast."

"How is your health?"

"Good, so what is it that you want to tell me?"

"Has Frank White got a hold of you yet?"

"No, I was wondering where he was."

"We got a letter two days ago, saying he was sick and was trying to get in touch with you."

"I'll give him a call."

"Your Uncle Paul bought eight hundred acres that butt up to your property."

"What's on it?"

"Trees and brush the deer like to hide in there from what your uncle said."

"Ok, I must put some trails through it." "How's the other property?"

"Everything is finished and looking beautiful, and the plants are doing just fine."

"Has someone been running the vehicles?"

"Oh yes, the boys would like to drive them, but I won't let them."

"Well, if you or Uncle Paul wants to drive them, you can."

"How is everybody's health?"

"Good, Christine came home; she looks terrific?"

"Is she home now?"

"No, she went shopping in Poplar Bluff."

"Tell her that I'm thinking of her and ask her if she is ready to join the Army."

"I think she is finished, with the military she is going to school," she said laughing.

"And how is my cousin Val and his new hot rod."

"He has been going to school every day on his bicycle." "It's a bit more scratched and banged up, but it is his pride and joy."

We talked a little more about the property; then, we said our goodbyes, and I called my parents' house, "Hello, this is Jim."

"Oh, Jim, let me get your father."

"Jim, are you doing, alright?" asked my father.

"Yes, I've just haven't called for a while." "There is something I need to tell both of you."

"Let me put you on speakerphone." "Ok, we are all set up." What he said sounded a little like an echo, but I could understand them.

"Let me tell you what has been going on; I have been given a command in the middle of Germany, and they promoted me to major."

"That's good," said my father.

"Well, it has its benefits and drawbacks." "This unit I am in command of was in terrible shape, but it is slowly getting better."

"How is your health?" asked my mother.

"It's good, I'm a bit tired because of what I've had to do with this unit, but I will be alright." "I talked to Aunt Adeline, and she told me that I had bought another eight hundred acres for a total of eighteen hundred and fifty acres." "She said that there are mostly trees and brush there, but there is some wildlife deer and such."

"That's a lot of property, how much more are you going to get?" asked my father.

"That depends, most of this land is on the west side of the house." "The land goes almost to the highway."

"So, you want more land to the east and south of you?" asked my father.

"Yes, you know you all should go out there." "You could stay at the house." "I think you would like it."

"You know I don't like to travel," stated my mother.

"Well, it's nice there."

"We'll have to think about that," said my father.

"I need to tell you something I met a girl I fell in love with." "We are getting married, her name is Maria, and she has a seven-year-old son by the name of Frederick that I will be adopting."

"When are you getting married?" asked my father.

"September twenty third, don't worry, you will like her." "The wedding will be held here in Germany." "Do any of you know if Allen Olivera ever went into the Army?"

"No," they both said.

"Have you seen him lately?"

"No," they said.

"I'll have to give him a call."

"Is he supposed to go into the Army," asked my mother.

"Yes, he asked me to talk to some very important people to get him in." "How are my investments coming along?"

"They're doing good?" said my father.

"Do you intend to roll them over into other investments?"

"Yes, unless you don't want me to."

"No, you do what you think is right." "How is everyone else doing?"

"Everyone is fine," said my mother. We talk for a little longer, and then I called Allen.

"Hello Evana, it's Jim."

"Hello, Jim."

"I'm calling to find out if Allen went into the Army."

"Yes, he did; he is at Fort Ord right now." "Well, how have you been doing?"

"Good, I'm getting married." "I'll have a formal wedding here in Germany." After talking to Evana about the details, I said my goodbyes to her and called Frank in New York.

"Hello, I'm Major James York I wish to talk to Mr. Frank White."

"Oh yes, Major, we have been trying to find you I'll connect you."

"My God, James, where have you been?" "I've been trying to find you?"

"I've been very busy, Frank; I'm in a place called Bamberg Germany, and a lot has happened." "Are you still writing the second book?"

"Yes, I need to interview you and observe you for a while?"

"Why don't you come here and stay for a while?" "I have a home here, with a spare bedroom, if you are well enough." "I heard you were sick."

"I'm still recovering from pneumonia; hopefully, I will be able to come in a month or so."

"I'll give you my address and phone numbers."

I gave him my addresses and phone numbers and was about to say Goodbye when he said, "Wait a minute; there are things I need to let you know."

"What is that, Frank?"

"The first book finally dropped to second, but it will be back up there because your movie opens tomorrow."

"It will be a while before it comes to Germany; I'm guessing, watch it and let me know how it is."

"I'll do that." "You have quite a few checks worth a lot do you want me to bring them with me when I come or mail them."

I didn't need the money right away, so I said, "Just bring them with you, how much is it?"

"It's in the millions, and by the time I come, you should have your first royalty check from the movie."

"That sounds great, Frank."

"Well, I'll let you go, James."

"Goodbye, Frank."

19

MY COMRADES

At morning formation, I said, "From the first day I came to this unit to present, I am pleased and impressed at how much you have improved." "It's been a lot of hard work, and if you keep up the work, you will get rewarded soon."

Tuesday, I had a meeting at battalion in Schweinfurt. This time I didn't take Lieutenant Dizon since we were on full duty. When I walked into the conference room, it was like walking into a freezer; no one would have anything to do with me, but I didn't care. "We any closer to war Major?" said an arrogant Captain McMullen with a smirk on his face.

The others chuckled, then I said, "When war comes, you won't be laughing." The door open and in walked Colonel Greenhill, and we all stood. After making a few statements, he went around the table, wanting to know the conditions of the units and whether we were having any problems. I was the last person he came to, and I said, "The renovations to the missile site are complete." "The barracks and mess hall will be completed this week. I have no problems with my unit to tell you the truth my men's performance since I've taken over has improved by one hundred percent."

"Yeah, right," said Captain McMullen sarcastically while the other smirked.

"Well, the fact that I am on full duty should say something."

"Yes, and I heard you have no more drugs in your unit good job, but at what cost," mocked Captain McMullen.

"At all costs, can you say you don't have any drugs in your unit?"

"Even to shoot your own man?"

"An idiot would know if the shooting wasn't justified, I would be in the stockade by now."

"Enough of that, I don't want to hear anymore," said Colonel Greenhill.

"I.G. inspection is in four weeks, make sure your unit is in shape."

We talked for another thirty minutes, and just before Colonel dismissed us, he said to me, "See me after the meeting."

"Yes, Sir."

"Sir Major York reporting as ordered," I said as I saluted him.

"You don't need to be so formal Major; now sit down while I talk to you." "I'm a bit annoyed with you, Major." "I'm trying to be patient with you, but I'm starting to lose it."

"What is it about me that disturbs your Sir?"

"Didn't we agree that you wouldn't bring up this ridiculous feeling you have about war."

Now I was getting angry, and he saw it, "You, Sir, have a problem with assuming things, don't you?"

"I assume nothing I heard the conversation before I came into the room."

"If you truly heard what got said, then you would have known that it was Captain McMullen who brought it up to mock me." "The only thing I said in my defense from the mocking of those men was when war comes; they won't be laughing." "If you wish me to resign my commission, I'll be happy to."

"No need to resign I didn't know about McMullen or the others I guess I do assume without asking first."

"Is that all, Sir."

"Yes."

"Then, I will be going, but I wish to ask you one question." He nodded, and I continued, "What are you going to do if war does come?" Before he could answer, I left.

I informed Lieutenant Dizon what happened. By the end of the week, everyone knew about the I.G. inspection and what I expected. Mr. Zimmermann's crew finished with the Barracks, and they were working on the mess hall. I had talked to General Abrams. After explaining to him the conditions of the off-post housing, he allowed me to have the housing also done. He also said he was going to fly out Thursday to see how much change I had done.

Wednesday out on the site, Washington came up to me and said, "Major, I need to tell you something."

"What is it?"

"Some of us black folks are having trouble with the white soldier folks from the other units."

"Racial problems?"

"Yes, Major."

"How many in our unit is involved."

"Not sure, maybe seven."

"Gather up the ones you know and have them meet me in the mess hall in ten minutes."

I went and got Lieutenant Dizon, and Top and eight, not seven men came into the mess hall. "I understand there have been problems on the post can someone tell me the whole story." Specialists John Montgomery told the story with the help of the others. "Does anyone know what unit they are from?"

"I believe Major it was the Third Infantry Division and the Second Armored Cavalry," said Specialist Booker.

"Have anyone gotten physical with any of you?" asked Lieutenant Dizon.

"No, but we are thinking of getting physical with them," said Specialists Montgomery, which got some laughs and agreement.

"Top, did you know this was happening?"

"No, Sir." "How long have these rednecks been harassing you all?" asked Top.

"It has been going on ever since I've been here sergeant, but this last month it has been worse," said Private Washington.

"Alright, I'm going to talk to Colonel Cromwell and then go to the two units that you mention and talked to company commanders." "But before I go, I'm going to talk to Colonel Greenhill and General Abrams and get some advice I've never run into a situation like this before." "In the meanwhile, stay in groups of two or preferably more, and if this does get physical, I want to know right away." Everyone seemed to be satisfied and left, and I said to Top and Lieutenant Dizon, "Any advice?"

"I think the course you are going to take is the right thing to do," said Lieutenant Dizon.

"I think, Sir, if this does not stop quickly, it will turn into violence," said Top.

"I agree with you, Top so what I am going to do is make a few phone calls then you and I are going to visit some people."

"Yes, Sir."

"Lieutenant Dizon, take care of things here while I'm gone."

"Yes, Sir."

"I wish to speak to Colonel Greenhill?"

"Hello James, is there a problem?"

"Yes, Sir, I need a little advice." "We have a racial problem here; some white soldiers from a couple of other units on the post have been harassing my black soldiers."

"What have you done so far?"

"I've talked to my men told them when they go out to go out in groups of two or more." "I said I would talk with Colonel Cromwell and the company commanders of the two units."

"That sounds good."

"To tell you the truth, I've never run into a situation like this, and if something not done, there will be violence."

"Well, I think what you plan to do is correct; keep me posted."

"Yes Sir, I plan on calling General Abrams not to go over your head but to get his opinion." "I'm a little nervous about this one."

"Understood James."

"I wish to speak to General Abrams."

"One moment Major."

"James, do you need something?"

"Yes, Sir, I need your advice on a problem I have."

He talked, reassuring me that I was on the right path and said Thursday he would shake things up when he comes. Top and I left to speak to Cromwell as we went Top said, "Don't be surprised if the Colonel doesn't believe you or thinks it is no big deal."

"If he dismisses it, it won't make any difference; General Abrams is going to raise some hell when he comes."

"I wish to talk to Colonel Cromwell."

"Major York is here to speak with you, Sir." As I waited, I saw Major Preston peering from his office with a smirk on his face.

"The Colonel will see you now, Major."

Top and I went in and sat down, "Colonel, I have a problem."

"Is it Major Preston again?"

"I don't know, but I hope not my black soldiers are having problems with some of the white soldiers on post."

"What kind of problems?" he asked disinterestedly.

I stared at him for seconds, then said, "Racial problems."

"You shouldn't worry about them, colored boys. They complain about one thing or another; they just never learned their place," he said as a matter of fact.

"Let me guess you're from the south."

"South Carolina."

"You haven't read my book, have you?"

"Why no, I'm afraid I haven't."

"Let me tell you there is going to be violence if this trouble does not stop are you going to do something or not?" I asked a little irritated.

"I'll check into it, Major." "As far as violence, my MPs can handle any trouble," he said, irritated himself that I pressed him.

"When?"

"This is my post Major I'll do it when I'm not too busy."

Top and I got up to leave, and I said, "It's your post, but maybe not for long." Before he could say anything, I departed, and I told Top to stop at the MP barracks.

"I wish to talk to Captain Mills."

"Major, First Sergeant, please come into my office." I told him what had happened and what the reaction of Colonel Cromwell was, then he said, "I could have told you that he is a racist haven't you notice that all his staff are white."

"Do you think Preston is involved in the racism with my men?"

"I wouldn't put it past him."

I thought for a second and then said, "Expect if this doesn't get taken care of, there will be violence."

"I hope not," he replied.

I thought for a few more seconds again then said, "Keep it to yourself, General Abrams will be here tomorrow." We went to the two company commanders in question, and both denied their men harassed any black soldier even though they couldn't have known for sure.

"How accurate are we in knocking down planes, Bill?" I asked the next day.

"One hundred percent, Sir."

"Is that consistently."

"Yes, Sir."

"How long have you been at a hundred percent?"

"Since Tuesday."

"Fantastic."

"Keep on practicing, but you can cut back on the number of times you practice."

"Yes, Sir."

As I walked towards the motor pool, Lieutenant Dizon met with me. "What time do you think the General will be here?" he asked.

"About nine-thirty or ten o'clock."

"I'll go and recheck in each area."

"Good idea, Top is making sure everything is right back in the post."

At nine-fifty, I could hear the thump-thump of a Huey coming, so I headed to the helicopter pad, as did Lieutenant Dizon. We maintained our distance while the Huey landed and when the blades stopped out came General Abrams and Colonel Greenhill and a couple of other officers. Lieutenant Dizon and I approached them, and I said, "It's a joy to see both of you."

"From the air, this place looks excellent its credit to both of you."

"Thank you, Sir," we both said.

"Well, let's take a tour I'm anxious to see everything."

"As am I," said Colonel Greenhill.

We toured the site and Lieutenant Dizon, or I explain different points of the site improvements.

As we were walking, General Abrams asked, "Any more problems with the racism?"

"We do need to talk Sir, perhaps we can sit down in the post mess hall, and I will explain just what is going on."

"Sounds good to me," said General Abrams. We finished with the site and drove over to the barracks where we met up with Top; Marc stayed at the missile site. We walked through the barracks and then headed over to the mess hall.

"Now, tell me about your race problem."

"Washington, take a break with your KP duties and come over here," I said. "Grab a chair and sit down and tell General Abram and Colonel Greenhill what has been going on with you and your friends."

"You mean from those white soldiers?"

"Yes." For the next ten minutes, he told everything, added some things he didn't mention before, and then went back to the kitchen.

"Let me tell you what happened when I tried to resolve this problem and Top if I leave anything out speak up."

"Yes, Sir."

"I went first to see the Colonel who got testy when I asked him what he intended to do." "He used demeaning language toward my black soldiers." "When I asked him when he would act, again, he informed me that this was his post, and would get to it when he got around to it."

"Oh, he did, did he," said General Abrams.

"Do you have anything to say, Top?" I asked.

"Just that he seems to me to be disinterested in what you said, Sir, and a lot annoyed that you brought him this problem." "I also have a feeling that Major Preston is somehow involved with this."

"Major Preston is his brother-in-law to remind you." "After his office, I went to see the company commander of the MPs captain Mills." "He was sympathetic to my problem and my experience with Colonel Cromwell and informed me about his bigotry." "I then went next to the two company commanders of the units in question, and both were annoyed that I would insinuate that they had men who were racist."

"They were totally in denial they had a problem," said Top.

"After we eat, I will go see Colonel Cromwell and raise some hell."

Someone brought food to us, and as we started to eat, I heard a voice speaking in broken English behind me that I recognized. "Sergeant Cookie, is time to eat?"

"For you, yes," the Sergeant said.

I turned around and dressed in his uniform was Frederick waiting for his food.

"Frederick, why aren't you at school?"

"School was only half-day, no lunch."

"Why didn't your school tell your mother or me?"

"Do not know."

"Why didn't you go home?"

"I did, but no food at mama's house, and I could not get into your house, it lock, and I am hungry."

"You sit at this table and eat, and I will take you home." He nodded as he was stuffing food into his mouth. "How did you know Sergeant Cookie would feed you?" I asked.

"I Private Winkie, a soldier like you, daddy."

Everyone chuckled, and I said, "I guess you're right." He wolfed down his food, and Sergeant Hill brought Frederick a couple of chocolate chip cookies and a bag full of more.

"What do you say, Private?"

"Thank you," he said with a mouth full of food.

"He speaks English pretty good," said Top.

"Yes, I talk good English," Frederick said.

We all finished eating, and I asked the General if he wanted me to come with him to Colonel Cromwell's office. He said, "No, it would be better if you didn't go beside you need to take this young soldier home."

"Very well, Sir."

"I'll meet you in an hour in your office."

"Yes, Sir." I took the jeep that Top brought in from the site. I brought Frederick to my home much to the delight of Frederick not only because he was going to my house but because he got a ride in a jeep.

"Now you stay here until I come home and don't gobble down all these cookies there is better food for you in the refrigerator."

"What gobble?"

"It means to eat."

"Do you have homework?"

"No."

"I love you; I have to go now." I kissed him and left.

It had been an hour and a half, and still, the General and Colonel hadn't returned. "What do you think Top, you think there was bloodshed when they met up with Colonel Cromwell?"

"There was nearly blood drawn when you went to see him."

"That fool Colonel and his idiot brother-in-law major of his should be kicked out of Germany."

"I would agree with you, Sir." "I would suggest you talk to the General and Colonel on your guest list, Sir."

"I'm glad you reminded me, Top."

Two hours after they had left, the General and Colonel showed up. "We thought there might be bloodshed; because you were gone so long," I said.

"There nearly was bloodshed." "Colonel Cromwell has a thick head, and reality doesn't sink in well." "However, when I told him I would send him and his brother-in-law to Greenland and give you his command, he changed his tune real fast."

"Just as well, Sir, I'm shooting for General," I said lightheartedly.

"I wouldn't be surprised at the rate you are going if you get promoted to general," said Colonel Greenhill.

"So, what got done to resolve this problem, Sir?"

"Well, after we got Colonel Cromwell's head straight, we went over to the two units in question." "Although it wasn't as hard to get their company commander head straight, it did take time." "I let them know that if another incident happens again, I won't be happy." "We also talked to your Captain Mills and let him know what happened."

"What did he say?" I asked.

"Well, he wasn't very hopeful." "If there are any more problems, let me know, and those responsible will pay."

"On a happier topic, I wish to ask both of you about people I should invite to my wedding; it's in three weeks, you know."

"How many people can we suggest?"

"As many as you wish."

"Did you send one to General Arnold and the President?"

"Yes, Sir."

"How about if you give me five invitations, and I will hand them out," said Colonel Greenhill.

"Alright, Sir."

"Let me have ten?" said General Abrams.

"Alright, Sir, we can swing over to my house before we return to the site." When we got to the house, Frederick was in his underwear asleep on his bed. I placed a blanket over him, grabbed fifteen invitations then gave them to the Colonel and General.

We drove back to the site, and just before General Abrams got into the Huey, he said, "You're doing a fine job, James." "I've forgotten to tell you; you should receive two more shipments of men."

Lieutenant Dizon came over to me and said, "How did things go?"

"I think well." "The General was impressed with the site and barracks area; he also raised a lot of hell with Colonel Cromwell."

Friday came and went, on the weekend I was allowed by Maryann and Helen a little time with Maria, and it was terrific. Maria had given notice at her work and had a week left and two weeks still at the apartment. When Monday came, I was out on the site early; I had already informed everyone what happened last Thursday. The moral seemed to be up, and everything seemed to go smoothly. It was about three-thirty. I had just got back to the barracks when Frederick came into the building crying in hysterics; he got brought into the office by Washington, where I was talking to Top. "What's wrong, Frederick?"

"Some bad men who live upstairs were mean and hit me using bad language because I bumped into one of them," he said in German.

"What did these men look like?"

"They were dressed in black and had guns."

"Guns, were they carrying anything else?"

"Cameras."

"How many men do you think are in the apartments?" asked Top.

"I do not know for sure maybe fifteen or twenty maybe less," he said sniffling.

I looked at Top, and he said in German, "Did they speak German?"

"Yes, but they were not German; they speak funny."

"Washington, go find eleven men and bring them here; make sure you and the other eleven men have their helmets."

"Yes, Sir."

"Top when Washington gets back, go to the site and pick up enough M-16s and two forty-fives and enough rounds for each weapon bring some of the M-79s also."

"Yes, Sir, but don't you think we should call the German police?"

"I'm calling them next." "Chris take Frederick down to the mess hall, let Sergeant Hill know that I want him to take care of Frederick."

"Frederick Sergeant Cookie will take care of you." "Lieutenant Faust, please, this is Major York; it's an emergency."

"Yes Major, you just got me in time I was about to go home."

"You need to get all the men you can muster and have them heavily armed and come to my office."

"What is it Major, another drug raid."

"No, I've discovered a heavily armed spy cell from another county." "There are anywhere from twelve to twenty spies, and I don't think they will give up without a fight."

"I'll be there in forty minutes or so."

Chris came in and said, "Sir, you better come out here."

The hallways were full of my men with their helmets on someone asked, "Is it war, Sir?"

"Everybody, get into formation, and I will explain." They all jumped into formation, and more men were coming as I started to talk, "It's not quite war yet, but it is the step before it." "This past month, some men dressed in black taking pictures of our site; perhaps some of you have seen them." "A large heavily armed spy cell has been discovered we are going to assist the German police in taking it out." Most likely, there will be gun fired; they won't quit easily."

"When do we go, Sir?" someone said.

"I'll take the original twelve that Washington picked; another six for traffic control, plus another six for medical." "Swartz, aren't you the medic?"

"Yes, Sir."

"The rest of you will be on standby." "Chris called everyone and tell them what's going on." "Ricker, Hurley, do you know where the restaurant where my Maria works?"

"I do, Sir," said Ricker.

"Take the sedan and go get her and bring her to Frederick." Just then, two German trucks drove up and out popped Captain Faust.

"Join me in my office." I got a blank piece of paper and a pencil and started to draw a picture of what the situation was. "This building is an apartment building of maybe of twenty-four units stacked five stories high four units per level." "The armed men in question are on the third floor in maybe two or three units."

"What's the address?"

"Six twenty-seven Zollnerstraße."

"This is my operation, Major."

"Of course, we will give support; you direct it as you wish."

"Are you sure about this, James?"

"Absolutely." "My men will set up roadblocks on both ends of the street, and they will have a medical station." "They will only get involved in the fight if fired upon or you order it."

"Very well."

"Don't underestimate them, Lieutenant."

"I don't intend to, but I don't think there is going to be a big gunfight where they will get killed."

"Just don't forget there are innocent people in some of those other apartments." "Do you want some of my men to cover the back?" I asked as Top came in.

"Yes, perhaps two."

"Ok, let's go."

My trucks blocked both ends of the street. Two of my men went with the Germans around the back. We went down both sides of the road, taking cover behind the cars that were parked. The Germans hugged the buildings leading up to the apartments. As the German police slipped into the building, I sent two men across the street to guide the German civilians down to where medical got posted. The first floor got cleared without a problem. People from the second floor were getting evacuated when there were some gunshots and then followed by some automatic rifle shots coming from an AK-45. Civilians and German police came rushing out of the apartment complex. There were some gunshots in the back of the apartment building, which I knew came from an M-16. "Hooper, Ellis, Orion go back up those men in the back," I said. "Top, Clark, you're with me; you take over here, Washington." We made it across the street just as some glass broke from a window, and automatic gunfire was raining down. Immediately my people fired back, Washington using the M-60 Top had brought. "Call for back up and medical," I said to the German police on the other side of the street. "Kelly, go get the MPs."

"Yes, Sir."

"Where is Captain Faust," I asked one of the German police.

"He and four others were shot."

"Follow us back in the building."

We went into the building and made it up to the stairs to the second floor. I saw three men in black tormenting, one man who was on the floor wounded. We shot two of the three men; the third ran up to the third floor, we rushed up to the second floor. Three of the German police appeared to be dead, but two were wounded Captain Faust being one of them.

"Take the wounded downstairs," I said to one of the German police." "Clark, check the apartments on this floor." There was one frighten little old lady that Clark escorted downstairs. Top and I headed up to the third floor only to get a volley of gunfire we returned fire driving them back, but they got reinforcements and stopped us.

"Clark, you stay here and back up the Major," said Top. They had made a barricade, and every time we took one out, another took its place. Top had been gone for some time when he came back, he said, fire in the hole, and there were two explosions, and dust and smoke came rushing down to the second level. We started to go up to the third level again, Top carrying an M-79 and plenty of grenades. We still had a barricade, and those men weren't ready to give up. The gunfire was so thick that we couldn't move forward, so Top fired a grenade into the barricade. That pushed them back to the fourth floor by this time German police reinforcements came. I was shocked to find that there was one civilian hiding in his apartment. We advanced to the fourth floor there were no barricades there, they tried to get into some of the apartments but were unsuccessful, so they got quickly forced to the fifth floor. From what I could see, there were only eight or ten of them left, several times, we tried to get them to surrender, but their only response was gunfire. People were cleared out of the fourth floor as we headed up to the fifth those men didn't stay long on the fifth opting to make a stand on the roof. As the German police evacuated the fifth floor, I was glad that there were no hostages.

"There is a metal door to the roof," Top said.

"Got any more grenades?" I asked

"I sure do," he said with a smile.

"Let's wait until the building is clear of the civilians." There was a lot of gunfire coming from the roof and street with an occasional explosion, which concerned me. A company of MPs had arrived with Captain Mills.

"What's the situation?" asked Captain Mills.

"There are about eight or ten heavily armed men on the roof, which I believe to be a spy cell." "They are well trained, and I feel they are willing to die rather than be captured and don't care who they kill."

"Why didn't you call us before you started this party?"

"Well, I should have Captain; it was a mistake I won't make again." "The German police made it their operation and weren't all that happy we were involved, but we should have called you anyway."

"How did you find out about these people?"

"I got a tip, and I spotted some of them photographing my missile site." "How are things outside?"

"A lot of wounded, maybe some dead." "I have some of my men backing your men."

"Captain on the third floor, those apartments need to be secured." "I believe there are sensitive documents in them."

"I'll get my men on it."

"You might want to get CID here also." "I'll wait for you before Top blows the door."

"Alright."

I checked the four apartments on the fifth floor for a phone and found one. I then called the barracks and got Chris on the phone. "Chris have someone get some trucks and bring more people out here to relieve some of these men they won't need weapons they can use what we have here."

"How is it, Sir?"

"Bloody, let Frederick and Maria know I'm alright, then call Maggie at the clinic, tell her to standby for wounded." "Then call Colonel Greenhill and General Abrams and tell them what's going on."

"Yes, Sir, I've done this already."

Captain Mills came back, and I had a couple of German police when I told Top to blow the door. We cautiously went up the stairs, which was a much narrower staircase than the rest. The metal door was mangled but was still attached. I looked out and spotted some men, then I was detected, and they fired at me.

"Top, load a grenade in the M-79 and hand it to me."

"Yes, Sir."

"What are you going to do?" asked Captain Mills.

"Create a diversion." I stuck the M-79 in the general direction of those men and fired. When the explosion went off, we all shot out and hit the ground shooting. One of the men in black made a mistake and stood up, and the M-60 cut him in half. There were only about four or five left, and they were hiding behind something that looked like some large vents. We were hunkered down behind the stairwell after we got up from off the ground.

"If you don't surrender now, we will blow you off this roof," I said. We got a hail of gunfire, and I said to Top, "You have the honors Top." He loaded another grenade into the M-79 and fired at the vents. There was an explosion, and one man flew over the side of the building and onto the street. Top loaded another grenade and readied himself as we were firing at them.

"This is your last chance." "We will fire another grenade if you don't surrender." We got more gunfire for what was said, Top fired again, and we rushed them all were dead, but one who was wounded and tried to shoot, but Captain Mills shot him. The rest of the MPs and German police came up onto the roof, and we went back down to the street. "It's over, pack it up," I told the men. "Washington, come over here."

"Yes, Sir."

"Did we lose any men?"

"No, Sir, but we had five wounded three not so bad, but I don't know about the other two men; the Germans and MPs weren't as lucky, Sir."

"Alright, where are the wounded men?"

"I don't know, Sir; they had a military ambulance at the end of the street."

"Go and clean up and get back to the barracks." "Send someone back here to pick us up."

"Lieutenant Dizon is just down the street, Sir."

"Have him come down here." There were stains of blood on the street, and a lot of smoke was coming from the building.

"Quite a mess isn't it," said Lieutenant Dizon.

"Yes, it is, let's go see if it was worth it." We went upstairs to the third floor and started going through one of the rooms where they were working. We found plenty of pictures of the post and places where the soldiers hung out. There were plenty of notes in a language I didn't know we didn't get through half of it when CID showed up.

"CID Lieutenant Perry."

"There are some photos over there some notes in a language I do not know," I said.

Lieutenant Perry went over to what I pointed out and said, "It looks like Czechoslovakian." "They have been taking pictures of the post." "Major, I don't want to be rude, but I need everyone to step out."

"Alright, but there are two other apartments."

"Stay out of those apartments also."

We all stepped out of the apartment, started to talk when up came Colonel Cromwell and his brother-in-law Major Preston matter than hell. "You're going to burn Major, and I am going to enjoy it," said Colonel Cromwell.

Major Preston smiled and said, "Finally, we can get rid of you and get back to normal."

"You think so, uh," I said.

"Yes, and that stupid General can't protect you now."

"You two will never know," said General Abrams as he and Colonel Greenhill came up the stairs. "You two go home and pack your bags." "I'm transferring both of you because I'm stupid."

"Now General, I never called you stupid," said Colonel Cromwell.

"Colonel, you and your brother-in-law better get out of my face before you leave Europe as privates." They left, and the General turned to me and said, "I do hope you have an explanation, James."

"Yes, Sir." As I was about to talk, German investigators came up the stair and into the room where CID was, and an argument broke out.

"Sir, perhaps they can share the investigation," I said. General Abrams agreed, and I said, "Let's go somewhere where I can tell you what's going on."

"Sounds good to me let's go to your office."

"Top, you can go with me," said Lieutenant Dizon. We drove back to the barracks and into my office.

"Sir what about Maria and Frederick," Top said.

"Oh, my goodness, Sir, Top can tell you what happened to start." "I need to take care of Maria and Frederick; I'll be right back."

"Very well," said General Abrams.

I went down to the mess hall with Washington. When I walked in, Frederick jumped into my arms, saying, "Bad men gone."

"Yes, sweetheart, you did a first-class job telling me." I let Frederick down, then embraced Maria. I finally said, "I'm afraid you can't go back to your apartment officials are all over there," I said in German.

"What about the Volkswagen."

"I'll take care of it give me the keys." "Private Washington, drive them home here is the key to the house." "I will be home soon." I kiss them and then sent two men to get the car.

"Sorry about that, Sir, they were frightened," I said.

"It's alright, James, the First Sergeant, told us almost everything."

"Yes, Sir." "I know you don't want to hear it, but I think this was a step before the war starts."

"Frankly, I don't know I need to see what CID comes up first." "Have you had any reports of spying?" the General asked Colonel Greenhill.

"No, I haven't, Sir."

"Well, the only thing I saw that you could have done differently was perhaps you should have stayed out of it and let the MPs and CID handle it, James."

"Sir, I don't think the MPs or CID would have taken it seriously." "Even if they did, the German police wouldn't have accepted the MPs, and you know how many casualties the Germans had."

"I would have to agree with the Major I've been here in Bamberg for some time, and the German police don't trust the Americans except the Major who has built up a trust with them," said Top.

"Very well, I want to go back and talk to CID," said General Abrams.

"Top, Lieutenant, take care of things here."

"Yes, Sir."

"Sir, can we stop off at the infirmary so that I can check on my men."

"Of course."

"Better take your hat off, Sir, the head nurse is a stickler for it, and she doesn't take shit from anyone regardless of rank."

As we walked in, the place was abuzz with activity. I spotted Maggie and started to walk over to her when General Abrams said, "Maggie is that you."

"Small world isn't it General."

"You know each other?" I asked

"Yes, I met her in Nam best damn nurse they had."

"You come to see your men, Major?"

"Yes, Maggie."

"If they aren't getting worked on, they are on the fourth floor."

We went up to the fourth floor, and we ran into Captain Mills. "How are your men, Captain?" asked General Abrams.

"I lost three; seven wounded some of those will be going home."

"Well, we are here to visit them."

"I'll join you, Sir."

"Sorry to hear about your loss," I said to the Captain. I was relieved to see my men weren't injured very severely, that most of them would be back to duty by tomorrow. After General Abrams said a few words, we left to go to the apartment.

"Lieutenant, what can you tell me about these men who were here." Asked the General.

"Well, it's strange, Sir; the weapons and ammunition are Russian, the radio we found was East German, the notes are in Czechoslovakian." "Their pictures are of the Bamberg, the post, and other American installations."

"Are there any pictures of my missile site?" I asked.

"Yes, Sir, there is."

"I want a full report." "Let's go," General Abrams said.

"Wait, Sir, I want to talk with the German investigators."

"Hello, I'm Major York, this is General Abrams and Colonel Greenhill what have you found?"

"They had counterfeit passports, and they are all professional."

"What do you mean, professional?"

"They were trained for this mission they had."

"How can you tell this?"

"Sergeant Smith can read Czechoslovakian most of what they wrote is American troop movements and opinions of what they observed." "The rest the American investigators told you, I assume."

"Do any of you know English?"

"No."

"Then, our investigators will need to know what is in those notes."

"They can have them."

"Perfect one more question, do you know the condition of Lieutenant Faust?"

"He will be sore for a while, but he is alright he should be out of the hospital by tomorrow."

"Thank you."

"Think nothing of it."

"Lieutenant those notes in Czechoslovakian get them translated they are significant." "The German investigators said that their passports are counterfeit and that they were professional, and those notes describe the American units amongst other things."

"Lieutenant, make sure I get that report as quickly as you can."

"Yes, Sir."

"James, I'll drop you off at your barracks, then we need to be going."

After the General and Colonel left, I went to see Lieutenant Faust. "I wish to see Lieutenant Faust?"

"It is late, and visiting hours are over; are you a relative."

"Yes, I'm his twin brother."

"You are an American soldier."

"Yes, I was with him when he got shot."

"I'm sorry but visiting hours are over."

"You will show me where he is, or I will go into every room to find him."

"Alright, but don't stay too long."

"I won't."

"I bet your wound hurts like hell."

"You could say that." "I heard you got the bastards."

"Yes, with the help of others, including your men."

"Was it worth it?"

"Yes, they were from the Eastern Bloc countries, and they were spying."

"I'm going to tell you something, but I don't want you to say where you got it." "Frankly, I don't think you should mention it to anyone." "You can call it whatever you want, but I have a talent for knowing when something is going to happen before it does." "In five months or less, there will be an attack from the East; we will be at war."

"Does this come from your superiors?"

"No, it comes from me." "The generals got told, but they do not believe me, although they may change their minds after today."

"How many men were killed tonight?"

"Three American MPs I don't know about your men. There is a lot of wounded."

"It's my fault I should have been more cautious."

"You couldn't have known; your investigators said they were highly trained professionals."

"You need to be going," said one of the nurses.

"You take care of yourself, you and your men did just fine." I went next to the site to see if everything was alright, then to the barracks where Top and Marc were just about to go home. "Our wounded should be back tomorrow, give them at least a day off more if you think they need it."

"Yes, Sir, you better get home, Maria, and Frederick will be worried."

"Yes, I'm heading there next."

Over the next few days, protests got lodged. They said they would do an investigation but thought they were a bunch of rouge men not connected to the governments. The German government demanded compensation, most likely; the American military will also ask. To me, everyone on the Eastern side was shifting the blame or making excuses. I gave a National Defense Service Ribbon, which was a standard ribbon, for Frederick. We were able to get everything out of Maria's apartment, which delighted Frederick he got his toys. Monday at morning formation, I praised the men for what happened the past week. "Sir, is there going to be any recognition for anyone?"

"Let me get back to you on that question; it did pass my mind, but I have to get some clarification if I can give recognition or not."

I was walking to the armory when my site clerk yelled, "Sir, you have a phone call."

"Major York."

"James, this is Colonel Greenhill."

"Yes, Sir, what can I do for you?"

"General Abrams called he said even if there was a large spy ring, there is no sign of any other spying." "It is considered an isolated event." "He said there is no sign of threats coming from the Eastern countries, so your opinion that war is coming has been rejected."

"He's, wrong, Sir, and many will feel foolish when we get attacked."

"If we are attack James, we will see James."

"I have a question for you, Sir."

"What is it?"

"The action my men took last week was impressive; can I award them anything other than promotion?"

"I will give you permission for the Good Conduct, and Army Achievement medal for those you believe deserve it."

"What about the wounded can they get a Purple Heart?"

"I can't authorize it, and I would advise you not to ask General Abrams because he is going to tell you the same thing."

"I wasn't going to call him Sir, thanks for allowing the two ribbons."

"You ready for the wedding on Saturday?"

"My goodness, I've forgotten all about the wedding my mind has been on what happened last week." "I'll be ready well as ready as a guy getting married for the first time would be."

"Very well, James, I'll let you get back to what you were doing."

"Yes, Sir." I got up to go to the armory when I received another phone call before I got to the armory door.

"Major York."

"James, this is General Abrams, how are you doing."

"Fine Sir, maybe a bit nervous I just talked to Colonel Greenhill he reminded me of Saturday."

"He told you about our findings."

"Yes, Sir."

"I assume you disagree."

"You must have heard my conversation with Colonel Greenhill."

"It comes from Washington."

"Yes, Sir, but they are wrong."

"I knew you would say that." "Not to change the subject, but I need to fill that Colonel's position in Bamberg." "I was going to give it to you, but I'm not sure war isn't coming despite what you think."

"That's alright, Sir; I'm shooting for General anyway," I said jokingly.

"You just might get that someday." "Do you have any suggestions on whom to replace Cromwell with?"

"Does it come with the Colonel rank?"

"Yes."

"Major Henderson; he is the company commander over the Green Berets at Fort Bragg, and he is a black man."

"Tell me about him."

"He is a good man, Sir, friendly when he is off duty, all business, no-nonsense crack soldier when he is on; you would like him."

"Is he the one in your book?"

"Yes."

"I'll see if I can get him."

"I'll let you go, James."

"Yes, Sir, and I will see you on Saturday."

"Yes, James."

20

MY WIFE AND CHILDREN

Wednesday at noon formation, I had all the men stand at ease. I started praising them about last week and all the hard work they did in getting this unit in shape. "All this deserves a reward; two complete weight sets and nautilus machines got delivered to the supply room, as well as a color television set." "These things you would have gotten regardless of last week or your work on the site." "So how else can I reward you this is what has bothered me these last few days, so I called Colonel Greenhill and asked him if I can award you with a ribbon." "His answer in part disappointed me." "He said that conflict is not a combat situation even though he thought you deserved it." "He did, however, agree to allow me to award two ribbons. They are the Good Conduct and the Army Achievement Medal; they aren't considered combat ribbons." "I have also done something I should have done long ago; everyone who is a specialist is now a hard stripe." "Washington, you have been promoted to corporal." "Chris, I promoted you to sergeant, as is Booker, and Clark, you are sergeants."

"Lieutenant Dizon, you are a captain, and Top you are promoted to sergeant major." I've talked to both Colonel Greenhill and General Abrams about this; he has allowed your promotions." I gave promotions to about half the unit and said, "More promotions will get given out in the future." "I wish to invite all of you who aren't on duty to my wedding." "The ceremony is at four-thirty Saturday at the Bamberg Catholic Cathedral. Followed by a reception at the hall next door, no gifts I have everything we will ever want." "I will post a notice next to the dayroom; I would like to see you there." Top informed everyone of the physical training there would be with the weights and placed them into groups, and the men got dismissed.

Friday, Maria, Frederick, and I went to a German court with a German lawyer for Frederick's adoption. "Frederick Muller, do you wish to be adopted by this man," said the judge.

Frederick looked upset and said, "My name is Frederick York, and he is my daddy."

"Yes, young man, you are Frederick York now, and he is your daddy."

Saturday came, and Maria went to Top's house, and I wasn't allowed to see her something to do with tradition. We tried to get Frederick into a suit, but he threw a fit wanting to be dress in his military clothes, so we let him. General Abrams, Colonel Greenhill, and their guests were here, as was General Arnold, the governor of Missouri, and California. Some congressmen and senators from both states and even the First Lady Mrs. Nixon. A few officials from Bamberg and even Lieutenant Faust were coming. Of course, I invited Captain Mills, Maggie, and Frank White. I was surprised that I was getting nervous, "Calm down, there is nothing to be nervous about," said Captain Dizon. I had gotten dressed in my Dress Blues with my saber Top, who would give away Maria and Captain Dizon, who would be the best man. I had four other men who would be dressed in blues also. Maryann, Helen and two other friends of Maria's were going to be bridesmaids.

I had figured there would be about five hundred or more people attending the wedding. I knew we were going to have a lot of flowers, caterers, photographers, and a band. I don't know what else there was going to be Maryann and Helen, and I guess others took care of everything, and I just paid the bills. Marc, Top and I drove to the cathedral, I got my first look at the decorated church, and I was impressed as was Top and the Captain. We were ushered into a room to the left of the altar by a member of the clergy. Our attire was looked over and corrected by what seemed to be a butler. "I haven't asked yet, who is going to do the ceremony?" I asked the clergyman.

"Archbishop Gruber, Cardinal Luecht, was going to do it, but he got called to Rome."

"It ought to be a colorful wedding," I said more to myself.

"Yes," replied Top.

We were sitting talking for about thirty minutes when we heard what sounded like angels, "I wonder who is singing?" I said. It turned out to be a children's choir from Munich. I also noticed the church was filling up with more people than I thought there would be, and I was happy to see many of my men dress in their greens. "None of you force the men to come."

"We were going to, but they wanted to come, especially when we told them about the food and booze," said Top.

Top was sent to the back of the church to escort Maria and give her away, and Captain Dizon and I went out to the altar and waited. I looked around and saw General Abrams and his wife, General Arnold, and his wife and the first lady. So, it started, the choir started up. Then there was the notice that the bride was about to enter, then the doors open and in walked Maria all dress in a satiny white flowing wedding dress. Everyone stood up to view the bride as she passed by them. Maria looked like a princess coming down the aisle; my mouth hung open at her beauty. When she reached the alter Top handed her to me and then stepped to the far right, I wanted to take her into my arms right then and there but had enough self-control not to ruin the wedding for Maria. Catherin, Top's daughter, was the flower girl, and she was all into the ceremony's spectacle. Frederick was Frederick fidgety and all, wanting the whole thing to get over with, but he stood his ground. When the archbishop asked for the ring, Frederick had to be nudged by Catherin much to his annoyance. Still, he lifted the pillow that the rings were on, high enough for Maria and me to get the rings. The ceremony finally ended, and I got to kiss Maria and boy did I kiss her. The only thing that stopped me is Frederick pulling on my trousers, wanting a kiss too. We stood for pictures for a minute or two. The music started with the choir singing, and we headed down the aisle, followed by everyone else in the wedding party. Once we left the cathedral, the wedding party had to go around the side and back into the church for more picture-taking.

"Mama, why we go back to church?" Frederick said with his broken English.

"Take pictures," Maria answered.

"How long?"

"Not long, sweetheart," I said. Pictures got taken for a half-hour, and Frederick was having a fit, to tell you the truth I wasn't pleased with it. Usually, there would have been rice thrown on us after we left the church. Since the reception hall was right next door, we decided to wait until we departed the reception. When we left the church and entered the reception hall, we were seated at a table up in front of everyone Maria and me in the center and everyone else to either side of us. Food and champagne got severed to everyone except the children; they got apple juice. There was extra food on a long table for those who wanted more and a bar for those who didn't wish to drink just champagne. Captain Dizon gave a toast then Maria, and I stood up and exchanged a sip from each other's glass.

We enjoyed our food for a few more minutes, and then we were informed by Captain Dizon, "James, Maria, it's time for the dance."

"What dance?" I asked

"No one can dance until you two dance first," said Captain Dizon."

Now dancing wasn't something I had learned in Fort Bragg, and as I look at Maria, who it was obvious she wanted to dance, I said, "I've never danced before."

"I show we do waltz." We got on the floor; then, Maria showed me where to put my hands much to everyone's amusement. She said in German, because it was more comfortable, "Move me around like leaf floating to the ground on windy day but to music."

"I'll try." The music started at the instruction of the Captain, and it was the Blue Danube. "I know this song."

"Yes, I know."

As I started dancing, I got more confident and started singing the words to the Blue Danube in German. "You sing very well." Others got up and danced, and I was shocked to see Chris dancing with the first lady, as everyone else was shocked.

The waltz ended, and one of my men said, "Major, you going to play something less tame, and perhaps wilder."

"You mean something a little more rocking?"

"Yeah," many of the men said.

I turned to Maria and said, "They want some rock and roll music; how do you feel about that."

"They are our guests, let them have what they want."

Maria and I went over to the band, and I said, "Can you play any rock and roll and maybe jazz mixed with classical?"

"Yes, we would be happy to play all types of music." As we walked away, they started to play some rock and roll music, which many of my guests liked. Maria and I decided to visit the guest to thank them for coming. We approached first Generals Abrams and Arnold, which were on the other side of the room. When we got there to my surprise sat Major William Henderson now Colonel William Henderson and Sergeant Major Booker.

"I was hoping you would take the post command position, but I didn't know you would bring Sergeant Booker with you."

"It was part of the deal."

"I'd like to have a few words with both of you in the next few days."

"It must be by Monday; we're going back to North Carolina in three days to pack up our household."

"Then, I will talk to you tomorrow."

"What about your honeymoon James?" asked General Arnold.

"That must wait for about two weeks, Sir." "Maria has a sick aunt in the hospital that is very old, and she needs to be with her."

General Abrams looked at General Arnold and said, "It makes no difference; it's open to when he wants to use it."

"I'm a little confused, Sir?"

General Arnold handed me an envelope. I looked in and said to Maria, "Its orders for one-week leave, and this is a hotel room in Vienna Austria."

"It's very kind of you, Sir."

"You deserve it, James, and you can use it when you can get away."

"Thank you, Sir." "We better talked to the other guest." After we talked to everyone, we went back to the dance floor to dance one more dance.

As we dance, I saw Catherin drag an unhappy Frederick out on the dance floor, we danced over to him, and I said, "Frederick give it a try you might like it."

"You don't."

"Oh, that's not true any time I can hold your mother this close I am happy." What I said met Maria's approval, and Frederick stopped resisting. By the time the music stopped, and Maria and I sat back down, Frederick and Catherin were still on the dance floor, enjoying himself. It was time to cut the cake ceremony, and I knew what was going to happen. Frederick was very interested in this; he had been impatiently waiting to eat some of the cake. His favorite sweet was Sergeant Hill's cookies. He had asked him if he brought any, which Frederick got a disappointing no. He did get a promise that he would make some more and give it to him. We cut two pieces of cake; each grabbed one, interlocked our arms, and then as predicted, the cake was smashed into my face as well as hers. That was the first time Frederick saw anything like that. He was in hysterics with laughter as well as everyone else looking at him and later tried to do the same to Catherin, but she had no part in it. It was time to go. We had already arranged with Top and Maryann to bring Frederick home, and Captain Dizon announced we were leaving.

Everyone went outside to see us off, and we were showered with rice as we got into the limousine we had rented. The limousine headed for home where we had our bags packed for an overnight stay at a fancy place near Munich, we also were taking Frederick. Maria and I changed into something more comfortable. Although it would be hard, we decided to put Frederick into some lederhosen if we could. He would never wear anything but his uniform. We came home late the next night we undressed Frederick and put him to bed. Tuesday, Maria and Frederick left to be with her sick aunt. I had thanked those who came to the wedding at morning formation. Then I headed to see Colonel Henderson and Sergeant Booker.

"Sir, you think we can go someplace away from here, so we can talk without being heard."

"Yes, do you know a place?"

"Yes, a small beer joint." We went to a small place in a small village near Bamberg.

"What's with all the cloak and dagger?" asked Sergeant Booker.

"What I'm going to say I've gotten in trouble for, but I think you two will believe me. Sergeant, do you remember I had a knack for knowing something was about to happen before it did?"

"Yes."

"Colonel, do you remember that last exercise I went through at Bragg?" "I decided to take the harder trail above the canyon because I knew there was going to be a trap. Then I realized the enemy was coming up from the other direction, and I tricked them.

"Yes, I remember that."

"I knew because I had a feeling that told me."

"Alright, but what are you now trying to tell us."

"We will be at war in about five months; it will come from the east."

"You tell this to General Abrams and Colonel Greenhill."

"Yes, and they don't believe me."

"Do you have any other proof other than your feelings?"

"Did you read the report on the spy ring?"

"Not in detail, it said something about an isolated incident."

"Well, you should read it more carefully, and I don't believe it is an isolated incident." "I was lucky to run across these spies; they were good." "There has also been an increase of MiG's flying over Bamberg."

Colonel Henderson stared at me, then Sergeant Booker said, "I believe him, Sir, he has never been wrong."

"I tend to believe you, Major, but what can I do."

"Get the units prepared for it you have an armor unit that their equipment is out in the open and bunched together."

He nodded then said, "I'll do what you say and more, but I am not going to bring up war and bring down the raft of General Abrams."

"Good, you're going to have trouble with some of your units."

"What do you mean?"

"There are many bigots in those units, and they aren't going to be happy you are now the post commander."

"Yes, I know about this General Abrams told me, but I will root those red necks out." We talked some more and had a few beers and food then went back to the post.

When I walked into my office, there was Frank White.

"Where are you staying?" "I have room at my place?"

"I'm in a very nice place that I'm very comfortable with besides I'm in and out too much, and I will be meeting with many people."

"Well, if you change your mind, my place is free."

"It does not cost me anything the company is picking up the tab."

"Ok, you miss some excitement a few days ago."

"So, I've heard a spy ring or something."

"Yeah, a lot of men were wounded and died."

"How many did you lose?"

"None, I had five wounded the ones who died were from the MPs and German police and, of course, those spies."

"I'll want to know the whole story."

"You can talk to any of my men, the one who would know the most is Sergeant Major Jack Bennett; he is out on the site."

"He the one who gave the bride away?"

"Yes, he's a good man."

"Alright, how do you want to work this?"

"You can talk to anyone about anything except classified information." "If my men or I am too busy, don't push, the Army comes first." "How long will you be here?"

"Oh, maybe a month or two, and then maybe I will check on you once every other month."

I stared at him for a few seconds, then got up, shut the door, then asked, "Can you stay longer?"

He looked at me, confused, and said, "If there is a good reason."

"Do you have to tell Penguin the reason why?"

"No, but it better be a good reason."

I started pacing and said, "You remember in the first book I and others told you I had a knack for predicting what was going to happen before it happens?"

"Yes, your premonitions."

"In less than five months, Europe will be at war." "We will get attacked from the east; it will last for a short time." "It will be short, but deadly a lot of good men will be lost or wounded."

"Who do you think will win?"

"We will, of that I have no doubt but at a high cost in my opinion."

"I take it your superiors don't believe you even after the spy incidence."

"You would be right." "My staff believes me as does Colonel Henderson and Sergeant Major Booker, who know me."

"I'll make arrangements to stay here at least six months I might have to fly back to New York a time or two."

"Just don't mention the battle to come to anyone."

"I won't." He handed me the checks from the book and movie royalties, which added up well over five million.

"Let's go down to supply and get you a helmet." I got him his helmet, drove him out to the site, and introduced him to Top and some of the other men. I sent my dad a million to invest, another million for the bank in Missouri. The rest I opened an account through the military.

Maria and Frederick left to visit her aunt on Tuesday, and the house was lonely without them. Wednesday, I saw Frank in the morning, but he disappeared, and by Thursday, he was nowhere around, so I assumed he went back to New York. I had been talking every night with Maria and Frederick by phone, and that helped my loneliness. I had expected the last of the men that General Abrams promised today, and by ten, they showed up. There were seven of them one of them, a short babyface young man, caught my attention. There was something about him that bothered me, so I decided to see him last. "Chris, go out into the dayroom and place the files, so that shortest and youngest looking one is on the bottom."

"Yes, Sir."

I called the site and instructed Top and Captain Dizon to come in. Chris came back with the files, and I took the bottom one and looked at it. His MOS said supply, his IQ, and MOS scores were either average or just below average. Physically the young man's height was barely five feet, but he looked shorter, and his weight was under a hundred pounds. His age said eighteen, but he seemed much younger all this confused me. I have never seen a person in the military with these conditions before. I decided to call Maggie, "Maggie is there any way you can break free from there and come here?"

"What's the problem, Major?"

"I just got seven new men, and one looks like he is too young."

"Why don't you bring him here?"

"If he has been fooling everyone to get this far successfully, I want to put the pressure on him to tell the truth; besides, I don't want to look like a fool in public if I'm wrong."

"Well, I can be there in about an hour."

"That will be fine, Maggie." "I'll have some coffee brewing."

"You do that, Major."

I started in with the other six men and was on the second one when Top and the Captain showed up. I then finished with the second man and sent him to supply. After he left, I turned to Top and the Captain and said, "Go get the next man and when you go into the dayroom, check out the smallest man with the babyface and blond hair."

The next man I talked to and sent him downstairs to supply then turned to Top and Captain Dizon and asked, "What did you think when you saw that small soldier?"

"He looks kind of young," said Top.

"He looks very young," said Captain Dizon.

"Yes, that is what I was thinking." "Maggie is coming; she should be here soon; meanwhile, we will leave that young man for last just play along with me when he does come in; I'm going to press him."

"Yes, Sir."

Just as we got through with the last man, Maggie came in. I explained to her what is going on. Top gave her some coffee and offered her some cookies that she refused. "Chris, go get the last man."

"Yes, Sir."

"Sit down." "This is Captain Maggie McCall, This Sergeant Major Jack Bennett, our top sergeant. My Executive Officer, Captain Marc

Dizon, and I am your commanding officer, Major James York." I opened his file and said, "Your name is Jonathan Kruger."

"Yes, Sir."

"Most men, when they get older, would change their first name to Jonah."

"I call myself Jonah."

"You do, do you."

"Yes, Sir."

"What is your birth date?"

"It's right there, Sir."

"Answer the Major son," said Top.

"June fourteen, nineteen…. fifty-two."

"That can't be son to old want to try again?"

"Nineteen, fifty-eight."

"Too young."

"Nineteen fifty-five."

"Well, now the math works."

"Yes, Sir, I don't celebrate my birthday much."

"That sounds like a lot of bull shit," said Maggie.

"What is your real age?" I asked.

"Eighteen, Sir."

"I think your lying, and I hate liars." I could see he was getting very nervous but didn't say anything. "How old do you all think he is?" I asked everyone in the room.

"I would guess thirteen or fourteen," said Captain Dizon.

"No more than thirteen," said Top.

"I think he is younger than that," said Maggie.

I stepped in front of my desk, put the meanest look on my face, grabbed his arm, jerked him up, and then yelled, "What is your age."

A tear rolled down his cheek as he slumped down back in his chair, but he still didn't say anything. Finally, as I stared at him, Maggie said, "I think I know a way to know his true age."

"How's that?"

"He may not like it."

"I don't care, do it anyway unless young man you're willing, to tell the truth?" He didn't answer, so I motioned for Maggie to start.

"Jonathan, I'm a nurse, an excellent nurse as any of these men will tell you, so I know how a man is and how a boy is as far as medicine." "There are three things I'm going to have you do." "You can stop me anytime by telling the truth, do you understand." He nodded yes, as his eyes watered up again. "Open your mouth wide open." She took a flashlight she had and looked in his mouth and nodded as she turned off the flashlight. She stroked his cheek with the back of her hand, then pulled out some alcohol, and a tissue applied alcohol and rubbed the top of his lip that looked as if he had the beginnings of a mustache. A smug of black color got deposited on the tissue, and Maggie showed it to me. "Alright young man strip to your waist."

"What?" he said, frightened.

"Take your shirt and tee shirt off." Reluctantly he did as Maggie said, and then she instructed him to place his hands on his head. She had a bottle that looked like nail polish remover that she put some on a cotton ball then told him, "This may tickle." She gently rubbed the cotton ball under his arm and then gave a tug at the hair he had there, and the hair came off. "Make me a muscle." She felt what muscle he had and then felt his chest. Tears were rolling down his face. He knew he had got caught, but he still wasn't talking until Maggie said, "Son, as I told you, I'm an excellent nurse I've been doing this for a long time." "You have no facial hair that mustache wasn't real." "You don't have your wisdom teeth yet, and they come in between thirteen and fifteen, the hair under your arms came from the hair on your head, and you foolishly glued it in with superglue." "Your muscles haven't started to develop yet, which points to you haven't reached your teen years yet, and your breasts are puffy, which means you haven't gone through puberty." "Now, to confirm everything you could admit to your age or I could have you completely strip in front of everyone." "I could check your penis, testicles, and bottom." He was crying a lot now, and Maggie said, "Come on, Jonathan, you have got caught what are you twelve or younger?

"Eleven."

"Eleven how in the hell did he get this far in the Army at eleven?" asked Captain Dizon, shocked.

"I don't know, but I will find out why." "Why don't you two go back to what you were doing, and I will talk with you later."

"Yes, Sir," both Top and the Captain said, then left."

"Maggie, thanks for your help."

"No problem, I'd get the hair off him; he most likely has hair between his legs." "Just use nail polish remover and cotton I'm sure Maria has some." "When you get him cleaned up, bring him by, and I'll give him a full exam."

"Will do, Maggie."

"Put your shirt back on, son."

"What are you going to do to me," he said sobbing.

"You're not in trouble if that is what you are worried about."

"Does it mean I'm out of the Army?"

"I'm afraid so." He completely broke down in tears, and I said, "Why are you upset, don't you think your parents are worried about you."

"I don't have a father the money I was making in the Army; I sent to my brother and sisters, so they could have something to eat."

"Doesn't your mother work or get help from the state and some churches that will help?"

"My mother doesn't work, nor will she what little money she gets from her boyfriends; she spends most of it on drugs and alcohol."

I went and sat down on the couch with him and put my arm around him and said, "So let me guess you left because there would be one less mouth to feed, and you could send money home."

"Yes, but I don't know what I'm going to do now."

"You let me worry about that I'm good at fixing things." "I would assume if I sent you back home, you would just run off again?"

"I would have to there aren't any jobs where I come from."

"Do you have any relatives that might take you, your brother, and sisters in?"

"My mother has some poor cousins, but they won't have anything to do with us; they say we are trash."

"You're not trash, what about your father's side of the family?"

"I not sure I think I have grandparents somewhere in Arkansas."

"Arkansas, where do you live?"

"I live in a small house near a place called Ellsinore, Missouri."

"Off-highway sixty?"

"Yes."

"That's where my ranch is, I live there."

"You do."

"Yes, do you know a family by the name of Korenek?"

"I know Valentine Korenek; he goes to my school."

"Let's go get something to eat; then I will take you home and get you clean up." "Hopefully, I will come up with something to help you." I grabbed his gear, put it into my sedan then walked down to the mess hall. When I saw what there was to eat, I looked at Jonathan and said, "Do you like this stuff?"

"No, not really."

"Put your tray back; we'll eat at the canteen."

"Sergeant, do you have any of those cookies of yours."

"You know I always do, Sir."

"Let me have a few for the boy, Sergeant."

"Yes, Sir, are you adopting another one."

I looked at Jonathan then said, "Now Sergeant, that is a good idea." The Sergeant gave me a bag of cookies, and I headed to the canteen to get what he wanted.

He and I got a hamburger, french fries, and a soda pop; then, we sat down to eat. "Jonathan, you're a little boy what you need to be is a child now." "All that responsibility is gone now." A tear went down his cheek, and I put my arm around him again.

"Would Nurse Maggie have made me take all my clothes off?"

"Yes, but why does it bother you?" "Are you bashful?"

"Well, I guess not, but she is a girl." We left the canteen and headed to my house; I had already told Chris I wouldn't be in for the rest of the day.

I got him home and found Maria's nail polish remover and cotton but decided to talk to Jonathan first, so we sat on the couch. I put my arm around him and said, "I can't send you back home knowing you will run off again; I don't think you will be as lucky as you were this time." "How would you feel about me being your father it would mean you would have another mother and brother?" "You would also have to get used to our customs." "The benefit of staying with me is you will never go hungry, you will always have nice clothes and things, and you will be loved more than you ever have been."

"What are you saying you want to adopt me?"

"That is the goal, and the best part for you is that you can be the little boy that you are supposed to be this would be the last big decision you would have to make until you were an adult."

"What about my brother and sisters in Missouri?"

"I was getting to that." "I haven't forgotten your brother, and sisters, tonight I will be making a lot of phone calls to have your bother and sisters removed from your mother." "I'll place into a good home long enough to find your grandparents in Arkansas."

"They will separate them."

"No, I think I know a person who will take them in."

"Who."

"My aunt and uncle." "I'll need to ask you some questions about your mother, are you willing to answer some questions, and do you want me to be your father?"

His chin started to quiver, and tears flowed down his cheek, he shook his head yes then gave me a weak, "Yes."

"It's alright to cry your eleven years old." He buried his head into me and got out all the pinned-up troubles he had out of him. I picked him up and put him on my lap, and he curled up in a fetal position and continued to cry for about twenty minutes.

I cleaned off the fake hair, which took about an hour to get all the hair and glue off. I got Frederic's tub toys, and he said, "I don't need any toys for a bath."

"All boys your age plays with toys in the tub remember you are eleven years old."

We went into the bathroom. I got some liquid soap from under the sink in the kitchen and poured some in the tub's which amazed Jonathan.

As he was playing with the toys, I washed his hair three times, which had a ton of grease. His hair came out much blonder and longer looking with all the washings. "When you are finish playing, you call me, and I will get you out."

"Ok."

I put something more comfortable on got a notepad pencil out and placed it next to the couch. Jonathan played in the water for about fifteen minutes. He wasn't having that hard of a time converting back into a child. Finally, he called out and said, "I'm ready to get out." I ignored him, and he said a little louder, "I finished playing; I'm ready to get out." Again, I ignored him; he was quiet for a minute then said, "Daddy, I'm ready to get out."

That's what I was waiting for, and I went to the bathroom and said with a smile, "I thought I heard someone yelling from here, but I didn't know who you were calling."

As I helped to dry him, I bent down and kissed him, which surprised him. "What's the matter haven't you ever been kissed?"

"No."

"Well you better get accustomed to it we kiss a lot in this house," I said as I gave him another kiss.

"Why do you kiss me?"

"Why does anyone kiss anyone?"

"Because they love them, but you hardly know me."

"How long does it take before you love someone?"

"I don't know; I guess not long."

"You're right, and I love you, why do you think I am doing all of this for you." I went through his duffle bag and found some jeans, a shirt, socks, and some old beat-up tennis shoes. "Tomorrow, I will take you shopping downtown for more clothes and things." He nodded his approval. I finally got him dressed, and I combed his hair like Fredericks except Fredericks' hair was a lot longer. I showed him what he looked like in the mirror, then I said, "Now you look like an eleven-year-old boy or maybe younger." "I'm going to have you grow your hair long." "You think that will be alright with you?"

"Yes, I like my hair longer."

"Why don't you go into Frederick's room and see if there is something you would like to play with, I'm going to call your new mother and brother."

"Suppose they don't want me."

"They will love you."

I called Maria and told her everything that happened, about the boy's background and what I wished to do. "Do you wish me and Frederick to come home?"

"Of course, I miss you terribly, but I can handle Jonathan." "You come home when you were planning to."

"Alright, let me talk to him."

"He doesn't speak German yet."

"I will use my best English, and Frederick will help."

"Alright." "Jonathan, come here."

"Yes."

"Here, say hello."

I handed him the phone, and he said, "Hello." As Maria talked to him, I saw tears come down his cheek and then he said, "Alright, mama, I love you too. He handed me the phone, I kissed him, and he smiled and went back to play.

"You are alright with bringing Jonathan into the family?"

"Of course."

"I don't know what you told him, but it did a lot of good."

"I just told him I loved him."

"How is Frederick taking the news that he has a brother?"

"He is excited to have a brother," I told her how much I loved her and then talked to Frederick and said goodbye.

I called Jonathan to the couch, then asked him questions about his mother and his life back in Missouri. Everything he told me was useful, but what was most helpful was where his mother kept her drugs, the numerous boyfriends she had, and what they did to him and his siblings. As he told all of this, he broke down several times, but I think it was a good thing to lift that burden off his back. "Daddy, I'm hungry?"

"Well, it's too early for dinner, but I think you could have some milk and those cookies Sergeant Hill gave you." He went back to playing as I started dinner.

I got halfway finished with making spaghetti when there was a knock at the door. "Come on in; it is unlocked."

In walked Captain Dizon and Top, "We have come to see how things are going," said the Captain.

"Well, everything is going fine." "I'll tell you what's going on in a second; you guys want to eat with us."

"No," they both said.

"How about a beer?"

"Now you're talking," said Top.

I opened the refrigerator and pulled out two beers. "You're not drinking with us?" Top asked.

"No, I have a lot of phone calls to make tonight."

They both sat down, and the captain asked, "Where's the boy?"

"You two remember what he looked like?"

"Sure, we do," they both said.

"Jonathan, come out here."

"Yes."

"They want to say hello."

"Hello," Jonathan said. Top and the Captain's mouth hung open, shocked at the transformation of Jonathan.

"You're sure this is the same boy?" asked Captain Dizon.

"Yes, that's him quite a change, isn't he?"

"Daddy, can I go outside to play?"

"Daddy?" Top said, stunned.

"I'll explain in a little bit." "You can go out until dinner time try not to get too dirty,"

"Can I take some of Frederic's toys outside?"

"You better not, but I think he has some toys out there already."

Jonathan went outside happily. I turned to Top, and Marc then said, "That boy has been through hell." "He has carried the burden of not only what he has gone through in the Army. He also has the responsibility of caring for his younger siblings." "His mother abuses drugs and alcohol with many boyfriends." They, with the permission of the mother, has abused him and his siblings." "They live in filth with little food and raggedy clothing." "There are no relatives that will take the kids in on the mother's side." "The mother and her family are considered white trash if you know what I mean." "His father is dead, and there are no relatives except for maybe grandparents in Arkansas someplace, but Jonathan said that they are old and poor."

"Alright, but why is he calling you, daddy?" asked Captain Dizon.

"I hope to raise him and if I can adopt him." They were going to say something, but I said, "If he goes back, he will run again, and I don't think Jonathan will be as lucky as he was this time." "I will call some people tonight and have his siblings place in a home where they can be together, and I'm going to find their grandparents." "I plan to ask them if they would allow me to adopt Jonathan and share custody." "I'll also with the help of the state to help support his siblings."

"Don't you think the boy should be with his siblings?" asked Top.

"Ideally, yes, but you know how I get these feelings, and they are right I don't think their grandparents can handle four children or could afford them even with the state and my help."

"Suppose the grandparents won't take any of them?" asked Marc.

"I am hoping my aunt and uncle will take them in until a home can get found where all three could live, a worst-case scenario would be I would adopt all four, but I don't feel that would happen."

"I give you credit for what you are doing, Sir, but when you step in it, you like to step in it with both feet," said Top.

"You are going to have troubles with the brass, but somehow I think they will listen to you and go along," said Marc.

"I think some of my ability to know something before it happens is rubbing off on you, Marc," I said with a smile.

"Maybe," he said. "We better be going, Top."

"I'll be in tomorrow morning for the formation and to make the phone calls, but afterward, I will be taking Jonathan shopping for clothing and things."

"We will see you tomorrow morning then," said Marc.

I walked them out to their vehicle and said, "Look at him doesn't he remind you of Frederick playing in the sand, I'll bet you he hasn't played like a little boy in a very long time."

They drove off, and I said to Jonathan, "Time to come in the house to get cleaned up and eat." Of course, he was dirty like any other little boy, and I cleaned him up and put a bib on him then fed him. After he ate, I let him watch TV while I cleaned the kitchen. I then went to the couch and told Jonathan to shut the TV off and sit by me. What amazed me about him is how fast he was bonding with me and accepting me as his father after only a few hours. I only hope when Maria and Frederick come home, he adjusts to them also. "I need to know how you fooled everyone when you came into the Army." He told me the whole story of a lot of luck, some excellent acting, and avoiding being around those who would know, also a lot of sloppiness from the Army. Once General Abrams and Arnold found out, there will be many heads that will roll. I let him watch TV until nine then told him, "It's time for bed, sweetheart." "You will sleep with me until your mother and Frederick come home, then you can share the room with Frederick." "I must get up at midnight then again at four in the morning to make some phone calls, so I will set the alarm clock to get up, but you can stay in bed and sleep." "When I leave to go to work tomorrow, you stay in the house until I get home, which hopefully will be before noon." I pulled back the blanket and flopped him on the bed. I then set the clock then hopped into bed myself, and Jonathan snuggled next to me; I kissed him goodnight, and within ten minutes, he was sound asleep.

"Hello, Aunt Adeline, its James."

"James is everything alright."

"No, not really. I need you and Uncle Paul's help."

"What is it, your Uncle Paul is right here?"

"Do you know a family by the name of Kruger?"

At first, there was silence, then she said, "Yes, it's a low life woman who has four dirty children who go hungry most of the time and run around in clothes that are dirty and raggedly."

"How do you feel about the children?"

"Oh, they are sweet little children; I wish I could do more for them; the oldest tries to take care of his brother and sisters." "Why are you asking me about them?"

"Are you aware the oldest has been missing for some time?"

"No, Val, have you seen that oldest Kruger boy?"

"Jonathan, No, but I saw his brother and sisters."

"What's this all about, James?"

"I have Jonathan with me." "Somehow, he got into the Army to support his brother and sisters, and he ended up in my unit, and I discovered him."

"But he just a little boy, how can this happen?"

"He's a beautiful, perfect little boy, he is smarter than what most people think, and he is very fortunate also." "I am hoping to adopt Jonathan, and I wish to find a home where all three children can be together." "What I'm asking are you and Uncle Paul willing to take in the three children until I can find a home for them." "I will make sure it will not cost you anything?"

I could hear her talking to my uncle then said, "We do have our foster license, and we would be pleased to take the little dears in."

"Fantastic, I'm going to call my lawyer in Popular Bluff, then I will call the sheriff and anyone else that they tell me to call."

"Sounds like a good idea."

"Any new property to buy?"

"I'll let your Uncle Paul talk to you about that."

"Hello, James."

"Yes, Uncle Paul."

"There is some property that doesn't border your property, but it borders mine; it's about two hundred acres."

"Is there water on the property, and is it wooded or pasture?"

"It has a small spring much smaller than yours, and it has some grass and woods."

"You plan to graze your cattle on it."

"Yes, if you buy it."

"Go ahead and buy it and send me the paperwork." I finished talking to them and then went back to sleep after setting the clock to three o'clock. At three o'clock, I spoke to my attorney and told him the whole story and what I wanted to do. He was shocked at what I told him and said he would take care of everything, including the children in Ellsinore. I also let him know that I was calling the sheriff. The good news was because of who I am and the wealth I had, I should have no problem in adopting Jonathan and that he would take care of the paperwork. I next called the sheriff and talked to a detective by the name of Peter Thompson. I informed him of the story of Jonathan and added the drug, alcohol, and child abuse that Jonathan told me. I gave him the name and phone number of my attorney and my aunt and uncle. He told me that they were having drug problems and thought Jonathan's mother was involved. They said they would deal with her soon and take the children to my aunt and uncle's place.

I was tired, so I set the clock for five-thirty and laid back down. It seems like I just dozed off when I had to get up. I threw some water on my face, shaved, and got dressed in my fatigues and boots. I kissed Jonathan, which woke him, and he asked, "You going to work daddy?"

"Yes, sweetheart, you go back to sleep, and I should be home before noon if not, I will call you." "If you get hungry, you know where the cereal and everything else is."

He nodded and rolled over, and I left for the barracks and got there a little after six.

"You look worn out," said Top.

"I was up all night, making phone calls back to the states." "I'll tell you more after I get something to eat."

"I'll come with you."

"You look like you had a rough night, Sir," said Sergeant Hill.

"Yeah, your right; you got any tea?"

"You go ahead and sit down, and I'll bring it to you."

I sat down to bacon, scrambled eggs, and pancakes then dove into them. "I'll be glad when Maria is back." The mess Sergeant came over with some tea, buttered toast, and a couple of aspirins and sat down.

"Thanks." I took a couple of gulps of the tea, took the aspirin with water then went back to eating.

"You know about Jonathan Sergeant?"

"That he is a little boy Sir, did he like the cookies?"

"Yes, to both, and I plan to adopt him." Captain Dizon came in and grabbed a cup of coffee. "Marc, I was just about to tell these gentlemen what happen last night."

I told them the whole story about my relatives, Jonathan's relatives, the lawyer, and the police. "Today, after I talk to Colonel Greenhill and General Abrams, check out what paperwork I have. I'll do a walkthrough of the site; then, I plan to take Jonathan shopping for clothes and things." "After I finish shopping for him, I plan to go to the JAG office."

"Well, it looks like things are going pretty smooth for you, did you talk to Maria about it," asked Top.

"Yes, she is thrilled, as is Frederick."

I finished my meal and had a morning formation, then I went to my office and did some paperwork for an hour. After I finished, I called Colonel Greenhill. "Sir, do you have a few minutes."

"Yes, what's going on, James?"

"I have a problem that I am handling but want to run it by you, and I intend to call General Abrams since he is involved."

"I received seven men recently; are you aware of this, Sir?"

"Yes, you should be at full strength now."

"I'll need to get one more man, Sir." "Six of the men seem to be just fine; however, the seventh man there was a problem."

"What's wrong with the seventh man James?"

"That's just it, Sir he is not a man he is an eleven-year-old boy."

"What!" he yelled, shocked.

"Let me tell you what I have found out and what I have done." I told him the whole story of how he got into the Army, his background, and what I had decided to do.

"I think you should send him back to the states and let the authorities deal with him."

"He would run again or get put in a detention facility." "He has been through too much for me to let that happen to him."

"I could order you."

"Now Colonel, you know those kinds of threats don't scare me, and you know what I would do if you pushed me."

"Alright, James, you do what you think is right; it's out of my hands."

"Sir, he is a wonderful boy, and I'm sure you would love him as much as I do."

"Alright, James, I'll let you call General Abrams."

"General Abrams, please, this is Major York."

"One moment, please."

"James, how are things going?"

"Good until you sent me those seven men," I told him the whole story, including my conversation with Colonel Greenhill.

"I can understand how you feel, James, but I also think what Colonel Greenhill said is correct."

"Consider this, Sir, if I decided he had to go back to the states as the Colonel said and what happens is what I predicted, what do you think the press would do?" "It's going to be bad enough that he somehow got this far in the military, but to throw him away heads will roll."

"Heads are going to roll anyway." "What kind of a child is he?"

"He is a beautiful, wonderful boy starving for affection and happy the weight of the world is off him."

"Alright James, I probably wouldn't have handled it the way you have, but I think you are right for yourself and the Army, I'll send you another man." "When are you going on your honeymoon?"

"About a week, Sir, I'll have to make arrangements for Jonathan, though."

"Don't worry about that I'll fix that and send you the papers."

"Thanks, Sir."

I hung up then stood up and stretched. I grabbed my hat and headed for my car when Sergeant Hill came with a bag of cookies. "These are for Jonathan."

I looked in the bag and said, "Thanks, but I will save half for Frederick he and his mother should be back Sunday."

"Good idea, Sir."

I got out to the site by about ten-thirty, "How did it go with the Colonel and General?" asked Captain Dizon.

"With the Colonel, it went as well as I could expect, but the General was a lot better."

"Well, it's the General that counts."

I smiled and said, "You can say that again."

I found Mr. Shafer and asked, "You still running practice simulations using the new math program."

"Yes, Sir."

"How often, and what are your scores?"

"About once a week, Sir, and we are at one hundred percent."

"Do it every third day, and if you drop below a hundred percent find out why and go back to doing it every day, I think we have about three months."

"Yes, Sir." I met with Top and told him that I wanted a meeting with NCOs E six and above and all officers ten o'clock on Monday morning and then left for home.

I walked into the front door, and Jonathan was on the floor with some toys watching TV. He got up, ran over to me, then gave me a hug and a kiss. "After I clean the kitchen, we are going shopping." I made the bed after this; I got Jonathan ready. We headed downtown, and as we went, I said, "I talked to a lot of people last night, and this morning about you."

"What did they say about you being my father?"

"They said the one who could cause troubles would be your grandparents." "Your brother and sisters are going to stay with my uncle and aunt. As soon as the police deal with your mother."

"I don't think my grandparents will try to take me away from you, and I'm glad that my brother and sisters will be together."

"We are going to see a military lawyer after we finish shopping." "Do you want to see what is going on at the missile site after all of this?"

"No, I didn't want to be in the Army anyway." "I didn't like it much except when I got to shoot the rifles."

I bought him many jockey underwear, pants, shirts, and then I saw some lederhosen, and I had him try on a pair. They weren't the short pants, but the long kind he wasn't too sure he wanted to wear them. I told him that most boys wear them in Germany, and besides, Frederick had a pair he wore except when he had his uniform. I was going to get Jonathan some shoes and socks at a German store but decided to wait and go to the PX, where they had better shoes. Along with what I bought him, I also got him something he could wear to go to church. We then went to the Toy store, and I felt that Germany had the best toys. Jonathan's reaction to the toy store was much the same as Fredericks, "You can pick out three toys one for inside the house, one for outside the house, and one for the bathtub."

The store owner knew me, so we talked a little. "He does not look like Frederick?"

"No, it is not Frederick; his name is Jonathan; he is German, but he grew up in the United States; he doesn't speak German, yet I plan to adopt him."

"So, Frederick is going to have a brother."

"Yes, and he is excited about it."

"Where is Frederick, is he in school?"

"No, he went with his mother to visit a sick aunt; they should be back Sunday."

Jonathan came back with a big box filled with smaller toys and asked, "Is this alright?"

"It's alright, but is it an outdoor or indoor toy?"

"Outdoor," he said then went looking for two more toys. Like Frederick, he was meticulous looking for the best toys, and the store had a lot. I could see him struggling with which one to choose. He came back with two other toys and said, "I don't know what to choose from."

"Is it an indoor toy?"

"Yes."

"I know it is hard, but you must choose."

He looked at them both carefully, and he said, "This one I'll put the other one back."

"He said he wants this one and will put the other one back."

"No, no, I will put it back."

"Mr. Gruber said he would put it back for you what do you say."

"Thank you."

"He said, thank you."

"He has to learn German sometime; I think I will start today."

Jonathan went running back to look at something for the bathtub, and about ten minutes later, he came back with a plastic tugboat. Mr. Gruber rang everything up and handed the toys to Jonathan, and Jonathan said, thank you, in German, which surprised me. After loading up the trunk, I asked, "You hungry?"

"Yes, I think there is a place up the street I saw daddy."

"That place isn't good; your mother used to work there, but I know a good place."

We drove to a place where the locals eat. I said, "Now Jonathan, they eat differently here, they don't pick up their food with their hands even if it is fried chicken or pizza the exception is fresh fruit from a tree or an ice cream cone."

"How do you eat it then?"

"With a knife and fork, it will be strange at first, but you will get used to it." We went in, and to play it safe we both decided to eat something German, Wienerschnitzel and Jonathan loved it.

Instead of going to the PX after lunch, we went to the JAG office first; the PX would be open until seven at night, but the Jag office would close earlier. "I'm Major James York I wish to talk to a lawyer."

"Personal or military Sir," said a clerk.

"Personal, an adoption."

He looked at me, then Jonathan, with his mouth open, and before he could say anything from far behind him, I heard, "I'll take care of this one, Sergeant."

"Captain Elizabeth Lawson Major."

"It's a pleasure; this is Jonathan."

"Please to meet you, young man," she said in German.

"He doesn't speak German, yet he is from Missouri."

"Oh, I had assumed he was a German child."

I looked at Jonathan and said, "It must be the Wienerschnitzel."

"You think, so daddy, do I look like a German boy?"

"Wait till you see Frederick you will think he has always been your brother I think you look and act just like him."

I turned to the Captain and said, "Do you know who I am?"

"Yes, I do."

"Good, this is not going to be an easy adoption; I don't think." "I do have the backing of General Abrams." "I have a lawyer in Missouri working on the adoption from his end." "I'll tell you the whole story, but I want to tell you that the story is confidential, so no press by orders of General Abrams."

"It would be anyway orders or not." I went on and told the whole story, which took about thirty minutes. "You are a very clever young man Jonathan." "I'm glad you came to me." "I see two cases here." "The adoption which I will call your lawyer in Missouri and protect him from any prosecution for deceiving the military." "I don't think they will prosecute because of his age, and they want to keep it quiet." "This action is going to cost you a bit of money, mostly for the adoption."

"I have the money."

"I don't see that much of a problem with the adoption; there is just a lot of paperwork the only stumbling block with the grandparents."

"I don't think they will cause problems," Jonathan said.

"I hope you are right young man."

"I'll give your lawyer a call Monday morning." "We will need to sign some papers before you leave."

After we finished with the JAG office, we headed to the PX to get him some shoes and socks, and then we went home. "We started bringing in the things we just bought for the house, of course, he grabbed his toys and put them in Frederick's room, and then he went into the bathroom."

After he had finished, he said, "Daddy, can I go out to play?"

"Yes, for a little while."

He grabbed his outside toy and said, "Daddy, do you think Frederick will let me play with his toys when he comes home?"

"Yes, if you let him play with yours and you show him, love."

"I will, daddy." He played outside until it was starting to get dark, and then I called him in. I washed him up, kissed him, and let him play with his indoor toy.

It was nearly nine o'clock, and I was reading the Stars and Stripes when Jonathan got up, put away his toy, sat beside me, and shut his eyes. "You tired, sweetheart, it's nearly your bedtime?"

"Yes," he said softly. I kissed him, picked him up, and laid his head on my shoulder. Then, I carried him to bed, tucked him in.

"Are you coming to bed, daddy?"

"Yes, shortly, sweetheart, now go to sleep."

After I finished reading the Stars and Stripes, I turned off all the lights, then crawled into bed and fell asleep.

Saturday after cartoons on TV, Jonathan went outside to play. Top and Maryann came over in the afternoon with their two daughters; one was about Jonathan's age. "How are things going with Jonathan?" asked Maryann.

"Good, I got a good JAG officer yesterday." "You two want a beer?"

"You are having one, Sir?" asked Top.

"Sure."

"I'll get them," Top said.

Top handed Maryann and me a beer and sat down, and I said, "Thanks, you know you two, Maria and I, and Marc and Helen, we should all go out together."

"I don't know if that would be appropriate, Sir."

"Why do you say that?"

"You're an officer, and I'm not, Sir."

"I could promote you to lieutenant."

"I wouldn't accept it; I'd make less money, and me going out with you isn't a good reason to be promoted."

"We have gone to the Sportsman Club together."

"You are an unusual officer."

"Have you ever read my book?"

"Yes, we did."

"Then, you should know that I being an officer was pushed on me."
"I don't consider myself to be much of an officer."

"You Sir are the best officer I have ever seen, and I mean it," said Top.

I had my head down in humility, then pulled it up and smiled, and said, "Maybe I can promote you to a warrant."

"We have another problem other than what Top said," said Maryann.
"What's that?"

"Who is going to take care of our kids?"

I looked at Top and said, "You know she is pretty smart; I never thought about that."

"That's why I married her," said Top.

"You'll get rewarded for that one, Jack," Maryann said, smiling.

We finished our beers, and I took their bottles and put them in the crate. I saw out the window Jonathan sitting on the swing with Top's daughter Elizabeth. "Look at this."

Maryann and Top looked, and Maryann said, isn't that cute."

Top and Maryann had to go, so I went outside with them, and Top said to Jonathan, "Young man, what are your intentions with my daughter?"

"Intentions, I'm only eleven I have no intentions."

"Well, if you do, let me know."

"Jack, leave him alone I think they are a sweet couple."

A confused Jonathan said, "Daddy, what are they talking about?"

"They are teasing you, sweetheart."

The next day we went to church, Jonathan was impressed with the cathedral, but he had no idea what was going on during the services. It wasn't the fact that everything was in German. From where Jonathan lived, it was Baptist country; it is that church he was most familiar with, even though he never went. When we got home, I help Jonathan out of his church clothes and into his lederhosen then told him I wanted him to stay in the house so that his mother and brother could see him clean. Jonathan was playing with his toys on the floor; I was reading when I heard the Volkswagen drive up, then stop. I had just stood up when the door busted open, and Frederick said excitedly, "Daddy," as he jumped into my arms kissing me. Maria was right behind him with a smile on her face, she looked at a bewildered Jonathan then opened her arm, he came to her with tears rolled down his cheeks and he exchanged kisses.

After Frederick and Jonathan let go of both of us, I went into Maria's arms. I embraced her as she did me, then I said, "Never again will I let you go for this long without me and the rest of us." Jonathan and Frederick just looked at each other, not knowing just how to greet each other. Finally, Frederick made the first move and went up to Jonathan; they both hugged and kissed each other.

"Jonathan, Frederick, it's eight-thirty, time to take clothes off and put them away," Maria said.

Both boys went into the bedroom. Frederick was the first one out he sat next to his mother then I asked, "Where is your brother?"

"Bedroom."

"Jonathan."

From the bedroom came, "Yes, daddy."

"Come on out here."

He peeked out the door, and I knew what the problem was and said, "Jonathan you look no different than Frederick and Maria is your mother now you need to get used to us, come on out here." He came out nervously and sat down next to his mother. Frederick got on my lap after a bit of time, he kissed me and cuddled up to me. Maria put her arm around Jonathan, he shut his eyes and leaned into her. Maria kissed him and stroked his hair.

"Daddy, do you see that Jonathan look like me," Frederick said, as Jonathan then opened his eyes and looked at Frederick.

"Yes, he looks like he was always your brother, doesn't he?" Frederick nodded yes, and I said, "I think he loves you too."

"I love him too."

I looked over at Jonathan, and I saw a tear seep from his eye. Then I said to Frederick, "Before you and Jonathan go to bed, you both need to pick up your toys." He nodded, then Jonathan and Frederick gave both Maria and me a kiss and then picked up their toys and went into their room. Maria and I tucked them into bed, gave them both a kiss and went into the living room to do a little kissing ourselves. Just before we went to bed, we check the boys who were sleeping in the same bed. Hours after we went to bed, I got woken when Frederick crawled between Maria and me, and then ten minutes later, Jonathan crawled in both snuggling up to us.

21

THE HONEYMOON

Monday, I had a meeting with the staff. I explained to them that immediately, I wanted to start the physical training of the men. We also talked about the I.G. inspection. I wanted everything as perfect as possible so that I would inspect everything that included barracks, mess hall, and site. The I.G. inspection would be when I got back next Tuesday. The last thing I discussed was what was going to happen when we get attacked. I told them where everyone is supposed to be and how the combat gear and weapons would get handed out. Frank showed up, and I filled him in on what was going on, especially with Jonathan, and he followed me around, keeping his distance. Tuesday, I went to the battalion meeting. The meeting was like the other meetings I got mocked by the other company commanders as usual. After the meeting, Colonel Greenhill took me into his office and asked me about Jonathan, so I told him what had happened so far, and he never commented on it. However, he did inform me what General Abrams did and what happened because of it. "There are some officers who resigned from the Army, some who went to the stockade." "All responsible got busted in rank and fined," said the Colonel. "What does the boy think of the Army?"

"Jonathan wants no part of it; he is a very timid little boy."

Colonel Greenhill then said, "What do you think of me, James?"

Without hesitation, I said, "I think you are a good officer, smart but overburden by the demand of this command."

"Are you saying this because you want to be polite, and I outrank you?"

"Colonel, you know me, I say what I mean and do as I say."

"Would you like to know what I think about you?"

"I would guess you think I was a bit of a loose cannon that lets his imagination run wild regarding my premonitions." "But you have seen what I have done and think for a person of my background I've worked miracles, so you think I deserve my rank and you can put up with me." "On a personal level, you like me on a military level; you just don't know." "Is that pretty much it, Sir?"

"I couldn't have said it better."

"Sir, I'm going to tell you something that I have already told General Abrams." "If war doesn't break out in three months or less, I will be leaving the Army."

"That would not be necessary, James."

"If I can't trust myself to be correct, someone might get hurt, and I need to come out of the game."

"Well, it would be your choice, but believe me when I say I would miss you."

When I got back to Bamberg, I called my aunt in Missouri. "Hello."

"Hello, Aunt Adeline, this is James."

"James, I'm glad you called a lot has happened."

"I have the children at my house."

"How are they?"

"They have adjusted just fine and seem to be happy." "The children were filthy and skinny, and I took them to the doctor the people around here have been giving me tons of clothing and toys."

"Use what money you need from my account."

"The state has given me a lot of money to take care of them."

"That's good."

"It didn't go well when the police raided the house; one policeman was killed two wounded." "They shot and killed two of the four men in that house, and I'm afraid the children's mother also got shot, but she will live." "Once she is out of the hospital, the sheriff said she would never get out of jail again."

"I'll let Jonathan know, any word about the grandparents."

"Not yet, but they are still looking." "You know James; I think it would be a good idea if Jonathan talks to his brother and sisters."

"I would agree, but there is a seven-hour time difference." "However, on Friday, we're leaving for our honeymoon, so I will call you and put Jonathan on the phone before we leave." "The call should come through around three o'clock your time."

"That sounds good, James." I finish talking to her and then hung up and told Frank what happened.

I got home about four-thirty and told Maria in German what happened; she told me how to handle it by minimizing the negative and stressing the positive. I sat down in my easy-chair and called for the boys who were in their room. "Yes, daddy," they both said.

I kissed both boys and said, "Frederick go sit on the couch with your mother." I lifted Jonathan and put him on my lap then said, "Jonathan, I have some good news and some not so good news."

"What is it, daddy?"

"Your brother and sisters are at our aunt and uncle's house and are doing fine." "They are clean, have some nice clothes, and are not hungry anymore; they are getting all the love our aunt and uncle can give them." "You will talk to them on Friday morning at around seven o'clock in the morning."

"That's good news, daddy."

"Well, yes, as I said, there is some not so good news also." "The police went to your house, one policeman was shot and killed, and two were wounded." "There were four men in the house with your mother." "Two of those men got killed, and your mother got shot." "She did not die, and they expect her to live. The police said that because of the dead policeman and the two wounded and all the other things your mother did, she would be in jail for a long time." Frederick knew enough English to understand what I said to Jonathan; he came over almost in tears, hugged Jonathan then kissed him.

"It's alright, Frederick." "I only have one mama now, and she is on the couch." "That other person deserves to get hurt and go to Jail."

I kiss Jonathan again, put him down, and said, "You two boys go play now until dinner." They ran back to their room, and I turned to Maria and said, "He loves both of you as much if not more than me."

"Yes, we love him; also, he will fit in very well."

"Have you started to teach him German yet?"

"Yes, and he teaches us English."

"Very good."

Wednesday, I got the trip arrangements that General Abrams said he would send with a pleasant note. That day Captain Lawson from the JAG office showed up. "I have some papers for you to sign, Sir."

"Alright, how are things going?"

"Good, smoother than I thought they would." "These papers give you full custody of Jonathan." "I talked to your attorney back in Missouri, and he had some news about Jonathan's mother and siblings."

"I already know about his siblings and mother; I talked to my aunt, but what about the grandparents?"

"We haven't found them yet, but we do know their age, which is in their late sixties or early seventies." "I will tell you the state of Arkansas or any other state won't let someone that age take care of four children unless they are rich and can get some support."

"So, what will happen to the three siblings?"

"It's a good question, worst case scenario they will remain in foster care until adopted."

"That means they would be separated?"

"Yes."

"I won't allow that to happen." "What is the best-case scenario?"

"The Grandparents will convince a judge that they can care for the children with no ill effect on them."

"I'll want to talk to the grandparents if they wish to raise the children, I think I have a plan that might work that I don't want to talk about until I talk to them."

"Either way, it looks like Jonathan is your son."

Thursday, I made sure everything was going the way I wanted it to go. Jonathan was very close to Maria as if she was always his mother. He loved his brother I never heard any harsh words, to tell the truth, it was quite the opposite. Friday Maria and I got up at six o'clock in the morning showered and ate something light. I had planned to drive to Vienna, which was about six hundred miles away. The boys were asleep in our bed, and just before seven o'clock, Maria woke up Jonathan and I called my aunt. "Hello, Aunt Adeline."

"Hello, James."

"I have Jonathan with me, do you have the kids nearby?"

"Yes, they are all excited."

"Well, I'll put Jonathan on."

"Hello," Jonathan sat in a chair with tears of happiness streaming down his cheeks as he talked to his siblings. As he was talking to his sibling, Frederick came out of the bedroom, sat next to Jonathan, and Jonathan put his arm around him, snuggling up to him as he spoke.

Jonathan had finished his phone call, and I said, "Is everything the way you wanted it, sweetheart?"

"Yes, daddy, my brother and sisters are happy now."

Frederick came over to me, wanting me to pick him up, which I did, and he said, "Daddy, why do you call Jonathan sweetheart?"

"Because that is what he is, and you are my pumpkin." I kissed him and put him down, and Maria took them both to bath them.

We were on the road by a little after eight heading south towards Vienna; we stopped once in a city by the name of Passau, which was about halfway for food and gas. I pointed out to the boys the river that ran through this city is called the Danube, which also runs through Vienna. Frederick looked carefully at the river and said, confused, "Daddy, the river is not blue."

"Why would it be blue?" asked Jonathan.

"There is a song called the Blue Danube; I'm sure you have heard it; it goes like this." I started to sing the song in German, which surprised Maria.

"I have heard that song before," said Jonathan.

"Daddy, why is it not blue?" Frederick demanded to know.

"Well, because all of the blue in the water ran out into the blue Mediterranean."

"Oh, we studied about the Mediterranean in school," said Frederick seriously. Maria smiled and shook her head as we got closer to the Austrian border.

We reached Vienna by late afternoon, and I found the hotel, which was beautiful. "I have reservations for the York family."

"Oh yes, Mr. York, we have been expecting you; you and your family are our VIPs," said the clerk as he called for someone.

Out came an older man, and he said, "I am Heinrich Schmidt, the manager of this hotel."

"It is an honor to meet you, Sir," I said in German.

"Oh, you indeed speak German very good," he said as he shook my hand.

"Thank you, but I don't think it's that good."

"I will get someone to carry your bags to your suite, Sir, and tell you what we have planned for you; please follow me." He took us to a fantastic suite with a living room that overlooked the city.

"All expenses have been paid for at the hotel." "You will have use of the limousine and driver who will give you a tour of the city and the events that you got scheduled to go to."

"Is there dining nearby," I asked.

"The hotel has a fine restaurant that you can dine in your room or the restaurant, your driver will take you any place you wish, or you could walk just down the street where there are several places."

"Thank you."

I was going to tip the man who brought up the baggage when the manager said, "We do not tip here, Sir."

"Alright." We settled in while the boys were excited, looking at their room and out the window. "I wonder what he met when he said the driver would take us to the scheduled events."

"I would not know," Maria said with a sheepish smile.

"I think you know more than what you are telling me," I replied with a smile. "I'm hungry."

"So am I, and I think the boys are also."

We had a nice dinner at the hotel we were sitting in our room, and the boys were playing on the floor with some toys we brought when we got a knock at the door.

"Sir, I just want to inform you we are to be at Vienna Mozart Orchestra in about an hour," said a man from the hotel staff.

"Alright, we will be ready." I've heard Orchestras before, but the Mozart Orchestra kept Maria and me awestruck. What surprised me the boys were entranced. It all ended too soon, and we were back in our room, the boys falling asleep, so we put them to bed. They were out in minutes, thirty minutes after some lovemaking Maria and I were sound asleep.

The next morning, we ate breakfast in our room, and then we got informed we would be going on a tour of Vienna. The boys saw a puppet show, which delighted Frederick and more Jonathan because he had never seen one. We did a little shopping and going to museums. Near noon, we went to a small restaurant for lunch. I notice that the driver, who was also our tour guide, never ate with us. He maintained his distance whenever possible, several times we invited him to dine with us, but he didn't. The restaurant had a piano that wasn't getting used, and Frederick said, "Daddy, you see piano?"

"Yes."

"Play me song." I had told him and Maria that I could play some time back. I was about to say no, it wouldn't be proper when Maria and Jonathan begged me to also.

"Alright, Frederick, if you can get permission." Frederick got up with a smile on his face and asked the waiter who asked the manager.

The manager came over to me and said, "Of course, it would be alright to play the piano; this is Vienna."

"Well, okay, what do you wish me to play?"

"You choose but something special for Vienna," said Maria. I started playing Edelweiss, singing softly but loud enough for Maria and the boys to hear. I sang it in both English and German for everyone's sake.

When I finished my family, the restaurant staff and the rest of the customers applauded my efforts. Frederick said in German, "One more daddy."

"Alright, pumpkin, just one."

"Daddy play Heidenröslein."

"Okay, Frederick."

"Jonathan, you might not know this song," then I played and sang a bit louder than before. As I played suddenly to my surprise, Frederick and Jonathan started singing the song, and they sounded like angles. They were as good as any boy in the Vienna Boys Choir. I stopped singing and kept playing, letting the boys do the singing.

When the boys and I finished, we got another round of applause, and as we went to sit down, a man came up to us and said, "That was very good, and I should know my business is in music."

"Thank you."

"May I join you?"

"I guess it will be alright," I said with a smile.

"Let me introduce myself; I'm Franz Schliemann; I'll be going with you to your next destination."

"Oh, wonderful, our driver is not a joiner."

"I'm James York; this is my wife, Maria, and my two boys, Jonathan and Frederick.

"Your two boys sing very well."

"Yes, they did, as well as any boy in the Vienna Boys Choir."

Mr. Schliemann smiled and said, "Perhaps you're right; you have heard of the choir then."

"Yes, they are the world's best I wanted to be in the choir when I was young."

"Well, you certainly play beautiful, and if your voice was as good if not better when you were a child, you could have been."

"Unfortunately, I am an American I would have never been allowed even to audition."

"That is not true, Mr. York, many boys in the choir, are not from Austria."

"Is that right, perhaps if I had known my life would have been different." "Well, I hope to see them sing maybe at the church Sunday."

We finished eating and piled into the limousine. "Where are we going?" I asked Mr. Schliemann.

"To the Palais Augarten."

"I wonder where I have heard of that place before." We came to a stop at an enormously big white building that was very beautiful. All five of us got out, but the driver stayed in the car. We went into the building and entered a lovely ornate reception area with a grand staircase and several hallways and doors all around.

"Surprise honey," Maria said as the boys giggled.

"Surprise," I said, confused.

With a smile, Mr. Schliemann guided us through some doors to another large ballroom where I now knew why I'd heard of the Palais Augarten what and the surprise it was. In front of me was the Vienna Boys Choir singing a welcoming song. I walked up to them and asked, "May I talk to them."

"Yes, of course.

"It is an honor to be before you, as a young boy in America, I wanted to be a Vienna, Choir Boy." "Do any of you truly know how lucky you are, there are thousands, maybe millions of boys who would like to be with you right now."

One boy stepped forward and said, "I am Hanns Schnee." "I am glad you speak German my English is not the best, but I wish to tell you ever, boy here knows how special it is to be a Vienna Choir Boy." "We now wish to sing to you any song you wish."

"There are many songs I could think of, why don't you just pick one I will be happy with anything you boys sing."

Frederick and Jonathan were standing next to the piano, where Mr. Schliemann was about to play. He started with a prelude of the Blue Danube, and Frederick said to Jonathan, "The Blue Danube."

Mr. Schliemann stopped and said, "Do you know this song, boys?"

"We know the song, but not the words, but daddy does," said Jonathan.

Mr. Schliemann started again, and the choir sang it beautifully. When they finished, I said, "That was wonderful."

"Boys, we have a change of plans, Jonathan, Frederick come with me," Mr. Schliemann said to the choir and my boys. He placed Frederick and Jonathan amongst the choir boys. Then he said, "Mr. York, would you sit at the piano and play Heidenröslein."

"Sure, do you want a prelude," I said with a smile."

"Yes."

I played, and everyone sang the song, including Frederick and Jonathan, who were having a ball. Jonathan and Frederick blended in perfectly with the choir, which brought happiness to Maria's and my heart. "Mr. York, we at the choir have a present for you to help you never forget us." He nodded to one of the boys in the choir, and he went to a chair where there was a box, and the young boy handed it to me.

"Thank you," I said. The young boy smiled, and I opened the box with Maria and the boys looking. I couldn't believe my eyes; it was the dark blue sailor shirt, pants, and hat that the choir boys wore.

Then Mr. Schliemann nodded at another choir boy. He brought him another box, opened it up, and pulled out a document in a picture frame. He read it, and it said, "That James York is an honorary Vienna Choir Boy." I was speechless as Maria grabbed my hand and smiled.

"I am truly grateful all of this will be framed and hung on my wall wherever my family and I are."

"We wish to give you now a tour of the palace, and then we will serve some refreshments after I wish to speak to you and your family privately," said Mr. Schliemann.

"That would be wonderful; I would like to see everything."

"Hanns Schnee will guide you, and I will meet with you later."

As we toured the palace, I asked Hanns questions about what goes on with the choir, which most people don't know. It was very insightful, and some of it surprised me. He told me, "When many of us boys go home for a visit, other boys who were friends tease us, call us names, and harass us because we are choir boys."

"Those boys do that because they are jealous when you are old enough you will realize you were part of the most famous choir in the world few could say that, and few will ever have the opportunity you have." "Just look where you live how much better is your life here."

"Yes, Sir, that is what my parents say also."

Our tour ended in the dining room with Mr. Schliemann and some of the other staff members. He had some sweet pastries milk for the boys, coffee, and tea for the adults. My boys stayed around the other choirboys, Jonathan doing his best to talk to them.

"I know no normal tourist would get the reception my family and I got who arranged all of this?" I asked to no one in particular.

Mr. Schliemann answered, "You must be an important man." "The President of the United States and Austria called here and made the arrangements and told us all about you."

"You know I am a soldier then."

"Yes." Afterward, we all met in Mr. Schliemann's office. "Of course, James, you are too old to be in the choir even though I feel if you were a child, you would likely have gotten accepted; I say this with all honesty."

"Thank you what you said, it means a lot to me."

"Even though you cannot be in the choir, your children can do you notice that they sang and blended in perfectly."

"Yes." I looked at Maria, Jonathan, and Frederick, and I explained in German what Mr. Schliemann said. "What do you boys want?"

"Hanns Schnee's heart is devoted to singing in this choir daddy like you if you could, but even though I like to sing, my heart is not devoted to it, nor do I think it will," said Jonathan.

"I don't understand what Jonathan said, but I sing just for my family. I would not be happy here; besides, I want to be like daddy a soldier, and I would not be happy without Jonathan," said Frederic.

I looked at Mr. Schliemann, and he said, "Well, if the boys change their minds, give me a call."

"We thank you for your offer, and if it were me like Jonathan said, I would be leaping for joy." We headed back to the hotel; I should have pushed the boys a little more. By the time we got back, I felt Jonathan was right; if your heart not in it, there was no point, I couldn't live my dream through them.

The next day after breakfast and church Maria and I did some more shopping while the boys took-in another puppet show. At two, we were all going to see the famous Lipizzaner Stallions. Since we had a late breakfast, we ate lunch at about one, and then we went to see the Lipizzaner Stallions. I tried to explain to the boys that it wasn't going to be an ordinary horse show. I don't know if they understood, but from the start to the end, the boys were excited at the spectacle as were Maria and me. Both boys would continuously say excitedly, "Did you see that daddy, did you see that mama."

In the end, Jonathan said, "The horse show was not like I thought it would be; it was more like a circus."

"Have you ever seen a circus, Jonathan?"

"I've never been to a circus but saw pictures before."

"I too, daddy," said Frederick.

I looked at Maria, and she said, "I've never seen one, either."

"Well, the first chance I get, I must do something about that."

Monday, we had an excellent breakfast and lounged around a little. I wasn't in a hurry to leave, but as time went on, Maria and I started to pack the car little by little. I had sent a letter to General Arnold, Abram, and the White House thanking them for an incredible honeymoon. We all left after lunch and headed home. Maria and I talked as the boys slept in the backseat of the car. We stopped twice, once for a snack, and once for dinner before we reach home late Monday night. I unloaded the car as Maria bathed the boys and put them to bed, and it wasn't long before we went to bed.

I was already at my office when Top came in, "Well, how was the honeymoon?"

"Fabulous."

"The kids didn't give you any problems?" Captain Dizon asked as he came in.

"No, they were just fine." "It wouldn't have been as good without the boys." "We brought some things back for you, Viennese pottery for both your wives and a pair of short leg lederhosen for both of you," I said with a smile.

"Great Sir, I'll wear it to formation tomorrow," said Top with a smile.

"You do that, and we all will go to the stockade," said the Captain.

"No need to worry, Marc, that lederhosen may look like something else," I said.

"Well, I must tell you, Sir; I am relieved," Marc said with a grin.

"We will do the inspection ten minutes after formation?"

"How is the exercise program working?"

"Except for a few individuals liking K.P. rather than getting with the program, good Sir."

"We did have one fight over the machines." "Someone wasn't taking his turn in order." "I took care of it, it gave me another person for K.P.," said Top.

"Officers taking advantage of the equipment?"

"Yes, Sir," said the Captain.

"What about the NCOs?"

"They are taking part I made sure of that," said Top.

The inspection went well except for a few bunks, and the latrine needed to be a little cleaner. At the site, everything looked good. I announced what I wanted to get corrected at the formation. I also let them know Friday I would inspect again. The week had passed, everything seemed to be going smoothly on Monday morning I did a quick inspection of the barracks, mess hall, and then the site. The I.G. inspectors should be at the missile site by nine, and at nine-fifteen, the inspectors rolled onto the site, and I greeted them. Colonel Greenhill was with them, and he said, "Major, are you ready for the inspection?"

"Yes, Sir."

As we walked to the parts room, the Colonel asked, "How was your honeymoon?"

"Fantastic Sir, the whole family had the time of their lives."

"That's good."

The inspectors checked the parts room and had no negative comments. Sergeant Booker in the radio room answered their question. He showed them his flawless paperwork; they were impressed. We went over to my office and the site mess hall then to the armory. "I notice your weapons are not in the trailer," said an inspector who was a Captain.

"That's right; they are easier and quicker to access and maintain."

"How do you move them if you go out into the field."

"Then we move them to the trailer by the time everything else got packed up the weapons are ready to go. But I will be honest with you; I would prefer the men to carry the weapons with them."

"Storing them in here is not regulation."

"Captain, you know how small that trailer is if we got attacked right now and the weapons were in that trailer it would take forever to get them to the men."

"I understand your reasons; I'll tell you what I'll note that they weren't in the trailer and state why."

"That's alright with me; General Abrams saw this and approved it."

"He did, did he," said a Major.

"He's telling you the truth," said Colonel Greenhill.

We went to the command center next; they asked some questions, and I said, "Do you wish them to run a simulation?"

"Yes." I nodded, and the men proceeded. The simulation was three Soviet MiG's their best and fastest planes just crossed the border to attack us. After the calculations, three missiles got sent up, and three aircraft got shot down.

"One of the inspectors, a Colonel, said, "How did you do that those planes were faster than your missiles?"

"Your right Colonel and that is the problem with the Hawk missile, so I found some men who knew calculus, and they were able to calculate how far you had to lead the jet sort of like skeet shooting."

"Interesting and unique," said the Colonel.

They asked about the berms around the missiles and high-power radar system, and I explain it to them. They checked the rest of the things on the site, and we left for the barracks.

We met with Top, who stayed at the barracks and went through the rooms. They only looked at lockers that were open and then checked the latrine, my office, dayroom, and supply. Lastly, they went down to the mess hall I sat at one of the tables with Colonel Greenhill and Top. "Top, are you having a hard time finding K.P.s?" I asked.

"Yes Sir, the rotation is short, not enough men in the lower ranks."

"How do you feel about paid K.P.s?"

"It would sure solve this big problem I have, Sir."

"How do you feel about it, Colonel?"

"I have mix feelings about it; on the one hand, I know how much the men hate pulling this duty." "I know they are more useful in doing their jobs, but on the other hand, there is the cost, and if you do it, then the other four units will want to do it."

"If I found the money, would it be alright with you?"

"Yes, I wouldn't have an objection, but good luck trying to find the money I don't think even General Abrams could help you."

"Top I want a mural painted above the serving line and a smaller one above the barracks' entrance." "We will see how many will volunteer and then have a contest and pick the best."

"Yes, Sir."

By two, everything ended, and I went up to Colonel Greenhill and asked, "How do you think we did?"

"I didn't see any negative marks I think you did well." "This coming Friday, we will have a staff meeting to discuss the whole battalion's results."

"Yes, Sir."

The next day I called General Abrams, "James, I thought I would hear from you sooner; how are things going."

"I have been busy since I got back from my honeymoon with the I.G. inspection, but everything has been going well."

"And how was your honeymoon?"

"It was just fabulous the whole family, including myself, had a ball thank you so much for setting this up for us."

"Well, to tell you the truth, it wasn't just me General Arnold and the President had a hand in it."

"Yes, I know I sent them a thank you letter also."

"Well, I know you didn't call me to talk about your honeymoon, what do you need?"

"Do you think the Army could spare another twelve hundred dollars a month?"

"For what I must justify it."

"Paid KPs I feel one of the big reasons why so many men leave the army is K.P. it is one of the worse jobs a soldier can do, and I don't know if anyone likes doing it."

"Nice justification and you're most likely right, what do I get for the twelve hundred dollars."

"Three German KPs, seven days a week, ten hours a day."

"What about your men putting money in the pot for them."

"I'm going to ask them about that, Sir, regardless of what you say, but you know they don't make much."

"Yes, I know they don't pay them much money, and they deserve a raise. Give me a week, and I will see what I can do."

"That would be just fine, Sir."

At noon formation, we went through our routine, and then I talked to the men. "I need some volunteers to paint two murals." "I know some of you are a good artist doing it will get you a case of beer and two pizzas." "Any questions?"

"Where are these paintings going to be, and what is the subject matter," asked a corporal.

"One above the severing line in the mess hall and a smaller one above the entrance of the barracks." "Any subject matter you can come up with if it reflects Charlie, and it is appropriate."

"Can we sign it?"

"Yes." "Any more questions?" No one said anything, then I said, "Do we have any volunteers?" Five men raised their hands, and Top took their names. I said, "Alright, this is how it is going to work. When you go in tonight, pick up some paper and a pencil from my office, and I want you five to draw the murals on this paper and give it to Top by Friday." "Top, Captain Dizon, and I will pick the best one, then that person can pick two others to help him." "Are there any questions?" No one answered, and I went on to the next subject, "I want to know how many of you people like doing K.P. that includes NCOs and Officers also." No one raised their hand, and then I said, "We all know how much of a miserable job it is, I was thinking about getting paid K.P.s how many of you would be for that."

"Everyone raised their hand, but a lieutenant said, "How much is this going to cost, Sir?"

"Worse case about five dollars a month from each of you, best case it won't cost you anything." "I talked to General Abrams, and he said he would try to do something he is going to let me know in a week." "Is there anyone who has a problem with this plan?" Again, no one raised their hand, and I said, "Very well, I will keep you posted as to what is happening." The rest of the week went fine, and on Friday, I dressed in my dress greens and left the house. Maria and Frederick were teaching Jonathan German, and they were learning better English by teaching him. After formation, I headed for the battalion meeting. In the conference room, the other men talked about the I.G. inspection and wondered who did the best.

Captain McMullen asked, "Well, Major, how well did Charlie do, or did they bring down the battalion again?"

I looked at him and smiled and said, "Charlie held its own."

"Impossible," the Captain scoffed.

Thank goodness, Colonel Greenhill finally came in, followed by his aid with a report for each of us. Each I.G. report told us the strengths and weaknesses of our unit and the battalion in general. Colonels Greenhill's report showed the whole battalion. "I'll give you a few minutes to skim through the report before I comment."

Someone knocked at the door then came in; it was the same aid who brought in the reports. "Sir, your wife is on the phone."

"I have to take this call; I will be right back." I looked at my report and noticed that there were no negative remarks. They did comment on my shotgun approach at knocking down a Soviet Jet, but even though they thought it a little unorthodox, it seemed to work well. They also mention the armory and again said it wasn't regulation but thought it was a good idea. If General Abrams approved it, then it was alright with them. I glanced at the strengths, it was flowing with comments of praise, and each department got the highest rating possible.

"Sorry about the interruption gentleman I assume you have looked at your reports." He started going over each report according to how we were sitting starting at Headquarters, then Alpha, Delta, Headquarters, Bravo, then Charlie. Before he was about to give Charlie's rating, I noticed that Alpha got the best score so far. Bravo and Headquarters did about the same, and Delta was just under them. "Charlie, I am pleased to say didn't have any negative marks, they have a perfect score." "The compliments were too numerous to count, but one of them I will mention. At their command center, they were the only unit that could run a simulation and knock down a Soviet plane with a hundred percent accuracy."

It did my heart good to see the other commanders speechless with their mouth hanging open. Then Captain McMullen said, "Wait a minute how could he shoot down a Soviet Jet with a Hawk."

"I'll tell you how, Captain, if it is alright with you, Major?" I nodded yes, and he continued, "He and his men have developed a program that the men can calculate the speed and predicted the path of the aircraft and the speed of the Hawk." "He can lead the jet and hit the target, is that right, James?"

"Yes, Sir."

"Because of this, I am sending a team from Charlie to Crete." I could hear all the commanders moaning at this. The Colonel said, "However, I am sending one man of your choice from Alpha, Bravo, and Delta to learn what they do." "Good Job James."

"Thank you, Sir."

I drove back to Bamberg and went directly to the site where I knew Captain Dizon and Top would be. We met in the site mess hall, and they could see by the expression on my face that I had good news. I gave them the report, and they skimmed through it. "How did we do compare to the other units?"

"We have a perfect score; the others didn't even come close."

"A perfect score I've never been in a unit that got that," said Top.

"That's not all Colonel Greenhill is sending Charlie to Crete, so we need to get a team organized. I'll leave that up to you, Marc and Mr. Shafer, to pick the best team. Alpha, Bravo, and Delta units are going to send one man each to see how we can shoot down a Soviet jet."

22

WAR

The days went by, and the team that got picked to go to Crete. They were in Crete for four days, and they were due back in one or two days.

General Abrams found the money for the paid KPs, and I was about to have a meeting with Top and Sergeant Hill about hiring some German KPs. "More than likely, the people who will want this job will be older German women," I said.

"My problem, Sir is the language barrier, I don't speak German," said Sergeant Hill concerned."

"Do any of your men speak German?" I asked the other cooks.

"Just a few words, Sir," one of the cooks said.

I thought for a few seconds and said, "I will have a list made up of key fraises." "I will also have a list of people to call who can speak German." "Hopefully, we will hire someone who can speak English well enough to translate for you." "At the interview, Top or I will be your interpreter." "All this alright with you, Top?"

"Yes, Sir."

"Sergeant, what happens to the left-over food the men don't eat?"

"It depends, some of it gets kept, and some will get thrown out."

"We will divide it out amongst the KPs for them to carry home. "I also want you to feed them; three meals won't cause a shortage."

"No, Sir, that's will be fine."

"On another subject Top, Captain Dizon and I have picked the picture of the mural I wish your opinion."

I showed him the picture, and he said, "This is fine, Sir."

"Here is the other two we considered."

He looked at them and said, "No, I prefer the first one, Sir."

"They will start painting tomorrow."

"Yes, Sir."

"I'll go downtown with Frank and get the ball rolling on the KPs; we will have the interviews Thursday afternoon."

"That's fine, Sir."

"Ok, let's go, Frank." "Top informed the painters that they would start tomorrow, and the art supplies are in supply."

"Yes, Sir."

We went to a couple of employment offices and ran an ad for KPs. They told me that I should have no problem finding people to interview. When Thursday came around, about twenty-five people showed up for the interview, and Sergeant Hill started talking as Top or I translated. The first thing Sergeant Hill said was, "This work you will be doing is not easy. It requires you to be here ten hours a day Monday through Friday and eight hours Saturday and Sunday if any of you can't do these hours you may leave." About twelve left after he said that, and he went on and explained what was to get done, we lost another three after that. He told how much they would get paid, and they could get paid in marks per hour or dollars as well as the food they could eat and take home. We lost another one who was mumbling not enough for what you must do. That left us nine to interview Sergeant Hill then asked if there were any questions. One woman raised her hand and said, "Do we get any days off for things like being sick, holidays, and personal business?"

I looked at Top and Sergeant Hill and said, "What do you think?"

"It is a stressful job." "I know I would like a day off," said Sergeant Hill.

"I agree, Sir," said Top.

"Well, I think it should be a set time," I said.

"This is an excellent question, and to tell you the truth, we never thought about this, so we will do this." "You will have ten sick days a year anymore after that you will not get paid if you take too many days and can't prove you are sick then you will be let go." "You will be allowed three personal days off, and you will be off Christmas, New Year's, Easter, and one other of your choice." "Any more questions?"

There weren't any more questions, so I turned it over to Top and Sergeant Hill to do the interviewing and left. I went to the barracks. After doing the paperwork for about an hour, in came the men who went to Crete. I called Mr. Shafer into my office and asked, "Well, how did it go."

"Excellent, Sir."

"How accurate were you?"

"One hundred percent, that's why we got asked to stay longer." "The military personnel in Crete wanted us to shoot down an object that would be going as fast as the Soviets fastest jet, and we did."

"Fantastic, how did the men from the other units act?"

"They were cocky at first, but when they saw what we did, they changed their tune."

"So, what did the people in Crete think of our method of knocking down planes?"

"Well, they were impressed but thought it would be too hard to learn, which it would, but they also feel there is a lot of luck involved in shooting down a jet, so they think it isn't worth it."

"They are fools; you did just fine."

The following week the new KPs were doing fine, and the men were happy they didn't have to do KP. I had gotten a visit from the JAG officer Captain Elizabeth Lawson. She told me they found Jonathan's grandparents, and she said that there was no worry the grandparents wouldn't fight the adoption. I intend to call them today.

"Hello, is this Mrs. Kruger."

"Yes, I'm Mrs. Kruger."

"I'm Major James York."

"Oh, let me get my husband."

"Hello, I'm Joe Kruger, what did you say your name is?"

"James York, Sir."

"How is Jonathan?"

"He is happy, healthy, and a loved little boy."

"Oh, that's great that woman my son married was pure trash; we have always had a feeling that she killed him." "You know we are not contesting you adopting Jonathan."

"I know this; I also know you are taking in his siblings." "What I wish to do is share joint custody with you; I don't want Jonathan to lose his grandparents."

"Let me talk to my wife, give me a few minutes." He had been away from the phone for about five minutes when he came on; he asked, "Mr. York, may I ask why you didn't try to adopt his brother and sisters?"

"Sir I am a Major in the Army we have a home, but it is tiny, and I have another son beside Jonathan." "If I get moved, I don't know what kind of housing I will get. However, if it meant that Jonathan's siblings have to be separated, I would have quit the Army and adopted them all."

"I understand you are very wealthy, why do you stay in the Army."

"It is true; I am wealthy." "I have a large ranch in Missouri, but I have a desire and a duty to serve my country, so I stay in at least for now."

There was a hesitation, then he said, "I want to work you a deal that will benefit Jonathan and his siblings." "I wish you to adopt all the children, and we will share custody the three children will stay with us; we will have parental custody of the three and you of Jonathan." "The reason we wish this is we are old, and there will come a time when we are too old to take care of the children, and when that time comes, they should all be together."

"Well, I am all for it, but I think you should talk to the children to see if they want this." "I need to talk to my family." "I will call you again Saturday around four or five o'clock in the afternoon your time, and you can talk to Jonathan also."

"That would be wonderful; we'll be waiting for your call."

When I got home that night, I went for a walk with Maria leaving the boys to play in front of the TV. "This is something new we have never gone for a walk before," said Maria.

"I have something to talk to you about."

"What is that?"

"I talked to Jonathan's grandparents; we can adopt Jonathan."

"That is wonderful, but I see there is more you want to tell me."

"Not tell, ask, they wish us to adopt Jonathan's brother and sisters."

Maria was thinking, and I looked at her. In English, she said, "I think where everyone will sleep, girls won't be a problem, and I think we can squeeze one more in with Jonathan and Frederick."

"No, you don't understand the three children won't be staying with us except for a visit; they will stay with the grandparents." "If the grandparents can't take care of them anymore, they will come to us permanently."

"We will be like Godparents?" Maria asked.

"No, we will be their father and mother since we don't have enough room; they will stay in America with their grandparents; it will be easier for the children."

"Then, we should adopt them."

"I should also tell you I must pay child support."

"We have a lot of money, don't we?"

"Yes, more than enough?"

"Then, we adopt them."

"We have to talk to Jonathan and Frederick about this first."

"Yes, you are right."

We went back to the house, turned off the TV I had Frederick on my lap and Maria had Jonathan. "We need to talk and discuss some things Jonathan I talked to your grandparents today, and they said we could adopt you." Frederick got excited as did Jonathan, and I said, "But there is something else we need to talk about."

"What is it, daddy?" Jonathan asked.

"Your grandparents want us to adopt your brother and sisters." There are two reasons, one I feel they should have a mother and father also and two if your grandparents get too old or just can't take care of them anymore, then they will stay with us."

"Do you and mama want to adopt them?"

"Yes, sweetheart, if it is alright with you and Frederick."

"Yes, it is alright with me; I can still be a family with them."

"What about you, pumpkin?"

"Frederick, it will mean you will have another brother and two sisters," Maria said.

"Can I still sleep and play with Jonathan?"

"Yes, pumpkin, you can, with anyone you wish, in our family."

"Then, I adopt them."

I smiled at what Frederick said, then I said, "Your grandparents are going to talk to your brother and sisters about it, Saturday we will call, and you can talk to them."

Saturday, I called, "Hello Mr. Kruger, this is James."

"We've been waiting for your call," said Mr. Kruger.

"The boys just got up, how do Jonathan's bother, and sisters feel about the adoption."

"Oh, they are thrilled they want to talk to you."

"Go ahead and put them on."

"Hello, are you my daddy?"

"Yes, princes, what's your name."

"Sarah."

"Well, Sarah, you know you have a new brother; his name is Frederick and a new mama, whose name is Maria."

"Is my new mama like my old mama?"

"No, you will love her." I talked to Jonathan's other sister Elizabeth and his brother William. Then Mrs. Kruger got on the phone, and I said, "I'll put Jonathan on the phone."

He started talking to her all excited, and Frederick, who was sitting next to him, asked Jonathan to give him the phone, which he did. "I Frederick Jonathan brother, you going be my grandma too?"

"Yes, Frederick."

"Good, I no have a grandma or grandpa except for my daddy's." He gave the phone back to Jonathan, and Jonathan talked to both of his grandparents and siblings.

"When he finished, he gave me the phone back, and I said, "I will get in touch with my lawyers to get everything set up."

"That would be great; we will keep in touch with your attorney in Missouri also."

The following week I got a hold of my attorney in Poplar Bluff and the military lawyer who were aware of everything. By Friday, we had a court date in Würzburg on the American Army post. The ceremony lasted only about fifteen minutes; then, it was over, and Jonathan and William, Sarah, and Elizabeth were my children. We got in our car the plan was to have a pleasant day in Würzburg, see Maria's aunt, then go home. We drove off looking for a park near the river, and as we traveled, Frederick said, "Mama Jonathan is crying."

Maria looked then said in German, "What's the matter, Jonathan?"

Jonathan didn't say anything but only cried more. Maria looked at me, concern, and I said in German, "I think I know what the problem is." "Everything that happened to Jonathan happened so fast that he became overcome with emotion."

I found a park and found a place to pull over there was a bench, and Maria got out and grabbed Jonathan and held him and rocked as she spoke to him softly as he cried. I took Frederick, who was confused and sat down on the bench with him. "Daddy, I not understand why he sad he should be happy?"

"Jonathan has been through a lot of pain in his life now he knows he is in a loving family, and the relief of not having that pain anymore has been a lot for him to handle."

I don't know how much he understood, but he said, "Will he be happy again?"

"Yes, he will, but you must show him a lot of love."

Frederick went over to him, gave him a hug and a kiss then said, "I love you, Jonathan."

"I love you too, Frederick," Jonathan said, trying to recover from his emotional breakdown. After a little while, we walked through the park and then went to see Maria's aunt. Her name is Brigitte Hershberger; she was a short old heavy-set woman with an infectious smile. Her health wasn't the best, but she was happy to see the whole family. She lived in a small little old house on the outskirts of Würzburg. She took an interest in Jonathan and couldn't get over how much he looked like Frederick. When he uses his best German, which was short sentences, she gave him a big hug for the effort. She gave the boys some sweets, which they gobbled down quickly. I said to Maria in English, "Why don't we bring her to live with us."

"I tried to get her to come, but she not want to leave her home or friends; she has many."

After spending some time with the aunt, we headed for a place to eat and then headed home. The weeks passed, I had planned for Jonathan to be schooled at home and had already made up my mind that both boys would start the American school next year since Frederick could speak English well. Both boys and Maria had gone down to the clinic to get checkups and shots, which the boys hated. I was working out more and more with the men who were starting to look good for the most part. I had noticed that there were fewer MiGs overflies I hadn't seen any for the last two weeks, nor did we track any. I asked at the C. O.'s battalion meeting if they had any flyovers, they said no but mocked me saying where is your war. As I got up on a Wednesday morning, I had a feeling of dread. I turned to Maria and said, "Keep the boys in the house today."

"Why?"

"I have a feeling please just do as I say, stay in the house."

"Alright, but you got me worried."

"I'm worried too, but I think everything will be alright." "Call Maryann and Hellen and tell them to stay at home too and call the other wives," I told Maria.

As I got closer to the barracks, the dread I felt got more intense. Top saw me, and right off, there was something wrong he came up to me and said with concern, "What's wrong, Sir."

"Get everyone out on the site regardless if they are off or sick. Get the armory open, and everyone is to be in combat gear also issue the men a weapon and ammo, get the people you need to help you." "Then call all the off-post personal and get them in here."

"Yes, Sir." After I said this, all hell broke out; people were scrambling all over the place. I went down to the mess hall and told them they should get ready to set up a field mess, but for today, we would be using C rations. I also told Chris to go with Top and give him a hand while I took as many as I could to the site. Forty-five minutes all the men were out at the site except for mess hall people who were on their way. "Team A into the command center, B team set up with machine guns in sector A." We had sandbagged pits all around the perimeter. The men who weren't in critical areas were in the sandbag pits.

"I was up at the command center and said, "You see anything yet."

"No, Sir."

I went in to look myself, and on the eastern side of the border, the screen was blank, but on the western side, there was plenty of activity. "Don't you think it is unusual for there to be nothing on the eastern side of the border?"

"Well, yes, Sir," said Mr. Shafer.

"Keep watching the border."

"Yes, Sir."

Captain Dizon came over to me, and I asked, "How are the men?"

"Frighten, you think we are going to get attacked."

"I don't think I know and very soon." "Get the LAWs out, put half in sector A and the other half up at the gate."

I went over to my office and called Colonel Henderson.

"Colonel Henderson here."

"Sir, this is James York, do you remember what I told you that was going to happen."

"You mean the war."

"Yes, you don't have much time; it's a matter of minutes but no more than two hours."

"Is there any sign of them yet?"

"No, but there is no aircraft flying on the other side of the border."

"Alright, James."

"Believe me, Sir, it is coming."

"I believe you, James."

I then called Maggie and let her know she didn't question at all. I went back outside, looked up into the cloudless blue sky then up to the command center. "Anything yet?"

"No, Sir."

"Keep watching." It was nine in the morning; I decided to check all the key areas and machine gun pits. I had installed a Siren that we used in case of an attack. It was a little after ten when the Siren went off, and I rushed off at a full run to the command center.

"What do you have?"

"The whole border lit up with aircraft flying in formation, and they are coming fast."

I had communications with radio Headquarters, Alfa, Bravo, and Delta units, informing them what was going on. I found out Grafenwöhr, where there was an American Army post, was hit, and I ordered my men to pick a target and open fire they were less than five miles from my position. We didn't get two missiles off when the planes came in eyesight. We had shot down ten jets before we and the post got hit. Even though we got attacked, our missiles, radars, and command center were intact, so we knocked down eight more jets with only seven missiles, and one rocket knocked down two planes. As the missiles got fired, I had the missile launcher pull out of here and hid in the thicket. It was the second launcher that I saw about a dozen Soviet attack helicopters blew one of them up. I ran down and grabbed a LAW as did Top, and we both shot two helicopters that were about to blow up our high-power radar. Top and I grabbed two more and fired at two more helicopters, but there were three, and before we could shoot down the third one, someone shot a LAW and knocked down the third one, and when I turned to look it was Washington. "Washington, you defend everything from this end Top, and I will go to the gate and defend it from there."

"Yes, Sir."

As Top and I ran across the site, I saw one high power radar damage and two men trying to fix it. There were men on the ground with the medic doing his best to help them. An attack helicopter came straight at Top and firing its machine guns Top knock a man who was petrified with fear to the side as I jump the other way. Then there was an explosion, and the copter went down in flames; Washington got another one. I could hear explosions that were coming from the Army post area, maybe the city too. We had five missiles; I didn't know why they didn't use them to knock down five more jets and get out of there. At least, I didn't know until the big slow Soviet bombers came into sight, and then our last five missiles went into action by that time Top, and I had gotten the other LAWs. Jets were coming down low strafing us Top notice they were coming in the same pattern each time, so he aimed a long distance in front of them and fired, clipped one in the tail. It went down, taking out part of the armory. "Nice shot," I said.

"I thought so." We knocked down two more helicopters before they backed off. The missiles were able to knock down five bombers.

My men captured the pilot in the jet that Top had knocked down. I lost two more missiles launchers before we got everything hidden in the thicket of trees. The action around us had slowed considerably. I checked on the wounded men; fortunately, no one got killed. There were five who were injured severely enough for medical attention. Others were also injured, including Top and me, who was grazed and didn't need any real attention. We could still see and hear explosions and mushroom clouds from bombs being dropped by this time NATO Jets arrived, better late than never, and the air battle started. The Soviet bloc planes were getting the worse of it from what I could see.

"Sergeant Walker get a vehicle and a driver to transport the wounded to the clinic."

"If it is there, Sir."

"If it isn't, bring them back and we will take care of them."

"Sergeant Booker is that radio working in communications."

"It was Major, but if it isn't, I'll make it work."

"Good take the men and equipment you need and radio headquarters and find out where they want us to go and answer what questions they might have."

"Yes, Sir."

"Top, have you seen Captain Dizon."

"I think he is with the prisoner."

"Michael, tell headquarter we have a prisoner and what are we to do with him."

"Sergeant Walker, did we lose any vehicles."

"Yes, Sir, two, but I have men working on them."

I walked over to where the prisoner and Captain Dizon were. "You find anything on him." He had a wallet and a letter I got told.

I looked at the letter, and it looked like Czechoslovakian I went up to him and said, "Do you understand English?"

He acted confused and said, "No English."

I then decided to use German and said as Top came over, "Do you understand German?"

"No German."

I know he was lying by the expression on his face. From what I knew of the Czechoslovakians who should have no problems understanding the German language. I decided to place my best-acting face on and said in German, "Top let me have your pistol I might as well shoot this poor bastard if he can't answer me?"

"Yes, Sir."

He handed me a forty-five pistol, and I said in German, "I have to shoot you since you can't understand me."

I cocked and lifted the pistol, and he said in German frighten, "I understand, I understand, don't shoot."

"Very well, you will talk to this man, or he will shoot you?" I said as I pointed to Top.

I let Top get any information out of him, figuring that he would know what to ask because of his long experience in the military. I decided to go over to the radio shack to see what progress Booker had done. As I went, it seemed most of the damaged varied, all that got left of the mess hall and office was part of a wall. I surveyed the site around me, and I thought it was amazing no one died.

"Sir Sergeant Booker wants you."

The radio and parts building had been shot up good with gaping holes all through it, and it was on fire as were most buildings. "I have headquarters on the radio, Sir," said Booker. "We'll try to keep the fire away for as long as we can, and this radio won't last that long."

"Headquarters, this is Major James York."

"James is that you?" asked Colonel Greenhill."

"Yes, Sir."

"What is your situation?"

"Five wounded bad enough to need medical help." "I have no deaths." "All my missiles got fired, I lost a few missiles launchers and high power, but my mechanics are working on them." "I don't know how many we can save." "All my buildings are destroyed." "We knocked down twenty-one jets, five bombers, and eight or ten attack helicopters." "We also caught a prisoner." "The American post got hammered before the NATO jets came; I don't know what their condition is."

"Can you gather your men and equipment, then send half to Alpha and the other half to Bravo." "You command one Captain Dizon can command the other, they have missiles there, Delta got wiped out." "I've sent someone there to see if anyone has survived, but I don't think so."

"Yes, Sir, what do you want me to do with the prisoner, Sir?"

"Bring him with you, when you get set up come to Headquarters."

"Yes, Sir." "Sir, Colonel Greenhill, can you hear me."

"Booker, the radio is dead."

"There is nothing I can do with it, Sir; I don't have the parts."

"Alright, let's get out of here." We went back to where Captain Dizon and Top were and told them what our orders were.

"I would love to check on our families, but I don't think the phones are working."

"They aren't, Sir," said Captain Dizon.

I thought for a second then said, "Captain, I want you to stay here pick yourself a first sergeant split the unit and get them ready to move out. Top and I are going to the post to check on our wounded. Then we are going to go to every home of our people and reinsure the families."

"Yes, Sir."

We drove over towards the post along the way many German buildings were on fire, and debris littered the road as we went, and German emergency vehicles were everywhere. For the most part, the fighting was over, but we could see occasional explosions and a MiG or two, but that wouldn't last long with all the NATO planes in the air. The post seemed entirely wrecked. Many buildings were crumbled or on fire, bomb craters everywhere, and there was equipment mangled. Men were running all over the place, some with stretchers, some with guns. We rode up to where the clinic should have been. It was a mess, but large tents were getting erected, and nurses and doctors were tending wounded on the outside. Top and I went looking for our men. There were hundreds of men either injured or dead on the ground. As we searched, Top and I split up, and as I looked, I heard a weak voice calling, "James, James over here."

I couldn't make out who it was but found out when I went to him, "James, thank God you're alive," said Sergeant Major Brooks.

"How bad are you?"

"I'm not good; I think this will put me out of the Army."

"Nonsense, you've been worse off than this."

"Yeah, I guess you're right, I have, haven't I?"

"Of course, but how did it happen you getting slow in your old age."

"I'm not that old, a fool private froze, and I knocked him out of the way and took the bullet met for him."

I shook my head and said, "Are you bucking for another MOH."

"Now, you can't tell me you wouldn't have done the same."

"I guess I would have, but of course, I'm not as smart as you."

"That's a laugh; you predicted this war." "There are going to be many people who will be doing a lot of apologizing to you." "I don't see you remaining a Major for long, either." "By the way, your people did some nice shooting with those missiles."

"Thanks, have you seen Colonel Henderson?"

"He was here a little while ago."

"Well, if I don't see him, send him my best wishes."

I felt a hand on my back when I turned around, and it was Maggie. "Thanks for the warning you saved a lot of lives by calling."

"That's alright, Maggie; I'm surprised you were able to get so many doctors and nurses to follow you."

"Ha, I run this clinic they do as I tell them."

"I believe you." "You know where my men are?"

"Yes, follow me."

"You take care, Greg."

"I'll do my best, and you keep your head down."

As we walk away from Brooks, I asked Maggie, "How bad is he?"

"He will live, but he is going home."

"You want me to leave you my medic and the two men I sent with my wounded to give you a hand."

"No, I was promised people from the German hospitals when they could send them."

We reach my men and Top was already there after checking them out I ordered my medic and the two men who were with them back to where the rest of the men were, and then we headed to the families. Top and I stuck together, and we didn't stay long with the families. They were terrified but were grateful that their men were safe. The last two families were Top's, and mine Top insisted we see mine first. I went into the house, Maria and the boys rushed into my arms, I hugged and kissed all of them then said, "What's with these tears you two are my little soldiers," I said to the boys.

"We thought you might have gotten killed," said Jonathan.

"I don't like the noise of the bombs they frighten me," said Frederick

"Well, we are chasing those bad people away."

I grabbed Maria and said, "Can't stay long, my men and I have to be moving out if you need help talk to Maryann and or Helen."

"You be careful, she said with tears in her eyes."

I kissed her and the two boys and said, "I'll contact you when I can, don't worry."

We then went to Top's house, after Top reassured his wife and his children he said,

"Maryann will keep an eye on Maria and the boys."

"I sure will," Maryann said.

"You, Helen, and Maria might want to organize the families and help out in the post; it is a mess."

"I'll see what we can do."

We head back to the unit, and when we got there, Captain Dizon had everything organized. "Sir everyone is ready to move out," said the Captain

"Have everyone gather around me."

"Yes, Sir."

All the men gathered, and I said, "I want first to say how proud I am of all of you." "Your performance was beyond excellent you are all heroes as far as I'm concern." "We have talked to your family members who are doing fine and Top, and I reassured them that you are alright." "We are going to go to Alpha and Bravo units and help defend them."

"Sir, I wish to remind you of something we only have one high power, and we need to keep all the radars together," said Mr. Shafer.

"Thanks for reminding me." I looked at Captain Dizon and said, "I think Colonel Greenhill doesn't understand how a missile unit works." "I'm changing the orders all the radars will come with me. Captain Dizon, you are to go to Bravo and bring back anything that can be salvageable and bring it back to Alpha that includes Bravo's men. The wounded and dead try the hospital; otherwise, bring them to me."

"Yes, Sir."

"Let's move out." As we moved out down the road heading toward Schweinfurt, we had to weave in and out of civilian traffic, but we managed to keep moving. As we got nearer to Schweinfurt, there was a dark cloud of smoke hanging over the city, and we could see fires. Schweinfurt got it much worse than Bamberg; God only knows what we would find when we got to the military bases. I could see more and more NATO jets flying over heading east and north; then, we saw the bombers. We finally came to the point where we split, and I went to Alpha while Captain Dizon went to Bravo. The Alpha site and barracks got destroyed, and as we rolled through the gate, I saw men walking around stun, some of them wounded. Men were lying on the ground; I don't know if they were dead or alive. I did see some intact missiles, but most of the launchers got destroyed as the radars were, but maybe there was enough to get parts from them. The command center was gone, and all the buildings were much as it was at Charlie.

I stopped and grabbed one of Alpha's men who was bleeding and asked, "Where is your commander, soldier?"

"What," he said, still shocked.

"Where is your commander?"

"Over there, someplace," he said, pointing to his left."

"Corporal Swartz, come over here and take care of this man," I said to my medic.

"Yes, Sir."

"Top, let's go find the commander."

"Yes, Sir."

We found him where his office was sitting on the ground, shuffling through some partially burn papers. "Captain McMullen."

He looked up and said, "What are you doing here."

"Temporary taking over your command."

"Says who."

"Says me, who outranks you and Colonel Greenhill now get up we got to get this place organized and take care of your men." He stood up and walked with us. I was surprised he didn't fight with me. "Top before we deal with the equipment take the men you need and gather Alpha's men put the wounded to the left of me and the dead to the right, the men who are still physically fit have them sit down in the center."

"Sergeant Hill set up a mess hall."

"Where are your C rations at Captain?"

"They were in the basement of the barracks."

"Sergeant Hill, when you get your mess hall set up, see if you can scrounge any more food."

"Yes, Sir."

"Where are your first sergeant and medic Captain?"

"They were killed along with a quarter of my men in the barracks."
"What an arrogant fool I was, I should have been prepared, like you, so many killed or wounded."

"You can't cry over spilled milk Captain, all you can do is make the best of what you got and learn from your mistakes besides, you're not the only one who was caught with their pants down." "Where is your armory?" He pointed to a bullet-riddled trailer like ours leaning on its side. "You got the key to open it." He fished around his pants and found a ring full of keys, and he opened the trailer, and I went in and started pulling out everything. As we were working, I decided to start talking to him; I felt it might help him get himself together. "How many missiles did you fire off?"

"We only got off three before they blew up the command center."

"Did you hit any?

"No." "I wonder how Bravo and Delta faired."

"I have Captain Dizon, and half my unit at Bravo." Colonel Greenhill said Delta got destroyed; my men at Bravo are going to bring everything here?"

"So, we are going to set up a working unit here."

"For now, we will have a meeting at what's left of Headquarters. My thinking is we will be heading out to the Czechoslovakian border to give support for the Air Force and other ground units."

It looked like at least three-quarters of what was in the Armory was still good. The wounded and fit men of Alfa were pouring into where I said to put them. My medic was doing the best he could with what he had but was having a hard time keeping up with the wounded, so I said, "Corporal, do you need more help?"

"Yes Sir, I could use some help, where is their medic?"

"Dead, but I will get you, someone, at least it will be a set of extra hands."

"Yes Sir, I'm running low on medical supplies, also."

"I'll see what I can find."

"Sir, I'm Second Lieutenant John Oakley; many of us would like to be doing something instead of sitting."

I walked over to the Alpha company men and said, "How many of you people want to do something?" All fifty raised their hands, and I turned to the Lieutenant and said, "That second duce and a half has three officer's tents in it set them up over there by the wounded then move the wounded in them."

"Yes, Sir."

Lieutenant Keith Kallstrom came over to me and said, "Sir, we got all the dead line up over there; however, there are some body parts still laying out there."

"If that body part was yours, Lieutenant, would you want it buried with you?"

"I suppose so, Sir."

"Take a quarter of the men and retrieve those parts as difficult as it will be." "Then divide the rest send half out there to see what they can salvage, leaving the missiles for last I want the other half with me to see what we can get from their barracks."

"Yes, Sir."

"Lieutenant Oakley, when your men get finished with the tents, have them give my men a hand salvaging what's left out in the field, leaving the missiles for last."

"Yes, Sir."

The men I got loaded up in a duce and half, and we went over to the barracks where I saw Sergeant Hill. "I see you've found some things."

"Yes Sir, we just got about all the C rations, and I intend to go over to their mess hall to see if I can find anything there."

"Very well, hopefully, it will be easy getting to supply."

"Just be careful, Sir." "I don't know how stable that place is; we found some dead bodies also, Sir."

"Understood, Sergeant."

"We went down and pulled out the bodies first, then we got busy loading up the truck and driving it back to the site several times over the next few hours." As we were going through the barracks, we had pulled out nearly fifteen dead men, and we placed them in a line near the street.

When we finally got back to the site, some men and supplies from Bravo were there, including Bravo's commander Captain Tom Riggs.

"Captain Riggs, how many men do you have left?"

"Over half my men were either killed or are wounded just like you warned us."

"Are they all here?"

"No, Sir, more are coming."

"You the XO," I asked a Lieutenant standing next to Captain Riggs.

"Yes Sir, Lieutenant Douglas Jones, Sir."

"Lieutenant, I want you to take that jeep and go get Captain Dizon let him know I need him and tell him to put someone else in charge."

"Yes, Sir."

"Get back here as quickly as you can."

"Yes, Sir."

"We better eat something before we leave."

"I don't think I could eat to tell you the truth," said Captain Riggs.

"Neither could I," said Captain McMullen.

"I can't afford to have any of you, getting sick; you will eat."

By the time we finish eating, Captain Dizon arrived, and I said, "Stay here and take command I'll talk to you when I come back the two commanders, and I are going to Headquarters."

Captain Riggs and McMullen grabbed a forty-five, then we threw the prisoner into the vehicle and left. As we drove into headquarters, I was surprised at how the place escape most of the damage. There were some windows blow out, bullet holes, bomb craters but overall in good shape. We went to battalion headquarters and found out the Colonel was elsewhere on the post, but a Captain sent a man to find him. The MPs took the prisoner after telling them he was a Czechoslovakian, what he told us, and he could speak German. We waited about thirty-five minutes when Colonel Greenhill came in, accompanied by two Generals.

"James, this is Brigadier General Provost and Major General Pearson." "This person is Captain Riggs of Bravo Company, McMullen of Alpha Company, Major York of Charlie Company who I have given command of all three units."

"Yes, we know you, James, from what we understand your unit has saved our ass," said General Pearson.

I didn't say anything I knew they were aware of my forewarning of the war and ignored it. We went into the conference room, sat down, and rolled out a map showing the countries. The invasion was stopped dead cold, which surprised me because the battle plan of the east was a blitzkrieg type of attack. They did push into Germany, Austria, Italy, and even Greece quite far, except where Charlie Company was where they only came in about twenty miles. Berlin was all but gone Vienna got surrounded. For every one MiG that would fly over, they would face two NATO planes, but eastern bloc planes still got through, and then I heard a Schweinfurt

Siren. I heard a couple of explosions then one big one then silence. "Must be going after the ball bearing factory," said Colonel Greenhill.

"Or my missiles unit," I said.

"Well, I reassure you troops, and supplies are moving in fast from all over Europe and North America," said General Pearson.

"How long will it take you to be up and running James?" asked General Pearson.

"A day with the help from what's left of Alpha and Bravo."

"Good when you get everything working, come here and set up, so you can defend this post," said General Provost.

I stared at him for a few seconds. I then said, "It's a bad idea and a waste of men and equipment." "We should be up on the front, pushing into Czechoslovakia, helping defend the air and ground troops."

"Well, I can make it an order or relieve you of your command," said the General."

"As Colonel Greenhill can tell you, your threats don't scare me." "No desk jockey brigadier general is going to tell me to do something stupid and get more men killed." "Before you do that, I will resign my commission and walk away from the military, and you can shove your orders, up your ass."

General Provost turned beet red with anger. I was about to turn and walk out when General Pearson said, "Wait a minute, James, you have more balls than I thought you had." "Everything you said happens to be correct, regardless of how you feel, Ed." "We screwed up the first time when we got warned I won't take that chance again." "What do you have in mind, James?"

"You have tanks, artillery, and men here west of Grafenwöhr that are taking a pounding."

"Yes."

"That's where we will go." "We will give that tank outfit enough of an edge to break through the enemy lines and push them back."

"What are you going to do with the extra troops?" Colonel Greenhill asked.

"Use them as infantry to help protect us."

"Sounds good, James," said General Pearson.

"Thank you, Sir."

"I wish to apologize for what I said to you, James, your plan does have merit," said General Provost.

"I don't carry any grudges general."

"That's good, but I'm a desk jockey?"

"I was mad, and things that get said in anger are mostly not true." "Colonel, has the condition of Delta been confirmed?"

"Yes, there were a few wounded and taken care of and a small number alright do you want them they are here at headquarters?"

"No, keep them here to help you here." "I have enough men to handle what I need to do."

We got out of there and headed back to the site as I drove, I said, "We need a couple of people to check on the families of the men you pick one person each and send them out to do this."

"Yes, Sir."

We got back to the site, and the men had loaded one missile launcher. I went over to Captain Dizon and said, "We need to have everything working and loaded by tomorrow night."

"Yes, Sir."

"Do you know if either unit has any vehicles working?"

"It looks like we have two here, maybe three or four at the other site." "Where are we heading to?"

"The front near Grafenwöhr."

"What are we going to do with all the extra troops?"

"They will be our infantry to protect us." "Captain McMullen and Riggs will oversee the infantry you will take over the missile unit, and I'll be over all of you."

"You trust those other two Captains?"

"No, but I will keep an eye on them and ride their asses."

"Perhaps I should go back to the B company and light a fire under their ass."

"Sounds good to me." "We will need to get all the equipment and supplies we can get; it will be a while before we get resupplied."

Captain Dizon was at B company a couple of hours; we had loaded another missile launcher when supplies were starting to roll in again. I decided to cut the crew in half having the first half get some sleep while the second worked there would be four-hour work periods and rest periods. Sometime during the night, I got a few hours of sleep.

Parts department crammed the trailer with as many parts as they could fit into it. The wounded and dead bodies from both units were taken care of by our men. Just about breakfast time in came Captain Dizon and the rest of his men with all the salvage equipment and supplies they could get. "You and your people get any sleep?"

"No, Sir."

"Get them fed, then get some rest we move out at six tonight."

"Yes, Sir."

We had two other launchers to fill, which would mean we would have a few missiles left over. The mechanics check all the vehicles repaired what they could; all the men were armed and were give combat gear. When everything got packed away, I had a meeting with the three captains, Bravo's First Sergeant, and Top. "Captain Riggs, you take over the riflemen that will be on the right of the unit, Captain McMullen, you take over the riflemen on the left."

"Yes, Sir," they both said.

"You two First Sergeants decided what men you want to oversee; you two are the most experienced combat soldiers we have here."

"Yes, Sir," they both said.

We left at six at night and headed east towards Grafenwöhr. I figured it would take us about fourteen or fifteen hours to get there, which means it will be approximately eight in the morning. We headed out at about ten miles an hour as we were going down the road, I was surprised, a few foolish people were driving on the road. I decided to get some sleep, then replace Top driving and give him some rest. When I woke up, I switched seats with Top. I knew he was asleep when I heard him snoring. I was driving for an hour and a half when I started to see a lot of military traveling on the road.

A half-hour after seeing the military on the road, the unit got flagged over by a Lieutenant Colonel who came towards us. I woke Top and said, "We have company."

"Major, who are you and where are you going?"

"Major James York commander of most likely the only Hawk unit in this sector I'm going to the front to protect our tanks and troops from air attacks.

"I know you; you're that Medal of Honor major from Vietnam."

"I am Sir."

"I heard your people shot down a lot of those commie planes."

"Yes, Sir."

"Outstanding."

"What kind of unit do you have, Sir?"

"Armor infantry; I'll let you go; you got another four or five-hour drive."

"Good luck to you Sir,"

"You too, Major."

When the sun came up, the road was full of military vehicles. I pulled our convoy over to a wide spot and gathered all the men. Then I said, "We are very close to the front the likelihood of an attack is very high if this happens, take your vehicle off the road and hide it the best you can." "Everyone is to seek cover and protect yourself until it is clear." "Let's load up and head down the road; we should be there in about two hours."

About an hour and forty-five minutes later, we got flagged over to the side of the road. "What is your unit major?" asked a Lieutenant.

"Third of the Seventh Artillery, we are a Hawk missile unit."

"Thank God you're here; we've been expecting you." "General Fitzgerald will want to see you." He guided me to an area with many tents, and there was a large tarp over a table.

The Lieutenant talked to the General, and then I was motioned forward, saying, "Major James York reporting, Sir."

"Glad to see you York, I'm General Fitzgerald." "Come join us; I will introduce you to everyone, frankly, I didn't think you would make it."

"We are intact, Sir, and biting at the bit for a little payback."

"You'll get it."

He introduced everyone and then showed me a situation map and said, "We have stymied them here about five clicks out of Grafenwöhr."

"Why haven't you had a counter-attack and pushed them back you have plenty of tanks and infantry?" I asked.

"We would love to, but our air defense is not enough." "Most of our jets are up north or south of us and there using jets to escort our bomber." "We've taken quite a pounding from not only their MiG's but also those dam attack helicopters they have." "The other nations are sending more troops and planes, but that takes time."

"My men can give you the air protection, at least from the jets, and I think I have an idea about those helicopters."

"What is the range of those missiles Major?" ask a full bird colonel.

"Forty-five or fifty clicks, Sir."

"How many missiles do you have, and how many can you knock down?" he asked.

"I have a little more than sixty-five missiles, and we can shoot down at least one plane per missile then must be resupplied." "Perhaps you could help get more, Sir," I said to the General.

"You're telling me you never miss Major," said the Colonel.

"He doesn't his unit shot down twenty-six planes with twenty-four missiles," said General Fitzgerald.

The Colonel was baffled, so I said, "A missile shot down two planes, and we shot one down with a LAW."

"What's your plan with the attack helicopters?" asked the General.

"Can you supply me with a lot of LAWs?"

"As many as you want." "You would have to do a lot of fancy shooting to knock those out of the sky."

"General three men shot eight or ten copters out of the sky with a law we were about seventy-five percent successful."

"It's like skeet shooting, Sir; besides, they have to hover before they shoot rockets, and that makes it even easier." "The only trouble is my Sergeant Major, and I are two of the three people."

"Are you two needed at your missile outfit?"

"No, Sir, I have an excellent Captain." "I'll need about six men who know how to shoot a LAW and who has skeet shot before also transportation for the men and LAWs."

"I'll do you better than that said a Lieutenant Colonel I'll send a rifleman outfit with you."

He sent a Lieutenant to get the men and equipment, and then I said, "My unit needs an area to set up."

"There is a good area about two clicks up above how long will it take for them to set up?" asked the General.

"A couple of hours would be nice."

"Good, then we attack in three hours."

"Not good, Sir, it would be better if we attack about three o'clock."
"Why?"

"The sun will be in the enemy's eyes."

"Perfect, three o'clock, it will be."

"Colonel, the enemy believes in a blitzkrieg type of attack." "It would be nice once the shooting starts to reverse the tables on them, it's only about seventy-five clicks to the border."

"We must do it in three leaps; we must give your missile unit time to set up each movement."

"Yes, Sir, but you can move as far as you can, keeping the enemy on the run, and then my unit will catch up."

"Sounds good."

"Please have the men that will be with me meet me at the missile site with the equipment," I said to the Lieutenant Colonel.

"Will do," he replied.

I headed back to my men with a Lieutenant. The Lieutenant showed me where to set up the site. Captain Dizon came over to me, and I said, "Lieutenant Rose is going to show us where to set up. When we get there, I want the unit set up as fast as possible then we will have a meeting."

"Yes, Sir."

We traveled down the road for about thirty-five forty minutes and entered a field that had a rise to it. The camp went into a frenzy setting up, and in about two hours, everything got set up, including a mess hall, latrine, and tent housing.

"Mr. Shafer, I want you to run a simulation we need a hundred percent accuracy then give them a rest." "About three o'clock P.M., the fighting starts Captain Dizon; you will oversee the missile unit." "Captain Riggs and McMullen will take over the ground defense." "First, Sergeant Harper, you will be the Top of the whole unit." "Top, Corporal Washington and I will be going with that rifle unit to knock some of those attack helicopters down with the LAWs. Any questions."

"Sir, I'm good with a LAW, can I go?" asked Captain McMullen.

"You know how to skeet shoot?"

"Yes, Sir."

"I'd like to go with you too, James," said Frank White.

"I suppose I couldn't stop you, but wear a helmet and flak jacket." "Captain Riggs, you're in charge of the defense of the missiles."

"Yes, Sir."

"Let's get going." "We walked over to where Washington was, and I called "Washington.""

"Yes, Sir."

"It's time to be a hero again, Washington."

"Where are we going, Major?" asked Washington.

"To shoot down some helicopter."

"Oh, I like doing that."

I talked to the six men from the rifleman company who knew how to use a LAW. We told them how to knock down a helicopter with Top and

Washington putting in their input. We headed out to where our tanks and infantry were. There was a lot of activity going on in anticipation of the big push. Lieutenant Colonel Sayer came over and said, "When we move, stay as far away from the tanks as you can we can't see you that well."

"Will do, Sir," I said for everyone. We all strapped two LAWs to our back and carried one, and at three o'clock we moved out, and we didn't have to go far when our tanks opened-up across a valley hitting some tanks, of course, there was some return fire. Then the jets came, but Charlie took care of them, knocking Jet after Jet down, and we moved forward. Later, copters arrived, we started to knock them down as we used up the LAW, another got handed to us, then we all moved forward. We began to move out quickly now, NATO jets flew overhead, as we got closer to Grafenwöhr. By night, we were on the outskirts of Grafenwöhr, and the infantry entered the city.

Captain McMullen, Top, Washington, and I got some rest as we heard the gunfire and explosions in Grafenwöhr. I woke when Top kicked my leg, he handed me a box of C rations and said, "Breakfast you better eat sun will be up in about an hour, and we will move out."

I stretched, then got up and relieved myself, came back, opened my C rations box, and picked at it. I put it back down and drank some water."

"Sir, if you're not going to eat that, can I have it," asked Washington. I handed him my box as did Top and the Captain, and he ate it all. We moved out and headed into the city; we didn't have any resistance; they were retreating. There was plenty of dead and damage from the conflict. We moved through, then out of the city heading to the border. The jets came, again and again, the missile flew, and the planes fell. Like before, the helicopters came back, and we shot them down. We started to get artillery fire, and we stop while we called for an airstrike. Two hours later NATO jets lit up the front, we moved out, by sunset we stopped again, I got informed that my unit was moving up and we wouldn't move until they got set up. We were only about ten miles from the border, and I knew that we would be in Czechoslovakia tomorrow. We wouldn't be leaving until near sunup, so I decided to check on my unit. I drove out to where the site was with Top, and of course, Frank was my shadow. The place had gotten set up, and when I stopped at the command center Captain Dizon, Captain Riggs, and First Sergeant Harper joined us.

"Looks like you got everything operational."

"Yes, Sir, just a few minutes before you got here," said Captain Dizon.

"How is your supply of missiles?"

"We were almost out, but we got a large shipment of missiles and supplies."

"Have you been attacked?"

"Well, they tried to attack us with a few of those attack helicopters, but we knocked them out of the sky with the LAWs."

Sergeant Hill joined us and said, "You three hungry?"

"You got coffee?" asked Top.

"You know, I do."

We went over and got something to eat, and Captain Dizon said, "We know we shot down some planes because we saw them, but what is our percentage."

"From what I have seen, I would say one hundred percent none of their planes have touched us."

"We heard that MiGs from the north and south had to leave their area to try to stop you."

"Well, we will be in Czechoslovakia tomorrow." "I don't want you to be any further than ten clicks from us."

"Sounds good to me." "How far east do you think we will go?"

"I don't know, but I'd like to go all the way to Moscow."

"You think we will go that far."

"It will depend on how they are doing north and south of here." "Sergeant Hill, do you have something I could carry back food for Washington and McMullen?"

"Yes, Sir, I'll get you something."

We got back, and when McMullen and Washington saw the food and coffee, they had grins from ear to ear, chiefly Washington, which Sergeant Hill gave a double portion.

As the two men were eating, Lieutenants Colonel Sayer approached us, "Major, we'll be moving out in eight hours."

"It's a little early, but I think it is a great idea to leave at that hour."

"Yes, they will think we will be here, but by sunup, I hope to be on the border."

"I wish I had known this before I would have like to tell my unit, but there is no worry they have a crew on twenty-four seven."

"I'm going out there shortly and will inform them."

"That would be great, Colonel."

We moved out at three in the morning and caught them with their pants down. Their MiG's tried to find us, but my missiles knocked them down and when the sun came up. We moved across the border more jets, and helicopters came, but when my missiles weren't knocking them down, NATO was. Even though it was hard because of the attack helicopters, we manage to keep them off the tanks and infantry. Near three in the afternoon, our tanks were pounding the military post in Strakonice. We drove them out with heavy fighting, and we occupied the Czechoslovakian post by dusk. Our jets kept the MiG's off us until my Hawk unit caught up and set up. All through the night, we got hit with everything they had. I lost some men, two that were shooting the laws. Two tanks got put out of commission, but we held at least for now. As I rested between a lull in the fighting, I worried about Maria and the boys. The battle would get heavy and die down. About two-thirty in the morning, when the fight was the heaviest, there were several massive explosions about two hundred yards from me. We were defending an area on the left flank, keeping light armored vehicles and infantry from advancing when a Lieutenant approached, "Sir Colonel Sayer has gotten hit."

"Is he conscious?"

"Yes, Sir, and he is asking for you." "You need to know you're the ranking officer now."

"Top you got this?"

"Yeah, go ahead, we got this."

We went across the compound towards those loud explosions had been, keeping low so as not to get hit. "The Colonel keeps drifting in and out," said a medic.

"Sir Major York reporting."

"You're in command now."

"Yes, Sir."

"I made a bad mistake in my arrogance; I push too far inland."

"I probably would have done the same, Sir."

"Protect my people the best you can."

"Will do, Sir." At that, he passed out again. I thought for a few seconds then said, "How many men and equipment have we lost?"

"About four hundred men are out of action, three tanks, several trucks, and more importantely, our radio has gotten damaged."

"We're not going to advance anymore until we get reinforcements."

"Sir, I don't know how long we can hold this position; we have enough ammo, but we lack men.

I looked around, and I asked, "You know where the missile unit is?"

"Yes, Sir."

"Go there and tell them what the situation is here and tell them to contact command as to our position and condition." "See if the missile unit can make it here, their C.O is Captain Dizon."

"Yes, Sir."

I said to the medic, "Keep me apprised of the Colonel's condition."

I went to one of the Lieutenants of the Abrams tanks and asked, "Do you have a tank to tank communication?"

"Yes, Sir."

"Let them know I'm in command, and I want a line of fire along that tree line."

"Yes, Sir, but if we can't see what to hit, we won't be very effective."

"Yes, I know, but the enemy doesn't know that, and it will scare the hell out of the enemy."

"Sounds good, Sir."

I headed back to Top and the rest of them as the barrage commenced. The desired effect I wanted to happen, happened there seemed to be fewer attacks, and the attacks that were coming were less intense. Every once and a while, a tank would fire, and I knew something must have gotten hit because there would be a massive explosion.

By five, the Lieutenant came back from my unit and found me. "They are on their way, Major."

"Did you get a message out to command?"

"Yes Sir, it was Captain Dizon who sent it."

"Alright, grab a rifle and join the party."

"Yes, Sir."

Before seven, Charlie came and started to set up to the rear of the compound Captain Dizon, and Riggs joined me. "It looks like you dished out a lot of hell to the enemy."

"Yes, and we received a lot of hell." "Captain Riggs deploy your men where needed along the line."

"Yes, Sir."

"We should be up in about thirty minutes."

"What did command say when you contacted them?"

"Help is coming."

"When Booker gets his radios working, have him look at this tank's radio system, their communication crew got killed."

"Yes, Sir."

It didn't take long when jets and even bombers came at us, but our missiles knocked them down, and they only got a few shots off. They kept coming, and I was concern that our missiles would run out faster than they could reload them. We got hit by a massive counterattack, which concerned me we may get overrun. Then our jets show up, and they lit up the enemy's lines with napalm. More and more of our jets showed up either strafing the ground or knocking planes and copters down. The bombers came soon; it was all over, and the line was quiet.

Top, McMullen, and I walked over to my unit, and I talked to Captain Dizon and Sergeant Hill. "Do you have enough food to feed all these men, Sergeant?"

"Will make do, Sir."

"I sent our medic to help with the wounded," said Caption Dizon.

"Good." "You and the men did a fine job."

I went over to the wounded to check on the injured and to see how Lieutenant Colonel Sayer was doing. "How is the Colonel doing," I asked the medic of the tank outfit.

"He'll live, but he needs to be sent to a hospital soon."

I walked over to him, squatted down, and said, "It looks like you're going to get a little R and R time."

"Yeah, in a hospital." "How's the unit?"

"I won't lie to you; we lost some good men and equipment, but we held our position, and the Air Force pounded the hell out of them."

"Outstanding."

"Reinforcements should be here in a couple of hours, and you should be medivac out of here when they come."

I was getting some sleep when Top woke me and said, "Huey coming in."

I got up and went to see who it was when I approached it was General Abrams and some staff. I saluted and said, "Sir, it's a pleasure to see you."

"How are things going, James?"

"A lot better than when we started." "As soon as we get reinforcements, we'll be ready to move out and kick some more ass."

"That's a negative James; we aren't moving any further than this for now." "The Russians are trying to negotiate a cease of hostilities saying it was an act of a few rogue generals."

"What did our negotiators say?"

"Bull shit."

"Good response."

"Yes, we won't accept anything less than full reparations."

"Good."

"Let's go someplace and talk."

"Well, we have a mess hall set up."

"That will be fine."

We all sat down, and General Abrams said, "I understand you took over command here."

"Yes Sir, Lieutenant Colonel Sayer was badly wounded."

"What do you think of him?"

"He is all Army, a good soldier."

"What do you think he did wrong?"

"Wrong, Sir?"

"Yes, wrong, you got caught so far forward that you had no support."

"I guess the Colonel bit a little more off than he could chew."

"You didn't confront him?"

I stared at him with my jaw clenched, and I then said, "We are in constant battle, he is a Lieutenant Colonel, I am a Major." "I didn't question him as I didn't question you when I warn you of war."

"No need to get mad; you understand me wrong." "I wanted to know if you informed him of his error."

I calmed down and said, "He might have gone too far forward, but by doing so, it drained off MiG's and helicopters off other combat areas." "I'm betting you the Russians are willing to end the conflict because of how far we did push in."

"Your right." "We all blundered at not listening to your warning nor seeing the evidence." "For myself, I want to apologize for doubting, and I want to assure you that you will hear from others." "Schweinfurt and Würzburg heavily attacked most of my generals and officers down there was either killed or wounded."

"Was Generals Provost and Pearson among the casualties?"

"Yes, they were both wounded; Pearson was bad enough to be sent back to the states." "For many reasons, you will get promoted."

I smiled and said, "I was just getting used to major now I must get used to lieutenant colonel."

"No, James, you're getting promoted to lieutenant general."

"You don't have to do this."

"This promotion doesn't come by me, but I approve it, it's from General Arnold approved by the President."

"I'm assuming I'll be losing Charlie Company."

"Sort of, you will take control of all American Army forces in Europe; you will be under me."

"Do I have to make my headquarters in Würzburg?"

"No, where do you want to make it?"

"Schweinfurt at the third of the seventh battalion headquarters."

"You want to take over command the third of the seventh also?"

"No, I don't want to take Colonel Greenhill's command from him."

"He's retiring it got planned long before this war started, and the Colonel and I talked about giving the command to you."

"I'll do both, but I will make some changes for me to do it."

"Do anything you think needs to be done to fix the Command."

"Will I have you to lean on if I need help?"

"Of course, the relationship between you and me won't change."

"So, when is all of this going to happen?"

"Unofficially, you are already a General; formally, it will be in a ceremony sometime after this war is over." "I want to move you out of here and have you stay with me in Frankfurt."

"No, I'll see this through to the end; it's where I'm supposed to be."

"Alright, James, if that is what you want."

We toured the post, and General Abrams and his staff saw the destruction of the enemy's line. Shortly after the general left, our reinforcements came, and the wounded got evacuated. Things were busy on our site with the new arrivals, but I got a chance to sit down with Top, Captain Dizon, and some of the other men. "So, are we going to advance, Sir?" asked Captain Dizon.

"No, General Abrams said that there are negotiations to end the conflict; you disappointed."

"No, I'm not the war type."

"Are you the company commander type?"

"Well, someday maybe," he said with a smile.

"That someday better be today; the command is yours."

"What?" a confused Captain Dizon said.

"You are quitting the Army, Sir," asked Top.

"No, I was promoted to Lieutenant General." "I'll be taking over the European command." "I will still be under General Abrams." "I am already a General, but there will be a formal ceremony after this war."

"I'm surprised the General didn't take you out of here," said Top.

"He wanted to take me out; I told him no, I started this party with you; I'll finish it with you."

23

REWARD AND NEW COMMAND

e were in Czechoslovakia for five days when we got orders to withdraw to our post. As we drove through the German cities and towns, thousands of people lined the streets cheering, it was heartwarming to see this, and the men were eating it up. Reconstruction was well on its way, and you could see the activity of construction in the affected places. I was hoping as were many that the phones got restored so I could call my family when we got back to Schweinfurt. "Frank, did you get enough notes and photos," I asked him who happen to be riding with me.

"Oh yes, I need to tell you when we get back to Bamberg I have to go back to New York for a while."

"That's alright; I'm going to be a little busy for a while anyway."

"You just make sure you don't get yourself into another war."

"I'm hoping this will be my last; I don't like death and destruction."

We made it back to Schweinfurt in two days to the battalion and a German welcome. All the Captains and I went up to Colonel Greenhill, then we saluted, and I shook his hand.

"Well done, James, or I should say, General York."

"It won't be official for a while; you're still in command, Sir, and it wasn't just me who did a good job; it was all the men."

"Would you like to say a few words to all these people?"

"Sure." "I will first speak English, then in German." "There has been a lot of death and destruction on both sides of the border. For the families of men, women, and children that got killed, I send you my condolences, and they are in my thoughts and prayers." "It is a misconception that soldiers such as me enjoy war." "The truth is most soldiers in all armies would rather

484

there would be peace." "Insane people create war, and when this happens, someone must stop them, and in this case, it was NATO, French, English, American, and German forces that stopped them dead in their tracks." "I assure you they wanted to take over all of Europe and beyond." "I can assure you that the American soldiers in my command fought gallantly under dangerous and harsh conditions." "In my opinion, everyone is a hero." I then spoke in German and told them similar things but stressing Germany. We walked into the battalion building, and I said, "Colonel, my men and I would like to contact our families if the phones are up."

"Of course." The Colonel had a Lieutenant make available phones for the men to use while I went into his office. As I sat in his office, I was eyeing his phone more than what he was saying, and he took notice and asked, "James, you want to call your family."

"I sure do, Sir."

He handed me the phone, and I called Maria and the boys. "Hello, Maria."

"James, we were worried about you, are you alright?"

"Yes, I'm fine; I'm in Schweinfurt; I should be home today or tomorrow." "Are you and the boys alright?"

"Yes, we are fine; the boys cried every day you were gone, nights were the worse time."

"You know that I love you and the boys too much to die."

"We love you too."

"Maria, where are the boys I can't be on the phone for too long."

"They are right here."

"Hello, Daddy, I miss you; I want you home," said Jonathan.

"I know you do, and I will be home soon sweetheart, have you been good?"

"Yes."

"And have you been protecting your brother and mother."

"Yes, we sleep in mama's bed every night."

"That's good, let me talk to Frederick now I love you."

"Alright, daddy, I love you too."

"Daddy, you ok."

"Of course, pumpkin."

"I don't like bombs, daddy them scare me."

"They scare me too."

"Them do."

"Yes."

"Maybe we move to American."

"We will go to America someday, but I made sure you would be safe in Germany; that's why I have been away so long." "Have you been protecting your brother and mother; you are a private with a medal, you know?"

"Yes, I wear my uniform every day."

"Well, there won't be any more bombs, and I will be home tonight or tomorrow."

"That good daddy."

"I love you, Frederick let me talk to your mama now."

"Hello, James."

"Maria, I want you to relax and be happy, and I will be home soon." "More people need to call their family, so I must go." "I love you."

"I love you too, James, goodbye."

"Thanks, Sir, it was good to hear them."

"No problem."

"Alpha, Bravo, and Delta companies are gone." "I'm taking Charlie back to Bamberg for a few months taking some of the men from the Alpha and Bravo do you have room for the rest of the men here?"

"Yes, I would assume you are going to rebuild Alpha, Bravo, and Delta."

"Yes, and no, the Hawk missile is too old and slow; we need something better more mobile." "I'll be speaking to General Abrams about it in the next few days."

"You were told I am retiring."

"Yes, you deserve the retirement you served loyally for many years."

"I understand you're taking over the Third of Seventh directly, including taking over the all of the European command."

"Yes, in part, I'll have a finger in it, but someone else will have the day to day operation."

"Do you think you can find time to meet with me in a few days?"

"I'm going to take a couple of days off, and then I will come down."

"Great."

"I'd like to phone the post commander of Bamberg."

"Sure, go ahead."

"Colonel Henderson, please."

"Henderson here."

"It's James Colonel."

"James, I'm glad you survived."

"Have you heard anything about the condition of Greg?"

"He was well enough to ship home." "I think he is at Walter Reed."

"Good, the main reason I'm calling you is I'm bringing my unit back to Bamberg, the site we are on won't be adequate for my equipment do you have any room on your post for us."

"Is it temporary?"

"Yes."

"On the other side of what's left of the quartermasters building."

"Great, I'll be seeing you then."

"Ok, James."

I finished talking to Colonel Greenhill and looked for my three Captains, Top and First Sergeant Harper.T We all met in one of the mess halls, but we had to wait for First Sergeant Harper and Captain Dizon, who hadn't finished talking to their families. Twenty minutes later, the two men walked in, and I said, "Gentlemen are your family's safe and doing well?"

"They're fine, Sir," everyone said.

"That's good; I plan to get rid of the Hawk and replace it with something better I will give you more details later." "For now, because of housing, I'm sending Charlie back to Bamberg, and I'm sending what men Captain Dizon needs from Alpha and Bravo." "With what men are left Captain Riggs, and Captain McMullen will organize their units from here, I will be back in three or four days." "Colonel Greenhill said they would house the extra men before I leave, I will make sure they get housed." "Are there any questions?"

"Sir, will you get us equipment and men?" asked Captain Riggs.

"Yes, as quickly as possible."

"Can we give our men a day off, Sir," asked Captain McMullen.

"That's up to you, but I would put some guards on the equipment, and Charlie needs to set up." "Top you're no longer the first sergeant of Charlie First Sergeant Harper is." "You will be with me; I need your expertise." "I'll need detail reports of what you observed in five days, and that's from everyone."

"Gentlemen, if there aren't any more questions, let's get to it." "Captain Dring, do you have the housing for what got left of Alpha and Bravo units?"

"Yes, Sir, we moved the men from the barracks next door to the main post, and those men will get housed there," said Captain Dring.

"Good, I'll be back in three or four days."

"Top, you about ready to go?"

"I've been ready for days."

I turned to Captain Dizon and said, "Set up your unit near the quartermaster building on the parade ground when you get there." "Top and I will meet you there do you want me to transport anyone with us."

"No, Sir, we should be there in about two hours."

"Very well, we will meet you."

Top drove, and as we went, I checked my arm where I had got hit. "Your arm giving you trouble, Sir?"

"Yeah, and I think I'm running a fever; it might be infected."

"I will take you to the clinic when we get back."

"Might be a good idea, but Maggie will give me hell."

"Yeah, I know, that's why I'll go over to the barracks and mess hall to see what damage it has."

"Chicken."

"Yep." We arrived at the Bamberg post. Most of the rubble from the damaged buildings got removed. The buildings that could get repaired were getting worked on, including the clinic. Top dropped me off, and I notice there were still large tents set up, but there was part of the hospital still operating, and I went in.

"Maggie here?" I asked a nurse.

"Yes, I'll go get her Major."

Maggie came out with a concerned look on her face and said, "You wounded."

"Yes, in the arm, and I think it's infected."

"You look like you're running a fever, too, come with me." We went into an examination room where she had me strip to my waist. She then took off the dirty bandage and looked at it. "It's infected, alright." "I'm going to have to clean it out, and it's going to hurt like hell."

"It's ok."

She gave me some pills to swallow and then a couple of shots. Then she went to work, and it did hurt just as she said. It reminded me when I was only nine or ten, Doctor Taylor, a dentist, worked on my teeth for five days straight without any painkillers like Novocain. After about forty-five minutes to an hour, Maggie had finished cleaning and sewing up the wound. After she bandaged it, she said, "You need to stay here overnight."

"I can't."

"I figured you say that I'll get you some pills to take, and you make sure you see me sometime tomorrow."

"I'll do that Maggie can I shower with the bandage."

"Yes, and you need a bath; I guess you haven't been home yet."

"No, and it will be a couple of hours before I will be able to Charlie is coming in."

"What are their conditions?"

"I'm not sure it's Captain Dizon's unit now."

"Why?"

"I got promoted I'm a Lieutenant General commander of all European forces under General Abrams."

"Well, it was a smart move by Abrams."

"It wasn't his idea; it came from the Pentagon and White House." "Unofficially, I'm a general now; they will make it official at a ceremony."

We walk out, and Top was waiting for me, and Maggie said, "What's the matter you old goat, you so afraid of me you couldn't come in and say hello." "You shot anywhere?"

"Yep, I'm afraid of you, and yeah, I've got grazed not bad." "I'm too ugly for a bullet to do me any damage."

"You can say that again," Maggie said with a smile.

"How's the barracks and mess hall? I asked.

"Shot up a bit, but useable they are working on it."

"Thanks to Colonel Henderson," I said. We drove over to where Charlie would set up and waited, and it wasn't long when they rolled in.

"How do you want us to set up, Sir?" asked Captain Dizon.

"It's your unit, Captain; set them up the way you want." About forty minutes later, they got set up, and I walked over to the Captain I was about to say something when a car drove up, and out hopped Colonel Henderson.

"Maggie said you were wounded."

"It's not any big deal; it was a flesh wound that got infected."

"Well, you look like hell, as does the rest of your men."

"These men are Captain Dizon's men."

"What do you mean?"

"I've been promoted."

"Good for you, from corporal to lieutenant colonel."

"Not colonel, lieutenant general, I'm the commander of all European forces under General Abrams." "If you don't shut your mouth, a fly will go in it."

"You're kidding."

"About the fly, yes, about the lieutenant general no."

"So, you're my boss," he said with a smile.

"In a roundabout way." "Do you know how many generals are members of the Green Berets?"

"Not many."

"Captain, what are your plans?" asked the Colonel.

"Set up and place a guard, Sir."

"You're not going to man the equipment?"

"Not until tomorrow, I'm going to give my men a rest, Sir."

"I'll tell you what I'll get some MPs down here, and they will watch your equipment, and I will also arrange for your men to eat at another mess hall for a couple of days."

"That's very kind of you, Sir," said Captain Dizon.

"Thanks, Will," I said.

"That's the first time you have ever called me Will."

"You always outranked me."

"Well, I'll be going to get everything arranged."

Colonel Henderson left, and I said to Captain Dizon, "As soon as you get everything button up here, we will take you home."

"Thank you, Sir."

The equipment got set up, the men sent to their quarters then Captain Dizon, Top and I went home.

I drove the Captain and Top home and went home myself. I just got out of the sedan and shut the door when Maria and the boys came running into my arms, smothering me with kisses. We finally went into the house, and I went to change my clothes and clean up.

"You look better, showered, and shaved."

"I most likely smell better too."

"You do."

"Where are the boys?"

"They are in bed, sleeping."

"Oh, I will check on them and give them a kiss."

I finished with the boys and sat down with Maria and said, "There is a lot I need to tell you, our lives are about to change."

"What is it?"

"I've got promoted, and I don't work at the missile base anymore."

"That is wonderful."

"We must move."

"Oh, where to."

"Schweinfurt as soon as I can get housing."

"I will miss Maryann and Helen."

"Maryann is coming along, and also Helen."

"Oh, that would be wonderful." "When do you have to go back to work?"

"Two or three days, but I will be doing a little work from home."

"Good, we need you here." We snuggled on the couch until we went to bed.

The next day I got up late with the two boys still curled up in the bed with us. I got a notepad and started writing everything that happened from the spies' incidence to the present. I then wrote recommendations for medals, especially a silver star for Washington and a Medal of Honor for Top. Everyone got recognized for their courageous performance. About ten o'clock while writing the report, I took a break and called General Abrams. "Sir, I want to talk to you about something on my mind."

"What is it, James."

"I'll get right to the problem, Sir; it's the Hawk missile system; it's outdated clumsy, and it needs to be more mobile; it needs to get replaced."

He was silent then said, "Are you on a secured line?"

"I'm calling you from my home phone."

"I'll talk to you about this in person when can I see you?"

"You name the time, when, and where."

"How about day after tomorrow I'll fly down to Schweinfurt, and I'll be there sometime in the afternoon."

"That's okay, Sir.

I went back to writing my report and then about one o'clock Maria, and I went to the clinic so that Maggie could look at my arm. "Well, look at you, you look halfway human, and I bet you smell better."

"He does," Maria said.

We finished with the clinic picked up some groceries and treats for the boys then headed home. We went downtown to have dinner and have some fun a couple of times. It was sad to see a building here and there burned out, but most places were getting restored. It was time for me to go back to work. Maria and the boys weren't happy about it but accepted it. I sent Top to check on Alpha and Bravo. I also asked him to check on where the unit's reports were. "James, I was just about to go to the mess hall to get some coffee, would you like to join me?" asked Colonel Greenhill.

"Sure." We sat down, me with a cup of tea and the Colonel with coffee.

"I want to take you over to my house some time today."

"It must be this morning because General Abrams is coming this afternoon to have a meeting with me."

"Then, we will go right after I finish my coffee."

"Sounds good to me."

"I'll get a car, and then we can go; it'll just be a few minutes."

"That's alright, Colonel, I want to tell Top where I'm going anyway."

I saw Top talking to someone, so I walked over to him. "Sir, this is Sergeant-Major Patrick Mattson. He was a hard-looking man about Top's age slim with short hair; his arm was injured and in a sling. "Pat, this is Major soon to be General James York."

"Yes, I know you, Sir," he said with a raspy voice.

"I see you are injured, was it during one of the bombings?"

"Yes, Sir, it's bad enough to be sent home."

"He is giving me his house when we move out here."

"Very good, I just have to find a place for myself. The Colonel is taking me over to his house for some reason; I'll be there for a while."

"Yes, Sir, I'll be busy here anyway, Sir."

"Alright, nice to meet you, Sergeant Major."

"The pleasure is mine, Sir."

The Colonel picked me up and off we went. We were soon in a nice-looking neighborhood. We turned down a street that ended in a cul-de-sac. There was a large white two-story house with an attached garage, a picket fence, and many flowers. "You have a nice house, Colonel if I didn't know better, I'd think I was in the states."

"You like it."

"Yes, very much."

"Then, let me show it to you."

We went in, and to the left was the beautiful living room with a fireplace. To my right was the dining room very fancy we walked down a hall to the left we came upon a great kitchen with a breakfast nook. In front of the kitchen was a family room, and off the family room was an office. I noticed a piano in the family room, and I said, "You play, Sir."

"No, it was my wife and boys who played."

He showed me the garage that was a two-car garage smaller than my father's garage from what I remember. In the garage were a cream color Mercedes and a red VW bug. "Nice Mercedes."

"You like Mercedes James."

"Oh, yes, they have nice lines."

We went back down the hall to a side hall where he showed me a bathroom and laundry room to the left side, the right side had a large rumpus room, and he said, "My boys liked to play in here just before they left for school in the states."

"It was a great play area for any age." We went out the back door to the right was an enclosed patio with a hot tub and all this connected to the kitchen. Outside was a patch of lawn, an area for a vegetable garden, some fruit trees, flowers, and what surprised me a big sandbox with swing slide. "I didn't know you had children young enough to play there."

"I don't; it came with the house, and I never removed it." We went back into the house and went upstairs. To the right was a large master bedroom with a bathroom and some large mirrors. Next to the bedroom was a sewing room or nursery, then in front of us was another bedroom. To the left, as you walked into the bedroom was a bathroom that connected to another bedroom. "These were my boy's rooms," the Colonel said. We went out of the bedroom and turned right, and there was another bedroom with a bath connected to it. "Well, Major, what do you think of the house?"

"It's extremely nice, Sir."

"And what do you think of the way we furnished it?"

"You and your wife have good taste."

"Well, this house and all its furnishing are yours at least in a couple of weeks; it will be yours."

"You're kidding, aren't you, Sir."

"No, Marie is in the states at our home, and she is getting new furniture for it." "She should be back in a few days; then we will pack our things and ship them home."

"I don't know what to say other than thank you, Maria and the boys will be thrilled as I am now."

"Frankly, I owe you a lot if it wasn't for you; it could have gone horribly for this war we had."

"Well, the men had a lot to do with it, Sir."

"Yes, but it was you who trained and guided them."

When we drove back to the post, I said to Colonel Greenhill, "I would like you to join me in the meeting with General Abrams." We ate, and Top joined us, and I said, "How are the other units Top?"

"They are doing fine, Sir, what's left of them."

"They will be getting new equipment and more men of that I'm confident." "I want you and the Colonel to join me at the meeting.

"Yes, Sir."

About an hour after we ate, a Huey came carrying General Abrams and some aids. I went up to him, saluted and shook his hand as well as the others. The General and we all decided to walk instead of taking a vehicle back to the battalion building. "I didn't want to talk on the phone just in case someone was listening; that's why I cut you off."

"I figured that and took no offense." "I'm going to bring in Top and Colonel Greenhill into the meeting."

"Alright."

"Frankfurt hit bad?"

"Yes, but they are rebuilding."

"What about the French and English sectors?"

"Yes, they got hit badly, what saved them, and all of us was your incursion into Czechoslovakia." "I want to show you something." He pulled out a newspaper and handed it to me, and I opened it and seen that Frank and Penguin has been creating a little mischief.

"I had nothing to do with this, and this is the first I've heard of it."

"Well, it's in all the papers, TV and radio." "Not only in the United States but from around the world."

"You mad about it?"

"No, it's mostly truthful but a little sensationalized."

"Yeah, it's exciting, isn't it, but it wasn't too exciting when I got hit," I said mostly to myself.

"You were wounded?"

"I was shot in the arm when we were still fighting in Bamberg."

"I hope you put that into your report?"

"No, I didn't put anything about me in the report."

"Well, you should have." "I'm sure someone else in Charlie will."

We walked into the building, and Colonel Greenhill showed us to the conference room. General Abrams took his briefcase, opened it, and handed two sets of orders. "Your first orders are your promotion; I'll talk about that in a moment." "The second set of orders is you are to take over the European command." "Regarding your promotion, you got officially promoted." "However, don't change your rank on your uniform yet." "General Arnold wants to pin your stars on in a formal ceremony, which will be in five weeks at the parade grounds in Bamberg." "At this ceremony, there will be many dignitaries." "These dignitaries come from not only the United States but from NATO, most European countries; I even heard the royal family might show." "Also, there will be representation from all units in the European command and those involved in the fighting." "As regarding the Hawk missiles, first, I want to know why you think they are outdated after all they seem to knock down all the planes that you aimed at."

I looked over at Top, and Colonel Greenhill and said, "The Hawk is too outdated, slow and cumbersome." "While it is true, we hit everything that we aimed at, it was because of a couple of soldiers who were highly skilled at math, and they had a hard time keeping up." "The most important thing is we never shot down the new faster Russian MiG's nor do I think we could, I'm sure the Russians know this also." "These missiles and equipment are large and easy to hit, it is amazing, and by the grace of God that they didn't wipe us out before we fired any missiles." "There are only twenty-four missiles per unit." "It takes four men to load one missile on a launcher, and that takes time." "When all the missiles got fired, it took most of the day to reload the launchers." "That tank outfit that I commanded had to wait for cover before they moved." "We couldn't move because every time there was a movement, it took time for the missile unit to be ready to move." "Top, Colonel Greenhill, do you have anything to add?"

"The parts of the missile launchers, radars, and command center don't last long." "They have to get constantly replaced, and that means when they run out of parts in the parts room, I have to send a man to find that part which takes time," said Top.

"I confirm everything that got said," said Colonel Greenhill.

"It's like sending the men to war using flintlocks against automatic weapons," I said.

"I thought you might say something like this, and I believe you," said General Abrams. "The reason I questioned you about this is that there are those in Congress who will oppose spending money after what you did." "You must explain to them why they need to fund a new missile program." "We have several new missiles systems that are ready to go into production." "You must pick the best and convince those paying for it that it is worth it." "You will leave for the states a week after the ceremony."

"I intend to take my family with me, Sir."

"If you wish."

"There is another problem, Sir, that needs to be addressed and solved."

"And what is that."

"Helicopters, Sir." The General nodded, and I said, "We still use Hueys, and they are no match for the enemy's attack helicopters." "We were attacked by what I would guess was neither the Soviets best helicopters nor the best pilots." "Would you agree to that Top?"

"Yes, I would, Sir."

"The ones that attacked us had a major flaw in that they had to hover before firing." "We were only successful in knocking them down seventy percent of the time, and you had to be good at shooting a LAW to do it." "We need a faster and more powerful copter than the Huey, and I intend to use it as part of the new missile unit."

"You must explain it to Congress also." "Two new attack helicopters are coming out that you will see; from what I understand, they are better than anything the Russians have." "What in the missile unit are you going to use them for James?"

"Transport and cover."

"Excellent, you should be getting replacements of men and equipment no later than next week."

"I'm going to need some staff officers and a new Colonel since Colonel Greenhill is leaving."

"Your staff is coming, and you can promote someone from the Third of the Seventh."

"Unless there is anything else, I'll be leaving."

"I'd like to know; can I still promote or demote anybody under me?"

"Yes, full bird down, a general has to come from the Pentagon."

"I just wanted to promote someone to Major."

"Who Captain Dizon."

"He deserves it, but he just made Captain." "The person I'm thinking of is Captain Maggie McCall."

"She does deserve it, Sir," said Top."

"Yes, Maggie, she is not just an ordinary nurse; she is special, promote her," said General Abrams.

General Abrams left as did Colonel Greenhill. I met with Captains Riggs and McMullen and talked to them about the men and equipment they were going to get and Bamberg's ceremony. On the way back to Bamberg, I said to Top, "I want to get together with you and Captain Dizon about my vision of what the missile system is going to be like."

"Wouldn't it be better if you to talk to some battalion officers' Sir?"

"No, I don't trust desk jockeys I trust you and Captain Dizon."

"Yes, Sir, when do you want this meeting."

"Tomorrow, I'll give Captain Dizon a call tonight," I said. "When is that Sergeant Major leaving?"

"About three weeks, Sir."

"How soon after he leaves are you going to move?"

"I think the following week, Sir."

I drove Top home and then went home myself; after dinner, I gathered everyone together and said, "I have a couple of surprises."

"What is it?" everyone, including Maria, begged to know."

"Well, we will be moving to Schweinfurt in about three weeks." "Now, this house is a special house, and we will look at it just before moving in." Frederick didn't look pleased about it, and I said, "What's wrong, Frederick?"

"I will miss my toys and swing and sandbox."

"You can bring your toys, and I don't think you will miss your sandbox and swings."

He looked at me, disbelieving, and said, "I will also miss Catherin."

"Yes, I'll miss my friends also," said Jonathan.

"Top and Maryann will be moving just around the block so they will be nearer about the same time." "And the rest of your friends will be coming in about a month or two after we move." That seemed to cheer them up.

"What does the house look like?" asked Maria.

"It's a surprise you must wait to see it."

They were disappointed but accepted it, and then Frederick said, "Daddy, you said you had two surprises."

"Yes, I did, didn't I." "Well, in about two months, I must go to the United States for some time to do some business, and I have room for three more passengers if you know anyone who would like to go."

"Me, mama and Jonathan do," said Frederick excitedly.

"Jonathan there will be a good chance that we will be going to the ranch in Missouri you must watch out for your mother and brother they don't know about the snakes, ticks, chiggers, and fleas."

"Yes, daddy, will I be seeing my brother and sisters?"

"I hope so."

I called Captain Dizon and talked to him about the meeting, and the next day I said, "Sergeant Hill, why don't you join us.

"Yes, Sir, let me get my coffee first."

"Sergeant Hill Schweinfurt battalion post has two mess halls one is in fair shape the other is a mess you will be taking over the worse of the two." "I intend to close that mess hall until you and all the men you need, transform that mess hall into the best mess hall."

"When are we moving to Schweinfurt, Sir?" asked Sergeant Hill.

"About two months."

"Can I look at this mess hall?"

"If Captain Dizon can spare you, it would be a good idea." "Now, to get to why I set up this meeting, I want to bounce off you, my vision of what the Third of Seventh will be." "It will be the core of the European command once I get the Battalion fix to the way I want it I will work on the rest of the European command." "Headquarter, Alpha, Bravo, Charlie, and Delta will all get stationed in Schweinfurt; the Hawk missiles system is ending." "It will be replaced with what I hope to be a more mobile, faster, more accurate, and concealable unit that can be fired by fewer men." "Also, a new helicopter unit will be attached to the battalion." "The helicopters will be used to transport, supply, and to protect the missile units." "The men will get highly trained not as intense as the Navy Seals, Green Berets, or even the Rangers, but they will get trained to survive in the field."

"These missiles you're thinking of must be a lot smaller," said Captain Dizon."

"Yes, the Hawk missile is too heavy, bulky, and easy to spot."

"Who's going to do this training of the men, Sir, you're going to be too busy with the European command?" asked Top.

"You're right, Top, so I'm going to get help from Special Forces and some of our allies." "I'll set the program and let them take care of it." "So, what do you think of my plans?"

"Well, Sir, the plan sounds good, but you need to know I don't think many of the men will get brought up to the standards of what you expect," said Captain Dizon.

"It's a concern I also have," said Top.

"Are the cooks and older soldiers going to have to go through this training?" asked Sergeant Hill, concerned.

"No, some departments will be as they are now." "However, new soldiers for certain departments will get handpicked." "I won't throw anyone out of the Battalion, but I may reassign some of them." "Of course, there will be reasonable modifications as time goes on." We finished our meeting and Top, and I went to Schweinfurt. "We will start with the Battalion headquarters and take a clipboard, so we can write down the changes I want."

"Yes, Sir."

"Lieutenant, where is Colonel Greenhill?"

"I saw him earlier, but I don't know where he is now."

"You see him tell him I want to see him." "Who oversees the maintenance of this building?"

"Lieutenant Bellman and Sergeant McPhee, you can find them at the Headquarters building."

"Top, would you go get them?"

"Yes, Sir."

I went outside and found the German foreman of those working on the buildings and asked him if he could remodel the inside of the building, and he said yes. When Bellman and McPhee showed up with Top, I discussed what I wanted to do with the building. "This building will house battalion and my office and the offices of my staff, come up with something." I had Bellman and McPhee work with German foreman and Top, and I went over to Headquarters building and found Captain David Dring. "How many open beds do you have?"

"None right now."

"How many will you have once I move the people who aren't part of the missile unit?"

"Maybe three hundred to three hundred and fifty, Sir."

Top and I went to the next four barracks, then talked to their commander and informed them that they would be moving in about two months or less. We were at the hanger at the far end of the post when Colonel Greenhill came. "I hear you've been looking for me."

"Yes, I need you to give me recommendations on who would be best to replace for you."

"I'll give you a list of names and qualifications."

"I'm going to be remodeling the battalion buildings and moving some of these units out of here." He nodded, and I said, "I also want to get this hanger ready for the helicopters and move the motor pool somewhere else."

"Warrant Philip Adams runs the motor pool; we should talk to him."

"Sounds good to me."

"Mr. Adams, I'm General York."

"Yes, Sir."

"I am getting several helicopters here, and I am going to need this hanger to work on them."

"How many helicopters are we talking about, Sir?"

"I'm not sure I haven't seen the specifications of them yet, but it could be sixteen to twenty-four to start at."

"Sounds like these helicopters are going to be something special."

"They are."

"Well, I guess we could set up a motor pool outside."

"Helicopters or no helicopters, you will have four extra motor pools anyway because you will have a large increase of vehicles posted on this post."

"Yes, Sir, we will make do."

"Is it true there is a plane booby trap under this hanger?"

"Yes, Sir, in a flooded hanger under this one."

"Colonel, do you know why it never got disarmed."

"No, it was flooded before my time."

"I want to get that hanger cleared so we could use it for parts and or supply room depending on the size."

"We could sure use it, Sir," said Warrant Adams.

"I'll make some phone calls and see what I can do." I got on the phone and called General Abrams first, who told me he knew of the hanger but didn't know much about it. He said that he would send an explosive expert team next week to deal with it. Two weeks passed, and I had moved the men in the four barracks to the main post in Schweinfurt and Bamberg, we had a lot of equipment and men come into the battalion. The explosive team was working on the hanger by first draining the hidden hanger to get a better look at it. When I went home on Friday night, I told Maria, "Tomorrow we are going to look at the new house to see what we need."

"What time?" asked Maria with a smile.

"You name the time, and we will go."

"I think we should go after breakfast, so the boys don't get dirty."

"That's a good idea." The next day the boys and Maria were excited and ate fast so that we could go. We drove to Schweinfurt, and when we got near the cul-de-sac, I said, "Everyone put your hands over your eyes so you will be surprised." They all did as I said, and when I drove up to the house, I said, "Alright, we are here."

As they looked their mouth hung open in disbelief, Maria said, "It is beautiful, it looks like a palace."

"Let's go in mama; I want to see inside," said Jonathan."

"Ja daddy, we go in," said Frederick.

"Let your mama have a good look at the house."

"Alright, we can go in now," said Maria.

I walked up to the door and unlocked the door and in we went. "Daddy, there is still someone living here; their furniture is still here," said Jonathan.

"Everything that is here is ours. Colonel Greenhill has given it to us."

"Really," said Maria.

"Yes."

We walked past the formal dining room. I notice in the china hutch was full of beautiful china, crystal, gold, and silver silverware, and everything one would need to put on a fancy dinner. We then went into the family room, and I was thrilled to see that the Colonel and his wife left the piano. In the office, they left all the furniture. Maria went into the kitchen, on the kitchen table was a letter, it read, "Dear James, I want to thank you for all you have done for my wife and me." "You have saved my ass several times." "Just before we left for the states, I received a promotion to brigadier general." "I don't know if you had anything directly to do with it, but I don't think I would have gotten promoted if you never came to the battalion." "You will notice I left a few extra things for you and your family I would check the garage after you read this letter if you haven't already." "Good luck with your command, James, General, and Mrs. Greenhill." We all went out to the garage and Maria, and I was surprised by the yellow cream Mercedes, and the red Volkswagen. I heard two squeals of excitement coming from the two boys on the far side of the garage. Maria and I went to investigate what was all the excitement about and seen two new shiny bicycles with bows and tags on them. One read to Frederick from Santa, and it had training wheels; the other said to Jonathan from Santa. "Are they ours daddy they have our names on them?" asked Jonathan.

"I guess they are; they say it's from Santa."

"Who Santa?" Frederick asked

"Saint Nicolas," I said in German." "In America, he is called Santa Clause.

"How did he know we are moving here, daddy?" asked Frederick.

Before I could answer, Jonathan said with all seriousness, "Santa Clause knows everything I think it is magic or something." "I don't understand why he never came when I lived in Missouri."

"Maybe your birth mother chased him away or something." "He is making up for it now, given you all a loving family, nice things to wear and play with, and now a bicycle," said Maria. Jonathan seemed to accept this explanation. I was surprised that at the age that Jonathan is, he still believed in Santa Clause; I hope it lasted for a while.

"Daddy, can I ride my bicycle," said Jonathan.

"Me too, daddy," said Frederick.

"Maybe after we look at the house," I said. They were disappointed but didn't argue about it.

We went to the patio that was off the kitchen. I showed my family the hot tub that was there. Frederick asked, "What it for?" I looked at Jonathan and Maria, and I could see they weren't sure what it was for either.

"Well, it is sort of like a bathtub, but hotter, we can all go in at the same time, and it bubbles, and it feels terrific." We went outside to the backyard and then Maria, and I saw a blur of two little boys running to the sandbox.

I looked at Maria and said, "I said they wouldn't miss the sandbox."

"It's a beautiful backyard," said Maria.

"Yes, it is, boys, let's see the rest of the house." We all went into the house but through the back door near the laundry room. After showing the bathroom and laundry room, we went to the playroom. I said, "This room is for playing whenever you wish, but it is best when the weather outside is not very good or too dark outside." We went next upstairs and into the bedrooms. Maria was thrilled with the master bedroom and bathroom. When we came to the next room, I said, "Mrs. Greenhill used this room as a sewing room, but it could get turned into anything like a baby nursery."

We went next to the boy's room, when I explained to them whose bedroom was whose, Frederick said, "No, daddy, I sleep with Jonathan."

"I'd rather sleep with Frederick." "I don't like being alone," said Jonathan.

I looked at Maria then said, "Well, you can sleep together if you want, but you still have your separate room." They both agreed to that, and we all looked at the guest room before we went downstairs. The boys beg me to let them ride their bicycles, so I opened the garage door and said, "You two be careful of cars."

"Yes, daddy," they both said, and off they went.

Maria and I went back into the family room and sat down, and I said, "What do you think?"

"It's wonderful."

"We won't' have to move very many things."

"I better see if they left the pots and pans," Maria said. "They did and silverware, dishes, bowls, and glasses and a few other things."

"What are we going to do with the things we don't need, including the Volkswagen?" I asked Maria.

"We will find someone who could use them."

"I guess we could move tomorrow." "What do you think?"

"Yes."

I called Top, Captain Dizon, and a few others to see if they could use the car or any other things we were getting rid of, and they couldn't. When we went to church the next day, I spotted a few nuns sitting in front of the church, and I had a great idea. I whispered to Maria, "Why don't we donate everything to those nuns."

She smiled and said, "That would be good; it would make them happy."

When the mass concluded, I approached the nuns, and in German, I said, "Sisters, may I have a word with you."

"Yes, of course."

"My family and I are moving there are many things that we do not want, including our Volkswagen would you like them?"

"A Volkswagen, yes, yes."

"We will bring the things we have to your convent in a few hours. We loaded up everything we didn't want, then Maria drove the VW and I the sedan, and we went to the convent. The mother superior came out, and I said, "This is it; someone has to sign for it." "Do you want me to help you carry the rest of the items into your convent?"

"No, no, I will sign for it, and we will not need the help what do you wish me to sign." I pulled out the registration and told her where to sign; she thanked us repeatedly, and we left for the old house. After we loaded up our things, we took it to Schweinfurt and went back with my sedan and the Mercedes to get the rest. It was ten o'clock and way past the boy's bedtime, by the time; we got the boys into bed. Maria and I didn't get to bed until eleven-thirty, and we were exhausted. Wednesday Top took the day off, borrowed a truck, and moved his household to Schweinfurt much to the boys' delight. Of course, Maria helped Maryann as much as she could, and she was happy that they were here.

I had moved most of the other personnel in the barracks to the main post in Schweinfurt and Bamberg. I had a talk with Colonel Henderson about what I was planning to do, which he approved. He let me know what he got ordered to do for the awards ceremony, and it was going to be one big day. I could already see an army of workers setting up things on the parade ground. Captain Dizon had moved the missile equipment back to the site since he had temporarily fixed what needed fixing out there. Eventually, that site would get returned to how it was before the missile site got constructed. On the weekend, we did what shopping we could do in Schweinfurt; then we drove to Würzburg, which was heavily damaged, for the rest of the shopping and to visit Maria's aunt. I also had this weekend to decide who to promote to Colonel to take over the battalion. I had narrowed it down to two people a Lieutenant Colonel Jason Novick and a Major Ralph Upton. Novick had just been promoted and came over from the states about a week ago; he had an excellent record, a good education from a fancy university, and was an older man. Major Upton had been in the unit for a year and was in the thick of battle. He had a good education; it was from a state college, and his record was mostly good, He had one comment that he was argumentative with superiors. Monday morning, I would make my decision. Monday, I went into my office reading the Stars and Stripes. When I looked up, there sat Top and Mr. White drinking coffee. "I see your back from making mischief in the states."

"Mischief, everything that was said was true just like you like it, and we got great publicity." "There has been a rush to buy the first book, and they want to make another movie about you."

"I would assume you have another check for me?"

"I have three checks for you, one for the first book, one for your second book that I will write after this formal ceremony this Wednesday, and one for the next movie." "I have a couple of contracts for you to sign."

"What kind of deal did you get for me?"

"A lot better one than you had before and a lot more money."

"Are you going to do the third book?"

"Yes, but I'm going to do it a little differently because I have other projects to do."

He handed me the three checks, and I looked at them. They added up to about seven million dollars, "Frank, do you have a place to stay?"

"Not yet."

"If you can put up with my boys, you can stay at my house."

"I will accept."

"I'll drive you home at the end of the day." Top had to do some work, but Frank stayed as I called to have Lieutenant Colonel Novick and Major Upton report to my office. They both reported about thirty minutes later, and I said, "This is Frank White who is writing a book about me if either one of you doesn't want him here, I will send him out."

"It's alright with me, Sir," said Major Upton.

"It's fine with me also, Sir," said Lieutenant Colonel Novick.

"Very well, I'll come right to the point I must pick a new Colonel to run the battalion, and it's between you two who I will decide."

"I thought you were going to take over the battalion, Sir," said Major Upton.

"I am to a point I have the whole European command to consider now and won't be able to give it the attention this battalion needs." "I agonized over which one of you to pick you both have your strong points and weak points, so I'm going to ask you both a few questions and make my decision now." "Lieutenant Colonel Novick, what did you do when you were in the states?"

"I worked in the accounting office at Fort Dix."

"How long did you work in an office environment?"

"About ten years almost ever since I joined the Military."

I looked at his file again and notice he just squeaked through boot camp, and he wasn't a good shot. "Major Upton, looking at your file, you have a problem of being argumentative with your superiors, especially Colonel Greenhill, you want to comment."

"I'm not argumentative; I am just expressing my opinion strongly."

"Had your opinion ever turn out wrong?"

"A few times."

"Did anyone ever tell you why their opinion was better than yours?"

"Yes Sir, I understand you, Sir, have expressed yourself strongly a time or two."

"You're right, Major, but the difference is I'm always correct."

"Yes, Sir."

"How do you react if a captain disagrees with you?"

"I'd listen to him and tell him why my way is the best."

"Lieutenant Colonel Novick, you and the Major both are college-educated, but you went to one of the best universities in America, and you did very well in school."

"Yes, Sir, I was on the honor roll every semester."

"Yes, I know, so why did you join the Army when you could have gone out in the private sector?"

"It was kind of a family tradition which my family expects of me besides, I would have to find and interview for a position in the private sector, and I'm not good at that."

I looked at them both then said, "I'm going to tell both of you exactly why I've made my decision." "Lieutenant Colonel Novick, you outrank the Major, you don't question superiors' opinions and have a fine education. However, it was behind a desk; things around here are going to get intense physically." "You have also just made lieutenant colonel, and you haven't had any combat experience." "I like an officer who has the balls to challenge his superiors when he thinks he is right." "For that reason, Major Upton, I'm promoting you to colonel effective today, and you are in command of the battalion under me."

"Congratulations, Colonel Upton," said Lieutenant Colonel Novick.

"Jason, it doesn't mean you won't get promoted." "I'll keep an eye on you, and in time if everything goes well, I'll promote you."

"Thank you, Sir."

"Your dismissed, Colonel Upton, stay here for a minute." "Thursday, I will go over everything that will happen to this battalion and all Hawk battalions." "I would suggest you get these men into shape." "Talk to Captain Dizon about this; he can tell you what seems to work." "A day after the awards ceremony, Charlie will be setting up in the field past the hanger, and their personnel will be moving into the empty barracks." "Their cook, who is the best cook in the European command, will take over the mess hall that has been closed and reopening it." "Once he has done this, I'm promoting him to warrant and putting him over both mess halls."

"Don't you think that we shouldn't bunch all three units together?"

"If this were to be a Hawk unit, you would be right, but it won't be soon." "I will tell you of the changes after the awards ceremony; then, you will understand why I'm doing this."

I informed my clerk to type out orders for Upton promotion, and he was to pick them up in an hour. I went down to the hanger and talked to the men who were disarming the booby trap plane. "You have been working on this for some time what is taking so long?"

"It's a slow process, Sir, we have to move inch by inch." "Then, when we find something because of the deterioration over the decades, we have to be extra careful, or someone will get hurt."

"I don't want to rush you, but how much longer will it take?"

"Maybe a week, Sir."

"Is there a plane down there?"

"Yes, a couple of planes and some parts."

"This whole floor is supposed to be able to lift bringing up those planes make sure when you finish the mechanism hasn't gotten rigged to blow also."

"Will do, Sir."

Wednesday came, and everyone was to be in their dress greens. While Maria got dressed, I made sure the boys were bathed and got dressed. Frederick insisted on wearing in his uniform, and I didn't stop him. We all piled into the Mercedes, and off to Bamberg, we went. When we got there, MPs were directing cars where to park. When the MP saw who I was, he said, "Sir Colonel Henderson wants to see you before the ceremony starts."

"Alright, where is he?"

"Over by the damaged clinic, Sir."

After I parked, my family and I walked over to the clinic, and I found the Colonel. "Colonel, I was told you wanted to talk to me."

"Yes, James, you will be marching in with the Third of the Seventh just like I have it diagram here." He shows me where each company would get led by their First Sergeant, and Top would lead them all. All the captains will be on the side of their units. Battalion personnel would be up in front of us alongside them would be Colonel Upton. I would be in the center of the four companies left of the captains.

"Where is the Third of the Seventh now?" I asked.

"Down by the theater."

"What about my family, where do they sit?"

"I'll take them to their seat right now."

"Very well, I better get down to the theater." I gave Maria and the boys a kiss and left for the battalion. There was a Lieutenant giving instruction, lining up units, and sending them down to the parade grounds. The viewing stand was filling up, and the military band was playing. NATO troops were forming up on the parade ground by the music that started playing. Finally, the American forces began forming up on the field. When it was our turn, we all lined up in our proper places and marched down towards the parade grounds. We marched down to the parade ground in front of the viewing stand. The men got brought to attention saluted the dignitaries and got placed at rest. Colonel Henderson made a speech and then called up other dignitaries to talk, including the president and the Queen of England. Everyone who spoke after praising their troops ended up honoring the Third of the Seventh and me.

General Arnold took the podium; I got ordered up beside him, then he said, "It's no secret who saved us all." "It was the Third of the Seventh under the direction of Major James York." "We were all warned by him, and we should have known better." "For this reason, Major York has been promoted to the rank of lieutenant general and given the command of the American European forces under General Abrams."

He congratulated me and sat down. The president stood up and said, "Congress has awarded you, for the second time, the Congressional Medal of Honor." "You also got awarded the Silver Star and Purple Heart, amongst others."

He shook my hand, introduced the prime minister of France and a French general who made a speech that I didn't understand. Then the French general pinned a French Cross for Military Valor and kissed me on both cheeks. I heard the laughter of Frederick, who wasn't far away. It annoyed the general, and I said, "Excuse the boy he is nine years old and doesn't know French custom."

The prime minister smiled and translated to the General, who indicated he understood, and it mattered not. Next, someone representing NATO came up spoke, and presented me with the NATO ISAF Medal. There were other dignitaries from various countries, making short speeches and awarding me with multiple awards. The prime minister of Britain already talked, and the Victoria Cross got awarded. The Queen of England and Prince Charles got up and spoke. After praising the performance of all forces and my men and myself. The Queen said, "General James York, I give you a decree that you and your family are to present yourself in ten days to Buckingham Palace to be knighted by me." I looked at her shocked then looked at Generals Arnold and Abrams, who had smiles on their faces. I switched back to the Queen, who said, "James, I can see you are concerned about what your superiors will say, don't be. I've already talked to your president and Generals Arnold and Abrams, and they said it was alright."

"Your Majesty, your gracious offer is wonderful, but there is something you need to know about my family history."

"Is it that in all reality you are Lord James York of Worcester, your great grandfather being the Earl of Worcester?" I nodded surprised she knew, and she said, "Don't be surprised I'm aware of your genealogy, are you ashamed of your royal heritage?"

"No, your Majesty; I'm quite proud of it." "I have to admit I don't know what is proper when it comes to royal customs; I thought you couldn't get knighted if one had a title."

"Of course, you can, and you shall if you accept."

"Yes, your Majesty, I accept wholeheartedly."

Colonel Henderson then got up and said, "We will now hear from General James York, who will say a few words."

"Mr. President, Prime Ministers and your Majesty distinguish guess. I wish you to forgive me for the poor etiquette I had never gotten trained in this kind of manner. I had just had a strong feeling and said, "I will first speak in German." "I have always had a love for Germany." "My wife and my children are Germans, and I am of German heritage." "Not very long from now before the turn of the century, Berlin will be one, and Germany will be one never to get divided again." "To the brave German troops who fought for the fatherland, I salute you." "For the German people who suffered from the attack, I salute you." "For one united Germany, I salute you, Germany forever." The German troops, police on the parade ground, and the German public and officials in the stands went nuts cheering. Then the military band played the German national anthem. "I wish to speak of the British, French, NATO, and all other troops and Countries of Europe that took part in defending this unjustified attack." "You all fought bravely many times you came to our aid." "It is obvious how well you did by the way you stopped any advancement of the enemy." "Well done, we are all proud of you, and your people are proud of you." "To my American comrades, we had many casualties, but you kept on fighting." "Though the road was rough, you persevered, when I know most of you for what you had to face had not gotten prepared by the time war broke out." "When hostilities broke out, I was in command of Charlie company, which has a few hundred men we had a few wounded." "I can't say the same for the other units, which suffered greatly." "I contribute to Charlie's success to the fact of my suspicion that we would get attacked, and I trained these men accordingly." "Now that I am in the second command of the American Forces, I plan to do the same to each unit." "It's not that I think there will be another war here, but because if you are a soldier, you never know where you will be sent or will be needed." "I will speak to you more about this when I visit your units." "They have promoted me to general I who was a fat private, but I know a general or commander is only as good as the men under him." "I am proud to have served with you all, and I will continue to be proud to command you." "God bless you all, and God bless the United States." Colonel Henderson handed me some papers I looked at them and said, "Just when you thought you were going to get rid of me, I have got asked to hand out some awards." I turned to Colonel Henderson and said quietly, "There's too many I'm going to let the company commanders hand out the lesser metals." "I will announce the most important ones."

"Sounds good to me go ahead let them know what you are doing."

"There are a lot of names on this list, and it would take hours before we would get finish with them." "What I am going to do is hand out a few awards now, and your company commanders will hand out the rest later." "Mr. President, would you do me the honors for these next awards."

The president came down and stood beside me. I said, "Sergeant Major Jack Bennett, Lieutenant Robert Wolf, Sergeant Stephan Schrader front, and center."

Then the president said, "You men have placed your life in harm for your comrades." "For this reason, with my blessing, Congress has awarded you with the Congressional Medal of Honor."

After placing the medal around their necks, the president then went back to his seat, and I said, "Captain Dizon, Corporal Washington front, and center." "Your actions during this conflict have been outstanding, and you both have gotten awarded the Silver Star among other awards." "Corporal Washington, I told you once if you showed me your best, I would promote you, and you have." "For this reason, I am promoting you to Staff Sergeant; if you keep on going as you are, you will be a first sergeant soon." "I handed out many other awards and promotions then said. The rest of you men, your company commanders, will award you the awards and promotions that you have earned." "I do, however, have one more award and promotion that gives me pleasure to present." "This soldier has served tirelessly for years with distinction without regard to this person's own needs."

As I was talking, a note got passed to the president. He spoke to General Abrams, who interrupted me by whispering to me, "The president has just got notified that Congress approved a Medal of Honor for the Captain." "He wants to present it."

"I then should promote her to lieutenant colonel instead of major and give her a Silver Star and a Bronze Star."

"You're a general you can do as you wish."

"Yes, it is nice, Sir." I then said, "There has been a change of plans for the good." "I have a few more words about this last soldier before I call this person up." "This person has saved many lives and helped others in ways I can't imagine from many nations, both military and civilians." "This person has done this without considering her own needs." "This person is Captain Maggie McCall." "Captain McCall front and center."

An unsettled captain proceeded front and center, and I stepped out of the way, as the President took the podium. "General York, who knows you, has praised you far better than I could ever praise you." "He has told other members of Congress and me of your service to your country, and we are impressed." "I just received moments ago from congress a messaged awarding you with my approval, the Congressional Medal of Honor congratulation captain." At that, he placed the medal around her neck as those around her cheered her. Then he said, "General York, Captain is not finished with you yet."

With a smile on my face, I said, "You Captain has gotten overlooked for years, but I intend to correct that." "I am awarding you the Bronze Star and the Silver Star for not only what you did in this conflict but also what you have done throughout your military career." "I am also promoting you to the rank you should be at, lieutenant colonel. Congratulations, Maggie; I wish there were more like you." There broke out an eruption of applause, and Maggie took the podium. A shocked and emotional Maggie got up to talk. With a shaky voice, she spoke of her love of country. Maggie also spoke of the soldiers that she served alongside with throughout her career. Of course, to the amusement of everyone, she chided Top and me. That night there would be a party with dignitaries, officers, and their families and significant metal winners attending.

24

RETURN HOME

Frederic insisted he wanted to wear his uniform to the party. However, I did something about that. I had bought what looked like a cadet dress uniform from a military school when he saw it, he had forgotten all about the fatigue olive green uniform. We went to the reception I was pleased to see Sergeant Washington was there, but I didn't get a chance to talk to him nor Top. I was ushered around to various dignitaries. I spoke to the British representative and the French representative. I asked, "Do you think you could loan me a squad of British Commandos and a squad of French Legion?"

"What is the reason you want them?" asked the French representative.

"I would like to know that too?" said the British representative.

"One of the units that I command I wish to change drastically; they need some of the skills that your men have." "I also am going to talk to Israel about using a squad their Mossad, and I'll bring in a squad of Green Berets."

"General, you will have the cooperation of France," said French representative.

"And Britain," added the British representative.

"Thank you; I will contact you both." I then was ushered away by the queen to have a private talk. "You know your Majesty I'm just about the same age as Prince Charles he's just a few months older, and I'm very jealous of him," I said with a smile.

"Why would you be jealous, General?"

"Even if you were not a queen or in the royal family, you would have made me a fine mother."

"I'm sure your mother is a good mother."

"Well, I don't know about that; I don't believe she comes near how great of a mother you are." We talked for a few minutes more, and I got steered off to the president who was talking to General Abrams. They talked about how soon General Arnold was going to retire, what my plans were for the European Command. They also asked when my family and I intend to stay at the White House, and I explained to him that I would have to stay two or three days at Buckingham Palace. When the conversation switched to someone else, I looked around for Maria and the boys. I got concerned they were being neglected, but I was relieved to see that Maria was being taken care of by the other wives. The boys were socializing with the other children that were there. The party finally ended; we loaded up in the Mercedes, and we headed back home.

I talked with Colonel Ralph Upton on the direction I wanted the third of the seventh to go and what I wanted him to do when I was gone. Then my family and we left for England. We arrived at Heathrow Airport late in the afternoon. It was cloudy with a drizzle of rain. A limousine got sent to pick us up and take us to Buckingham Palace, so we didn't have to go through customs. Maria and the boys were fascinated with all the buildings and how large London was. The chauffeur was kind enough to explain what the more important buildings were.

As we drove into the courtyard of Buckingham Palace and went inside, we didn't get to meet the queen; instead, we got shown our rooms. The boy's room was in the nursery, which they were apprehensive about not staying with us, but when they saw their room and the toys in them, they changed their minds. When we had settled in and got served lunch, it was just Maria, the children, and me. The boys ate their lunch fast, so they could go back to their room and play some more. A man came up to Maria and me while we were eating and said, "Sir, the queen wishes to see you and your wife when you finished eating to share some tea and biscuits with her."

"Alright, we should be done in a few minutes."

After lunch, a servant took us to the queen's quarters, and the queen motioned for us to sit. "I hope your room is adequate."

"The room is quite wonderful your Majesty, thank you," I replied.

A servant served us tea and cookies, which they called biscuits, and the queen said,

"General, are you going to your estate in Worcester?"

"I'd like to, but the President of the United States is expecting my family and me at the White House after the knighting."

"I think I have a solution that will let you visit your estate and be at the White House on time."

"What is the solution, your Majesty?"

"We could fly out to Worcester and have the knighting there."

"I wouldn't want to impose on my relatives, your Majesty."

"It wouldn't be an imposition I've already talked to them, and they would be thrilled to see you and to have the knighting."

"Then, we would be grateful for you arranging all of this."

The next day we all loaded up in a large helicopter, which excited the boys. It wasn't long before we landed on the estate just outside of Worcester. We were greeted by Earl Edward York, a distant cousin of mine and his wife Lady Catherin and several servants and townsfolks. When Edward shook my hand, his jaw dropped in shock and said, "You could be a twin to our great grandfather, there is a painting in the manor of him you must see." As we walked into the manor, I saw a picture of my great-grandfather, and he did look like me to my surprise. In a short ceremony, I got knighted, served lunch, we got a tour of the estate, and as the sun had set, we headed back to Buckingham Palace. The next day after breakfast, we said our goodbyes and headed to the airport and Washington, D.C.

Washington was just the opposite of London when we landed; it was hot and sultry. Washington had a heatwave, but I've always liked the heat, and it was a welcome change of weather, at least for me. A limousine took us to the White House, where we stayed until my business got done. Maria, Frederick, and even Jonathan, who had never been to Washington D. C. before, were fixated on everything around them. It turned out the president and his wife were doing business elsewhere, but he still provided rooms and use of the White House. I arranged for Maria and the boys to get a full tour of Washington D. C. while I took care of business at the Pentagon. "General York to see General Arnold."

"One moment, Sir." The clerk used the intercom and announced I was here and said, "Follow me, General, I will show you to his office."

"James, I was expecting you, or should I say, Sir James," General Arnold said with a smile.

"James is good enough, Henry." "I'm no different than I was before."

"We have a meeting in about twenty minutes with some important people; while we wait, tell me how things are going back in Europe." We talked about my plan with the European command. He finally said, "That's ambitious; you think you can transform the troops without changing them all to Special Forces?"

"Yes, and I'm not trying to change them into special forces but get close to a hundred percent out of them."

"Well you will have my support, and I wish you well, we need to get to the meeting now."

After introductions, we all sat down the secretary of defense was there as were two men from Congress. There were four other men, two from a company that would be building a new missile system and two from another company developing a new helicopter. The first one to speak was Mr. Charles Beckett, who was with the helicopter company. "General York, I am told that I have to get your final okay for us to get this contract with the military." "Let me show you what we came up with," Mr. Beckett said, handing me pictures and specifications of a large transport helicopter.

I studied everything carefully, noticing that it was massive much bigger than a Huey with two fifty caliber machine guns attached to both sides of the copter. "How does it compare to the Russian Havoc?"

"It's just as maneuverable; ours can carry more people or cargo and go higher."

"I notice you didn't mention anything about its firepower." "I think I would like more than just two machine guns."

"It's not cost-effective to add any more armaments," said one of the men from Congress.

"What state do you represent, Sir?"

"The great state of South Carolina."

"How many soldiers from South Carolina are you willing to lose, and what will you tell their loved ones when they are gone because you wouldn't give them the best protection?"

"The general is right," said another congressman.

"James, just what changes would you make?" asked General Arnold.

"I'd put two more fifty calibers machine guns in the front and a rocket system under the carriage." "The one thing in Vietnam that bothered me the most and caused a lot of injury and death was bullets coming up through the floorboards I experience this myself."

"We have solved the floorboard problem General with a product called Kevlar it's light and can protect from any ground cover," said Mr. Beckett.

He showed me this Kevlar, and I said more to myself than to anyone, "I wonder if this stuff could get fused in flak vests and helmets."

"Sounds like a good idea, James," said General Arnold. "Mr. Beckett, what is the cost to add the things General York wants?"

"Between thirty and fifty thousand dollars per helicopter."

"It's not that much more for a lot of protection, Senator," General Arnold said to the Senator from South Carolina."

"I won't fight it, General," the Senator said.

"Let me show you the other helicopter General," said Harold Cahoon, who was the other representative of the helicopter company.

I studied the specification and the photos, and I was impressed. It was a two-man attack helicopter deadlier than any other country had. However, I wanted to know how much protection it had, so I asked, "Does this model have Kevlar also?"

"Yes, it does," answered Beckett. "Both models have an advanced radar system also."

"I could use sixty of those and about twenty-five or thirty of the troop copters to start; when can all of this be ready."

"That number about six months we do have some available if you want to see them operate," said Mr. Beckett.

"How long will it take to modify the troop copter?"

"About two or three weeks."

"Okay, I'm going on leave, so in four weeks, have your demonstration at Camp Pendleton in Southern California." "I'm sure the Marines will want to see this also."

"Let's move on to the new missile system," said General Arnold.

They gave me the first three specifications and photos of three different systems by a Mr. Jeff Ladd. I didn't look long, all three were too bulky and not much better than the Hawk, so I rejected them and said, "Mr. Ladd, you do know what I require of this system." "It has to be compact and be fired by one or two people and be packed and moved by hand on one of my men." "It also has to be both air to air and ground to ground anything thing else is worthless."

Mr. Burl Gordon, who came with Mr. Ladd, looked at me, opened his briefcase and handed me specifications and photos of another missile system. I studied them very carefully, shook my head, and asked, "What is the range of this missile?"

"About forty miles."

"And how much does it weigh?"

"About fifteen pounds."

"How much does the radar system weigh, and what is the range of the radar?"

"It weighs about thirty pounds, and the range is about forty-five to fifty miles."

"Why didn't you show me this one first?"

"We wanted to show you the best at the end," said Mr. Gordon.

"What is the price of the first three systems?"

"They range from about seven hundred and fifty thousand to a million dollars."

"And the last system?"

"About six hundred thousand."

"I'm thinking you were hoping to sell the more expensive system." "I think these gentlemen from the Congress will be happier with the last system, and frankly, I like the last one the best." "How long will it take you to deliver this system?"

"Depending on how many missiles you want six to nine months."

"Then, I believe we have a system I can live with." When I finished talking to the people from the missile company, one of the men from Congress asked why I think we needed a new system when the Hawk worked so well. Like I told General Abrams, I told him how inadequate the Hawk was, and he accepted what I said but wasn't happy. We talked a little more, and the meeting broke up with everyone leaving happy except maybe the one person from Congress. Afterward, I went to see Sargent Brooks, who I was pleased to say doing well. It was late in the day when I arrived at my room in the White House.

When my family spotted me, they came rushing up to me, all excited, especially Frederick. "Daddy, you should be with us today, I see Dinosaurs," said Frederick with a heavy German accent.

"Yeah, daddy, it was great." "I've never seen anything like that before," said Jonathan.

"We saw big statue of man with beard sitting down, and we went up in this big tower," Frederick added excitedly.

"It sounds like you had a lot of fun today." "How was it for you, Maria?" I asked.

"I like all wish you could be with us today."

"I had a long meeting with the military today, but tomorrow we will leave for our home in Missouri." "We will be there for three weeks." "Then, we will see Grandpa and Grandma York for three days after that we will go to Disneyland for two days."

Jonathan was thrilled, but Frederick said, "What Disneyland?"

"Do you know who Mickey Mouse is?" I asked.

"Mickey Mouse, he one who is little mouse that talks."

"Yes, and we are going to his home."

"Why?"

"It's the happiest place in the world you will see."

The next day we headed to the Washington Dulles International Airport and a flight to Springfield-Branson National Airport. We rented a car to Ellsinore, which I plan, dropping off in Popular Bluff.

We drove into the Ellsinore home late in the afternoon after stopping off and buying groceries. The place looked great; the trees were in bloom, and the wildflowers were everywhere. I had called my Aunt the night before and told her we would be in about this time, and she had the windows open airing out the house. There was a note on the door that read give her a call when I get in. We brought the groceries in, and the boys wanted to go outside and play. I said to Jonathan, "Be careful with your brother, you know about the snakes and other things, and Frederick doesn't."

"Yes, daddy."

The boys went outside, and I said to Maria, "I better call my aunt."

"Hello."

"Aunt Adeline, its James."

"James, are you at the house?"

"Yes, we just got in."

"Well, I want you all to come for dinner."

"We bought food before we arrived; you don't need to cook for us."

"Nonsense, I want to see your wife and children besides if you aren't tired, I'm sure your wife is." "I'm sure she doesn't want to cook."

With a smile, I said, "Alright, you win, I'll be over in a little while meanwhile if you see two strange boys wandering around your place and one of them has a strong German accent just hold them there."

"I'll do that I'll see you later."

I showed Maria the house, including the secret room and the guest cottage and the loft apartment. She was quite impressed with everything, and she admired the vehicles in the barn. We took the rented car and went down to the pond, where we found the boys chucking rocks into the water. "Daddy is it our pond?" asked Jonathan.

"Yes, and the land on the other side belongs to us also." "You boys get into the car, and I'll take you to another part of the ranch." They got into the car, and I headed to where the forbidden tree was. The place was a little bushy again with new growth, but the tree had grown and had blossomed, and with the rest of the area, it had plenty of wildflowers. I explained to everyone where the boundaries of the property were, well as best I could. What surprised me was that it appeared my uncle wasn't using the land for grazing and watering his cattle.

"Well, hello."

"Hello, Aunt Adeline, this is Maria, Jonathan, and Frederick." My Aunt gave Maria, myself, and Jonathan, a big hug. She wasn't the type of person who gave kisses. With Frederick, she picked him up much to his delight; he always liked to be fussed over.

"Val is out in the barn boys if you want to talk to him," my Aunt said. Val was closer to Jonathan's age, but his maturity was closer to Fredericks, so they should all get along well. My Aunt, Maria, and I sat down to talked, "Tom and Mike should be home any time now, and your Uncle Paul should be home soon after that." "I'm afraid the girls are still at school and won't be home for another two weeks," my Aunt said.

"Well, we will be here for about three weeks before we go to California," I said.

We talked about Europe, notably Germany, which brought Maria out of her shyness. Maria was talking to my Aunt about German cooking when Tom and Mike arrived in my truck. They came in through the front of the house, and I said, "Well, I see that old truck of mine is still running."

"Yours I think you're getting senile in your old age didn't you give that truck to us," Tom said with a smile.

"That's the way I remember it too," said Mike, smiling also.

"Now you boys know that is James truck," said Aunt Adeline.

"No, they might be right; I am getting older."

Maria wasn't surprised by their antics, and when I introduced her to them, Mike said, smiling, "You did pretty well for yourself."

Tom's reaction was a bit different he grabbed her, kissed her, and said in French with a Missouri accent, "Bonsoir comment Allez-Vous."

Maria took it all in good humor and said to me, "He is a better kisser than you."

"He might be, but he's trying to speak French, and you're German."

"It not matter if French or German I know good kiss is," she replied with a smile.

"I guess I'm just going to have to get some kissing lessons from you."

Tom and Mike went to take a shower, and while they were cleaning up, Uncle Paul arrived, he got first greeted before he came into the house by Val, Jonathan, and Frederick. After my uncle cleaned up, we all sat down for some dinner and conversation. "Mr. Schumacher is selling his place," my uncle said.

"I thought when you're a Mennonite, you don't own the property; their whole church owns it."

"Normally, that would be true, but many of the Mennonites left for Minnesota." "Mr. Schumacher tried to stick it out, but with a failed crop and the new ruling on schools in the state, they are leaving."

"What's this new rule on school?"

"Your children have to go to a school with certified teachers and follow a certain state program on how kids are going to get taught."

"How much does he want for the property?"

"About two hundred fifty thousand dollars."

"Wow, that's a lot."

"Well, the price for property around here is going up, and I think he is including his equipment and livestock." "The property has been up for sale for some time; he may be willing to lower the price."

"Well, I don't want the sheep, do you?"

"No, but I know a few people who might take them off your hand if you don't charge too much."

"Maybe I will give Mr. Schumacher a visit tomorrow afternoon." "Aunt Adeline, would you follow me to Popular Bluff so that I can turn in that rented car."

"Of course."

The boys asked to spend the night at their Aunt's house, but I said maybe tomorrow you need to spend at least one night in our home. The next day we dropped off the car and picked a few things up mostly toys for the boys, including Val. When we got back, the boys wanted to go play, but I told them, "No, we are going to visit our neighbor; they prefer to speak German."

We cleaned up, took the 1928 Model A Ford sedan then drove over to Mr. Schumacher's farm. "Günter, where is your father?"

"In the house, with mother." We all got out, and I knocked at the door and got greeted by Mr. Schumacher.

"Hello Mr. Schumacher, may we come in."

"Please do Mr. York."

We went into the house and sat in his living room, and Mrs. Schumacher and some of their children joined us. "This is my wife, Maria, my son Jonathan, and my son Frederick."

"Please to meet you, but James, you don't need to speak German if you don't wish to," Mr. Schumacher said.

"To tell you the truth, Sir, my family is more comfortable speaking German."

"Very well, what brings you over to my home today?"

"It is my understanding that I am losing you as a neighbor."

"Yes, this is true if I can find someone to buy this place," he replied sadly.

"I got told you had a bad year with your crops and sheep; if you need money, I will give it to you; I don't wish to see you go."

"It is not just the money I've had bad years before." "The problem is the government wants to educate my children in their ways, and this is not acceptable to what we believe."

"You want two hundred and fifty thousand for your place, isn't that a little high?"

"This place is in excellent shape, and it comes with the equipment and livestock."

"Yes, it is one of the best properties in the area you've done a good job developing this land, but could you come down a little on your price?" "You don't have electricity, phone, or indoor plumbing, and the next people who live here will need those things."

"Are you thinking about buying this place, James?"

"Yes, although I will hate to see you and your family go."

"Well, since it is you, I think I could lower the price a little, how about two hundred twenty-five thousand dollars."

"You know if I buy your property, I will change it into forest land and orchard land is this alright with you?"

"If you buy it, the land is yours; you can do what you want with it."

"I'll buy your land, but you must know there's a developer who wants to build houses; he will most likely pay your full price."

"The wise thing would be for me to sell to him, but you have been a good neighbor, so I offer it to you first."

"Then I will buy your property would you object me driving you to Poplar Bluff, so I can pay you and transfer the deed?"

"No, I'll get the deed, and we can go."

Maria and the boys stayed at Mr. Schumacher's home, talking and playing. At the same time, Mr. Schumacher and I headed to Poplar Bluff. "I'm surprised you would ride with me in the car."

"I can drive a vehicle I intend to buy a vehicle to move my family to Canada."

"I thought your religion forbids the use of a vehicle."

"They do, but I have to get there somehow when I get there, I will sell it and use the money for something I'm more accustomed to."

We went to the bank and then the title company to transfer the title, and after all this, Mr. Schumacher asked, "Do you think you can take me to a place where I can buy a vehicle."

"I know just the place."

Mr. Schumacher bought an old bus with a rack on top and a trailer hitch. He got on the bus and drove to his home, and I followed behind him. Mr. Schumacher seemed to operate the bus just fine, which surprised me because of his upbringing. He was a bit slow, too slow for me. Perhaps some of his slowness was because he had not driven for some time. "My family and I will be out of here in three days, Mr. York."

"You take as much time as you need, and if you need some help packing, my family and my aunt's family are willing to help."

"No, we don't need any help moving, and we will be out of here in three days." "If you don't mind, I wish to take one of the wagons."

"Of course, take what you want I will be here for the next three weeks if you need help." He nodded, and I got the feeling he wanted to be alone, so we loaded up in the car and headed back.

When we got home, the boys immediately shot out of the house and headed for my Aunt's house to play with Val. After doing a few things at the house and on the property, Maria started cooking a few items for dinner tonight. It was getting late, so I called my Aunt, "Aunt Adeline, would you send the boys home, it's dinner time for them."

"They are already eating here, why don't you and Maria come also."

"No, Maria has already cooked, but we will come later to pick up our two moochers."

Maria and I ate, and after we cleaned up, we headed over to my Aunt's house in the Model A. "Well, I got the deed to the Schumacher property," I told my Aunt and Uncle. "I have given him as much time to move as he wanted and told him just before he leaves to drop off the keys."

"How much did you pay for the place?" asked my uncle.

"More than I wanted two hundred twenty-five thousand." "If I hadn't bought it, Mr. Schumacher would have sold it to some developer, and I don't want a bunch of homes next to me."

"What are you planning to do with the livestock and those buildings, they are constructed well?" my Aunt inquired.

"Sell or give away most of the livestock." "The farm has some chickens and turkeys over there I would like to keep and would if I stayed here." "I might let the turkeys run wild, but I think everything else I will get rid of." "The buildings I will install electricity and plumbing." "I was thinking of hiring someone to work all my property and give them rent-free for their labor and a small wage." "You think I'll be able to find someone who will go for that deal?"

"People need work, I would think you wouldn't have too much trouble finding someone who qualifies," said my uncle.

"Mr. Schumacher has a large orchard with various fruit trees, and with my smaller orchard, I wouldn't want the fruit to go to waste." "It would be a good business for someone to make jams."

"It won't go to waste; I'll see to that, James," my Aunt said.

Three days passed, and Mr. Schumacher stopped by and gave me the keys to the property, and we said our goodbyes. It was Friday, and I already had a list of people who wanted the livestock. Including my Aunt and Uncle, who wished to have the chickens and turkeys, which my Aunt talked me out of letting the turkeys run wild. Everyone agreed to come Saturday to pick up what they bought, or I gave away. The chickens and turkeys would be brought back to my Aunt's house. Then put in her much smaller chicken coop until the much larger coop on the Schumacher property could be disassembled and reassembled at my Aunt's place. I also had an electrician and a plumber coming to give me a quote on the house and outbuildings on Saturday.

We all went over to the property right after breakfast. Mr. Nichols, who bought the horses, was there waiting for us with his large horse trailer. "Did you have to wait long, Mr. Nichols?" I asked.

"No, I just got here."

He paid me, and I gave him all the horse tack, which pleased him. When Mr. Nichols left my uncle, and I went into the house where my Aunt and wife were. There wasn't much in the house; we went through room by room, the kitchen had a pump, and I said to my Aunt and uncle, "Does that pump remind you all of the good old days?"

"Don't remind me," my Aunt said with a smile.

We went upstairs, and it got cleaned out also there was a trap door to the attic I opened it and climbed in, and to my surprise, it was full of things the Schumacher's left behind. I handed everything in the attic to my uncle. Then came out of the attic to take a closer look at what there was. The first thing we all notice everything was handmade. "I wish I had an address to send this to them, but I don't."

"I'm sure they knew they were leaving it behind James, so you can dispose of it as you wish," my Aunt said.

"Why don't you and Maria see what you want and what you don't want?" "I will decide what to do with it." "Uncle Paul and I will check on the boys and see what got left behind in the barn and sheds."

They both nodded, and we left to check on the boys. Mike and Frederick were gone Tom, Jonathan, and Val was still trying to round up the rest of the chickens and turkeys. "Did Mike take a load of birds back to the house?" Uncle Paul asked Tom.

"Yep."

We went over to one of the sheds, which was locked, I found the correct key on the keyring that Mr. Schumacher gave me and opened it, and we both went in. It took time for us to get used to the light and we saw some old woodworking equipment. "Do you know anyone who would want this stuff?" I asked my uncle.

"No, I can't think of anyone.

"Well, I don't want to throw it away." "I'll have to think about this." As we headed to the next shed, the electrician showed up. My uncle looked at the other sheds as I explained to the electrician about the house and outbuildings and what I wanted. I signed some papers and let the electrician take some notes as I joined my uncle.

Uncle Paul was talking to Mike, who was back with Frederick, so I joined them and said, "How are the birds taking to their new home?"

"Oh, just fine; plenty of bugs and things for them to eat in there."

"Are you going to take the rest of them with the next load?"

"Yes, then we can get busy tearing down this bigger chicken coop and rebuilding back home."

I looked at Frederick, who was filthy and said to Mike, "Has your helper been pulling a full load?"

"Oh sure, he's as good as Val." Frederick got all puffed up, we all smiled, and Uncle Paul and I went over to the barn. There were some more things in the barn I didn't want and a lot of feed for the birds, which I told my uncle he could have if he wanted it. About an hour after the electrician left, the plumber came, and I explained what I wanted, and I found out it was going to cost, but it had to get done.

Three days later, the boys were at my Aunt's place working; I think they were playing more than working. I was on the porch with Maria eating lunch after working on the property. I had just given Maria a kiss when I looked up and saw a car coming and said, "It looks like we have company."

In came a beat-up old station wagon, I knew, as did Maria right away it was Jonathan's grandparents and siblings. They stopped, and before the Krugers could get out of the car, the three excited children got out and ran up to us and asked, "Are you our mama and daddy?"

"Well, if you three are Sarah, Elizabeth, and William, we sure are." Excitedly they rushed up and into our arms to be smothered with hugs and kisses.

"Where is Jonathan daddy?" asked Elizabeth.

"He and Frederick are building a chicken coop over your Aunt Adeline's house."

"Aunt Adeline Korenek?" asked William.

"Yes."

"How far away is her house?" asked Elizabeth.

"Not far just down that road," I said, pointing to the road behind the house.

"Can we go and see Jonathan?" asked Elizabeth.

I looked at Mr. and Mrs. Kruger, and Mrs. Kruger said, "They are your children."

"Yes, you can go, but remember that Frederick is your brother too." "You tell your brothers they need to come home to meet their Grandpa and Grandma." Excited, they ran off down the road and Maria, and I went over to greet Mr. and Mrs. Kruger.

"I believe you would be comfortable in the guest quarters." "We can put the rest of the children upstairs with Frederick and Jonathan," said Maria.

After putting their things away, they came in to have refreshments. As we were talking, the children came rushing back into the house. Jonathan went into his grandparent's arms teary-eyed. At the same time, the rest of his siblings and especially Frederick, were eyeing the sweets. "Alright, you can have one with some milk," Maria said.

After Frederick got his milk and sweets, he went over to Jonathan's grandparents, who had just released Jonathan. Frederick asked in German, "Are you, my grandma and grandpa, too?"

"He wants to know if you're his grandparents, too," Jonathan explained.

"Of course, we are," said Mrs. Kruger. At that, Frederick gave them both a big hug and kiss. He then ran outside with the rest of the children who were already out.

"How is both of your health?" I asked the Krugers.

"We're a bit slower but in good shape," said Mr. Kruger.

"And you're doing alright with the children?" I queried.

"Yes, they are wonderful children considering what they went through," said Mrs. Kruger.

As the days passed, I bought toys and clothing for all the children, and after five days, it was time for the Krugers to leave. It was a sad day, and everyone was crying. A few days after the Krugers departed, the electrician and plumber had gone, and we inspected what they did. Some small things need to get fixed, but everything was just fine. With my Aunt and uncle's help, we found the right family by the name of Sands to maintain the property. I told Mr. Sands, "Fred, my aunt, uncle will be in charge while I'm gone." "They will be seeing how well you are doing, and if you need anything, you just let them know."

"Alright, General, I'll do that."

It was time for us to leave for California, so on a Friday, we departed for the San Francisco Bay Area much to the disappointment of the boys who wanted to stay.

25

CALIFORNIA

I assured the boys that their trip to California would be even more fun than Missouri, and they accepted that. We landed in the Bay Area in the late afternoon, and I rented a car and headed to Fremont. I would have stayed at my parents' house; they had a large enough home. My father would have welcomed us to stay; it would have made my mother tense; she didn't like people to stay at the house. So, I decided to get a room in Fremont near where my parents lived. After we settled in at the motel, we left for my parent's house after a warning of what to expect from my parents. When we stopped in front of the house, my father was sitting in front of the window. When he spotted us, he got up and went to the front door. As we went to the door, the boys saw the orange tree full of oranges, and Frederick said, pointing at the tree, "Daddy them oranges?"

"They sure are, pumpkin."

"Can we have some Daddy," asked Jonathan.

By this time, my father and mother were standing on the porch, and I said in German, "Ask your grandfather and grandmother."

"Grandma, grandpa, can we have some oranges?" asked Frederick in German.

"They don't speak German, Frederick," I said.

He looked at me, and Jonathan said, "Grandma, grandpa can Jonathan, and I have some oranges?"

"You can have as many as you want, but be careful the tree has thorns," my mother said.

Each boy took two oranges, and I turned to Maria and asked, "Do you want any?"

"No, not now," she said shyly.

After the boys got their oranges, we all went into the house. "This is my wife, Maria, my sons Frederick and Jonathan."

"I hope everyone speaks English because we don't speak German," my mother said.

"We talk English grandma Jonathan talk gooder," said Frederic.

"You do."

"Ja, I gooder in German than Jonathan."

"How long are you going to be here?" my dad asked me.

"A couple of days, I think then I told the boys I'd take them to Disneyland, and I have business down there."

"Does it have anything to do with that war in Europe?" asked my father.

"It could."

"How bad was that war?" asked my mother.

"Oh, grandma it bad daddy shot," Frederick said.

"Were you wounded?" asked my father.

"It was a flesh wound, but Frederick was correct; it was terrible, Europe almost was lost." "That Green Beret soldier I was in the prison camp with was shot bad; he is still at Walter Reed Hospital."

Jonathan was sitting near my mother, but Frederick was sitting next to my father on the floor. My father looked down and said to him, "Freddie, what do you think of America so far?"

Frederick got up all serious and got very close to his grandpa's face and said, "Grandpa, my name Frederick no, Freddie, can you not hear my daddy good?"

My mother and father smiled then started chuckling, and my father said, "Maybe your grandma and I can't hear too well anymore."

"That alright, grandpa, I speak louder."

"Frederick, some people in America, say Freddie instead of Frederick, however, I think your grandpa is teasing you by calling you, Freddie."

He smiled and sat back down, looked up at his grandpa and said, "Oh grandpa, you teaseded me."

"Jonathan, you seem to speak English perfectly, have you been learning English in school?" asked my father.

"Grandpa, I'm from Missouri." "I spoke English since I was a baby, my mother, father, brother, and a tutor has been teaching me, German."

"What's the matter with you, Jim told you about Jonathan, don't you remember?" my mother said to my father.

"This is the boy who was in the Army?" my father asked me.

"Yes, he is my son now."

"It's hard to believe that he could get into the military."

"He looked different then."

"Maria is this your first trip to America, too?" my mother asked.

"Yes."

"What do you think of the United States?" asked my father.

"It big, very beautiful."

As the conversation continued, I could see, Maria was very uncomfortable and shy with my parents. Frankly, I wasn't all that comfortable myself. I didn't know why perhaps the old saying you can never go back home is correct. It was almost as if we were a neighbor from down the street. Maybe it was just all in my head, but something just didn't feel right. We talk for some time, and then I said, "Would you like to go get something to eat; I'm paying."

"Oh, I would have to get dressed up I don't know if I would want to go through all that fuss," my mother said.

"You look just fine were not going to some fancy restaurant anyway," I said.

"We not dress either," said Maria.

"Well, it's either that or to cook for them, Marie," said my father.

"Alright, give me a second," she replied. I had noticed she was quick to respond when she knew the prospects of cooking for my family.

"What kind of food would you like to eat my family and I will eat anything?" I asked my mother.

"Oh, whatever you want."

"Dad, do you eat Chinese food," I had asked him this before, but I wanted to see if he still didn't like it. I and my family like it; it was one of our favorite food.

"It's not my favorite, and I'm surprised you will eat that kind of food after what you went through at that prison camp."

"What I ate in the prison camp is a lot different than what's at a restaurant." "Well, I'll find something to eat on the menu." I looked in the telephone book and found a Chinese restaurant that served American food, and that's where we went.

We all ordered Chinese food except for my father. Then we talked about how my finances were coming along that my father was handling. In the end, we drove my parents back and left for our hotel. I had wanted to visit my grandmother, but she went on vacation with her sister, and so the next day, we headed to my aunt's house in Pleasanton. It was Saturday, so my uncle was home; their reaction to seeing us was the opposite as my parents. I'm not saying my father wasn't responsive; however, my mother was, in my opinion, distant and uncomfortable that we were there. My uncle gave Maria and me a drink, and he teased the two boys who ate it up.

"I assume you saw your parents?" my aunt said.

"Yes."

"You plan to see them again?"

"I'm going to try just before we leave to say goodbye."

"Did you know your mother and I are fighting again?"

"No, I didn't know, but I'm not surprised."

"She treats your grandmother terrible; she just like her father."

"Well, I don't know about that." "The only thing I know is every time Julia and Ed are around her; there is a problem." I turn to Maria and explain to her who Julia and Ed are.

"No, it has nothing to do with them; it's your mother."

"I'm just glad I don't have to deal with it; I'm too busy in Germany and Missouri.

"How is Adeline?"

"She is doing fine; she works hard at her home, but she is healthy."

"How many acres do you have now?" asked my uncle Art.

"About three thousand, maybe more."

"Any deer there?" my uncle asked.

"Yes, if you can get some tags, let me know you can stay in either the house or the other two guest houses."

"I might just do that, is it hard to get tags?"

"I don't know I've never hunted there."

"The house and guest houses are nice; you could also go, Aunt Dorothy," Maria said.

"What are you going to do in Los Angeles?" asked my aunt.

"See mouse house," Frederick said.

"I plan to take them to Disneyland, and I have some military business at Camp Pendleton."

"Pendleton, that's a Marine Base, what are you going to do there?" asked my uncle.

"I know it's a Marine Base; I can't talk about what I'm going to do."

"Well, if you're going down that far, you might as well go to the zoo in San Diego," my aunt said.

"I might just do that if I can drag them away from Disneyland."

"Is Disneyland good as James say?" asked Maria.

"Oh, you will like it; it is something you have never seen; I'm sure," my aunt said.

"Except the castle, it got modeled after a castle in Germany," I said.

"I would like to go to the zoo," said Jonathan.

"Me too," said Frederick.

"We'll see if you change your minds when we get there," I replied.

We talked about the war in Europe and what my role was. Of course, the boys told them I was wounded, but I quickly explained the wound wasn't that bad. I did tell them about the queen of England and staying at the White House, and Maria made some comments about both places. As we talked, my aunt started preparing food, and I asked, "That's not for us, is it?"

"Yes, it is."

"You don't have to do that." "I still want to talk to Evana and Alex to find out how Allen is doing, and then the following morning, we are heading south by air."

"When does your flight leave?" asked my aunt.

"Eight-fifteen in the morning."

"You'll have plenty of time." At that, we talked about other things; most of it was embarrassing things about my childhood.

We ate and talked some more, then about one-thirty, we went back to Fremont to speak with my cousins. We all walked up to the front door, the boys standing behind Maria and me. I rang the doorbell, and after a few seconds, my cousin Evana answered the door. "Hello, Evana."

"Jim, how nice to see you come on in."

"This is my wife, Maria, and sons, Jonathan and Frederick."

"So, nice to meet you all."

"Let me get Alex; he is in the backyard."

Alex came into the living room with a smile on his face, shook my hand, and said, "You're looking good."

"Thanks," I then introduce everyone again. Alex shook Maria's hand and greeted each of the boys.

"Sit down," he said.

I motioned for the two boys to sit on the floor and Maria, and I sat on the couch. At first, the subject of the conversation went about the same as it did with my aunt and parents. Then after we talked about Sandy, I said, "How's Allen doing?"

"He finished his military schooling and just shipped out," said Alex.

"Where did he go?"

"Europe," both Evana and Alex said.

"He will be in my command; do you know where in Europe?"

"He said it is classified; he couldn't talk about it," said Alex seriously.

"Classified that don't make sense, what kind of military schooling did he have."

"Something to do with accounting, I think," Alex replied.

"Well, I'll find out when I get back."

"Maybe he can live with us that would be nice," Maria said.

"No others would think he was getting favoritism, and there would be trouble for him." "However, I feel it would be alright to have him over for a visit and dinner." I turned back to Alex and Evana and said, "I don't think it would be wise to mention that we are related." "I sure hope he doesn't say anything."

"Why are you embarrassed by him," asked Evana concern.

I could see that Alex was irritated, and I said, "Of course not, I wouldn't have gone through all the trouble to get him in the Army if I was." "The problem is the same as before if he is promoted or gets a good assignment, which I'm sure he will, many will think it was because of me and not because of his merit." "I won't be in Europe for the rest of my life." "I either will quit the Army or get transferred, and God knows what will happen with the next commander, Allen gets." "I'm not saying I won't help him I will as time goes on, but I don't want anyone knowing what I am doing including him he needs to know he is doing it all by himself." "I hope you understand how I feel?"

The irritation on Alex's face had disappeared. He said, resigned to the truthfulness at what I said, "Well, you do what you think is best, but I have to tell you I think Allen might talk about you."

"If that happens, I'll figure something out to deal with it." We talked for another hour. Some time while we visited, Evana brought out coffee and tea and some sweets. Then we finally left to say goodbye to my parents.

"Well, how is my sister?" asked my mother.

"She's okay; I see you two are fighting again."

"I don't know why she thinks I said or did something bad to my mother."

"Well, I can tell you what I think."

"And what's that?" asked my father.

"I think Ed and Julia are putting things into Wella's head." "Those things may be true, and she is misinterpreting what is said, but most likely they are lies, and then Wella tells Aunt Dorothy who assumes they are true, not knowing what's going on."

"So, what do you think we should do about it?" asked my mother.

"If you think I'm correct, you have to take a risk." "As soon as you and Aunt Dorothy are talking, you need to confront the situation again." "You need to tell her what you think is going on." "She may get mad and start fighting with you again; I just don't know." "If she disagrees with you, you can ask her what she thinks the problem is and then deny it if you didn't do it but be prepared to tell why it's not true." "Just to say it isn't true isn't good enough; she won't believe that."

"Why do you think Ed and Julia are doing that?" asked my father.

"Well, I think they know my grandmother is old, and they are eyeing the things she has." "They want them for themselves and not for you and Aunt Dorothy." "They especially don't want any grandchildren getting anything, and you know she said I could have the china cabinet and everything in it." "I guest Julia thinks because she is the sister that it belongs to her."

"James, why you no call her aunt?" Maria asked.

"She has done things and said things to me that I don't like." "I am very uncomfortable around her and her husband."

"You mark my word if something happens to my grandmother; she will take everything she wants out of that house," I said to everyone.

We finally left for the motel after saying our goodbyes. The next morning as I drove to the airport, my thoughts were, I wished I could have visited my best friend Charles Kahler, but I just didn't have the time and my brother David and Jerry who weren't around. As we few, I was motivating the boys and Maria about visiting Disneyland getting Frederick and Jonathan singing the Mickey Mouse song. About forty-five minutes later, we departed from the plane at LAX airport, and the boys and Maria were all excited. We hailed a cab, and I said, "Take us to the Disneyland Hotel."

"Say, aren't you that Army hero guy from Europe?" asked the cab driver.

"I don't think I'm a hero, but I was over there." I was getting many stares wherever I went. At first, it was uncomfortable for my family, but they were getting used to it. The only rest from it was the time we spent at our place in Missouri.

The boys were wide-eyed and excited when we got to the hotel. I believed that Maria was also but didn't show it as the boys had. We were given the penthouse on the eleventh floor. As we entered the room, the boys ran to the windows wooing and awing the park's sights.

Then Jonathan said, "Daddy, let's go now to Disneyland."

"Ja Daddy, we go," repeated Frederick.

I looked over at Maria and said, "Are you ready to go into the park?"

"Ja, we go now," she said with a smile.

"Daddy, we drive to get inside?" asked Frederick.

"No, we are going to take a special train."

"Special train?" Maria asked.

"You will see."

The boys were thrilled with the Monorail, but Maria was uneasy about riding in it until we started to move. What happened next, I didn't expect. We had gone on a ride that thrilled everyone, and Jonathan asked, "Are all the rides free to ride on, daddy?"

"Yes, as many times as you wish." At that, Maria and I looked at different things in the various shops when the boys disappeared.

Maria and I went into panic mode, and we started looking. At first, I was angry with them for wandering off, but quickly that anger changed when Maria said in German worried, "Do you think someone kidnapped them?"

I thought about that for a second then said, "If it were one of the boys that could have been a possibility, but since it is both boys, I think they got impatient and went to find some rides to try."

We searched for almost an hour when Maria said, "Maybe we should contact the authorities."

"I'm beginning to think your right, but let's check one more area first before we do that."

We went over to Tomorrow Land, and by luck, we spotted the boys getting out of a speedboat attraction. Worry changed to anger, and the boys saw us. With smiles and squeals, they came running over to us, and Frederick said all excited, "Mama, daddy, we went on boat ride twice and flew up and down in an Elephant."

"Yeah, we also went twice on a car ride, you got to try it," Jonathan added excitedly.

I looked at Maria, the anger was off her face, then I took the boys in hand, and we all went over to a table with four chairs. "Now, boys, what did you do wrong?"

"We took off by ourselves without you," said Jonathan uneasy, as he answered, Frederick, held his head low.

"Yes, Jonathan and you both worried your mother and me."

"I'm sorry," said Jonathan.

"Me too," Frederick added.

"You boys could have gotten kidnapped, so let's not run off like that again, alright." They both nodded yes, and we were off riding the same rides they had just rode at their insistence. It wasn't long before the night events were catching up with all of us, so we went back to the hotel, ate, and then retired to our room for the night, and soon, the boys were sound asleep as were we.

The next day I made reservations in San Diego that had a heliport. I arranged for a military copter to meet me there the day I was supposed to be at Pendleton. I had arranged for a tour guide to take my family around when I went to the base. When I got back to the room, the boys were bathed and dressed and were anxious to go back to the park. "We'll eat breakfast first, then we can go," I said.

"But daddy, we eat at Disneyland," said Frederick pleading.

"Disneyland isn't going anywhere; we can go after breakfast." We ate, and we tried to get the boys to slow down, but they were anxious to get back inside the park, so we were on a ride before our food had time to settle. The day went very well. The boys were excited about all the rides they went on. It was cute to see how Frederick reacted to the Disney costume caricatures that roam the park. It was as though, they might be real, but he just wasn't quite sure. Jonathan pretended he was too old for the caricatures, but I also detected his fascination with them. Of course, Maria was fascinated with everything and was having the time of her life. We took a ride to the ocean and Maria, and I walked along the beach while the boys played chicken with the waves and of course, they got wet.

We also spent a short time at Knott's Berry Park. The boys had fun, as did Maria and me, but they wanted to get back to Disneyland. The day came when we had to be going to San Diego, it was rough the boys wanted to stay, but I told them they would have fun at the next place, and we packed up and went to the airport. I thought we were going by jet, but we went by a prop type plane. The plane wasn't pressurized, and my ears were feeling it, and when I looked down, I saw a crack in the floor, and it looked like you could see the sky through it. Maria and the boys didn't seem to be having any trouble with the flight. They also didn't notice the cracks on the floor. The trip took about twenty minutes, and I was sure glad when we landed. It took me a few minutes for me to recuperate from the flight. We got our things and hailed a cab then went to the hotel. I had told Maria and the boys I wouldn't be able to be with them when they went to the San Diego Zoo and Sea World, but a tour guide would be taking care of them. They were disappointed but understood and, in an hour, after we had gotten to the hotel a young lady who spoke German came, she was their tour guide. We all agreed about ten the next morning the tour guide would come and take Maria and the boys to the zoo first then the next day to Sea World. The following day, at nine-thirty in the morning a Marine helicopter landed on the pad at the hotel two Marines came and got me then Maria, and the boys saw me off. It bothered me that I couldn't spend the day with Maria and the boys, but I knew they would be taken care of and fun.

When the copter landed at Pendleton, I got greeted by General Arnold, a Marine general by the name James Amos, the people from helicopters and missile companies and others. "Have you and your family been having a good time, James?" asked General Arnold."

"Yes, up until yesterday, Sir."

"What do you mean by that?"

"My family is having a great time, but on the flight from Los Angeles to San Diego and the fight here, my ears started hurting horribly."

"How do you feel now?"

"I'm alright."

"After we see the new equipment, I will take you to see the doctor."

"Yes, Sir." I didn't even try to argue with the General I was dreading the trip back to the hotel and perhaps medical could do something.

We went to the firing range, and they had a different missile system from what we talked about in Washington. It wasn't much different from the Hawk missiles we already had. "What the hell is this?" "This missile system is nothing that we discussed in Washington, and it won't work?" I growled.

"Now calm down James, this system is cheaper, and some think what you are asking is just not needed."

"Bull shit, I was there; they weren't this system is worthless." "This demonstration is a total waste of my time; you'll have my resignation tomorrow."

At that, I got up and started to walk off, and General Amos said, "What about the helicopters?"

"With this system, we don't need them that will make whoever came up with this stupid idea happy they will save a lot more money and lose a lot more lives." Everyone was shocked at my anger, chiefly the civilians representing the various companies.

"Wait a minute, James," said General Arnold. "Are you going to give up your career over this?"

"Career, you know damn well that I couldn't give a shit about my career or being a General." "All I care about is the men, and I'm telling you this system will kill them, or don't you believe me again."

"No, I believe you, but this comes from the White House."

"Then I would tell the White House there are a lot of people who like me and would listen to what I have to say." "Tell them also if they want their party back in the White House and Congress, they better do what's right, or I will talk to a lot of citizens of this country." At that, I walked away, caught a cab back to my hotel in San Diego.

I was fuming with anger as I left, and it was no different when I was back at the hotel. Maria and the boys were still gone, so I went to a nearby bar and had a few drinks. Afterward, I went back to the hotel, and I laid down and took a nap. I got awoken when Maria and the boys came back from their day out. "James, I'm surprised you're back so soon."

"We need to talk about something that happened, and you need to know about it." The boys knew something was up and didn't interfere even though they wanted to tell me about their day. A concern, Maria, the boys and I went out to dinner somewhere where I could talk without any eavesdroppers around me.

"What is it, James, what has gone wrong?" Maria asked.

I told them the whole story of what happened then said, "I told them I'd give them my paperwork to resign from the Military tomorrow."

"Are you sure this is what you want?"

"I don't need the hassle, and we have more than enough money."

Frederick and Jonathan were whispering to each other, then Frederick said, "I quit Army too, daddy."

"You don't have to, Frederick," I said.

"You no army man, daddy, then I no army man."

The rest of the dinner went by quietly with an air of dread was over everyone, and we headed back to the hotel room feeling the same way. As we walked through the lobby, there was General Arnold and Amos, and there was a senator from California that I recognized. I said, "You people come to get my resignation," I said, not pleasant.

"No, James, this is Senator Alan Cranston." "We've come to talk to you," said General Arnold.

"I know the senator, and if you are here to try to change my mind, you're wasting your time I won't compromise, not on this."

"General you've won, we all talked to the president, and he has agreed to give you what you want," said Senator Cranston.

I looked at Maria and the boys and said, "Maria, would you and the boys go upstairs to our room."

"Yes."

Maria and the boys left, and I directed everyone to a part of the hotel where we could have some privacy. We all sat down, and I said, "Alright, gentlemen, let me hear it."

"As Senator Cranston said the missile system you want, and the helicopters are what you will get," said General Arnold. "The missile system and helicopters are at Pendleton just in case something like this happened."

"We can demonstrate everything tomorrow," said General Amos.

I stared at them then suspiciously and said, "Alright, send a car for me tomorrow, not a helicopter I still have an ear problem." "I must warn you if this turns out to be a ruse to keep me in the Army, I will quit on the spot and do as I threaten to do." "Senator off the record, what is the real reason for the president to agree to what I wanted?"

"Off the record, uh, well, okay, I'll tell you, the President is of the same party as I am with the pressure from the military and his party, he caved in." "Besides, he knows that the people of this country admire you a lot, and you can get most of the people on your side."

I looked at General Arnold and said, "Have a car here at seven in the morning."

"Yes, I will do that, and before you see the demonstration, I will take you to sick call."

"Very well, gentlemen, I wish to be with my wife and boys; I will see you tomorrow." At that, they all left, and I went upstairs to my family. I told Maria everything that happened and said, "I think they are afraid I could get the people not to vote for them."

"So, you are going to stay in the army?" Maria asked.

"Yes, for now."

"Good."

"Oh, you like a man in uniform, uh." "What about you, Frederick, are you going to stay in the army too?"

"If you want me," he answered, not convinced he should.

"It is not what I want; it is what you want."

"I think maybe I stay, but I won't be in the army as much as before."

"That's okay; it is your choice." I changed the subject and said, "Let me hear about your day." Frederick talked excitedly about the dancing bear, and Jonathan talked about the snakes for which Maria wasn't too fond of seeing. She liked the birds, especially the flamingos and the butterfly building. I explained to Maria and the boys what to expect tomorrow at Sea World and the boys were excited about going there.

We all got to bed at a reasonable time, and the next morning I got my wake-up call at five. Maria started to get up, but I stopped her and told her to rest. I got ready and went downstairs to get something to eat and to wait for my ride. At five minutes to seven, my driver showed up. The driver tried to talk to me while he drove, but I never spoke. When we got to the base, we drove up to a building, and the driver said, "Wait here, Sir General Arnold will join you."

I nodded, and he went into the building about five minutes later, he came out with General Arnold, who sat in the back seat with me. "I'm taking you to sick call first." I nodded, and he stared at me and said, "Are you mad at me, James?"

In a slow trance-like state and bewilder, I said, "No, why would you say something like that, I was just in deep thought."

"I thought you were mad at me about yesterday morning."

"I know it wasn't your fault; it was those damn politicians."

"Were you going to quit?"

"Yes."

"That would have been a great loss."

We drove up to a large white building. General Arnold told the driver to wait. A navy nurse approached us, I told her what the problem was, and I immediately saw her. She examined my ears then flushed them out with some warm liquid, which made me nauseous. Then she swabbed the ears with an antibiotic, gave me a shot and some pills and said I had an ear infection. Her diagnosis seemed apparent to me, so I asked, "You think I can fly back to Europe tomorrow?"

"You should wait for three or four days, but if you have to fly, I think you will be alright, but I can't guarantee you won't have some trouble."

"Alright." I got up and left, and I met General Arnold.

"You alright?"

"I have an ear infection." Everybody who was at the site yesterday was there today, plus others I figured were from Congress. This time they had the right missile. There were also the two types of helicopters that I was going to get. The plan was the men from the missile company to get in the helicopter, fly over the ocean, and then land on the beach. They would set up and shoot a target in the air two miles away over the ocean and a second target towed by a boat that would be about two miles away.

The demonstration went off flawless, and I was impressed at how quickly those men from the missile company could get out of the helicopter, set up and fire hitting their target. Then it was time for the men from the helicopter company to show their stuff, and it was terrific. Two smaller attack helicopters took off like a bat out of hell with cannon fire, machine guns, and missiles; they blew up some targets further down the beach. They then flew over the ocean and blew up a target that got towed in the sky. The larger helicopter took off with men and equipment few out over the ocean, then came in and landed the men in the helicopter, jumped out and unloaded the equipment out of the helicopter. When the show was finish, I first walked towards where the missile system and talked to the men representing the company. "How often have you missed the target while operating this system?"

"We have never missed," said one of the men.

"How many times have you operated this system, and how many years training have you had on it?"

"I've operated it about a dozen times, and I had a month training on it."

As I was talking to those men, the executive from the company came over to me. He said, "So what do you think of the system?"

"It appears to be just what the doctor ordered." "When can you deliver the system?"

"Some next week, the rest will be delivered in about two or three weeks."

"Can you spare some of your men to train my men on the system?"

"Of course, they will come with the system." "We will make sure your men are well trained."

I then went over to the helicopters and talked with the men operating the equipment and the company executives. General Arnold joined me there, and I asked the executives, "Is that larger helicopter capable of carrying a Jeep?" I asked.

"Yes, with room to spare."

"Good because the Jeep is getting replaced also," said General Arnold.

"How is it loaded?" I asked.

"Show the General how a vehicle gets loaded," the executive said to one of his men.

The copter's nose rose, a ramp came down, and I said, "Fantastic." "When can you send the helicopters, and will you send someone to train my men?"

"I can start delivery in about three weeks on both helicopters, and there will be men to train your men." "What did you think of the attack helicopter?" the executive asked.

"It was outstanding," I replied, and General Arnold confirmed.

Then General Arnold said, "If you finished inspecting the equipment, let's go get some coffee."

I smiled and said, "That sounds good, but I will have some tea instead of coffee if you don't mind."

"That will be just fine."

I got a diver to take me back to the hotel, and again I got there before Maria and the boys. When everyone came back from their outing, Maria asked me, "Was everything good?"

"If you're talking about the Army, everything went fine the way it was supposed to be." "If you're talking about my health, the doctor said I have an ear infection."

"Can you fly on an airplane?"

"I must we will leave for Germany tomorrow."

The next day we lingered around the hotel and had breakfast then did a little shopping that Maria enjoyed. However, the boys weren't very thrilled about doing. The boys retold me about all they saw at the zoo and at Sea World and in the afternoon, we went to the airport we got on the jet after a short wait. As we sat waiting for the plane to get filled up and move out, I had anxiety about what was going to happen to my ear.

26

REFORMING THE EUROPEAN COMMAND

ortunately, the jet got pressurized, so although I felt a little discomfort, it was mild nothing like before, and I slept through part of it. We got into Rhein-Main airport after a little more than eleven hours, and we were all tired. I drove the car while the boys slept until we reached Würzburg, we stopped to get something to eat, especially some tea for me so that I could stay awake. "We will be home in about an hour, and then I want you boys to go right to bed and get some sleep," Maria said. The boys were tired and didn't give their mother any trouble, and after about forty-five minutes, we left again for home.

We finally got home, and I said to the boys, "You two get to bed."

"I'll help you," Maria said.

"No, it's alright your tired too just make sure the boys get to bed." In no time, I had everything in the house. The boys were undressed and fast asleep, sleeping together, of course. I was also tired, so I decided to get a few hours' sleep myself. As I went into my room to get ready to go to bed, I saw Maria had the same idea, and soon we were both asleep. I had set the alarm clock so that it would wake me in four hours, but Maria woke me.

"You didn't have to wake me." "I had set the alarm clock," I told Maria.

"Yes, I know it went off a half-hour ago." I showered and got into my dress greens and headed for my office.

"Nice to have you back, Sir," said a clerk.

"Well, thank you." I got a lot of that as I walked upstairs and down the hall to my office. When I got to the office, I said to my aid that was there,

"Schedule a meeting with Colonel Ralph Upton for eleven hundred hours. Also, schedule a meeting all the company commanders for tomorrow at eleven hundred hours." "I want to also have another meeting with my general staff here the next day at the same hour."

"Yes, Sir." "Most of your general staff have moved down here."

I worked on the paperwork that had piled up on my desk for about two hours and then walked down to one of the mess halls to get something to eat. "Officer in the building," shouted someone.

"You were gone so long I thought you might have quit, Sir," Top said from a table from the back of the mess hall.

I sat down with him and said, "I almost did quit."

"Are you just tired of it all, or did you have trouble with the new system?"

"Politicians tried to pull something that would have cost a lot of lives." "I'm having a staff meeting tomorrow at eleven." "I want you to be there, and you will hear the whole story."

"I'll do that, Sir."

"How is the battalion doing?"

"Confused at what you are planning, but otherwise, they're fine."

"How are your wife and children," I asked Top."

"They are doing well." "Sir, I need to tell you something?" I swung my head around I knew whatever he had to say wasn't going to be good. "About a year to eighteen months, I will have my thirty in, and I'm retiring I'm just getting too old for this."

I was silent for a few seconds and then said, "I can't say I blame you, and I won't try to change your mind." "To tell you the truth, even though I have fewer years in than you do, I feel the same, so I don't know how much more time I'll stay." "Where are you going to move to?"

"North Carolina, I have a place there, it's a good place to raise kids."

"Have you told your wife and kids yet?"

"My wife, yes, my kids no."

"Do me a favor, don't tell them just yet I want to break the news to Frederick and Jonathan they are going to be upset." "And remember Top North Carolina isn't that far from Southern Missouri."

"And Southern Missouri isn't far from North Carolina either, Sir."

I smiled and said, "Maybe when we are both retired, you will stop calling me, Sir."

"Not a chance, Sir."

We got to the site where everyone was at a large field behind the hanger. Many of the men from Charlie came over to Top and me, and there were also men from Alpha, Bravo, and even the new men from Delta too; Captain Dizon said, "Good to see you, Sir."

"That's very kind of you, Marc." "I hear there is confusion as to what is going to happen with the battalion."

"Yes, Sir, some."

"Everyone will know tomorrow after the staff meeting in the morning." There was some more small talk then Top, and I went back to the brigade headquarters.

"I'm going home why don't you and your family come over to my house after dinner, and we'll talk about the trip."

"You sure Maria and the boys aren't going to be too tired for company, Sir?"

"No, Maria and the kids would be thrilled." I let Maria know about Top and his family coming, and she was pleased. We had a pleasant visit with Top and his family, and I told them about the non-military things like our stay with the queen and our property.

The next day I was in my office, and I was putting my notes together when Top walked in with a cup of coffee. "Good morning, Sir."

"Good morning, Top."

"Want me to make you some tea or chocolate."

"That would be nice of you Top there are some of those special chocolate chip cookies in the box help yourself."

"I think I will, Sir, thanks."

"No need to thank me you can raid the box any time you want.

"There is something I've meant to talk to you about, Sir."

"Go ahead."

"Ever since you made me a command sergeant major and placed me under your command, I haven't had anything to do."

"I'm aware of that."

"Perhaps I should ask for a transfer back to the states since I'm going to retire anyway."

I stared at Top for several seconds, which made him uncomfortable, and then I asked, "Why do you think I want you at that meeting?"

"I don't know, Sir."

""What's going to happen to this battalion you will be the one directing it to make sure things go the way I want them to go." "Also, you will be training your replacement before you go." "You are going to be busy, and I can't let you go back to the states yet."

"Yes, Sir."

"There is something else I'm going to promote you."

"Sir, we had this conversation before I can't get promoted any higher unless you promote me to be an officer." "I don't want to be an officer, Sir."

I stared at Top again for a few seconds then said, "You know Top how you won't stop calling me Sir even though I have asked you not to, you said that is the way it works in the Army, and you are right." "Well, I'm a general, and you know better to question a general." "I'm promoting you to warrant, and you have no choice in this matter; besides, you'll get more money for your retirement."

"Yes, Sir."

I looked for a second at Top and said, "I hope you're not mad at me." "I consider you a close friend first, and a man in my command last."

"No, Sir."

We talked about several subjects, and then when it was time to go to the conference room, I went with all my notes and a blank tablet. I had Top to the right of me, and Colonel Upton to the left the company commanders. Their executive officers surrounded the rest of the conference table. "Gentlemen, what I am going to talk about today and show you is confidential I don't want it talked about outside this room at least not for now." "The wisdom in Washington wanted to give us almost the same missile system as the Hawk, and the helicopter was going to stay the same." "When they announced this to me, I told them I was resigning my position in the Army." "To make a long story short, they quickly changed their minds and gave me everything I wanted." I had a bulletin board behind me, and I placed a large picture of the new missile system behind me and then passed around a smaller version of the same picture. "As you can see that this missile system is more mobile than the old Hawks." "This new missile system can be hidden easier, it's faster, and it's more accurate than the old Hawk missile system." "Also, fewer men are needed to operate it, and it can be used ground to ground or ground to air, and missiles can get replaced much quicker than the Hawk." "Any questions?"

"Sir, how are we going to be trained with this system." "Also, how is the system going to be deployed?" asked the Delta executive officer.

"Upon delivery, there will be twelve trainers, three per company to train the men on the missile, radar, and maintenance." "Everything is scheduled to happen by the end of next week." "As far as deployment, I will speak on that later in this meeting."

"Sir, if it will take fewer men to operate this system, what are we going to do with the rest of the men?" asked Captain Dizon.

"Each missile system will have its primary operators with two backups, and any left-over men will get retrained for support."

I placed the two pictures of the types of helicopters that were coming on the board and passed around smaller versions with written details of each. "These are the helicopters that will be coming to this battalion and throughout the European command." "As you can see, they are more powerful and effective than anything the Russians have, or anybody else has." "We will be getting a fleet of over twenty helicopters to start." "We should get everything within two weeks, and there will be trainers coming with helicopters." "Are there any questions?"

"Sir, why all the helicopters?" asked Captain McMullen.

"I'm glad you asked, it will lead me to the next part of this meeting." "No longer will there be four separated companies, but there will be four teams." "There will also not be any specific missile sites." "Teams will be transported out into the field with the transport helicopters back by the attack helicopter to random sites throughout the western front." "Support departments must change their way of supplying the men in the field, and you will learn what these changes will be later." "Are there any questions so far?"

"Are you saying that each team is going to use the same equipment when they get rotated?" asked Colonel Upton.

"Yes, if this missile system were the old Hawk system, it wouldn't hold up long, but this new system will make it possible for this type of deployment." "This type of deployment is designed to make it almost impossible to destroy because of its mobility and accuracy, unlike the Hawk system, as we saw in the last conflict." "I have considered the men who will be out on the field; it will not be easy for them, especially in the winter." "Because of this, the men who must be in the field operating this system will be specially trained." "I am bringing in special forces from Israel, France, England, and the United States to train them."

"Sir, you expect our men to become Special Forces?" "I don't know if that is possible," said Captain Tom Riggs.

"No, but maybe halfway in between what they will learn will help them when they are out in the field." "Remember also that in the beginning, not all will get trained in the field." "The support department will continue almost just the way they are except for how they will deliver their support."

"I feel the whole battalion should have this special training," said Colonel Upton.

"I would agree with you, but I know there are some who won't do well, and I don't want you to get rid of them." "However, as the men rotate out of the unit, other men will get replaced with more qualified personnel." "Eventually, this unit will be specialized." "I meet with my general staff and General Abrams tomorrow, and I will bring this up." "Other than those who must be in the field anyone in the battalion that wants to go do the training, you can allow it."

"Yes, Sir, when do you want to assemble the battalion?"

"How about fifteen hundred hours tomorrow and make sure everyone is there, including the cooks."

"Yes, Sir," said Colonel Upton.

"Top your job will be to separate the wheat from the chaff, choose those who have a possibility of going through this physical training, and make recommendations for new departments for those who can't." "You're also to train a person for your replacement." "I have now promoted you to a CW5." I could see the disapproval on his face, and I said, "Top you deserve it, don't let it bother you; it's only going to be painful until you retire." "Before the special forces personnel come, I want you to evaluate those who aren't necessary for the field but want the training whether they can complete the training."

"Yes, Sir," Top said without commit."

"Are we still friends, Jack?"

Top smiled and said, "Of course, Sir." When I got back to my office, I called the various governments to use their special forces. All governments agreed, and the personnel was to arrive next week. After I finished, I found Colonel Upton and informed him of the Special Forces coming and to find housing for them.

I had a great night with my family and was at work the next day early. I had planned to briefly describe what was going on with the Third of the Seventh, talk about the specialized training the men will need, and then hit the rest of the European command.

I was heading to the conference room when I met General Abrams in the hallway. "James, after the meeting, I want to see you privately."

"Alright, Sir." I knew that what he wanted to talk to me had nothing to do with the transformation of the European command. So, I was utterly baffled at what he wanted to speak to me about this time.

After formalities, I told them what I wanted to do with the missile units, which they were impressed. I said, "During the conflict, I had the opportunity to see how our tank battalions functioned." "I was impressed by what I saw; however, I'm not that versed in the operations of a tank battalion." "General Brown, about two weeks from today, we will inspect the tank units if you and your staff have any ideas about how to improve these units, I will hear them then."

"Yes, Sir."

"I have an issue with the heavy artillery units." "I remember reading and seeing movies how the United States Military made a big mistake on the Hawaiian Islands during World War Two." "They bunched up all the planes the Army Air Core had, and it was the same with the Navy with their ships." "We all know what happened, and the same thing happened to our heavy artillery." "They were all bunched up together, which made it an easy target for the enemy planes and missiles."

"What would you suggest, James?" asked General Abrams.

"We need to spread them out and camouflage them."

"We don't have the room, and I don't believe the German government will give us anymore," said General Brown.

"We have the four missile sites where the Hawk missiles were." "I'm not convinced the German government won't loan us more land."

"General Westboro heavy artillery is your field of expertise do you have anything to say?" asked General Abrams.

"Well, what General York said is true the equipment got bunched too close together, and it was the cause of losing so much equipment."

"How much of the field artillery can get stored at the abandoned missile bases?"

"With just the four abandon missile bases about sixty percent."

General Abrams looked at me, and I knew what he wanted. I said, "General, you know that there is another Hawk battalion other than the Third of the Seventh." "Eventually, what's happening to the Third of the Seventh will happen to the other battalion."

"When will that happen, James?"

"It will start to happen next week with the other battalion."

"What do you mean by start to happen?"

"As I told you, the special forces units will be here next week." "Representatives from each unit in the other battalion will be here to see the new missile system and the training required." "Once the training is over, the other battalion will be converted over to the new missile system."

"Are you saying that the men in that other battalion will be training with this unit?"

"No, I don't know how I will work it yet." "I will send the Special Forces over to that battalion, or I will send them home except for maybe one or two of them from each country." "Then the other battalion will be trained with by Third of the Seventh."

"Well, it sounds like a plan to me," said General Abrams.

"Thank you, Sir, I want to now talk about the infantry." "The infantry here in Europe is weak, lazy, indifferent, and unprepared to enter another fight." "It's as if they came to Europe not to do a job, but to go on vacation doing only the minimum to get by this is got to end."

"Do you think it's that bad, James? General Abrams asked.

I shuffled through some papers then said, "According to the reports I have received nearly three thousand infantrymen were either killed or wounded." "General too many GI's found out the hard way that they should have taken their training more seriously." "I found it out in Vietnam, and they need to find it out here before it's too late again."

"Do you think there will be another conflict, James?"

"Here in Europe, there will be small conflicts that the United States will be involved in but not to the scale as what just happened, and around the world, there will be major and minor conflicts."

"Ok, what do you plan to do with the infantry." "Are you going to do the same as the Third of the Seventh?" asked General Abrams.

"No, their mission in a conflict is different than this battalion. I plan to first clean up each unit from the bottom on up of any drug or alcohol problem." "Then I think some of that advance infantry training with P.T. should get them in shape."

"Alright, go ahead with your plan."

"I'll start tomorrow, Sir."

General Abrams thought for a second and said, "We will talk about when you will start after this meeting."

"Well, unless anyone has anything else to say or add, this meeting is finished." No one said anything, and everyone left except General Abrams and me.

"James, let's go to your office."

"Alright."

I was confused about what this was all about, and I even got more confused when we passed my head secretary. The General said, "No visitors no calls unless it is an emergency."

"Yes, Sir."

General Abrams pointed for me to sit on the easy chair, which I did, and he sat on the couch. "James, how do you feel?"

"I feel just fine, Sir."

"I mean your wounds from Vietnam, and are you still having those flashbacks?"

"On occasion, a sliver comes up under my skin." "The last was several months ago." "I may have a flashback once or twice a year, but not like I use to." "What's this all about, General?"

"Do you remember a person by the name of Kien in Vietnam?"

"Yes, Colonel Kien," I said cautiously.

"He's a general now, and we would like you to see him for several reasons, including missing MIAs." I just stared at him as he talked.

"By we, I would guess General Arnold has something to do with this?" "What would he want to see me about?"

"Yes, this does come from him and others; we are not sure what he wants."

"What does he know about me?"

"I would guess everything." "I'm assuming because of your fame; the Vietnamese know a whole lot about you."

"Will you let me do it my way?"

"Yes."

"He won't give up anything unless we give him something."

"Yes, we know that."

"Will you let me decide what to give him?"

This time he studied me, then he said, "Yes, within reason."

"Alright, I'll do it."

"Do you know how to speak French or Vietnamese?"

"No, but I know someone who does?"

"We want to keep this confidential."

"I understand, the person I'm thinking of is reliable."

"Good, go to the Vietnamese embassy in France as soon as you can get away." He then handed me a piece of paper and said, "These are the things we want, memorize the paper, and then destroy it."

"Yes, Sir."

"You pull this off, and it will be huge for you, hell you might even get my job." He got up, as did I, and he said, "I have to go, good luck."

"Yes, Sir," I said, thinking of how I was going to pull this off. That night I made some excuse to Maria, went back to my office and called the Disney Corporation. I was able to talk to Donn Tatum, who ran Disney. "Sir, do you know who I am."

"Everybody knows who you are General, what can I do for you?"

"What I'm going to ask is confidential."

"Yes, what is it?"

"The Disney studios made a movie a long time ago called "A Light In The Forest," do you remember that movie?"

"Yes, of course."

"I need a sixteen-millimeter version of that movie dubbed in Vietnamese and maybe a quality cartoon also. For now, I can't tell you why, but it is important for our nation." "I will pay for whatever it costs, and it needs to get done as quickly as possible."

"I will do it, and it won't cost you anything." "It will get done in about three to four weeks, and I will ship it to you." "The only thing I ask is to let me know what this is all about when you can."

"I will do that, Sir." "Unnoticeably, this needs to get done because it is in the national interest."

"No one will know." I gave him the address to ship it and how to mark the package, and then I went home.

The following week the special forces from the various countries started to show up. Once they were all present and settled in, I had a meeting with them in one of the mess halls. I had with me Colonel Upton, Top, Sergeant Acer, and I told the men what I wanted, "I don't expect these men to be as well train as you are, but what I wish is to give them skills for them to survive in the field." "I wish you all to discuss what you all think they need to know and can do." "I know each of you has your specialty that you can give them the edge in a difficult situation." "Write up a plan, but remember these are not men who have the capability as you, so be patient and go as easy as you can." "Colonel, Top, Sergeant Acer, do you have anything to add." All three of them said a few words, and then I asked, "Are there any questions from any of you?"

"Sir, who will be over us during this training?" said an officer from Great Briton.

"You answer to me, General Brown, Colonel Upton, I ask you to listen to Mr. Bennett and Sergeant Acer." "All other officers treat them as they are due, but they are not over you."

"Is it my understanding that when we get finished with the training, you want some of us to stay to train some more personnel?" said a man from the French Foreign Legion.

"There are two missiles battalions when you get finished with this battalion; the men of this battalion will train the other battalion." "What I wish is one or two men from each of your countries to stay behind as advisors to keep the training on track."

"We will need to know the mission of this unit and the type of equipment involved, Sir, in customizing the training," said a lieutenant from the Green Berets.

"Colonel Upton, as well as Mr. Bennett, and Sergeant Acer will give you that information."

"Sir, you're a special force officer why do you need one of us to keep these men on track once they get trained?" said a Sergeant in the Green Berets.

"I'm very busy with other demands of other units."

"General, as you know that where we operate is very different." "Do you want us to train these men for all conditions around the world or just Europe," ask the Lieutenant from Israel.

"I feel they should get trained in all areas." "Gentlemen understand you will get the mission of this battalion and know what kind of equipment will be in use, but the details of how things work are classified." "I would assume that NATO would inform the various countries anyway sooner or later." No one asked any more questions, and I left with them getting organized and deciding on how to proceed with the training. Top and Acer weeded out the weaker men. Then replaced them with others who were more suitable to the demands of the military training. The following week the new missile system came in all wrapped up, and I could see it would have to get assembled. Two days later, the new helicopters arrived the same way. I had Colonel Upton have his men, and those that came with the equipment put everything together. The Special Forces wrote a plan and trained the men who were going to be operating the missile equipment. General Brown and I visited infantry units, and after having meetings with the battalion commanders, I instituted my plan for reforming those units. After spending a few days back in Schweinfurt, General Westboro and I went to the heavy artillery battalions. In most places, we found areas to spread the artillery out, and those who didn't have or lacked a significant amount of camouflage got told to order them. When I got back to Schweinfurt for a few days, I checked how the combat survival training was going. Also, how the equipment set up and training was progressing, and everything was going smoothly except for a few changes. I called General Brown and said, "Don all the units we didn't hit; I want you to look at them take whoever you wish with you." "Leave the supply depots to me." "I want to light a fire under them."

"What about the MCC?"

"MCC, you are going to have to tell me what that is."

"Missile Control Center it's located near a small town called Bad Mergentheim." "The barracks for the control center is in that town."

"I'll go to this MCC myself give me the instructions on how to get there." In the next few days, I hit every supply depot that we had. I went in disguise by dressing as a specialist four, so I could see for myself what was going on. When I found something, I gave them hell; then, everything started to quickly move out of those depots.

A few days after shaking up the supply depots, I was home with Maria and the boys. I said, "Maria, I'm going to a town called Bad Mergentheim; have you ever heard of it?"

"Yes, it is a health resort, I believe."

"There is an American base there." "I will visit there for a few days."

"We miss you; will be last place you be away from us?" Maria asked.

"I'm afraid not in the weeks to come I have a few more trips I have to take."

"We will manage I have strong men to help."

I looked over at the boys and said, "I see you do." I traveled alone to Bad Mergentheim using the instructions that General Brown gave me. I passed a lot of beautiful farmland and forest as I was driving, I passed an installation which I assume was the MCC. About twenty minutes later, I came to the town of Bad Mergentheim. Bad Mergentheim looked like a place that someone who never had been to Germany would think a German town should resemble. I checked into a small older hotel in the middle of the village. My room was clean with a bath that overlooked the street below. After settling in, I asked the old woman who owned the place, "Do you know where there is a good place to eat?"

"There is a good place right down the street not far from here."

"Can I walk to it?"

"Oh, yes, it's not far?"

"Thank you."

The old woman sent me to a quaint little restaurant that the locals frequented, and the food was excellent. After I finished eating, I walked back to the hotel. It was about six o'clock at night, so instead of going back to my room, I decided to go to the American barracks to see if I could catch them off guard. The barracks was located up a hill just out of the town next to a German Panzer installation. I drove up towards the building; there was a German guard at the Panzer installation entrance. I went to talk to the German guard there first. When he looked into the car, he snapped to attention because he recognized me right away.

"What can I do for you, Sir?"

"I wish to ask you about the American soldiers."

"What do you wish to know?"

"What do you know about them?"

"We have orders not to go out of our way to associate with them."

"However, they have come up to us on occasion and asked to buy penicillin pills that are issued to us."

"These pills, I would assume for protection from venereal disease."

"That is what we use them for."

"Why do you think you were ordered not to associate with them?"

"To get the real reason, you would have to talk to our post commander."

"If you ask me, I would guess the Americans are very unruly, and they tend to get into trouble a lot."

"Thank you; you have been helpful."

I went to the American barracks I didn't try to hide the car I parked right in front of the building and went in. To my left was what looked like a dayroom with a few men in it. On a couch next to the door, was a child with a young soldier. I walked into the dayroom; at first, no one paid any attention to me. The child and young soldier were horse playing, and it was the boy who pointed at me. The young soldier looked up and yelled attention, which got the attention of everyone else.

"It seems like the only one who acts like is a real soldier is this young boy." "What's your name, son?"

"He's a German Sir and doesn't speak English."

"What is your name, young man?" I asked in German.

"Oliver."

"Oliver, I've never heard a German boy named Oliver."

"My father wasn't German."

"Are you here all by yourself?"

"No, my brother David is here."

"Did your brother and you come by yourself?"

"My sister's boyfriend John brought us; he is an American Soldier."

As I was talking to Oliver, one of the men in the room slipped out. A staff sergeant walked in and said, "Sir, I'm Staff Sergeant William Filipe." "I am the acting first sergeant and in charged tonight."

"Acting first sergeant, what happened to the real first sergeant?"

"We don't have one, Sir; I'm the ranking sergeant."

"I see, do you know who I am?"

"Yes, Sir, your General York."

"And who are you, soldier?"

"Specialist Four James Grant, Sir."

"What do you do here, Specialist Four James Grant?"

"I just transferred here Sir they have me running supply."

"You and Sergeant Filipe follow me."

"Oliver, be a good boy and show me where this soldier John is."

As we went upstairs, I said to Oliver, "You know Oliver, I have a son about your age at home."

"You do; does he speak German?"

"Yes, he is German; his name is Frederick."

"Does he have any toys?"

"Yes, I sometimes think too many."

"He is lucky I don't have any except for two broken ones."

"Well, maybe I can do something about that." We walked into someone's quarters sitting at a table with a halo of smoke hanging over their heads were six men playing cards, and it wasn't a nickel, dime game. Sitting on one bed was another boy who I assume was Oliver's brother. "Go sit with your brother Oliver." When I said this to Oliver, those men playing cards spotted me, only one stood up at attention. I said, "You soldier may be the only one who won't get in trouble in this room," I said to the soldier who stood up. That got the others to stand, and I said, "Sergeant, go and open the window so that we can get some of this smoke out of here."

"Yes, Sir."

I looked around the room; it had a lot of civilian furniture. "Are all the rooms like this?"

"Most are, Sir."

"I'll talk to you about this after I finish here."

"Who is John?"

"I am Sir."

"Weren't these two boys placed in your care?"

"Well, yes, Sir."

"You think your gambling is taking care of them?"

"Well, Sir, they are alright."

I walked over to the table where they were gambling and looked at the cash, and it was a considerable amount more than these men would typically have. "Does John play cards every time he brings you here?" I asked the boys.

"Yes," said David.

"Sergeant, has the private bring these boys here often."

"Yes, Sir."

"John, you must be a far superior player than these other men, is that right you men?"

They started to laugh, and one said, "He keeps us supplied with plenty of cash, Sir," said one of the three men.

"Sergeant, what does private John do here?"

"Maintenance at the site and he runs the little PX we have here."

"Where is this PX at?"

"Downstairs, Sir."

"You follow me," I said to John.

"Specialist Grant, take these two boys down to the dayroom and stay with them."

"Yes, Sir."

"You boys go with this soldier; his name is James." "I'll bring you both a surprise when I get finished talking with John."

The Sergeant, Private John, and I went to their tiny PX. "Open the door," I told the Private. Nervously he fumbled for his keys and opened the door, and we went in. "Where are your books?" "I want to see the accounting of what you have done here?"

"I don't have any books, Sir."

"What are you talking about you were told to keep an accounting of everything when you got this job," said Sergeant Filipe angrily.

I looked at the Private and then said sternly, "You have a choice you can tell me the truth, and maybe you won't go to prison, or you can deny doing anything wrong, then I will have a full audit of this P.X." "If I find out that you have been stealing money I promise, you'll do your young life in a military prison." The Private was sweating, and I knew I was right, so I demanded, "Make your decision."

"You don't need to do an audit I borrow some money from the PX."

"Sergeant, restrict him to the barracks, he will be getting transferred out of here, so you better start packing now get the hell out of here." He left, and I said to the Sergeant, "Place a note in his file."

"Yes, Sir."

I looked around the small PX and took four candy bars, pulled out my wallet, and then paid for them. We then went to the dayroom, and I handed each boy two candy bars. There were a few men still in the dayroom, so I said, "Let me have this dayroom for about half-hour I wish to have some privacy." They all agreed and left. I shut the doors and told the boys they could play with the pool table. "Let's sit down here and talk." I sat on a chair, and the other two men sat on the couch. "Where does this furniture these men have come from?"

The Specialist and Sergeant looked at each other. Finally, the Sergeant said, "Captain Harrison, the company commander, gets the furniture, Sir." "He finds old hotels in this town and other towns that are going to be torn down or remodeled, and he makes a deal with the owner from what I understand."

"And where does he store this furniture?"

"Downstairs in the shelter where I have a supply room, Sir, that's where I clean them up and fix what's broken," said the Specialist.

"How does he get the furniture here?"

"He orders our men with our trucks to disassemble the furniture and brings it here," said the Sergeant.

"I see, and then he sells it to the same men?"

"Yes, Sir, or anyone else who will buy the furniture."

"What happens to the money he makes?"

"I don't know, Sir."

"How much time does he spend here or at the MCC site?"

"He checks in here in the morning about eight, and then he will spend about a half-hour at the MCC."

"How well does he get along with the men?"

"If they leave him alone, he leaves them alone."

"I see; do you have other officers here?"

"Yes, a First Lieutenant and two Second Lieutenants."

"How is the First Lieutenant?"

"He is a drunk and a bully," said the Specialist.

The Sergeant confirmed what the Specialist said, and I asked, "Do you have any good officers?"

"Not really, the two Second Lieutenants are inexperienced and afraid to anger the First Lieutenant, and especially the Captain, they also try to be equal to the enlisted men."

"I see, nothing is to be said about this to anyone understand?"

"Yes Sir," they both said

"Sergeant, you're with me tomorrow."

"Yes, Sir."

"I'm taking these boys home."

"Oliver, David, I'm taking you home."

"My mother and sister don't get off for another hour," said David.

"It's alright we can drive around, and you two can show me Bad Mergentheim until your mother and sister gets off work."

We went all around the town, and when we got to the toy shop. We got out and looked through the window at what was there. Oliver's eyes were as large as saucers looking at all the toys sighing; he knew he would never have. Even David committed to things he would like. He was more direct in his disappointment of not having them by saying, "Mama and Frieda don't make enough money to have anything in there."

As we traveled to where their sister and mother worked, I asked, "Do you two have school tomorrow?"

"Yes," said David.

"What time do you two get out of school?"

"About three."

"When you and Oliver get out of school, I will come and pick you up, and we will do some things together is that alright with you two?"

"Yes," they both said with a smile. The boy's mother and sister worked at the health spa. We had to wait before they got off work. Oliver had fallen asleep, and I told David not to wake him. Then David spotted his mother and sister we went out to greet them, leaving Oliver sleeping. They were both beautiful, even though they just came off work and not made up.

David reached his mother and sister before I did and told them about the Private, which didn't make his sister very happy. "This is the General."

"General, this is my mother, Elisa, and my sister Frieda."

"Hello, my name is James York." "Frieda, don't be too upset about your soldier friend." "He was not taking care of your brothers very well." "The reason why I am punishing him is that he is a thief."

"What will happen to him?" asked Frieda.

"I will just move him someplace else and put a note in his file."

"Frieda, he was too old for you anyway, but I will miss him taking care of the boys even if he didn't do it very well," said Elisa. "I don't know what I will do for tomorrow," she added.

"Don't worry about that I have plans for David and Oliver tomorrow and I will have someone watch them," I said.

"Where is Oliver?" asked his mother.

"Asleep in the car," I replied. "I'll take you all home, so you don't have to walk." They were tired, so there weren't any arguments about me driving them home. We drove to a run-down apartment building that looked worse than where Maria had lived. It was very trashy with broken windows and shady people around. Oliver's mother started to wake him, but I said, "There is no need for that I'll carry him to bed."

"Alright, but I warn you my home might not be clean."

"That is alright I've been to some terrible places."

They had a ground floor apartment, and it was a two-bedroom one bed in each room there wasn't much in furniture a table to eat on with miss match chairs and clothing thrown everywhere. I laid Oliver on the bed in one of the rooms, and his mother took care of the rest while David started to get ready for bed. Frieda disappeared into the other bedroom. I stepped out into the kitchen area, which was cluttered but seemed like it got cleaned not long ago. While I was alone, I looked in the old refrigerator and few nearly bare cupboards. "Would you like some coffee, General?" asked Elisa.

"No, coffee isn't my favorite beverage; besides, it would keep me up all night." "I just wanted to tell you before I left, I will pick up the boys right after school."

"That's very kind of you, General."

"Well, goodnight."

"Goodnight, General."

Instead of going back to the hotel, I went back to the MCC barracks and told the Sergeant that I needed to make some phone calls. He showed me to Captain Harrison's office, and I shut the door and called General Brown. "This better be important; I just went to bed," said General Brown.

"Bill, this is James York, sorry to disturb you, but I need to talk to you, and I'll be too busy tomorrow."

"That's alright, James, what is it."

"I'm in Bad Mergentheim there is trouble here," I told him the whole story of what I've found so far.

"What do you wish for me to do?" asked General Brown

"First, send some MPs tomorrow, then find a Second Lieutenant by the name of Allen Olivera." "Ask him if he has a sister by the name of Sandy, and his parent's name is Alex and Evana." "If he says yes, that's the one I want." "Promote him to a first lieutenant, pack him up, and send him here." "Next, give me a list of some names I can send out here to replace Captain Harrison."

"I'll get right on that James how long are you going to be there?"

"Maybe another two days, and Maria isn't going to like that."

The next day I went to Captain Harrison's office early before he had arrived. Sergeant Filipe was talking to a Specialist Five when I walked into the office, and I said, "Sergeant, have you been up all night?"

"Yes, Sir."

"Why don't you get some sleep I'll send someone to get you when I need you and, on your way, stopped off at the mess hall and have someone send me something to eat I only drink tea, chocolate, or water no coffee."

"Yes Sir, this is Specialist Five Crieg, he is our company clerk."

"Any relation to the composer, Crieg?" I asked the clerk.

"Maybe I'm not sure, Sir."

"Do you know how to type up promotion papers?"

"Yes, Sir."

"Type me up some papers for Staff Sergeant William Filipe promoting him to first sergeant E eight." "When you get finished making enough copies, bring them to me, and I will sign them."

"Yes, Sir."

"Don't tell anyone, including Captain Harrison, that I'm in his office."

"Yes, Sir."

I had eaten, and everything got taken away when I heard through the door, "Who does that staff car belong to?"

"He's in your office, Sir."

The door opened, and there stood Captain Harrison staring at me. "You don't know how to address me, Captain?"

He snapped to attention and said nervously, "Yes Sir; I do, what can I do for you, Sir?"

"You can sit down I have some questions for you but first call Lieutenant Steward and bring him in here."

"He should be in here in about twenty minutes, Sir."

"Alright, I see on your record; you are married."

"Yes, Sir."

"And where is she?"

"I left her at home when I left this morning."

"Does she know about the black-market job you have?"

He stared at me for a few seconds and said with fear, "I don't know what you mean."

"Yes, you do, using military personnel and equipment for your furniture scam could put you in prison for a long time."

"What I do in my spare time doesn't hurt anyone."

"First, you don't do it in your spare time, and what you're doing is illegal."

After a few seconds of silence, there came a knock at the door. The company clerk stuck his head inside and said, "Sir, here are the orders you wanted, and there are some people here to see you."

"Have them wait, when Lieutenant Steward gets here, send him in."

"Yes, Sir."

"So, are you going to have me arrested?" asked Captain Harrison.

"You will learn your fate when the Lieutenant gets here," I said as I signed the orders.

It wasn't long when an arrogant looking First Lieutenant came into the office. "Find yourself a chair Lieutenant and sit." "This small unit has a problem fortunately for you two most of your men have been putting out more than a hundred percent to keep this place up and running."

"Lieutenant, are you married?"

"No, divorced, what has this to do with me," Lieutenant Steward said annoyed.

"You're a drunk and a bully I wouldn't be surprised if you are high now."

"I don't have to put up with this," he said as he stood up to go.

"Sit down Lieutenant before I knock you down." He wasn't happy, but he sat back down, and I said, "You two don't deserve to wear those uniforms, and with one of the enlisted men here all three of you are a detriment to this unit." "Fortunately, for you three, I'm feeling generous."

"The fact Captain you are married, I'm not going to have you jailed or demoted, but all three of you are going to get transferred." "You two are going to be removed from Europe effective immediately." "When you leave here, Captain with the MPs you will be taken back home, I suggest you get on your knees and kiss Mrs. Harrison feet that she is your wife, or you would have been in prison for a long time." "Specialist, get in here."

"Yes, Sir."

"Send in the MPs and then go get Private John Morgan with his things."

"Yes, Sir."

"Sir Lieutenant Mike Bush here as ordered."

"Lieutenant, how many men and vehicles did you bring?"

"With myself, Sir, there are six of us; we have three vehicles."

"Good General Brown sent an extra vehicle."

"Lieutenant, you are to take these two officers to get their things and get them out of here along with Private John Morgan."

"Yes, Sir, General Brown gave us their transfer orders."

"Very well, carry on."

"Gentlemen, you will follow me," said the MP Lieutenant.

I followed everyone out, and when I came out of the office, there stood Allen Olivera. "Allen, go wait in the office for me." "I'll be back in a minute." I and some of the men of the barracks stepped out of the building long enough to see the three men taken away much to everyone's approval. I got rid of one problem, and now I had to get things in order, so I headed back in. When I joined Allen, he stood up, "No need to stand Allen; this will be informal." "Did anyone tell you what's going on?"

"No, all I was told I was getting transferred, and I got promoted to a first lieutenant."

"It was me who promoted you not because we are cousins but because I know what you are capable of." I then went and told him the whole story of the three men I threw out of here. "You are an officer you can associate with the men as you please, but don't bully them for the most part they seem to be a good bunch of men." "This unit is a little lax on how they do things, and that's all right if the men perform well." "You should also know that some of the men have civilian furniture in their room courtesy of Captain Harrison's black market; let them have it." "You are the executive officer of this small unit, but you are green listen to your men, your NCOs, and especially the first sergeant he is a good man." "There are two other second lieutenants that I could have promoted but didn't because they are followers and didn't report what was going on here." "They aren't bad men but lack leadership; they know their job at the MCC, take from them what helps you." "I will also be sending a Captain who will replace Captain Harrison." "Someone with a little more military experience than you have, he will also help you."

He nodded approval at everything I said and then asked, "Where is the First Sergeant, is he out at the MCC?"

"No, he worked all night, and I told him to get some sleep." "He's going to be working with me today."

"How long will we be without a Captain?"

"I hope by next week I can send someone here." "This assignment, others would kill to get, do well, and you will make Captain yourself in no time." "I don't think you should advertise that we are cousins; it could make things rough for you."

He nodded again and said, "Where will my quarters be?"

"Good question lets go ask the clerk, so we can get you settled in and then we can go out to the MCC."

"This is Lieutenant Allen Olivera he is the new executive officer he needs some quarters what do you suggest?" I asked the clerk.

"Well, Sir, you can have Private John Morgan's room, for now." "It has some nice furniture in it until we can clean Lieutenant Steward's quarters if you want to live off the post, but that will cost you, Sir," the clerk said to Allen.

"That will be fine, where is the room?"

"Let me get someone to show you," said the clerk.

"Put a sign on his door saying that's his room, so he is not disturbed unless he wants to be," I said to the clerk.

"Yes, Sir."

We followed the supply clerk to Allen's room and went in it was a mess, so I told the specialist to clean it up, then I said to Allen, "Throw your things on the bed and let's go out to the MCC."

"Alright."

As we drove, I said, "This is a resort town, and since there are few Americans here, the people treat the Americans well."

"How is the beer here?"

"I didn't drink any beer in this town, but I've never found beer anywhere in Germany tasting bad. Ask some of your men they can most likely tell you better than I."

"I'll do that."

"You know, even though you need to keep your distance from me you are still welcome to visit, Maria would love to see you."

"I'll do that if I have time."

"Well, time or no time Christmas is always better with family."

I got a visitor's badge, but Allen had to go through some paperwork and a picture to go in since he was part of the unit. We toured the facility until two o'clock, then I had to go, so I asked Allen, "You want me to drive you back, or are you going to get a ride?"

"I'll get a ride from someone else?"

"Then I must go now other duty calls," I called the barracks and had them wake Sergeant Filipe. By the time I got back to the barracks and picked up the Sergeant, we had a ten-minute wait for the boys.

"Are you married, Sergeant?"

"No."

"Why not?"

"I guess I haven't found the right one yet, and besides, as a staff sergeant, I don't make enough to support anyone."

"Well, you'll have to find the right person, but I can do something about the pay problem." I pulled out the orders I signed to promote him, handed it to him, and said, "You acted as a first sergeant and doing a good job, so I promoted you to E eight.

He was speechless and then overwhelmed, said, "Thank you, Sir."

As I shook his hand, the boys came out of the school, and we called them over to us. We took the boys to get something to eat first, and while we ate Sergeant Filipe with part German and English was interacting at times teasing the boys. They both loved the attention, especially Oliver, and this pleased me a lot. "The boys have little or no toys, and only shabby clothing do you think we should take them to a few stores Sergeant, of course, everything will be on me."

"I think that would be a good idea, Sir."

We finished eating and went to the store. I explained to the Sergeant what the living conditions the boys were as we went. We stopped at the toy store first much to the delight of the boys. "Both of you can pick out two things for yourself." The boys, both with smiles on their faces, went racing through the store. They reminded me of my boys, and it was beautiful to watch them.

"It's like watching children opening presents during Christmas," said the Sergeant smiling.

"Yes, it's the best part I think after this we should get them something new to wear their clothing looks shabby.

The boys came up with two items in hand, and both looked at me with big eyes and said, "Are these alright to get?"

"They are alright with me, but Sergeant Filipe is also part of this, so maybe you should also ask him."

"Sergeant are these alright?" asked Oliver.

The Sergeant looked at me, wanting a translation, and I said, "They want to know if the toys are alright to get."

"Yes, yes," the Sergeant said in German with a smile.

I paid for the things the boys wanted, and then I said to the boys, "We are going to get you both something new to wear, alright?"

They both nodded, and I put their things in the trunk, then since the next store was only a block and a half away, we walked to it. We passed a bicycle shop, and the boys stopped to stare at what was there. "I wish we could have a bicycle," said Oliver longingly.

"Oliver, it is not polite to say that," lectured David.

"Maybe Saint Nicholas will bring you one," I said.

David gave me a look of a boy who didn't believe in Saint Nicholas. Oliver said, "Christmas is a long way off, and Saint Nicholas doesn't visit us very often."

"I've known Saint Nicholas to deliver presents sometimes early to good boys who believe," I said, looking especially at David.

We went into the clothing store and got greeted by a store clerk, and I said, "These two boys need some new clothing from the top of their heads to their feet, in other words, everything and they will need to try on their new clothes."

"Do you have something in mind?" asked the clerk.

"No, something boys wear today."

"Something every day or something more formal like church?"

"Something every day, but nice."

The Sergeant and I picked out some clothing, and we went back to the changing room to try on the new clothes. "Do you boys want to wear your new clothes or take them home?"

"Wear them," said Dave, and Oliver nodded. They changed out of their clothing and into the new things admiring what they had, looking in a mirror.

We got the boys next, some new shoes, which both were excited about, and I said, "Well, don't you think you should thank Sergeant Filipe?" They hugged and thanked both the Sergeant and me. After paying for the clothes, we went to a park and walked with the boys pointing at what interested them.

"My mother and sister should be home by now," said David.

"They get off early today you didn't tell me," I said.

"I told you now," he replied.

I informed the Sergeant, and we got something for the boy's mother and sister then headed for their home. When we got there, Elisa and Frieda were picking up the house, the Sergeant couldn't take his eyes off Elisa, and she noticed. When they saw the boys, all dressed up and their new toys, Elisa was shocked, and then I said, "Why don't the Sergeant and I take all of you to dinner."

"You don't have to do that, General," said Elisa.

"I think the Sergeant would be very disappointed if we didn't go."

"Well, give Frieda and me a little time to get clean up."

I looked at the Sergeant and said, "We're taking them to dinner."

"Sounds good to me, Sir." I sat with Frieda and the boys while Sergeant Filipe couldn't leave Elisa alone, and she was enjoying it. After a longer than usual dinner, the boys started to get tired, so we headed back home. Elisa and Frieda had the day off work the next day, and somehow Sergeant Filipe asked Elisa if he could come by, and she said yes. After dropping off Sergeant Filipe, I went back and called Maria.

"Hello, sweetheart I miss you when I get back, I am going to take off a few days so that I can spend some time with you and the boys."

"When you come home, we miss you?" asked Maria.

"Maybe tomorrow night or the next day." "I would guess the boys are asleep?"

"Yes, they are asleep."

"Look, Maria, I need to tell you something that happened here and what I wish to do if it is alright with you." I told her the whole story of the boys, their mother, and sister and how they were living. Then I said, "What I want to do is move them out of that terrible place put them into a house that I will buy in a good neighborhood."

"Won't they need furniture also?" asked Maria."

"Yes, I guess you're right."

"Then you better stay until they have everything they need."

"Maria, I love you, give the boys a big kiss for me."

The next day I got up early, ate and found Gertrude Hoffenzimmer a realtor, who spoke English better than me. I let her know about the boys and their mother and their sister and said, "What I want is a good three-bedroom house in a good neighborhood." "Also, furniture and sundries to fill it and a good used Volkswagen to get around."

"I know you are a General, but this will cost a lot of money."

"I'm wealthy and can afford it."

"Ok, I'll show you a house that I think will meet your needs."

The first house we saw, I liked the neighborhood had plenty of children with well-kept homes. The house on the outside looked neat and well-kept. When we went in, it was an ordinary three-bedroom house with a pleasant kitchen, and it even had a fireplace, but it had no thrills, but it was in good shape. I looked at the backyard, and it was big with a swing set and a sandbox I turned to the realtor and said, "I'll take it when can I get the keys."

"Lets us go back to the office, and I will call the owner."

"We have to make this quick so that I can get the furniture and sundries."

"Why don't you write me a check and then go get the furniture and things, and by the time you get back, I should have your keys." It was ten-thirty when I got to the furniture store. What I did was first planned for the delivery, and that was a chore. However, when I explained that I would pay extra and the amount of furniture I was going to buy, they agreed to deliver tonight. At the same store, I could get everything that I thought the house needed, including a TV. Everything would come by ten that night.

The next place I went to was a used car lot, and I bought a used blue Volkswagen that was in good shape, and I had a mechanic look at it. When I got the keys, I parked it on the street and went back to the realtor's office. "Well, do you have the keys?"

"They are on the way coming, they didn't want to come today because the owners have to come from Würzburg, but when I told them who you were and what you were trying to do, they agreed to come."

Sure enough, about thirty minutes later in walks, two older adults and I got up to greet them. "I am General York, and I am so happy you both took time out of your busy life to come to this office."

"I'm Carl Hoffmire, and this is my wife, Liesel." We shook hands and sat down to some small talk as the realtor drew up the papers that the

Hoffmires signed. The realtor handed them a check and told me that the spare key would be under the doormat, and within a half-hour, everything got done, and we all left to do what we had to do.

I went to the barracks to see if the sergeant was there, it was five o'clock, but he wasn't there, so I went upstairs to see if I could find that supply clerk or Allen. I saw Allen in the TV room watching some German TV, a nude movie, "I didn't know they can put things like that on TV where kids can see it."

"Yes, it is common here in Europe, but the Germans don't make a big deal about nudity, and the children aren't interested in it." "My two boys never watch it most of the time they are outside, playing with their things, or doing their homework."

"I don't think American kids would be," he replied.

"Do you know how to drive in Germany?

"Yes, I got my license just before I came here."

"Good, can I drag you away from that I need you to drive a VW someplace."

"Sure, let me get my hat." We drove out to the VW; I handed him the keys and told him to follow me.

When we got to the house, we parked out in front and got out of our vehicles. I said, "I'll explain to you what is going on in a second." I tried the house key in the garage door, and it worked, so I had Allen drive the car into the garage, then we went into the house. As I showed the place to Allen, I explained to him about the boys and their mother and sister.

"You mean you are going to give them this house?" Allen asked disbelievingly.

"No, I'm just going to let them stay here rent-free so that they can get on their feet." "When they move, I'll sell the house."

"Sounds to me that is going to take some time."

"Yes, I believe you are right, but I have plenty of money." "Are you up to do some grocery shopping with me?"

"Sure."

Along the way, I stopped at that bicycle shop the boys looked at yesterday, and I said to Allen, "A quick stop first."

"Can I help you, Sir," said the shop clerk.

"Yes, I need three bicycles if you can fit them in that car."

The clerk looked at the car and said, "Well, if you assemble them, I can fit the three bicycles in the car."

"I'll need tools to assemble them."

"I have what you need for sale."

"Alright, I need two bicycles for two boys, one about nine the other about twelve and another bicycle for a girl about sixteen."

"No problem I will get them and load them in your car." It was a tight squeeze, but they got put in the back seat area, and the clerk sold me the tools and a pump for the tires.

We went next to the grocery store and got enough groceries to feed an army with cleaning supplies, and we went back to the house and put them away. Allen and I put the bicycles and accessories in the house; they were still in the boxes. "You want me to help you put them together?" asked Allen.

"Yes, but I'm getting a little hungry." "You want something to eat."

"Sure, I can eat."

We went to a Hofbräu and ordered pizza and beer. It was about seven o'clock, and I figured I had about three hours to wait for the furniture. There were some GI's at the Hofbräu, but we sat at another table and ordered a pepperoni pizza and some beer. We were there for about an hour then went back to the house to try to put the bicycles together. We were finishing up on the last bike when the furniture showed up, and Allen said, "Why don't you take care of the furniture, and I'll finish here."

"Alright," I told the men who delivered all the furniture where to put everything, and within an hour, everything was in place. It was eleven-thirty when we got back to the barracks, I asked the Sergeant in charged that night if Sergeant Filipe had come back.

"Yes Sir, about ten minutes ago, he is up in his room."

"I'm going to bed," said Allen.

"Thanks for the help," I replied.

He mumbled something as I went down to Sergeant Filipe's room and knocked on the door. Half-dressed he came to the door and said surprised I was there, "General, what can I do for you?"

"Can I talk to you privately?"

"Sure, come in."

"So, how did your day go today with Elisa?" I asked

He turned beet red and said, "Well, just fine, Sir."

"Are you going to be seeing her tomorrow?"

"Yes, her and her family."

"What do you have planned?"

"Sir, why are you asking me these questions about Elisa?"

"Just be patient with me a little longer, and by tomorrow you will know why I am asking you, now what do you have going on for tomorrow?"

"I plan to take them to lunch then shopping; they don't have much, then maybe to the park."

"You're getting close to her, aren't you?"

"I like her and her family, but I'm afraid to get too close because I could get transferred anywhere."

"Do you want to be transferred?"

"No, I like it here."

"I don't blame you this is a nice post, don't worry about being transferred you won't be you will be here for some time." "You might not like what I'm going to say, but again you need to be patient with me." "I'll be going with you to lunch and shopping afterward." "However, the park is out I have other plans for you, Elisa and her family." "The shopping will not be for groceries, which I'm assuming is what you were going to do, but it will be for clothing for the family." "Don't worry about the cost I will cover it."

"Sir, they need food; there is little in their home."

"Yes, I know, and you will understand tomorrow why I'm dictating how tomorrow is going to be, and I assure you will be pleased." "We will take two vehicles tomorrow you will take Elisa, and I will take her children."

"Yes, Sir."

"I will be here at eleven-thirty tomorrow, wait for me."

"Yes, Sir."

The next day I was in the barracks at the precise time I said I would. I could see the Sergeant wasn't very happy that I was tagging along, but he would change his mind when he saw what I had done. We went to Elisa home, and this time it was kept up a little better than before. I don't think Elisa was all that happy to see I had come, but I told her that by me coming, it would be well worth it by the end of the day, and unconvincingly she excepted I was there. She was happy that we went into two cars her going with the Sergeant and me with the children. Frieda sat in the front seat with me, the boys in the back, and she wasn't pleased about going, and I said, "Frieda, by the end of the day, you will be happy that you came, I promise you that." The lunch was excellent. I sat with the children and only spoke to Elisa to tell her how I felt the Sergeant felt about her, which embarrassed the Sergeant but delighted Elisa. When Elisa found out we were going to the clothing store rather than the grocery store, she said, "Your money would get better spent on food than clothing."

"You will have enough food, but you all can use some special clothing, something you would like," I said. Elisa gave in, which delighted Frieda for the first time. The girls enjoyed themselves trying on one thing or another and finally settling on a couple of outfits. Then they didn't expect was that the Sergeant and I guided them to the cosmetics and jewelry area of the store. I took care of the boys, getting them a few more things to wear.

"General, are you going to take us to the toy store again?" asked Oliver.

"You wear out your new toys already, Oliver?"

"No, but I could always use some more toys," he said with a smile."

"Well, you know late last night I ran into St. Nicolas, and I told him about you two." "I think he might do something for you two."

"You think so?" he asked excitedly.

"Yes." David was rolling his eyes, and I said, "Oliver and I will make a believer out of you yet, won't we, Oliver."

"Yes."

"Elisa wants to drop everything at the house first before we do the next thing you have planned," said Sergeant Filipe.

"Alright."

"Where are we going, Sir?"

"Just follow me, and you will see and understand what's going on."

We drove to the apartment, and before I got out of the car, I could see something was wrong. I noticed that the window appeared broken, and the door to the apartment was wide open. Everything was tossed and wrecked all over the place, even out the door. Elisa and Frieda were in tears, and Sergeant Filipe was trying to comfort them. The two boys went running into their bedroom and came out crestfallen all their toys, and things got taken.

"I'll go asked the neighbors if they saw what happen," I said.

"There is no use even if they did see something, they won't tell anyone this is not the first time someone broke into my apartment," said Elisa.

"Let's see what can be salvaged and put it into the cars you can't stay here tonight," I said. While everyone else was going through their things, I did pound on a few doors until one opened. As Elisa predicted, no one saw or heard anything, but I did get one man to call the police to make a report. I then went and helped everyone gather their things together while they were doing this the police came, and I said to Elisa, "Tell the police what happened."

"You should not have called them there is nothing they can do," Elisa said.

"They can write a report, and you may need that report someday."

After Elisa finished with the police, she returned to the apartment and said, "It's just as I said there is nothing they can do."

She then started crying again. I said, "Elisa, I'm a believer that when God closes one window, he opens another have faith.

"I will try."

We loaded up the cars, and I said to Sergeant Filipe, "Follow me, we have to make one stop before we get to where we are going."

"Sir, perhaps because of the circumstance, maybe we should cancel the activity you had planned."

"Sergeant, you need to have faith in me too."

"Yes, Sir."

We took off, and we stopped off at that same toy store that the boys got their last toys. "Boys go in and get some more toys to replace the ones you lost, Frieda; if there is anything you would like, please get it," I said.

We all went in, and Elisa said, "Well, at least the boys won't go without their toys; thank you, General."

The store clerk was about to close when we came, but after I told him what happen, he agreed to let the children look. We loaded up the cars, and I told everyone, "If what is about to happen doesn't put a smile on your face, then nothing will." We drove off with the Sergeant following me. It took about twenty minutes to get to the house, and I parked out in front with the Sergeant parking behind me. We all got out, and everyone was confused about why we were here, so I said to the Sergeant, "I will translate what I'm about to say in English if you can't figure it out, Sergeant." "Elisa, Frieda, as I was telling Oliver and David, I ran into St. Nicklaus last night." "We had a long talk about you and your family." "St. Nicklaus suggested since I could afford it, I should do a few things for you and your family." "I pulled out all the keys and handed them to Elisa and said, pointing at the house, "This place is yours rent-free for as long as you need it." She was speechless as was Frieda the boys were squealing with delight, and I said, "Shall we go in."

"General, this is too much you can't do this for us," said Elisa.

"Elisa, I love your children, and besides, I already have a house to live in, I can't live in two houses." "I should tell you this house is only the beginning lets go in." We all went into the house, and she was stung when she saw the furniture, and I said, "There are three bedrooms, one for the boys, one for Frieda, and of course, one for you."

"I finally have my bedroom," Frieda said with joy.

"Yes, Frieda, now go find your rooms." As they found their rooms, I could hear the squeals and screams of delight. "Well, Sergeant, do you approve?"

"Yes, Sir," he said with a smile.

They finally all came out to the living room, and Elisa gave me a big hug and a kiss, and I said, "Elisa, I'm a married man, besides there is more, look in the kitchen." She opened everything and looked in the refrigerator, and I said, "I told you, you didn't need groceries."

"I must at least give you a hug," said Elisa.

"There are swings and a sandbox in the backyard," said Oliver excitedly.

"Yes, your right Oliver," I said. "Elisa, you need to look at the keys on the key ring."

"This is a car key," Elisa said.

"Where do they keep cars?" I asked with a smile.

"The garage," Elisa said. She and her children went to the garage and looked in, and again they all started squealing with joy.

"St. Nicolas has been here," Oliver said excitedly.

"Well, I told you I saw him didn't I," I replied. We unloaded the cars, and I said to Sergeant Filipe, "If your relationship with Elisa turns into a marriage, you let me know we would love to come."

"Yes, Sir."

"Elisa, I have to go home, my wife and children miss me." I got a hug from everyone, and then I headed back home."

27

FRANCE

I got home feeling good late, Maria was up still, and I got a warm welcome. I went into the boy's room and kissed them before retiring to bed with Maria. The next morning, I told Maria before the boys got up, "I'm going to work this week, and then Friday, I'll take off for five days, and we all will do some enjoyable family things."

"That sounds like fun," Maria replied. As always, Maria is continuously uncomplaining when it comes to my work. After a boisterous morning with the boys, I went to work late. I got caught up with some paperwork and talked to General Brown about getting a list of captains to replace Captain Harrison. I then sent an aide to inform Captain Dizon I wanted to talk to him at ten o'clock tomorrow morning. I went home to a great dinner, and that's when I told Maria about Elisa and her family. I said to her it would be nice to visit Bad Mergentheim for a day or so to see the town and how Elisa and her family are doing. As always, she was agreeable with that, and we made plans to go on Saturday.

The next day at work, I was looking at the possible replacement captains for the MCC. It was ten minutes before ten when I was to talk to Captain Dizon. I had noticed the name Captain Paul McMullen on the list of captains for the MCC. I started to think about him, and I remembered when I first met him, he was an arrogant S.O.B. from company A. He was a man that was up in age at least older than the rest of the company commanders. Well educated, if I remember right, he went to a big-name college Yale or Harvard. He appeared to be a desk jockey, slightly overweight, and too sure of himself. Even though I remember him being this way during and after the conflict, he seemed to humble himself, and I had no more trouble. In many ways, he reminded me of my cousin Allen. There was a knock at the door, and my thoughts of Captain McMullen vanished, "Yes, what is it?"

In popped my secretary, saying, "Sir, Captain Dizon is here to see you."

"Send him in?"

"Marc, good to see you."

"The pleasure is mine, Sir."

"We will have to get together sometime; I'm sure Maria would love to see you and your family."

"Yes, Sir." I knew we would never socialize as we use to, but it was a formality of conversation, and it needed to be said.

"Before I get to the business at hand, tell me how the training goes."

"Very well, Sir, we are almost finished with it." "Then, with the help of some of the Special Forces, we will train the other units."

"Sounds great just as I planned it." "Tell me how Captain McMullen is doing?"

"He struggles, but he hasn't given up, Sir."

"Forget me being a general and speak from the heart." "As you can remember, the Captain was a real S.O.B. and extremely arrogant when I first met him." "He seemed to humble himself after the conflict how is he now has he reverted to his old ways?"

"No, Sir, he is a different man than when we first met him."

"How well does he command Alpha Company?"

"He is a good company commander his men get treated well, and he insists that they give one hundred percent when they do their work and training."

"In your heart, Marc, do you truly think he should be out there training with his men?"

Marc thought for a second and said, "Sir, as I told you before, he tries hard, but he is having a tough time." "He is more of an administrator than a field combat officer, in my opinion."

"That's just what I thought he is an intelligent, good officer now that he has gotten humbled." "Do you know what the MCC is?"

"I believe it's the missile control center, Sir."

"Yes, they need a captain there." "I'm thinking of sending him there."

"To replace Captain Harrison, Sir?"

"Yes, you heard then."

"Yes, Sir." "From what I understand, it is a good posting an administrator's job Captain McMullen would do well there."

"That's what my thinking is, but I will give it a little more thought before making my decision." "Let's go down to the conference room; the next topic is secret, and the walls have ears."

"Yes, Sir."

We sat down in the conference room, which was soundproof, and I looked at Captain Dizon and asked, "If I remember right, you speak French."

"Yes, Sir."

"Can you read and write French?"

"Yes, Sir."

"Good, let me tell you what is going on and what I plan to do." For the next half hour, I told him of the Vietnamese General who was the prison camp commandant and what the Pentagon wanted me to do. I told him my plan at the Vietnamese consulate in Paris, the movies that the Disney Corporation sent me, and how I was going using the films. "What I would like is for you to accompany me to Pairs and be my interpreter."

"Yes, Sir, when will this happen."

"Next week Thursday." "You can't tell anyone why you are going to Paris, not even your family."

"Alright, Sir, are you going to Vietnam alone?"

"Yes, I think it will be best if I do."

"Suppose you have a flashback, or they try to throw you jail again?"

"I'll just have to take my chances and try to control any flashbacks that I get." We talked for another ten minutes, and then I walked him back to his unit. On the way back to my office, I stopped to speak to the Green Beret lieutenant about Captain McMullen to get his view on how his training was going.

"To tell you the truth, Sir, his men are doing just fine, but I feel he would be a burden to his unit." "I'm not saying he hasn't been trying; he just isn't cut out for this type of unit." "He is more of a desk jockey."

"That's what I thought."

"How is his executive officer?"

"He is doing just fine, like the rest of his men."

"Thanks for the input."

"No problem, Sir."

After work, I went home and had dinner, my mind was on Captain McMullen, and Maria knew I was mauling something over in my mind. "What's wrong, James?"

"I have to transfer an officer, and I am trying to think of the best way to tell him, he is married."

"Why don't you just go over to his house and be honest with him that's always the best way."

"Yes, your right; do you wish to come with me."

"Yes, Jonathan can watch Frederic."

"I'll need to call the Colonel first about this; it's his battalion," I called the Colonel and told him what I was going to do. He understood he was going to come to me about it. I also told him I was promoting his executive officer to captain. Again, he approved of the move; in fact, he wanted to do the promotion himself. Maria and I went over to the Captain's house we had never been there so when the Captain came to the door, he was shocked to see us. "Can we talk about some things, Paul?"

"Yes, Sir, come on in."

We sat down on the couch, and I said, "Perhaps your wife should join us," I said.

"Nancy, come join us."

Once we were all together, I said to Captain McMullen, "How is your training going?"

"It's rough, but I'm handling it."

"I heard you're having a rough time." "I don't think you can handle it without hurting yourself or someone else."

"I beg to differ, Sir."

I stared at him doubtfully, and he noticed then Nancy said, "Paul, you know he is right; the training is killing you what will happen when you go out into the field."

"Now, Nancy, I have a little more in me than you know."

"Paul, I'm going to transfer you."

With his head down, he said, "Yes, Sir, where to Sir."

"Don't be upset, Paul; it's not as gloomy as you think." "Your record will say you served with honor, and the post I'm sending you to is one of the best posts in Germany." "Have you heard of the MCC?"

"Yes, Sir, missile control center, it's somewhere west of here."

"It's in the small resort town of Bad Mergentheim I had to fire the company commander because he was running a black market and wasn't doing his job." "You'll have a good first sergeant and your X.O. although green, he is very much like you; you will find that you will have much in common." "The men are good workers; I don't think you will have any trouble with most of them." "You can get help from your officers and N.C.O.s to learn the job which I'm sure you will learn fast." "You will get isolation pay also, but I do need to tell you something the men are a little informal when they aren't working. In their quarters, they have civilian furniture, which I prefer you let them have if they keep it clean." "It's a small unit smaller than Alpha, but they have a small movie theater and small P.X." "The barrack is outside a German Panzer company." "Since there are only a few Americans there, they get well received in the town." "If I had to get posted somewhere, Bad Mergentheim would be one of the places I would want to be."

The Captain's disposition wholly changed, and he said, "It sounds pretty good when do I go, Sir?"

"Your X.O. will be promoted to captain tomorrow, and I need you there as soon as possible."

The next day Captain McMullen's X.O. was promoted by Colonel Upton Captain. McMullen and I were there to look on; another first lieutenant got made X.O. After the ceremony, Captain McMullen shook everyone's hand, and he was off. I went back to my office, called General Abrams, and told him what I was up to then let him know Captain Dizon and I would be going to Paris that following Thursday. Friday came, and for the next five days, I promise Maria and the boys I would take time off and spend some time with them. We went to Munich, where they had a festival of some sort that I knew the children would like. It wasn't long after we got there that the boys disappeared into the crowd and Maria and I for the next hour and a half went looking for them. Overall, we had a good time; the boys were excited at all that had been going on in Munich.

The next day we headed to Bad Mergentheim. We got our room at the same hotel I stayed in before, then got something to eat. "Perhaps we should go up to the American barracks and find out if Sergeant Filipe is still dating Elisa," I said to Maria.

"Does it matter if he is dating her or not?" she replied

"No, but it would be less awkward if we found out before we went over to their house."

"Yes, I see what you mean."

We went up to the barracks, and I found out that Sergeant Filipe wasn't there, but he was still dating Elisa, so the person on duty told us. As we were about to leave, Allen showed up, and I said, "This is my wife, Maria, my son Jonathan, and my son Frederic." "This is Allen Olivera, your cousin."

"It's nice to meet you," replied Allen.

"You must come to Schweinfurt to our home so that you can have some home cooking," Maria said.

"I'll do that."

"Have you met your new C.O. yet?" I asked Allen.

"Yes, he seems like a good man; he is still moving in, though."

"He is a good man, have you moved out of the barracks yet?"

"Oh yes, I did that last night, I just came back to get some more of my things."

We talked for a short time more then went to the park that I took Oliver and David to. After the park, I took the boys to the toy store.

They were to pick something for David and Oliver, of course, Frederic wanted something also, and that meant Jonathan would be getting something too. After that, we all went to another store to get something for Elisa and Frieda; I also picked up a bottle of wine. As we drove up to the house, I saw Sergeant Filipe and Elisa outside tending the front yard garden. Neither he nor Elisa recognized me because we were in the Mercedes when we drove up. "Are you learning a new trade if the Army doesn't work out, Sergeant," I asked after getting out of the car? I opened the door for Maria, and the boys got out by themselves. The Sergeant and Elisa stopped what they were doing with smiles on their faces. I introduced everyone we went to the house the boys were out in the backyard and came running in when they found out I was there with my family, and Frieda was in her room. She also came out with a smile on her face.

"Daddy, what about the presents?" asked Frederic.

"Alright, you and Jonathan go get them."

I handed Frederic the keys to the car, and he said to David and Oliver in German, "Come with us, we have something for you."

They all went running outside, and after a short time, David and Oliver came back in with smiles on their faces. Jonathan and Frederic brought in the rest of the things for everyone else. The boys ran out again and got their new toys to share with David and Oliver, and that is the last I saw of the boys until we left. I asked Sergeant Filipe about Captain McMullen, and he told me about the same thing as Allen did. Elisa said,

"The manager tried to get me to pay for the broken window and make me pay for leaving early."

"You didn't pay him, did you?"

"No Sergeant Filipe took care of it."

I looked at Sergeant Filipe, and he said, "I told the manager that if he pushed too much to collect this, I would take them to court and report them to the health department."

"And what did he say?"

"He got very nervous and said he would forgive the rent and damages, and then I made him sign a note saying he would do this."

"Excellent Sergeant." We spent about forty-five minutes to an hour visiting and then called the boys and left. We spent the rest of the time doing family things Wednesday I told Maria that I had to go somewhere, and I didn't know how long I was going to be gone.

I was waiting for Captain Dizon to arrive at my office; the plan was to catch a military flight from the Rhein-Main airbase and fly to Pairs. We wore civilian clothing, and he came about thirty minutes after I arrived, and I said, "There is a plane on standby at Rhein-Main."

"Yes, Sir, I'm ready whenever you are." We loaded up the car I had the movies in a large leather briefcase that locked. The captain insisted on driving to the airport; it was going to be about a two-hour drive. We could have taken one of the copters, but I wanted my staff car, so when we got back from France, I could see General Abrams and tell him how it went. Another reason I didn't take the copter; it would have drawn attention, and no one wanted that.

We got to the airport a little after ten in the morning, and the first thing I did was find the commander of Rhein-Main airbase. I got directed to Colonel Robert Brady, "We need to get to Pairs France as soon as possible."

"Yes, Sir."

"This flight has to appear to be no big deal; perhaps you can give a few men leave for three days to go there."

"Yes, Sir, when do you want to go?"

"Now, if possible, if not as soon as possible."

"I can have the men and plane ready in two hours is that ok."

"That would be fine; do you have a place to eat around here?"

"I would suggest the café you might draw unwanted attention in the mess hall."

"That would be fine." "We have some baggage, where can I stow it, one item is secret, and care has to be giving that nothing happens to it."

"You can leave your baggage here, and I have a large safe to put the other bag in." I looked at the safe and thought it large enough.

We had gotten the directions to the café and went there to get a bite to eat, of course, I insisted everything was on me. Captain Dizon protested, but I told him I would get reimbursed. We sat in the café, had breakfast, and talked about everything except the trip. Captain Dizon got warned while we were driving to not to address me as Sir or mention my rank so as not to draw attention. When it was time to go, we went back to Colonel Brady's office to get our things. "There will be six men going to Pairs with you, Sir."

"Did you give those men any money to be able to be in Pairs?"

"No, Sir."

"Do you have cash on hand?"

"Yes, Sir."

"Give those men six hundred dollars, put in for reimbursement to General Abrams or me." "After we leave this office, you're not to call me, Sir, or mention anything about my rank."

"Yes, Sir."

We got on the plane with six jovial men. The aircraft wasn't your typical military plane, but it was like a commercial plane. The flight was going to be about a forty-five-minute trip. As we were in the air, one of the six men turned to us and asked the Captain, "I don't recognize you, but your partner looks familiar did the Colonel give you leave too."

"No, we are going on a business and leisure trip for the military," said Captain Dizon before I could answer.

"Sad for you two for some reason, the Colonel gave us a three-day leave, and on top of that, he gave us six hundred dollars to spend."

"I'd be careful with that money I hear Pairs is expensive," I said.

"Oh, I will, but we have our own money too."

We flew into the Paris airport the six men went one way, and Captain Dizon and I went another to find an adequate hotel to stay in."

We hailed a cab, then Marc said something in French to the cabbie, and we were off. I had kept my briefcase with me, but everything else went into the cab's trunk. The taxi drove up to a nice-looking hotel, and we went in. Captain Dizon talked to the hotel clerk, who seemed rude to him, but we got a room.

"Any other time I would have knocked that clerk out," I said.

"Yeah, me too, and I understood what he was saying, so it was worse for me." "We must expect that kind of rudeness; that's how the Parisians are from what I understand."

"Let's just hope it doesn't interfere with our mission," I replied.

We settled in, and I asked the Captain to check if they had a safe to store the briefcase. He called downstairs to the clerk, and he told me they did. Before we went to lunch and to see the sights, I brought the briefcase downstairs, and the Captain had them lock it up. The plan was about ten o'clock the next morning we would catch a cab and head to the consulate. We decided to walk, and as we went down a side street, we spotted a small café, so we sat at a table outside the café. The waiter came and took the order from Captain Dizon. As we received wine and some cheese to snack on, an older man in shabby clothing went down the street, begging money. When he came to the café, he begged a few people at the other tables who treated him terribly. Then he came to us, and I said to the Captain, "Ask him what he wants."

"Sir, what are you asking for."

"Money to get something to eat and a place to sleep for the night."

The Captain told me what he said, and I told him to ask him why we should give it to him when he would most likely use it for liquor.

The Captain relayed what I said to the old man, and he said, "It is true that I would get something to drink, but I would also get something to eat and a place to sleep." "I drink to forget the horror of war that I was in."

"What war?"

"He said the French Vietnam war he still has nightmares."

"You are a hero in France then, aren't you?"

"He said no, I was just a common soldier."

"In my eyes, you are a hero."

As the Captain translated, the waiter came out and started to yell at the man, and Captain Dizon explained to me. "Tell the waiter that this war hero is my guest."

The Captain translated, and the waiter stopped getting after him, and the Captain ordered him dinner and some wine.

"Should I tell him about your background?"

"Tell him about my time in Vietnam and the war here in Europe but not my name or anything extra." The Captain told him, and the response shocked me.

"He knows you were in both wars and who you are."

I smiled and said, "Tell him not to make a big deal about it." After we ate and drank, we went down to a bank, and I opened an account with three thousand dollars in his name. I then gave him three hundred dollars, headed for a clothing store, and bought him some warm clothing. After the garments, I got and paid for a room for him for a week and called a French General I knew and told him about the French veteran, and the General assured me he would help him. In tears, he talked to the General and said to us that they were to meet the next day. We shook hands, and the Captain and I left it was a risk for me to contact the General, but I felt it necessary.

We slept well, and the next morning we cleaned up and ate. I wasn't in a hurry to get to the consulate, but I knew I couldn't put it off for long, so about ten o'clock, I got my briefcase, and Captain Dizon call a cab. The consulate was across town. The Vietnamese were in an unadorned brown building with the Vietnam flag out front. There were two guards out front in their khaki uniforms and pith helmets. When we exited the cab, I said to the Captain, "I will talk, you translate."

"Yes, Sir."

We walked up to the guards, and I said, "I'm General James York; this is Captain Marc Dizon, my interpreter." "I'm here to see the consulate General on important business." One of the guards went to a phone, spoke in Vietnamese, and then said in French, "You can come in but not the Captain."

"Tell them that is unacceptable either we both go in, or we don't go in at all, and they can deal with General Kien."

They then called again and said in French, "No, only you."

"Let's go; we can find a phone and call for a cab."

"Sir, I can wait out here; it won't bother me."

"No, what they are trying to do is bully and manipulate me, and I won't have that besides, they contacted the United States, we didn't contact them if they want me, they will give in."

We started walking away; one of the Vietnam guards must have called inside again because before we got a block, one of the guards called us back. "We can both go in, Sir," said Captain Dizon.

We walked past the guards and went through two doors inside, and two other guards stopped us and wanted to frisk us. He said something in French and pointed to the briefcase, and Captain Dizon said, "He wants to see inside the briefcase."

"Tell him no, it's for the Consulate General's eyes only."

The guard said something else, and the Captain said, "He said you might have a bomb or weapon in there."

"Tell him does he think that I would risk my life; however, if he can't trust me, I can always leave."

He was upset when the Captain told him, but he gave in and guided us to the Consulate General's office. The consulate general stood up behind his desk and said in English, "Please sit down now what can we do for you?"

I stared at him for a few seconds. Then said, "As you already know, General Kien wishes to see me I'm here to tell you I'm willing to see him, but I won't play any games for the United States or Vietnam."

"Alright, General, there won't be any games, and I will arrange for you to meet General Kien."

"Do you know what he wants, and when do you think I will go?"

"No, I have not been informed as to why he wants to see you." "I think I can have you on a plane to the Socialist Republic of Vietnam in about ten days if that's acceptable to you."

"Yes, that will be fine."

"May I ask you something?"

"Yes, go ahead."

"How do you feel about going to Vietnam?"

"Do you know what I went through in Vietnam?"

"Yes, in part."

"Going to Vietnam isn't my most favorite thing to do." "I've was asked to go because the U.S. military asked me and, more importantly, by a friend."

"I see, then you feel resentment toward the people of Vietnam and General Kien."

"I hate only certain things that happen in Vietnam to my men and me that I cannot forget."

"I see, well, I will contact you when your plane is ready to go." I lifted the briefcase and unlocked it, I pulled out the movies and said, "Before I meet with General Kien, I wish him to have these."

"What are they?"

"A movie called A Light In The Forest and a cartoon called Fantasia." "Do you know who Walt Disney is?"

"Yes, a capitalist who made the cartoon mouse."

"He made these two films, and his company changed them so that it is in the Vietnamese language." "I would assume that you and your staff will look at them first before sending it; just make sure you get it to him before I go."

"Why are these movies so important for him to see?"

"The cartoon isn't, it's just entertainment, but the movie General Kien and I had many discussions when I was his guest." "I wish him to see it before we meet so we can have more discussions." "Besides, it would be entertaining for your people, especially the children."

"I will see if it has any political propaganda in it before I send it."

"I assure you General Kien would be angry with you if he found out, and he didn't get it." He gave me that malicious laugh that many power-hungry fools got when they weren't sure if I was right. "I will wait the ten days to hear from your government of my departure."

He nodded and without a word from Captain Dizon or me, I got up and departed the consulate. We walked down the street, my briefcase lighter now. We didn't have to walk far before we came to a café we went in, and Captain Dizon ordered something light for us. We talked about what just happened, and the Captain was utterly amazed at what we pulled off. "To tell you the truth, there was a time when I didn't think my plan would work, Marc."

"Yeah, I know what you mean, Sir," said Captain Dizon.

"Let's watch the military courtesy until we get back to Germany."

We caught a cab back to the hotel where I left the briefcase in our room and then we decided to do some shopping for our families before we took the plane back to Rhein-Main airbase the next day.

The next day we relaxed and ate, then afterward, we caught a cab for the jet that was supposed to be there at three-thirty that afternoon. The plane came late, and we had to wait for the six men who went on leave. They knew what time they had to be here, so it made me angry. I was about to tell the pilot to take off when one of the six men who looked like hell showed up. "Where are the rest of the men?"

"I don't know we all split up in pares Bill should be here in a few minutes he had to take a leak."

Moments later, Bill showed up stumbling, getting on the plane. "If the others don't show soon, we will leave them," I said.

"Who do you think you are to leave our friends behind," said the first man while Bill came on the plane laughing.

I looked at Captain Dizon and said, "We're not in Germany yet."

"We will be," replied the Captain.

"Yeah," I said.

The other four finally came in the same shape as the first two. Of course, the first two men told their friends of my displeasure, and they gave me smirks and whispered insults. The co-pilot came back with the Stars and Stripes and said to me, "You might want to see this."

It was a picture of me, and I smiled at him and said to Marc, "Look at this." When we're in the air, I said, "Gentlemen, I think you should see this article in the Stars and Stripes."

They took the newspaper, stared at it, and then stared at me and then back to the paper. One of the six men said, "Sir, we didn't know who you were."

"Does that make a difference?" I asked angrily. "Your actions will have consequences, but I will leave that to Colonel Brady." "You might want to know it was I who got all of you your leave and the six hundred dollars." I then told the pilot to radio Rhein-Main and asked them to have Colonel Brady meet us there.

The rest of the flight was in silence except for the whispers of the six men. Captain Dizon and I got off the plane first, and I talked to Colonel Brady and told him what happen, which didn't make him happy. Then we got to our car and drove to General Abrams's office. "James, I've been waiting for you," said General Abrams elatedly.

"Yes, Sir, this is Captain Marc Dizon."

After the General greeted the Captain, he asked me, "How did it go while in Paris?" For the next thirty-five to forty minutes, Captain Dizon and I told him what went on. "You took a big chance, James."

"Maybe not as big as you think." "If I hadn't strongly approached the Vietnamese, they wouldn't have respected me." "You need to remember Sir, they contacted us; we didn't contact them; they must want something awful bad from us."

"I think you are right." "I will be coming down to Schweinfurt in a couple of days I'll tell you just what we want from Vietnam again." We talked for another thirty minutes, and then the Captain and I excused ourselves and headed for home.

28

VIETNAM REVISITED

We got home late, and after dropping off Captain Dizon, I finally walked into my home and in Maria's arms. Maria and I discussed my experiences in Vietnam in the past, and two days after I came back from France, I told her of my pending trip back to Vietnam. She was distraught that I was going, but I told her I had to go, it was vital for the United States, and reluctantly she accepted it. General Abrams was to come to my office tomorrow, so I made sure to be at my office early.

It wasn't until about ten that morning when General Abrams showed. My secretary showed him into my office, and I stood and shook his hand. "I hope your trip here was pleasant, Sir."

"It was, thank you." "How's your family?"

"Happy and contented."

"Have you told Maria about your pending trip?"

"Yes, and she isn't happy about it but accepts it."

He looked at me then the door he came in and said, "Let's go for a walk." I got up and showed the General to the door. His aids and my aid wanted to follow, but we both told them to let us be alone. "I called the Pentagon and talked to General Arnold." "The Joint Chiefs are pleased with you not only with what you did in France but with the whole European command."

"France was nothing, and what good did come from it was just pure luck," I said. "The changes I did to the European command weren't anything you wouldn't have done."

"I beg to differ with you." "You have a knack of looking at something and turning it into a positive way." "That is a quality that doesn't come around very often; I envy your talent."

"Well, that's very kind of you, Sir."

"Did you know General Arnold is going to retire?"

"The last time I talked to him, he talked about retirement." "Do you think you will replace him?"

"I don't know it's not up to me; they could pick anyone; besides, I'm getting kind of old myself." "I think they would want a younger man."

"Well, I'm pulling for you, Sir."

"Well, let's talk about Vietnam." "The four things we want is access to look for our MIAs; we would also like to trade pack and establish a consulate somewhere in their country." "If they are willing, to establish a military base there." "That last one might just be wishful thinking for now since it hasn't been that long since the war."

"They aren't going to give us anything unless we give them something, Sir."

"This, I know, I think they want some equipment, that's why General Kien wants to see you."

"I would agree, what can I give them?"

"I'm authorized to tell you anything that we don't use anymore you can offer them." "I have a list of things you can offer them, but memorize it, don't take it with you."

"I'm thinking about the Hawk missiles and Hueys; I'll bet you they will give anything for them."

"I hope you are right."

"Are there any plans for me if they decided to keep me."

"That got discussed; we will extract you, but I don't think they would be so stupid to do that." "In the eyes of the world, they would be considered a rouge country, and not many countries would have anything to do with them." I stared at him for a while, then he said, "You have second thoughts about going."

"No, I just hope I don't get flashbacks when I'm there."

"You do well on this assignment, and the Pentagon and I will consider you our golden boy."

I smiled and said, "I thought I was already your golden boy."

"Well, I guess you are," the general said, laughing. Getting serious, the General said, "James, I can't tell you how important this mission is." "We don't have a lot of bases in that area, and since the Vietnamese don't like the Chinese, it's an opportunity to get a foothold in that area."

"Yes, Sir, you should know the reason I agreed to go was the MIAs."

"I understand." We talk some more, and I tried to get him to come to my home for lunch, but he said he had unfinished business back at his office. We then headed to General Abram's helicopter so that I could see him off.

For some days, I was dwelling on the trip. I decided to call General Abrams and ask him if I can talk to Colonel Henderson, and he permitted me. I drove out to Bamberg and went to Colonel Henderson's office. "Colonel Henderson in?" I asked his clerk.

"Yes, Sir, let me check to see what he is doing, Sir." The clerk stuck his head into the Colonel's office and told him I was here and said to me, "Please go in, Sir."

"So, good to see you, General," said Colonel Henderson.

"It's James Bill, and it's good to see you too."

"What can I do for you?" the Colonel asked.

"Are you too busy to go for a walk with me?" I said seriously.

"For you, I'm not that busy."

We walked towards the parade grounds in silence, and then I turned to him and said, "I've come to you for some advice and reassurance, but what I tell you is confidential."

"Alright, James, what is it?"

"Without going into detail, the Pentagon is sending me to Vietnam to meet with General Kien."

"How do you feel about it?"

"I don't know, perhaps apprehensive."

"So, why are you going then?"

"Because it's in the United States' best interest, and there are a lot of people who would like to know what happened to the MIAs."

He thought then said, "I wasn't at those prison camps with you." "I did talk to Sergeant Brooks about what went on in those camps in detail, and I read the book." "I can tell you, in my opinion, if you show anxiety or are anxious in front of the Vietnamese, they will see it and use it against you."

"Well, I was able to control it in Pairs."

"Yes, you did, for a few hours, you will be in Vietnam for days."

"Yes, I know."

"Well, you're not the same man you were when you were in Vietnam."
"I would suggest if you start to get anxious just focus on something pleasant like Maria and your boys."

"Now, that sounds like an idea that might just work."

"You hungry?" asked Colonel Henderson.

"I could eat." We went to a restaurant in Bamberg, and the conversation changed to more pleasant things.

Eleven days had passed, and there was still no word from the Vietnamese. I called General Abrams at his house, "Sir, it has been Eleven days and still no word, have you heard anything."

"No, but I'm not too concern." "I think what they are doing is trying to shake you by not contacting you."

"Yes, I think you're right; it sounds like something they would do."

Three days later, I got a call from General Abrams, "Well, I got a letter from the Vietnamese." "It was brief you're to be at the airport at Rhein-Main nine o'clock tomorrow; they will have an Air France jet waiting for you."

"They are trying to reestablish power and control after I made that trip to France, that's why they are doing it this way."

"I feel you are correct," he replied. "If tomorrow is too soon for you to get here, I will contact them and tell them to reschedule the trip."

"No, I won't play the game to see who has the biggest balls as they did in the peace talks; I'll be there tomorrow."

That night I went home and told Maria who had a distressed look on her face. My suitcase was already partly packed, Maria, and I finished packing it then we set it aside. The children were informed about my pending trip after dinner; of course, Frederic asked me to bring him something back.

I took a helicopter to the airport and got there by eight in the morning. General Abrams and one of his aides were there to see me off as well as Colonel Brady. I was given advice and took what I knew would work. When nine rolled around, the Air France jet hadn't come, and it annoyed me, and when ten rolled around, finally the Air France landed. Now you would think things would go quickly, but the Vietnamese were still playing games and didn't disembark nor call for me. This time they pushed my last button, and forty minutes later, they finally paged me to embark on the jet, but I didn't move. "James, it's time to go," said General Abrams confused why I didn't go.

"No Sir, it's not time, they can wait." They kept on paging me, but I ignored them. Finally, I told Colonel Brady, "Tell the pilot of that Air France that I will be there shortly when I finish writing a note for General Kien." "Telling him how rude some of their people were."

"Yes, Sir."

After the Colonel did as I said, it wasn't long when three Vietnamese men came hurrying towards where I sat. One of them said, "General, you don't understand there is no disrespect." "We just had some complication that prevented us from greeting you sooner."

"Bullshit, if you or your people do this again whatever your government or General Kien wanted, they won't get it, you understand." The shocked and frighten Vietnamese men shook their heads, yes, and I got up with my things with a scowl on my face and followed them to the jet. As we were walking, I turned around and winked at General Abrams, and he started chuckling.

I got on the plane; they wanted to take my luggage, but I said no, and I stored it above my seat. The flight was a long one; we stopped in India for refueling and a change of pilots. I had slept not wanting to talk to anyone; besides, I was going to make sure I was well-rested by the time I met General Kien, and I had hoped that the sleep would help with the jetlag. I thought I was going to land in Hanoi, but we disembarked in Saigon now called Ho Chi Minh City. The Air France jet finally came to a stop, and one of the Vietnamese personnel came up to me and said, "Please this way, Sir."

I grabbed my bag, the man who directed me to disembark tried to take it from me, and I said, "I'll take my bag."

"Sir, if I don't take your bag, I will get in trouble." I stared at him and released the bag, and the man took it, and we proceeded to leave the jet. There was a receiving line with General Kien standing at the bottom of the stairs. There were two lines of soldiers dressed in khakis, all bearing rifles and a small military band playing as I walked down the portable stairs of the Jet.

I saluted and then shook General Kien's hand, "It's good to see you, General York, and you are a real general this time."

"I am, and it's nice to see you in a more pleasant situation." He chuckled and indicated we should go down the receiving line. I ignored the soldiers and the band. When we were clear of everyone, I noticed that the place hadn't changed much from when I first came to Vietnam as a corporal.

We got into a black Mercedes limousine, and as we went, I choose not to look at my surroundings. "So, can I assume you're uneasy about being in my country?" asked General Kien.

"I've put my feelings about Vietnam in the past."

"So, you have no anger towards anyone in Vietnam?"

I laughed and said, "I wouldn't say that, either." "Did you get the movies I sent you?"

"Yes, I did, and I saw them." "That native picture is the one we talked about?"

"Yes," I replied.

"The movies you sent were so good my government is allowing them to get released to the people."

"Good, your children will love the cartoon."

"Yes, I believe your right." We stopped in front of a large building, then got out and went in. There were a lot of people and guards in the building. I followed the General to a large room where there were refreshments and other official-looking people. When I arrived, the same military band that was playing at the jet started to play again when they got to the building.

"Please General help yourself to the food," said General Kien to me. I helped myself to some of the food, but I didn't overdo it.

General Kien introduced me to some of the people who were there. One person who spoke English and was a little drunk, I think, said, "I understand you have become quite a capitalist General."

His statement irritated General Kien, but before he could say something, I said, "Tell me something, Mr. Sang, do you live in a hut as your farmers do."

"No, of course not."

"I didn't think you did, and as I can see here, you don't eat the same food nor wear the same clothing as them." "To me, Sir, you're more of a capitalist than me, especially since you live in a socialist country." That shut Sang's mouth and had shaken him, and he moved away.

"He will get punished for insulting you," said General Kien.

"No need it wasn't as big an insult as what happened at the consulate in France."

"What do you mean?" I told him the whole story from the beginning as to what happened at the airport and what I thought the reason was for the treatment. He was visibly shaken and angry; he believed me totally, and he said, "They will be dealt with harshly."

General Kien stuck to my side, and after a while, he said, "Perhaps you will want to get some rest since your long flight I will take you to your room and we will talk tonight."

"In private, I hope," I replied.

"Yes, there is much I wish to talk to you about." I was taken to my room when I laid down it didn't take me long to fall asleep.

When I woke up, it was dark out, I looked out the window, and I could see a courtyard down below and beyond a busy street. I got dressed and left the room, wandered down a hallway until I found a flight of stairs. A soldier said something to me, but I didn't understand him. I must have looked confused because he left the room and brought out a woman who spoke better English than me, and she said, "General, I see you have woken up."

"Yes, I thought I'd go outside and get some air."

"That would not be wise without an armed guard; some people still have anger at the United States because of the war."

"Yes, I can understand that it was a nasty war." "There are Americans who still feel anger also."

"I can have a guard accompany you if you wish, but I would not go far or stay out too long at night."

"Alright, General Kien is meeting me sometime tonight anyway."

"Yes, he will be here shortly." She called for a guard and said something to him, and he showed me to the door.

We went out to a lit courtyard, and I walked around. I believe it was the same courtyard that I could see from my window. I found a door to the street, and I motioned to the guard that I wanted to go out. He didn't want to, but with an unhappy look on his face, he opened the door, and we stepped out. I looked up, and down the street, it was in or around Ho Chi Minh City for sure. There were some buildings and stores with their lights on everything seem clean. The vehicles and people that went by didn't pay much attention to me. After about five minutes, I motioned to the guard to go back into the courtyard. It was about another twenty minutes later when General Kien joined me.

General Kien said something to his guards they cleared out the courtyard and he posted guards on the outside of all the exits. We then found some chairs and sat down, and I said, "How are things going for you?" I asked.

"There has been much progress, but we have had our troubles."

"Where were you when the Chinese invaded?"

"I was in command of the resistance; how do you think I made general." "We stopped the Chinese cold." "The Chinese Army didn't know what hit them."

"From what I heard, they said they just wanted to punish you for something, and then they withdrew."

"You believed them?"

"No, I think you kicked their ass, and they were afraid they were going to be caught up in a long war like we were."

"Exactly, that's what happened."

"You are having trouble with Cambodia. Since you don't have the best relationship with China, you are running short on supplies."

"We still have the support of the Soviet Union and other countries."

"I know the Soviet Union is going to collapse; they can't afford to take care of their own, let alone you." "I also know their equipment isn't made very good." "Those other countries you talk about what can they offer you."

He laughed then changed the subject, "So what is the feeling of your country's government towards our operation in Cambodia."

"Officially, they do not support your attack on the Khmer Rouge and your support for the socialist of Cambodia." "Privately, my government hates the Khmer Rouge and hopes you are successful."

"So why don't they openly support us?"

I looked at him surprised he even asked and said, "You are a socialist country; we are capitalist." "I believe because of politics; they can't support you verbally." "If I were the president of my country, I wouldn't hesitate to support you."

"Are you saying your country would support us quietly?"

"Perhaps it is a topic we should talk about another time." "I will tell you the United States has already supported you in a roundabout way by not taking a stand against you at the U.N."

He was quiet for a few seconds then said, "I would like to talk to you more about this, but it's getting late, so let's talk tomorrow."

"That would be alright but tomorrow let's not beat around the bush let's talk plainly." "You asked me to come here for a reason let's just talk about what that reason is."

"That will be fine with me," he replied.

The next day, when I woke up, I felt much better, and they tried to prepare breakfast, something I would get at home. As I was eating, someone tapped me from behind, and I turned around there, smiling was a young Vietnamese man, which I quickly recognized. It was the fourteen-year-old boy now older who was a prison guard when I was kept captive. "General, I could not resist coming and seeing you."

"I'm so happy to see a familiar face, and I am happy you survived."

"Then, you do remember me?"

"Of course, you're Huu Phuoc, my friend, you were very kind to my friends and me." "Pleases sit down and let's talk about you." I got him something to eat, and we talked for some time. I had asked him how he could come into this building, and he told me he had General Kien's permission. After the American war in Vietnam had ended, he had left the military. He was working in an office in Ho Chi Minh City. We were having a pleasant conversation when General Kien showed up.

"I see you have found a familiar face General," General Kien said, smiling.

"I would have been offended if you hadn't allowed Phuoc to come to see me thank you."

"There is no need for thanks, I knew you were fond of Phuoc back in Hanoi," General Kien said. We talked and laughed at the things of the past for another half hour to forty-five minutes, then Huu Phuoc said he had to leave, and I got left with General Kien.

"Let's go for a ride so we can talk freely," said General Kien. We got into a car, and he drove off, we didn't go far out of the city when we came to a large military compound. We parked and got out and started walking; I saw a lot of American equipment left behind; most were a lot of parts. As we walked, the General was quiet at first, then he said, "You know your right about us losing support from the Chinese."

"I would also guess you are not getting much meaningful support from the Soviet Union anymore," I said.

"Why would you think that?"

I smiled and said, "I thought we agreed to talk truthfully." "I assume you know that after that little war we had in Europe, the Soviets who already needed money now had to pay the west a lot of money for the damages." "Russia already long before the war was having a hard time supplying the rest of the Soviet countries now it is worse." "They are trying to hold on to what they have left even though their people aren't happy, so they can't be too concerned with those who aren't part of their union." "It doesn't take a genius to see that the Soviet Union will start to crumble within ten or twenty years."

"You're right, but if you tell anyone I agree with you, I will deny it."

"I understand, so just what do you want from the United States."

"The campaign in Cambodia, as you have said, has given us troubles." "My government is committed to this war; we must be they are our neighbor, and the Khmer Rouge are not acceptable, but we are in no mood for a long war." "Without equipment and supplies from others, we could sustain the campaign, but it would be a long war, with many deaths on our side."

"So, you wish the United States to help supply you?"

"Yes, we have a lot that you left behind, but most don't work because of a lack of equipment to maintain or repair it."

"I want you to understand that we are willing to give you more than what you will ask, but we also have things we wish."

"Let's have a private lunch, and so we can talk."

"Sounds good to me."

We had a good lunch and a pleasant conversation, then he said, "I would like to hear what the United States wants first."

"How much power do you have to make decisions?"

"I have been given full authority to make any fair deal."

"What we want is fair, the United States wishes four things access to look for our men who are missing in action." "We would like a trade pack, and we would also wish to establish a consulate somewhere in your country." "And since my country doesn't trust the Chinese, we would like to establish a military base in your country."

General Kien stared blankly out into space and was quiet for what seemed to be forever. He said, "I can give your country permission to look for your lost soldiers in Vietnam, and we would help you." "However, for those lost in Cambodia and Laos, your country would have to ask those countries." "We would also be willing to exchange diplomats, and we will allow you to have at least two consulates." "I would welcome a trade pack, but the details should get worked out with our diplomats." He then went silent for a few seconds, then said, "What kind of base would the United States want?"

That was a good question; General Abrams didn't tell me what kind of base the United States wanted. I figured that a naval base would be the best with that we would get a place for our ground troops with the Marines, planes with the naval airpower, and a naval port. "We would like to have a naval base somewhere in your country."

General Kien had to now think for a few seconds then said, "I believe that a small naval base would be alright, but again the diplomats will need to work out the details."

"General Kien, I trust your word, but my government doesn't know you as I do." "I feel that these agreements need to be in writing."

"That would be acceptable."

"What is it that you would want from the United States?"

"We need parts to repair and maintain what helicopters we have."

"Are you talking about the Huey?"

"Yes."

"You will have them, and I will do better than that. We will supply you with fully operating Hueys, which are in good shape."

General Kien was surprised that I had sweetened the deal, and he was happy about it. "Well, that is very generous of you; we also need some trucks."

Trucks were on the list of things that General Abrams said I could offer, so I said, "Yes, we can supply you with some trucks." He then gave me the rest of the list of things that he wanted. Most of the things I did agree to supply them with an overall, he seemed to be satisfied with what I said. When he got finished, I said, "I have something else to offer you that you haven't asked for."

"And what is that?" asked General Kien.

"Could your Army use some missiles?"

"Missiles, what kind of missiles?"

"Hawk missiles."

"Aren't they ground to air we don't have any need for them now."

"Originally, they got designed as a ground to air." "Then we sold some to the Israelis, and they modified them so that they can be used as a ground to air or ground to ground." "When they fought the Egyptians, they used them with great effectiveness." "The United States knows how they have modified them and is willing to show you."

"How much will this cost us, and how mobile is this system?"

"I don't know the cost, but it shouldn't be too high. We don't use this missiles system anymore." "The missile system comes in two ways on tracks, much like a tank, and they are on trailers."

"What are the drawbacks of this system?"

"Those who operate it must be good at it for maximum effectiveness." "Once the missiles get fired, it takes six men to reload the missiles, and the command center is on wheels and is as big as a two-and-a-half-ton truck."

"Did you use them in the war with us?"

"I am not sure, but I think we might have had a few here, but I don't think we used any of them." "However, that conflict in Europe they were used quite heavily with great results."

"We would welcome the missiles." "I would assume you would send technicians to show us how to use the equipment and maintain it."

"Yes, but that should be worked out with diplomats."

"I think we should announce the agreement we have reached between our countries."

"Let me call Washington D.C. before we make that announcement."

"Alright, let me show you a phone you can use," General Kien said.

I was left alone in a room with a phone, and I decided to call General Arnold in Washington. "General Arnold, please, this is General York."

"He is in a meeting General."

"Interrupt him this is more important, tell him who called."

"Yes, Sir, I'll go inform him."

Five minutes later, General Arnold came on the phone, "James, how's it going in Vietnam?"

"Better than expected, Sir."

"What did they give us?"

"Everything, Sir."

"I'll expect a full report, James."

"You'll have it, Sir." "Sir, they want to go to press and announce the agreement; is it alright to do it?"

"It's alright, but use your best judgment when talking to the media."

"Will do, Sir." I hung up the phone, left the room, and said to General Kien, "Make arrangements with the press."

"We will have a state banquet tonight, and then tomorrow, we will have the signing of the agreement and a statement to the press."

"I would like to read over the agreement before I sign it."

"What's the matter you don't trust me?"

"I trust you; I just don't trust your government," I said with a smile.

That night we went to a large decorated hall. Speeches got made in the Vietnamese language. I knew I would have to say a few words of meaningless claptrap just to satisfy the Vietnamese, but I didn't care. The festivities ended a little after ten, and I headed back to my room with the treaty that was in both English and Vietnamese. I read it repeatedly to see if there was anything changed in our agreement. Also, worded in a way that there was no commitment to what was agreed. I'm not that much of an educated man, but I know when something is bullshit or not. The only thing that General Kien put extra in the agreement was a clause. It said if either side becomes dissatisfied with what the agreement stated that each government would come back and meet and work out their differences. This addition seemed logical it showed that to me, they don't want any hard feeling because of a misunderstanding. The next day General Kien and I joined in the same room where that the party was. There were many media in the hall, which surprised me because I didn't think that a country the size of Vietnam would get that much attention. "I wish to ask you something, but I don't want to disrespect you or your country."

"You won't disrespect me or my country, go ahead and ask."

"For the size of your country and what we are to do, why is there so much media here?" "After all, there are many agreements like ours that doesn't get this much attention."

"Yes, you are right; there are many agreements like ours, but there are not too many agreements between two countries that were at war not long ago." "You are another reason why they are here; it is your presence in Vietnam, but we do have some media from France and other countries." General Kien's response satisfied me. When we got up to talk to the press, he said, "We will give a statement and then answer a few questions before signing the agreement." "Do you want to speak first?" General Kien asked me.

"No, you go first, then I will speak," I said.

He spoke eloquently, giving the United States and me an enthusiastic appreciation for the agreement made with Vietnam. He went into briefly some of the things they would be getting from the United States. He mainly went into the medical items Vietnam would be getting, which went over well.

Then it was my turn, "I want first to say that I am not as eloquent as General Kien." As I was speaking, someone was translating. "I wasn't going to come to Vietnam because of my past experiences." "When my Government told me one of the most important things they wanted was to search for our missing in action, and that got me to change my mind."

I talked some more, and I concluded by saying, "I wish to thank General Kien and the Vietnamese people for the kindness they have shown me." "Now I think you have heard enough from both of us, do you have any questions for us?"

General Kien stood beside me. The first question was from a Vietnamese reporter who spoke in his language; it got translated to me. "General Kien, with past conflicts, do you think the Vietnamese government can work with the United States and the United States with the Vietnamese government?"

"Yes, the fact that General York is here with the permission of his government." "General York and I have gotten along so well even though I commanded the prison camp he was in during the war."

"General York isn't it true that the only reason the United States has ventured into this agreement is the hope to dominate Vietnam." "Also, to have a base to threaten the peaceful people of China?"

This question irritated General Kien, but I told him, "It's alright, I will answer him." "May I ask you where you are from?"

"I am from the Soviet Union."

"No, no, what part of the Soviet Union."

"Russia."

"Is this the same Russia who built a wall dividing Berlin Germany?" "Is this the same Russia who built a fence dividing Europe placing mines along that fence killing men, women, and even children?" "Is this the same Russia that sent thousands if not tens of thousands to the gulags simply for having different views of the Russian government." "The United States doesn't want to dominate anyone, especially Vietnam, unlike Russia." "And Sir, we have a base in Korea, Japan, Philippians, and other places just like Russia has bases in the Mediterranean, Africa, Cuba, and other places." "We are there as a deterrent to protect our friends and interest." "There is no threat to China; they are capable of taking care of themselves, and we have no interest in interfering in the Chinese interest."

That shut the Russian reporter up. The next reporter asked me another question, and then another reporter asked General Kien another question. That's how it went until General Kien ended the news conference. We left and went to another room; General Kien said, "I'm sorry about that Russian reporter you handled it very well."

"I'm used to ignorant pig-headed people, so don't let it bother you."

"Let's get some lunch," suggested General Kien.

"That sounds good to me." As we were eating, I said, "I'm anxious to get back home, I miss my family, so when we are finished with business here, I would like to get a flight back to Germany."

"I'll have a flight for you tonight." "When do you think we can get a shipment of supplies?"

"I would guess as soon as they see the list of things you want." "When I get back, I will get things rolling." "Do you think you could do me a favor before I leave?"

"Yes, what is it you want?"

"I would like to get something that is Vietnamese for my wife and children, a boy who is twelve years old and a boy who is eight years old."

"I'll get something for your family right after lunch?" he said with a smile.

When I boarded my flight, it was nearly nine that night. When the jet left the runway, and out into the ocean, I let out a breath of relief, it was over. After a stopover for refueling, I finally got back to German. I was tired, but I got a ride to General Abrams's office, so he could debrief me and get the ball rolling on the supplies to get shipped. "Congratulations on your success," said General Abrams.

"You're welcome, Sir." There were several officers and clerks recording everything as I sat in a large conference room.

"We will record everything so that we can send a report to the Pentagon," said Colonel Perkins.

"So, James, tell us just how well it went," said General Abrams.

"We got everything we wanted." "It's my opinion that Vietnamese need us, and Vietnamese need us bad." "Vietnam and China are not friends anymore." "Russia, because of the war in Europe, their trade with Vietnam has dropped off dramatically." "To tell you the truth, the Vietnamese just don't think most of their equipment works very well." "So, they are hoping that we are willing to fill their needs." "I learned that the conflict with China drained a lot of their supplies, and now they have no choice but to fight the Khmer Rouge."

"It seems like if they are desperate, perhaps we could charge what we want for our supplies and demand a lot more," said Colonel Jackson.

"That would not be wise; hurting or no hurting the Vietnamese would withdraw from the deal." "The best way to deal with them is to give them more than what they want, build a relationship with them, let them depend on us, and slowly we can get more," I said.

"I would agree," said General Abrams.

I told them everything, then I said, "General Abrams, when do you think all those things can get sent to Vietnam?"

"As soon as this report hits Washington from what General Arnold told me." "The first shipment was loaded before you left, in anticipation of what they want, and you would be successful."

"That would be great; I stuck my neck out and told General Kien that we would be sending his equipment and supplies quickly."

29

PROMOTION THE EUROPEAN COMMAND

I got home about five o'clock the boys were out on the street with their bicycles they dropped them and came running. "Daddy, daddy, what did you bring us," yelled Frederick with joy when I was spotted.

"Bring you; I brought you me, isn't that good enough?"

"That good, you say you bring something," Frederick said, frankly.

"Yes, I did, didn't I; well, we must see what I have in my bags."

"See Frederick, I told you daddy wouldn't forget," said Jonathan.

I went into the house, and Maria was in the kitchen, "Say, lady, you think I can get a kiss while your husband is gone?"

She came out of the kitchen and said with a smile on her face,

"Of course, you can you're probably a better kisser than he is."

"Oh, is that right," I said as I held her in my arms and kissed her.

I spent the next two days at home, getting some rest. Then I went to work doing paperwork, which wasn't my favorite thing. I also spent some time with General Brown, who briefed me on what was going on with the European command. The second day I checked out the missile battalion with Colonel Upton. Then I went and checked the rest of the forces the following week.

It was the end of the day when I got a call from General Abrams. "James just wanted to let you know that I got a call from General Arnold he said those supplies and equipment were shipped by air and sea to Vietnam." "A diplomat and his team have also been sent to set up one or two embassies."

"That sounds excellent, Sir." "It should make General Kien and the people of Vietnam happy."

"Everyone in Washington is very pleased with you." "I'm going to go there for a meeting tomorrow; I won't be around for a few days."

"That's alright, Sir; I can handle things."

"I know you can." I went home delighted that the supplies got sent and I was feeling so good I thought it would be an excellent thing to take Maria and the boys to dinner.

When I got home that euphoria, I was feeling left. Maria had gotten visibly shaken, holding the two boys who were crying, and tears were streaming down their faces. "What's the matter?" I asked, concerned.

"Jack and Maryann going to America tonight," said Maria, upset.

"Catherin too," Frederick said, still crying.

"And you, Jonathan, are upset because Elizabeth is going," I said sympathetically. He nodded, and I said, "They are moving to North Carolina, which is only about five hundred and thirty miles away from where we live in Missouri."

They all stared at me, and Frederick asked, "Is that very far, daddy?"

"No, just a few hours." "Now, let's all go over to Top's house to say goodbye to them." I had been so busy I had forgotten to break the news to my family of their leaving. Saying goodbye wasn't easy; I even got emotional with his going. Life goes on; we exchanged addresses then said we would visit each other, but who knows what will happen. I didn't know when I would leave the military, I had plans to retire years ago, but something always came up. Top was on my mind for many days I talked to Captain Marc Dizon about how I felt, he, Top and I were all good friends. He told me he was also hurting, but it isn't as if he died. Marc was right, of course, as the days went by feeling within myself and at home did ease up.

I was working on plans for maneuvers for the whole European command when I got a buzz on the intercom, "Sir General Abrams is here to see you."

"Send him in." "General, it is a pleasure to see you."

"The pleasure is mine, James." "Let's go for a walk, James, if you can."

"I can, but the last time we went for a walk, I went to Vietnam."

"No, I'm not sending you anywhere," he said with a chuckle.

As we walked, I asked, "How're things going with Vietnam?"

"Great thanks to you." "They have been receiving equipment and supplies, and we opened up two embassies, one in Hanoi and the other in Ho Chi Min city."

"That's good.

"You were right; they are desperate for our help; we're getting more done now than when we were at war with them."

"How are things in Washington and with General Arnold?" I asked.

"That's what I came down to talk to you about it." "I looked at him, and the General asked, "How are you handling things here?"

"Just fine, I inspected most of the units, and I only had to make minor changes." "I was working on plans for maneuvers this summer, and I will then get to see how well everyone performs."

"Yes, I know, who is, in your opinion, is your right-hand man?"

"General Brown," I said without hesitation.

"You think if you were to leave, he could take over your command?"

I looked at him surprised he asked, then said, "Yes, you are thinking of transferring me?"

"Yes, and No, the truth is you already have been transferred." He reached into his pocket, handed me a star, and said, "Congratulation, you have been promoted and now in full command of the European forces."

"What about you?"

"General Arnold retired yesterday. I'm taking his spot as a member of the Joint Chief of Staff in the Pentagon." "Don't get too comfortable in your new command because I'm getting old and will be retiring soon, and they want you to fill my spot." "When they offered me the position, they said if I was thinking of retiring in less than a year, they give the position to you."

"There are others with more experience than me."

"That is debatable, but for sure, there isn't any including me that have had more success and foresight."

"Shit, they name a tank after you."

"Yeah, they did, didn't they?" "The truth I'm retiring in a year, but I wanted just to experience being a Joint Chief and commander of the whole Army, besides it's nice for retirement."

"Well, you're more qualified to be there than I."

"Well, you better get qualified in about a year."

"Yes, Sir." General Abrams handed me orders and said there would be a big ceremony for the change of command.

As I went home, the boys were outside playing, they waved, but they continued to play there would be time later to tell them. Maria, who was five months pregnant, was sitting on the couch resting. I would hire someone to do her chores, but she didn't want anyone to do it. I sat down next to her, put my arm around her, and gave her a big kiss. "You are home early," she said, pleasantly surprised."

"Yes, there is some news that I feel you need to know."

"What is it," she said curiously.

I pulled out of my pocket the star that General Abrams gave me and said, "I got promoted and a new assignment."

"That's wonderful, honey, but what's your new assignment?" she asked happily about the promotion but concern of the assignment.

"I am in command of the whole European Command; General Abrams was promoted and is going to Washington, D.C."

"Are we going to have to move?" she asked, even more concerned.

"No, I'll command from here General Brown will be taking my spot he will be moved up to Frankfurt."

"That is a relief. I'm in no shape to move now," said Maria.

"Well, I have more for you to know." "While I was talking to General Abrams, he told me that he would be retiring in little more than a year." "When he retires, I'm supposed to take his place, that means we would have to move to America."

"To our home?' she said with hope.

"No, not right away, the Washington D.C. area is where we will live."

"Oh," she said disappointedly.

"We will be about two hundred and thirty miles from North Carolina," I added.

"She smiled and said, "We will be able to visit Maryann and Jack."

"Yes." We told the boys after they came in, and they were excited not at my promotion or assignment but at the possibility of going to live in the United States.

I turned my uniforms in to get my new rank sewed on before I went to work the next day. General Brown wasn't in his office, so I sent one of my aids to look for him. I got busy with paperwork, and in about forty-five minutes after I started, General Brown came into my office. "You have something for me, James."

"Yes, Bill, I need to talk to you." "You have been doing a lot of work that I haven't had time to do, and you have done it well."

"Thanks, James."

"How many more years do you think you will remain in the Army?"

"At least eight."

"If I had to leave my command, are you capable of taking over."

"I'm capable, but I'm not as capable as you." "Are you leaving?"

"Yes, I've been reassigned." I grabbed into my pocket for General Brown's star and handed it to him. "You have gotten promoted to lieutenant general, and you are replacing me."

"Thanks, but where are you going, James?"

"I'm still your boss; I got promoted too, and I'm replacing General Abrams." "General Abrams is replacing General Arnold."

"This is a big surprise; I'm a bit overwhelmed."

"Yes, it was for me too, but it is better than finding out when we have our combined ceremony next week."

"We will need to get together, so there is an easy transition."

"Yes, we will start today." "I will tell you what I've been doing, make suggestions on who to promote, and the standard I wish to continue."

"Let me clear my calendar, and I'll be back in twenty minutes."

When he came back, I said, "Let's cover promotions first." "It's up to you; I will make suggestions, though." "There is something you need to know; things need to go well because in a little more than a year, I'm supposed to replace General Abrams, and you will replace me." "If I replace General Abrams, I expect the European command to be still as excellent as it is now."

"It will be James; I can assure you of that."

"To replace your position, I have no preference any Brigadier will do if you can work with him, and he isn't a desk jockey." "To replace the Brigadier, I would suggest Colonel Upton, and to replace Colonel Upton; I would suggest Captain Dizon." "It will be up to you, but those two have done an excellent job and are go-getters." We worked way past quitting time and agreed to meet the next day at ten to get other business done.

Over the next couple of days, we hit everything I did and what I expected. The buzz of the change of command was going around the post, and I assume the whole European command. We worked on the maneuvers for the entire European forces when my secretary came in and said, "Sir, you have a phone call."

"I said I didn't want to be disturbed."

"It's from a Lieutenant Olivera; he said it is an emergency."

607

I stared at him for a few seconds wondering what he wanted then said, "Alright." "What's the emergency, Allen?" "I'm swamped with work?"

"There has been a bad accident, First Sergeant William Filipe, his wife Elisa, and their daughter Frieda were all killed."

"What about the boys?"

"They are in shock but are alright." "I'm staying with them; I don't speak German, but I figure out they want you." "Captain McMullen is working on arrangements for Sergeant Filipe, his wife, and daughter." "I told him I would take care of the boys and contact you."

"Alright, tell the boys the best way you can; I will be there soon."

"I'll do that, Jim."

I hung up the phone, and General Brown said, "Troubles?"

"Yes, its Sergeant Filipe; he, his wife and daughter have been killed in an accident, his boys are alright they have me as next of kin."

"When are you going?"

"As soon as I inform Maria."

General Brown left my office, and I called Maria. "Maria, something terrible has happened." I went into detail as to what happened then said, "David and Oliver have been asking for us to come can you handle two more boys."

"Of course, I can handle two more boys, but I think you should go alone to get the boys." "I don't want to take Jonathan and Frederic out of school, and I don't think it would be a good idea for me to travel."

"Alright, give a kiss to the boys, and I will be home as soon as possible."

"I'll do that; I love you."

It was late afternoon when I got to the boy's home. I rang the doorbell Allen opened the door, and almost the same time the boys spotted me they came running into my arms crying. "Let me talk to Allen he is my cousin, and then we will talk," I told the boys in German. Allen and I sat down he explained what happened.

"Sergeant Filipe and Elisa were having trouble with Frieda." "Frieda took off with some boy they didn't like, and in their frustration with Frieda Sergeant Filipe and Elisa left the boys home and went to a Hofbräu to drink beer and talk." "They went looking for Freda, found her, and on their way back, they got killed in an auto accident."

"I'll stay with the boys until I can take them home with me," I said.

"I'm sorry for what happen, but I'm relieved that you are here." "I had a hard time trying to communicate with them."

"Well, it will be alright now you can go back to your quarters." Allen gathered his thing as he did, he said, "Congratulations on your promotion and assignment."

"Thanks."

Allen left, and I called the boys out of their room. We all sat on the couch; I had arms around them. "What will happen to us now that mama and papa Wilhelm are gone?" asked Oliver.

"Well, you and David will have two more brothers."

Oliver looked confused, and David said, "He's adopting us."

"Is that true you are going to be my papa?" asked Oliver, hopefully.

"Yes, I love you both very much." "You will both have to learn English, and there will be differences in how you will get raised."

"We tried to learn English in school, but we didn't do well," said David.

"Don't worry, your new mother and brothers will help you," I said. "Jonathan felt the same way about learning German."

"When are we going to go live in your house?" asked Oliver."

"First, it's not my house, it's our house, and we will go as soon as I take care of things here and get permission from the authorities." "There will be happy times and sad times in the next few days, but everything will get better." "I promise you." I took the boys to dinner. They didn't eat much; their mine was on all of what happened. When we got back to their home, I had them both bathe. They bathed as I called Maria and told her how the boys were. I let the boys stay up until nine, then I sent them to bed and tucking them in. I gave them both a kiss; then, as I started to shut the door, they said they wanted it left open. Before I went to sleep, I checked in on the boys Oliver had gotten out of his bed and crawled into David's bed, much like that of Frederic and Jonathan.

The next morning, I fixed breakfast and then called Captain McMullen and asked him what he had done for the deceased. "The funeral is tomorrow." "I felt it best that Sergeant Filipe got buried with his wife in Germany." "He has no family back in the states other than his siblings, who he wasn't close with." "He and his family will have full military services."

"Thank you; give me the time and place for the funeral." He gave me all the information, and I hung up the phone. The boys got dressed to go with me to town. I went through Sergeant Filipe and Elisa's things to find any critical paper I would need when I saw the German lawyer.

We got to the lawyer's office, and after some polite conversation, he asked a few questions to the boys, "Do you want him for a father?" Both boys said yes, and then he said, "You must live with him."

"We wouldn't want to live with anyone else," the boys said.

"General, do you plan to adopt them?"

"Yes, I've talked to my wife, and we both agreed to adopt them."

"You might have a problem, you because you're an American citizen."

"I hold dual citizenship; I am also a German."

"You are?"

"Yes."

"That will make it a lot easier for you; with this paperwork of the parent's desires, I don't think you will have any problems." "Legally, you can take them back to your home in Schweinfurt."

The next place we went to was a realtor to sell the house. The realtor said it would be listed tomorrow, and I said I would have it clean out this weekend. Next went to the local church to talk to the pastor. "Father, I would like to sell or give away the items in the boy's home that they don't want."

"I will send Father Schmitt and some of the nuns to their home."

"I will need to have them come by in a couple of hours." He agreed, and we left to have lunch, and then we went to their home.

"You boys stay here in the living room, and I will bring things in here to see if you want them, if you don't, I will give them to the nuns." I started in their parent's room and brought them out. The boys just stared at the things their parents had, and I said, "I know this is hard, but it will get better." The boys sighed, then got busy sorting and about forty-five minutes, and most of their parent's room cleaned out the people from the church came with a truck. By eight o'clock at night, we finally clean out the house, except for the car, and I was going to give that to Allen. I then took the boys to a hotel; they were exhausted.

I got the boys dressed the next day in their best clothing, and we went to the funeral to say it was rough for the boys would be an understatement they couldn't stop crying. After the funeral, they rolled up on their beds in the fetal positions, still sniffling until they fell asleep. I let them sleep and went downstairs to use the lobby phone to call Maria, and I talked to Frederic and Jonathan also. Then David and Oliver woke up, it was six o'clock at night, and I said, "Let's go get something to eat." They didn't want to eat, but I coax them, and we went to a quiet place.

"When will we leave for Schweinfurt," asked David.

"You mean home?" I said, knowing what he meant but wanting him think Schweinfurt as his new home.

"Yes."

"We will load up the car tomorrow morning and then go."

The next day I don't know how I did it, but I got everything into the car, including their bicycles, which got broken down. We left Bad Mergentheim, and as we traveled, Oliver asked, "Why do we need to learn English when everyone knows how to speak German."

"Because we will soon go to live in America, and not many people speak German there."

"When will we go to America?" asked David.

"Maybe a little more than a year." "How do you feel about that?"

"I don't know; I haven't been to America; I hear it is big."

"Yes, it is big and different, but I think both of you will like it."

We reached Schweinfurt in the afternoon, and I headed straight for home. I was surprised not to see the Frederic and Jonathan outside playing it was Saturday I parked out on the street. The boys and I got out and headed for the house Oliver said as we went, "It's a big house." I smiled and continued to the house. Frederic and Jonathan were in the playroom. Maria was in the kitchen when I came in with David and Oliver.

Maria, Jonathan, and Frederic all came to greet us, and at first, everyone froze and stared at each other, not knowing just what to do. Then Frederic went over to Oliver, hugged him, and kissed him then said, "Welcome to the family." Then Jonathan did the same to David by this time, both Oliver and David were in tears. Maria came over and comforted them then brought them into the family room with Jonathan and Frederic following them. I opened the garage and started to empty the staff car. By the time I unloaded the car, both David and Oliver were laughing and giggling with Frederic and Jonathan. It got decided that David would be in Jonathan's room, and Oliver would be in Frederic's bedroom; hopefully, the boys could stay in their rooms. The boys took everything upstairs to their bedrooms except for the bicycles. After they did that, all four boys went to the garage to fix their bikes. I sat down with Maria and nestled with her while the children were outside. That night the boys stayed in their rooms, but Oliver and Frederic slept together in the same bed, as did David and Jonathan. I hired a tutor for David and Oliver to learn English and to help them with their studies. Over the next few days, Oliver and David adjusted just fine and fitting in as if they had always been there.

30

THE PENTAGON

B ecause Maria was pregnant, General Abrams agreed to have the change of command in Schweinfurt. At the ceremony, I had my family in the stands. Jonathan was explaining what was going on to Oliver and David. It was time for me to give a speech I thought I gave the same quality of speech that I always do, but I found out it was a lot more, and the news people hung on every word. General Abrams came over to me and said, "That speech you made was quite impressive." "I've never heard you make a speech that powerful."

"You think so; I thought I was just average." "Maybe I just got lucky, or in my old age, I just come off smoother."

"Old age, shit, you still have your mother's milk on your breath," General Abrams said, laughing.

There was a party after the change of command, but the press wanted to talk to me first. I received several questions about my speech. One reporter said, "Isn't it true the only reason why you got this command and promotion is because you went to Vietnam and made an agreement with them?"

"I would say that my going to Vietnam didn't hurt, but I feel there were many other reasons I got the command."

"And what were those other reasons?" asked the same reporter.

"Well, I transformed the European command, and I am also the next one to replace General Abrams."

That seemed to satisfy the reporter, and the questions went on. One German reporter asked, "I have information that you are adopting two boys from Bad Mergentheim, is this true, and what can you tell us about it?"

"The answer is yes, the boys are from Bad Mergentheim I haven't adopted them, yet I'm going through the red tape of the adoption process." "I knew these boys and their parents from before they came into my family." "Their parents and sister passed away in a bad accident." "They have no other relatives since my family, and I were close to them, my wife and I decided to adopt them."

"That's very generous of you; I heard that you also before their parents died you bought them a furnished home and a car."

"Yes, you seem to know a lot."

"That's what I do for a living General." "How are the boys now?"

"My family and I love the boys very much, and I believe they love us; they have fitted into my family very well." They changed the subject, and after a little time the news conference was over, and I could join the party with my family.

I was in all the papers, but I wasn't interested. General Brown took off some time to move his family to Frankfurt, and I got busy with the European command. The weeks went by, and the boys were doing well; it was difficult, and there were bumps in the road, but the boys melded into the family just fine. Learning English was hard for the two boys, but slowly they were learning with help from all of us. As soon as General Brown moved, he got busy working on the European command. I had to meet with NATO and with the governments of the western European nations from time to time. About every two months, General Brown contacted me either by phone or in person. NATO wanted updated equipment, and after giving it some thought, I agreed to give it to them with all sensitive equipment removed, though. It wasn't that I didn't trust them, but in their hands, there was a high chance that the other side might get their hands on the sensitive equipment. It was May when General Abrams came to see me, "James, I have an assignment you're not going to like."

"What's that, Sir?"

"An American diplomat wants you to accompany him when he meets the Soviet President in France."

"You know how I feel about the Soviet government, and I'm sure they are aware of how I feel about them."

"I'm aware of your feelings, and I'm sure you're right; they most likely do know how you feel about them too." "I told all this to the diplomat, and he still wants you he's pushing hard James."

"Does he have any power to force me to go?"

"He knows a lot of people who could hurt you."

"I see, is the diplomat arrogant?"

"No, I didn't find him arrogant." "He might have a good reason for wanting you with him."

"Maybe he does have a good reason, but I'm not going to like it."

"Then, you will do it?"

"Yeah, for you, but if it were anyone else, I'd say no."

I was to go to the American consulate in Paris and first meet with the American ambassador, who would be with a diplomat from the states. I informed Maria about this and said I would be away for a day or two. The day before I was to leave, I was sitting on the patio with Maria she was reading a magazine, and I was just staring off into space. My eyes focus on the boys who were playing in the yard. My thoughts were when I first met Frederic; he was a charterer very adventurous and outgoing he had grown quite a bit. However, he was very much a little boy still, as was Oliver, who was a bit younger than he was. Then there was Jonathan trying to be a soldier to support his sibling back in Missouri. He had grown at least a foot taller, and his voice was getting deeper. But even though he was fighting growing up, I don't think that would last long; he was very interested in girls, unlike Oliver and Frederic. David was only a few months younger than Jonathan was and somewhat smaller his voice hadn't started to change yet, but I knew it would. Girl wise, he tries to be like Jonathan, but I think he is still a bit more of a little boy than Jonathan is. The next day I headed for Pairs France. I didn't take Colonel Dizon; he was made battalion commander of the third of the seventh and was much too busy to go.

I took Lieutenant Tomas Lynn, who spoke French as well as Colonel Dizon. We flew by helicopter first to the airbase in Frankfurt then took a plane to Pairs. Lieutenant Lynn wasn't as relax around me, as Marc was; it most likely was because of my rank and position. I tried to get him to relax a little, but I wasn't successful. We landed in Paris just before lunchtime, and we headed directly to the consulate. We were escorted directly to the Ambassador, who was with the diplomat, which I eyeballed. "General York, my name is Trent Richardson have you and your aid eaten yet?" asked the ambassador.

"No, we haven't, Sir."

"This is Andrew Seaman from Washington." I shook both their hands, but it was apparent that I was uptight with the diplomat. "Well let's go to the dining room for lunch we have some of the best cooks I have ever had."

"Sounds great, Sir," I said.

When we sat, Andrew Seaman sat across from me, and the ambassador was to the right with the lieutenant to my left. I was mainly talking to the ambassador when the Seaman asked, "General, how do you feel about meeting the Soviet president?"

If looks could kill, the diplomat would have been dead, and I answered, "You know damn well how I feel about this."

"Well, I hope you can be civil when you meet the president."

"I will treat the Soviet president the way he treats me." "I'm not so stupid to give him something use it for propaganda, but I'll know how he is by his demeanor." "I will be like what Winston Churchill said, "Walk softly but carry a big stick."

"Well, I hope you will be a little diplomatic."

"I'm a general, not a diplomat why you ever arranged this; I'll never know, but whatever happens will be on you, Sir."

"This meeting with you was requested by the Soviet government."

"Why?"

"I don't know, but they are wary of you; I think they want to find out what you plan to do with the American forces in Europe."

"You could have told him that yourself, you know I don't move unless I'm attacked or get orders from Washington."

"Yes, you're right, I do know, but they want to hear it from you." Mr. Seaman took a deep breath to try to relax and said, "Look, General, you don't have to be angry with me." "It was the President who wanted me to get you to meet with the Soviet President."

"I don't mean to express my irritation towards you; it is my anger with the Soviets government that I have." "My anger stems from their involvement in Vietnam and more so the last conflict here in Europe; I lost some close friends because of them." I tried to ease up on the diplomat, and the rest of the lunch went by more pleasant. We were to have a private meeting after lunch between the ambassador, the diplomat, and myself. I gave my credit card to Lieutenant Lynn and said, "This will take some time, so go get something for each of my children and my wife."

The meeting went on for an hour. The diplomat and the ambassador explained what to expect from the Soviet President and how to react. Most of what they said, I already knew. "General, we urge you not to take anything he might say as offenses."

"Why are you and more important the American government kowtowing to the Soviets?"

"There are many treaties we would like to get signed, and we would like them to help us with other nations they have influence over." "We hope with our friendly meeting we are about to have that the Soviets will be a little more cooperative," said Seaman.

I stared out into space for a bit of time. The ambassador got concerned because it was apparent what I was doing and said, "General, are you alright?"

I slowly turned to him and said, "Yes, Ambassador Richardson, tell the President it's not going to matter if we get what we want." "Within eighteen months, the eastern bloc countries will fall, and soon after, the Russian government will fall."

"How do you know this?" asked Mr. Seaman.

"The same way I knew of the conflict we had not long ago."

The diplomat looked at me unbelieving, but Ambassador Richardson said, "Mr. Seaman, if the General says this is going to happen, believe him he is never wrong."

"Alright, I'll tell the President."

We walked out of the meeting and went into a lounge area where we had brandy, a drink, I didn't care for but drank it out of respect. I believe they gave me the brandy to relax me, but it didn't work. The Soviet President finally came a little late, which I figured he would do to make a statement. We all went out to greet him, and he shook the ambassador's hand, then the diplomat I was last, and we shook hands. The first thing I noticed was that his grip was more than normal, so I gave him back as much as he gave me, and I also held it longer than usual. I then notice him staring into my eyes, trying to see something. "I'm looking forward to talking to you, General," said the Soviet President.

I didn't comment on what he said but said instead, "I see you speak English very well." The truth was he spoke English better than I did.

"Yes, it's too bad you can't speak Russian."

"I have no reason to learn; I am a soldier, and from what I understand, an excellent one, as you know." By saying that I indirectly insulted him, which got done to gain control and what pleased me, I could see his discomfort at what I said on his face.

I listen to what the ambassador and diplomat were saying and the response from the Soviet President. This talking went on for an hour, then the Soviet President said, "I would now like to speak to General York in private." "We can tomorrow talk more about these treaties and your interest in and those countries you talked about."

"General York is this alright with you?" asked the Ambassador.

"I am willing to meet in private."

Everyone left the room except the Soviet President and me he motioned for me to sit down in a chair and he and I sat down. "General, I am aware of how you feel about my people and country, but perhaps we can have an honest talk."

"Sir, you have no idea what my feelings are." "The truth is I think highly of your people." "However, it is your government and its policies I detest."

"My government works for our people."

"Your government is forced on your people."

"Well, I could debate you on this, but I won't."

"Well thank you, Mr. President, I'm no politician and don't want to get into it with you."

"You're more of a politician than I think you realize."

"What is it you want from me?"

"You have deployed highly advanced equipment and doing threatening maneuvers what are your intentions?"

"My intentions Mr. President are to follow orders just like your Generals." "Those maneuvers are for training purposes only as I would assume the maneuvers your military do are for training also."

"I've been following your career for some time." "I feel you do what you wish, and this hostility you have towards us is a threat towards us, and I assure you that we will be more than a match if you try to do anything."

What he said got me angry, but I held it in and said, "I notice you never asked me why I detest your government." "I will tell you; it was your attempted invasion of Western Europe in which I stopped you cold." "Then I reversed the invasion with inadequate equipment and poorly trained men." "I lost many friends because of it and was wounded myself." "I also believe you don't know what I did in Vietnam." "I will tell you." "I gathered information and turned that information into propaganda." "So, when you tell me that it wasn't the Soviet Union who was behind the invasion of Western Europe, I need to tell you I know when I hear bullshit." "So anytime you want to invade the West again, we will see who comes out better."

The Soviet President didn't know what to say, so he was silent for a few moments. He finally said, "We are not a violent people General we just want peace and respect."

"Peace is in your actions, and respect must get earned, so why don't you cooperate with Ambassador Richardson and Mr. Seaman." "I see nothing harmful towards the Soviet Union."

"Despite me being President, I must face my government." "I have to convince them that all that your government asked will benefit the Soviet Union, so I can't be quick to sign anything, and I have to get some things also."

"I leave that up to the diplomat, ambassador, and you."

"Well, General, I hope that you will someday be able to have a friendlier feeling towards the Soviet government." "It is my strong feeling that someday you will be the leader of the United States."

I started to chuckle and said, "Mr. President, I think the chances are about the same as you becoming a capitalist." "Sir, are you aware of my ability to know something that is going to happen before it happens?"

"Yes, I have heard that you have this ability."

"Then what I tell you, I mean you no disrespect." "You will know if it is possible or not, but within eighteen months or less, the Soviet bloc will collapse, and even Russia soon after will also collapse."

"Are you ever wrong?"

"No, and anything that you might try to do to stop this won't help."

"But you are saying Russia will still go on."

"Yes, so you can see my feelings towards your government won't matter."

"If this is all true, why should I agree to anything the United States wants?"

"What agreements you make with the United States now will be honored when the collapse comes." "The actions you and your government do now will make it more likely the United States will be willing to help you through any difficult times." "Of course, only you know what I have told you to be true or not."

"Who have you told this to?"

"General Abrams, Ambassador Richardson, and Mr. Seaman."

"I would appreciate it if you wouldn't say anything more about this." "Do you think that General Abrams will say anything?"

"I won't say anything, Sir, and as far as General Abrams, it was a long time ago when I told him, and he hasn't said anything so far."

We talked for a few more minutes; it was apparent that he got shaken because of the possibility that I was right. We then got up and left the room the ambassador and diplomat joined us to say their goodbyes to the Soviet President. They could see that the Soviet President looked shaken, and I knew Mr. Seaman and Ambassador Richardson would want to know what went on, so I stayed. "I think we need to talk," said Mr. Seaman angrily after the Soviet President left.

"Alright, Lieutenant, you better find us quarters while I'm talking with the Diplomat and the Ambassador."

"You can stay here, General."

"No, I would not feel comfortable staying here; this whole thing is giving me a headache."

We went back into the same room that the Soviet President and I talked about the fall of Russia. I barely sat down when Mr. Seaman tore into me, "What in the hell did you tell the Soviet President to upset him?"

"I told him the truth, and I express it to him in the same matter as he spoke to me." "Frankly, Mr. Seaman, I don't care for your tone when you talk to me, I would suggest you back off," I snarled.

"So, what are you going to do if I don't back off."

I said, "Normally, I would break your jaw, but I told General Abrams I would be nice to you." "For your information, the Soviet President said he wasn't going to agree to anything you want." "He doesn't like your ass-kissing tactic; he thinks people like you, Mr. Seaman are weak." "I didn't let him get away with anything, I was honest with him, and he respected that." "He has agreed to what you want after he negotiates with you tomorrow." "Now, I am out of here." "I don't want to deal with you people anymore."

I then turned and was leaving when Mr. Seaman said, "If you are trying to say the success of this negotiation is all because of you." "You think way too much of yourself."

"You sniveling fool, just keep doing what you are doing, and he will leave without agreeing to anything."

"Just leave you arrogant bastard; I don't need you anymore."

"Shut up, Andrew, the General is right, and I have had enough of you," said the Ambassador.

"You can't talk to me like that."

With a stern look on his face, the Ambassador said, "General York, would you please step out for a moment and wait."

"Yes, Sir." I stepped out and heard a lot of muffled yelling by both men. Then after a time, the door flung open, and Mr. Seaman stormed out of the embassy.

"General, please come back in and let's talk."

"Yes, Sir."

"I sent Mr. Seaman home." "For this negotiation, he's not prepared."

"He might cause you trouble; he supposedly knows people."

"I've heard that also, so before he gets home, I will make a few phone calls tonight to head him off." "I will also write a report on everything that has happened."

"Alright, for your sake, I hope he gets contained."

"You're not concerned for yourself?"

"No, before he could do anything to me, I would retire." "I've been thinking about retirement for some time."

"Well, if you retire, it would be a big loss." "The reason I've asked you to stay is I would like you to be with me here when the Soviet President comes tomorrow."

I sighed and said, "Alright, Sir."

"You can stay here for the night."

"No Lieutenant Lynn has made arrangements by now."

"Well, be sure you're here by nine in the morning."

"I'll be here before nine."

We exited the room Lieutenant Lynn was waiting for me, and we left. As we drove off to the hotel, the Lieutenant asked, which surprised me, "How did it go, Sir?"

I smiled and answered, "It started very rough but ended up very good." "I will see how things will go tomorrow."

The next day we had an early breakfast and headed to the embassy. When we got there, I told the Lieutenant, "Go enjoy yourself and be back here about one or one-thirty this afternoon."

"Yes, Sir."

I went in and met with Ambassador Richardson. "General, it's a good thing you are here the Soviet President will be here in about forty-five minutes if he is on time."

The Soviet President showed up with an aid, and when he saw me, he was surprised. "Mr. Seaman won't be joining us, Mr. President," stated Ambassador Richardson.

"Why," the President asked.

"He was unsuitable for these negotiations, as you know," I said.

"Alright, it will be better this way." "I would rather have you here than him," said the President. We all sat down, and the Soviet President said, "You know, Ambassador, if it weren't for the General here, I wouldn't have come back." "Although he isn't friendly with my government, he is honest with what he says, and I like that."

"He's a good man, Sir." The negotiations went on for more than two hours at times it got hot I kept quiet except when things started to go awry for the United States then I jumped in to put things back on track. Finally, they hammered down a satisfactory agreement. The final deal was going to be a sign in Moscow between the President of the United States and the Soviet President. It was going to be a big deal broadcasted all over the world.

I left the embassy, and I told the Lieutenant, "Let's go back to Germany." "I don't want to stay here a minute longer."

We got back to Schweinfurt late, and after dropping off Lieutenant Lynn, I went home. I had written a report to General Abrams, making sure I told him about the diplomat. Months went by, we had maneuvers, which went off better than I thought. A few weeks after the military exercises, General Brown and I decided to do some surprise inspections. I found that all the units we visited were better than what I could hope. Our last place I was going to was the American base in Bamberg, Germany. I wasn't only going to do a surprise inspection but also to promote Colonel Henderson to Brigadier General with the blessing of General Abrams and the Pentagon. I chose one barracks to inspect, and as I did with other inspections, I just did a walkthrough. I was about to leave when I heard someone yelling for me. I turned around and saw a private with something in his hand; he was getting restrained. I walked over to him and said, "I was a private once let him go, what do you want?"

"Besides a promotion, I like you to sign the book you wrote."

"Book I wrote." I thought he was talking about the two books that got written about me. He handed me the book. I looked at it and started giggling then said, "Let's go into your dayroom so I can explain a few things." "I will sign this book if you want, but you need to know private that this book is not written by me, nor is it about me." "This book is about my Great Grand Father, who I got named after Sir James York." "I was told that he dictated the story of his life to his grandson, who was a writer." "So, what will it be private?"

"I still want your signature, Sir."

I signed his book and said, "Captain Daley, any private that has that balls to approach me deserves to get promoted to corporal."

"Yes, Sir," said the Captain.

I got the address of the unit to send the private both of my books signed. Next, we went back to Colonel Henderson's headquarters, and I said, "Bill, I need to apologize to you."

"What for?" asked Colonel Henderson.

"What's going happen next you deserve to have a big ceremony, but I'm not going to put you through that so here."

I handed him a box, which he opened and saw a star. "I don't know what to say; it's unexpected."

"Don't say anything you deserve it, and I need to do this now; I don't know how much more time I have left in the military, so it's now or never." I shook his hand, talked a little more, and excused myself, and we went back to Schweinfurt.

A few months had passed. Maria was due to deliver at any time I had hired someone to be with her. Oliver and David were learning to speak English very well. I was busy doing something in my office when in walks General Abrams. I stood up and said, "Sir, are you here to send me on another embassy trip?"

"No, not this time, James," he said with a smile.

"Then what is it, Sir?"

"Your part in the negotiations with the Soviet president was truly appreciated by the President and most of Congress." "Mr. Seaman got demoted, and when that happened, he quit."

"That was nice of Congress and the President." "Those in Congress who didn't like what I did, why did they object?"

"It wasn't you; they just don't like the Soviets." "All of Washington is pleased with how you are handling the European command; in fact, some are saying you are doing better than me."

"I think those who think that are blind as to just what you did."

"Well, thanks, James, but I have to be realistic; you have done better than what I've done." "Your insight on the collapse of the Soviet Union was investigated." "The government has found just about all you are saying is correct."

"As I know, they would find," I said. "But you could have told all of this by letter or phone, so what brings you here?"

"Are you ready to move back to the United States?

"I am, but Maria will need a few months she is to deliver any time now, I'm waiting for a phone call."

"That's alright, I'm retiring, and it is time for you to take my place at the Pentagon."

I took a deep breath and asked, "How tough is it."

"You are going to be busy; there is a lot of desk work and decision making that will affect the whole United States if not the world." "Don't worry, James; you can handle it."

"When do they want me to be there, Sir?"

"I'll be in and out of my office for the next three months." "I'd think you can take at least four months."

"Alright, Sir, I'll work with General Brown to take my place."

"Yes, you will need to promote him; you're getting promoted to General of the Army as of today. You'll get a full ceremony when you come to Washington."

He handed me orders and a five-star pin, and I said, "Well, after this, I won't have to alter my uniforms anymore," I said, laughing. "I guess I'm going to have to find a house for my family and me."

"You won't have to look for a home you and your family can have my home in Maryland." "It is in a great area for your family with parks nearby, and it is a larger house than you have now."

"Sounds good, Sir, your house will be just fine."

"You know James ever since you met me; you had given me the courtesy of calling me Sir when you didn't have to." "You're the General of the Army James; you can call me by my first name Will."

"You still outrank me." "Please understand me; I call you Sir because I respect you." "It would be like calling my father by his first name."

"I understand." We talked some more, and I had asked him where he was going to retire, and he told me, Indiana. He finally left, and I leaned back in my chair, rubbing my eyes. I went home early Maria was sleeping, and the boys were in school, so I got my uniforms and sent them to be altered for the last time. When I got home, I told Maria, "As soon as you have the baby and the baby can travel, we will move to America." She was thrilled as were the children.

When I went to work the next day, I attracted a lot of attention but ignored it. I called General Brown and arranged for him to meet me the next day, and the following day General Brown showed up and said, "I've heard rumors that you will be leaving us soon."

"It's true, Bill." I pulled out my own four stars, handed it to him, and said, "You're the only one qualified to take my place."

"So, you are going to take your place in the Pentagon."

"Yes, for a while, then I will retire and go live at my place in Missouri." "I'll be working with you for the next few months; then, I will leave."

Two days later, I was in my office getting ready to have a telephone conference with General Brown. I got a phone call from an excited David, "Daddy mama having baby."

"Where is your mama now?"

"Home, come quickly."

"Alright, David, I am coming home right now."

As I left my office, I told my secretary, what happen and to call General Brown and let him know. I got home, and the boys were frantic. The only ones who were calm were the nurse and Maria. I had the nurse drive my boys to the hospital while I took Maria. Maria was brought into the delivery room while we waited out in the waiting room. The boys' excitement waned by the second hour of waiting, and they started getting fidgety, so I asked the nurse to take them home. She was in labor for nine hours, and we had another boy. As I looked at the baby, the doctor who delivered the baby asked me to come to his office. "I wish to talk to you about Maria."

"Is she alright?"

"No, if she has another baby, she will not make it through the delivery." "She is going to have to be careful; she will be delicate."

"What happened to get her to this state?"

"It's nothing that happened during the delivery; Maria shouldn't have had another baby." "I think she had something happen to her in the past, or it's something in her genes; I'm just not sure." "When she awakes, we need to talk with her," the doctor said.

"How long do you think she will be unconscious?"

"At least until late tomorrow morning, why don't you go home and rest."

I went home, the next morning I told the children what was going on and of course, they were frantic. I tried calming them down as best I could, and I left to see Maria. Maria was awake but very weak after kissing her, she said, "Have you seen the baby?"

"Yes, he's beautiful and healthy." "Has the doctor seen you?"

"No, is there something wrong."

"Well, we will talk about it when the doctor comes."

"Is it the baby?"

"No, just relax and rest."

We waited and talked about possible names for the baby and of our other four boys. Finally, after about forty-five minutes, the doctor came. He said, "Mrs. York, I'm going to speak to you frankly having this baby has done a lot of damage to your body." "I would urge you not to have another baby it would damage you so much you wouldn't survive." "When you recover, you will never be the same as you were before, your health will be very delicate; you must be careful."

"Maria, did you know that you would have trouble having this baby?" I asked.

"Yes."

"Then why did you want to get pregnant."

"Because I knew you wanted a child that was from you."

"Yes, I wanted a child but not at the risk of your health; I love you."

We talked some more, then the doctor said, "Maria needs some rest." "I think we need to go."

"Yes, Sir." I kissed Maria, went out the door then asked the doctor, "Do you think Maria and the baby will be well enough to move to Washington D.C. in three months?" "I would think so, but I wouldn't put any stress on Maria while you leave." I went and checked on the baby and then went home. The boys immediately clamored around me, still upset about their mother. I told them how their mother is and what we must do to make sure she stays healthy when she gets home. Then to get their minds off their mother's condition, I told them to come up with a list of names for the new baby and not share it with any of their brothers until I came home. I decided to go to work to get my mind off my troubles.

The first thing I did was to call General Brown. We talked about Maria and the baby then the command. I only stayed a few hours and then went home the boys gave me their list, and I had them sit down as we went over the list of names. There was one name that came up with all four boys, and that was William. Jonathan said Billy, and I told him that Billy was short for William, which he accepted. "It looks like you all want William."

"No, daddy, Wilhelm," said Oliver.

"Ok, we will call your brother Wilhelm if your mother agrees." "We haven't heard what she wants yet."

I gave the nurse a little time off and took all the boys to the hospital to see their new brother and mother. The boys lined up at the window to look at the baby, making commits at how small he was. Of course, they immediately started tapping at the window, calling him Wilhelm. After a while we went to see Maria, the hospital didn't want all the boys in the room at one time. They didn't want Frederic and Oliver in the room at all. After I had a somewhat forceful talk with the head nurse, she relented, and we all went into her room. After kissing their mother, they all lined up. David said, "We see Wilhelm."

"Who?"

"Wilhelm, mama," said Frederic.

"Who is Wilhelm?" asked Maria

"The boys named the baby unless you have another name," I said.

"Oh, so you named your brother I was thinking of naming the baby after your father," Maria said to the boys.

"I don't think it would be good to name the baby after me," I said.

"Ja mama Wilhelm is good name," said Oliver.

"I see, well Wilhelm is a good name don't you have a brother who is named Wilhelm James?"

"Wilhelm, yes, we called him Bill." "He passed away many years ago."

"Well, Wilhelm will be your brother's name then," Maria said to the boys.

Maria came home three days later with the baby I kept the nurse and hired a house cleaner. I also went back to work, transferring the European command to General Brown. As the weeks passed, Maria did get stronger but not like she was. I finally got rid of the nurse but kept the housekeeper. General Abrams said I could send some things to their house in Maryland. I hired a moving company to ship most items we wanted back in the states. Maria and I had finally gone to court and formally adopted David and Oliver. As time moved on and I got convinced, Maria would be alright, so I decided to go to Washington to get everything ready. When I flew into Washington, I got swamped by the press, so I talked with them for a few seconds. "General, I have heard that you made General of the Army sometime back." "Why didn't you come to Washington sooner?" asked a reporter from the New York Times.

"My wife just gave birth, and it wasn't an easy birth." "We need time before we made the trip; meanwhile, General Abrams is still serving in the Pentagon and will stay until I bring my family here."

"When will that be General?" asked the same reporter.

"Within the next two weeks."

More questions got asked on various subjects, then from a reporter from the Washington Post asked, "What are your feelings on budget cuts with the military?"

I then started in with my feelings about any budget cuts, and I had all the people in the press captivated with what I had to say. I took a few more questions then said, "I'd love to stay and talk to you all day, but I have to get some business done." I then left and met with General Abrams, who took me to his house.

"Well, what do you think of the house, James?"

"Just like you said, it's larger and nicer than what I live in now."

"Here are the keys I want you to come with me to the Pentagon so that I can introduce you to everyone."

"That's alright with me, tomorrow I must make some arrangements for my family, but I have some time now." We went over to the Pentagon, where I got introduced to the other joint chiefs. I had time after I visited the Pentagon to get some of my business done in Washington. Over the next two days, I got almost everything done, including hiring a housecleaner, having a company unload the container, and buying a large enough vehicle for my large family. I headed back to Germany on the third day and didn't arrive until six-thirty the next morning. I caught a helicopter to Schweinfurt, and by the time I got home and into Maria's arms, it was just after eight.

The days went by, and we finally boarded a Jet to Washington. The flight was exciting for all the boys, especially David and Oliver. Still, it was also a long trip, and so that excitement diminished. I always watched Maria and the baby as we traveled to see how they were doing. It was dark when we landed, and everyone was exhausted. The only one that fared better than any of us was the baby. I guess he had his schedule and wasn't going to let the flight bother him. I decided we would stay in a hotel for the night then go to the house. I got adjoining accommodations the boys stayed in one room and Maria, the baby and I stayed in the other. It didn't take Maria and me long to fall asleep to our surprise; the baby was cooperative with letting us sleep.

The next day we woke up late and ate breakfast, then headed over to the house. Everything from the container was scattered all over the place. I had three weeks to get everything in order, and I needed every bit of it.

The boys ran through the house, exploring. I set up the playpen, then Maria, and I did a little exploring ourselves.

I called the maid service and told them they could start the next day. Then I got busy with the house while the boys were outside checking out the backyard. Frederic and Oliver came back in, and Frederic said, "Daddy, this house has no swings and sandbox."

"Aren't you two getting too old for that?"

"No," said Oliver.

"Well, I could get you one, but just down the end of the street is a park, and I would guess there are a sandbox and swings there."

Both boys went running out of the house, and I went to see where they were going. David and Jonathan were in the front yard staring at some girls across the street, which they took notice. "David, Jonathan, nothing will happen unless you go across the street and introduce yourself." They looked at me, smiled, and walked across the street to the delight of the giggling girls.

Back in the house, I went to get busy. I saw Maria moving things around, and I said, "Maria, let me take care of this, your job is to take care of the baby."

"I'm not completely helpless," she said.

"I know I just don't want anything happening to you."

She smiled and said, "I know, but I know how much I can do." She went and started doing lighter things while I did the more substantial stuff.

As Maria and I worked in the house in came Frederic and Oliver with two other boys about the same age as them, they had gone to their room to get their toys. After some time, I went out and got some Chinese food and Maria, as well as the boys, couldn't get enough of it they love it so much. After we ate dinner, Maria gave me a list of groceries to get in the store, so I went shopping while she and the boys watched the baby. By the next day, I had set everything up, the maid came and cleaned the house. I was working in the garage when Maria said, "Someone is here for you."

Thinking it might be a neighbor or someone from the Pentagon, I went into the house. There standing in the living room was Frank White. "Frank, what brings you here, socializing or business?"

"Both."

"Did you forget to give me some extra money or something?"

"No, I'm here to congratulate you and talk to you about a third book and movie deal." "I've heard people in both parties thinking you would make a fine president."

I started laughing and said, "I'm not a very educated person; no one would vote for me, and do you think a third book would sell, let alone a movie."

"Yes, a third book would sell, and this country is in love with you, you are as popular if not more so than Eisenhower."

"Well, you go ahead and write your book, my job now is General of the Army." "Where are your papers?" "I'm sure you want me to sign, the same rules apply." "I'll talk to you when I can; you can follow me around until you can't."

I signed the papers, and we talked for about an hour then finally he said, "I most likely won't be starting this book for a year, or more so I won't be in your hair right away."

31

MARCH TO THE PRESIDENCY

I got a call from General Abrams, "James, I know you were coming in tomorrow, but can you come in today."

"Yes Sir, can you send me a car."

"I've already sent one."

"I see your psychic, too; I'll be waiting for my ride." I told Maria and then changed into my military dress greens.

It wasn't long when my driver drove up to my house. I started to get into the front seat when the driver said, "Sir, it is customary for you to sit in the back seat."

"It is?"

"Yes, Sir, it's for your protection."

"Protection from what," I said, then slid into the front seat. Realize when I'm not working, I'm going to be driving in the front seat. What's the difference unless there has been a threat to me?"

"No, Sir, there hasn't been any threat."

"Then let's go."

"Yes, Sir."

We zipped across Washington, and I was at the Pentagon in about thirty minutes. They took me to my office, which I been before, and I was looking at things on my desk when General Abrams came in and said, "James come with me."

I left the office, went down the hall to an elevator, and asked, "Where are we going, Sir?"

"To the situation room with the other joint chiefs and the Secretary of Defense." We went down two stories and then exited and went down a hallway and into the situation room amongst a lot of security. I got introduced to everyone who already knew me. We all sat down. General Abrams said, "James, the reason I called you in a day early is that we have gotten ordered to make plans for the invasion of the island of Grenada. You will be directly involved."

In the middle of a table where I sat at was a model of the Island I stood up, looked at it then said. "Is this island in the Caribbean?"

"Yes, it's at the southern part of the Caribbean just northeast of Venezuela," said Admiral James Watkins.

"Just what I predicted a few years ago," I said mostly to myself. I was then brief on the reason why the President wanted to invade.

Each officer in the room gave what the officer thought would be the best plan for invasion. "What would you do, General York?" asked Secretary Caspar Weinberger.

I looked at the map for a short period then asked, "What is the strength of the enemy manpower and weapons?"

"Our intelligence people tell us that they have about five thousand men, mostly Cubans." "They have about ten tanks, about the same in other track vehicles, and maybe five pieces of artillery," said General Robert Barrow Commandant of the Marine Corp. "They also have mortars, machineguns, etcetera," he added.

"What about their Air Force and Navy?"

"They have a few outdated jets and cargo planes," said Admiral James Watkins. "Their Navy consist of twenty patrol boats." "The last, we saw a couple of Frigates again operated by the Cubans."

I looked at the relief model of the island again and finally said, "General Gabriel the Air Force won't be needed, to small of an island and not enough of the enemy." He nodded agreement. I went on, "The Navy needs to take out the Frigates, and patrol boats also neutralize what Air Force they have without destroying their airstrip which we will need." "The Marines need to land just outside of St. George, Sauteurs, Greenville, and Gouyave and take control of those towns." "When the Marines take Gouyave, they need to move up to Victoria and take control of that town. The Marines must sweep the smaller islands around Grenada, but I don't think they will run into any troops." "The Rangers will parachute here at this end of the island near St. Paul, the center of the island near Lower Capital, and at the other end of the island near St. John." "After the Marines take the towns, the Army will fill in behind them, and the Marines can fan out to other parts of the Island." "You won't have many causalities with this plan, and the whole thing should be over in days."

They all looked at me with blank looks on their faces as if they were shocked at what I said. Finally, Secretary Weinberger said, "It sounds like the best plan I've heard in the last two days." "We just now must work out the details, and we can put the plan in motion." "The President wants to move fast on this, this will mean we will be working until late at night so who wants coffee?"

"I don't drink coffee, but I do tea or chocolate."

"You got it."

"Do you all mind if I call my wife to tell her that I will be working very late." No one objected, so I went upstairs and made a call from my office.

Finding my office and getting back was some task, it's easy to get lost, but when I got back, I saw a table full of pastries with coffee, tea, and hot chocolate. I went up to General Abrams and said, "I'm going to have to get a map of this place."

"You have one; it's in your desk, but you will get used to everything in due time."

It was nearly eleven at night when we finally put together a detailed plan. I had to be at work tomorrow at seven when we would hear the final go-ahead from the President.

I was up at six and had a light breakfast before my staff car came. At precisely seven in the morning, I was walking down the hall to my office. I found the Pentagon map, and I was happy to see a full gym I could use. General Abrams didn't show up until eight, "James let go down to the cafeteria and get a cup of coffee."

"Coffee, Sir?"

"Tea or chocolate then," he said with a smile.

"Much better, Sir."

We went down to the cafeteria and got what we wanted and then sat down. "This will be my last day, and then I'm leaving." "I'm sorry I won't be here to help you settle in."

"It's alright, Sir; I'll muddle through."

"That's my boy." "You did well yesterday; I like how you took charge and came up with an excellent plan."

"Thanks, Sir, I just do what my gut says is right."

"The one most important thing I could tell you is to remember that you are as equal as the rest of the joint chiefs." "This assignment isn't an assignment you have had in the past where you decided something, and it got done." "Here, you have to negotiate with the other joint chiefs and then negotiate with the government."

"Yes, I'm aware of this, Sir, and it sounds like a pain in the ass."

"Yes, it is a pain, but you are a good talker, and you have the respect of the joint chiefs and, more important, the respect of the nation."

Just then, Admiral James Watkins came into the cafeteria, got a coffee and a piece of pastry, and sat down with us. "Gentlemen, the President should be contacting us in about a half-hour I'm guessing," said the Admiral.

"Well, James, you think you are ready for the Pentagon?" asked the Admiral.

"Well, Admiral, you saw how I reacted at our business yesterday what would you think?'

"You did very well."

After we talked a bit, Admiral Watkins said, "Well, I'll see both of you in the conference room." General Abrams and I went back to our office. He handed me a schedule on how things worked day to day unless something extraordinary happened like this Grenada conflict. We were talking when there was a knock at the door, and my secretary said, "The President just came into the Pentagon."

"We better go to the conference room, James," said General Abrams.

When we walked into the conference room, most of the joint chiefs were already there. After a few minutes after everyone arrived, in walks, Secretary Caspar Weinberger with the President, and we all stood up and shook the President's hand. He was a tall man who was trying to hide his age by the work he had done on himself. I've seen some of his movies and thought they were of good quality. "I'm pleased to meet you, General York, I understand that this is your plan," said the President.

"Yes, Mr. President, these gentlemen here think it has some merit."

We talk for a short time about the invasion; the President asked when we could put the plan into action, then Admiral Watkins said, "Immediately with your okay Mr. President."

"Let's do it then there are Americans being held captive I want their safe release, and the original government restored."

The President left, and we put the plan into action, under cover of night. It was another late night and early morning before we got our first report. Our forces had landed on the island and that the Navy had contained what Navy and Air Force they had. By early afternoon, they had rescued most of the Americans on the island, and hundreds of the enemy got captured. By late afternoon most of the joint chiefs decided to go home since everything in Grenada was going smoothly. After embracing my wife and finding out what the boys were up to, I laid down to sleep. We went shopping for things that Maria and the boys needed then I finally got to eat at home.

I was at work early the next day. I found out that the operation in Grenada was complete. The troops were doing a sweep of the island to make sure the entire enemy got taken out. We had lost three soldiers in this conflict with eight wounded, not seriously. Overall, the operation went very well, and everyone seemed to be happy. Over the months, I got used to working at the Pentagon. I had many visits to the White House as well as gave many press conferences. It seemed I was a target of the press. They wanted to know what we were doing at the Pentagon. What surprised me they wanted to know my opinion on subjects that somebody who was a joint chief would not have an answer. Maria and the baby were doing fine, and the boys were in school. David and Oliver were having a little problem with their schoolwork because of their language barrier. I had hired them a tutor to help them, and they have shown progress.

One morning while I was working at the Pentagon. I got a call from the White House secretary. The President wanted me to come to the White House for lunch and discuss some things with me. I got to the White House and got guided to the dining room. I was the only joint chief who was there, but there were other people, some of them, if not all I recognized was from Congress, and of course, the Vice President was there. I've been to the White House before. Mostly with the other joint chiefs and always on military business. I was shown to a seat and sat down, and the President introduced everyone. The one person I notice who wasn't there was the First Lady. After we got served and the servants left, the President asked me, "General York, you're very young to be a General; just how old are you?"

"I just turned thirty-five, Mr. President."

"Am I prying if I ask what party you belong to?"

"No, Sir, you're not prying, but I need to explain what I am going to tell you." "I am a Democrat mostly because that is what my father is and my aunt, who lives next door to me." "However, both my aunt and father are conservative as am I." "Most of the time, my father has voted for

Republicans because most in your party are conservative, I'm guessing." "For myself, I vote for the man, not the party if the man says and does what I like, then I vote for him."

"So, if your father changed parties, you would too?"

"No, parties aren't important to me as I said I vote for the man."

"Why don't you change to Independent?" asked the Vice President.

"I guess, Sir, a party, doesn't matter to me; I'm not a politician."

"So, can I assume General if there were a good reason you would change parties."

I thought for a second wondering where he was going with this conversation then said, "Yes, if I had a good reason, I'd switch parties." Everyone smiled, and then the subject changed, and I never did find out where they were going with their questioning. I finally left, still scratching my head, wondering just what went on today.

I had been working at the Pentagon for more than a year. We had made the trip to North Carolina to see Top and his family, but the boys quickly found out that it wasn't the same as it was when we were in Germany. Top's children had their own life and had moved on much to the disappointment of Jonathan and Frederic. Maria and I even noticed the difference between Jack and Maryann; it was almost as if it was uncomfortable for us to visit them; we left. I knew we wouldn't be going back again. From time to time, I heard from Allen that he had made captain sometime back when Captain Paul McMullen retired. He wanted to be in a combat unit, and I had considered it but told him no for now because of his problems with his feet, but I would consider it later. He was transferred to Korea and placed in command of a unit there. Jonathan and David were in high school, and both were doing well, especially in sports. Oliver and Frederic were in junior high, and their interest I noticed had changed somewhat they too were doing well in school. Both David and Oliver's English had improved so much that they talked almost as well as Frederic. The baby was getting big and was healthy; my concern was Maria; she seemed to get tired very quickly. We had gone to the doctors, and they said just about the same as the doctors in Germany. I tried to get Maria to slow down some at home, but there was no holding her back. Frank had been shadowing me for some time now, taking notes and this time pictures of the whole family and me. We just ignored him, and that's just what he wanted. He would question me on one point or another, and I answered him when I could. I had planned to take the family to our home in Missouri the coming summer.

David and Oliver had never been there besides Jonathans' birth siblings we hadn't seen in some time.

I was in my office reading the newspaper when I got a visit from the House Democrat leadership. "General, would you let us take you to lunch we would like to talk to you about something."

When they asked me, I immediately flashed back to that strange White House visit many months back. Regardless I was curious at what they had to say, so I said, "Yes, I will go with you." The conversation went much the same as it did at the White House, and I was about confused the same as I was when I was at the White House.

The press was continually asking me to talk about something. When I am at an event, the media are recording everything I just said or did.

By summer, it felt good to get away for three weeks, and I was happy to go to Missouri. I was never a city person, and I didn't like the hectic pace of Washington. So, going back to Missouri was well welcomed, and before we left, I made a call to my maintenance man to open the house for me. We got into Springfield early; I rented a vehicle large enough for my whole family then drove to Ellsinore. By midafternoon, we entered our property. The first thing I noticed was everything that had grown and seemed well maintained. The boys disappeared while Maria, the baby, and I went into the house.

There was no word from my aunt and uncle and their family. I didn't know why they knew I was coming so as the children played, and Maria was resting, I walked over to my aunt's house. I knock on the door, and a much larger Val came to the door, "James, you're here," he said with a big smile.

"Yes, you have grown."

"You think so."

"Yes, where are your mother and father?"

"Mama isn't feeling well; she is lying down." "Daddy is at work."

"And your brothers?"

"Michael doesn't live here anymore, and Tom is at work too."

"Well, you can come over to my house when you want." "I'm sure your mother wants to get you out of her hair."

"Alright, I'm doing something right now, but I will be over later."

I went back home and told Maria about my aunt, and she said, "I will make her a big pot of homemade soup; it will do her some good."

"Alright, but just don't push yourself."

"Oh, I'll be fine."

Maria took the soup over to my aunt while Val found the boys, and I stayed with the baby until she came back, and then I checked my property. Maria told me that my aunt had a cold or flu. My property was well maintained and grown just the way I wanted, and it was ready for people to use it if they wanted to. I had stocked the pond with fish years ago, and Val and Tom had been fishing and swimming in it. I went over to the maintenance man's house the following day and talked to him. "You've been doing a fine job I will be using the property more now that I'm in Washington."

"Yes, Sir, do you think I could hire some people to help me out on your property?"

"How many?"

"Maybe two or three?"

"Sure, that would be alright, and I'll give you a raise you deserve it for the fine job you've done."

"Thank you, Sir."

That night Maria made dinner for my aunt and her family, and I delivered it to them. I didn't want Maria to spend too much time with my aunt until she is over her sickness. A week past and my aunt was well enough, so Maria spent some time with her. I had noticed that my aunt's voice was getting raspier, but I contributed it from smoking for years and didn't think about it much. The following week Jonathan's siblings came, and I first noticed the children didn't want to be here. They had their own life, and my family was like strangers to them, even Jonathan. So, Maria and I talked to their grandparents about the situation. "It's obvious that they don't want to be here what do you wish to do."

"We can't afford to take care of them by ourselves without support," said Joe Kruger.

"We adopted them, and we will continue to support them, but if they don't want to be part of this family, I won't force them." "I am also concern about your health; can you still handle these children."

"My wife and I are fine; we can handle the children."

"Perhaps I should talk to Jonathan about the situation."

"That sounds good," said Joe.

I found Jonathan with David and said to David, "Let me, and Jonathan be alone for a bit."

"Alright, daddy."

Jonathan and I started walking, not saying anything; then, after a short time, Jonathan asked, "Is this is about my brother and sisters?"

"Yes."

"If they don't want to be here with us, that's alright. I just want my brother and sisters taken care of."

"Let's have a whole family meeting." We had the meeting, and we all agreed that the next day Jonathan's siblings would go back to Arkansas.

We stayed in Missouri another week. The boys had a good time except for when Jonathan's siblings were here. Still, overall, they enjoyed themselves, especially Oliver and David. Even though the boys had a good time in Missouri, they were happy to return to their home in Maryland and be with their friends.

In the following weeks, I spoke to Maria about taking the children to Disneyworld in Florida just before the boys went back to school. She was all for it and was interested in going herself. When we told the boys that we were going on another vacation at first, they didn't want to go until we let them know we were going to Disneyworld, and that changed everything. At the park, the press was there to ask me some questions. "General York, this is your second vacation this summer. Doesn't this impact your work at the Pentagon?" asked a reporter from Florida.

"No, nothing is pressing for me in the next few weeks at the Pentagon." "I normally wouldn't have taken two vacations in one year, but this is something special for my boys, they haven't been here before, and I'm only going to be here a few days." "I want you to understand that years past, I haven't taken any vacations." "I hadn't been to my home in Missouri for many years, so I need to go there, and as I said, this is for my boys just before they go back to their school."

"We hear, there has been talk about you running for president what can you tell us," asked a reporter from the New York Times.

"I have only been working in the Pentagon for a short time to think about that."

"From what I've gotten told, you had meetings with both the Republicans and Democrats on this subject," said the same reporter.

"I don't know about meetings I've had lunches with people from both parties, but I haven't given it much thought." "Besides, do you think the people would vote for me?"

"General, you are an extremely admired person in this country, perhaps as popular if not more so than Eisenhower." The questions were on these subjects and other things that deal with the military, and then I excused myself. The children and Maria loved Disneyworld. We got a babysitter for the baby. Oliver was utterly mesmerized by the park he had never seen anything like it before. Frederick was a tour guide for David and Oliver because he had been to Disneyland; he took charge of showing them everything. The vacation to Disneyworld was a lot of fun, but it was time for the boys to go back to school and for me to go back to work.

More than a year had passed since we went to Disneyworld; David and Jonathan only had two things on his mind, sports and girls, not necessarily in that order. Oliver and Frederic were playing less with their toys and interested in sports, mainly soccer or football as they call it in Europe. The baby was walking and doing some talking, Maria looked pale, and that concerned me. I had taken Maria to the doctors many times, and they had tried many things, but nothing worked; they all told me the same thing as before. As the months went by, I had more and more interviews with the press across the country. Most of the questions have been pushing me to run for president. In November of nineteen eighty-eight, I got a call from my father he told me that my aunt was very sick and in the hospital. Maria was too frail to go to Missouri, and the boys were in school, so I took emergency leave and went by myself. When I got there, I notice all my cousins were there, and my uncle was absent, and I asked Christine, "How is your mother?"

"She isn't doing well."

"What's wrong with her?"

"You don't know."

"No."

"She has lung cancer; they don't think she will survive," she said as tears streamed down her cheek, and I got crushed at the news.

They only would let two people into the room where she was, and I assumed that Uncle Paul was there, but when my Uncle Ray and my father came out, I asked Christine, "Where is your father?"

"He is home; he hasn't slept for two days, so we made him go home to rest."

I talked to my father and uncle while two of my cousins were in the room with my aunt. My Uncle Doug and Aunt Mary came to the waiting room, and after that, my mother and brothers arrived. I offered my home to any who wanted to stay there, and most did. I didn't get to see my aunt until the second day when I saw her; I broke down something I hadn't done in some time. It came the time when I had to get back to Washington. I told my cousins to let me know if anything happens. Two months later, I was told by my father again that my Aunt had died, and the news stabbed me to the core. I attended the funeral, but I was too upset to talk to anyone, and it took some time to cope with it all.

The same year that my aunt died, we invaded Panama, it also went fast without any loss by our side. We invaded Panama on the premise that the current government was nothing more than a drug cartel and were going to take over the channel. After a few years, Oliver and Frederic were getting ready to go to high school, and David and Jonathan were picking colleges. It turned out that both boys went to Harvard. Jonathan wanted to be a lawyer, and David wanted to get into medicine. While David and Jonathan were in college that summer Maria, the rest of the boys, and I went to Missouri. My uncle wanted to talk to me about his property, and I needed to check on my property. Maria stayed mostly at the house, and I went over to talk to my uncle. My uncle had remarried, and after a few years, he wasn't doing well, so he decided to move into Poplar Bluff. "James, I'm giving you the first option on my property if you want to buy it."

"Don't any of your children want it?"

"No, it reminds them of their mother too much."

"I will buy your property, but this property will always be Korenek property even though I hold the deed." The papers were signed, the money he wanted, paid, and I owned another six hundred and fifty acres. I told all my cousins that they were welcome to move back to the ranch if they wanted, but none wanted to.

In nineteen ninety-one, we made plans for the Iraq war. This war would be my last. I was making plans to retire and have General Colin Powell, who was already working with me, take my place. The war went off just about what I had figured it would, and we kick their ass. Three days after the conflict, I got a visit at home from the Democratic Party. "General, we want you to run for the presidency on the Democratic ticket," said the senator from Missouri.

"Sir, after the last war the President is very popular, what chances do I have."

"You're right, he is popular now, but there are cracks, and the cracks are getting bigger," said the congressman from California. "We believe that you will win the White House," he added.

"Show me that the president's popularity will fall, and if my family is ok with this, I'll run, but I won't be a puppet of anyone."

"We don't want you to be a puppet of anyone, Sir." "We will give you all the help you need to ease the stress on your family, especially your wife," said the senator from Missouri.

I talked to these people in front of Maria, and she jumped in and said, "James, I think you should run the people want you."

"Well, gentlemen, you heard the boss." With smiles, they told me that they would handle everything, and then they left.

In the following weeks, I retired from the Pentagon, and General Powell took over. I planned to stay in Maryland until Oliver and Frederic graduated from high school and then move to Missouri. I had been hounded by the press to make a statement about the presidency I knew this would happen my campaign people purposely leaked to them. At first, I was to play dumb. I got visits from the Republican Party, trying to pump me on what was going on. I was making statements to the press on various subjects much to the delight of the Democratic Party. The President's popularity was waning while mine was soaring. A few people had interred the race for the presidential race of the Democratic Party. However, I got told to wait, and yet I was still going around making speeches. The press took polls without me and with me in the race, and those polls showed that if I didn't run, the Democratic Party didn't have a chance to win. However, polls with me in the races showed the President was falling far behind. A couple more people joined in the race, and my campaign manager said we would announce your running Wednesday in St. Louis. When Wednesday came, we had a news conference, and I got up to make a speech before the announcement. I had a speechwriter but never totally used the speeches that they wrote. I did use it for an outline at times, but the words I use were from me. As I stood in front of the press after my speech, I said, "A president can't just focus on one issue, but he must focus on a whole array of issues." "This President, with much of my help, did very well in pushing Iraqi out of Kuwait, but he has been weak on everything else." "For this reason, I am running for the position of president of the United States."

"General, from what state do you say you are from?" asked a reporter from Missouri.

"I'm from two states I was born and raised in California, and I live now on a ranch in southern Missouri area." "I turned my property into a park that church groups and scouting can use."

"General, I mean no disrespect, but you have no education other than high school." "Why do you think you have enough education to hold the office of the Presidency?" said a reporter from New York.

"That's a good question; let's see if I can give you a satisfying answer." "It's true I haven't been to a university over the years I've been a little busy." "When I got my first command in the military, I brought up this concern to General Arnold." "He told me if it concerns me that much, I could take courses through the mail for which I did." "I know it's not the same as going to a university, and I wish I could have gone, but that was impossible because of my job." "You might want to consider the past presidents who have gone to the big-name schools how well they performed during their time in office." "I'm a common working person who served the people." "Consider Abraham Lincoln; he was self-taught, yet he was one of the best presidents we had."

"He was a Republican," said someone from the crowd.

"You don't have to be a Democrat to be great."

The questions went on much the same, but I didn't have a problem talking about anything. The only thing my campaign manager suggested was to shorten my answers somewhat.

In the following months, I was hitting every state and the territories in the United States. Because my grandmother is from Spain on my mother's side, I can speak some Spanish. That helped me when I went to states and territories where a lot of people talked Spanish. It came time for a primary debate, something that I had no experience with but had gotten drilled on for a month. The press predicted that I would be overwhelmed because of my inexperience. There were five of us behind podiums, and I was second from the right. The first two questions I wasn't even involved in answering. Then I was asked, "Is there room for the military budget to get cut to help balance the overall budget?"

"Yes, I believe it's possible if it doesn't harm our troops."

"Then General, why haven't you cut the budget when you were at the Pentagon?" asked another candidate smugly.

What was said got me mad, and I said, "Well, Sir, if you knew what you were talking about you, would have known that I cut the budget three times even though I had to negotiate with the other joint chiefs." "I'm surprised you didn't know that since you are a senator." I made him look like a fool, and he didn't know what to say, I knew I scored some points because they started asking me more questions.

"General Congress is constantly fighting, and almost nothing has ever gotten done because of the partisan bickering what would you do to get things moving through Congress?"

"As these gentlemen know, when I was a joint chief, I had to negotiate with the other joint chiefs who often don't agree with each other." "After we reach a consensus, we have to negotiate with the President and members of Congress." "My fellow joint chiefs and I were rather successful at doing this." "What you must understand as you negotiate is that you are not going to get one hundred percent of what you want, there must be some give and take." "A good negotiator has to be a good listener and have the stamina to push until he can't push anymore." The questioning went on about the same, and no one tried to challenge me the press said I was a great surprise and a clear winner of the debate. There was one more debate before the Ohio Caucus and the New Hampshire primary. In that debate, I held my own, there were a couple of other candidates that did well, but the other two were terrible. To my surprise, I won the Ohio Caucus and the New Hampshire primary, and by a large margin. One of the candidates dropped out of the race right after the New Hampshire primary, and about two weeks later, when a new poll came out, another candidate dropped out, leaving three of us. We had another debate, and I got brutally attack with lies and half-truths. When I got a chance to respond, I went on the attack myself and dispelled everything they were saying. One of the candidates accused me of conspiring with the enemy while I was a prisoner of war. All this got this candidate is to bring out my fellow prisoners to dispel this lie, and that candidate's poll numbers plummeted. By the time the Florida primaries got finished, I had won all but two states. By a close margin, I had lost Georgia mostly because it was one of the other candidate's home state, and West Virginia, which was another close state. I figured they couldn't get over I had a Mormon chaplain when I was a prisoner. The one thing I hated to do was fundraising, but money was necessary if one is to run for office. Maria and the boys joined me on some of these, and most thought my family was charming. After the Florida primary, which I won, money started pouring in, which made things easier. The President was running campaign adds against me, which my campaign manager warned me would happen. So, ninety-five percent of my campaign money got used for the primary. Five percent of the money got used to combat the President for now. I had many visits to the Jay Leno show, David Letterman show, and even Oprah Winfrey show. On the Oprah show, I got asked where I grew up, which was East Oakland, California, and about my time in Vietnam, especially with Colonel Henderson. I finally said, "You have been asking me a lot that involves African American people. You should know that I never look at a person as being from one race or another; people are people."

"I'm happy to hear you say that, but I, as a black woman, who a lot of people listens to want to know what kind of man you are."

"And what kind of a man do you say I am."

"Well, let's asked someone from the audience."

"It's alright with me."

Oprah called on an older black woman and asked, "So what do you think of General James York?"

"Well, for a white man, he seems to be not as races as I've seen; I'd vote for him."

"Well, what do you think, General?" asked Oprah.

"First, let me thank this lovely lady for her vote." "I must tell you that although I don't consider myself as races, I want to tell you that I have been around people who were." "Some of the statements that these people said I didn't say anything about nor walked away."

"Has there ever been a time you were the one who was using this kind of language?"

"No, but I do remember a time I think I was six or seven." "I was at school I and another boy, who happened to be an African American, were pushed into a fight by other boys." "His name was Willy; no one got hurt; just a few punches got thrown." "Afterward, I felt terrible about it, and later I found him and apologized." "That was the last time anything like that ever happen again."

"You were just a child, but it still bothers you after all those years?"

"There was no reason for my actions he had done me no harm."

The show went well, my poll number went higher, by the time I won Texas and Missouri another candidate dropped out. The last candidate dropped out when I won California. I then concentrated on my running mate and my campaign against the President. Three weeks before the Democratic convention, I chose Bill Clinton, the Governor of Arkansas as my running mate. He was a southerner, which would help me in the southern states, and he had ties to the northeast. He probably would have been a strong president, and I was advised not to go with him, but something told me I should, and immediately it paid off. He was a man who could appeal to a Republican and Democrat, and his wife Hilary was also a political animal. Maria and I had them over to our ranch for a weekend a week before the convention. They were both a lot savvier about politics than I was, and they advised me on many points. They were both liberals, but I felt that my conservative ways would make a decent mix with him. Privately I told Bill and Hilary about the condition of Maria and that I wanted to limit her time on the trail. She would be at the convention but would only come out when I got confirmed as the Democratic candidate. Bill thought that would be a good idea. At the convention, there were several speeches made. Hilary gave a speech, which impressed Maria and me, and finally, Bill made another great speech. It was time for me to talk, and I, with help, made the best speech I had ever made. Then it came for the convention vote; it wasn't long before I obtain the nomination by this time the whole convention floor had exploded with noise. It was time for Bill, Hilary, and their daughter to come out with Maria, my boys, and myself onto the floor stage to cheers of jubilation.

David and Jonathan went back to school while I took Maria and the rest of the boys back home. Hilary and Bill headed Southeast while I headed Northeast. I had a bus and planned to hit every state in the Northeast. Then hit the Midwest down to Texas and over to California. Bill and Hilary, when they get finished with the South, will head over to the Northwest, and we will both meet in California. When I got to Texas, I found that the Texan people were one tough people to persuade. Still, I didn't want to give up so soon, so I decided to take a couple of extra days to try to make some inroads in the President's backyard. I finally left and hit New Mexico and Arizona and then went to Southern California. I found that one of my most significant assets was having the entire volunteer campaign workers that I had. I believed that it was they who would ultimately help me win or lose a campaign.

I met Bill in San Francisco Hilary had gone home. "I need you to hit Texas; I made some dents in that state, but I think you could do a lot better." "Meanwhile, I will go through the center of the country and then down South." "I might stay a day in Missouri with Maria and the children before I return on the trail again."

"Sooner or later we will have to debate the President and Vice President," Bill said.

"You think they will debate?"

"Yes, but they will resist at first, and that will hurt them."

"How are they as debaters?"

"The Vice President isn't bad, but I can handle him." "The President is not as good at it; that's why he will resist by saying he's too busy."

"I'm glad he isn't a great debater that will give me an even field."

"I saw your debates in the primary; you're not that bad."

We campaigned in the Bay Area. I visited my parents and some of my siblings and then headed to Sacramento. I liked hitting small towns and getting out talking to the people one on one, and the press ate it up. As I traveled to each state, I stopped in small towns and cities and also at military installations. After campaigning in Missouri and staying for a day at home, which I enjoyed, I headed south. In the South, I got a good reception; there were always a few who didn't care for me, even some hecklers, which I surprised them by confronting them. On occasion, I found out the heckler was sent by the President's campaign, something I would use against the President in a debate.

In North Carolina, I did visit Top. However, it wasn't an enjoyable visit. He wouldn't even let me into his house, so I finally confronted him. "What's the matter Top, every time I see you and your family, you seem more and more distant why?"

"I've moved on; the Army was just a job; it's nothing against you."

"The military was just a job." "What the hell are you talking about, it was your life." "Nevertheless, I'm not talking about the military; I'm talking about our friendship." "Are you going to tell me that wasn't real?"

He put his head down and was silence then said dismally, "I should not have ever left the military I've been miserable ever since." "I have been so miserable I started to drink very heavily." "I also started to get violent and doing things; I don't want to even talk about to anyone." "It got so bad that I lost my wife and family."

"Where are they at now?"

"Wife and my children are living with her family."

I thought for a second and then said, "What you need is to be back into the Army I think I can arrange that."

"I'm too old, Sir."

"I'm not talking about putting you in combat, but maybe a basic training unit would fit you well." "I'm going to leave an aid here to get you some help with your drinking and anger." "What's the telephone number to Maryann, and I will give her a call?" I told the aid, what to do, and I called Maryann and talked to her for about an hour. I convinced her after

I told her what I was doing for Top to give him a second chance. After that, I called Maria and told her what happen, then gave her Maryann's number.

I finished up in Florida then headed North by the time I got to Washington D.C. the President finally woke up and started to campaign, so he was out of town. I stopped in at the Pentagon and talked to General Powell, who replaced me as joint chief, and he agreed he would reinstate Top and have him in a basic training unit. A couple of weeks had passed, and the President was taking a beating for not wanting to debate. However, he finally caved in and agreed to do two debates, as did the Vice President. The first debate got held at Penn State; Bill would have his turn three days later. At first, the questions were easy for me to respond to, the President stumbled a little, but not much, and I didn't try to challenge him. I would give him the respect that he gave me, but if he got nasty with me, I plan to slam him. I got told he might try to get a zinger in just before the debate was over, but I got prepared for that. We had our differences, and they were apparent. I got a question about jobs, economics, immigration, drug problem, and other countries. I had no issues at all, answering any of the questions, but the President tried to make me look bad. I saw his frustration about halfway through the debate when he said something; I didn't think he would bring up. "General, did you or did you not shoot one of your soldiers and threaten to shoot others when you were in command?"

"Mr. President, I didn't think you could sink so low." "However, to answer your question, yes, I was tough on someone who harmed others but was not so rough that I went to prison or stopped from my promotion to the highest rank." "Now, you would think that if I had done something wrong, I would have been relieved of my duty, but no, this didn't happen because you are making up something from nothing to smear me." "Mr. President, where is your honor, where is your sense of decency?"

"Well, my sources say you did."

"Your sources are as corrupted as your policies."

Things got very hot for a while; the President was stumbling badly. The commentator finally got control back. He asked me, "General York give me three good things you can say about the President."

"Well, without reservation, I can say he married a wonderful woman." "He also comes from a wonderful state, and his decision to kick the Iraqis out of Kuwait was a correct move."

"Do you have anything else about his presidency."

"You asked for three things, but it is difficult to say anything about his Presidency." "He got so consumed with the Iraq war that everything else was a low priority."

"Mr. President, can you say three things good about General York."

He struggled to say anything, and it showed he then said, "Well, he was a good general, I guess, he did give us a good deal in Vietnam."

"That's only two, Sir."

"I can't think anything else all I just want to talk about the issues."

From that point on, the President had trouble the rest of the night, and I had no problem controlling and dominating the debate. Three days later, Bill had his turn, and from the beginning, it was apparent he had control. After the debate, Bill said, "They will come at both of us, and because of this we must get prepared.

After the debates, both Bill and I got big-name support from both the businesses and the Hollywood field. With that support came money to obtain more TV and radio advertising.

Three weeks had passed, and the next debate was coming, again I studied a lot for it. I knew the president would come at me hard. I have been having some trouble with overzealous campaign workers. They made statements that were offensive that neither Bill nor I had ever authorized. I knew it would come up in the debate. Bill said, "I would suggest James that in your opening statement, you bring it up before the President does." "Also, apologize and let him know you are fixing it. Doing this will take away anything he could say about it."

"That's pretty smart, Bill that's what I will exactly do."

When the debate came, the President and Vice President were friendlier as far as appearance. However, as I was shaking his hand, he whispered, "I'm going to bury you."

But I whispered back, "Go for it." Since the President gave an opening statement first the last time, I went first this time. I said, "Mr. President, Mr. Vice President, thank you for both of you finally finding time to debate." "I wish to first apologize to the President for some unauthorized statements made by some people who weren't part of my campaign organization." "This problem was corrected, and we are now investigating who started this." "I assure you that when I get to the bottom of it, all will know who did this." I could see that the President and Vice President were very shocked that I made this statement. I went on and talked about my formal education before they could use it against me. Of course, I spoke of other things that I would do once I was elected.

The next person who talked was the Vice President, who got visibly shaken. Bill, with a smile, went next, followed by the President, who was also shocked. Overall, the debate went very well, admittedly. The President and Vice President did a lot better, but the critical thing was Bill, and I wasn't hurt. Bill slapped me on the back and said, "We are going to make a politician out of you yet." The elections were only two weeks away, when the time came, we joined Bill and his family in New York to see what the results would be. Maria and I were tired, so we took a nap, but the boys being excited stayed awake.

It was dark when I felt someone shaking me; it was Oliver, "Daddy, it's time to get up."

"Uh, Oliver, did I win."

"No, not yet."

"Wake me when I win."

"Come on, daddy, it's time to get up."

"Alright, but let your mother sleep."

I got up, splashed some water on my face then went down the hall to Bill and Hilary's room. "Well, Bill, how are we doing?"

"The Republicans started strong, but their lead is shrinking fast in most states reporting except for Maine."

"I knew I should have spent more time there."

"You can't win them all besides the President has a home there, and they have always been Republican," said Hilary.

As I sat there with everyone else in walks Jonathan and David with Maria and I said, "Why aren't you two at college studying?"

"We didn't want to over study, Daddy," said David.

"We will see how you two do on your exams."

"We know the material good, Daddy," said Jonathan looking at David nervously and knowing I wasn't buying it as Bill was laughing.

We lost Maine and Vermont but won everything else in the New England area, including the big state, New York. Later, we lost West Virginia and Kentucky. However, after a long-fought battle, we picked up Pennsylvania, Florida, even though the President's brother was governor, and we won Virginia. By the time results were coming in from the Midwest, I had gained most the states east of the Mississippi, there were a few states that were still undecided but leaning for me. It only took an hour after the

Midwest polls closed for results to come in, I won Missouri and Arkansas easily. What surprised me was Texas; we were very close, but it would take some time before we heard who won that state. As the night went on, the President won North Dakota, Montana, and in a very close race, and he won Utah. I won New Mexico, Nevada, and Arizona, but Arizona was very close. Idaho was too close to call, the President won Alaska. However, it looked like I was going to win California, Oregon, and in a tight race, Washington. I also won Hawaii and Portia Rico. Near midnight and when Wilhelm was asleep, I got declared the winner immediately we were given extra secret service personnel. At twelve-thirty in the morning, I got a call from the White House, "Congratulations General, if you need anything over the next few weeks, I'm here to help you."

"Thank you, Mr. President."

"There are some things I wish to discuss with you if I may."

"Alright, why don't you come to the White House next week."

"Yes, Sir, I will."

Maria stayed with Wilhelm she was much too tired to join me at the reception held for Bill and me. When we got to the reception Bill, and I made a short speech thanking everyone and then joined the party.

32

Life Ending Retirement

The next day Maria wasn't looking right. I had a doctor look at her, and he said after giving Maria some medication, she needed complete rest. We went back home to Maryland while Bill and his family took a short vacation. The following week I met with the President. "Mr. President, I have a problem." "I am a conservative Democrat, as you know, this is as scarce as hen's teeth in the Democratic Party." "The Republicans don't care for me because I'm a Democrat."

"If what you say is true, then you and Bill will have an interesting time."

"Yes, I chose him because I knew he wouldn't be a yes man and face it, not all ideas that liberals have are bad." "Do you have any ideas about how to deal with both sides of the aisle?"

"Listen to them with an open mind." "There will always be those who will play politics with you, and those in Congress will also test you."

"I would like to use you either in my cabinet or as an ambassador, something like President Carter does so well."

"I'm getting too old for a cabinet position beside it wouldn't look right, and I don't want to leave the United States." "So, an ambassadorship is out, but if you need me to take a trip to help this country like Jimmy Carter, I would be willing if my health is alright." "I would also be willing to give you all the advice you need if you want." The meeting was pleasant, but you could see he was uncomfortable talking to me. The months past the President moved out. It was time for my family and me to move into the White House and the swearing-in. There was much talk in the news about Maria's lack of activity, so in a morning briefing, I told the press why and after this, the reporters let Maria alone. Maria seemed to get weaker and became sick more often. The boys were acutely aware of how delicate their mother was and helped her as much as they could. It was getting near when Oliver and Frederic were going to graduate from high school. Oliver wanted to major in business and didn't want to go to the same college as his brothers, so maybe Yale for him. Frederic surprised me; he wanted to go to West Point to follow in my footsteps. I had thought he got over the Army long ago, but I was wrong now he talks nothing else.

I had talked to Bill about trying to pass a bill in Congress. Requiring the congresspeople to stay working until they can resolve their disagreements when it threatens the stability of the United States. He said, "It sounds good to me, but there are some that will fight it." "Why do you think we need this law anyway?"

"There will come a time maybe not in this Congress, but it will come that because Republicans and Democrats can't get along will jeopardize the stability of the United States." "Those who try to fight it; I think we need to head them off at the pass."

"You must get both sides to agree on this." "I think if you pick Republicans and Democrats to write this bill, then you have a good chance getting it to pass."

"I like that; I will schedule a meeting with four members of the House and four from the Senate." While that was going on, I had Bill get on the illegal immigrants' problem. I had him form a committee with both parties to tackle it. As time went on, I could see there were those who, no matter what I say, were negative at whatever I said.

Maria wasn't doing well, so I didn't want to stray too far from her. However, being president does not permit this. I had to go overseas for several reasons and each time I worried about Maria even though there wasn't much I could do. When dignitaries came to the White House, Maria could muster the strength to be pleasant. Our sex life was non-existent; I was afraid she was just too fragile. At first, we spent time in Missouri, but the Missouri trip took too much out of Maria. By the time that Jonathan passed the bar, Frederic graduated West Point and was a lieutenant. David had another two years of medical school while Oliver had just one more year before he finished.

Wilhelm was still in grammar school and was doing very well. He worried about his mother all the time and would climb up on my lap asking all sorts of questions about her. I could see he was missing that touch only a mother could give I had gotten a nanny, but it wasn't his mother. I had been President for three years, and before the State of the Union, I had taken an assessment of my presidency. I had many successes, mostly because of my policy of including both parties in the bills I wanted past. I still had some significant things that were always getting fought over in Congress, such as the immigration bill that Bill Clinton wrote. There were other things I still wanted to do, such as a medical bill and an education bill. I had to decide whether to run for a second term or not. I was popular, and I did not doubt that I could win. The trouble was Maria; it would be the same for the next four years, so I knew I would have to sit her down and talk to her. "If you don't run, we will go live in Missouri?"

"Yes, on our ranch."

"Will I have the same care at our home in Missouri as I do here?"

"I'll make sure that you have the best of everything."

"Like you do now."

"Yes."

"Then, if you want to run, run, I am taken care of very good here."

"When you make your decision, remember, you have to think of Wilhelm too; he has been going to school here for a long time."

In March, I let those who needed to know that I would be going for another term. I didn't have to do a primary like the one I did the last time, which took a lot of pressure off me. I and others in the Democratic Party hit all leaders the contenders that were of the Republican Party, especially those who were giving me trouble in Congress. By the time the Republican Party had their convention and picked their man, we had been hitting his shortcomings for some time. I wasn't too worried about who they chose; he was a weak person, and it had gotten placed in the peoples' minds that he was a wrong choice and couldn't win. This approach frustrated the Republican Party, and they took a lot of their money and time to combat this. By the time the election came, I had no problem defeating the Republican nominee. This time around, Maria took no part, but the children filled in. I'm always asked about her health and have always been honest about it. The media has been pushing for an interview with her, but I have refused each time. I got most of my bills passed with some compromise, and I was satisfied. About the second year of my term, I started to move things back home in Missouri. I had begun to promote Bill Clinton as the next president by giving him more noticeable things to do. Bill was making a lot more speeches and making a lot more visits to the media. I figured Bill had served me well; his way of doing things was a lot different from mine, which I didn't care for much. Where I believed in comprise, Bill believed in divide and conquer, which ended up in animosity between the parties. The people didn't like this method, but Bill and the rest of Congress would have to learn the hard way. I delt with an increase of Muslim radicalism that I warn that would be a problem in the future. I was also dealing with modern-day pirates around the horn of Africa.

Maria had spent a lot of time in the hospital towards the end of my second term. Her sickness was taking a toll on her; she was aging much more quickly than her age was, but still, I loved no other she meant everything to me. Before the end of my presidency, Wilhelm graduated high school and wanted to teach he chose Stanford in California for a school to go. He decided he would not go until we got settled in at our home in Missouri.

All of Wilhelm's brothers had graduated and were working. Frank had just about finished my last book on me. He was going to retire after the book was published, and maybe a movie was made. I had done some campaigning for Bill Clinton, but because of Maria, it was limited Bill understood, and I didn't go as much as I would like to, he had no hard feelings. I had hired a cook who also did the housekeeping and a nurse that would tend to Maria's needs. By the end of January, we moved to our home in Missouri. I tried to make the trip for Maria as easy as possible, but it was still rough for her. For the first week or so, she stayed in her bedroom. It was winter, and there was snow on the ground; I did take a walk around the ranch. Everything had grown a lot larger, especially at my aunt and uncle's place where I planted a forest. My maintenance men had done an excellent job with the property. I wish Maria could see how beautiful everything was, but I couldn't take a chance. When spring came, and the snow melted away, I felt Maria was doing better she was sitting during the warm part of the day out on the porch. I decided to get an electric golf cart so that I could drive Maria around the property in comfort. I had it custom made so that it would feel like Maria was floating on a cloud.

It was the end of May when I got a golf cart. It was an excellent time to take Maria out for a ride on the property because of all the wildflowers that were out, which Maria loved. Wilhelm reluctantly went to college in California, so it was just Maria and me not counting my hired staff. On a warm day, I loaded Maria in the cart and started to drive Maria around the property slowly. We stopped several times so that Maria could admire the area. On one of these times, Maria said, "Do you love this old, sick woman that you are sitting next to?"

"I love no other."

"I am not so pleasant looking anymore."

"I wouldn't say that you look beautiful to me."

"There is an old saying which is love is blind."

"Yet, I see." We drove on, and I asked, "Maria, do you miss Germany?"

"No, my home is with you and our children."

When we stopped again, there was a flowery meadow with a lone tree in it, and Maria pointed and said solemnly, "There is where I wish to get buried."

"Don't talk that way you still have a long life."

"She didn't look at me but just repeated herself and said, "There is where I wish to get buried." When I got back to the house, Maria was exhausted and went straight to bed. I knew that would be the last time Maria would ever see the property. There were a few days that Maria felt good, but that was getting less, and I had to call a doctor.

It's unusual for a doctor to come to one's house, but I was able to find one for a price. He and the nurse went into Maria's room and were in there for some time. The doctor and nurse finally came out and sat on the couch, and I sat across from them. The doctor sighed and said, "This sickness that Maria has is very rare." "It affects the females in her family and shows up whenever it decides to it could skip many generations or maybe not." "Maria is getting weaker every day, and I have given her medication to help her, but it is just a bandage there not much I can do." "You could put her in the hospital, but I think she would be miserable, and there isn't much we could do."

I was silent for a few seconds then asked sadly, "How long?"

"Does she have?" I nodded, and he said, "It's hard to say maybe one or two months maybe less." "I've given your nurse prescriptions to make Maria comfortable." The doctor then got up and said, "Call me when you need me."

He then left, and the nurse said, "It's none of my business, but perhaps you should inform your children." That night I didn't sleep at all, but I kept getting up and checking in on Maria. I didn't want to talk to anyone I just wanted to be left alone for the next two days I went on long walks. Maria got a lot of medications that let her sleep. Still, when she was awake, I was right there with her comforting her.

I had been putting off calling the boys, but I knew I had to, so after Maria went to sleep, I first Called Bill Clinton to see if he could arrange for Frederic to come home. "Bill, I'm sorry to disturb you, but I have an emergency, and I need your help."

"Don't worry about disturbing me; we are friends; what's the problem."

In near tears, I said, "Maria is dying." "I need Frederic home; he got stationed in Germany." "I don't know how long he needs to be with his mother, the doctor at best only gives her two months." "I'm sorry to hear this let Hilary, and I know when it's time." "Frederic will be on a plane for your home in forty-eight hours."

I thanked Bill and started to call the other boys. The only thing I said to them in tears is, "Come home." Their answer without them even questioning me was I'll take the first flight home.

The first one home was Jonathan, and that night Wilhelm drove into the yard, and the next day David and Frederic showed up, and lastly, Oliver came. They were shocked at what I looked like, which was someone who hadn't eaten for a long time, unshaven, dirty, and depressed. They tried to console me before they went in to see their mother. When they saw their mother, they fell apart; fortunately, she was asleep when this happened. It had been solemn around the house until Maria woke and they all went in to see her. It was the first time I noticed her smile in some time. Each boy kissed her and then took turns holding her hand. "The ranch looks real beautiful mama when you are better it will be fun walking with you seeing everything," said Frederic.

She smiled and said to all the boys, "I want you boys to visit your father often when I am gone, he will be lonely." All five boys started crying, and tears seeped from my eyes.

Maria had a habit of waking at certain times; it never varied. After four weeks, since the boys came home, Maria didn't wake up at her usual time. We were concerned but waited to see if she would wake up a little later, but she didn't. I called the doctor after the nurse said it would be a good idea. About an hour after I called, the doctor came. The boys and I were hanging around the doorway as the doctor examined Maria twenty minutes later, he came out. He said to all of us, "I would say your goodbyes now she will be gone shortly." The boys surrounded Maria's bed, I at the foot of the bed next to Frederic. It was Frederic broke down first as I put my arm around him, and then we all broke down. Ten minutes later, Maria took her last breath. The doctor said he would call for an undertaker to pick up Maria before he left. They came and picked up Maria's body within an hour after the doctor called. We all look forlorn as she drove off the property. All the boys walked off in different directions to grieve, without saying a word. I went back into the house and sat in her room, staring off into space as tears flowed down my cheeks.

I must have been in her room for hours because when Jonathan shook me out of my trance, it was dark. "Are you going to eat?" Jonathan asked.

"I'm not much in the mood to eat anything."

"Neither am I, but I don't want to lose anyone else, so I think you should eat something, we are all worried about you."

I left Maria's room with Jonathan; most of the boys were in the living room eating a sandwich. The nurse and cook were in the kitchen fixing something for Wilhelm. I looked at the nurse and said, "I won't need you anymore." "I'll pay you for six more months, and you can stay here until you can find another place."

"Thank you."

The boys and I went to bed late; I don't know how the boys slept, but for me, I toss and turn all night. It got to a point when I just sat up in the bed, and I started thinking a perfect complement for Maria would be to place a statue made of marble, bronze, or copper. I decided to talk to the boys about it in the morning and see how they felt about it. I did doze off to sleep before it was time to wake up. The next morning as we ate, I talked to my boys about my plans, "I'm thinking of having a life-size statue made of your mother and put it at the gravesite, how do you all feel about that?"

"It's a good idea, Daddy," said Wilhelm.

"I think the statue should include all of us mama would want this," said Jonathan.

"My brothers and I should get represented as children; she would like that too," said Frederic.

"Well, those are all good ideas," I said. "Now we can have the statue made of marble, bronze, or copper," I added.

"Marble would be nice," said Oliver.

"No, I've seen some marble headstones and statues, they over time deteriorate when they are outside to a point where it doesn't look like the person," said David.

"Then it will be copper or bronze," I said.

"Copper also deteriorates daddy," said Oliver.

"Then it is settled it will be bronze," I said. The boys nodded in agreement, and I added, "We all have to do something very unpleasant, and that is to go to Poplar Bluff and pick out a coffin."

The funeral was going to be in eight days from when we made arrangements. Typically, Maria would get buried within days of her death. However, preparations need to be done so she could get buried on the ranch. We were all at home getting ready for dinner when I got a telephone call; it was the President. "James, let me give you Hilary's and my condolences we will be there for Maria's funeral."

"Thanks, Bill, how did you find out I haven't told anyone except those I had to?"

"It's in all the papers and on TV." "How are you and your boys holding up?"

"Not good, I can't speak for my boys, but this is the toughest thing I've ever gone through tougher than the prison camp that I was in."

I had commissioned a person in Pennsylvania to do the bronze. It wouldn't be ready for the burial, but I should have it installed in about three months. We had so many people coming to the funeral we had to find a bigger place to hold it. There were over five thousand people who attended the funeral, many from Washington D.C. and the military. Even Top and Maryann came, it was nice to see them together, and Bill and Hilary came. There were also representatives of Germany, France, England, and Prince Charles who came representing the queen. At the funeral, it got announced that refreshments would get served in my home. My cook, with the help of a caterer, put it all together. The funeral and graveside services went wonderfully. At the house, the boys and I were somber as people came up to us to give their condolences. Hilary, who was with Bill, said, "If there is anything we can do for you, just call." Top and Maryann, who got visibly shaken, also told us all we had to do is ask if we needed anything. Top talked to Frederic for some time; I would assume because he was in the military. It was nearly six pm when everyone finally left.

As the days passed, the boys left; first, Frederic had to go back to Germany, then Wilhelm, who went back to school in California. A few days after Wilhelm left, David and Jonathan left, then a day or two later, Oliver left, and I was left alone except for the cook. Maria's nurse had left after the funeral she had gotten another job to replace the one she lost with Maria. A month later, a slab of red granite got placed over the grave with all the pertinent information of Maria. There wasn't a day that I didn't visit Maria's grave and talk to her; I was utterly empty inside. I had lost a lot of weight. The boys visited me as often as they could, and they knew I was suffering. When the statue of Maria was delivered, it took all day for them to install it. It reminded me of those times we went on picnics in Germany. The person who designed the bronze also included a bench so that I could admire the statue. I sat there, admiring the bronze as tears streamed down my cheeks at the thought of Maria's memory. As time went on, I took five pictures of Maria's statue and sent one to each of my sons. I had the maintenance people spread wildflower seeds around the area with instruction to keep this area as perfect as possible. A year and a half had passed since Maria had passed. I had many groups such as the boys and girls scouts also church groups visit my property. They now made arrangements with the head of maintenance for a place to camp. This location was in high demand, and each group had to schedule a time to use it. I was asked a lot about the statue, which I freely explain to them about Maria.

My head of maintenance came to me and asked, "Mr. York, don't you think we should charge these groups who camp here?"

I thought for a second and then asked, "Have any of these groups damage the grounds."

"Nothing serious, but there are water and toilet use, and we have a problem with wood for fires."

"Is there any dead wood lying around?"

"There is always dead wood, but it is away from the campgrounds."

"I'm not for charging any of these groups, but you can have them put a small refundable security deposit if they do some major damage." "Meanwhile, hire someone maybe high school kids as temps and have them pick up the deadwood so that these campers can use it for firewood."

"Yes, Sir, I will do that."

I had noticed that the Ellsinore area was changing somewhat, and new people were moving in. I was glad over the years I had bought as much land I had. Many developers asked me to sell them some of my property for a lot of money, and I had refused each time. They built a new grammar, middle, and high school. The gas stations were gone, and new ones got rebuilt, getting made larger. The general store closed and got replaced by a supermarket and hardware store.

I was sitting in my living room playing my piano when someone drove into my yard and out of the car exited Val and Christine, and I said, "You two have just made my day."

"We went to the old place you have changed it a lot," said Christine.

"Come into the house, and let's talk about it." They both came into the house and sat down I had my cook make something for them and then I said as I sat down, "You two are going to stay here for a while so you can see the whole property."

"I was hoping you say that," said Val.

"I'm no rancher, but I always loved the beauty of this area, so I planted a forest where you use to have your cattle." "I even have a large pond stocked with fish that I feed water to." We talked into the night, and I gave them the two rooms off the deck in the back of the house. The next day we walked the property, and Christine commented on her approval of how I landscape the land. I offered to have their parents' graves moved to the ranch near their old house, but they said no, they preferred to stay where they are. They were with me for two days, then left. I told them they could use any of the houses they wanted on the property any time they wanted. They both said they had moved on with their own lives.

The winter had come, and it was a heavy snowfall this year. I had bought a snowplow, and I kept the roads open for me and anybody else who wanted to use them. Christmas was coming, and the boys said they would come to my home to be with me. I had decorated the house the best I could with my cook's help, and she baked a lot of treats and things. I had given her a two-week Christmas vacation. Frederick, Jonathan, and Oliver brought a girlfriend with them. All the boys and their friends were trying to be festive. I was quiet, not joining; I couldn't get my mind off Maria, and the boys notice. "Daddy, I miss mama too, but I don't think she would want you or us to grieve this way she would want us to move on," said David.

I nodded and said, "You are right, but it is tough for me." "I am very lonely for your mother, but I will try for you boys' sake." I got coaxed to play the piano; it has always been able to cheer me up.

After the piano, Frederick's girlfriend came over to me. She asked, "Forgive me for getting into your business, but why don't you start dating, you wouldn't be so lonely?"

I smiled and said, "I want no other woman other than Maria." "If I did date someone else, it wouldn't be fair to her because I would be thinking of Maria every time I look at her." She nodded, she understood, and I tried to be more festive.

After the holiday and all the kids were gone, it was just me again the winter went by slowly, but spring did come, and it was welcome by me. I went to check on all the campsites fixing what needed fixing. Of course, I visited Maria's gravesite. Eventually, campers came, for the most part, I stayed away from them. I had my maintenance people build piers out into both ponds, and of course, I stocked both ponds with fish. One day in June, I took my daily walk to Maria's gravesite. I usually make this walk early in the morning, but I had been a little lazy and got down there nearly eleven in the morning. As I approached the gravesite, I saw a child he was about ten or eleven years old. He was on the bench, looking at the statue and looking melancholy. He was a pleasant-looking child with long blonde hair very girl like he had a few small freckles across his nose and green color eyes. He looked up at me but didn't say anything, so I sat down beside him, and after a few seconds, I asked, "What do you think of the statue?"

"They look like they are happy; I wish I knew them."

"Well that boy is Frederic, and he is Oliver, that's David, he is Jonathan, and the little one is Wilhelm." "That woman is their mother, Maria, and that person is me; I'm James York." "You are also very right; they were happy then." "It's a picnic we had many years ago." "Do you see that red stone slab over there?"

"Yes."

"Under that stone is Maria, those boys' mother, and my wife."

"Did your family always have a happy time?"

"Oh yes, most of the time, but there were bad times too, like when Maria died." "Of course, you know that in all families, there are good times and bad."

"No, I didn't know where most of your time happy?"

"Yes, and still are with my sons."

He sighed and said, "I wish I had a happy family."

"You don't have a father and mother?"

"No, they died three years ago."

"Who do you live with?"

"A foster family."

"Why haven't you been adopted your very beautiful?"

"I don't know, maybe because I act more like a girl than a boy, or maybe no one wants me because I'm too old."

"Are you here with your foster parents?"

"Yes."

"Come on, let's go talk to them."

As we walked back to where he was camping, I asked, "How old are you, and by the way, you didn't tell me what your name is?"

"My name is Eon Wright, and I am almost eleven."

As I walked into the campsite, the foster parents came up to me and said, "Did he do something wrong?"

Their question wasn't said not as a concerned parent but as an annoyed person, and Eon noticed and was afraid. "No, he is a well-behaved boy, and we are friends." That comforted Eon, and then I said, "I'm James York, the owner of this property."

"We know who you are Mr. President we voted for you, you were a great president," said Eon's foster father.

"That's very kind of you, but that was in the past now." "What I've come here is for me to talk to you about is adopting Eon."

Eon's mouth dropped open, and they said, "Why would you want to adopt him you don't know what he is like," said Eon's foster mother.

"Oh, he has told me some things."

"Well, he just a gloomy sissy boy," said Eon's foster father, smugly.

What he said made me mad, but I didn't say anything. I could see it upset Eon because he hung his head down, but I said, "It doesn't bother me the way he is." "Will you give me the name and telephone of his social worker?"

"Gladly," said Eon's foster father.

"I'll be seeing you soon," I said to Eon. I also got the address to where Eon's foster parents lived. I went back to the house and called his social worker. The social worker knew me and planned to come out in two days to sign some papers to get the process going. She seemed anxious to find a home for Eon; she let me know a lot about him. I had told her over the phone how the foster parents treated Eon at the camp and how sad he was.

Two days later, Mrs. Chang, the social worker drove up to the house I went out to greet her as she got out of her car. To my surprise, the backdoor open and out came a bright-eyed all smiles, Eon. "Well, this is a surprise I thought it would be a while before Eon would come."

"Will this be a problem, Mr. York?" said Mrs. Chang concerned.

"No, I'm overjoyed that Eon is here." "Let's go in and talk."

"Are you hungry, Eon?" I asked

"No, Mrs. Chang got me a hamburger."

"Can I get you something, Mrs. Chang?"

"No, I'm fine." "The reason I brought Eon here now is that the home he was in was unsuitable, and I couldn't allow him to be there anymore." I didn't ask her any questions about the foster family; I just nodded, I understood. "Now, I don't see any problems with certifying you. I don't need to do a background check, and I know you are financially good." "Your age is a bit older than we would like, but since Eon is nearly eleven, we think it will be alright." "Now Mr. York, didn't you say you had a housekeeper and cook?"

"I have a housekeeper who cooks; she is on a two-week vacation."

"How many bedrooms do you have?" she asked.

"I have a loft over the barn, two guest bedrooms just outside the door, and three bedrooms inside." "Eon's bedroom will be upstairs on the left."

"Well, is there anything you want to ask?"

"When can I adopt him?"

"About three to six months."

"Wow, when I was in the military, I adopted my boys within weeks."

"You've adopted before?"

"Yes, four of my boys are adopted."

"We may be able to shave some time off those three to six months, especially with your background."

We went outside and got Eon's things out of the car, which wasn't much. "Looks like we are going to have to do some shopping Eon."

"What for?" Eon asked.

"Well, more clothing and more important, some toys." Indeed, he did get new clothing, and many toys and his brothers got notified that they had a new brother. They thought I was crazy, but they without exception all accepted Eon as their baby brother. Eon was an affectionate little boy who fit in very well. When it came time for the adoption, Jonathan and Oliver went to the hearing; the rest were sorry but couldn't get away from their jobs.

Frederic and Oliver had eventually gotten married, and David and Jonathan were engaged. Wilhelm dated but wanted to graduate and be established and working before getting serious with anyone. Eon seemed to be happy and was a joy to me. One day when Eon was twelve, I was sitting with him down at the statue when he asked, "Daddy, when am I going to have a statue of me."

I never thought about it, but he is part of the family, and I know Maria would want it, so I said, "I'll call the people who made this statue." When

I got back at the house, I called people who made the statue, and they said they would come out the following week.

On Wednesday, the following week at nine in the morning a Jennifer Carson showed up at my front door, "Hello Mr. York. I'm Jennifer Carson; I got a call from the company I work with about the statue I created for you." "They said you wanted to modify it. I was under the impression you are satisfied with what I had done."

"Come on in Ms. Carson, I will explain." We both sat down, and I said, "What I want to do to the statue you made is to add to it." "I have another son, and I want him in it also."

"That takes a lot off my mind."

"Why don't we go out to where the statue is, and I will show you what I have on my mind."

Eon was in school, but I would rather it be a surprise to him anyway. As we got to the site, Ms. Carson examined the statue and said, "It looks in great shape." "What do you want to do with it?"

"I was thinking perhaps having you make a statue of my youngest son Eon holding my hand."

"Yes, I could do that, but understand you won't have the same patina as the rest of the statue."

"That's alright; he's new to the family anyway." She took measurements and pictures I gave her of Eon that I had of him when I first got him and then left.

The months went by, and finally, Eon's statue came, and they assembled the statue and then left before Eon came home from school. "Daddy, I'm home."

"How was school today?"

"Good."

"You have homework."

"Yes, some math, and I have to get started on an essay." "I'm going to get something to eat first, then get started."

"Why don't we go for a walk first?"

"Where to?"

"You will see." Eon grabbed an apple, and off we went.

It soon became apparent to Eon that we were going to Maria's gravesite. "Did my statue come, Daddy?"

"You will see."

When we got near the statue, Eon ran off to see it. "It's me when I was younger, Daddy."

"Yes, do you like it?"

"Yes, we should take pictures and send them to everyone."

"Sounds like a good idea."

The years went by, and Eon got older to a point he was getting ready to pick a University to attend. He wanted to be a teacher and teach in Ellsinore. Wilhelm was working and is engaged to a girl from California. David finally got married, but Jonathan was still not ready to get married. Frederick's wife had died on the autobahn she was one month pregnant all the boys and I went to the funeral in Germany. Frederic wanted her buried in my place in Missouri, so Maria had some company. I didn't add another statue; it was up to Frederic if he wished to have one. It wouldn't be part of the central statue.

As the years passed, I was getting older and feeling it. I was lonely now that Eon was going to school in Cape Girardeau; he had another two years. I hadn't heard from Jonathan for some time, and that concerned me. I tried to call him, but he never answered his phone, but I left messages.

One sunny day I was in the barn with my vehicles when a teary-eyed Jonathan came into the barn embraced me and said, "Daddy, I'm very sick."

"How sick, Jonathan."

"As sick as mama was." I took a sobbing Jonathan into the house to find out what the problem was. "I have Lou Gehrig's disease; do you know what that is?"

I did know what it is, and I knew there was no cure for it, and it stabbed me to the depths of my soul. "We will do everything possible for you; you will stay here; it's not a time for panic." "Have you called your brother David yet?"

"No, I didn't want to bother him."

"He will be hurt if you don't tell him I'll call him and let him know after all he is a doctor; maybe he can help."

When I called David, I didn't have to go into detail; he said he would be home the next day. I also let all the boys know, and they said they would come soon. Frederic was the distraught he grew up with him at a much younger age. He said he would get some leave to be with Jonathan if he could but to keep him in the loop as to what was happening. We did all we could for Jonathan. However, in the end, we could only keep him comfortable, and on a warm spring day on nearly the anniversary of Maria's death, Jonathan slept for the last time. We buried Jonathan near his mother, and a part of me died. I never got over the death of Maria, and now Jonathan, I felt I am tired of life and wish it would end.

I got a letter from Frederic; he had been promoted to captain some time ago and said he was getting shipped to Afghanistan. However, I shouldn't worry; he would be cautious. I lost my wife and my son; I couldn't bear to lose another son. Happily, Frederic survived Afghanistan unscathed. He got stationed in Missouri at Fort Lenard Wood; he was near enough to visit on weekends. He was stationed there for eighteen months when he was shipped much to my dismay to Afghanistan again. I tried calling the President, but he wouldn't take my call, and neither would the Pentagon. Just before he left for Afghanistan, Frederic said, "Don't worry Daddy, I'll be alright I'm a York." When he said that, I had a feeling that kind of feeling I had when I knew something was going to happen. For the first four months of Frederic's deployment, seem to be going fine, but I still had that strong feeling that something was going to happen in fact that sense was much stronger than it had been. Every Wednesday without exception, Frederic either called me or talked by a computer that my maintenance man set up for me. I warned him about my feeling, but he kept on saying he was safe; he'd be fine.

It was the second week of the fifth month, and I got a visit to my home from an Army Major and a Chaplain. "Sir, we are here because of your son," said the Major.

"Is my son dead?"

"No, Sir?" said the chaplain. "He is badly injured he is being shipped to Germany first then to Walter Reed."

"How long will he be in Germany?"

"We aren't sure, but I would think months," said the Major.

They left, and I let Frederic's brothers know what was going on and that I was going to Germany to be with him. They all agreed they would see Frederic when he came to Walter Reed.

I flew to Germany and got a modest room. I had gotten to Germany ahead of Frederic. It would be a couple of days before he would have arrived. When he did come, they had him sedated, so I sat in his room until he woke up. "Daddy, what are you doing here?"

"You're my son; I'll be here until you get transferred to Walter Reed."
"Are you in pain?"

"I can feel some pain, but they have me doped up, so it's not bad."

"Well, the good thing is you have all your limbs."

"Yes, but this is going to put me out of the Army."

"How do you feel about that?"

"I would have rather retired from the Army like you." "I don't know what I'm going to do now."

"You are smart and well educated when you are well again, you will come home and decided what you want to do." "Meanwhile, you will manage our property." "I'm getting old and have little interest in it."

Frederic was in Germany for two and a half months while they worked on his arm and legs that got injured from an IED that was exploded near him, killing two others and wounding him. His right leg was the worse; the doctors in Germany weren't sure he would walk again; this would have to get determined at Walter Reed.

Frederic was in the hospital at Walter Reed being examined and taking tests. After about a month, he and I got told that they would do all they could to restore his abilities. But they said he would do a lot better at a hospital in Colorado by the name of Craig its best facility in the nation, but it would cost. "I don't care what it will cost, make the arrangements for him to go there," I said.

After spending three months at Walter Reed, Frederic got transferred to Craig Hospital, and I was with him all the way. All his brothers showed up to visit him, and David said he researched Craig Hospital, which was an excellent place for Frederic's situation.

Frederic was at Craig Hospital for eight weeks, and it was intense. What stabbed me through the heart; was with all three hospitals that I was with Frederic, I witnessed the pain that Frederic went through. I heard him often screaming as he got pushed to do one thing or another. After eight weeks, Frederic could walk, and the doctors assured him and me that as time went on, he would get stronger and walk better. However, the scars would always be there, and Frederic would continue to have a limp and have some difficulties with his bad arm.

We went home, and I got Frederic busy running the property explaining what I had envisioned for the place. I had bought most of the old buildings in Ellsinore to turn them into restaurants, stores, and offices. The population around this area grew, and the property was getting developed. My land was becoming more popular and in demand.

People not only came to camp but also for the day, and so with Frederic's suggestion, we set areas aside for these people.

As the years pasted, Frederic got stronger as I got older and was less involved in running the ranch. I had grandchildren by this time, and the boys and their families did come home from time to time. As for me, I stayed strictly on my property. I got invited to visit the White House several times, and sometimes I went. As time went on, I didn't go to the White House because of my health or I didn't get invited. They wanted to build a library where all my military and White House memorabilia would be on display. I didn't think anyone would visit it, but I said, "If you are going to build it, build it in Ellsinore near the buildings that belong to me and make it blend in with the rest of the buildings."

The years passed, I broke my ankle and tore my Achilles tended and was using a walker. My health was failing me, and Frederic tried to stop me from visiting Maria's gravesite, but I went anyway. It was one of those days, in the warm summer morning, that I was heading to Maria's graves site. I wasn't feeling very well, and I was a bit tired when I sat down on the bench opposite the statue. I was thinking about all the good times I had with Maria and dozing a little in the warm sun when I saw someone coming from far off. He was dressed in buckskin and had a familiar look to him; he sat down beside me, and I figured he was a camper. He was quiet for a moment then asked, "You mourn for your wife?"

"Yes, she was the love of my life; I miss her very much."

"That's how I felt about my first and second wife."

"I'm sorry you lost both of your wives."

"I never lost them."

"Uh?" Just then, I felt someone's hand on my shoulder, I look up, and I couldn't believe it, it was Maria. She sat beside me, and all I got out of my mouth while I put my arm around her was a shocked, "Maria, my love."

I swung my head around to the other side, expecting to see the man in the buckskin, but it was Jonathan. I put my other arm around him also and started weeping in joy. As I sat there, I began to nod off to sleep with joy in my heart that Maria and Jonathan had come back to me.